Facsimile page with Frank Lloyd Wright's
handwriting: his additions and revisions
for this definitive edition of his autobiography

my away thd sovereignty

sm or through any other ,
vidual, It bears a ~~royal~~
e, ~~strong~~ and operative,
Democracy,
~~I~~ It applies to Nations. *because*
ould act as a check upon
of ~~any~~ Nation.
e to our Civilization.
~~as~~ for ideas; A whirlpool
at ease. *There wars*

money or blows

had written and hearing
ow the visit had affected
ank, come now, what do
sians have done remark-
But the 'Revolution' has
is destroying us ~~and~~ will
f human beings on hard
for military purposes).
~~t, will~~ rend us." "Then,"
turns and

I believe in a capitalist
ntry .
~~oF FORM.~~

TO THEM NO TUMBLED

he who
ries ago, built a city for
city that is nowhere yet
that city of the Future
dacres, will be the sixth
slutest to newered
e certain that nothing
eno The omnipotent
the immediate loves
e that happen to me &
United States of America .

BOOKS BY FRANK LLOYD WRIGHT

The Future of Architecture (1953)
The Natural House (1954)
An American Architecture (1955)
　(Edited by Edgar Kaufmann)
The Story of the Tower (1956)
A Testament (1957)
The Living City (1958)
Drawings for a Living Architecture (1959)
Writings & Buildings (1960)
　(Edited by Edgar Kaufmann and Ben Raeburn)
The Solomon R. Guggenheim Museum (1960)
The Drawings of Frank Lloyd Wright (1962)
　(Edited by Arthur Drexler)
Buildings, Plans and Designs (1963)
The Work of Frank Lloyd Wright (1965)
The Japanese Print (1967)
The Early Work of Frank Lloyd Wright (1969)
The Industrial Revolution Runs Away (1969)
Genius and the Mobocracy (1971)
An Autobiography (1977)

ABOUT FRANK LLOYD WRIGHT

by Olgivanna Lloyd Wright

Our House (1959)
The Shining Brow (1960)
Roots of Life (1963)
Frank Lloyd Wright: His Life, His Work,
　His Words (1966)

AN AUTOBIOGRAPHY

To my co-author Olgivanna
from her own "author"—
Frank Lloyd Wright.

AN AUTOBIOGRAPHY
FRANK LLOYD WRIGHT

HORIZON PRESS NEW YORK

CONTENTS

ILLUSTRATIONS

17

18

F.Ll.W. and daughter
Iovanna in the garden, Taliesin
Iovanna on the hill at Taliesin
Architect's cabin, "Ocatillo," Arizona
General view of "Ocatillo," Arizona
"We start from 'Ocatillo' [for New York]"
S. C. Johnson and Son, Inc., Racine, Wisconsin

19

BOOK ONE □ FAMILY

PRELUDE

Light blanket of snow fresh-fallen over sloping fields, gleaming in the morning sun. Clusters of pod-topped weeds woven of bronze here and there sprinkling the spotless expanse of white. Dark sprays of slender metallic straight lines, tipped with quivering dots. Pattern to the eye of the sun, as the sun spread delicate network of more pattern in blue shadows on the white beneath.

"Come, my boy," said Uncle John to his sister Anna's nine-year-old. "Come now, and I will show you how to go!"

Taking the boy by the hand he pulled his big hat down over his shock of gray hair and started straight across and up the sloping fields toward a point upon which he had fixed his keen blue eyes.

Neither to right nor to left, straight forward he walked, intent upon his goal—possessed.

But soon the boy caught the play of naked weed against the snow, sharp shadows laced in blue arabesque beneath. Leaving his mitten in the strong grasp, he got free.

He ran first left, to gather beads on stems and then beads and tassels on more stems. Then right, to gather prettier ones. Again—left, to some darker and more brilliant—and beyond to a low-spreading kind. Farther on again to tall golden lines tipped with delicate clusters of dark bronze heads. Eager, trembling, he ran to and fro behind Uncle John, his arms growing full of "weeds."

Arrived at the point on which he had fixed, a long way up the slope, Uncle John turned to look back.

A smile of satisfaction lit the strong Welsh face. His tracks in the snow were straight as any string could be straight.

The boy came up, arms full, face flushed, glowing.

He looked up at his Uncle—see what he had found!

A stern look came down on him. The lesson was to come. Back there was the long, straight, mindful, heedless line Uncle John's own feet had purposefully made. He pointed to it with pride. And there was

23

the wavering, searching, heedful line embroidering the straight one like some free, engaging vine as it ran back and forth across it. He pointed to that too—with gentle reproof.

Both stood looking back. The small hand with half-frozen fingers was again in its mitten in the older, stronger hand; an indulgent, benevolent smile down now on the shamed young face.

Somehow, there was something . . . not clear.

Uncle John's meaning was plain—NEITHER TO RIGHT NOR TO THE LEFT, BUT STRAIGHT, IS THE WAY.

The boy looked at his treasure and then at Uncle John's pride, comprehending more than Uncle John meant he should.

The boy was troubled. Uncle John had left out something—something that made all the difference to the boy.

FAMILY

THE BOY

Back in Wales in the Victorian Era, there lived a hatter, stalwart maker of strange, black, high-pointed cones. The witches wore them when riding on their broom-sticks. The Welsh wore them for hats. The hatter was proud of his work and peddled his hats at fairs. He would throw one down on the ground and, "Stand on it!" he would say to anyone likely to buy.

On Sundays he preached, a firebrand of a man, questioning how man should be just with God, rejecting the answers most men, and women too, gave him.

He was tall, this Richard Jones, dark-eyed—an impassioned, unpopular Unitarian. The daughter of an old Welsh family, Mary Lloyd, heard him and fell in love with him.

"For there is the just man who perisheth in his righteousness, and there is the wicked man who prolongeth in his wickedness.

"But he that knoweth God and serveth him shall come forth of them all."

So she believed, and went away with him against her parents' will. If her wealthy family looked askance at her staunch man, what did that matter? She loved him and, so, trusted him.

They had seven children, whose family name became Lloyd-Jones.

Then his outspoken liberality offending conservative popular opinion made America seem a hope and a haven to the Unitarian, and he came with a delicate wife and their seven to The West. He came to find a farm where his stalwart strength might make a home and a place to work in a land where speech was free, because men were.

So the hatter-preacher in his fifty-third year became the Wisconsin Pioneer, with his Thomas, John, Margaret, Mary, Anna, Jenkin and Nannie.

Little Nannie, dying on the way, was left behind in strange ground.

They came by canal-boat and lake-steamer to Milwaukee on their way to Ixonia, Wisconsin. Six years the pioneer couple lived there, where they invoked four more children, Ellen, Jane, James, and Enos, to join their little band before they found the valley by the Wisconsin River.

"The Valley," they all lovingly called it in later years, and lovable it was, lying fertile between two ranges of diversified soft hills, with a third ridge intruding and dividing it in two smaller valleys at the upper end. A small stream coursing down each joined at the homestead and continued as a wider stream on its course toward the River. The lower or open end of the Valley was crossed and closed by the broad and sandbarred Wisconsin, and from the hills you could look out upon the great sandy and treeless plain that had once been the bed of the mighty Wisconsin of ancient times.

When the virgin soil was broken by the grandfather and his sons, friendly Indians still lingered in the neighborhood.

By the eldest son, Thomas, a carpenter, a small house was built on a gently sloping hillside facing south. Balm-of-Gilead trees and Lombardy poplars were planted by the Mother and her brood around the little house and along the lanes: lanes worm-fenced with oak-rails split in the hillside forests which clung to the northern slopes and hill-crowns.

The southern slopes were all too dry for wood, and were bare except where rock ledges came through. The stables were roofed with straw like the old Welsh thatch. The small simple house, however, was "modern," clapboarded and shingled by Thomas and his brothers. The kitchen was a lean-to at the rear. An outside stairway led to a cool stone cellar beneath. A root-house was close behind, partially dug into the ground and roofed with a sloping mound of grass-covered earth.

Here in "The Valley," the family tree on Richard Lloyd-Jones, Welsh pioneer, with its ten branches and one scar, struck root in the America of his hope. It was now his haven.

Up to this time he had preached, even while traveling on the ships or the canal-boats or at the inns where the family stayed. Usually he was listened to with respect. There was fervor, exaltation in him. He read the Bible his own way with strong Welsh accent, but no one could mistake his meaning. It was often new to his lettered betters and would change their thought. He was pioneer, not on the earth alone, but in mighty reaches of the spirit where the earth grows dim.

He had a Church during his years in Ixonia but again, "where speech was free because men were," the Church proposed to try him. He said, "You need not. If I am intrusive, I will get out. I cannot quell my spirit."

For family crest, he had the old Druid symbol: /|\ "Truth Against the World."

Grandfather preached as Isaiah preached. "The flower fadeth, the grass withereth—but the word of the Lord, thy God, endureth forever." His children had to learn that chapter of Isaiah, the fortieth, by heart so they could recite it.

The boy, his grandson, grew to distrust Isaiah. Was the flower any less desirable because it seemed to have been condemned to die that it might live more abundantly? As they all went to work in the fields, the grass seemed always necessary to life in the Valley, most of all when it withered and was hay to keep the stock alive in winter so the preacher himself might live.

The flowers have closed their eyes beneath the stars, opened to the sun, dropped their seeds into the bosom of friendly earth these thousands of years away from Isaiah and bid fair to be unfaded when the "word of our Lord," as Isaiah heard it, has been much modified in the mouth. . . .

Might it not be then before all, that this very grass and these flowers, too, are in truth themselves the very word of GOD.

There seemed base ingratitude in the boastful thunder of that hateful text.

When storms swept the Valley from bank to bank of its ranges of hills, then black against a livid sky—lashing the trees, drowning the helpless small things, in the destruction that was wrought and the wreck that followed, the boy would see Isaiah's "Judgment."

Ah, yes! In this prophet Hell enlarged itself and opened "her" mouth without measure!

Woe! Woe! that word "woe" struck on the young heart like a blow—"O Woe unto them that are mighty to drink wine and mingle strong drink!" Nor was there to be pity on "the fruit of the womb." Little children were to be trodden under foot.

Isaiah's awful Lord smote the poor multitudes with a mighty continuous smite, never taking away the gory, dreadful hand outstretched to smite more; never satisfied with the smiting already done.

And yet, according to Isaiah, were you willing to argue the matter, to reason with "Him" (none seemed to know whether Isaiah or His Lord was meant by "Him"), your sins would be white as snow. Why?

Verily this Holy Warrior was a prophet making GOD in his own image. Turning his own lusts into virtues because they were on the side of pain instead of on the side of pleasure.

What a curse to put upon the mind of any child!

How much too much to thrash him!

How much less than too little to lead him!

His grandson would see the stalwart figure, legs straight in stirrups, of this spiritual brother of Isaiah, his dreaded, beloved Welsh Grandfather, white-bearded and hoary-headed, sitting up straight upon his horse, Timothy, like a Patriarch; stick with shepherd's-crook hung over the left forearm, the Bible of his faith firm against his side. And his grandson would see that he was thus able to whack his horse on the flank without losing his hold on the BOOK.

Weekdays Grandfather believed in the gospel of hard work. Relentlessly he taught his children to add tired to tired and add it again, until the fountain of energy he himself was, working out through his offspring, began to cut away the forests and establish a human decency where the wilderness had been. A human smile, where before had been the Divine Countenance.

The Indians, in passing, sometimes brought venison and laid it on his doorstep and he had tobacco for them. For he smoked a pipe. And this pipe was a great source of shame to his family in after years. Their one shadow of reproach to him. Though he was hard, and, should a child by some slip pour much more sorghum on his plate than intended, Grandfather would righteously make him eat it all ("his eyes should not be bigger than his stomach"), yet this cruelty they respected. The pipe they could neither explain nor forgive.

After all, it was the little Grandmother who loved him and tempered his harshness. She had taught him to smoke as a cure for his asthma.

The asthma he outgrew but his pipe stayed with him while he lived.

Grandmother's gentle spirit had welded together with their father's the strong wills of his ten children in a united affection that was never broken.

Some ten years in the new home and the Grandmother passed painlessly away, carried out into the open air of the arbor which the Grandfather had built with his own hands for her. As if he, too, were transported, Grandfather, the better part of his life gone now, got on his feet and led these children in a prayer which they ever after remembered as the most beautiful they had ever heard.

Eleven years later, eighty-seven years of age, he lay down on his bed to sleep. In the night—painlessly—he, too, slipped away.

But not then was his spirit "quelled."

Grandfather's spirit lived on in a typical immigrant establishment on virgin American soil. A little Welsh clan, by himself set in this little corner of that enormous new ground dedicated to Freedom, and parceled out among all the breeds of the earth, stayed there with the ground.

The ground! What does it not hold impartially in its depths, breadths and beauty for the pioneer like Richard Lloyd-Jones, in league with the stones of the field, himself like the ridges of primeval rock that ribbed the hills in contrast to the verdure rolling over them. He planted a small world within the world that is again within other worlds, without end.

He did not consider the lilies—how they grew.

The little Grandmother was all that to him.

Beauty comes to all strong men, in some guise, sometimes in disguise.

His children, his flesh and blood, were like him but with something of the element added to them of the prayerful consideration for the lilies that was the gentle Grandmother's. Sympathy "for the flower that fadeth," gratitude for the "grass that withereth" came a step nearer to them in their mother.

"Mother's Pine" stands on the Hillside lawn, a living child of hers. The little Grandmother planted it there. A small thing. Careless mowing in the yard had injured it. They were going to pull it up and throw it away. "No, leave it to me," she said, and, bringing her sewing basket, knelt by the tree on the grass and covered the injury with pitch. She sewed a firm canvas band tight around the damaged trunk.

That white pine is seventy-five feet tall today! Twice, the lightning struck it, but it is still a noble specimen of its fast disappearing tribe.

Occasional Lombardies, of which she was fond, stand isolated in clumps where once their ranks along the lanes up the hillsides were unbroken.

Her balm-of-Gilead has scattered around the Valley to meet you in unexpected places.

Lilacs and the bouncing-Betty of her dooryard have colonized on their own along the roadsides in great masses good to see.

Willing worker in this intensive human-hive of work, song and prayer in rural Wisconsin was the Sister Anna. Her son, the grandson who doubted Isaiah, it was who went in quest of weeds while his Uncle John preached a sermon to the lad with his feet, in the snow.

Sister Anna herself, fourth child of Richard Lloyd-Jones and Mary Lloyd, his wife, was five years old when the immigration from Wales took place. She walked with a free stride like a man, had much dark brown hair above a good, brave brow; a fine nose and dark, dreaming brown eyes. Much fire and energy gave her temper beneath a self-possession calm and gracious.

Education was Sister Anna's passion even while very young. All this family was imbued with the idea of education as salvation. Education it was that made man out of the brute and saved him from the beast. Education it was too (and that was her mistake) that unlocked the stores of Beauty to let it come crowding in on every side at every gate. Although she believed Education the direct manifestation of God to reach it, Sister Anna loved—Beauty. Soon she became a teacher in the countryside, riding a horse over the hills and through the woods to and from her school each day. Old men in the neighborhood still speak of Sister Anna as their teacher, with admiration and respect.

THE MOTHER

Her school lay sometimes in one direction and sometimes in another, but always miles away. When her horse was needed in the fields she walked, but usually she rode, coming from the still shadows of the wood to the far prospect from the hilltops or overlooking the warm yellow-green sunshine on the meadow-stretches. All blazed with bewildering color in autumn, and was more beautiful than ever when asleep under wintry coverlets of snow, the shapes of the hills then like huge primeval monsters lying peacefully beneath them. Often she made those journeys after dark alone. Farmsteads were few and miles between.

Often too it rained. She had to go just the same, covered with a blue soldier's cape that had brass buttons and a hood. Bareheaded, otherwise, she went. She knew the ferns, the flowers, by name, the startled animals that ran along the road. There were berries by the roadside too, wild cherries, plums, and grapes. She might reach out and take them on the branches, hanging the branches to the saddle bow, eating from them as she rode.

How it happened that Sister Anna's ideals then are modern now, who can say. Unless first-hand contact with nature in the primitive struggle, and the rugged faith of the father ("at destruction and famine thou shalt laugh, neither shalt thou be afraid of the beasts of the earth for thou shalt be in league with the stones of the field") gave it to her. This "league with the stones of the field" must have imparted power to her imaginative vision.

The boy of this story was her first child, Frank.

Sister Anna came by him as the law prescribed. She married a man who satisfied her ideal of "Education." A man from Hartford, Connecticut. A circuit rider. A musician now going about the countryside near Lone Rock, Wisconsin, teaching folk to sing.

She was twenty-nine when she married him. Seventeen years her senior, the music-master was a product of education, one of a family of intellectuals to which James Russell Lowell belonged, and Alice and Phoebe Cary, from which distant branches he got his middle names.

He was William Russell Cary Wright, tirelessly educating himself, first at Amherst, then to practice medicine, soon found by him to be no genuine science. Then the law, but again—disillusion. He was just about to hear the "call" his preacher ancestors back to the days of the Reformation in England had all been hearing. And Sister Anna was the one to help him hear it. Soon after they were married he too became a preacher. He had his music still, which always consoled him, and music was his friend to the last when all else had failed.

After their son was born something happened between the mother and father. Sister Anna's extraordinary devotion to the child disconcerted the father. He never made much of the child, it seems. No doubt his wife loved him no less but now loved something more, something created out of her own fervor of love and desire. A means to realize her vision.

The boy, she said, was to build beautiful buildings. Faith in prenatal influences was strong in this expectant mother. She kept her thoughts on the high things for which she yearned and looked carefully after her health. There was never a doubt in the expectant mother's mind but that she was to have a boy.

Fascinated by buildings, she took ten full-page wood-engravings of the old English Cathedrals from "Old England," a pictorial periodical to which the father had subscribed, had them framed simply in flat oak and hung them upon the walls of the room that was to be her son's.

Before he was born, she said she intended him to be an Architect.

In due course of nature, in a little inland town among the hills, Richland Center, Wisconsin, the father preaching and sometimes lawing, still teaching music, her son was born.

That meant invocation ceased and "Education" took hold.

When the boy was three with a baby sister a year old, the father was called to a Church at Weymouth near Boston.

About this time the father's father died at his home in Hartford, Connecticut, aged ninety and nine. He went upstairs to his room, wrote by candlelight a letter to each of his three sons, addressed each in his own handwriting, went to bed and, like the mother's father, painlessly slept to final sleep.

Leaving the Lloyd-Joneses prospering in their Valley, our little family went east, nearer to Hartford, Connecticut, the father's native place. Went on to activities still religious but to different scenes, a different atmosphere—that of a Boston suburb.

A modest, gray, wooden house near a tall white-brick church in drab old historic Weymouth.

The tall, handsome mother in that house with her boy and the little girl Jane, named after the mother's sister back there in the Valley. A donation party of the previous evening had left twenty-three pumpkin pies on the pantry shelves where there was nothing much else to eat after the party had gone away. No wonder if the mother longed for the Valley for which she seemed always to pine.

BACH

At this time a nervously active intellectual man in clerical dress seated at the organ in the church, playing. Usually he was playing. He was playing Bach now. Behind the organ, a dark chamber. In the dark chamber, huge bellows with projecting wooden lever-handle. A tiny shaded oil lamp shining in the dark on a lead marker that ran up and down to indicate the amount of air pressure necessary to keep the organ playing. A small boy of seven, eyes on the lighted marker, pumping away with all his strength at the lever and crying bitterly as he did so.

Streams of sound went pouring out into the Church against the stained-glass windows *fortissimo*. The boy worked away for dear life to keep air in the bellows, knowing only too well what would happen to him should he give out. Then came a long-drawn-out, softer passage. It was easier to pump—the Vox Humana—faraway beauty, tenderness and promise in it stealing over boy-senses. He stopped, tears and all, entranced. Listening—breathless—he forgot, but suddenly remembered just in time to work away again with all his might to keep air enough for the Bach as it broke into the sound-waves of triumphant, march-like progress. The heroic measures brought him back again to strength and for a while he pumped away with fresh energy, hopefully. But as on and on the wondrous music went, more and more the young back and arms ached until again the tears began to flow. Would father never stop? He felt forgotten, and he was. Could he hold out? Pulling all his energies together now, despair gaining on him, eye on that leaden marker. Should it ever drop? But it will . . . it will . . . for he can't . . . No . . .

Just then the music abruptly ended. The stops knocked back into their sockets. The cover of the keyboard slammed down. His father called him. "Frank! . . . Frank!" There was no answer.

The figure of the father darkened the small doorway, took in the situation at a glance, took the boy by the hand and led him home without a word.

When they got there his mother, seeing the state the boy was in, looked reproachfully at the father.

It was always so. The differences between husband and wife all seemed to arise over that boy. Mother always on the defensive, father taking the offensive.

So the lad grew, afraid of his father.

His father taught him music. His knuckles were rapped by the lead pencil in the impatient hand that would sometimes force the boy's hand into position at practice time on the Steinway Square piano in the sitting room. And yet he felt proud of his father. Everybody listened and seemed happy when father talked. And Sundays when he preached the small son dressed in his home-made Sunday best looked up at him absorbed in something of his own making that would have surprised the father and the mother more if they could have known.

His pupil always remembered father as he was when "composing," ink on his fingers and face. For he always held the pen crosswise in his mouth while he would go to and from the desk to the keyboard trying over the passage he had written. His face would soon become fearful with black smudges. To his observant understudy at those times he was weird.

Was music made in such heat and haste as this, the boy wondered? How did Beethoven make his? And how did Bach make his?

He thought Beethoven must have made most of his when it was raining, or just going to, or when the days were gloomy and the sun was soft with clouds. He was sure Bach made his when the sun shone bright and breezes were blowing as little children were happily playing in the street.

Father sometimes played on the piano far into the night, and much of Beethoven and Bach the boy learned by heart as he lay listening. Living seemed a kind of listening to him—then.

Sometimes it was as though a door would open, and he could get the beautiful meaning clear. Then it would close and the meaning would be dim or far away. But always there was some meaning. Father taught him to see a symphony as an edifice—of sound!

At the Centennial in Philadelphia, after a sightseeing day, Mother made a discovery. She was eager about it now. Could hardly wait to go to Boston as soon as she got home—to Milton Bradley's.

The Kindergarten!

She had seen the "Gifts" in the Exposition Building. The strips of colored paper, glazed and "matt," remarkably soft brilliant colors. Now came the geometric by-play of those charming checkered color combinations! The structural figures to be made with peas and small straight sticks: slender constructions, the joinings accepted by the little green-pea globes. The smooth shapely maple blocks with which to build, the sense of which never afterward leaves the fingers: *form* becoming *feeling*. The box had a mast to set up on it, on which to hang the maple cubes and spheres and triangles, revolving them to discover subordinate forms.

And the exciting cardboard shapes with pure scarlet face—such scarlet! Smooth triangular shapes, white-back and edges, cut into rhomboids with which to make designs on the flat table top. What shapes they made naturally if only one would let them!

GIFTS

A small interior world of color and form now came within grasp of small fingers. Color and pattern, in the flat, in the round. Shapes that lay hidden behind the appearances all about.

Here was something for invention to seize, and use to create. These "Gifts" came into the gray house in drab old Weymouth and made something live there that had never lived there before. Mother would go to Boston, take lessons of a teacher of the Froebel method and come home to teach the children. When her housework was done mother and the two children would sit at a low mahogany table with polished top, working with these "Gifts."

Fra Angelico's bright-robed angels, some in red, some in blue, others in green, and one—the loveliest of all—in yellow, would come and hover over the table. From their golden harps simple rhythms were gently falling on child minds like flying seeds carried on the wings of the wind to fertile ground. Giotto standing in the shadow at the mother's elbow would have worn a smile beneath his Florentine cap; musing smile prophetic of seedtime and harvest other than his but eternally the same. Again—architecture.

His mother's son has been in Miss Williams's private school for some years, no doubt with the usual Snobbyists and Goodyites. For several years, the minister's son was kept in this fashionable school with the few little Lord Fauntleroys Weymouth afforded.

Let the delicate psychology of biological unfoldings in boys under eleven, important, but so much the same, stand as on record by able artists with a taste for psychological anatomy. In public schools the susceptible little animals encounter and learn things that mothers promptly try to make their boys unlearn and protect them from. So well was this done with him that until marriage in his twenty-first year, personal biological experience was exactly nothing at all, left probably too innocent for his own self-guidance.

34

But nothing much of this period remains very clear to a boy who dreamed as this lad did. His imagination made a world for himself as he would have it, except where rudely intruded upon by forces that would and could have it otherwise. Music he adored . . . and the Gifts. Meantime he was learning to play the piano. Going to his mother's kindergarten. Learning to paint and draw a little. Learning to sing a little. Reading much all the while.

Boylike, he discounted his sister. So he played alone usually. There would be an occasional excursion to Nantucket—or a clam-bake at Narragansett. What he was taught in school made not the slightest impression that can be remembered as of any consequence.

For many of the early years of his life when the minister's son was told by his mother that he must not eat a certain thing, "for it would make him sick," he would always say, "Well! Let's see if it will then!"

For the first twelve years of life he got a ginger-cookie now and then, gingerbread with a glass of milk, molasses candy, popcorn aplenty, but "store candies" only when mother didn't know it. No pie. No cake—except at other houses as he grew older. Sometimes, driven to it in the bitterness of thwarted desire, he would hurl this withering sarcasm at his defenseless mother, "Huh! bringing up your children on graham bread, porridge and religion, are you?"

Probably confirmed by the influence of the father's unhappy essay in medicine, this mother distrusted doses and doctors. Her idea of food was that everything in cooking should be left as simple as possible, natural flavor heightened but never disguised. Her brown bread, stews, baked dishes, roasted meats were delicious without sauces. The frying pan had no place in her sense of things. "Eat the skins of your baked potatoes," she would say. If potatoes were boiled, it would be with jackets on, to enhance the potato-flavor. And she would slice apples for pie or sauce without peeling a certain number of them. She believed the life-giving part of grains or fruit or vegetables was in the color the sun put in them. That was concentrated in the skins. The apple barrel from the Valley was open between meals or just before bedtime.

If mother picked flowers, she would take the stems long, or the branches, and would arrange them not, as was the mode, in variegated bunches, but freely and separately—never too many together. And she always loved best a glass vase for them showing the stems in water.

In the matter of clothes, she cared little for bright colors. She liked black or white or gray or purple with cream-colored or black lace at hands and throat. Long, flowing lines. She never believed in corsets. Never wore them. She used to say that a beautiful head of hair was Nature's most precious gift to mortals, and seldom wore more than a scarf on her own head unless she were on duty in her place as Minister's wife.

When she read to her children, as she was fond of doing, it was from Whittier, Lowell or Longfellow, or fairy tales. Usually poetry.

The most lovely thing in the world, she said, was a mother nursing her baby.

Though living in this atmosphere of emphasis on the natural, physically well made and strong, knowing little fear except shyness where his feelings were concerned, her son was too much in the imaginative life of the mind. He preferred reading to playing with other boys—and no wonder! He would rather listen to music than eat his food. He liked to read, listen to music, draw and "make things," rather than sleep. Above all he liked to dream by himself. And this dreaming he did, with mother's encouragement, regardless of the taunt, "graham bread, porridge and religion."

The mother saw which way her man-child was going. She was wise and decided to change it. Change it she did.

TRUTH AGAINST THE WORLD /I\

That Eastern pastorate was wearing out by now. The father had been a Baptist in that land consecrated to Unitarianism. But Unitarianism in the air and the mother's Unitarianism of a more colorful kind at home must have had its effect, for the preacher resigned—a Unitarian.

To the mother, accustomed to the free stride of her life in the country, the meticulous righteousness of the world now her world, the punctilio of her position, the hard-shell "Godliness" of the provincial Baptist, and the consequent consecration of meanness, probably made every "donation party" an argument for going back home—"out West."

The minister's pay was a pittance, of course, in keeping with the parsimony and poverty of the ideals of life—intolerance and infallibility—it paid for.

The Unitarianism of the Lloyd-Joneses, a far richer thing, was an attempt to amplify, in the confusion of the creeds of their day, the idea of life as a gift from the Divine Source, one GOD omnipotent, all things at one with HIM.

UNITY was their watchword, the sign and symbol that thrilled them, the UNITY of all things! This mother sought it continually. Good and evil existed for her people still, however, and for her. The old names still confused their faith and defeated them when they came to apply it. But the salt and savor of faith they had, the essential thing, and there was a warmth in them for truth, cut where truth might! And cut, it did—this

"truth against the world." Enough trouble in that for any one family—
the beauty of TRUTH! The family did not so well know the truth of
BEAUTY. These valley-folk feared beauty, seeing in it a probable snare for
unwary feet, and making the straight way their own feet might mark in
the snow less admirable in their own sight and as an example for irresponsible youth.

Now came back to the ancestral Valley from the East, by way of
Sister Anna and her "preacher," the "Unitarianism" worked out in the
transcendentalism of the sentimental group at Concord: Whittier, Lowell, Longfellow, yes, and Emerson, too. Thoreau? Well, Thoreau seemed
to them too smart. He made them uncomfortable.

This poetic transcendentalism was to unite with their own richer,
sterner sentimentality, with results that will be seen.

The luxury of the Lloyd-Joneses was not laughter, but tears.

Until you had water in the eyes of them you really hadn't got them.

Quick in emotional response to human need, sorrow or suffering,
good deeds thrilled them always.

The little preacher-family in Weymouth was desperately poor in
this scrabby, stony vineyard of the Lord. And but for the children of the
mother and the music of the father, body and soul by this time would
have been far apart. Maginel, a frail little thing, was born in this lean
period. She was, for months, handled carefully on a pillow. Her mother,
alone, saving her by giving her own vital energy, manipulating and
exercising her for hours.

She came to be added to the responsibilities of the preacher.

Salvage for the Mother? Private schooling for her boy, the Gifts, the
household, and the transcendentalism of Concord that was reaching
back to the Valley in letters she wrote and books she sent, the books of
Channing, Emerson, Theodore Parker, and, yes, Thoreau.

Salvage for the Father? A strange Italian, looking like Paganini
came to play. Remenyi, grotesque nose and eyes came, too. Later in the
West, to the house at Madison, came the handsome Ole Bull. And, always, there was the church organ in the quiet, deserted church.

So the preacher-father and teacher-mother came back West, forty
miles from the Valley, to a modest house on the shore of Lake Mendota,
in Madison. Now education of the male child was to begin in earnest.

But this child was to be saved not by, but from, the "word-of-God"
as it was thought to be something written in mighty books or spoken by
learned men from platform or pulpit. He was to learn the living, breathing thing it is: "The flower that fadeth, the grass that withereth."

ADDING TIRED TO TIRED

A letter to Sister Anna's beloved brother James brought him from the home Valley to the modest Madison town-house by the blue lake.

He drove down the entire forty miles leading a cow tied behind his wagon so that Anna's children might have good fresh milk. There stood Uncle James, tall, strong and brown, with a great shock of waving brown hair on his handsome head, thick brown beard on his face. When he smiled his eyes went nearly shut and witty wrinkles came to their corners. His nephew trusted him at first glance.

The golden curls had been cut off. The mother wept as she cut them. Curls there still were, but shorter and their glory gone. This "going to work" of her boy costing mother something more than the shedding of the curls. It could be seen now.

Uncle James put his arm around his sister to comfort her. She whispered something to him the boy did not hear. He patted her shoulder and laughed a reassuring laugh. How he always laughed! So clear! Ringing out, it always made you want to laugh too. He promised her something as he took the boy by the hand. "Ready now, Frank? We're going west. Going to make a farmer of you, my boy." Mother gathered the child in her arms and wept.

And so the boy went. He went away from mother, books, music and city boys and father and little Maginel and Jane, idle dreams and city streets to learn to add "tired" to "tired" and add it again—and add it yet again. Then beginning all over again at the beginning, he learned to add it all up some more until it seemed to him he would surely break or drop.

A low attic bedroom lit by a single window in one of the white-washed sloping walls, heated by a stovepipe running up through the floor and ceiling above from the room below.

Sharp rapping now on the stovepipe—loud. Again, sharper, louder. The boy rubbed his eyes, shocked by the banging outrage.

A voice below, "Four o'clock, my boy, time to get up."

How could it be? He had just gone to bed! But he remembered soon and sleepily called, "All right, Uncle James—coming!"

He looked down at the things Uncle James had put there by the bed the night before, got up and put them on. It was early spring and he shivered. Two pieces, a "hickory" shirt, blue-jean overalls with blue cotton suspenders. Coarse blue cotton socks and clumsy cowhide shoes, with leather laces. These last were worst. And there was a hat. That hat!

Forthwith, hating hat and shoes he learned to do without both.

Uncle James was waiting for him at the foot of the stairs with that life-giving voice of his and winning smile. After splashing water on his face from the basin on the bench—you got it by dropping into the cistern a bucket tied to a rope—he was ready. His Uncle took him off to the barn. The strange smells sickened him but he dutifully began milking as shown, until his hands ached.

That very morning he learned to look out for certain cows who, feeling you come in beside them, would lean over and crush the breath out of you against the wall of the stall. Beating them over the back with the milking stool only made them push harder.

Milking done, came breakfast. Potatoes, fried. Fried cornmeal mush, fried pork, green cheese and cornbread. Pancakes and sorghum. Buttermilk, glass of fresh milk. Coffee or tea, but not for the boy.

No cream.

When Gottlieb Munch (for Mensch), red-faced, yellow-haired hired man, would pour sorghum over his big piece of fat pork, he would take the boy's appetite away.

After breakfast, helping Uncle James's wife, Aunt Laura, to feed the calves. Teaching the darned, crowding, pushing, bunting things to suck the milk by holding the fingers in the pail for them to suck. A nasty business. And often a desperate calf would give the bucket a bunt and send milk flying all over him from head to foot until exasperated by the senseless bunting and pushing he would lay about him with the pail to keep from being trampled down.

Aunt Laura would laugh then.

After this, carrying sticks of cord-wood to the cross-cut saw, pausing to run errands, maybe, if your Uncle saw you were getting the worst of it, and told you to go. Then dinner. Boiled fresh beef, boiled potatoes, boiled carrots, boiled turnips, home-made bread and butter. Jam, pickles, prunes, sorghum, honey and green cheese, or pie or cake. Tea or coffee, but not for the boy.

No cream.

Afternoon—holding the split oak-rails while Uncle James nailed them to the fence-posts, hands full of slivers, going off to get the cows for the first time, at five. Home to supper at six. Fried potatoes, as regularly as the sun set. Home-made bread and butter. Cornbread, cornmeal mush and milk, honey and home-made preserves. Fried salt-pork or smoked beef, "creamed," they said. Milk.

No cream!

After supper, milking again.

In bed about half-past seven, too tired to move.

Again outrageous banging on the stovepipe, almost before he had really fallen asleep.

It had begun—this business of adding "tired" to "tired," and adding it again—and adding it again.

And so, as it was that day with the eleven-year-old it was next day and the day after and the day after that until the clothes he drew on in the morning to the violence of that rapping on the stovepipe were sweat-stiffened. They went on stiff and stayed stiff until he limbered them up by working in them.

On Saturday night he got a bath by carrying soft water from the cistern, heating some of it on the stove. He threw the stark things aside for his city clothes on Sunday morning. And already in April, for the first years, he would begin to look forward to September seventeenth when school would begin for him. Longing for the time to come. How sore! If mother only knew.

She came before long. Seeing him, she clasped him to her bosom and burst into tears. The boy wondered why she was so sad to see him.

Then after she went away work went on some four or five weeks and he began to wear down. His back ached so. His fingers were stiff and sore. Knees and elbows; feet, too. He was ashamed to let it be known—but one afternoon, he decided to change it himself. Having a difficulty with Aunt Laura over the free use of a hammer he seldom put back in its place, he got it, threw it in the creek for good and all, and departed. He took a kitchen-knife with him, intending to get home somehow, anyhow.

He started across the hill toward the river to find the ferryboat that would take him to Spring Green. He was footsore. Crestfallen, his legs stiff. Guilty, his back lame. Ashamed of running away, his hands bleeding in places.

Uncle James knowing what was good for the boy had given it to him until, well—here he was, running away: home or somewhere—what did he care where, if he couldn't go where he could find comfort?

Yet, his nephew adored Uncle James. Uncle James could do everything, and so well that the others liked to stop and watch him do it. Break colts to harness for the neighbors. Handle a kicking cow that Gottlieb, the hired man, would be afraid to touch. Swing an ax with such ringing accuracy that the clean-cut chips whizzed furiously around your head as you tried to dodge them. Could run all the machines. Always knew how to fix what was the matter with them—and there was always something the matter with them. Was always laughing at the same time and never afraid of anything. As the boy thought of him now he wanted to turn back and "stick." But he was too sore in body and mind. So he limped along. The home by the blue lake and mother seemed very dear and all he wanted, but—how far away!

As the road ran over the hilltop above Uncle Enos's, soft, white sandrock cropped out in long, thin ledges beside it. Fascinated by whatever there is in sand that bewitches boys, he scraped away at it with his knife and took the soft piles of pure white in both his hands. To the right were pink ledges. He scraped those. To the left, yellow and he scraped those. Put a layer of yellow over a layer of white, then pink and then white, and, even in his misery, it occurred to him to cut through the pile with his knife and take one half away and look at the color streaks in the section he thus made.

This diversion ruined his enterprise though he did not know it. His anguish grew less and he thought about going back before Uncle James came home and found him gone. But he had started something now, on his own. So he went on to the ferry.

He was sitting on the barge-board of the old ferryboat, legs over the side in the flowing water, waiting for a start. He sat there for some time, watching the eddies marking the sand along the shore. Then, feeling something, he looked up and saw Uncle Enos!

He liked Uncle Enos, Mother's youngest brother.

Uncle Enos was fond of him. They had wrestled and played together often.

Word had gone out from Uncle James to look for the boy. It would soon be getting dark. Uncle Enos's instinct had been the right one. In a kindly tone he asked, "Where are you going, Frank?"

No answer.

Tears . . .

Uncle Enos took the boy by the hand and led him to the grass on the bank overlooking the river. The boy cried it out, telling his woes and his resentment.

"Yes, yes. I know, my boy. Work the soreness out by keeping right on working! You will grow stronger by keeping at it, no matter how it hurts. Soon you'll be so strong you'll like it and can do things like Uncle James. The only way to do. Just keep on when you are sore and tired and stiff and think you're discouraged. But you never *are* discouraged. No . . . And by keeping on, still more, and again more, you'll see you can do most anything and never feel it too much." He gripped the biceps in the soft arm. "As much muscle as a blackbird's got in his legs," he said. Then stretching out his own arm, "Feel this,"—and the boy felt his Uncle's iron upper-arm with admiration. "Your muscles will be like that, Frank, if you keep on at it. Then you can laugh, too, like Uncle James, and never be afraid of anything. Work is an adventure that makes strong men and finishes weak ones."

"Aunt Laura? . . . Well, Aunt Laura is a bit hasty. Not very well just now. Something is going to happen. You needn't mind her too much.

Think of your mother and Uncle James. How disappointed they both would be if you went on with this. Shall we go back now?"

"Yes!"

Under cover of darkness, hand in hand, they made their way back. The boy went ruefully up to his bed in the attic.

Next morning—as though nothing at all had happened—the rapping on the stove-pipe, perhaps not so loud, but relentless just the same and it began all over again.

Something Uncle Enos had said stuck in his mind. "Adventures make strong men but finish weak ones."

But Uncle Enos had said "work" was that adventure. The connection of adventure with "work" got lost in the impressionable mind for the time being. But later he was to find it.

The rebel ran away again before long. Got farther this time. Brought back by Uncle James himself. Unregenerate, he slipped to hiding in the strawstack as soon as they got inside the farmyard gate. All night, not answering by any sign, he lay there hidden in the straw, listening to the anxiety and confusion in the dark, as one or the other of the household would call him from different directions, near or far away.

Thus, the truant boy took his revenge for the hurts that were his—by hurting them. A reprobate element of character, of course, this "eye for an eye, and tooth for a tooth." Worthy of Isaiah. This ulcerous Mosaic-root of human misery had shown itself in him before.

He fell asleep.

Fearing some evil had befallen him, so glad were they to find him in the morning that his punishment was in Uncle James's hand, and light. Aunt Laura stood aside for the time being.

That was the last of running away.

What Uncle Enos had said, and Uncle James had said too, began to come true. Work *was* adventure, when you were fit for it. And there was a small boy's mind fixed upon that spring-water stream flowing over the soft mud-bottom as it passed below the house. And whenever he could get into that stream, his was "recreation" in building dams of sticks and stones across it, sailing his shoes along the banks, wading and playing in it tirelessly whether he might or might not. Fascination for a child . . . running water!

Whenever it rained, running out into the rain for a shower bath, naked, was irresistible. Mother had started it when he was several years old by taking off his clothes and setting him running out of doors in thunderstorms.

"Uncle James!"

How many million times his earnest young disciple's voice had called that name from first to last. The young novice's questions were so incessant, Uncle James finally hesitated to take him to town as he usually did, the small legs dangling from the spring seat of the lumber wagon, just because he wanted a little peace!

The restless, inquisitive one, further, was a simpleton looking for a little, white bird which no one could make him believe he would not see. He had seen many red ones: scarlet tanagers, yellow thistle-birds and orioles. He had seen black and black-and-red ones and many colors mixed. Brown ones. But none all white. No, never one. Why was there no white bird? Uncle James would assure him that there were none in that region except doves and hens. But they wouldn't do. Much to his Uncle's annoyance he believed a white one existed. He continued to look for it just the same. But he never saw one and has never seen one yet.

The boy dreamed now, again. Sitting a long time, never moving, a look on his face that Uncle James came to recognize and he would call him, "Frank! Frank! Come back! Come back, Frank!" But the open sky was overhead, the woods surrounded the fields in which work was forever going on in a routine that was endless. Endless, the care of the animals, horses, cows, pigs, sheep.

His early lot was cast with the cows.

TO HER!

Cow! What a word! And, cow-bell! The cows! My boy. The cows! Always—"the cows!"

The Valley cows were red—Durhams—until Uncle James later got a black-and-white Holstein bull, envy of all the township. And so the herd, from year to year, grew to black and white. In three years the cattle in the Valley all changed from red to black and white.

Why is any cow, red, black or white, always in just the right place for a picture in any landscape? Like a cypress tree in Italy, she is never wrongly placed. Her outlines quiet down so well into whatever contours surround her. A group of her in the landscape is enchantment.

Has anyone sung the song of the patient, calf-bearing, milk-flowing, cud-chewing, tail-switching cow? Slow-moving, with the fragrant breath and beautiful eyes, the well-behaved, necessary cow, who always seems to occupy the choicest ground anywhere around?

She is the dairy farm, the wealth of states, the health of nations.

How many trusties and lusties besides her lawful calf have pulled away at her teats these thousands of years until the stream flowing from them would float fleets of battleships, drown all the armies the world has ever seen.

How the cow has multiplied the man!

And yet, so battened upon, she is calm, faithful, fruitful.

As companion, she endures all—contented, even indifferent.

But the Minnesingers down the ages have given small place to the cow in poetry or song.

She is just a Cow.

Yet, to go through the herd lying on the grass as the dew falls, all quietly chewing their cud in peace together, is to find a sweetness of the breath as it rises, a freshness of Earth itself that revives something essential to life lying deep in the instincts of the human race.

Is the cow now mother to the man to such an extent that his "instinct" begins to be aware of her in this exhalation from her nostrils?

And the dung that goes from her to the fields by way of sweating youths and men saturated, struggling in the heavy odor and texture of her leavings! This indispensable wealth that goes to bring back the jaded soil to a greenness of the hills, bring fertility to life itself—for man!

Yes, where her tribe flourishes there the earth is green, the fields fertile. Man in well-being and abundance.

She is Hosanna to the Lord! For where she is, "at destruction and famine man laughs," as he salts her, fodders her, beds her, breeds her and milks her. Thus tended she contentedly eats her way from calfhood clear through to the digestive tract of humanity—her destiny. Her humble last farewell to man—the shoes upon his feet!

"Come, my boy, the cows," or that dread cry like an alarm of fire: "The cows are in the corn!"

His special duty was getting the cows back home and taking them out to grass again. There were no fences about the woods in those days. Few roads, even, and no cow-paths except near the farmsteads, so that each time he went out to find them and bring them in was an adventure. The plaintive tinkle of that faraway cow-bell!

How many small boys in the homes of the brave on these grounds-of-the-free were, or for that matter at any moment since are, listening to the measured tinkle of that faraway bell—anxiously hearkening, stopping to listen, hearing it again. This time—yes—nearer! By losing it altogether and starting to listen all over again.

The tinkle of the cow-bell has steadily called the boys of Usonia. And, in some form, will call them always.

Usonia—Samuel Butler's appropriate name for the United States of America, roots in the word "union." If the United States is "America,"

44

then Georgia is South America and New York is North America, the Canadians are Americans, the Mexicans too. South America too is jealous of the term "America."

Now he went through the moist woods that in their shade were treasuring the rainfall for the sloping fields below or to feed the clear springs in the ravines, wending his way along the ridges of the hills gay with Indian-pinks or shooting-stars, across wide meadows carpeted thick with tall grass on which the flowers seemed to float. The field-lilies stood there above the grass like stars of flame. Wading the creeks, sometimes lost in the deep shade and deeper shadows of white-oak woods, he would go to find and bring home the cows.

He had to start early in order to get them home before dark, but sometimes it would be after dark before he brought them back. Sometimes he found them not at all and Uncle James would have to get on a horse and go after them.

It was his duty to help milk while the herd was standing in the yard if very warm, or at the stanchions in the cow-stable roofed with straw, if cooler. At this milking, each milker would sit balanced on a one-legged stool, bare head against the warm flank of the cow, drawing away at the teats with a slow rhythmical squeezing pull of the hands to the music that was the sound of milk-streams striking into the foaming milk in the pail. Occasionally a gushing stream of warm milk caught in the mouth, a trick learned from Gottlieb.

Everyone had to milk, even Aunt Laura, who wasn't very well.

The cows all had names—like Spot, who broke into the granary, ate her fill of ground feed, drank all the water she could, and died—a glorious heroine's death in her tribe, no doubt.

The death of Spot was a blow to him for she was a kindly old cow with a long tail. It was a help. There were other tails to hang to and they served, but none so willing for the pupose as Spot's.

In these adventures alone—abroad in the wooded hills to fetch the cows, he, barefoot, bareheaded urchin, was insatiable, curious and venturesome. So he learned to know the woods, from the trees above to the shrubs below and the grass beneath. And the millions of curious lives living hidden in the surface of the ground, among roots, stems, and mold. Soon he was happy in such knowledge. A listening ear, seeing eye and sensitive touch had been naturally given to him, his spirit was now becoming familiar with this marvelous book-of-books, Nature-Experience, the only true reading. The book of Creation.

One eleven-year-old was turning to inner *experience* for what he heard, touched or saw.

Sunrise to sunset there can be nothing so surpassingly beautiful in any cultivated garden as these wild Wisconsin pastures.

Night shadows so wonderfully blue, like blue shadows on snow.

Pendent blooms of the chokecherry to become black clusters of berries that puckered your throat.

Solid depths of shade, springs—a glittering transparency in the cool shadows.

Sunlight, aslant through the leaves on the tree trunks, plashing with gold the leaf-covered ground beneath.

White birches gleaming in cool shade.

Wild grape festooning trees and fences.

Sumach, braided foliage and dark red berry-cone clusters.

Fragrant herbs, and dripping leaves in soft rain.

Milkweed blossoming in the fields, to scatter snowy fleece on every breeze.

Sorrel reddening on the hills, far and wide.

The world of daylight gold would go through violet passing to the deep blue of the night.

He would dawn now as the day, and studious experiences began in the swarming insect life, in the warm living breath of fern beds. In the marvel of mosses. In leaf-mold.

In the damp grasses under bare feet.

In the strange life going on in them.

There was the feel of mud between the toes and burning sand under the feet, the cool, fresh grass on the open slopes.

He knew where the lady-slippers grew and why, where to find yellow ones and where those rare ones, white and purple, were hidden.

He could lead you surely to where Jack-in-the-pulpit stood in the deep shade of the wood; to wild strawberries in the sunny clearings of the hills, to watercress in the cool streams flowing from hillside springs.

Always he was the one who knew where the tall, red lilies could be found afloat on tall meadow-grass. Where nuts and berries abounded, there he would be.

The spot of red made by a lily on the green always gave him an emotion. Later, the red square as spot of flame-red, became the crest with which he signed his drawings and marked his buildings.

Soon the young ear could tell what flew overhead. What sang and where and why. He studied, by the hour, the tumblebugs, black-beetles: scarabs, rolling their marbles of cow manure in the host sun of the dusty road. Mysterious folk!

The ant-hills were busy cities. Catkins cutting circles making patterns on still water. He would go catching sleek frogs, or poking stupid toads, chasing crazy grasshoppers. Listening at night to the high treble of the frog-song as it rose from the marshes. He delighted in devil's darning needles, turtles, too: their fascinating structure, color pattern, strange movements—ever curious about them all. He was studying un-consciously what later he would have called "style."

And there were enemies: skunks, snakes, and hornets.

There were always too many toes to stub. Mosquitoes. Flies. Cut-grass, nettles. Poison ivy. What that poison ivy could do to young blood and tender skin! Quicksand in the streams. And hornets' nests in the barn-rafters, their wonderful house-nests sometimes hanging from the bushes. The lightning: always the lightning.

Cruel winds that seemed to be the enemy of every growing thing swept the valley sometimes. But he learned their value later.

"Wild Rose!" A legendary woman, gone wild, living in a hut in the hills and wandering about. He had not seen her. All seemed afraid of her, and liked to frighten him.

Such, teeming in the sun, quiet under clouds, drenched with rain, were the then-time pastures of the cow.

The trees stood in it all like various, beautiful buildings, of more different kinds than all the architectures of the world. Some day this boy was to learn that the secret of all styles in architecture was the same secret that gave *character* to the trees.

Work was hard, sometimes interfering with dreaming studies or studious dreams. At other times, dreams went undisturbed beneath or above the routine. These dreaming moments must have had charac-teristic expression in him for he would again and again, as before, hear Uncles James calling, "Come back, Frank! Come back!"

SUNDAY

Sundays were salvation for the "tired to tired" added during the week.

Uncles and aunts, some of them graying, some white-haired now, would sit at chapel in the old-fashioned rocking chairs provided for them round the platform on which the pulpit stood. The pulpit on which the family Bible lay was covered with a purple cloth and, Sundays, was usually smothered in wild flowers, brought in from the roadsides by the children.

Of course, the "help" were included.

And sometimes the neighbors came.

When Uncle Jenkin preached there was genuine luxury. Tears. Going gently to and fro in the rocking chairs below the pulpit tears were shed and, unheeded, trickled down. His sermons always brought the family to emotional states—but then—so did readings from the tran-scendental classics or the singing of the children. Tears, too, when all rose in family strength and in the dignity of their faith strengthened themselves to sing—"step by step since time began we see the steady gain of man." The faltering, the falsetto and the flat would raise that favorite hymn to the boarded ceiling of the little chapel and go swelling out through the open windows and—to the young mind looking out toward them—reach far away to fade behind the hills. Surrender to religious emotion was fervent and sincere! There was heart in the favorite hymns for all, and for all . . .water in the eyes.

Uncle Thomas was poet of the group. He planted the fir grove beside the chapel so that the Joneses' Sunday picnics might have shade.

On the east side of the shingle-sided chapel, with its quaint belfry and opposite the evergreen fir grove, was the churchyard where simple white-marble obelisks did reverence to the memory of "EinTad" and "EinMam"—Welsh for father and mother.

Grouped around a tall slender obelisk were the family graves.

Every Sunday, spring and summer of these youthful years, up to September fifth, the boy would put on his city clothes and go to sit on a chair at these chapel gatherings.

It was his work to decorate the pulpit and the rostrum.

Early in the morning—while still cool—his cousins would go with him to get what flowers and branches he wanted. Tremendous riches were within easy reach along the roads as the team jogged along and stopped, jogged and stopped, and the wagon box was piled high with branches and flowers.

The result, broad masses of verdure and bloom freely arranged, mingled pretty much as they grew . . . only more so. Rostrum and pulpit, Sundays, were a gracious sight.

This little wooden chapel designed by Silsbee stands in fair repair in the Valley almost hidden by the sober, towering, green mass of Uncle Thomas's fir trees under which pine-board tables used to be bountifully spread for young and old of a united family. Uncles and aunts, ten. With husbands and wives, eighteen. Girls and boys all told, forty. An audience, with the neighbors and help, of about seventy-five. That is, unless something special was going on like Uncle Jenkin preaching, a wedding, funeral or camp meeting. Then the whole countryside would be there, lining the road for a half mile.

This family chapel was the simple, shingled wooden temple in which the Valley-clan worshipped images lovingly created. In turn the images reacted upon the family, still their own image. Those sunny simple religious meetings were, in reality, gatherings of the clan.

But in midsummer the meetings became an orgy of visiting divines and divinity from the cities. William C. Gannett, Henry M. Simmons, J. T. Sunderland and Dr. Thomas of Chicago were family favorites. From time to time many others. The visitors would come at preacher's vacation-time. Camp meetings, reunions, picnics and birthday celebrations would greet them from first to last.

Uncle Thomas with his gentle, rather downcast mien was always for picnics. "Come now, girls," he would say to his sisters, "let us go for a picnic. Do not bother at all, a little graham bread, a little cheese, a drink of milk. Let us all be together."

Preparations would begin. All the children, they had begun to swarm by now, would be called in to help. Soon the "graham bread, bit of cheese, drink of milk," would swell into roast pig, roast turkey. Maybe fresh corn-on-the-ear to be roasted. Roast chicken, delectably stuffed. Chicken, fried. Boiled ham, hard-boiled eggs. Sugared doughnuts. Turnovers. Cinnamon-covered Dutch rolls. White biscuits, brown bread and butter. Ripe tomatoes. And maybe fresh cucumbers, whole, to be peeled, eaten in the hand, like a banana but with salt. All kinds of sandwiches and pickles. Fat sugary green-apple pies and pumpkin pie. Green cheese and cream cheese. Sorghum and honey. Of course, home-made preserves of special kinds that ran the gamut from strawberry to watermelon rind. Interesting inventions in the way of pickles, all kinds of dark and light cookies, slabs of ginger-bread. Each household's favorite frosted, layer or plain cake. Plums or berries might be thereabouts for the picking. Coffee would be made on the fire. But milk, buttermilk and clabbered milk to drink would be set in the spring water. Abundance. Hardly anything left out that could, or ever had, gone into a Jones at one time or another and pleased or profited him.

Pharoah, no doubt, fared worse.

All this would go into baskets and each family go with its own basket and children into its family wagon. The first wagon ready would draw up and wait for the others. Dressed for the occasion they would, soon after waiting for all to get together, go off in a procession large enough to have been the funeral of some ancient prophet—even Moses himself.

But it was all just a Lloyd-Jones picnic.

Bright-colored cloths would be spread on green grass in some cool selected spot, probably in the shade of beautiful trees. If possible always near a spring or stream. All the preparations would be gorgeously spread out. Swings would be hung from the trees for the children. After the feast the children sing and speak "pieces." Father would play the violin and sing, leading the uncles and aunts in favorite hymns. Some of the older Lloyd-Joneses knew songs in Welsh: used to sing them in Wales. There would be *Esteddvod* then and there. The boy, "modern" note, would give "Darius Green and his Flying Machine" or the "Wonderful One Hoss Shay." All—grownups and children too—would have something or other to "speak" or sing. But the hymn-singing—in unison, of course—was the most satisfying feature of the day, unless it was Uncle Jenkin's preaching. All would join in, happy tears—under those circumstances—reaching their best.

At a distance you would hear the harmonicas and jew's-harps of the hired men, walking about with the hired girls. Preaching the psalm-singing hadn't the same delight for them as for the Lloyd-Joneses.

These sons and daughters of Richard Lloyd-Jones, Welsh Pioneer, now in his American Valley, had already gone far toward making the kind of life for themselves he would have approved. This united family had its own chapel, its gristmill (Uncle John's), and owned, cultivated or pastured pretty much all the land in sight in the Valley.

Lloyd-Jones family life was growing in human welfare and consequence.

This life of the Valley in spring and summer, and of Madison the city in fall and winter, was now established. It was to last five years more for the boy until he was passing sixteen. But the twelve-year-old comes home in September to the modest brown-wood house by the blue lake in Madison where were Mother, Father, Jennie and Maginel.

Madison is a beautifully situated city. From near or far away the white dome of the State Capitol on a low spreading hill shone white in the sun between two blue lakes, Mendota and Monona. Two more, smaller, not so blue, Wingra and Waubesa, were flung nearby on one side for good measure.

The State University stood domed on its own hill beside Lake Mendota; a collection of noncommittal, respectably nondescript buildings.

Its hill, too, was crowned by a dome—a brown and gold one.

Both domes were in debt for life to Michelangelo. But it was no unusual discredit. As anyone might see, they were doing the best they could to be domes. The young student saw both destroyed within a few years. The mortgage of time (not Michelangelo's) on human fallibility foreclosed.

The City was laid out as a sort of wheel with eight spokes radiating from the Capitol dome, one of the spokes hitting the campus below the University dome. The capital obstructing the center of communication.

Madison was a self-conscious town. A city, but provincial beyond most villages. The University gave it a high-brow air—the air, that is, of having been educated far beyond capacity.

There were a few good residences—good for their day. The Vilas home was the best of them. These better places bordered on the lakes.

As for the rest, it was Sun Prairie, Stoughton or any Wisconsin village of one to five thousand inhabitants on a somewhat larger scale only.

The intelligentsia, as was proper, ruled in Madison. The University, their badge of brief authority, shed a certain cloak of respectability upon the town.

There was influx and exodus of ambitious legislators from the various provinces of the State once a year, coming to immortalize their services by making laws and more "laws."

The Capitol then wrested the honors from the University.

At all times, there was a feeble "Town and Gown" rivalry. But it never became exciting enough to attract much notice.

The lakes Monona and Mendota it was that saved the city and its population from utter weariness by self-imposed importance in this provincial matter of intellectual-respectability.

ROBIE

One "William C. Wright," teacher, preacher and music-master, started a Conservatory of Music above some kind of store on Pinckney Street. The Madison ward schools were, at that time, good and at the Second Ward School—his ward—on the bank of the lake near the music-master's home—his son found Robie Lamp: red-headed Robie Lamp—"the cripple." Boyish enterprises grew out of the circumstance. More than ever shy, the boy had need of few friends but somehow always needed one intimate companion. He couldn't live, move enough and have his being, so it seemed, without a heart-to-heart comrade. No, not even at that early day in school.

Robie Lamp, fourteen years old, became his inseparable companion.

Robie's legs were shriveled, dangled dead as he moved along on crutches. He had a good large head well covered with coarse, bright-red hair. His face had the florid complexion and blue eyes of the Teuton. His arms and chest did the work of the legs that "went out on him"—to use Robie's Pa's phrase. So arms and chest were fine and strong although his hips were withered and twisted. The arms were much stronger because the legs were so helpless.

All there was of Robie was the splendid head, brawny shoulders, chest, arms and hands and—the Robie spirit.

"Lamp" was a good name for him, he was so effulgent. His well-earned nickname was "Ruby" but his eyes were turquoise ringed with white, clear and wide open.

Schoolboys teased the cripple—unmercifully.

Savagely, squat-on-the-ground, he would strike out at his persecutors with those powerful arms of his swinging the brass-shod crutches. His tormentors were careful to take his crutches away or keep out of reach but enough of them together could get him and in this autumn, at the moment when he comes in here, they were burying him in the fallen leaves until he was all but smothered, wherefrom he would emerge sputtering, raging, and crying.

Plucked up by his farm training of a season, the boy rescued him. Drove off the boys so cruelly picking on him; got the crutches they had wisely thrown far out of his reach; dusted him off; got him up on them and on his smile again. This was the first meeting with "Robie."

The boys were fast friends thereafter till Robie, forty-four, died in a little cream-white brick house with a roof-garden filled with flowers, designed for him by this rescuer of his.

At the boy's own home in Madison was the irascible, intellectual preacher father, with his piano and violin, now—and more frequently—writing and reading in his study. The household was peaceful at such times. Father was trying to make his Conservatory go and preaching occasionally. The modern refinement of the home grew under the yearning, ambitious mother's hands; the new-laid white, waxed maple floors; the cream-colored net curtains hanging straight beside the windows and partly over them; pictures (good engravings) hanging on the walls—framed in narrow maple-bands. The centers of the room floors were covered with India rugs—cream-colored ground with bright-colored patterns and border. Maple and rattan furniture. Everywhere, books. Simple vases were gracefully filled with dried leaves, and flowers in glass vases.

The "son-of-his-mother," as might be expected, had ideas about fixing things up. He was coming along by way of architecture, whether he knew it or not. Sometimes he did know it.

The flat, wooden door to his attic bedroom was marked in large loose letters, "SANCTUM." It opened with a latch and a string. This attic room with its sloping sides was decorated with dried leaves and the pod-topped weeds we have seen in the snow. In spite of Uncle John's "lesson," there they were. The woodcuts of the English cathedrals, which the boy saw soon as he opened his eyes to see anything, were on the walls and as many "things" as were not needed below. "Things" at this stage were just so many objects to compose—with which to "fix up" effects, the childlike desire to make "pictures" of everything, yes, including himself.

There were his own drawings and some "oil paintings" he had made during that pastorate in Weymouth as disciple of Miss Landers, a friend of mother's who vainly imagined oil painting a useful accomplishment maybe for any architect and certainly a social asset.

"Oil paintings?" One of them he carefully made invited your consideration of a cardboard cock-robin on a leadpipe branch looking nowhere, on guard beside his wife's four speckled eggs. She had thoughtfully laid them in a cast-iron nest tipped toward you under a baby-blue sky. Another was a "landscape" with one hairy tree and oilcloth water deep-sunk in a really fine plain-gold frame chosen by Miss Landers herself. This "painting" was committed in the bushy brush work of the "buckeye" of that period. The "buckeye," as you may remember, was profitably distributed about the villages for a dollar to two dollars each, or painted while you waited. A virtuosity. Sometimes because it was so slight, curiously effective. He always liked that frame.

But the paintings were Miss Landers's own innocent crimes to which the innocent mother had allowed her innocent son to become an innocent party. Innocent yet indubitably "crime." In due course suitably punished.

A certain earthenware churn—he stippled it with color and decorated it with plum blossoms scratched through the paint while it was fresh—was better. It was a later work and untaught. Really a kind of *sgraffito*, he afterward came to know.

But the son had given up this precocious "painting" by way of Miss Landers. He was learning now to play the viola in the orchestra his father was getting together from Madison pupils—boys and girls. Jennie played the piano.

Robie, too, was taking violin lessons of the father. "Ma" and "Pa" would always sit and listen while their Robie practiced. They saw in it a career for him perhaps.

A small printing-press with seven fonts of De Vinne type, second-hand, was set up in the old barn at first, and later a quite complete printing-office fixed up in the basement of the house.

Books read together: *Hans Brinker,* Ruskin's *Seven Lamps of Architecture,* a gift from the Aunts Nell and Jane. Jules Verne's *Michael Strogoff, Hector Servadac.* Goethe's *Wilhelm Meister.* The *Arabian Nights* as always—Aladdin and his Lamp—and many tales. Not much poetry. Whittier, Longfellow, Bryant. If they were not poets, they were at least, poetic.

A seductive touch upon dreaming life were the enchanted and enchanting pages of the *Arabian Nights*!

Enchantment, no less, the tattered illiterature of thrills—the Nickel Library—secretly read. Hidden at the reading for hours. The culprit appearing at mealtime—still elsewhere—would fail to answer in time. Mother would perhaps be anxious.

"What has happened to you, Frank? Are you feeling well?"

"Oh, Mother, I'm all right. I was just thinking."

"Thinking of what?"

"Oh, just how wonderful the lives of some people are—and what wonderful things happen to them. And we live along just the same every day. Nothing ever happens."

"Frank, what have you been reading?" Mother would ask, fixing him with her searching eyes.

He would come out with it then and he would lose that one too and never know if they got the Scarlet Rover in the ambuscade at the river-crossing or not.

IN MEMORIAM

Was the Nickel Library really bad? Why would Mother or Father or Teacher take the blood-and-thunder tales away and burn them if they caught us with them? Greasy, worn and torn like old bank-notes they would secretly circulate in exchange for a glassie or an aggie or two. One would go from pocket to pocket until it would have to be patched together to be read, fragments maddeningly missing at critical moments. Stark, they were, with the horror of masks and corpses— dripping with gang-gore—but cool with bravery in the constant crash of catastrophe. The *bravery* thrilled. The daring hero, usually some lad like ourselves, triumphant all the time. Going down, only to come right-side up through scrambled Indians and half-caste cut-throats, carcasses, bowie knives, and cutlasses.

The movie requires no imagination. The Nickel Library did. And (just like "the movies") all was utterly arranged in every detail to the perfect satisfaction of the girlish heroine whose virtue, meantime, was tested and retested from every possible angle, and ambush—she too, at the critical moment emerging manhandled but unspotted—with style all the while!

This ill-assorted pair—Frank, good legs, and Robie, bad legs—lived many lives.

One with the lake.

One, typesetting, printing, and composing. Inventing, designing.

Another with music in the evenings and reading.

The girl-friends of the boy's sisters came in often to sing and play.

Gay evenings! Young, eager, happy voices and clear-shining eyes. Gilbert and Sullivan lyrics were then not only popular—they were the rage. Born of true lyrical genius that never failed to charm the singers who sang them and those who heard them no less. Nor did they ever fail to yield new effects in the experiments made with them. How could *they* have come out of the hideous artificiality of the Victorian Era? Gilbert and Sullivan must have been Victorian "relief." A *genuine* gaiety.

These evenings were no concerts. They were happy riots. No one could tell where laughter left off and singing began. Nor where singing left off and laughter began.

Musical education, however, stopped short for the youth when he entered the University and his father had gone. Somehow, the undergraduate got the unpardonable idea that being musical was unmanly, and started in to harden up with the boys.

Naive perspectives were already opening outward into the world in many directions, but in one direction all the others were steadily converging: this direction encouraged in skillful ways by the mother. Her son was to be an architect. He was to get beautiful buildings built. Bridges and dams were fascinating him now. Any construction whatsoever would do to pore over. And he would make what he called "designs."

Both Frank and Robie had real passion for invention, and were banged, pinched, stained or marred or were "had" somewhere by perpetual experiment going on.

A water-velocipede was started—to be called the "Frankenrob." Drawings made for a "Catamaran" that cost too much to happen. The boys made a cross-gun, bows and arrows, and long bob-sled on double runners. They painted them—the joy of striping them in colors! They had them "ironed" by the blacksmith according to design. A new style newspaper—a scroll. Another kind of ice-boat. Fantastic new kinds of kites of colored paper. Kites with fantastic tails. A water-wheel. Who could remember how many schemes were hatched, patched up and scrapped during these winter-schooling periods of adolescence? And there was the excellent scroll-saw and the inevitable turning lathe. The boys were perpetually making designs. Drawing always. Always making drawings for fun. Especially by lamplight, evenings.

But—of the schooling itself? Not a thing he can remember!

A blank! Except colorful experiences that had nothing academic about them. Like dipping the gold braid hanging down the back of the pretty girl sitting in front into the ink-well of his school desk and drawing with it. Getting sent home in consequence.

There was the cruel torture of speaking once a month.

The mortification of the nickname "Shaggy" pursued him, earned by the still abundant curls that made any hat he put on his head deciduous.

Distant worship of several pretty girls. Goodie Storer, Carrie Jacobs, Floy Stearns. And Robie at this time began to contract his secret hopeless passion for little blue-eyed Etta Doyon, next door. Golden curls and brown eyes, the boy then preferred. Ella Gernon had both to perfection!

Etta's younger brother, Charlie, more innocent of heart, if possible, than the pair, wanted to come into the printing office with them.

Mr. Doyon was rich for that town and time. Charlie was told that if his father would lend "the firm" two hundred dollars to buy a larger Model Press and more type, they would let him in. Charlie got the money easily. The "papers" were offered by Mr. Doyon and signed by the boys.

Such was the origin of the firm of "Wright, Doyon and Lamp, Publishers and Printers." Charlie's share in the enterprise was "capitalist." All he had to do was to sit around and look as though he owned the whole thing, and owned the boys too, just because they owed his father money. And he would "pie" the type when things went altogether wrong for him.

Is anything more pleasurable to the mind than unsullied paper? The studious comparisons and selection of "stock" in textures and colors of cards and paper?

Letters are works of art, or should be.

The choice of type—a range of choice to tease the most ample taste.

The absorbing mechanics of actual press work.

What room for space invention—"composing"!

A real toy—the press—for growing boys as well as for grown-up rich men.

And what *is* the fascination to the average man or boy of seeing his name in type, even on a business or visiting card? Phenomenal! A secret is there of intense human interest.

But the schooling! Trying to find traces of it in that growing experience ends in finding *none*. What became of it? Why did it contribute so little to this consciousness-of-existence that is "the boy"? It seems purely negative and for that reason it may not have been positively harmful. Difficult for one to say. You can't let boys run wild while they are growing. They have to be roped and tied to something so their parents can go about their business. Why not a snubbing post or—school, then? A youth must be slowed-up, held in hand. Caged—yes—mortified too. Broken to harness as colts are broken, or there would be nothing left but to make an "artist" of him. Send him to an Art Institute.

But certain episodes were harmful and remain so to this day. "Speaking pieces," for instance. The accomplishments after all seem most devastating as one looks about either before or after.

At this period features in the spring and summer life at the Valley were the country cousins of the city boy—Dick, Tom and Ed. The city boy practiced on them too. They looked upon their cousin with faith and confiding interest. Fully conscious of their admiration. He beguiled them, showed off for them, used them, fooled them and loved them sincerely. But this life-of-the-imagination in him wrought havoc with them.

One time, the four all day together in the fields. The young Aladdin (that's me) suddenly got the idea of a "party." The party grew so real in his imagination, as he rubbed his lamp, that it became due for that very evening given by Mother at Grandfather's where she was then on a visit. It grew so real he began to talk about it to the boys, and as he talked about it the party grew in his imagination. As the day wore on he built it up, touched it up here and there to his satisfaction. There were to be presents for Tom, Dick and Ed. Things he knew they longed for. There were to be goodies of all sorts. And surprises were cleverly hinted at, to work up excitement. The possibilities grew as he talked until ex-pectations were boundless. Three mouths were watering. His own no less.

When they all turned toward home, they could hardly wait for the party to come with the evening.

Tom, Dick and Ed's parents had heard nothing of all this, but told by the boys, believed them, scrubbed them clean and dressed them up in their Sunday best. By this time the enthusiasm of invention had cooled in the hatching architect and a certain uneasiness came upper-most in him as he half-remembered what he had done. But he said nothing. The invited guests arrived early. Mother in the middle of her work received them, wondering—with "Hello, boys! Why! Why are you all so beautifully dressed? Where are you going?"

"We've come to Frank's party."

"Party?" said his mother, and looked at her son! One look was enough. And she soon found from the guests they were expecting pre-sents and goodies.

She rose to the occasion to her son's delight and gratitude. Perhaps he knew she would, who knows! Anyhow, she found something in the way of presents so there was only partial disappointment. She made molasses candy, gave them popcorn and ginger cookies, got father to play "Pop Goes the Weasel" on his violin and sing for them too. And sent them home in an hour or so—her precious son's reputation saved, she hoped.

Now he was facing mother as to his idea of this party. "Why did you want to fool your cousins, Frank?"

Indignantly, he denied wanting to *fool* them.

"Why did you promise them all those things when you knew they were not going to get them?"

"Well, why did they have to spoil it all by *believing* they were going to get them? It was fun already to think about getting them, wasn't it? Then why did they have to come to the party? Couldn't they just let it alone?"

And Mother understood. Nobody else. Clearly they were not up to the game.

A MAN

Time came a year or two later when the boy drove Pont (short for Pontius) and Pilate afield alone, on his own for the first time. That was a day for him! The day before he had been only a boy on the farm. Today he was a man among men. To be a man is to do a man's work. The job in hand now was driving the "plankers" to finally smooth the harrowed fields for the marking of the rows before corn-planting. The whiffletrees of Pont and Pilate were hitched to a clevis fastened to the planks at the middle of the side, dragging them crosswise along over the fields. You stood upright on the planks at the center or to one side as you wanted them to drag, and drove with short hold on the lines, close up to the horses.

All went well. Home at noon as good as the best. In the afternoon, toward four o'clock, coming down the sloping field the planker caught on a rotten stump half-hidden in the ploughed ground. The jerk broke the top off the stump. The "planker," thus suddenly released, jumped forward on to the horses' heels throwing the boy onto Pont's rump. Instinctively the lad grasped the breeching of each horse with his hands as they jumped, kicked and started to run. The clinging boy was so close to Pont he was lifted each time the horse kicked. And Pont was kicking continually as he ran. Pilate running close but, fortunately, not kicking.

If he let go his hold on Pont's breeching, or the straps broke, the plankers would go over him. To hold on and hope nothing would break was the only hope.

There were no cries, no words, as the team came tearing down the side hill, the boy rising and falling with the running kicks of the horse. Adolph Sprecher, the good-hearted hired man, at work elsewhere marking the field, saw the dangerous flight and with all his brawny might ran over the ploughed ground to head off disaster. Grabbed at the horses' heads, missed and fell. Got up and fortunately as the breeching was pulling Pont's check-rein on one side, causing him to run in a wide circle, he could cut across and he got him just in time.

The lad promoted to man's work dropped on the planks and lay there to get the breath back into the body that crazy horse had kicked the breath out of. All that Pont-horse ever needed to indulge in similar performances was a horsefly on the job in earnest. Many a tussle the amateur had under this professional protestant from first to last.

Adolph Sprecher, for some time, could not believe the boy was not seriously hurt. Begged not to tell Uncle James, he agreed, but broke his promise. The fact was—the boy stuck for another hour's work, went home and did his chores. Next morning, his body was so stiff and black and blue and sore that he simply could not make it go. Then the story came out.

His Uncle James had sent him with hired man number two, with confidence in Adolph. And for some time after this he was sent out in company. But he always liked best to be sent off alone—to be treated like a man. He was soon trusted and sent alone.

That summer he "bound" his station after the reaper.

In those days the reaper, pride of the farm, was a "rake-off McCormick."

A bright-red affair with a varnished wood grain-platform onto which bright-blue, green, yellow and red reels knocked the yellow grain as it was cut by the busy to and fro of the gleaming sickle. This machine, gaily painted, like a toy, no doubt for the same reason, would leave the bundles raked off neatly on the stubble behind, to be bound by four or five men spaced around the field as the crop of grain was light or heavy, and the bundles would be tossed aside out of the way of the horses as they made the next round.

Taking a wisp of the grain-straw in the left hand for a band, dividing it in two parts, deftly twisting it together at the head and in the right hand—stopping and reaching under the bundle with the hand—lifting the bundle in the arms, bringing the ends of the band together over it, dropping it to the ground under the knee as the band would be pulling the band up sharply—then twisting and tucking the ends of the "band" tight under with a thrust of the fingers, tossing the bundle away— bound!

The young harvester's fingernails would be worn to the quick and bleeding before the last band on the bundles of the season's grain was "tucked in."

There was the hauling of the grain in the ample grain racks that also served for hay racks. The pitching of the bundles with a long-handled three-tined fork. And the stacking. The stacking was expert, entrusted to few. The whole thing might come down. Sometimes it did "slide." There had already been hauling of the hay and the pitching of hay to the stack.

Aching muscles in the morning always had to be limbered up again by the first few hours of the next day's work.

Soon he learned to endure the routine of continuous labor by finding in it a sort of sing-song. "Humdrum"—but for one's imagination.

He would actually sing to the ever-recurring monotonies of rhythm. Hum variations or whistle them when he was at it or in it or of it. Here was the secret of endurance for the imaginative.

Any monotonous task involving repetition of movement has its rhythm. If you can find it the task can soon be made interesting in that sense. The "job" may be syncopated by changing the accent or making an accent. Binding grain and shocking it, or pitching bundles to the wagon and racks. Pitching hay, hoeing, dropping corn with a "checker." Cultivating corn as the green hills passed regularly four feet apart between the shovels—planted four feet apart each way.

All machinery makes some recurrent noise, some clack or beat above the hum that can be made into the rhythm of song-movement—a rhythm that is the obvious poetry in the mathematics of this universe. Maybe.

The body in performing heavy labors for hour after hour can get into a swinging rhythm with music to accompany it, rhythm to be whistled or sung aloud or kept in the mind.

Folk dances originate in this way, no doubt. Sacred dances no less.

Walking there after the plough, bare feet in furrow, was ideal opportunity to indulge this inner rhythm and adjust it to outward movement.

This sense of rhythm, entering into monotonous repetition, naturally led to arrangements of sound to go with it—sometimes a song with words.

The idea—no, it could have been no idea. It was instinct, or whatever it was, for him to suit this naive release of the within to inspirit the work in hand. Work would be better done. Without fatigue.

Milking was the perfect opportunity to turn monotony into music. The sound of the streams at first, soon to be modified by the foaming of the milk in the pail—a kind of music! And usually, the boy sang to this rhythm while he milked. Gottlieb—his red face turned down and sideways, yellow hair against the cow's flank—would sometimes sing with him. You see here, *within himself*, he had found release. He had found a way to beat "tired to tired." And Uncle James would not have to call, "Come back, Frank! Come back!" For he would be satisfactorily active while he dreamed.

60

More significant than all else at this time was this sense-of-rhythm in him.

Life impelling itself to live?

Notwithstanding this release coming up in him, and out from him continuously, he was doing a man's work on the farm and at the age of fourteen (Uncle James was generous) getting a man's pay—nineteen dollars a month and his board and clothes.

Yes, Uncle James was doing pretty well by him—because . . .

THE HORSE

Now the amateur "hired man" had come by experience to intimate knowledge of The Horse: to the ways of bits and bridling . . . saddling, haltering, harnessing. Eternal buckling and unbuckling. He knew whiffle-trees, neck-yokes and whips; tugs, breechings, and collars; straps, hooks, bits; hoofs and fetlocks; withers and hocks . . . all man's part in the horse! He saw—procreation. The rearing gorgeous pride of the Clydesdale stallion with his noble head and quivering nostrils. Sleek, meek mares. Young colts, if unluckily male, forthwith sex-degraded to geldings struggling against the inevitable with no sound.

The work horses: he was forever getting them up. Currying them. Brushing them. Getting them over while getting the stables clean under them and behind them. Always this cleaning up to do, behind them. Braiding their tails. Hitching them. Unhitching them. Sometimes ditching them. Switching them. Feeding them. Leading and coaxing. Driving them. Riding them bareback or saddled before and after they were broken. Seeing Uncle James break them, sometimes himself all but broken by them. Getting thrown off them. Getting run-away-with by them. Getting run over, kicked or stepped on. Angry and jerking a horse shamefully, feeling ashamed. Getting the horses shod. Putting the horses with alternate patience and exasperation to the plow, to harrows, seeders, markers, plankers, cultivators and lumber-wagons—sulkies, buggies and logging-trucks—milk-wagons, reapers and turntables. To threshing-machines. Saws. Hayracks. Hayrakes. And there he would work the horses, and take them away to again feed, water, curry them and bed them.

These gaily-painted accessories to the horse had to be greased, to get them to go. Getting the life-sized man-toys to stop was sometimes desperation.

Learning to swear in the style proper to the hired man and the horse's taste. So, this amateur young master of the HORSE.

Noble excitement comes to a growing boy in this fellowship with the horse. Most respectable of all man's animal associates it is, romantic, too. . . . But, there was . . .

THE SOW

Daily fodder to haul and boiling the pumpkins or something or other—for the hogs. This grunting boar with foaming mouth and ugly tusks, heavy brood sows, bellies almost dragging the ground, grunting always. The clean, pink little pigs. Ringing all snouts at four months so they could never root and spoil the sod. Catching and holding unlucky young boars—screaming infernos of despair as they were degraded into "barrows." Loading all—eventually—into the hog-racks and hauling them to market.

Perpetually someone was running to get the pigs out of the corn. Get them out of the garden. Get them out of the neighbor's fields. Getting them—well, always "*getting*" them out or "*getting*" them into—something, himself breathless, perspiring and oftentimes despairing. And then, this business of getting the heavy sows off their own little pigs. He knew they were lying on them by the infernal heart-rending squeals. Sometimes they would eat their newly born. The call of "P-o-o-i-g! P-o-o-i-g! P-o-o-i-g." The tenor of that call would do credit to Grand Opera.

Sickened at butchering by seeing the knife stuck deep in the fat throat, hot blood gushing and streaming from the pig marked for family "pork." Smell of their yard—devastating! Utter degradation in smells. Procreation, too, of the pig. This unreconciled assistant to the hog now knew these devastations full well. Fortunately less of it went into his experience than . . .

THE COW

His first farm familiars.

He was always afraid of the heavy-necked, bellowing Holstein Bull. Sex slave with ring in his nose but pride and terror of every farm just the same. First farm familiars—the Cows. Calling them—"So Boss! So-o Boss! So-o-o Boss!" A baritone call. For years and years—and years—would they never end?—getting the cows in from early pasture. Getting the cows into their proper places in the barn. Feeding them. Milking them early in the morning. Milking them late in the evening, eaten up by flies. Cruelly twisting their tails to make them stamp their hind legs and stand over to be milked. Getting the vile manure off their bags before milking them, to keep the milk clean. Getting the lazy creatures up. Milking them weekdays. Milking them just the same on Sundays. Milking them—always milking them. Getting bare feet soiled—"cut" the farm-boys used to say—in the warm, fresh cow-flops, in the stable or in the lane. Always cleaning away at the stables. Always cleaning up to be done—never quite done till next time and next time was always soon. Getting the slow-moving bovines out to pasture again. Adventuresome ones to get out of the corn. The whole tribe would get into the grain. Hooked. Beating a cantankerous old cow goring a young sister, the gored one bellowing agony, head stretched out, big eyes bulging in terror rolled back until the whites were all you could see. Fixing a wooden poke on the neck of the "leader"—the one first to jump the fence and lead the others to glory while it lasted. He would see the torture of the poor adventurer punished for her innocent initiative as that adventurer in all skins is always punished in some form . . . secretly he would take the cruel "poke" off without permission. Getting reprimanded when next the cows were in the corn, but taking the cruel poke off again—just the same.

Feeding the calves. "*Sukem* suke suke-suke, *suke*-suke-suke-suke." Tenor again. Soprano preferred. Catching and tying the luckless bull calves while, bawling in fear, they were degraded into steers—or hauled to market for veal after six weeks of here-on-earth. Seeing a fine steer knocked in the head with a maul—dropped with a thud like lead, throat cut in a flash. Helping to strip off the heavy skin for leather and dress the steaming carcass for beef. Getting the cows in, getting them out, day in and day out—summer after summer. Occasionally helping Uncle James to haul one out, when she got stuck in the mud of the creek. Haul the cow out with a team of horses hitched to a rope tied around her neck. No harm to her whatever.

Always procreation—in season. Always in season, some.

Chased by the bull but never tossed, this go-getter of the Cow knew cow-business now, habitually, as the cattle chewed their cud. Meantime, scattered about in all this was

THE HEN

O cock, with the scarlet comb! Squire of the Hens. Hundreds of them were all over the place. Crowing. Scratching. Clucking. Cheeping. Squawking. He would have to get up at night to look into the hen-house when a terrific squawking commotion indicated some prowling enemy in their midst. It was given to him sometimes to catch and strike off the heads of superfluous young roosters when their turn came to be eaten. It invariably came. Throwing the flapping convulsive fowl aside in headless tumble over wood-pile and dooryard in frantic letting go of life. Eggs. Always hunting eggs. Setting eggs. Sucking eggs as taught by Gottlieb. Chucking or ducking cross old hens who should have known better, into the water-trough to cool maternal ardor. Dropping them into the bottom of a barrel with water in it to let them "set" on that. Getting pecked by the lousy things. Getting actually covered with lice. This young fowler, admiring the cock and his brood but never liking them and detesting their procreation—perpetual. But he did like guinea fowl with the raucous cry and speckled gray plummage, formed like a quail. The peacock fascinated him—a spiritual element in all this because peacocks seemed introduced for love of beauty—ornament? That element hovers over everything . . . this sentiment for beauty. Man cannot drive it entirely away! No—even when he domesticates the animals it will linger there and it will cling even to . . .

THE HOE

Whosoever would sow must hoe.

And if he who hoes would reap—he must weed.

The Garden! A comparatively peaceful place that Garden—when not raided by unnatural domesticated enemies from over the none-too-good fence—chickens, little pigs and some few non-conformist sows. To say nothing of natural enemies underground—grubs, worms and the marching armies of insects. Insects! Will they eventually win the battle and exterminate man?

Weeding is an art, though the back breaks. The boy learned to twist his fingers around the weed-stems close to the ground and with a sidewise twist—thumb as a lever—bringing the narrow side of the hand to the ground—prying, while pulling, he would get them out with roots unbroken while the skin on his fingers lasted.

Thus the process would go on for hours a day, all the days the garden was young, until back and arms were stiff and fingers sore in the continued effort to clean the weeds out from between the plants known to be useful as the garden grew older.

And this amateur hired-man hoed. Hoed lettuce. Hoed radishes, beets, carrots, parsnips and turnips. Cabbages. Tomato plants. Onions. Always he seemed to be hoeing in the season of early summer. Hoeing and weeding, weeding and hoeing until the palms of his hands were thick and hard—as shiny as the hoe handle—both like glass. And finally

64

Grandmother and Grandfather Richard Lloyd Jones

Mother Anna Lloyd Wright

Father William Russell Cary Wright

F.Ll.W. at three

Mother at seventy-seven

The eldest son, Lloyd, at seven

Uncle Enos

Uncle James

Romeo and Juliet. "Amateur engineering architecture on its hill crown above the Hillside Home School"

"The valley from the hill crown at Taliesin; the family chapel at the middle of the middle-distance; the range of hills; a glimpse of the stream running down its length."

Aunt Nell, Aunt Jane, Mother

Hillside Home School, Spring Green, Wisconsin. 1902

Catherine and her son, David

Frances, blue-eyed daughter

Llewellyn, sixth child, at six

Catherine "the rogue" at the studio door

"Drawing shown to Lieber Meister [Louis Sullivan] when applying for a job"

The rebellious student at twenty, shortly after arriving in Chicago

Frank Lloyd Wright Studio, Oak Park, Illinois. 1895

Dankmar Adler, the "Big Chief,"
senior partner of Adler and Sullivan

"Lieber Meister" Louis Sullivan

H. H. Richardson. Photograph by Mrs.
Henry Adams while Richardson was
planning the Adams House at Washington

Cecil Corwin, the comrade of "Fellowship."
Chicago, 1890

"The Fisherman and the Genie," fireplace at end of Playroom of Oak Park House. 1891

Jenkin Lloyd Jones

Lloyd Wright, architect,
Los Angeles

John Wright, architect,
Michigan City

Larkin Building, Buffalo, New York. 1904. Office interior and side view. "A fireproof, air-conditioned building furnished throughout with steel. First in many ways—all-glass doors, double glass windows, complete air-conditioning, especially designed steel filing systems, steel desk furniture and seats, telephones and lighting system especially designed in steel, etc. Building demolished in 1950."

Cheney House, Oak Park, Illinois. 1904. "Designed when I was still with Adler and Sullivan in 1893—built several years later."

Willitts House, Highland Park, Illinois. "The house on the prairie a well developed type by 1901."

Unity Temple, Oak Park, Illinois. 1906. "So far as I know the first concrete monolith to come from the forms as architecture completely finished."

The Robie House, Chicago, Illinois. 1908. "A masonry structure of tawny brick and stone with red tile roof, eaves of copper, woodwork of oak throughout. This became known in Germany as *dampfer* architecture. It was a good example of the prairie house of that period."

Coonley House, Riverside, Illinois. 1907. Garden front above, living room below. "Mrs. Coonley came to me to build her house because she said 'my work wore the countenance of principle'—a good encouragement to me at that time."

Sister Maginel
(Mrs. Maginel Wright Barney)

Sister Jane
(Mrs. Andrew T. Porter)

Taliesin, Spring Green, Wisconsin. 1911

Taliesin. Living room

Taliesin. Garden court

they would have to come and cut down the triumphant weeds with a sickle or scythe and burn them up!

The wielder of the hoe would wonder why weeds couldn't be studied, possibilities found and then maybe cultivated. The "crop" eliminated. Perhaps the "crop" was weeds once upon a time just because the farmer didn't know what they were for. Tobacco was a weed once. And corn! Seems there never was wild corn. And potatoes. And tomatoes were once thought by Europeans to be poison. Love apples they called them. Cancerous? Nearly everything was a weed once upon a time. Maybe, sometime, there would be no "weeds" and then? But meanwhile weeds seemed fittest to survive in this unequal strife—in this contending, never-ending competition between Good and Evil or whatever the competition should be named.

What vitality these "weeds" had! Pusley, for instance. Chess (velvet weed). Pigweed. Dock and ragweed. Quack grass—king of all. Canada thistle—queen! Would the weeds become feeble, if they were cultivated, and "crops" become as vigorous as "weeds" if left alone to flourish on their own?

What of such science and art? Ask the professors?

Afield in June, he saw as reward of toil, forethought and some art and science the sweeping acres of clover-bloom floating in perfume, heard the hum of busy bees as the tall, round spires of the timothy stood above, slender spires bending to the sweeping of the breeze. Soon there would be the large round cones of the yellow grainstacks standing in the transparent stubble-fields in August, gathered together from the orderly ranks of yellow grain-shocks dotting the tawny stubble—in the midst of July green. The silvering rows on rows of haycocks in June to end in purple haystacks tomorrow. In September would come the wigwam rows of Indian corn-shocks; solid-gold pumpkins lying thick in the reddening sun over the fields between the "wigwams."

And at the red barns there he would be—handling the dangerous hayfork, choking in the dust of the great big hot haymows, "tailing" on the strawstacks, struggling to keep from being choked and buried alive in the chaff that fell from the end of the straw-carrier of the threshing machine, his features obliterated by grime, sweat and dust. And later, body dripping with sweat, on the haystacks he would be putting away the fragrant hay. Turning tedious grindstones under sickles, scythes and axes. Turning the crank of the fanning-mill to the limit of endurance. Working the wood handle of the old green pump, until arms were numb.

Did wet weather bring a rest from all these labors? Except for digging post-holes and rail fencing—yes.

Someone should do the barbed-wire fence in song and story. It would be the story of the march of our civilization. Together with the tin can, it has made man's conquest too easy. Enough.

On the farm there was always the glib Ax. The honest Bucksaw. And the persuasive Hammer. The pliers! The vise! No farm could have a farmer without this magic. And, almost forgotten, the tragic Monkey Wrench! Whose song is that? What disorganization could be wrought with a monkey wrench? What about the precious Jack-knife? Has anyone sung the song of that great gift to boyhood—the Jack-knife?

MAIN STRENGTH AND AWKWARDNESS

So it is that farm-boy life is continually at the mercy of hoofs, horns and blades. Gleaming plowshares, flashing scythes, poisonous stings, bites and briars. Boy-life there is one continuous round of fatal ups and downs, disastrous ins and outs. Too dry! Too high! Too low! Too wet! Too hot! Too cold! Too soon! Too late! Drought, Flood and Frost—major enemies the farmer must learn to defeat or he will go down like his crops with his animals.

Military warfare? Comparatively fancy business. The farmer must make constant demands upon refractory or dull animals and tools. His world is a desperate merry-go-round of ill or happy contrivances painted bright-red, poison green or red, white, blue and gilt, fascinating to him as toys are fascinating to children. Contrivances that will or will not work; main strength and awkwardness the never-failing final resource in every end.

And—continually there is this perpetual restless movement of perverse or willing perspiring, laboring animal-bodies strapped, tied to and straining at those machines. Machines that would kill them if not managed. Machines that ploughed and dug, cut, piled and tore, ground and bound if you mastered them—or killed you or somebody if you didn't— but gaily painted just the same. Machines all in some way dangerous, all rusting in vital spots, oil and oiling notwithstanding, or at some time or other all—damned! Scrap!

Such is the amazing, endless category of parts every one necessary to the stupendous complex whole into which a boy on the farm is thrown—to survive as he may.

Thus the encounter with the Cow, Sow and HEN! served by the humbled HORSE—and himself. Meantime, yes already all imposed upon by fascinating machines. The matter helped by them—perhaps. Who really knows? But the time is coming when man must know or perish.

PEACE! BEAUTY! SATISFACTION! REST!

The divine discontent of the Creative Spirit made havoc with all this, then and there—as things were. And as they are now. Anyone might have seen this and avoided it if he could. But the boy didn't know. No one warned him.

He was unsuspecting.

Fearlessly did this human item live the life of the imagination in all he did.

Sometimes when the day had been too hard, too tired to sleep he would get out of bed, sweaty jeans pulled on, rolled above his knees, and barefoot and bareheaded slowly climb the path up the hill behind the house. Climb to the long, quiet ridge that ran to the north high in the moonlight, ornamented here and there with scattered hazel-brush and trees. Climbing to wander, look forward and imagine, enjoy waking dreams in a high place.

Going over that ridge later in life, many times, he would wonder how a barefoot boy could safely take that stony way in daylight, not to speak of moonlight.

On either side of the ridge lay fertile valleys luminously bathed and gentled by the moon. The different trees all made their special kinds of pattern when the moon shone on them and their favorite deep-dark silhouettes when it shone against them. The flowers had no color, but their cups and corollas glistening with dew were like pallid gems. The barefoot's feet and legs were wet with the cool freshness of the dews fallen in the long grasses. Broad, shallow mists, distilled from heavy dews, floating in cool, broad sheets below were lying free over the tree-tops in long, thin, flat ribands. All would be quiet except for the drowsy singing undertone of summer insects. The ancient element of moisture seemed to prevail there as a kind of light flooding over all. The deep shadows held mysteries alluring and friendly to the boy.

No haste now.

He could listen to music religiously as though it were the last strain he might ever hear, and make more in the heart of his mind. Or he would hear the strains of Beethoven that had come to him from his father's playing as, early in life, in his bed he lay listening. Entranced, he would be uplifted.

The intimate fairy princess drew near then, she who was growing up somewhere preparing herself and looking forward, as dreamily, to him. Listening too. Sometimes fair and sometimes dark, she was always beautiful as only adolescent boys can picture girlish beauty. Great deeds would rise in him. Unquenchable triumphs until the evanescent scene faded into many-colored achievements and boy-sized glory. There was no feeling that the dreams could ever be desecrated by failure. Out of the character they arose into the mind as waking dreams. Magical, mystic, pale-amber and amethyst nights settled quietly on the spirit to refresh a mortal weariness as the dew came upon the flowers that stood beside his naked legs.

Looking back now, the dreams seem not great. But then how he thrilled with them and walked in the tall dew-laden grass among moonstruck flowers as on air. Feeling no stones beneath his naked feet. Half-consciously he would wander back, come down and climb into bed again to sleep—deep sleep with no dreams at all.

After one thousand two hundred and sixty todays and tomorrows like those yesterdays the boy was coming sixteen. Farm-days for him were over. He was about to enter the University of Wisconsin.

These farm-days had left their mark on him in a self-confidence in his own strength called courage. Muscles hard. Step—springing. Sure-footed, fingers quick as thought and quick *with* thought. Mind buoyant with optimism. Optimism that came through seeing sunshine follow clouds and rain—working out success succeeding failure. It had come to him self-consciously, out of his daily endeavors, as an underlying sense of the essential balance of forces in nature. Something in the nature of an inner experience had come to him that was to make a sense of this supremacy of interior order like a religion to him. He was to take refuge in it and grow in it. Besides, coming sixteen, for several years the youth had been doing a man's work. He had learned how to do much and do much well, do most of it happily, feeling himself master where he would. That gave him a whip-hand.

He was afraid only of people. The fearful unknown to him—people. Not to mention girls. The sight of a girl would send him scampering like a scared young stag, back into his wood.

THE FATHER

By now, family life at the small town house by the blue lake was not so well. No longer much agreement between the father and mother.

Father on this eve of the entrance of his son to the university was himself deep in learning to write Sanskrit. Mother for some years had been ailing. Poverty pinched.

The youth would see her self-denial at table. See her eating only what the others did not want. Drinking her tea without sugar and not because she preferred it so. When, rarely, a chicken from the small coop in the back yard would be killed and come to the table—pretending to

68

prefer the neck of the roast chicken so well you almost believed she did. The boy wondered.

Provisions often arrived from the farm—potatoes, vegetables, barrels of apples. The father's earnings were small and shrinking. Teaching music wasn't much of a livelihood in Madison. Irregular preaching there and in surrounding towns less so. And the father grew irascible over this and cross-currents of family feeling. The Joneses didn't much approve of Anna's privations. He, being a proud man, resented their provisions. His helplessness irritated him.

The lad was his mother's adoration. She lived much in him. Probably that didn't help either.

For some disobedience about this time, the father undertook to thrash the young man. It had happened in the stable and the young rebel got his father down on the floor, held him there until his father promised to let him alone. He had grown too big for that sort of thing. "Father ought to realize it," said the boy, as he went into the home, white, shamed and shaken to tell his mother.

This youth had hardly known himself as his own father's son. All had gone well enough on the surface now broken. The son had sympathy for his talented father as well as admiration. Something of that vain struggle of superior talents with untoward circumstances of life that was his father's got to him, and he was touched by it—never knowing how to show Father. Something—you see—had never been established that was needed to make them father and son. Perhaps the father never loved or wanted the son at any time. Memories would haunt the youth as they haunt the man. . . .

His father's son listening at the closed study door, father walking—walking to and fro studying, reciting as he walked: practicing for readings he sometimes gave at churches. Experimenting with changes of intonation and accent, evidently reading the poem, book in hand and occasionally trying over certain passages again and again. This time listening to "The Raven." Measured footsteps, father's voice reciting . . .

> . . . As of someone gently rapping,
> Rapping at my chamber door.
> "'Tis some visitor," I muttered,
> "Tapping at my chamber door;
> Only this and nothing more."

Interval:
Slowly walking—then—

> And the silken sad uncertain
> Rustling of each purple curtain

> *Thrilled me—filled me with fantastic*
> *Terrors never felt before . . .*

Silence
Now again . . .

> *Darkness there and nothing more. . . .*
> *Darkness there and nothing more. . . .*
> *Merely this and nothing more.*

Pause
Footsteps, measured as before. . .

> *Let me see, then, what thereat is,*
> *and this mystery explore. . . .*
> *and this mystery explore;*
> *'Tis the wind and nothing more. . .*
> *'Tis the wind and nothing more.*

Silence again.
Walking faster now . . .

> *"Prophet still, if bird or devil! . . .*
> *Prophet still, if bird or devil! . . .*

Quiet now for a time, then . . .

> *"Is there—is there balm in Gilead?*
> *Tell me, tell me, I implore.*
> *Quoth the Raven, 'Nevermore!' . . .*
> *Quoth the Raven, 'Nevermore!' "*

and the youth would tiptoe away so he could hear no more.

Sometimes, all gone to bed, he would hear nocturnal rehearsal and the walking—was it evermore?—would fill a tender boyish heart with sadness until a head would bury itself in the pillow to shut it out.

One day when difficulties between father and mother grown unbearable mother, having borne all she could—probably father had borne all he could bear too—said quietly, "Well, Mr. Wright"—always she spoke of him, and to him, so—"leave us. I will manage with the children. Go your way. We will never ask you for anything except this home. Savings of my earning as a teacher have gone into this home and I have put into it so many years of my life.

"No—we will never ask you for help.

"If ever you can send us anything, send it. If you cannot we will do the best we can."

Who can know what, in the eighteen years preceding, gradually and inevitably led to the heartbreak under simple words—spoken so quietly?

Like some traveler taking the long road to some point where another road branches to the left or to the right, the turn is taken with nothing to mark it as an event, yet direction, destination, perhaps all of life—changed. Destruction too may wait on that turn. All real crises in

70

Life, are they not finally so? Who may judge these silent changes so gradually taking place in the human heart like organic changes taking place in trees or plants, and like them, when manifest as complete, to be accepted?

What presumptuous folly to rise against them with "No!" Senseless hazard to encourage them! What mischief to advise; what idiocy to "judge"!

Father disappeared. Never seen again by his wife or his children. Judge Carpenter quietly dissolved the marriage contract.

Mother's people were deeply grieved, shamed because of her "disgrace."

She herself bowed down in grief. Although believing in the rightness of separation for their children's sake, she had not believed in her heart—it seems—their father would take advantage of her offer to release him.

Until he died fifteen years later, she never ceased to believe he would come back. There was never a thought of another man in her life, nor thought of another woman in his. Perhaps it was that their life together had worn its soul away in failure after failure added to failure: the inveterate and desperate withdrawal on his part into the life of his studies, his books and his music, where he was oblivious to all else.

So his boy himself, supersensitive, soon became aware of "disgrace." His mother was a "divorced woman." His faith in her goodness and rightness did not waver. Therefore seemed injustice to her. Did this injustice to her serve some social purpose?

The wondering grew in him to resentment. Became a subconscious sense of false judgment entered against himself, his sisters, Jennie and Maginel, innocent of all wrong-doing. His mother's unhappiness—was it a social crime? Why must she, as well as they, be punished? Just what had they all done?

He never got the heavy thing straight, just accepted it as one more handicap—grew more sensitive and shy than ever and began to be distrustful—of what he could not have told you. Then.

The mother was alone now with her son and his two sisters. She found a place for the budding architect with blue-eyed Allen D. Conover, Dean of Engineering at the University of Wisconsin, himself a competent civil engineer. He had an office of his own and a private practice in the city of Madison and probably really needed some boy to work for him. How can one be sure? Professor Conover was a cultivated, kindly man. He allowed the youth to work for him afternoons so that he might have mornings for classes. He gave him thirty-five dollars a month. This arrangement left the freshman free to study evenings. Architecture, at first his mother's inspiration, then naturally enough his own desire, was the study he wanted. But there was no money to go away to an architectural school. There were classes in engineering at the home university. That was the nearest to architecture within his reach.

So the youth enrolled at the University of Wisconsin as a prospective civil engineer.

Fortunately, too, by the limitation, he was spared the curse of the "architectural" education of that day in the United States with its false direction in culture and wrong emphasis on sentiment.

He walked to the University every morning—a couple of miles away. After recitations he walked back to the Conover office at noon to eat the lunch he carried. An afternoon's work done at the drawing-board, he walked home again to eat his supper and to study. Robie Lamp and he were still "chums" though other associations now drew the youth away from Robie, for Robert Lamp had not entered the university! It made such a difference in those days!

Retrospect of university years is mostly dull pain. Thought of poverty and struggle, pathos of a broken home, unsatisfied longings, humiliations—frustration. Mathematics excepted, there seemed little meaning in the studies. At least mathematics "worked." But mathematics was taught by Professor Van Velzer, an academic little man with side-whiskers who had no feeling for romance in his subject. A subject when rightly apprehended most romantic. Music itself is but sublimated mathematics.

Consequently the punctilio of the conscientious little professor of mathematics opened for his pupil the stupendous fact that two plus two equal four. Is it unreasonable to suppose that a professor of mathematics should be a poet? Or a civil engineer be a creative composer of symphonies?

Studying French? Miss Lucy Gay, a charming honest little person whom everyone loved and respected, taught him. He read "Romance of a Poor Young Man," "Le Cid," etc.

English Composition was taught him by Professor Freeman. A handsome gentleman, deeply afflicted, so it seemed, by a too strong expression of his own professional dignity.

The youth yearned to read and write his own language—yearned to speak it—supremely well. He had no chance, under the pompous professor. His compositions were all marked "good," "excellent thought," when he already knew them to be dishwater. And barring the correction of gross grammatical errors, what did he get from that "marking" business? Merely nothing with less subtracted for pleasure or good-measure. English to this day remains more or less a mystery. He was never taught just why English is English—just what it is that makes it English as distinguished from all other languages and what its peculiar and individual resources are to make it "speak." What its limitations are and how they may be turned to advantage he was left to find out for himself if he could, and without proper material to work with.

The hungry student read at this time, at home, Carlyle's *Sartor Resartus, Heroes and Hero Worship, Past and Present,* the father's calf-bound copy of Plutarch's *Lives,* Ruskin's *Fors Clavigera, Modern Painters, Stones of Venice* (gift of Aunts Nell and Jane), Morris's *Sigurd the Volsung,* and Shelley, Goethe's *Wilhelm Meister,* a little of William Blake, *Les Misérables,* Viollet-le-Duc's *Raisonné de l'architecture.* But he doesn't know in the least what he read in the school course.

Professors Conover and Storm Bull were the engineers under whom he worked and to whom he reported; they would look over his work in Stereotomy, Graphic Statics, Analytical and Descriptive Geometry. All as painfully spread by him upon his drawing-board in the drafting room in the old dormitory on the hillside campus. But it was with Professor Conover, in that practice of his, that the youth really learned most.

THE FRESHMAN PARTY TO GET THE YOUNG FRESHMAN A PARTNER

Charlie Ware saw May White, his own cousin, explained the matter, the diffidences, etc., and made the engagement after the formality of a call on May with the fool who was about to go fearfully in where the angels happily tread.

The morning of the party, a beautiful clear day, the freshman, chesty as a young cockerel went for a walk. He ran into Charlie.

"Say, Charlie, I ought to know what I do at this party anyhow, and how do I, or ought I, to do it."

Said Charles, "Nothing much to know, man. Get May. Take her in. Dance a few dances with her. Keep off her toes. Then get some of the fellows to dance with her. There you are! Dance with some of the other girls yourself. After the last dance—and, mind you—you dance that one with May. Then take May back to "Ladies' Hall."

But the freshman, somehow, thought it good form to kiss the girl when you left her at the door after the party. It was more of this he had been thinking than anything else. He mentioned this. Charlie laughed, "Oh," he said, "that's optional," and left the freshman still up in the air.

The class-party was to occur in Assembly Hall, a Gothic churchly edifice next door to Ladies' Hall. But a carriage was "good form." So, carriage it was.

Dressed. White tie. Black suit. Patent-leather pumps. White gloves in hand. Bouquet for lady. Boutonnière for black coat. So far so good—far too good. He had an uneasy feeling himself that it was much too good.

Got to Ladies' Hall, found May ready. May found her escort too embarrassed to say anything to her at all. But May had been informed. She got him safely back to the carriage. No sooner started, May White and Frank Wright sitting a respectful distance apart, than the carriage stopped at the Hall. Nothing whatever said. The young couple got out and the amateur led the way to the entrance.

They got in only to find a crowd of the "fellows" chaffing each other. No ladies in sight.

Blushing painfully, he realized he had brought May to the men's entrance. Helplessly he looked around. Where was the women's dressing room, anyway? May evidently didn't know either.

He went sick with shame.

Charlie Ware, from the other side of the room, took in the situation at a glance and rushed over, "Come with me, May!"

She straightway left the freshman stranded; standing out from the crowd, he felt, like the bull's-eye of a big target. Some boy took pity on him and showed him where to stow his coat and hat. Then he went back to look for his unfortunate lady. He couldn't find her.

Came the promenade. No lady!

Came the first waltz. No lady!

The waltz nearly over and he about to cut it all, when May's voice: "Why here you are! I waited a long time at the dressing-room door. Then I thought you didn't recognize me. You see, you don't know me very well so I came to find you."

He felt he should indignantly deny not knowing her among a thousand like her. But could only murmur—neither ever knew what!

They danced together. Charlie came when the dance was over and got May's programme filled. Got May's partner himself a dance or two for good measure—Charlie was what "Charlies" usually are. All of which went off without resistance or remarks from the green partner. Now he hung around and waited for that last dance with May, wondering if it was going to be expected of him to kiss her when he said "Good night."

He couldn't picture it. But although an amateur, he wanted not to be a duffer and disgrace Charlie. So he made up his mind he would go through with it.

He felt he ought to tell May her dress was pretty and that she danced well. He really admired her dress and white shoes and gloves and the way she wore her hair. All he could say was "We're having a good time, aren't we?"

"Are we?" said May—a bit miffed by now.

The pair got into the carriage after anxious moments when the escort would have given his college education to be well out of the affair forever.

But no more absurdities until—"We had a good time, didn't we?"

"Did we?"

That kiss seemed far away! Standing on the steps, time to say good-bye . . . "Well," he stammered—he felt miserably foolish—he felt . . . "Thank you," said he, and ran to the waiting carriage leaving his lady to open the door for herself. He had faith that she got in. But he didn't know.

When home, he lit his lamp, took off the togs so miserably betrayed. Threw them aside. Took *Sartor Resartus* to bed for consolation; but was inconsolable. He went over the whole affair and made himself brilliant—irresistible. He staged himself and played the part to perfection—too late! It was next term before he had courage to try again. A nice town girl, Blanche Ryder, took pity on him and asked him herself. Tactfully she saw him through.

TRAGEDY

About this time a vivid tragedy had its life-long effect upon the incipient architect. Passing by the new north-wing of the old State Capitol, he was just in time to hear the indescribable roar of building collapse and see the cloud of white lime dust blown from the windows of the outside walls, the dust cloud rising high into the summer air carrying agonized human-cries with it. The white dust cloud came down to settle white over the trees and grass of the park. Whitened by lime dust as sculpture is white, men with bloody faces came plunging wildly out of the basement entrance blindly striking out about their heads with their arms, still fighting off masonry and falling beams. Some fell dead on the grass under the clear sky. Others fell insensible. One workman, lime-whitened, too, hung head-downward from a fifty-story window, pinned to the sill by an iron-beam on a crushed foot, moaning the whole time.

A ghastly red stream ran from him down the stone wall.

Firemen soon came. Crowds appeared as though out of the ground and men frantically tugged and pulled away at the senseless mass of brick and beams to reach the moans for help of the workmen dying beneath them. Soon white-faced women, silently crying, were going about the ruins looking for husbands, brothers or sons.

A sudden movement of alarm and scattering of the crowd startled him, as someone pointed to a hand sticking out between chunks of brick-work on which the crowd itself was standing. After pulling away bricks, finally scarlet plaster, a mangled human being was drawn out— too late. One of the sobbing women knelt over it there on the grass. So it went all day long, far into the night.

The youth stayed for hours clinging to the iron fence that surrounded the park, too heartsick to move—to go away. Then he went home—ill. Dreamed of it all that night and the next and the next. The horror of the scene has never entirely left his consciousness and remains to prompt him to this day.

Only outside walls were left standing. The interior columns had fallen and the whole interior construction and roof was a gigantic rubbish heap in the basement.

The huge concrete piers in that basement and on which rested the interior cast-iron columns supporting the floors and roof, had collapsed and let the columns down. Of course that meant all the floors and interior walls as well.

Architect Jones, good and conscientious architect, had made those piers so excessively large that the contractor thought it no sin to wheel barrows full of broken brick and stone into the hearts of them. They were found rotten at the core where the columns stood. Poor Architect Jones! He was now guilty of manslaughter—tried by a jury of his peers and condemned. He never built another building. He was no kinsman.

The University of Wisconsin had its own beautiful situation on the hill by Lake Mendota, but the life of the University then was not as it is now. The herd of hungry students less by many thousands and more hungry. The buildings were few and badly furnished. Nor were the professors particularly able or distinguished. It was more like a high school today, only less sophisticated than the modern high school. It had the airs, dignitaries and dignities assumed by a university. But all values being relative, it served then as it serves now: to condition its students.

In love with the grand gesture and in common with the others—he got himself a black mortar-board with beautiful red-silk tassel hanging overboard: a pair of light-gray, skin-tight pants—in vogue then: toothpick shoes; dressed and acted the part with his hair still rather too long for it all. An incorrigible sentimentalist he.

But his heart was never in this education. It never seemed to be for him. Where was architecture in all this?

This "education" meant nothing so much to him as a vague sort of emotional distress, a sickening sense of fear of loss—of what he could not say. The inner meaning of nothing ever came clear. Besides there was something embarrassing in the competitive atmosphere. Something oppressive and threatening in the life of rules and regulations. Both rules and regulations hampered him.

So the university training of one Frank Lloyd Wright, Freshman, Sophomore, Junior and part-time Senior was lost like some race run under a severe handicap, a race which you know in your heart you are foredoomed to lose: a kind of competition in which you can see nobody winning anywhere. Nor quite knowing why anyone should want to win. Just for the degree? Just to be one of the countless many who had that certificate?

Things would seem to start but nothing would happen.

It wasn't like the farm. Doctrine, it was. Perfunctory opinion administered as doctrine. Being doctored in a big crowd and the doses never seemed to produce any visible effect at any vital spot; and anyway, he didn't feel that sick. Science Hall was in course of construction. So was the machine-shop and chemical laboratory. He didn't get into those new buildings for the University except in the Conover office.

His course didn't lead him into any shop at all, although he did get a beautiful red and white field-rod and a fine transit into his hands and went surveying with his classmates. And there was the testing of materials. But finally he did get to work on the buildings themselves by the way of his generous employer, Professor Conover.

At that time Science Hall was being built by a Milwaukee architect out of Professor Conover's office, the professor being superintendent of buildings for the University. So the young sophomore got a little actual contact with this construction. He was entrusted with the working out of some steel clips to join the apex of the four hips of the main tower-roof. . . . They wouldn't go together and the workmen, disgusted, left them hanging up there against the sky by the few bolts that would go in.

It was dead of winter—only the iron beams of the floors were on place in the floor levels below. All was slippery with ice, but he went up there, climbing the lattice on the chords of the trusses to the very top, with nothing between him and the ground but that forest of open steel beams. Got the clips loose. Dropped them down.

The office work with Professor Conover was a great good for him, as he realized then and since. That work was truly educational. But in the University, notwithstanding certain appearances, he was and remained outsider, yearning all the while for the active contact with the soil or for the tests of a free life of action. He was waiting for something to happen that never could happen. Now he realized that it never could for "they" were all there to see that it did not and should not happen.

Reading Goethe only made matters worse, for action, again action and more action was his urge.

The boy already wondered why "Culture"—what the University stood for wasn't it?—shouldn't consist in getting rid of the inappropriate in everything. Whereas "Education," as he encountered it, was as inappropriate as the rubbish wheeled by the contractor into the foundation piers of the Capitol. This he couldn't have told you then, but he felt it somehow—as waste—resenting it.

But his "Classical" course, whenever he compared it with the life on the farm, seemed to him the very *practice* of the inappropriate. So any human edifice reared up on it was likely to fall down like the Capitol?

Gestures were here, fine enough, but—how about *work*? Reality?

But the feeling about this best period of youth, lasting three and one-half years, is not so much that it was wasted.

How foolish to say anything is wasted in the living of any life!

Were one thing different, all were different.

So what weakness to regret any incident or turning of the way.

"Might-have-beens" are for the "Never-weres." Uncle James said that.

Nature is organic in Man's character-making as in other forms. His instinct was not to criticize her work unless he could know her method and discern her ends: thanks, for this, to the farm.

But Man's puny mind affronts "Nature" continually! He never knows what happens to him because of his philosophy; his "wisdom" usually something *on* life and seldom *of* life.

Motoring to and from Taliesin—seeing masses of the ten or more thousand students increasingly thronging grounds and buildings of the University, overflowing University Avenue, comes the same feeling of unhappiness. Something tragic in it all: a seeming futility or betrayal? The feeling is indefinable, but deep. Resentment against the mass product? Deeper than that. A conviction of betrayal of the individual.

Small wonder that we grow "old." Educated so soon beyond our capacity.

Now in his eighteenth year, dreaming architecture, seeing it more and more in everything, the feeling of depression regarding his one-two-thousand-five-hundredth share in the education afforded by the University of Wisconsin was growing unbearable. Added to this dissatisfaction with it and himself, there was a sense of shame in accepting the mother's sacrifices for so little in return. True, he turned over his Conover stipend to her, but the demands of college-education forever pressed, one mean form or another.

He had sold some of his father's books to meet them. The father had taken with him nothing but his clothes and violin—his mother's beautiful gold Swiss watch had now gone to Perry, the pawn-broker, by way of her son. Evenings he had made things, or during holiday vacations, with his scroll-saw, and sold them to his uncles to be used as "Christmas presents." Making these things was recreation in a sense. But his situation in "college" was all hopelessly inappropriate so far as he could see.

In spite of everything he was the heavy item of expense in that household. But for this miserable college education mother and sisters could get along well enough for a while. Mother would never consent to his giving up so near the time for graduation. Only another winter and spring term? A sacred sacrifice she was making. But the spring term of his senior year was just ended. Why go on with it?

For Mother's sake? Look at her. She was ailing and unhappy. Why not go to Chicago where Uncle Jenkin Lloyd-Jones was building a new church, get work in some architect's office, really help her and be getting nearer architecture himself?

He would plead—"There are great architects in Chicago, Mother, so there must be great buildings too. I am going to be an architect. You want me to be one. I am nowhere near it here. Professor Conover is fine but he isn't an architect. Here in the University I am doing nothing but draw and draw and see professional generalities glitter, spending money we haven't got or you have to slave to get.

"Do you believe in it yourself, Mother? In your heart I mean? It isn't real you know like the farm. Why won't you ask Uncle 'Jenk' why I can't begin to be an architect right now? Soon it will be too late. I was eighteen last June, remember."

Then, threatening: "I'll go anyway. It's time I put a stop to this foolish waste motion myself. You are willing to starve for it because all the Joneses, every one of them, is cracked about education. 'Education?' You sent me to the farm yourself for *experience,* didn't you? Well, it's experience I want now. You yourself spoiled me for this marking time. I tell you! I was sick of it long ago. It's no good for me. Can't you see, Mother? No good!"

Finally Mother, thus beset continually, did write to Uncle Jenkin who was making a great name for himself as teacher and prophet in his work in Chicago for a larger religion. Came back from the great preacher the answer, "On no account let the young man come to Chicago. He should stay in Madison and finish his education. That will do more for him than anything else. If he came here he would only waste himself on fine clothes and the girls."

Mother was shocked, but relieved too. Her son would now graduate. But for the son, that insulting misjudgment settled it. It didn't really apply to him. He intended to go if there was no more sympathy or understanding of him and the pathetic situation there at home than that letter showed, well—he would show the writer of the letter something . . . some day.

He left a few days later. Managing to get seven dollars left in his pocket, after buying the ticket to Chicago, most of the money got from old man Perry at the pawn shop for his father's—and his—favorite calf-bound copy of Plutarch's *Lives,* thumbed edges—by the son—at the life of Alcibiades. A finely bound set of Gibbons' *Decline and Fall,* which by the way he detested. Several other books from the father's library, and a mink collar that had been his mother's, but fitted by her to his overcoat!

Well . . . mother wouldn't know he had gone until he didn't come home tomorrow night. He had arranged all to deceive her that far ahead; but he would surely write her from Chicago as soon as he had a job. That couldn't be long . . .

He now put "University" behind him; a boundless faith grown strong in him. A faith in what? He could not have told you. He got on the Northwestern train for Chicago—the Eternal City of the West.

Here is the bravery of all life, in this tragic break with background, in this stand against clear sky—whatever fear, superfluous: This is my own earth! A song in the heart.

Say good-bye to "the boy" here.

Henceforward, on my own, I am "I."

Sentimental son of a sentimental mother grown up in the midst of a sentimental family planted on free soil by a grandly sentimental grandfather . . . the Welsh pioneer.

BOOK TWO □ FELLOWSHIP

INTERLUDE

Seed time.

The field is brown with the unctuous purple-brown of freshly turned earth.

The sowing has been harrowed home.

Life stirs at the root.

Sap rises to flow again into accustomed channels and course to new growth.

A faint tinge of green comes over the brown field. The wood is flecked with green and touched with delicate pink. The bobwhite has been calling the Spring for two weeks past. The boy, as he rakes the leaves and rubbish from the fresh green grass of the dooryard wonders as he notices that plum trees, apple trees, berry bushes, flower beds show no sign of Spring. He goes over to the beds to rake off the clean cane-stalks holding down the dead leaves when . . .

"Frank! Let them alone! Not safe to let them up yet."

The beautiful, warm, clear day.

A clear, high night. Stars. A slender moon in the sky when the boy went to bed.

Next morning Winter returned unexpectedly while he slept and spread a rime of thick, white frost afield.

The warm sun came out in the still morning. The tiny flecks of green and the pink tinge over the wood—went black.

Nipped in the bud!

"I thought so," said Uncle James, "I was afraid of it!" Let the bobwhite whistle another week. Keep the frost in the roots of the flowers and the fruit.

And the boy knew for the first time why "cover" was carefully spread over the flower beds after the ground had been frozen deep, and was spread around over the roots of the fruit trees.

To keep the frost in the roots until safe for them to wake!

The young sentimentalist has recourse to the oracle. "Uncle James! why don't the trees and flowers know when to come out?"

"Well, that's something I can't tell," said his uncle.

A vague fear settled over the spirit of the seeker after Truth. Had the spring been singing about something it knew so little as to be set back like this?

Did Uncle James know more about "Spring" then, than Nature knew herself? No, of course not.

He just knew how to play some trick on the ground that would make the trees and flowers wait—make them feel it was still Winter when it wasn't Winter, so he could be sure to have lots of fruit. Well, it was just like making the cows have calves to get the milk, wasn't it? Like making the pigs have little pigs so you could eat them?

That didn't explain anything.

And that wasn't Nature at all.

Not the real thing. That was just how men got their living out of Nature. Just craft. Perhaps art?

This boy wanted to know something deeper.

This young sentimentalist already in love with truth!

Is there a more tragic figure on earth—in any generation?

FELLOWSHIP

THE APPRENTICE

Chicago. Wells Street Station: six o'clock, late Spring, 1887. Drizzling. Sputtering white arc-light in the station, the streets, dazzling and ugly. I had never seen electric lights before.

Crowds. Impersonal. Intent on seeing nothing.

Somehow I didn't like to ask anyone anything. Followed the crowd. Drifted south to the Wells Street Bridge over the Chicago River. The mysterious dark of the river with dim masts, hulks and funnels hung with lights half-smothered in gloom—reflected in black beneath. I stopped to see, holding myself close against the iron rail to avoid the blind, hurrying by.

I wondered where Chicago was—if it was near. Suddenly the clanging of a bell. The crowd began to run. I wondered why: found myself alone and realized why in time to get off, but stayed on as the bridge swung out with me into the channel and a tug, puffing clouds of steam, came pushing along below pulling an enormous iron grain-boat, towing it slowly through the gap. Stood there studying the river-sights in the drizzling rain until the bridge followed after and closed to open the street again. Later, I never crossed the river without being charmed by somber beauty.

Wondered where to go for the night. But again if I thought to ask anyone, there was only the brutal, hurrying crowd trying hard not to see.

Drifted south. This must be Chicago now. So cold, black, blue-white and wet. The horrid blue-white glare of arc-lights was over everything. Shivering. Hungry. Went into an eating place near Randolph Street and parted with seventy cents, ten per cent of my entire capital. As I ate, I was sure of one thing, never would I go near Uncle Jenkin Lloyd-Jones nor ask his help nor use his name.

Got into the street again to find it colder, raining harder. Drifted south and turned left, shivering now in front of the Chicago Opera House on Washington Street, the flood of hard lights made the unseeing faces of the crowd in the drizzle, livid—ghastly. Under a great canopy that made a shelter from the rain were enormous posters— "Sieba"—Extravaganza by David Henderson, Grand Corps de Ballet. And there the dancers were, life-size almost, out on the sidewalk, holding their color in spite of the glare.

The doors were just open and a dollar let me go in to wait nearly an hour for the show to begin, where it was dry and warm. During that waiting . . . went back to the home by the lake—to see Mother, Jennie and Maginel . . . wondered what they would feel when they knew I had gone for good . . . never to come back? But they were all coming to me in Chicago. There must be clean, quiet "home" places in Chicago. Near the lake, maybe. I wondered if they were anxious about me, hardly realizing I wouldn't be missed until tomorrow night. Saw Mother's sad eyes and pale face as she sat quietly—waiting. She seemed always waiting now. A pang of homesickness already, but the orchestra filed out from under the stage.

Tuning up began, always exciting. Then the florid overture. I knew it wasn't good music—good music was not so sentimental (my father's term of contempt)—but I was glad to hear it. The Henderson Extravaganzas in those days were unduly extravagant. This one took the roof off an unsophisticated mind.

Went out after all was over, drifting with the crowd to Wabash Avenue. Cottage Grove Avenue cable cars were running there. My first sight of the cable car. So, curious, I got on the grip-car beside the gripman and tried to figure it all out, going south in the process until the car stopped, and "All out!" That car was going to the barn.

Got on one coming out headed north now. Not sleepy nor tired. Half-resentful because compelled to read the signs pressing on the eyes everywhere. They claimed your eyes for this, that and everything besides. They lined the car above the windows. They lined the way, pushing, crowding and playing all manner of tricks on the victim's eye. Tried to stop looking at them. Unfairly compelled to look again. In self-defense kept on reading until reading got to be torture.

There were glaring signs on the glass shop-fronts against the lights inside, sharp signs in the glare of the sputtering arc-lamps outside. Hurrah signs. Stop signs. Come-on-in signs. Hello signs set out before the blazing windows on the sidewalks. Flat fences lettered both sides, man-high, were hanging out across above the sidewalks and lit by electric lamps. Coming from extravaganza, here was the beginning of phantasmagoria.

Supersensitive ears and eyes were fixed by harsh dissonance but recovered themselves: reasoned and fought for freedom. Compelled again—until the procession of saloons, food shops, barber shops, eating houses, saloons, restaurants, groceries, laundries—and saloons, saloons, tailors, dry goods, candy shops, bakeries, saloons, became chaos in a wilderness of Italian, German, Irish, Polack, Greek, English, Swedish, French, Chinese and Spanish names in letters that begun to come off and get about, interlace and stick, climb and swing again.

Demoralization of the eye began: *names* obliterating everything. Names and what they would do for you or with you or to you for your money. Shutting your eyes didn't end it, for then you heard them louder than you saw them. They would begin to mix with absurd effect and you need take nothing to get the effect of another extravaganza. Letters this time. Another ballet, of A. B. C. D. E. F. G., L. M. N. O. P., X. Y. and Z., the première-danseuse intervening in fantastic dances.

It would have been a mercy not to have known the alphabet. One pays a heavy toll for the joys of being eye-minded. Ear-minded, too.

Got to bed at the Brigg's House north on Randolph Street, wrapped a sheet around myself—it seemed awfully like a winding sheet as I caught sight of it in the mirror—and slept. A human item—insignificant but big with interior faith and a great hope. In what? I could not have told you. Asleep in Chicago. Chicago murderously actual.

CHICAGO

Next day began on Chicago.

Hand in pocket after breakfast, I could feel sure of three silver dollars and a dime. Took the city directory and made a list of architects, choosing names I had heard in Conover's office or names that sounded interesting. All only names to me and missed the names of all names important to me. The name of the architect of my uncle's new church, "All Souls," I knew by heart—J. L. Silsbee, Lakeside Building, Clark Street, Chicago. But I wasn't going there. Tramped through street after street now seeing Chicago above the sign-belt.

Where was the architecture of the great city—the "Eternal City of the West"? Where was it? Hiding behind these shameless signs? A vacant block would come by. Then the enormous billboards planted there stood up grandly, had it all their own way, obliterating everything in nothing. That was better. Chicago! Immense gridiron of dirty noisy streets. . . . Heavy traffic crossing both ways at once, managing somehow: torrential noise.

A stupid thing, that gridiron: conflicting currents of horses, trucks, street cars grinding on hard rails mingling with streams of human beings in seeming confusion. Clamor! But habit was in the movement making it expert, and so safe enough. Dreary—dim—smoked. Smoked dim and smoking. A wide, desolate, vacant strip ran along the waterfront over which the Illinois Central trains puffed, shrieked and ground incessantly, cutting the city off from the lake.

Terrible! This grinding and piling up of blind forces. If there was logic here who could grasp it?

To stop and think in the midst of this would be to give way to terror. The gray, soiled river, with its mist of steam and smoke, was the only beauty. And that smelled to heaven.

Young engineer looking for work? "Sam Treat"—Treat and Folz—looked me over. "University man, eh?" The kindly intellectual face under a mass of gray hair smiled. "Sorry." Caught a glimpse of a busy draughting room full of men as I came out.

Well!—there was "Beers, Clay and Dutton." More tramping through brutal crowds that never seemed to see anything. Mr. Clay came out to look me over—a twinkle of kindly humor in his black eyes. I have remembered that HE seemed to see ME and was amused. Why? Was it the longish hair again, or what? Took pity on me maybe, for he asked me to call again in a few weeks if I found nothing. In a few weeks! I had just three dollars and ten cents left.

Over now to "S. S. Beman" in the Pullman Building way south on Michigan Avenue.

College "tooth-picks" made in vain if made for walking. Souvenir of sophomore vanity on right little toe "raising Cain" now. Perspiring freely. Found Mr. Beman not in! Foreman looked me over. I. K. Pond?

"University man? What college, Ann Arbor?"

"No, University of Wisconsin."

"No, nobody wanted at present, later perhaps—in a few months." In a few months! I felt the small change in my pocket.

The famous Pullman Building had come into view. It looked funny—as if made to excite curiosity. On the way down passed the Palmer House, that famous Chicago Palazzo. It seemed curious to me: like an ugly old, old man whose wrinkles were all in the wrong place owing to a 'misspent life. As I went on my way to "W. W. Boyington's" office I passed the Chicago Board of Trade at the foot of La Salle Street. Boyington had done it, had he? This?—thin-chested, hard-faced, chamfered monstrosity? I turned aside from Boyington's office then and there.

Chicago architecture! What was it? Not the Exposition Building, a rank, much-domed yellow shed on the lake front. No, nor the rank and file along the streets. The rank and file all pretty much alike, industriously varied without variety. All the same thought, or lack of it. Were all American cities like this one, so casual, so monotonous in their savage, outrageous attempts at variety? All monstrous and competing for the same thing, attention, in the same way? Another senseless competition never to be won?

So thinking, I got on toward Major Jenney's office. Head draughtsman Mundie came out. He was president of the Chicago Architectural Club as I knew. "Ah, university man. Engineer?" "Yes." Had I any drawings? No? First time I had been asked for any drawings. "Why don't you come around to the Club, meeting Saturday night? You might hear of something there. Bring some of your drawings along with you," he added.

Strange! I had not thought to bring any drawings with me. But some were in the bag, still checked at the Station. Mundie with his sunken eyes in an impassive frozen face was a little kindly warmth in the official atmosphere of the Chicago architect's office.

Too late to go to any more offices now. Got my bag to the Brigg's House not knowing where else to go. Hungry. Asked for a cheaper room. Clerk sympathetic—one for seventy-five cents, almost as good. For supper, what twenty. cents would buy at the bakery. I had found Kohlsatt's bakery-lunch. Tempting pastry piled high in plain sight, all that I had been denied or allowed to eat only occasionally. And things beside, I had never dreamed of. Here a hungry orphan was turned loose in a bake-shop? Lucky for me I had but little money.

To bed, dog-tired, not at all discouraged. No. On the whole everyone had been rather kind. Must be someone who needed me. Tomorrow, maybe!

Two days gone from home, Mother knew now. The thought of her was anguish. I turned away from it to action and repeated the performance of the day before in other offices, this time taking my drawings. Mundie was out. At five other offices, no success.

No lunch. No supper. During the day ten cents invested in bananas.

That night, a weird dream. Up in a balloon. Mother frantically holding to the rope, dragged along the ground, calling Jennie and Maginel to help . . . all dragged along. I shouted down to hitch the end of the rope to something, anything, and make it fast. But it tore out of helpless hands and I shot up and up, up—until I awoke with a sense of having been lifted miles to the strange ground of another world.

Awakened rudely to the fourth day. Got started again, pavement-sore now, gaunt. Something had to happen today. Tired again, three more offices. Same result.

There was still Silsbee's office. He was building my uncle's "All Souls" church, but he needn't know who I was. After noon I went there. Liked the atmosphere of the office best. Liked Silsbee's sketches on the wall. Liked instantly the fine-looking, cultured fellow with pompadour and beard, who came forward with quiet friendly smile—Cecil Corwin.

"Hello!" he said as thought he knew me. He looked the artist-musician. Through the gate in the outer office railing he had come humming from the "Messiah." I smiled and said, "So you sing?" He smiled, looking at my hair-cut, or lack of it. "Yes . . . try to . . . Do you play?" "Yes . . . try to." I had found a kindred spirit.

He sat down by me in the outer office. His sleeves were rolled above the elbow. His arms were thickly covered with coarse hair, but I noticed how he daintily crooked his little finger as he lifted his pencil. He had an air of gentleness and refinement. I told him my trials.

"You are a minister's son."

"Yes, how did you know?"

"Didn't know, something about you. I am one myself. The 'Old Man' " (moving his head in the direction of Silsbee's private office) "is one too. And there are two more here already, Wilcox and Kennard. If you come in here, there would be five of us."

We laughed.

"Well . . . could I by any chance come in?" I said anxiously. He looked me over. "I believe we could get along," he said. "Let me see your drawings."

He looked carefully at the sketches. "You made these just to please yourself?"

"Yes."

"You've got a good touch. Wait a minute." He took them and went in through a door marked "Private." Presently he appeared at the door with a tall, dark-faced, aristocratic-looking man, gold eye-glasses with long gold chain hanging from his nose. He stood in the door looking carelessly at me with a frown. It was Silsbee. "All right," he said, "take him on. Tracer's wages—$8.00."

He turned and shut the door after him.

"Not much, but better than nothing?" said Cecil. I agreed though I had been getting eighteen.

How far from my expectations! "$8.00." With my "experience" I should be able to earn three times as much. But no one thought much of my experience. Cecil saw the disappointment following elation. "Had your lunch? No? Come with me." We went downstairs a block away to Kinsley's. Cecil insisted on a good portion of browned corned-beef hash for me, and coffee.

"Thank you, no coffee. I don't drink it."

"Well then"—amused—"milk?" Ever since, feeling really hungry, nothing has tasted so good to me as browned corned-beef hash.

"Got any money left?" he said abruptly.

"Oh, yes!"

"How much?"

"Twenty cents."

"Had anything to eat yesterday?" This was getting rather too personal so I didn't answer.

"Come home with me tonight and we'll concertize with my new grand piano." It was Saturday. I was not to report for work until Monday morning.

So I got my bag from the Brigg's House and went home with Cecil. A nice home. Met his benevolent preacher-father, a Congregational missionary. His mother had died some years ago, but his sister Marquita looked after the father and her bachelor brother. She was "musical" too.

After a "musical" evening together, we went up to the room that was for me, and Cecil found how anxious I was about things back home, gave me paper, pen and ink to write. I did.

Then: "Would you lend me ten dollars to send to my Mother? I'll pay you back two dollars a week." Here started characteristic process continuing to this day.

He said nothing, took a ten-dollar bill from his pocket and laid it on the table. I put it in the envelope. We took it to the nearest box to post. A load went off my heart. I had a job, but better still, I had a friend. No mean one in any sense, as anyone might see. I could go now and see my uncle's new church, "All Souls." Cecil himself had been looking after the building of it so I asked him about it.

He said: Would you like to see "The Church," with curious emphasis on "Church." "We'll go down to Oakwood Boulevard and Langley Avenue after dinner and have a look at it." We went. Why the curious emphasis? I knew now. It was in no way like a Church, more like a "Queen Anne" dwelling. We used to say Queen Anne front and Mary Ann behind. This was. But interesting to me. Again, not beautiful—but . . . curiously interesting.

Taking advantage of the unexpected visit, Cecil went about looking after details in the nearly completed building. I went along Oakwood Boulevard to look it over in perspective. Was standing back, looking over from across the street when a hand from behind took me firmly by the collar and a hearty voice like a blow, "Well, young man! So here you are." I recognized the voice instantly, Uncle Jenkin Lloyd-Jones! I was in for it.

"I've been expecting you, young fellow. Your mother wrote— distracted. I'll telegraph you're found."

No!—Uncle Jenk—Please. I said, "I wrote last night telling her I had a job and I sent her some money too."

A job? "Where have you found a job?"

"Silsbee's office."

"Silsbee's? Of course. That was mighty good of him. Told him who you were I suppose?" said Uncle Jenkin.

"No!" I said. "I didn't!" He looked suspicious. But got the point quickly. "All right," he said. Then Cecil came up and greeted him. "Where did you get hold of my young nephew?"

"He's your nephew? I didn't know it," Cecil said in astonishment. That proved my case.

"Well—where are you going to stay now?" asked the maternal uncle. I didn't know. "You're coming to stay near here where I can keep an eye on you. Tonight you must come and stay with us."

"No!" said Cecil, "he's going to stay with me tonight."

"All right then, Monday night."

Isn't "opening to the way" usually as simple? Here came the chance end of a sequence that like the end of twine in a skein of indefinite length, would unwind in characteristic events as time went on. Not at all as I had expected! It seldom is as much or perhaps at all as we expect. But Cecil was already more in himself than I could ever have imagined. His culture similar to mine, yet he was different. So much more developed. So I began to go to school to Cecil. Soon we were together everywhere.

SILSBEE

Silsbee was doing Edgewater at the time, latest attempt at high-class subdivision; doing it entirely for J. L. Cochran, a real-estate "genius" in his line. A genius being, naturally, a man who can make much money easily? Silsbee could draw with amazing ease. He drew with soft, deep black lead-pencil strokes and he would make remarkable free-hand sketches of that type of dwelling peculiarly his own at the time. His superior talent in design had made him respected in Chicago. His work was a picturesque combination of gable, turret and hip, with broad porches, quietly domestic and gracefully picturesque. A contrast to the awkward stupidities and brutalities of the period elsewhere. He would come out to the draughting room as though we, the draughtsmen, did not exist, stand talking a moment with Cecil, one lank leg turning one long foot over sidewise, the picture of indifference or scorn as he stood on the other, grudging of words and shy of patience. All awed by him. Not so Cecil.

92

The office system was a bad one. Silsbee got a ground-plan and made his pretty sketch, getting some charming picturesque effect he had in his mind. Then the sketch would come out into the draughting room to be fixed up into a building, keeping the floor-plan near the sketch if possible. But the sketches fascinated us. "My God, Cecil, how that man can draw!"

"He can. He's a kind of genius I guess—but something is the matter with him. He doesn't seem to take any of it, or take himself, half seriously. The picture interests him. The rest bores him. You'll see. He's an architectural genius spoiled by way of the aristocrat. A fine education and family in Syracuse, but too contemptuous of everything."

I did see. I saw Silsbee was just making pictures. Not very close to what was real in the building—that I could see, myself. But I adored Silsbee just the same. He had style. His work had it too, in spite of slipshod methods. There was something finely tragic in his somber mien; authority in the boom of his enormous voice pitched low in his long throat with its big Adam's apple. I learned a good deal about a house from Silsbee and by way of Cecil.

Monday night I had gone to Uncle Jenkin's to spend a few days in the parsonage. Interesting couple came there to dine. Dr. Thomas, Rabbi Hirsh, Jane Addams, Dr. Mangasarian and others. I enjoyed listening.

A letter had come from Mother. She wrote regularly every week: seemed glad after all that I was at work. Told me to stay close to Uncle Jenkin. He was a good man beset by the countless trials of his position but he'd help me all he could. I was not to worry about her.

She had sold Father's library and a few hundred dollars had come to her from her brothers, her small share in Grandfather's farm. If I got along and needed her she would sell the Madison place, come down and make a home for me. There were the usual anxieties about diet, warm underwear, companions.

"I would have you," she wrote, "a man of sense as well as sensibility. You will find Goodness and Truth everywhere you go. If you have to choose, choose Truth. For that is closest to Earth. Keep close to the Earth, my boy: in that lies strength. Simplicity of heart is just as necessary for an architect as for a farmer or a minister if the architect is going to build great buildings." And she would put this faith of hers in many different forms as she wrote on different subjects, until I knew just what to expect from her.

Always very brave, she was, but I knew what she wanted—she wanted to come down to live with me. So soon as I could earn eighteen or twenty dollars a week I intended to have her come. Little Maginel was not very strong. Sister Jennie had gone to teach school in the country.

I have always been fond of Uncle Jenkin's son, my cousin Richard. He was good-looking, fair-haired, a brilliant "city guy," initiated and unabashed. His views of what went on around him were keen and amusing. Richard had ambition, a certain affection but small reverence. He was a good specimen of minister's son, too. His mother was older than his father and more intellectual, I believe. She adored her son and never tired of quoting him. He was quotable; I will say that for him, although Aunt Susan continually did overdo Richard. Mothers are apt to the habit of overdoing their sons.

"Uncle Jenk," his father, found a boarding place for me at the Watermans', a block away on Vincennes Avenue. I got my clothes into a wheelbarrow one night, late, and with Dick's help started down the deserted boulevard. It was so smooth I proposed to beat him the two blocks to the corner, I wheeling the barrow. We lit out. I did beat him but in trying to turn to Vincennes, over went wheelbarrow, clothes, helter-skelter into the grimy street, myself following head first in a cruel slide as though I'd been shot out of a cannon, Dick tumbling after did a cart-wheel into the wreck. Both of us were scratched and scraped, not hurt. Laughing—we were always laughing—we gathered dusty underwear, ties, Sunday clothes, shirts far and wide as the wind entered into the spirit of the thing and carried on . . . that boulevard dust in my things as near permanent as any dye.

The Watermans' was a quiet, decent place. I saw Harry, a morose lad nearly my own age, once in a while. But they were all rather pessimistic folk, saddened, it seemed to me, by something of a family nature. Did it follow me everywhere, or did I see it because of my own experience?

Dick and I went about together. Dick knew the ropes as Dick knew how to laugh. We would get to laughing and keep at it, the bait going to and fro between us until both were tired out.

There was quite a social life then going on at the church. Evening events, lectures and meetings of one sort or another. Sociables. Browning classes. I got "Rabbi Ben Ezra" into my system about that time and *The Ring and the Book*. Study classes of all kinds. All Souls had a circulating library, was a neighborhood center in which were many activities intellectual, social and literary. A kindergarten there too. A "church" that was never closed.

My uncle's soul seemed a sort of spiritual dynamo that never rested. His preaching, like Grandfather's, had force and fervor. And brains, but I began to suspect him of sentimentality. But he was evidently becom-

94

ing an active spiritual force in Chicago. His influence was rapidly on the increase.

Cecil was often taking me home and we went to the Apollo Club Concerts or any good concert wherever we could find one. To the theater sometimes. I had then, as now, a passion for the theater as for music.

Work in the Silsbee office was easy for me and I soon made myself useful. We took on a new man about that time, a few months after I had entered—George Maher. He had asked Silsbee for eighteen dollars a week and got it as he had "experience." After three months I had been only raised to twelve.

I soon found George no better draughtsman than I, if as good. So I made up my mind to try for a raise. If Silsbee could pay George eighteen, he could pay me twenty.

"The old man's here now—go in and talk to him," said Cecil. I went in.

Silsbee looked at me and frowned. Evidently he knew what my being there meant.

"Well!"

"Mr. Silsbee, I can't get along on twelve dollars a week. Don't you think I can earn fifteen dollars at least—now?"

"You've just had a raise, Wright. No! Perhaps—the first of the year."

I was sure injustice was being done me. So then and there, I "quit."

Mr. W. W. Clay, of Beers, Clay and Dutton, had interested me when I was job-hunting. I now went straight over to see him again.

"One of Silsbee's men?" he asked. A man in Silsbee's office could usually draw and design in his style and was in demand by architects less capable of design—

"Yes, sir."

"How much do you expect to earn?"

"Eighteen dollars."

He got up and went out with me to the foreman of the draughting room.

"Lockwood," said he, "take this young man on. We will pay him eighteen dollars a week. His name is Wright."

Cecil and I were still together noons and evenings. Mr. Clay, more than kind, seemed interested in me. But I soon found myself entrusted with work beyond me. Designing what I should be learning how to design.

I had made a mistake in the long run and I realized it. In a few weeks I went in to tell Mr. Clay so. He was astonished.

"Aren't we good to you here, Wright? Isn't the work interesting?"

"Oh, yes," I could truthfully say.

"Don't you like me?"

"Yes." And I really did.

"Well, out with it. What's the matter?"

I told him I didn't feel ready to "give out" designs. Wanted to learn how to make them. There was no one there skilled as a designer. I could learn very little.

"I see," he said dryly. He was hurt. I think he thought me a young coxcomb.

"What are you going to do?"

"I'm going back to Silsbee."

"Will he take you?"

"I don't know."

"Hadn't you better find out before you quit?"

"No."

"Why not?"

I had no answer.

"All right! Go out to Lockwood and tell him to give you your wages." But he thought that rather rough and went out with me himself. "Lockwood," he said gently, "give Wright his wages and let him out. Either he's got the big head or he's right. I don't know which." He shook hands with me, characteristic half-humorous look coming again into his eyes.

I went as straight back to Silsbee as I had left him. Told him the story. He smoked away without a word.

"You've quit already, have you?"

"Yes, sir."

"What for?"

"Well, I didn't want it to look as though you were taking me away from Mr. Clay, if you let me come back."

He smiled that bitter smile of his, went to the door and called, "Corwin!" Cecil came. "Wright is coming back. His wages will be eighteen dollars." The Silsbee private office door closed behind me as I came out.

Cecil and I went dancing around the big table in the center of the room in a friendly tilt.

During these later months at Silsbee's Cecil and I were inseparable.

Discussed everything in the heavens above, the earth beneath and the waters thereof. We would go to Madame Gallé's Italian table d'hôte and various other cozy restaurants. Or, if we had a little money, to the Tip Top Inn in the Pullman Building.

Theodore Thomas was giving his famous concerts in the old Exposition Building. We went there. In the rear of the audience there were tables and refreshments in comfortable German style. Loving concerts, I've never enjoyed any concerts more.

Adler and Sullivan were just beginning to build the Chicago Auditorium. The papers were full of its wonders. The architects were frequently mentioned. I wondered how I had come to miss that firm in my search for work.

Sunday mornings usually I went to All Souls. Perhaps to dinner at the parsonage above. I had noticed interesting people in the congregation but made no acquaintances, although a number of the people who knew me as the pastor's nephew asked me to come to them or invited me without that formality to dine. I didn't go. Preferred Cecil's company. If I couldn't have that, I would find something to do.

From the library of All Souls I got two books you would never expect could be found there. Owen Jones's *Grammar of Ornament* and Viollet-le-Duc's *Habitations of Man in All Ages*. I had read his *Dictionnaire*, the *Raisonné*, at home, got from the Madison city library.

I believed the *Raisonné* was the only really sensible book on architecture. I got copies for my sons, later. That book was enough to keep (in spite of architects) one's faith in architecture.

The Owen Jones was a reprint but good enough. I read the "propositions" and felt the first five dead right. I didn't know about the others. It seemed these five were equally sound applied to human behavior. They were. I got a packet of "onion skin," delicate, strong, smooth tracing paper and traced the multifold designs. I traced evenings and Sunday mornings until the packet of one hundred sheets was gone and I needed exercise to straighten up.

Eager to learn to box while at the University, I have practiced a little with Jimmie Kerr who had similar ambition. One of the items that rolled over the dusty boulevard when, moving, I upset the barrow, Dick and myself, was a set of boxing gloves. I used to put on the gloves with Harry Waterman. Used to walk sometimes nearly forty blocks downtown to work. A number of times, out of carfare, I walked the whole distance.

A PRETTY GIRL IN PINK

Study classes at All Souls were busy with Victor Hugo's *Les Misérables* under the guidance of the Pastor. Students were to complete this study with a costume party, characters of the tale appearing as Victor Hugo designed them. The affair was to be a sweeping one, music, dancing and a supper. Therefore a large hall was hired somewhere near Vincennes Avenue. I wasn't a regular member of the classes, but "Enjolras," young French officer, fell to my lot. My rôle was simple, so they said. All I needed was a pair of high-heeled shiny black boots coming above the knee, clanking spurs, not to mention white, tight trousers, scarlet military jacket with stiff collar, gold braid and epaulettes. I would need a small round red cap on my head. And, should have hanging alongside on a leather harness, a sword! I don't know where I got all the things—some customer's, I suppose. They were probably as correct as Victor Hugo himself sometimes wasn't. Cecil helped the great work on. When I was dressed and ready he said, "Maybe not anything like 'Enjolras,' Frank, but certainly something to look at."

I pulled out the sword, stuck it point down on the floor and made a leg. "You'll do," he said. "I almost wish I had agreed to come when your uncle invited me."

"Come on anyway!" I begged. But he wouldn't. So putting on my overcoat capewise to put the glory out, I buttoned it, sleeves hanging. Holding the sword by my side I walked down the boulevard to the hall, not to be conspicuous but late.

The scene, after I had stowed my coat and opened the door to the hall, was really brilliant. There they were—happy *"Misérables"* all of them.

But my plan had worked out wrong, for coming late I *was* conspicuous. The first dance over, the characters were standing around the sides of the large room regarding that large central area as I came upon it—an empty dancing floor! Many groups of prettily dressed French peasant girls and young yokels were standing about. Marat I saw, terrible as he needed to be, and perhaps wasn't. The best character there, seen at a glance, was my Aunt Susan, the preacher's wife, the Abbé. Suddenly a group of lasses in bright bodices, short skirts and pretty caps came rushing over the floor. In the lead Miss Emery. "Here you are at last," she said as she turned to introduce me to the others.

Older somewhat than I. "Finished" in a fashionable eastern school she spoke with pretty accent the broad "a." Too pretty to be natural and yet, somehow, it probably was natural—hers, after all. . . .

Glad to be taken in hand by her I danced with the church girls I knew but slightly. The infernal slab-sided sword was slung so low that if

I took my hands off, it got between my legs. If I took my mind off it, it got between my partner's legs with disastrous effect—some of the "effects" laughable.

No longer shy, I danced pretty well. But that sword sank me. I tried schemes to control it. I couldn't spoil the fine figure I was making by taking it off. I was going to hang on to that swinging, dangling, clanking sword if I mowed the legs off the whole "*Misérables.*" Some of the girls entered into the spirit of the thing while dancing and were helpful holding on to it themselves. While dancing or at psychological moments otherwise—that sword!

Miss Emery sat out a few dances with me or rather we went out into a half-dark auditorium opening into the hall. I felt quite at home in her company. Glad I came. But when I wasn't in trouble with that sword, she was.

Felt I was having a bully time. Outside the gathering, I could take off the superfluous weapon. She seemed to like to hold it—probably felt safer when *she* had it.

At ten o'clock came a lull in the evening. Refreshments served. There was a general rushing about to restore the various units to their several places with their parties. Rushing across the dancing floor to join Miss Emery's group, halfway over, a tall, pretty peasant girl in pink, blonde curls dancing my way while looking the other, was upon me before I could avoid her. Striking her forehead square against mine she was knocked to her hands and knees. I myself seeing stars managed to pick her up. Laughing it off bravely enough, she was still blinking. I saw the bump already on her forehead as I led her over to her parents to apologize, but she wouldn't have it. "All my fault," she insisted. The parents were Mr. and Mrs. Tobin, and this was their Catherine. Her father called her "Kitty." I had noticed her in church, a gay-spirited, sunny-haired young girl of probably sixteen, with a frank, handsome countenance. Her parents I remembered had once asked me to dinner. They asked me again now for Sunday—tomorrow. I said I would come. I hoped the bump, beginning to swell, would not be too painful.

Soon after I noticed they had left.

Next day, a bump on my own forehead.

The course of the party changed for me. At eleven o'clock, the hour for church parties to end, I saw Miss' Emery into her carriage and walked home alone along the boulevard.

An ancient oracle might have stretched a prophetic hand over that crash.

Next morning, turned by the party toward Victor Hugo again, I remembered the chapter in *Notre Dame,* wherein the amazing Frenchman had disposed of the European Renaissance as "that setting sun all Europe mistook for dawn." When I got up I went to the Church library.

Found a different translation. This chapter-heading, instead of using as in the original French, *Ceci tuera cela* (This will kill that), was "The Book Will Kill the Edifice." I took it home and read it again instead of going to church.

Victor Hugo loved diffuse discussion in abstruse style. But this essay was one of the truly great things ever written on architecture. Again I felt its force. My own gathering distrust was again confirmed. Splendid writing! How "modern" the great romanticist must have seemed in his time! Yet this chapter was omitted from later editions.

Again excited by the great poet into thinking about the difference between romanticism and sentimentality, I got started late, walking down Drexel Boulevard to the Tobin home. Late to dinner. Catherine opened the door, *Les Misérables* bump 'most gone. Easy to like hearty Father Tobin. He carried everything before him in a bluff, easy way; Mother Tobin was different—fine-looking, auburn-haired too. Both beloved by their children—but the mother ruled, evidently mistress of her nice new home.

Catherine, eldest, was sixteen. Charlie and Robert were twins. They were twelve. Arthur, youngest, a pretty, affectionate boy of seven, came and sat on my knee. Devoted to Jenkin Lloyd-Jones, all were disposed to lionize his nephew.

Diffidence disappeared in this home: a warmth I had lost since coming to the city. Girlish and lovely, "Kitty" vivaciously adopted me at once. She was in the Hyde Park High School. Also one of Professor Tomlin's pupils in music. Evidently Catherine had pretty much her own way in that household. Yet she seemed a sensible girl. Everything revolved around her. Not only was she accustomed to having her own way but having it without any trouble. At table I noticed she ate on her own particular plate with her own particular knife, fork and spoon. A hangover from childhood. The idiosyncracy seemed natural. The dinner went off gaily. After dinner Kitty came in dressed to go out, tall laced boots, gloves and short plaid walking jacket. A tam-o'-shanter topped her mass of ruddy curls.

She took me by the hand, simply, and said she was going to take me to see the new Kenwood houses. That meant to see some curious effects, because Kenwood was in process of becoming the most fashionable of Chicago's residence districts. So we went down the front steps hand in hand like children. She *was* one, although so tall and seeming to have such good sense. I was grown up pretty well in architecture, the sphere in which I lived in earnest. But where people were concerned, I had nearly everything to learn.

More months went by until, after a year with Silsbee, and coming twenty soon, earning the necessary $18.00 per week, I felt Mother should sell the Madison home by the lake and come to Chicago. Soon she did come.

The North Shore then attracted me, but Mother was afraid of the raw winds of the lake for me and for Maginel too. She didn't seem to want to be too near All Souls either, for some reason. So we went to see Miss Augusta Chapin, a friend of Mother's in Oak Park. A preacher and this time a woman. She was Oak Park's Universalist pastor. Miss Chapin was thick-set, a woman's woman of about forty, usually dressed in rustling black silk, a gold chain around her neck to hang a gold cross upon her breast. She wore, alternately, a very kind and very severe expression.

Miss Chapin and Mother worked out some temporary arrangement whereby we were to come in to the red-brick on Forest Avenue with her for some time to see if Oak Park was really the place to choose for our permanent home.

OAK PARK

Oak Park's other name was "Saint's Rest." So many churches for so many good people to go to, I suppose. The village looked like a pretty respectable place. The people were good people most of whom had taken asylum there to bring up their children in comparative peace, safe from the poisons of the great city. The village streets were generously shaded: had a village government of its own, too, accounting to some extent for its subsequent growth.

I remember Superintendent Hatch, a kindly dark-faced man, driving about in an open buggy from school to school. My sister Jennie, now, owing to Miss Chapin's kind offices, one of his teachers at the Chicago Avenue School.

I remember the old Scovill place, occupying a whole square of the town, standing up there shamelessly tall, to say the last word for the depravity characterizing the residence architecture of that period; this lean wooden house.

The quite village looked much like Madison to Mother. That settled it.

Opposite the red-brick on Forest Avenue, well within the center of the village, was the Austin lot, another whole square competing with the Scovill square. This one untouched natural wildwood. A newly built all-shingle home in the entering mode, Queen Anne, took the middle of a cleared space at the Lake Street front. To one side and to the rear of the house next to Forest Avenue stood an old-fashioned barn vertically boarded and battened. It had good proportion and was an interesting rusty color where the festoons of vines let color through. Built in a much earlier period, being only a barn, it had been allowed to live. I liked the barn better than the house. The old barn was honestly picturesque whereas the house only elaborately tried to be. But Forest Avenue residents thought it outrageous that Mr. Austin, Oak Park's leading citizen, should leave his old ivy-covered barn there on the best street in town.

Mr. Austin, short, slow-moving solid Scot, carried his head well down in his shoulders, a short neck, wore a quizzical look on his short, bearded face.

This Austin wood-lot was especially inviting to me in that aggregation of uninspired carpenter work: endless rows of drab or white painted wood porch houses set regularly apart, each on its little painted cardboard lawn. High front-steps went straight up to jigger-porches wriggling with turned balusters, squirming with wanton scroll-work. This prevalent porch-luxury was seldom of use, but still the roofs continued to shut out the sun from the parlors and sitting rooms. These enemies of Mr. Austin's barn all had the murderous corner-tower serving as bay-window in the principal sitting room. Where did that soul-destroying ornament come from? Never from earth. This popular fetish—for it was more than a "feature"—was either rectangular across the corner, round or octagonal, eventuating above in candle-snuffer roofs, turnip domes or corkscrew spires. I walked along the miles of this expensive mummery, trying to get into the thinking processes of the builders. Failed to get hold of any thinking they had done at all. The forms were utterly meaningless, though apparently much ingenious scheming and copying had gone into them.

Houses senseless. Most looked equally comfortless. No more so in Oak Park than anywhere else; rather better, because here in Oak Park there were more trees and vines and wider lots to cloak their ugliness. Those who lived in this ambitious Eastlake mimicry—called Queen Anne—were blissfully unaware of any serious losses or self-inflicted insults. And yet the monotonous iteration of this suburban-house parade like the sign-parade on Chicago streets compelled my attention willing or not.

The sign-parade—phantasmagoria—had at least some basis, some word-meaning. This procession—monogoria—had none whatever. My father's complaints and criticisms of music came to mind. "Sentimentality" spoiled music for him in the making or the playing. Did it apply here?

As I walked and walked about, helpless spectator, again a rank outsider, it would seem senseless reiteration: a monologue recited in monotone. . . .

Nobody home! Nobody home! "They stay here but they don't live here. We never knew life. But we are just as good as anybody's houses, just as good: Just as good as "they" are—Better, maybe.

Fooled? Maybe they are fooled. What do we care? Everybody is— everybody is! "They" are. We are. Everybody is. We suit them. They suit us. Why should we mean anything if they don't mean anything?

We're just as good as "they" are? We couldn't think if they wouldn't. They wouldn't think if we could. They buy what thought there is in us ready-made, buy what's in them, too. It's easier—because cheaper. How do you know—boy!

Houses are just like clothes, aren't they? We're just clothes too, so we have to be in fashion, don't we? Or we'll be laughed at! Won't we? Don't you see—boy? They'll be laughed at too—What then?

Fools are we? Maybe—but fools on the laughing side. Yet.

CULTURE

What matter? More painful than the Chicago sign-parade. Pitiful, because this was "Culture" while that was only mongering. Here was tragedy. Were these monstrosities like the people whose houses they were—like the men and women living in them? Was all this waste what they deserved? Or had education played tricks with them? If "they" were so far wrong in this expression of themselves, so lacking in feeling and perception of the natural—what were their other institutions like if you looked them square in the face? Were "they" really right about anything at all above the alimentary canal and reproductive tract? Weren't even those being corrupted, spoiled in confusion of spurious ideals with ignored needs? Why were "they" all satisfied with such pretentious attitudes and stupid gestures? Were all merely false-sentiment instead of sensible?

I used to take these doubts to Cecil. For wasn't Silsbee doing the same thing in the pictures he made for them, only he did it as an artist? Silsbee's houses were merely "arty" then? Probably—because what thought in them was just the same as this?

More than ever I began to be dissatisfied with Silsbee. He seemed to me making matters worse. Making a lie or any vain boast more pretty by his skill, therefore making this shameful swindle worse?

Going by, I would sometimes lean over the Austin fence, a mistaken affair of dead oak-tree branches with the bark on—therefore "rustic"; as I was leaning there looking into the woods on a Sunday morning, Mr. Austin came up and spoke to me. "Won't you come in?" he said. "You live next door? Young architect? Miss Chapin has spoken of you."

"I had wanted to get about a little in that oasis," I said. Pointing to the wood. I asked how he came to let it alone in the midst of all those harsh unsympathetic houses. He looked at me from under bushy eyebrows: "Don't you like their houses? Eh?

"They want me to move my old barn there, but"—looking toward it, eyes twinkling—"I like the looks of my barn better than I do their houses." He winked!

"I would rather live in it myself," I said.

"Come, let's look in it." He led the way.

Above, the old barn was fixed up as a playroom, or ballroom, being decorated now for a party to be given for his daughter, Sophie, returning from finishing school. There was a son, Harry, too—away somewhere at college.

Mr. Austin had turned his back on his new house to go to the old barn and never asked me what I thought of the house. The next Sunday he asked me in to meet Mrs. Austin. The interior of the house was livable and homelike. I could say nice things about it. The exterior was never mentioned between us. It seems it was an old home with a new outside. So it looked. Mrs. Austin, a placid invalid, sat in a wheel-chair by the window.

Mr. Austin and I went out back to the barn.

"Now what would you do with this room for an *occasion*?" he said.

I made a few spontaneous suggestions which happened to appeal to him—a decorative scheme of some sort; I have forgotten. "Will you come over and help carry it out?"

Then he took me several blocks away to a lot at the corner of Forest and Chicago Avenues, tanglewood of all sorts of trees, shrubs and vines belonging, he said, to a Mr. Blair, Scottish landscape gardener. Blair laid out Humboldt Park in Chicago. Mr. Austin had the greatest affection and respect for him. He never tired talking of the old gardener I never met, but kept this lot of his in mind.

Mr. Austin got into the way of calling for me regularly Sunday mornings to go for a little walk. I had found a quiet and, as circumstances proved, a staunch friend in Oak Park. A friend he remained while he lived.

CECIL

Months later Cecil and I, as usual, were talking over doubts gaining on me and making me less useful in the office.

104

"Frank, look out!" he would say. "Heresy in religion is bad enough, but nothing compared to heresy in Art and Culture. Read your Bible! Remember Jesus' instructions to His disciples?"

We happened to be at the Oak Park red-brick on a Sunday. I went after Miss Chapin's Bible. Cecil turned to Matthew and read: "Go not into the way of the Gentiles; and into any city of the Samaritans, enter ye not. . . . And into whatsoever city or town ye shall enter, enquire who in it is worthy; and there abide till ye go thence. . . . Behold, I send you forth as sheep in the midst of wolves: be ye therefore wise as serpents, and harmless as doves. But beware of men: for they will deliver you up to the councils, and they will scourge you in their synagogues. And ye shall be brought before governors and kings for my sake, for a testimony against them and the Gentiles." He put the book down.

"The Gentiles today, Frank, and the Pharisees, too, for that matter, are the people proud of these homes, satisfied by them. The architects who work for them are, literally, the 'scribes.' The 'professionals' today are in much the same social relation to the people as were the 'scribes' to the Pharisees in the time of Jesus."

He took up the book again. " 'Give not that which is holy unto the dogs, neither cast ye thy pearls before swine' . . . ('swine' meaning those whose appetites for gain or fame or pleasure rule their judgment) . . . 'lest they trample them under their feet and turn and rend you. Beware of the leaven of the Pharisees and of the leaven of Herod.' " He shut the book. Sat silent a moment. Then he said quietly, "Silsbee's right. Silsbee doesn't interfere with their beliefs or upset their ideas of themselves. He does the thing they have already accepted but does it better than others do it. That's all. In consequence he is considered radical enough by them and—God knows—has had enough trouble with them just on that account."

Now I had waited, to be sure of what I wanted to say.

"Yes but, Cecil, is Silsbee doing the best he can? I mean, could he do better if he would?"

"What does that matter if he's doing the best thing?"

"But he's not doing the 'best thing' if he is not doing as well as he knows how and *all* he knows how to do."

"Why not?"

"Because there is God, He can be trusted to use the best He has made or He wouldn't have made it. If He *is,* He can be trusted to make the modifications—not Silsbee. This God of my grandfathers—the first thing *He* would put upon every member of creation, conscious or unconscious, would be just that thing—*to do the best he knew how to do.* Not as he was *told* to do it, but as he *saw* it for himself. Else what meaning has 'He'?"

Cecil laughed. "That mother of yours is going to have occasion to weep for you, Frank."

"Maybe, Cecil, but not on that account if she is Grandfather's daughter. And she is."

"Have you ever talked these things over with her?" said Cecil.

"No, because only now it's just coming clear to me. I am not afraid of what she'll say, though."

"But *whom* are you going to build homes for? If you go against their wishes and try to give them what *you* think right and not what they think they want?"

"That's just where a wise Creator must come in, Cecil. I won't need but one man in ten thousand to work for—even one man in a hundred thousand would keep me more than busy all my life, because that man will need me as much as I need him. He will be looking for me. I've been thinking about old Mr. Austin."

"Yes," said Cecil. "Look at his house!"

"Well—looking at it. He got the best architect he knew. It happened to be Fred Shock, of Austin, and the old man did all he could with him and got disappointed. What he got isn't his house. He knows it. He's one man in Oak Park I could work for on the basis of the best I've got in *me*. He's getting the '*modified* Gospel,' when *he* ought to get it straight. If God is on the job, not loafing in heaven—there in Mr. Austin would be client one for me."

Cecil laughed, "Yes, and all you'd need would be to find him and for him to find you." Sarcastically, "A simple matter as things are?"

"Well, I did find *him* and I could make others like him find *me* if I had anything to show them. I know what Mr. Austin needs and what he missed. I believe he missed it because the 'Gospel is modified,' as you suggest. And yet you defend it and say it is the right thing. Man alive! Isn't making these modifications taking God away and sitting in his place? We are all given *choice* and let free to choose. We live or die as we are fit to do, to the extent of our natures only when *free to choose*. Not when somebody is allowing us to choose only what *they* think we want, cheating us out of what we might have but for their interference. Only by such choice, can we fulfill the Law."

"What Law?" said Cecil. "That irreligious, inhuman 'survival of the fittest'?"

"No," I said, feeling my way to the proper answer. "No. The process of nature-selection." I knew I had slipped . . . I tried again—"Well—no—keeping the truest and best of which man is capable where man can see and use it."

"If they can find it," said Cecil. "How are you going to put it in the show-window?"

"How do I know? That isn't *my* business either."

"Going to put that up to God too?"

"And why not?" I said. "Look here, Cecil, what's more—I see it now—that's just what's the matter with the Gospel as preached today in the churches: Jesus was doing the best He knew how. The truth was in Him. He preached it. But *He*, the Nazarene Carpenter (I wonder if the carpenter wasn't the architect in those days), was modified by His disciples in the next place.

"The disciples were sincere enough and did the best they could but they were 'modified' in the next place. Again their preaching was modified by disciples of those disciples. Again 'modified' to suit the 'needs of mankind.' Not as Jesus or His Father saw those needs. No. Only as preachers like your father and my father saw them. Haven't the sentiments of Jesus become sentimentalized—a sentimentality in mouths of His disciples? Where is there 'clear wine to drink' on any such basis, Cecil?"

"Who wants clear wine?" he said. "The water bottle stands beside the Chianti on the table. We use it unless we want the linings of our stomachs corroded beyond repair."

"That won't do! I'm not talking about Chianti. That, you said, was made from the skins of grapes anyway. I am talking about Champagne or Moselle or Burgundy or Port—who wants water in real wine?"

"All watered at some time to some extent," said Cecil. The discussion had fizzled out.

I began to wonder if, after all, Father's life had not been in spite of him such sacrifice to sentimentality. Tried to get it clear. What had the Lloyd-Jones emotional sentimentality done to Father? What would it do to me—to Mother? What was rank sentimentality, the degeneracy of fine sentiment, doing to the life of the world?

Next Sunday, it began with Catherine. Sometimes evenings I had taken her home from church. One chill evening, I tried to put my coat on her to keep her warm but she indignantly refused to let me. We compromised by walking with an arm around each other to keep *both* warm. Sometimes her mother would let us go together to Theodore Thomas's concerts in town. Her daughter began to wait for me to sit by her in church, and if I was late, to wait with a vacant place by her side. I would take her home to Sunday dinner after services.

I told Mother about Catherine. She had already heard—Uncle Jenkin probably. And, as now appeared, she had been anxious. The affair *was* conspicuous by now. Kitty had begun to fall off in her school studies. She was being unmercifully teased by her school-fellows. Young people at the church already took us for granted.

Cecil met her occasionally when she came to pick me up at the office. He thought her a gay, charming youngster. "She's awfully fond of me, Cecil," I said.

"Well," he said, "so am I. So is your mother. So are your sisters. Maybe others would be too, if you gave them a chance. I don't see that *that* gives her any special claim on you, does it? You don't know other girls at all, Frank. What do you know about women by merely knowing Kitty?"

He himself knew few girls and they were much older than I. Uninteresting, I thought. He was such an attractive person I often wondered why he didn't know more interesting ones.

"Why," I said, "does anyone have to know *many* if he finds himself at home with one?"

"Did you ever kiss one—except her?"

"How do you know I've kissed her?"

"I'm clairvoyant," he said. "Didn't you know?"

"No, but . . ."

Cecil interrupted me: "Exactly, *'but.'* You are going into this thing heels over head, 'at home with her.' *'At home,'* " he repeated excitedly. "Yes, that's what I was afraid of. Don't you know she's a child? *You're* a child? Before you can construct any family life worth having you must know what women are?"

"So you mean I have to kiss and *take* women, to study women before I know what I want? Is that what you are driving at? I can understand how a man might kiss a girl in a kind of game. But—how can a man *take* a girl he doesn't love and doesn't want to live with?"

He looked out of the office window, his gentle face dropped—didn't answer.

"Cecil, what is it? What's the matter, old man? I want to know."

"No use. Why talk? No one ever listened in this world—in these matters." Bitterly: "No, Frank, not since time began. I see where you're going. Your best friend can't stop you, nor can anyone else."

He was so earnest, really sad, I tried to understand the "danger." I sat trying to imagine and couldn't. It all seemed right to me not to have experimented, and lucky to have found the one I wanted, who wanted me, without all that wiseacre evil-thinking around.

Felt sorry for Cecil. He didn't know; of course he didn't know. Poor fellow! Look at the women he knew compared to the glowing Catherine. She was more of a woman than he thought, too. No child at all. Really a very sensible girl. She wanted me to save money and had offered to take care of it for me and already was doing it to some extent. She was sensible and careful about things, whereas—well—in that way I wasn't there at all, as anybody could see.

Then it flashed over me, "Look here. Have you been talking to Mother about this thing?"

"No. She talked to me about it."

"What did she say?"

"You might ask *her*."

My own mother talking over my own private affairs with my best friend, saying nothing to me? Angrily ashamed of the situation I began to feel both Catherine and myself betrayed. Now she seemed to need my care and protection. A feeling that had been merely warm and affectionate began to deepen.

"Well," said Cecil, "let's not quarrel. You couldn't manage an acquaintance with more than one anyway. You are a born 'soloist.' I know you. You'll have to go it alone in everything all through life. Only why go so desperately fast? You'll go far enough soon enough. Why try to put into a month what would last any reasonable fellow a year at least? I wish I had more of your steam and sensibility, Frank, and you had more of my sense and laziness.

"Don't feel I'm unsympathetic or saying anything against Catherine. For all anybody knows she may be just the girl for you."

On the way home to Oak Park that evening I was going over the scene I knew coming with Mother.

I got home and sat silent at supper with Mother, the girls, and Miss Chapin. Mother's looks inquiring silently. Upstairs in my room after supper she came up to see what had gone wrong with the day.

"What is it, my son?"

"Mother! Why go around to Cecil about Kitty and me?"

She didn't even look surprised. "Why, indeed?" she said and smiled.

It didn't seem a smiling matter to me, so I burst out with—"Why all this anxiety and fuss over a perfectly natural thing? What's it all about anyway? You are making Nature monstrous. Where *is* the sense in it?"

"Frank, have you thought of the consequences to this young girl of your singling her out to the exclusion of all others?"

She had begun on a vulnerable spot. Her first shot went home. "No, of course I haven't. But isn't she the best judge of what that means to her? I don't see how I can judge for her. And if she can't, how about her father and mother?"

"Her mother's in trouble with her over this already. It seems beyond her mother's control."

"So you went to see her mother too?"

"Yes. Catherine is accustomed to having her own way, and is giving her mother trouble. She seems to be unreasonable, as you are."

"Well, that proves, doesn't it, that it's all right for her? So why this worry, anxiety, anguish, curiosity, prying, praying and gossip, to make a perfectly natural thing scandalous? I don't get it at all. I've never seen *you* like this, Mother. It doesn't seem like you. You have always said, 'If you have to choose between the good and true, choose truth.' And, God! Mother—what in this matter *is* Truth?"

"Don't swear, my son."

This was too much! "Swearing? What is the name of the almighty God for if not to be called upon in extremity? I *mean* it. I think I see a conspiracy to force Catherine and me to give up everything fine and happy in our relationship and think of getting married. What a state of mind! Is only one thing possible to boys and girls in this world? Only one thing that everyone sees, thinks about, watches and believes? Who made things so damned fearsome and artificial anyway?"

"Frank, you are swearing again before your mother."

" 'Damned' is swearing, too? Then how get along on the farm? 'Damned,' a wonderful, necessary word! Can you dispose of your feelings about contrary things without that word? What other word have we got in English? Is 'damned' swearing just because all extremes are profane?"

Said Mother, "In your present frame of mind I see no use in talking to you, my son."

"Just what old man Cecil said. Why are all of you ready to weep, wring your hands and wail!" Mother quietly got up and left.

But, just the same, she had done what she had set out to do. "Have you thought of the consequences to this young girl of singling her out to the exclusion of all others?" Something had been left out of my education? The Social Instinct!

After this turmoil I saw the object of the contention but once. Something had been spoiled. I felt a sort of pity for Catherine and shame for myself. "Catherine, everybody is anxious and unhappy about us. Maybe I *am* doing you harm by being with you so much. 'They' say so anyway."

"How perfectly ridiculous," said she. "I've had pretty nearly everything myself but an out-and-out spanking. If I can stand it don't you think you can?"

"Of course, I can. But you don't see. They are right in one thing. You don't know any boys but me and . . ."

"I do, too; know dozens!" She started to name them.

"No. You know what I mean.

"Anyhow, I'm not coming down here so often and I am going to keep away in church."

This from her: "Well, let them have their way for a while—I will write to you."

"Yes," I said, "there can't be harm in that."

A week later I learned by a note from her she had been sent to visit relatives in Mackinac. For three months!

I began to see that in spite of all the talk about Nature that "natural" was the last thing in this world "they" would let you be could they prevent it. What did they mean when "they" used the word Nature? Just some sentimental feeling about animals, grass and trees. The out-of-doors? But how about the nature of wood, glass and iron—internal nature? The nature of boys and girls? The nature of law? Wasn't that Nature? Wasn't nature in this deeper sense the very nature of God?

Somehow I had always thought when I read the word "Nature" in a book or used it in my own mind that it was meant that interior way. Not the other superficial, external way.

"Fools!" They have no sentiment for Nature. What they really mean by "Nature" is just sentimentalizing the rudimentary animal. That's why they suffer all this confusion of ideas, make all these senseless rules—foolish regulations and unwise laws.

"What *do* 'they' work them out from? Do they really *know* anything good at all?"

Now thrown more in on myself by Catherine's being away, I brought the work in Silsbee's office to bar only to find it more than ever wanting, in any true meaning, to life, to the folk who owned and lived in those houses. All pose, that's what it was. Aimed to be unusual—pictorial. Yes, it *was* ordinary sentimentality.

ADLER AND SULLIVAN

Wilcox, preacher's son number four at Silsbee's, came excitedly to me one day, leaned on my table. "Wright," he said, looking around to see no one heard, "I know where you can get a good job if you want it."

"Where?"

"With Adler and Sullivan."

My heart jumped. Already I had formed a high idea of Adler and Sullivan. Architects foremost in Chicago Radical—going strong on independent lines. Burnham and Root their only rivals "Wilcox, how do you know?"

"Well, I've just been there myself. Sullivan turned me down. He's looking for someone to make finish-drawings for the interior of the

Auditorium. I can't make them. But you can. I told him about you. He asked me to send you over to see him."

"You did, Wilcox?' I . . ." Then I thought of Cecil. I called him. Silsbee was away. We sat in his private office to talk.

"Go on, Frank," he said, "you've got pretty much all there is to get here. Sullivan is the coming man in the West. He may be just what you need. Anyway, no harm to try. We won't get lost."

I swept some of my work together and went over to the Borden Block, top floor.

"Would Mr. Adler do?" Mr. Sullivan was about to leave for St. Louis, Architects' Convention.

"No. Mr. Sullivan wanted to see me—it will only be for a moment."

"Name?"

"Wright."

The easy-natured old clerk came back, held the gate open, and I went in.

Mr. Sullivan was a small man immaculately dressed in brown. His outstanding feature his amazing big brown eyes. Took me in at a glance. Everything I felt, even to my secret thoughts.

"Ah yes! Young man Wilcox mentioned. What have you there?" he said.

I unrolled the drawings on the table. He looked them over.

"You know what I want you for, do you?"

I said, "Yes—I think so."

"These aren't the kind of drawings I would like to see, but . . . no time now. I'll be back Friday morning. Make some drawings of orna-ment, ornamental details or something, and bring them back then. I want to look at them."

He looked at me kindly and *saw me*. I was sure of that.

"Of course I will," I said eagerly, and left.

The door to the big draughting room was open. At work there must have been twenty or more men as near as I could see. Whatever the number was, I was going to make one more. A large, tall, rather un-gainly young man with a pointed head, black, bristling pompadour and thin, black beard looked at me as I stood a moment at the door, his eyes a good deal like Mr. Sullivan's I thought. He looked too big for his age and the black beard seemed out of place on his face. Evidently he was foreman and young.

"Looking for Mr. Adler?" he said.

"No," I said. "Just looking at you." I walked away before his as-tonished expression could change. It was Paul Mueller, the office fore-man, growing a beard to look the part.

I went back to Cecil, elated.

"The job's mine."

"How do you know?"

"How does one know anything? He *saw,* I tell you, that I can do what he wants done. Making drawings for him is just a formality."

"Just the same," said Cecil, "I'd make them as well as I could."

"Of course I will, but it will be all the easier and I'll do it better now because I know I have the job."

Cecil gave up. It was hopeless.

"What will Sullivan pay you?"

"Forgot to mention it, but I'll ask for $25. And it will be all right."

When I got to Oak Park that evening, after telling Mother the good news I went to work on a drawing board in the room where I had T-square and triangle; but I used them only for guide lines. I was going to show Louis H. Sullivan what my free hand could do.

I took some of Silsbee's own drawings of mantels and drew them my own way, directly and simply with clear definition. Not "sketchy." Silsbee's way was magnificent, his strokes were like standing corn in the field waving in the breeze. So in some few drawings I imitated his style, just to show I could do that. Then I improvised ornaments such as I had seen on the Adler and Sullivan buildings. I had studied them a little since I learned of their work. Three o'clock when I got to bed. Next evening the same thing. Another evening I took the onion-skin tracings of ornamental details I had made from Owen Jones, mostly Gothic, and made them over into "Sullivanesque"—made a design for a dwelling.

When Friday morning came I had a lot of things to show. I got to Mr. Sullivan: took the work out in order:

"First: Silsbee," I said.

"I see. You've traced Silsbee's drawings to show me?"

"They are not traced. I drew them. You see? They are not on tracing paper."

"But you might have transferred them."

I laughed. "Too much trouble."

He looked me over with that glance of his that went clear through.

"Second: imitations of Sullivan."

"Well! You couldn't have traced those. Not half bad," he said to himself, scratching his scalp with the sharp point of his lead pencil. Some white dandruff fell on the drawings. He blew it off.

"Third: improvised Gothic from Owen Jones."

"Owen Jones? Who is he?"

I thought him joking. I said, "You know, *The Grammar of Ornament?*"

He looked puzzled. "Anything like Raguenet?"

"I don't know Raguenet."

"Oh, yes, of course," he said. "I do remember the book. So you are trying to turn Gothic ornaments into my style just to please me, are you?"

I said, "You see how easy it is to do it." I saw I had displeased him. Unconsciously I had reduced his ornament to a mere "sentimentality."

"Fourth: here are some things, perhaps original—I don't know: a house."

He was immediately interested. Said nothing. He was sitting on a high stool at his draughting board where he had been drawing. After looking over the drawings he made no comment but drew aside the cover sheet from his own board. I gasped with delight. "Oh!" I said, "and you asked me to show you mine?" He seemed to have forgotten me now and went on drawing. I was standing there thinking—"If Silsbee's touch was like standing corn waving in the fields, Sullivan's was like the passion vine in full bloom." I wondered what mine might be like if I developed one some day. I wanted to ask but, suddenly, "You've got the right kind of touch, you'll do," he said. "How much money have you been getting?"

"Not enough," I said.

"Well, how much is enough?"

"Twenty-five dollars."

He smiled, for I might have asked forty dollars and got it.

"All right, but understand you've got to stick until the drawings for the Auditorium are finished. But I don't mean you are to work for that salary during all that time. We'll come to an arrangement after you take hold. Can you come Monday morning?"

"I can come," I said, "for there is not much work at Silsbee's. He'll be glad to let me go."

That was how I got into the Adler and Sullivan office, how I first met the master for whose influence, affection and comradeship I have never ceased to feel gratitude.

Elated, I went back to Silsbee's and to Cecil. Cecil was glad and sad, too, as I could see.

"Go in and tell the old man," was what he said.

I went in.

"Mr. Silsbee."

"Well?" wheeling around from his desk.

"I haven't been doing very well for you or myself for some weeks."

"I've noticed it."

"I've asked Mr. Sullivan for a job."

"Did he give you one?"

"Yes, he gave me one that will last a long time, I believe."

"When are you going?"

"Next Monday, if you don't need me?"

He thought a moment. "This doesn't seem quite up to your standard, does it, Wright?"

"You were away when the chance came Mr. Silsbee. I was going to wait until you came back to come to you first, but I dreaded to wait for many reasons. The chance came unexpectedly. But if you need me I would stay."

"No! Wright—I don't need you. I wanted to know your reason for falling down on your principles—that's all."

"Mr. Silsbee—I was so sure my usefulness here was ended and you would be relieved."

"But is that the point?"

"No—not the point at all. I am wrong. Dead wrong. I should never have gone to Mr. Sullivan without first talking with you. It's clear enough."

"Never mind, Wright. You may like it with Sullivan. Not my style but maybe a genius, who knows?"

I hated to leave him that way. No matter what I felt about Silsbee's shortcomings I adored him just the same. I knew I left him like any tramp draughtsman when he had been really handsome to me. What could I say? I sat helpless. Nothing at all to say. If he saw my face, and I guess he did, he must have forgiven me. If he can see into my heart now, he will see what he saw in my face then. I got out.

I never saw Silsbee again.

LET THE DEAD BURY THEIR DEAD

Has every forward movement in human lives as it is realized, its own peculiar pang, I wonder.

The cause of this "pang" was definitely a fault of mine. I might have waited to talk with Silsbee at the proper moment and have quit with none.

As usual, I had taken too much for granted.

And, yet, do the trees know pain when top branches float leaves on the breeze? Shut the sun from the branches below so those branches must die?

Do perennial plants suffer too, when they rise up in spring, through the dead growth of last year rise to greater glory and abundance this year?

Does the snake slough its skin with regret, do you think?

Does each stage of our own interior growth cost enough vital energy in suffering so that our span is measured—the allotment of our lives' duration made by the number of pangs we can sustain as each successive forward step or upward movement happens?

Most human beings eventually die of the pangs of growth?

When we see a delphinium taller, more resplendent than the rest, a tree more superb than others, a human being in character and achievement outstanding from his fellows—are we to think: what magnificent resistance to suffering was there!

"Let the dead bury their dead" was said by the gentlest, wisest and most awful of all men.

Is this merely a human weakness or a human fault, then, that growth should have its pang? Or is it all merely the natural evil consequence of the so-called virtues which man in self-love is so earnestly making for himself?

I see that I left Silsbee as I left college, and as later, with anguish, I left home—for the same reason, with the same suffering, the same hope, obedient to a principle at work in me taking toll to this hour as I write. Old as man's moral life is this urge to *grow*. Listen to the Apostle Paul: "Brethren, I count not myself to have apprehended: but this one thing I do, forgetting those things which are behind and reaching forth to those things which are before."

I, too, whether I would or not, like Lieber Meister was going to ask of my generation in my own way, "Do ye reject the commandments of God, that ye may keep your traditions?" This in order that my generation should realize that traditions may be kept in the letter after the spirit had fled, only by such rejection.

Louis Sullivan—Lieber Meister—had come to this understanding. He was already at grips with the joys and sorrows of this affirmation—in action I knew.

Monday morning at the office of Adler and Sullivan, some little time before nine o'clock in the big draughting room. The "firm" then occupied most of the top floor of the old Borden Block, corner of Randolph and Dearborn Streets, now torn down. Paul Mueller was there in his shirt sleeves standing at his desk by the entrance. No one else. "Ach—Wright, where can I get you?" He looked about. Fixed upon one place—changed his mind several times—finally landed me against the south wall between two large windows. Good place but too closely surrounded by other tables. One of a crew now. Not like the studio-

116

atmosphere of Silsbee's. Might have been the rank and file of any large business office. Many clerks working.

"I'll have Anton 'stretch' some boards for you," he said, calling the office cub. Said the cub, Anton, "How many?"

"Ach! I didn't tell you. What you can find loose. What you can find *loose, loose,* Loose," he shouted. Mueller was awkward, energetic, emotional and under something of a strain as I could see. Too young, I was sure, to have any business with that beard or the job of foreman.

"What did Mr. Sullivan tell you to do?" he said.

"He didn't tell me."

"Wait, then—wait till he comes. I've got enough to do without what he wants. He wants you for the designs anyway. My work is construction. I used to work for Tsilsbee myself. Yes, Tsilsbee, he is a great designer." I loved the way he said "Tsilsbee" and wanted to hear him say it again. "Three years ago, Tsilsbee—he wanted an engineer. He took me. Then I came to Mr. Adler over here."

"How long have you been foreman?"

"More than a year."

"Like it?" I said.

"Ach!" he said, "too much to do. What is it? Mr. Adler wants me. . . . Yes, I like it."

Tony, office cub, found several draughting boards with the manila-paper stretch in general use there. I laid one good one on my table, delighting in the clean blank paper surface . A smooth untouched sheet of fine paper is one of the fairest of sights. My back was to the room so I did not see the fellows as they filed in.

Evidently they were a noisy crowd. They chaffed each other a lot as they settled down. A few remarks evidently intended for me. But there was some discipline in the office apparently, for they were soon quietly at work. Tired of looking at the paper I looked to the left. Got their names afterwards. Next table to mine Jean Agnas, a clean-faced Norseman. To the right Eisendrath—apparently stupid. Jewish. Behind me to the left Ottenheimer—alert, apparently bright. Jew too. I turned around to survey the group. Isbell, Jew? Gaylord, no—not. Weydert, undoubtedly. Directly behind, Weatherwax. Couldn't make him out—probably Jewish. In the corner Andresen—Swedish. Several more Jewish faces. Of course—I thought, because Mr. Adler himself must be a Jew. I had not thought of this nor well knew the difference. I thought of a Jew as more or less like any other naturals—like Irish, Welsh or German. I marked time, feeling alone in all that strange crowd, drawing carelessly on the margin of my "stretch." Had a notion to call up Cecil to say hello and hear his voice.

About 10:30 the door opened. Mr. Sullivan walked slowly in with a haughty air, handkerchief to his nose. Paid no attention to anyone. No good mornings? No. No words of greeting as he went from desk to desk. Saw me waiting for him. Came forward at once with a pleasant "Ah! Wright, there you are," and the office had my name. And evidently, in Sullivan's unusually pleasant address, also "my number." There was no friendly feeling toward me.

"Here, Wright," lifting a board up onto my table, "take this drawing of mine. A duffer I fired Saturday spoiled it. Re-draw it and ink it in." They all then knew what I was there for. He wandered about some more in a haughty sort of way seeming to have no respect at all for anybody there except perhaps Paul Mueller. My eyes had been following him when he was observable. Finally he stopped just behind me at Weatherwax's table.

"What the hell do you call that?" he said in a loud voice, without even bending to look. I had turned my head in time to see the man flush angrily and straighten up.

"What the hell do you call that?" Mr. Sullivan said, louder than before. The whole room now waiting for Weatherwax.

"What do *I* call it?" he said, evidently hot, as though struck by a lash. "Hell! It's a church, can't you see? *Christ!* What do you want?"

With trembling hands he was undoing the strings of his little black apron as he spoke. With violence he threw his pencil down on the board, grabbed the leather case of drawing instruments and deliberately walked out.

Mr. Sullivan, as though he had heard nothing, changed not a hair, looked a moment at the unhappy drawing while he blew his nose into a fresh handkerchief, then turned on his heel to the next table or two—I could see the cringing fear of him wherever he went—and walked slowly out of the room as he had come in, without another word. There had been no sound in the draughting room during the episode. Evidently all were used to something of the kind. When he had gone out there was a rustle, whispering and low talking which Mueller put down with warning looks in a loud voice.

My reaction to this was, "Afraid I won't last long here after all!" Evidently no one did where Sullivan was concerned. Then, I thought, "This is not the real Sullivan. I've seen a different one."

What was Dankmar Adler like? Just before noon he opened the same door through which Mr. Sullivan had entered. A strong personality, short-built and heavy, like an old Byzantine church. He was not gutty, just broadly and solidly built, one to inspire others at once with confidence in his power. I felt comforted.

He walked with deliberate, heavy-legged, flat-footed steps over to

Mueller's table and stood talking to him. The while his deep bass voice rumbled, he went about with his hands stuck under his coat-tails, looking with a friendly frown at drawings. A word of greeting occasionally. He would sit down at the board and make suggestions in a fatherly sort of way. Finally he got to me. Looked at me pleasantly from his deep-set eyes under the bushy brows.

"Hello!"—kindly. "Sullivan's new man?"

"Yes, sir!"

He sat down on the stool I had vacated to stand up to him. As he put one leg over the other, I noticed his enormous mannish feet. They spread flat like the foundations for some heavy building.

"Sullivan needs help, Wright. It's difficult to find anyone to 'catch on' to what he wants. I hope you will succeed!"

He got up abruptly almost as soon as he had sat down and, as though suddenly remembering something, went heavily out among the draughting tables like a barge making its way between river craft. Dankmar was the name for him.

INITIATION

Thus began association lasting nearly seven years. Mr. Sullivan had been interested and interesting. His drawings a delight to work upon and work out. His manner toward me markedly different from his manner toward the other men. Mark me it might, and mark me it did. I soon found my place in that office had to be fought for.

The work was going well. I could do it. The master was pleased. I had got his permission to get George Elmslie over from Silsbee's to help me and incidentally make it a little less lonesome for me there. George wasn't a minister's son but ought to have been. He was coming over in a few days. This evident favoritism of the master together with my own natural tendency to mind my own business, coupled with a distaste for most of the Adler and Sullivan men, had, in the course of a few weeks, set them against me. I was unpopular from that first day. And I was baited in various ways. My hair of course. My dress a bit too individual, I suppose. There would be casual conversation behind me with unmistakable reference to me. Studied interference with my work. The gang had evidently combined to "get" me. (Their phrase.) Mueller didn't see much of it all. He was an innocent soul. It was all kept pretty well out of his way. I couldn't say anything about it if I would. I wouldn't if I could.

There was a back room devoted to blue-printing, where Isbell, Gaylord and a few others would go at noon to eat their lunch and box a few rounds. Isbell was supposed to be pretty good, if talk meant anything, and Gaylord was candidate for pugilistic honors in the First Regiment Armory.

They wanted me in to "box." Evidently the longish hair, flowing tie and fastidious clothes gave them the idea I would be easy. A good spectacle.

I saw I would have to do something to square myself with that crowd.

I had boxed some at the University and had no doubt about my wind or ability to stand punishment—just in from my summers on the farm. But not much science. So, one noon, I went to see old Colonel Monsterry who had a fencing and boxing academy in the old Athenaeum next door; engaged for a course of twelve boxing lessons, all twelve to be given in the course of two weeks. I told the old Frenchman I wanted to learn how to hit hard and stop body-blows. I could already take pretty good care of my head.

But why not the foils? "It is so much more of a gentleman's game," he said.

"I'm not involved with gentlemen. I've got a battle on my hand with a pretty tough bunch. I want some rough training."

"All right," and he handed me the gloves. I put them on and put up my guard. "No," he said, "college boy! This way," and he put one hand down, the other out in front like a feeler and provocative. "Now, look out." He struck at me a number of times to see where I was. "Not so bad. Now, I'm going to hit you," he said. "Go ahead." He did, and the jolt jarred me to the heels. I thought if it was that easy to reach me I was far from that back room. Took the bout for an hour. Felt wonderful as I got out from under the shower into my clothes and back to the office.

Meanwhile the nagging went on while I had almost the two weeks of training. I knew it wasn't a case of getting into condition. I was in better condition than either of the office stars.

COMBAT

Daily practice with the old Colonel had, by now, taught me all he knew. I don't think it was much because he was a swordsman, not a boxer. But it might be enough. I could now take care of myself fairly well. I liked it and began to look forward with some pleasure to the coming event.

I looked at Isbell's heavy, prominent nose sometimes and thought—what a mark! He was a loud-voiced, blond-haired, stocky-built, conceited fellow, always keeping up a running fire of jibes and jokes when Mueller was out. Jaunty always and undoubtedly strong. Gaylord was awkward and slow, but stronger.

About two months had gone by since I had entered the office and steadily minded my own business. But taunting had grown, and was quite open now. As the noon rustle began just before the men went out, I turned to Isbell. "Boxing this noon?" He looked puzzled. "Sure. Coming in to look on?" "Yes, I might as well," I said.

"All right. Why look on? Put on the gloves! We won't hurt you."

I pretended to hesitate—"You fellows must be pretty close to professionals, practicing in there all the time. But—well, all right. I might as well."

I saw the look of triumph, winks passing between the office strong men. The other members of the gang were incredulous, smiling. I went in alone. But they had their gang, six or seven of them. Coats, vests and collars off, I drew on the gloves—dirty ones. Isbell wanted the first "crack" at me and put on another pair, also dirty.

I knew nothing about style, but struck him —on the nose—just as he fairly got up his guard. The blood came into his face and his blue eyes went hard and cold. He came after me heavily. I saw he was just a slugger.

So I let him slug.

Stopped him, when I could, took it when I had to. Standing up to him and backing away, continuously drawing him on. He was soon breathing hard, rather white. I had taken it easily, good wind anyhow always.

The crowd so fresh at first, a little flat now. Not just what they expected!

"Time!" called Gaylord. "Time? Not yet," I said. "This is a one-round contest." And I banged Isbell on the nose, hard this time, with my left.

The blood came. First blood for me!

But no applause.

Now Isbell was out for blood. We rushed back and forth, crashing around the room; the fellows raced out of the way knocking over everything that could come loose. Raging Isbell!

Again I got him on the nose. Soon he was a sight. My lip was cut and bleeding, but I sucked in the blood and swallowed it. I felt a wonderful lift. Still had the steam I started with.

"Izzy" was getting the worst of it and the gang saw it.

"Time!" yelled Gaylord. "Time, hell," I said, "this is a one-round contest," and I banged Izzy on the nose again: the abnormally large nose that had begun to swell. This was too much for Billy Gaylord. "Here, Izzy! Give me those gloves. It's my turn now."

"Yes? Your turn now?" I said. I was waked up and felt nothing could ever stop me. I stood eagerly striking one glove into the open palm of the other while Gaylord put on dirty gloves. "Billy" leaned way back, rocking to and fro, crouching low, weaving his arms in and out continually. Crafty. I couldn't wait for him for my blood was up by now and while Billy Gaylord had been comparatively decent, and I half liked him, this cutting in was a dirty trick. I was going to beat all the hell in him out of him, or die trying.

So I stepped up to him like a flash and slapped him down on the top of the head three times with all my might with my open glove. My foot was behind his and as he pulled back to recover he went over backward into the gang. He got up red and angry. "That's a hell of a way to box. Two fouls," he said.

"Fouls, nothing," I retorted. "Who said this was a boxing match? What are you doing in here before I finished with Isbell? Come on, damn you, foul *me*. And damn you all, anyway. You wanted to get me in here to do me up and have a laugh. Now come and get your laugh—take your gloves off, you coward." I threw mine away.

This wasn't quite what they looked for. The crowd now interfered.

"Aw, pass him up, Billy. He's crazy-mad and wants to fight. It won't do in here. Let's fix it up for some other time."

"All right," I said. "You fix it! A fine sporting gang you are. If one of you can't win, you put another in on top of that one." And I went out, too excited to want anything to eat.

The afternoon was quiet. Ominously quiet.

I knew I had lost my case by getting mad. If I had coolly taken Gaylord on, unfair as it was for him to cut in on Isbell, and had good-naturedly made a good showing with him, it would have probably been all over in my favor. By getting angry and sailing into them I made enemies of them all.

Then and there I made up my mind to stay in that office till I could fire every one of that gang, and later said so to Ottenheimer, ringleader: an active, intelligent, little Jew not present. He got the report from the gang next day and I heard him say, "Ooi, ooi, the goddamn son of a bitch! Leave him to me."

I might as well finish the story. I was now subjected to the refined cruelty of Ottenheimer's open taunts and skillful innuendoes. Ottenheimer evidently thought he had a drag with "the old man," that is to say, Mr. Adler. But it was easier to stand the isolation even though it had become downright enmity, now. I had George Elmslie at my side to talk to, a sort of understudy to help in my work. Mr. Sullivan wanted me to train an understudy so if something happened to me he would not be without work. I took George. George was a tall, slim, slow-thinking, but faithful Scottish lad who had never really been young. Very quiet and diffident. I liked him: couldn't get along without somebody—ever.

We were both staying in one noon to finish some work for the blue-printer some weeks after the boxing-bout failure. Ottenheimer, at the table behind me and over one to the left, staying to study for Beaux Arts exams he was soon to take. He was whistling and jibing as was his habit. He had thrown my hat down the stair-well just the day before. He was insolent always. "You're just a Sullivan toady anyway, Wright. We all know it." I had stood, without flinching, far worse than that.

But it was "time." I laid down my pencil, swung around on the stool and looked at him. He sat at his table, insolent, heavy-bodied, short-legged, pompadoured, conceited, red-faced young Jew, wearing gold glasses. His face, now red as a turkey-cock's wattles. "I think I've had enough from you," I said as I got up, walked slowly over to him and without realizing he was wearing glasses, or hesitating, struck him square, full in the face with my right, knocking him from his stool to the floor, smashing his glasses. I might have blinded him.

With a peculiar animal scream—I've heard something like it since from a Japanese mad with *sake,* but never else—he jumped for a knife, the scratch-blade with a wood handle lying on his board. Half-blinded, he came at me with it.

I caught his head under my arm as he came, and was trying hard to put him out, while with his free arm behind me, he was stabbing away at the back of my neck and shoulders. But his head was too close—tight against my side. Upsetting stools and overturning tables as George, white-faced and scared, looked on. I could feel the blood running down my back and legs into my shoes. They "cheeped" as though I were walking in puddles.

Finally, I wound my right hand in the back of his collar and with all the strength of despair, hurled him away from me. He went staggering, toppling backward clear across the draughting room to the opposite wall, struck with a heavy bang against the door leading to the next room and went down—but not out. He had dropped the knife nearby where he fell. He got up on his feet again and with that same curious animal scream grabbed the knife and came on—a bloodthirsty little beast. Quick as a flash, as he came toward me, I grabbed the long, broad-bladed T-square on my board by the end of the long blade, swung it with all my might, catching Ottie with the edge of the blade beside his neck just above the collar. The cross-head snapped off and flew the length of the room.

The knife dropped from his hand as he wavered a moment, then wilted, slowly, into a senseless heap on the floor like a sail coming down.

My heart sank. "Good God! George! Get some water quick." George seemed paralyzed. It had all happened in a minute. "Wake up! Quick man! Come on, George! Don't you see?"

Slow-moving George got back with some water in a dipper and I threw it in Otti's face. No sign. "More, George." I threw more water in his face—he sighed, opened his eyes. I stood there, waiting and trembling. "Are you badly hurt, Ottie?" No answer. Blinked—seemed to be "going out" again.

"Water!"

"No! Quit." From Ottie, "I'm all right."

Ottie got up by degrees. Stood white and shaking. "I'll pay you for this, Wright," he choked. "You'll get yours for this. You'll see."

He went back to his desk, shakily gathered up his instruments as I sat smiling, watching him. It was so good to see him move, for I thought I had killed him in that wild moment. I never saw Ottenheimer again. He had intended to go to the Beaux Arts in Paris before long. He went without ever coming back to the office.

The affair had taken place at noon, when everyone was out for lunch except Ottie, George and me.

My shoes were full of blood. "George! Call Cecil. I want to see how badly that little cuss cut me."

George called him. He happened to be in and came the five blocks in no time. He pulled off my coat and pushed my shirt down to the waist. "Man!" he said, counting, "you're stabbed on the shoulder blades in eleven places, to the bone, all of them. Lucky for you none on the spine. But near it on each side. I don't think any one of them is serious. Let's go over to Arthur's and get them dressed." Arthur, his brother, was a physician.

Today I wear the welts of Ottie's fancy work on my shoulder blades. But not because I turned my back on him.

The disappearance of Ottenheimer broke the persecution for a time. Isbell had been laid off. Gaylord rather friendly now.

Billy was a decent chap on the whole. But occasionally I would surprise sullen looks from Eisendrath and Weydert. I had them to deal with, later. Nor did Mueller or Mr. Sullivan know about the feud until several years after I had finally cleaned up the Adler and Sullivan gang by firing Weydert.

THE MASTER

At this time the Master's very walk bore dangerous resemblance to a strut. He had no respect whatever for a draughtsman, as he more than once confided to me in later years. Nor, as far as I could see, respect for anyone else except the big chief—Dankmar Adler, whom he trusted and loved—and Paul Mueller—probably me.

None of his contemporaries ever won from Louis Sullivan much but contempt—except H. H. Richardson. Richardson he condescended to criticize, and he was not so hard on John Wellborn Root—as on all the others. Evidently he liked him.

But Richardson at this time had a decided effect upon the Sullivan work, as may be seen in the outside of the Auditorium Building, the Walker Wholesale and other buildings. The effect is unmistakable, although he seemed to hold Richardson in no very high esteem.

I believe the Master used to talk to me to express his own feelings and thoughts, regardless, forgetting me often. But I could follow him, and the radical sense of things I had already formed intuitively, my kindergarten training by Mother, got great encouragement from him. In fact the very sense of things I had been feeling as rebellion was at work in him in his way.

He was absorbed in what seemed extravagant worship of Wagner at the time. I could not share but I could understand. He would often try to sing the leitmotifs for me and describe the scenes to which they belonged, as he sat at my drawing board. He adored and extolled Whitman, as I did. Explain it how you can, was deep in Herbert Spencer. He gave Spencer's *Synthetic Philosophy* to me to take home and read. He himself had just written "Inspiration." He read it to me. I thought it a kind of baying at the moon: too sentimental.

In those early days I never liked his writings. Here again was this insidious sentimentality showing even in him. What had been suspicion now began to ripen into rebellion against sentimentalism in general.

The Auditorium finished, soon other work came on—Pueblo Opera House (since down), Salt Lake City Hotel, foundations laid, but never built—one of the office tragedies. I worked hard on the plans with the firm.

From the very beginning my T-square and triangle by kindergarten table were easy media of expression for the geometrical sense of things I got there. But, at the time, Sullivanian ornament was efflorescence pure and simple. Mr. Sullivan would still talk of John Edelman. He had known him in Paris and visited him in New York. John Edelman—also of Boston—was his most respected critic, not to say teacher. I conceived a respect for Edelman, knowing no more than this about him. I have a number of drawings made by Louis Sullivan in Paris dedicated to John Edelman.

Whenever the Master would rely upon me for a detail I would mingle his sensuous efflorescence with geometric design, because, I suppose, I could do nothing else so well. And, too, that way of working seemed to me to hold the surface, give needed contrast, be more *architectural*. Again—less sentimental. But I couldn't say this to him and I wasn't sure then.

Often he would pick me up on this point—and try to "bring alive," as he said, what I was doing until I could make designs in his manner so well that toward the end of his life he would sometimes mistake my drawings for his own without being ashamed of his error.

A good pencil I became in the Master's hand, at a time when he sorely needed one. Because I could be this to him he had more freedom now than he had ever enjoyed before.

At this time Healy and Millet were his cronies. The three men had known one another in Paris. Sullivan spent much of his time in their company and in the company of Larry Donovan of the "Yale and Towne" hardware concern.

CATHERINE

About this time (now twenty) I wanted to marry. I told the Master so. "Who is the girl?"

"A young girl—still in Hyde Park High School—Catherine. She's seventeen years old. Met her at All Souls Church."

"Ah-ha! So soon?"

"They all think it too soon, and object!"

"They should," he said.

"I have no visible means of support for one thing."

"No? Well . . . we can fix *that*. How about a contract?" He called "Adler!" Mr. Adler came.

"Wright wants to get married—no visible means of support. What do you say to a five-year contract?"

"All right," said Adler. "You fix it, Sullivan!" And he hurried out—his usual exit as though suddenly remembering something that demanded instant attention.

Meanwhile, as fellowship was taking its course in the offices of Adler and Sullivan in the Auditorium Tower, let us go back to another fellowship—to the young girl in Hyde Park High School.

Already you have had a glimpse of our first meetings, the struggle with the circumstance of family that led to this announcement to Lieber Meister.

This phase of fellowship—the sunny-haired, tall, slenderly handsome high-school girl, now seventeen, the engaging Catherine herself.

She walked with a kind of light-hearted gaiety: mass of red curls, rather short, bobbing in the breeze. White skin. Cheeks rosy. Blue-eyed, frank and impulsive. Generous to see and to me.

"Kitty," idol of the Tobin household still had pretty much her own way about everything. And everyone except White Grandma.

After the stabbing I received as my share in that row at the office I had gone directly to her at Kenwood. There had been no mention of love—or marriage, no proposal. Why talk about it? It was all a matter of course, so far as that went—sometime.

But Catherine, recently back from the North where she had been sent, was quite changed. She was thinner and pale. Her blue eyes were not so happy now, her manner less gay than usual. She would fall silent. Listless.

For some time past, I myself had felt that we were in a false position. Catherine was doing nothing much in school. I knew "Kitty" was running the gauntlet there with the school girls who knew of her attachment to me. Knew because I saw the drawing of a large-eyed kitten—with the legend *"Perfectly Frank"* beneath. They had sent it to her from school.

At home, too, though holding her own with all but "White Grandma," she *was* under discipline. With no knowledge at all we had come to the boy and girl intimacy, no longer satisfied with sheepish looks and perfunctory visiting, playing or talk or music.

Freedom is necessary to any beauty in any such fellowship. Otherwise it becomes something mean and shameful by implication. It was shameful even to suspect we were being watched. So I decided to clear it all up.

The consequences of this announcement to Lieber Meister now enabled a boy and girl courtship lasting a year to end in marriage. Protests—sensible as well as sentimental ones, still. They were there. But, withstanding all, marriage!

Young husband-to-be just twenty-one, the young wife-to-be not yet eighteen.

Wedding on a rainy day. More resembled a funeral. The sentimentality I was learning to dread came into full flower. The heavens weeping out of doors—all weeping indoors. Mother of the groom fainting. Father of the bride in tears. Pastor performing—the now ceremonious uncle—affected likewise himself.

I now turned to Mr. Sullivan with a new idea. "Mr. Sullivan, if you want me to work for you as long as five years, couldn't you lend me enough money to build a little house, and let me pay you back so much each month—taken out of my pay envelope?"

Mr. Sullivan—it seemed—had some money of his own at the time. He took me to his lawyer, Felsenthal. The contract was duly signed, and the Master went with me—"the pencil in his hand"—to Oak Park to see the lot I knew I wanted. It was Mr. Austin's gardener's, the lovely old tanglewood. The lot was on the corner of Forest and Chicago Avenues. The Master approved the lot and bought it. There was $3,500 left over to build a small home on that ground planted by the old Scottish landscape-gardener.

"Now look out, Wright!" said Mr. Sullivan, "I know your tastes . . . no 'extras.' "

"I agreed. "None."

But there was $1,200 more to be paid toward the end. I kept this dark, paid it in due course as best I could out of what remained of my salary or I could earn overtime.

Mr. Adler said the contract at that time made me the best-paid draughtsman in the city of Chicago. But all the same, the children that followed during those years made creditors a familiar sight—or was it the "tastes"? To have both gratified was what made the sleeves pull and the coat split across the back.

The children grew up with similar "tastes" in an environment that invited these tastes to develop. Continually invited more creditors of course..

TRUTH IS LIFE

I had carved in the oak slab above the fireplace in the little living room, "Truth is Life!" A challenge to sentimentality, I thought. Soon after it occurred to me that Life is Truth. But I could not now make it say what I really meant. It was there.

I could not alter it. Anyway it seemed to me some improvement over the challenge of Grandfather's "Truth Against the World." But it wasn't.

THE MASTER AND I

Now went along these matchless early years of master and apprentice. Louis Sullivan, the Master, and I, the open-eyed, radical and critical, but always willing apprentice. We had already moved to the top floor of the Auditorium tower, where I had a small room next to him and a squad of thirty draughtsmen or more to supervise in the planning and detailing that was now my share. Mueller had the engineers and the superintendents reporting to him, at the opposite end of the long room with its row of windows to the north. Adler and Sullivan now stood well to the forefront of their profession. Commercial work, chiefly office buildings, theaters, and clubs, all came steadily in unbroken procession through the office. It was the most progressive and one of the most successful offices in the country.

Dankmar Adler had been an Army engineer. He commanded the confidence of contractor and client alike. His handling of both was masterful. He would pick up a contractor as a mastiff might pick up a cat— shake him and drop him. Some would habitually fortify themselves with a drink or two before they came up to see him. All worshipped him. He was a good planner, a good critic and all for Sullivan. He always called him "Sullivan," never Louis. Adler had implicit confidence in the Sullivan genius.

It seems he had taken Sullivan in as a draughtsman when the young man returned from the Beaux Arts. Later he took him into partnership to be what was known, even then, as a designing-partner. Architects all put the architecture on the outside—in those days. So there was one man to make it—another man to "handle" it. But Adler and Sullivan were not quite like that.

Dankmar Adler was a Jew. Louis Sullivan an Irishman. The clients all being Adler's, many objected to Sullivan. It did not matter. They had to take Sullivan or lose Adler. In those days Sullivan's attitude and ego may be seen in the fate of Weatherwax, the unfortunate draughtsman who went out of the office the day I came into it. But I had, from the first, seen a different Sullivan. He loved to talk to me and I would often stay listening, after dark in the offices in the upper story of the great tower of the Auditorium building looking out over Lake Michigan, or over the lighted city. Sometimes he would keep on talking seeming to have forgotten me—keep on talking until late at night. Probably liking the exercise. And I would catch the last suburban car for Oak Park and go to bed without supper.

As I have since reflected, he seemed unaware of the machine as a direct element in architecture, abstract or concrete. He never mentioned it. He was interested in "the rule so broad as to admit of no exception." For the life of me I could not help, then or now, being most interested in the exception proving the rule useful or useless.

But this outpouring to a worshipful and sympathetic though critical listener soon enabled me to understand him. Like all geniuses he was an absorbed egocentric—exaggerated sensibility, boundless vitality. This egotism, though, is more armor than character, more shell than substance. It is the usual defense for sensibility—a defense often become a habit. With all his synthesis and logical inclination, uncompromising search for principle, he was incorrigible romanticist. I have learned to see this as not inconsistent, except as the romanticist degenerates to the sentimentalist. Louis Sullivan himself did sometimes sentimentalize. What rich nature does not and when least suspecting the truth indignantly deny the "soft impeachment"?

But during all this period when General Grant Gothic was the prevailing mode, Chicago itself the center of the united fundamentalist ugliness of the United States, the synthesis of his common sense cut clean.

The buildings of the romantic Richardson and the susceptible Root were beginning to appear, but buildings like the Potter Palmer house on the Lake Shore Drive were still "Chicago." The Palmer home, Palmer House, Board of Trade were then popular architecture. Adler and Sullivan buildings stood clean and sharp by comparison. See the Borden Block, Gage Building and others in the Chicago wholesale district of this early period when John Edelman's influence may be seen in those early buildings.

THE AUDITORIUM BUILDING

The Chicago Auditorium was the first *great* room for audience that really departed from curious prevailing traditions. The magic word *plastic* was used by the Master in reference to his ornament, but the room itself began to show the effects of this ideal. The ideal began to enter into the Auditorium interior. Not consciously, I believe.

Mr. Adler himself had invented the sounding-board as architectural in the earlier theaters he had built. That is to say, the sloping surface, extending above the proscenium, opening into the audience room. This was "the sounding-board." Owing to this simple invention no public hall ever built by Adler and Sullivan was acoustically bad. The Master developed this sounding-board into the concentric, elliptical arches you may still see in that great room. While no advantage was taken of the arched elliptical form to carry the loads above, the inner shell itself being suspended from the level trusses above—still the form was appropriate, suitable to purpose and prophetic.

Opening night the great Chicago Auditorium was a gorgeous civic and social event to be remembered, Adelina Patti among the score of

130

opera stars that sang upon the occasion. The great room for opera was found to be perfect for its purpose. It was acknowledged to be the greatest building achievement of the period and to this day, all things considered, is probably the best room for grand opera yet built in the world.

THE VALLEY

Off to the beloved Valley for the honeymoon.

A few weeks later, young bride and groom came back to Oak Park, where the little new house, made possible by contract with Adler and Sullivan, was being built. On the way across town from the St. Paul R.R. station to Northwestern R.R. station, came the first *meum* and *tuum*.

I wanted to carve mottoes on the panels of the doors of the rooms of the new house. The decided Catherine, with better sense, accustomed to having her own way, too, said, "No. No mottoes." But the reason she gave was not good. "Didn't like mottoes."

I—new husband, lugging a heavy suitcase, tired and tried by the useless effort to keep the damn thing off my legs—was surprised to find my superior taste in matters pertaining to my own work disputed. I was caught red-handed in my own "sentimentality." It was forever claiming me and every time it did I would not only lose face, but patience: find someone or something to blame, usually the one nearest me. .

I put the suitcase down, wiped the sweat from my face, more indignant to be caught sentimentalizing than anything else. Picked it up again and refused the offer of help. Not in those circumstances. Thank you. We walked wide apart.

SIX CHILDREN

The little home was ready to move into and we moved into it.

Young husband more interested in the house than in his bride, so the young wife said to him again and again.

No—no children were provided for, but they came of course. The first one within the year. A son—Lloyd. Father still twenty-one. Then, two years later, another—John. The several grandmothers came in often to help, advise and keep domesticity working right side up. In two years another. A girl—Catherine II. Two years later, another! Boy, David. Those grandmothers were kept pretty busy around there for years to come. And the several grandmothers agreed none too often. This was something not at all in my reckoning. But just the same, two years later, another. A girl—Frances. Five years went by and Llewelyn came.

The young husband found his work cut out for him now. The young wife found hers cut out for her. Architecture was my profession. Motherhood hers. Fair enough, but it was division. The willow tree grew in the corridor between my establishment—the studio—and hers, the home.

With Silsbee, I had gained considerable light on practical needs of the American dwelling. Adler and Sullivan refused to build residences. The few imperative, owing to social obligations to important clients, fell to my lot out of office hours. They would, of course, check up on them in good time at the office. Sullivan's brother's own home on Lake Avenue was one of these, as were the southern house at Ocean Springs and the house next door there for the Charnleys.

The city house on Astor Street for the Charnleys, like the others, I did at home evenings and Sundays in the nice studio draughting room upstairs at the front of the little Forest Avenue home. But this draughting room soon became two bedrooms for the children—the children that had been left out of the reckoning in the building of that house. In this Charnley city-house on Astor Street I first sensed the definitely decorative value of the plain surface, that is to say, of the flat plane as such. The drawings for the Charnley house were all traced and printed in the Adler and Sullivan offices, but by preparing them for this purpose at home I helped pay my pressing building debts with "overtime" and paid out.

Other debts pressing toward the end of the five-year term, I accepted several houses for friends on my own account, one for Dr. Harlan, one for Warren McArthur and one for George Blossom. I did not try anything radical because I could not follow them up. I could not follow up because I did these houses out of office hours, not secretly. Mr. Sullivan soon became aware of the Harlan house and refused to issue the deed to the Oak Park house; the deed due because the little house was now paid for. But, although I had not fully realized this, I had broken my contract by doing this outside work. So protested. I asked the Master if I had been any less serviceable in the office lately.

"No," he said, "but your sole interest is here, while your contract lasts. I won't tolerate division under any circumstances."

Yet this seemed unjust to me. If I could work over-hours at home for Adler and Sullivan and keep up my work in the office what harm in doing likewise for myself to relieve my own urgent necessities? All the same I was wrong—I saw it. But, angered now by what seemed the unkindness of the Master—it was the first time he had said harsh words to me—I appealed to Dankmar Adler.

The Big Chief interceded, which more deeply offended the Master than ever and—more offensively still—he refused to issue the deed.

When I learned this from the Master himself in none too kindly terms and with the haughty air now turned toward me too much, I threw my pencil down and walked out of the Adler and Sullivan office never to return. Within a few months my five-year contract would have expired. This five-year term added to the previous time would make almost seven years with Adler and Sullivan.

Again in the wrong. More so than my Master. But again, out on my own, this time to stay.

Nor for more than twelve years did I see Louis Sullivan again, communicate with him or he with me, in any way. The deed to the little home duly followed, by Mr. Adler's hand.

From now on the young architect's studio workshop was on Chicago Avenue. The young mother's home and kindergarten continued, still kept on growing on Forest Avenue. The corridor—through which the great sprawling willow tree grew and covered the house with the shade of its spreading green—connected the two establishments.

I knew only a few of the neighbors' names. The young wife knew only a few of her husband's clients' names or what buildings he was building.

The children were well born and handsome. Each and all, they were fine specimens of healthy childhood, curly-headed, blue-eyed, sunny-haired, fair-skinned like their beautiful mother. They all resembled her. Every one of them was born, so it seemed, directly in his or her own right. You might think they had all willed it and decided it for themselves. They were seemingly endowed with the resistance and will of the father, inheriting his perverse qualities. They inherited their mother's good looks and good qualities.

That little home-department on Forest Avenue soon became a lively place. Things began to smash. Cries to resound. Shrieks. Quarrels and laughter. Someone or another or several or something in a pickle, and desperate all of the time. Destruction of something or other happened every minute.

Works of art and craft, crockery, toys—all went to smash together. Then followed destruction of Mother's peace and patience! I, their legitimate father, would hear all about it when I came in to be fed, or if I came in to go to bed early—which I seldom did.

The children were their mother's children and up to her except

133

when the two young parents themselves made eight children all together at playtime early in the morning. Warren McArthur, friend, early client of mine and something of a wag, dining with us one Sunday, caught one of the children and called to me—"Quick now, Frank, . . . what's the name of this one?" It worked. Surprised by the preemptory request I gave the wrong name.

Sometimes pursuing a kind interest in my state someone would ask: "And are there children?"

The answer "Yes, six" would leave the kindly interested one wide-eyed, wondering. I am afraid I never looked the part. Nor ever acted it. I didn't feel it. And I didn't know how.

FATHERHOOD

We two had a joint bank-account. Drew checks until they began to come back N.S.F.—in red. Then we knew the money was gone. Never mind! The first of the month was only two weeks off. There would be some more. Why worry? The father in the architect took the children's future to heart in that I wanted them to grow up in beautiful surroundings. I intended them all to be infected by a love for the beautiful. I then called it so in spite of growing prejudice against the sentimental. So I built a beautiful large playroom for them all on the upper floor at the rear of the little house. Before I could get it all paid for a benevolent sheriff came and sat in it all of one night. It was next morning before I could get the eighty-five dollars somewhere to send him on his way. I remember, to this day, that it was eighty-five dollars but I can't remember where I got it. Probably Wheaton, the old business clerk at Adler and Sullivan's, advanced it on my pay. He did such things for me. Sometimes.

But the children didn't know about such things then. Never mind, they learned all about such things later on.

But the playroom was a beautiful playroom and did its work well. The allegory at the end—the Fisherman and the Genii from the Arabian Nights: the Genii, first design, done in straight-line pattern. A lesson was to be drawn from the subject matter by the children. I forget what it was. Perhaps never to be too sentimental, or curious, or meddlesome, or there would be consequences.

The neighbors' children, too, came to kindergarten there. The home overflowed with children until one fell out of the window. Youngest son—Llewelyn. He was not hurt very much because his dress caught on the playroom windowsill and held him a moment.

There was little sickness, but when there was, gloom settled over everything. A sick child and the place ceased to live until improvement came and the child got well again. Fortunately little redheaded Doctor Luff lived only several doors away. And fortunately such sickness as came never lasted long. The six children were six happy, healthy, going, independent institutions not to say constitutions. And they all had their own way in the end. Yes. Always. They had about as much respect for their father as they had each for the others. And at times, later on in years, it was hard to tell which was father and son when together, whether by language, attitude or appearance of age.

That household was pretty much the children all the time—all together. But it was a double-barreled establishment. A three-ring circus on the one side. A stimulating excursion into the future here and now on the other side. Both were regardless. A good time was had by all until something or other would happen. And something or other always did happen. The establishments began to compete. The architect absorbed the father in me—perhaps—because I never got used to the word nor the idea of being one as I saw them all around the block and met them among my friends. I hated the sound of the word *papa*.

Is it a quality? Fatherhood? If so, I seemed born without it. And yet a building was a child. I have had the father-feeling, I am sure, when coming back after a long time to one of my buildings. That must be the true feeling of fatherhood. But I never had it for my children. I had affection for them. I regarded them as *with* me—and play-fellows, comrades to be responsible for. But their wills were set alongside mine, never across or against mine unless I was trying to protect myself from them. Though I did have to take in hand the upbringing of six-year-old Frances. I took her into the bathroom and punished her until her cries (Frances could open her mouth wide and cry enormously) were heard by all the next-door neighbors. I had closed the door but had forgotten to close the window. Finished with it, she rushed out of the house, slammed the door and went down the street to stay "forever" with "Blue" Grandma. The unusual indignity that outraged her had shocked and shamed me no less. And she was always bringing in some dirty stray cat, or stray mangy dog she had found at large in the streets and one no one wanted. She adopted them with a passionate clinging— pathetic or ridiculous according to the point of view. When her animals were turned out, Frances would stand stock-still, outraged, open her mouth wide and pour out the wailing only Frances or "de la Parma" knew how to wail.

And if there is any meaner feeling man makes for himself than when he strikes a child, what may it be, I wonder? The coward, ninety-nine times out of a hundred, is only releasing personal vexation or some cheap peevish resentment for upset "*authority*."

135

Spare the rod and spoil the child? Yes, another Mosaic root of human misery: the special invention—in self-defense—of that imposition called Fatherhood. "Fatherhood?" An *institution* I suppose in the interest of bigger and better domesticity.

These youngsters grew up alongside my coming of age and now call me Dad. I shouldn't be surprised if they were to call me Frank, nor ever would be.

They often started to do it, too, when they were little, but their mother would treat it as a form of disrespect, and insist upon "Papa," accent long on the first "a" making a more offensive word "*paa*-pa" than even when accented on the last and it became "pa-*paa*." There is a stuffy domesticity about the word applied to the male intolerable to me, as I have said.

"Father" is tolerable. After fifty? "*Paa*pa" never!

THE HOSE

I remember sitting on the terrace in front of the little Forest Avenue home waiting for Lloyd's mother to come home from Church. Two-and-a-half-year-old Lloyd left with me. Spring, I had turned on the revolving sprinkler to water the lawn. The two-year-old spied the revolving water-thing, wanted it. "No, Lloyd," I said, "you can't have it—keep away! You'll get your nice clothes all wet."

Unable to conquer desire himself I assisted by gently leading him back to the steps, sat him down there by me in full view of the whirligig, but out of the way of the water, where he could see and enjoy the swish and whirl. A moment and he got up to go after it again, regardless of warnings. Again I seated him. Again up and going. Threats now of dire consequences. He seemed not to hear any of them. He was fascinated. Though roughly seated again—he was up and going. "Come back, young fellow!"

But to return he was helpless. Angry, by now, I got up and brought him back myself. Should I punish him? Sunday, people coming home from church. So far as that went, yes, but what good?

By the time this thought got through my mind, there he was in the zone of the sprinkler. The lusty little redhead splashed, gasped and stopped a moment.

"Come back, Lloyd, or you'll be drowned," I called in a tone that might have blasted him where he stood. No sound from him. He went in further. Drenched thoroughly, he gasped again, turned his face aside and stood his ground.

"All right," I thought, "maybe this *is* the best way." I sat down on the steps to watch the struggle.

His mother had dressed him freshly clean. He had looked nice. Already a total loss.

He shut his eyes now, held his breath, his hand stretched out in the act, staggered in closer to grab the coveted thing.

Too much! Drenched, he fell in the mud. Bawling lustily now but not giving an inch, he got up and turning his face aside, stood there bawling loudly, angry.

He was a sight but there he was, only a few feet away from his desire, the water taking his breath every time he turned to go forward.

"Come back, lusty boy," I said. "Can't you see you can't get it? Come back here!" Myself angry to see him so. He didn't know I called, apparently, because another totter brought him so close I thought he had the whirling thing, but no—he fell. Gurgling, bawling and gasping, he lay there for a moment, but rolled over again onto his hands and knees, head down toward the whirling spray.

"All right," I thought cruelly. "Let's see what stuff he's made of!" I let him lie there half drowned, literally, to see what he would do. Features already obliterated with water, mud and anger, still howling desire, he got up on his feet, fell inarticulate with the water but he had what he wanted in his grasp. In both hands. I ran now to pick him up, mud from head to heels, gasping but hanging on to the whirligig, just in time to hear a piercing scream as his mother rushed in to snatch him from me, publicly reproaching me as she sobbed over her half-drowned infant. "My child," she sobbed. "My child!" And her own beautiful spring costume was a sight—too.

All right. He was good stuff.

That hose was the cause of many a divertissement. Myself coming home one Sunday, but not from Church, I found Lloyd and John playing the hose on the lawn, already too wet. None too pleased I called, "Boys, put up that hose!" No inclination to put it up. "Lloyd! John! Put up that hose or I'll put you all up a tree and leave you there." A challenge. John had the hose and, at this, swung it around toward me. Just a little warning to me, that's all. By now angry, I called—"Boys, put down that hose!"

Nothing of the sort.

Both boys took the hose and turned it on me. I had to jump back a few strides. "Look here, you . . ." but the neighbors were coming home and some of them had stopped to see what would happen next. This gallery excited the boys but restrained me.

I walked around to flank them from the shrubbery.

They were waiting for me and wet me down.

"Boys, come on, now, be good sports—put that hose down," I coaxed.

Not their idea of sport.

"Let's see you get it!" said John, by this time ringleader in the mischief. They danced around and around, finally came toward me with it. I jumped back out of the swishing water. The neighbors, a group on both sides of the street, were laughing, enjoying this show at paternal expense. Authority was getting a bad break. Already wet, I charged the pair. They turned the hose full on me and ran.

So it went.

EDUCATION

I took cold baths myself mornings and I would fling the boys into a tub of cold water, failing to drown their yells which would lift the roof. Then after they were rubbed dry—one hand in my pocket and a boxing glove on the other, I would take them on, gloves on both their hands and both boys working together until they grew too big even to be handled with both my hands gloved and free or later more than one of them at a time.

To each child, early in his life, I gave a musical instrument. To learn to play it was all I asked of their education.

Lloyd—Cello.

John—Violin.

Catherine—Voice.

Frances—Piano.

David—Flute.

Llewellyn—Guitar and Mandolin.

Their mother played the piano, reading. I played the piano a little myself, trying to improvise, letting the piano play itself.

Later this incipient orchestra was presided over by Lloyd, conducting with the bow of his cello. He would reach out so skillfully with it to rap the skull of the player of a wrong note that he would not even interrupt the rhythm of his playing. The howls and wails that mingled with the music gave a distinctly modern effect to every performance.

The connecting door to the Studio would open cautiously, when some rather important client would be in to go over the plans. And I would see curly heads and mischievous eyes challenging mine, knowing I could do nothing about it in the circumstances. There was a balcony around the draughting room reached from the connecting corridor with the willow tree in it. The children always loved to get up in that balcony and peer down at the goings-on. They would break out into a roar and scamper back before unkind words could overtake them.

One day a fashionable, fastidious client from the North Side. Mrs. Aline Devin. Her first visit to the studio. Sitting together at the big central office table, facing the corridor—I was just about to show her plans to her for the first time, always a strained situation—when I saw the door open a little and saw Catherine's dirty little face. A dirty little hand was on the door jamb.

I looked tons of "go away." But no fear. The door opened wider. In came the Catherine, one stocking down over one shoe—broadly chewing gum. Where did she get that gum? Gum was forbidden. The dirt was familiar enough.

She marched sidelong to the opposite side of the table, perfectly conscious of the effect she was having upon me. Her little jaws worked carelessly and freely while she deliberately regarded Mrs. Devin curiously—apparently unfavorably.

Then suddenly, stretching out her dirty little hand: "*Paa*pa! Mama wants a dime!"

I didn't have one. So I made merry over the break, escorted Catherine II to the corridor door and turned the key.

Fatal error.

There she was now up in the balcony above, looking down—freely chewing gum—as ever. . . .

"*Paa*pa! Mama wants a dime!"

Her mother finally came to get the persistent creditor dunning me for the dime I didn't have. I will say Catherine made herself charming, if dirty—all the while.

Mrs. Devin was highly amused. So must I have been, or worse, for I've never forgotten the moment.

Those children!

Worthy of a monograph, each!

NINETEEN YEARS

Life and work went on in Oak Park for nineteen years.

Food, clothing, shelter, education and amusement for my six meanwhile accomplished somehow. The older boys went from the Hillside Home School to college. The other boys from the Oak Park High School to universities. The girls went to private schools, Frances to Penn Hall and to Sophie Newcomb. Catherine was sent to New York to study music. All had musical educations of a sort, seemed talented individuals, yes and pretty much in their own right. They were happy only when they were on their own. They knew how to be, even at that very early age. I guess they knew how before they ever got here at all.

So long as we had the luxuries, the necessities could pretty well take care of themselves at home so far as we were concerned. Season tickets to the Symphony; the children always tastefully dressed in expensive things, best to be had. Their good looks made this agreeable extravagance. Catherine herself wore so well the clothes I designed for her that designing them was fun.

This love for beautiful things—rugs, books, prints or anything else made by art or craft or building—especially building—kept the butcher, the baker and the landlord always waiting. Sometimes waiting incredibly long.

GROCERIES, RENT

Our kind grocer down at the corner, Mr. Gotsch, came around once, I remember, with a grocery bill for eight hundred and fifty dollars. How many months old, I do not remember. But I do remember the kindly way in which he sat down to plead his side of the case with me. He showed me how much cheaper he could serve me if I would pay his bill regularly.

"Then," I said, "you are charging me for giving me credit, are you?"

"Of course," he said, "I must. I have children of my own." And I knew them—nice children. He went on to say: "If I didn't protect myself I would soon be unable to give them even a small part of what you are pretty freely giving to yours."

He didn't press the matter. He just showed me the folly of such neglect as mine. I felt remorse, even though I *had* paid in cash for my own neglect. I somehow got the money and paid him. I would resist the next adventure into art and craft, perhaps resist for several months. But this self-denial would not last. So, always, the necessities were going by default to save the luxuries until I hardly knew which were necessities and which luxuries.

It was my misfortune, too, that everybody was willing to trust me. I don't know why because my appearance or my way of life would not appeal to a businessman any more than my buildings appealed to the local banker. But I always found in those early days the merchants kind, indulgent to unbelievable extremes. This, too, tended to make me dreadfully careless. Only the banks would "N.S.F." us. So we came to distrust and despise banks. But they were really doing us the only favor they know how to do. The mistrust grew cordially mutual in the course of time.

But the group of children big and little in the little gabled house on the corner, the queer studio alongside, had unusual luxuries. Unusual advantages in education. Eventually, though I never knew *how* nor quite *how much* they all came to, I managed to pay for the necessary luxuries plus delinquency tax of course, which was—as Grocer Gotsch had said—considerable.

And I remember "rent" in the Schiller Building when offices were later opened there. Rent would sometimes be seven or eight months behind. I hear Mr. Dose, manager of the Schiller Building saying, when I would realize the enormity of the circumstances by being brought to book, would apologize and promise; "Never mind, Mr. Wright: you are an artist. I have never yet lost any rent owed me by an artist. You will pay me," said the heavy, severe-faced agent, my landlord.

Of course, I did pay him. After that, regularly if I could.

I don't believe anyone ever lost a penny either in rent or on credit account in all those haphazard years—except myself. It cost me handsomely in the end to allow the necessities to drift. How much? Say twenty-five per cent. Perhaps it was worth it. Who knows?

I remember walking into a little, thrifty, French investment broker's office one day and seeing on the wall the framed motto, "Spend what you earn." I told him he was corrupting the youth of this country. No such motto would ever get anybody anywhere. "Make the motto read: 'Earn what you spend,' and you will have everybody working hard for you and to better purpose." I might have said that he would also have everybody to whom the youth owed money working on the youth, to make him pay.

Nevertheless, always during those years there was a very real undertone of worry, owing to heavy drag of debt that fell to my share. I believe no one ever really forgets a money-obligation. It goes along with him wherever he goes. Pricking him sharply, from underneath at times, coming to mind wakeful nights. I believe, too, while debt is stimulating to some, it is stultifying to others. I suppose it is just a question as to how much punishment one can stand. The buying and selling of money has introduced a shopkeeping code into bookkeeping ethics of modern life, made preachers and teachers as well as profligate spenders all money-raisers, open or secret.

The secret information of the credit-detective systems, installment buying finance companies, their back-stair ruses and fine-print extortions, their refinancings. All this commercialite machinery takes terrible toll from any man who gets in too deep. Or he who lets his bills go by. We partly owe all these unpicturesque institutions to this tendency of youthful human nature to put off paying today until tomorrow. It gives jobs to too many sharks.

This chronic "weakness" has bred a whole new school of money-shark. This profit "system"—a meretricious, preposterous "absolute" among us now—has its teeth in the lives of nearly everyone today. The victim of "the teeth" will wake up some day to realize how costly these money-men are; and, by avoiding them make them, too, parasites of the system, go to work to earn an honest living.

BOOK THREE □ WORK

WORK

THE FIELD

Midsummer sun floods the field of smoothly rippling grain. The swath of yellow stubble left by the gay reaper on its rounds shows faint undertone of living green. The gaily painted reaper, pulled by three white horses, cuts its way around, round after round.

The stubble is interlined by the big wheel of the reaper as it is also patterned by subsequent grain-shocks. Adolph in a bright blue shirt is setting up the shocks. The bundles—six of them—he stands butt-end down firmly on the stubble and caps them by putting two bundles crosswise on the top.

The entire field is becoming a linear pattern of Work.

Coming along after the noisy red, blue, green, yellow and white man-toy—jerkily sweeping the grain into regular piles on the stubble— are four more men, each binding the bundles raked off on his side of the square of still standing grain. Each must finish binding his side of the square, his station, before the reaper comes around again or he falls hopelessly behind.

Rhythm in regular and patterned order is everywhere established in this work of the harvest.

After the stooping and rising men comes a bareheaded boy running barefoot to and fro in the stubble picking up the bundles. He gathers eight together in a pile. The shocker, coming along behind, grasps the bundles two at a time, standing all eight up together.

The twelve-year-old, brown as a walnut, sits down on a bundle in the hot blaze of the sun.

Nearby in the shadow of a shock is a brown stone jug filled with spring water. He goes to the jug, uncorks the nozzle, slips two fingers through the stone handle. He manages to lift the jug, letting it drop over on to his forearm as he has seen the men do. Head thrown back he takes a thirsty pull, water gurgling from the jug down his young throat, wipes the sweat from his tanned face and water from his chin with the blue gingham sleeve on his forearm. Head up, he listens for a moment.

The Meadow Lark!

Looks down at his bleeding fingers, nails worn to the quick by the too many straw bands already to his credit. Then, to carry on, he gets up and picks up the bundle on which he had been sitting. From the butt-end of the bundle a rattler unwittingly bound into the sheaf a few moments before by one of the binders and tossed aside, slips to the ground.

Smoothly, the snake swiftly coils in the stubble and—tail upended—rattles, darting a forked tongue—narrow hostile eyes gleaming.

The barefoot starts back, his own eyes narrowing at sight of the splendid enemy.

Instantly, clear consciousness of the whole scene comes full upon the boy: the golden blaze; the giddy whirl of the gay reaper; voices of the men—one singing; the distant rattle of the sickle mingling with the ominous rattle of the snake. The beautiful brown embroidery of its golden body makes the reptile belong. Some fascination holds the lad. A sense of something predestined—lived before. To be lived again? Something in the far distant past comes near—as repetition?

Held by this, he stands still, eyeing the snake as narrowly as the snake eyes him. Yes—as hostile.

A three-tined pitchfork stands against the shock sheltering the stone jug. He leaps for the fork, turns and with a thrust swift as the darting tongue pins the rattler to the ground. The piercing tines of the fork hold fast in the ground as the seething coils of the enraged serpent vainly struggle to get free.

Now what?

With the bottom of the stone jug he flattens the evil-spitting head and picks up the gorgeous thing by the rattles. Nine!

The reaper come opposite, stops. His uncle drops off the driver's seat and comes toward him.

"See, Uncle James! I've got him—nine rattles!"

"Why didn't you get away from him and let Adolph kill him?"

"Why?" the boy answers, missing the approval he felt he earned.

"Why? You are barefoot. You might get worse than hurt."

But the boy holds the limp snake as much higher as he can, looking at its length.

Rhythm and routine of the harvest field go on again all as before. But with no warning at all something dreadful had suddenly happened to challenge the order of the peaceful harvest field.

Work—the plan—for a moment was interrupted by something not

146

in the reckoning: something ever a part of Life but ever a threat to "the plan" as we shall see. Something that bothered the men who made the Bible. Is their *Devil* the only answer?

WORK

Come to the offices of Frank Lloyd Wright, Architect (gold letters on plate-glass door panel full-length), 1501 Schiller Building, where the arches loop beneath the top-story square mass of the parapet top glooming against the sky. An Adler and Sullivan building now called "The Garrick."

Late in the year Eighteen Hundred and Ninety-three. Fateful year in the culture of these United States. They are about to go Pseudo-Classic in Architecture.

The Columbian Fair has opened and closed its turnstiles to the crowd. Upon leaving Adler and Sullivan, Cecil Corwin joined me (not as a partner) and we opened offices together in this tower-floor of The Schiller, Chicago—a building, owing to Sullivan's love for his new home in the South, more largely left to me than any other so far. Accustomed to the view from a high place, I suppose feeling a little nearer Adler and Sullivan by being there, I wanted that space behind the big arches.

Cecil and I had a draughting room, each, either side the common central room for our "business." Defending this room was an anteroom or low vestibule, ceiling dropped down to the top of the doors. A straight line glass-pattern in colored glass, lights above, formed this ceiling— glass diffusing artificial light. The effect of this indirect lighting in the small anteroom was like sunlight. No light-fixtures visible. There was a large flat oak chest of drawers each side the door. Some of Hermon MacNeil's Indian statuettes standing on them. The walls were entirely plain. At either end were two plain square chairs. We liked to stand there and talk about the future—Cecil and I. We would greet a coming client or linger there to talk with one leaving, enjoying the atmosphere.

The outside entrance door to this anteroom, like the inner door to the business space itself, was a single clear plate of glass bordered by the usual wood stiles and rails, the usual width. A single clear glass plate from side to side ran top to bottom in between with our names lettered in gold on one side of the outside door at the top of the plate-glass. On the inner door, the word "Private." Also in gold.

These single-panel clear plate-glass doors were new—had style. Anyone could see directly not only into the anteroom from the elevator hall, but into the business space as well. So we had a shade on each door to pull up from bottom to top. But the shades were seldom used. The effect was so pleasant.

147

At the center of the inner business-space a huge, flat-topped table with four square chests of drawers for legs, leaving leg-space at the middle on four sides. Four comfortable chairs were placed one at the center of each side. We could thus sit on both sides with clients or contractors on the other sides. This table was seven feet square and in the center was a glass globe usually filled with flowers from our small garden. Sitting there I could see directly out as anyone could see directly in. This had various consequences.

I see one of the consequences as I write, in the yellow face and evil eyes of Shimoda, a Japanese draughtsman fired for cause and warned never to come back. The cause was speaking obliquely of a lady who got into the habit of leaving flowers in the glass globe on the big office table.

And yet, one noon, as I glanced up, there stood Shimoda.

A scared look came over the yellow face as I jumped to my feet. My time to be out so he was taken as much by surprise as I was. Probably he had come back with no worse intent than to see the boys, but I had warned him never to come back.

He turned to run but I could open those two doors quickly by now, owing to much practice. Before he could get away I reached him. A well-directed intimate kick landed him well down the half-flight on the main public stair running from directly in front of the entrance door down the half-landing below. He lay there in a whimpering heap and I turned back into the office and sat down—waiting.

But not satisfied with this salutary welcome he carried the tale to my reverend uncle of All Souls Church. Described the event with enlarged details—my big riding boots—insinuating I had them on that morning for no other business and no other intention than to kill him.

"Very rough business for me," said Yerrow Socks as his familiars always called him because "l" was not in his vocabulary.

For this characteristic carrying of the tale I did the work more thoroughly next time he came—which strange to say he did some weeks later, again thinking I was out of town—by continuing the work, this time, on down from the landing to the floor below.

This finally settled it and Shimoda disappeared from the American scene, not very much worse for wear.

No, Shimoda was not a good Japanese.

To this clear plate with the small gold letters—

FRANK LLOYD WRIGHT, ARCHITECT
CECIL CORWIN, ARCHITECT

—came my first client.

You notice the order? By seniority Cecil should have been first but he wouldn't have it so.

And, you see, opening an office was all that simple. It usually is in Chicago. Rent an office to your liking. Take out the door panels, all of them. Substitute a single beautiful clear plate of glass. Sit down and letter your own name in the size and style preferred. Hesitate a moment becomingly—then add "Architect." Get a thrill out of this, as you regard it for a moment with none too adequate realization of the implication. Get a sign writer to put it all in gold leaf on the glass, and—there you are. Another architect come to town. How many of the boys who have listened to the far-away tinkle of the cowbells, have had that same thrill—"professing" something or other? Opening an office?

Truth Against the World is a heavy standard. A flagrant banner. I had left it off the door. But it was sitting there inside. But individual preferences are a compelling circumstance. Babies are too.

Combine these several circumstances with the preferences and what have you? Or what is it that has you?

W. H. Winslow of the Winslow Ornamental Iron Works had often come to Adler and Sullivan to consult with me about the work of that office. "W. H." turned up now to give me my first job. I was to be the architect of his new home at River Forest. I could hardly believe I really had a "job." Difficult to believe the initiative I had taken was now a reality. But I soon enough found out that it was.

The Winslow house was to stand across the drive from Mr. Waller's own house in the Waller park in River Forest. Mr. Waller was the handsomest and most aristocratic individual I had ever seen. He had become my friend. He much admired the Winslow house. The building of that house should have a story, but it has none yet. Edward C. Waller and Daniel H. Burnham, the partner of John Root, were old friends. John Root had just died.

Mr. Waller brought about a meeting with "Uncle Dan," as they all called Daniel H. Burnham—inviting Catherine and me to meet Mr. and Mrs. Burnham at his home. "Uncle Dan" had seen the Winslow house and straightway pronounced it "a gentleman's house from grade to coping."

After dinner Mr. Waller led the way to his cozy library. He wanted to show his friend some work in it I had done for him. I saw him turn to lock the door after we were in. I wondered why. Then and there began an argument which I have never forgotten.

Sitting there, handsome, jovial, splendidly convincing, was "Uncle Dan." To be brief, he would take care of my wife and children if I would go to Paris—four years of the Beaux Arts. Then Rome—two years. Expenses all paid. A job with him when I came back. It was more than merely generous. It was splendid. But I was frightened. I sat embarrassed, not knowing what to say.

Mr. Waller got up, walked to and fro telling me what a great opportunity it all was for me. I sat there trying to find the right words to say.

"Another year and it will be too late, Frank," said Uncle Dan.

That was my cue. "Yes, too late, Uncle Dan—it's too late now I'm afraid. I am spoiled already. I've been too close to Mr. Sullivan. He has helped spoil the Beaux Arts for me, or spoiled me for the Beaux Arts, I guess I mean. He told me things too, and I think he regrets the time he spent there himself."

Uncle Dan: "You are loyal to Sullivan I see, Frank, and that is right. I admire Sullivan when it comes to decoration. Essentially he is a great decorator. His ornament charms me. But his architecture? I can't see that. The Fair, Frank, is going to have a great influence in our country. The American people have seen the Classics on a grand scale for the first time. You've seen the success of the Fair and it should mean something to you too. We should take advantage of the Fair."

He went on: "Atwood's Fine Arts Building, Beman's Merchant Tailor's Building, McKim's Building—all beautiful! Beautiful! I can see all America constructed along the lines of the Fair, in noble dignified classic style. The great men of the day all feel that way about it—all of them."

"No," I said, "there is Louis Sullivan. He doesn't. And if John Root were alive I don't believe he would feel that way about it. Richardson I am sure never would."

"Frank," he said, "the Fair should have shown you that Sullivan and Richardson are well enough in their way, but their way won't prevail—architecture is going the other way."

"But, it is essentially the uncreative way . . . isn't it?"

"Uncreative?—what do you mean uncreative? What can be more beautiful than the classic lines and proportions of Greek architecture? That architecture will never be surpassed. We should be taught by it and accept its rules. Without a good education in the Classics how can you hope to . . . succeed?"

"I know. Yes—I know, Uncle Dan, you may be quite right but somehow it just strikes on my heart like—jail. Like something awful. I couldn't bear it, I believe. All that discipline and time wasted, again waiting for something to happen that could never happen. I just can't see it as living. Somehow—it scares me." I actually began to look for some avenue of escape; the window was partly open. I knew the door was locked.

150

Mr. Waller now interfered, manifestly provoked at my obstinacy, if not my stupidity, indeed.

"Frank, don't you realize what this offer means to you? As you choose now, remember, so you will go on all the rest of your life."

"Yes, Mr. Waller—that's just it," I said. "I know. They all do. I have seen the men come home from there all one type, no matter how much they were individuals when they went."

"Individuals? Great architecture *is* severe discipline," said Uncle Dan.

"Think of your future, think of your family," said Mr. Waller.

I felt the weight of the occasion.

I saw myself influential, prosperous, safe; saw myself a competent leader of the majority rule. That much faith I had in it all. There would be no doubt about that, with Daniel H. Burnham's power behind me, if I qualified—and there was no doubt in my mind but that I could qualify. It was all so definitely set, too easy and unexciting as I saw it. And it was all untrue. At the very best a makeshift.

This was success as I had dreamed of it then? Was it? Right here, within my grasp? I, too, had already seen the effect of the Fair. But I could not respect it, though I believed Uncle Dan spoke the truth. I did fear and believe it was going to *prevail* as he said. I would have given a good deal to know my Master Sullivan's reaction to all this. But that was all over. I could not go to him now.

The two friends mistook my depression for a weakening in favor of the Beaux Arts.

"Well?" said both, smiling kindly—affectionately.

I felt like an ingrate. Never was the ego within me more hateful to me than at that moment. But it stood straight up against the very roof of my mind.

"No, Mr. Burnham, no, Mr. Waller—I can't run away."

"Run away, what do you mean?" said Mr. Waller.

"Well, you see, run away from what I see as mine, I mean what I see as *ours* in our country, to what can't belong to me, no, I mean *us*, just because it means success. You see—I can't go, even if I wanted to go because I should never care for myself, after that."

I don't believe either of the two great friends believed me. They thought I must be showing off—I saw that by their expressions, I thought. "It may be foolish. I suppose it is, somehow, but I'd rather be free and a failure and 'foolish' than be tied up to any routine success. I don't see freedom in it . . . that's all. Oh yes, I mean it. I really do. I'm grateful to you, both though; but I won't go." I got up on my feet. Suddenly the whole thing cleared up before my eyes as only keeping faith with what we then called "America" and I now call Usonia.

"Thank you both," I said again. "I know how obstinate and egotistic you think me, but I'm going on as I've started. I'm spoiled, first by birth, then by training, and"—this had now come clear under pressure—"by conviction, for anything like that."

Mr. Waller unlocked the study door, opened it and stood aside—hurt, I could see—to let me pass. I helped Catherine on with her things, and we went home. I didn't mention to her what had happened until long afterward.

The Winslow house had burst on the view of that provincial suburb like the Primavera in full bloom. It was a new world to Oak Park and River Forest. That house became an attraction, far and near. Incessantly it was courted and admired. Ridiculed, too, of course. Ridicule is always modeled on the opposite side of that shield. This first house soon began to sift the sheep from the goats in this fashion:

Mr. Moore, a lawyer on Forest Avenue near my own house, was going to build. I had learned of this, and I had given up hope that he might ask me to build for him, when, one day, sure enough—could I believe my eyes? I saw Mr. and Mrs. Moore standing outside the full length clear-plate in the outer door of the Schiller Building office. I opened it—excited. The Moores came in and sat down.

"How is it, Mr. Wright," said Mr. Moore, "that every architect I know or have ever heard of and some I never heard of have come in one way or another to ask to build my house and you live almost across the street from me but I haven't had a word from you?"

"Did Mr. Patton come?" I asked. He was the head of the American Institute of Architects, the A.I.A., at the time and lived in Oak Park.

"Yes, he was the first one to come. Why didn't you come?"

"I knew if you wanted me, you knew where to find me. And how did I know you wanted me? . . . You are a lawyer," I said. "Would you offer yourself to someone you knew needed a good lawyer?"

"I thought that was it," he said.

"Now we want you to build our house . . . but—I don't want you to give us anything like that house you did for Winslow. I don't want to go down backstreets to my morning train to avoid being laughed at. I would like something like this," and he laid some pictures of English half-timber work on my table.

Three children were now running around the streets without proper shoes. How money was needed in that little gabled house! (I had been insulted several times by guesses as to whether the house was "sea-side" or "colonial.") None knew so little as I where money was coming from. Could I take Mr. Moore on? Could I give him a home in the name of English half-timber good enough so that I would not "sell out"? It was worth trying anyway. I tried it . . .

They were delighted with the house, and so was everyone but me. Did I always resent the praise bestowed upon it because a mention of it made me think of my brave stand before Mr. Waller and Uncle Dan? But it was better to stand back and make way with a single house—wasn't it, than with a whole lifetime of them? Or was it?

So I consoled myself. At any rate it was the one time in the course of a long career that I gave in to the fact that I had a family and they had a right to live—and their living was up to me. The tragedy of the binomial theorem!

Yes, I often had occasion to remember and regret "giving in" in the years immediately following. I can look back now and see that young professional architect—I soon left off the affix as beside the mark—sitting at that big platform table—let's say the flowers were lilacs—listening to you expectantly. I suspect the ego in him invited or repelled you as you happened to be made yourself.

"You wish to build a house? . . . Oh? Like the one I built for Mr. Moore?"

There is a feeling of disappointment that gets to you. I hear myself saying, "But why like that house for Mr. Moore?" And the argument is on.

Anyone could get a rise out of me by admiring that essay in English half-timber. "They" all liked it and I could have gone on unnaturally building them for the rest of my natural life. It was the first time, however, an English half-timbered house ever saw a porch. The porch was becoming to the house.

But, by the time an hour or so passed, I was quite likely to have made that client see why and how it was the wrong thing, especially now wrong, to build anything more like that in our country, wrong in Usonia where men were free, and old enough to know that license, even in taste, is not freedom.

The offices in the Schiller (now the Garrick) saw the making of the Winslow plans; the plans for the Moore house. Mr. Baldwin, another Oak Park lawyer, had come in and laid a check for three hundred and fifty dollars on the table as a retainer. He had evidently heard from Mr. Moore. The Francis Apartments I built for an estate. The Husser and Heller home, the Lexington Terraces, the Wolff Lake Resort. A number of other buildings all characterized to a certain extent by the Sullivanian idiom, at least in detail. I couldn't invent terms of my own overnight. At that time there was nothing in sight that might be helpful. I had no Sullivanian models, even, for any of these things.

A remark of the Master's had come back to me by way of my client

Winslow: "Sullivan says, Frank, it looks as though you were going to work out your own individuality."

So he was interested in me still, was he?

Cecil had been working on some jobs of his own, Rush Medical College in particular. We were not partners. I did not see much of him now for I was intensely busy, and meantime he had found some new intimates. We sat talking in the business office we used in common. He looked discouraged, I noticed.

"What's the matter, old man Cecil?"

"Not much, in general, Frank. In particular, I don't believe I'm an architect, that's all."

"What's the matter with Rush? Don't you like it?"

He looked at me as he tilted gently back and forth in a creaking office chair—sadness and some whimsey in his look.

"You know. Why ask me?"

"Because it's a fine piece of work."

"Is it architecture?" he said quietly.

"Well, it's better than ninety-nine out of a hundred architects are doing—better than their barbering and make-up. And, Cecil, you are only beginning. You have such fine feeling for proportion—you know it—and good taste, and . . . Why are you looking at me that way? You are worth more to any client than any architect I know." Again I asked, "What is the matter with you?"

"All right, I'll tell you, young fellow. I've found out there's no joy in architecture for me except as I see you do it. It bores me when I try to do it myself. There's the truth for you. You *are* the thing you do. I'm not and I never will be. And worse than all, I'm not sure any longer, lately, that I want to be. There's joy in it for you—but there's obsession too. You live in your work. You will wake up some day to find that you can't do that, altogether, and then there'll be trouble, I foresee."

All this seemed to open a chasm where I thought all fair enough. I had lost sight of him. He had been lagging behind. Dear old Cecil. After all, was architecture everything? But worse was coming.

"I'm going East, Frank. I'm interested with Dr. Buchanan—we're going into something together. You can take over my room and, as I see, you'll need it."

This was unbelievable. I reproached Cecil because I had an uneasy sense of having betrayed him and so—inclined to blame *him*. Never would I have believed this *of* him. I was finding it hard to believe it even *from* him.

I argued, pleaded. All of no use.

"I might as well make a clean breast of it, Frank. I don't want to go on seeing you do the things I can't do. Already I'm where I can do less than I could when we came in here together, and I really care less. Caring less, this isn't so difficult as you imagine it to be."

It flashed through my mind that I was right. This abnegation on his part was genuine discouragement due to my own neglect—and I felt ashamed of myself. Why not take him in with me? But that was not what this meant. And I knew he wouldn't come.

But I said, "Why not join me, Cecil—I need you to help me and maybe I could help you out of this. How do you know?

"No, I'm not the man you need for a partner, Frank. I'm no business man at all. I despise business—it's too gabby and grabby and selly for me—and I'm no architect. I know it now. You do need me for a friend, and I'll always be one. You are going to go far. You'll have a kind of success; I believe the kind you want. Not everybody would pay the price in concentrated hard work and human sacrifice you'll make for it though, my boy." He added, "I'm afraid—for what will be coming to you."

There was no bitterness in this; I could see that a load seemed to have slipped off his mind. He got up. His expression changed. He looked happy again. I was miserable.

Cecil was something of a prophet.

Cecil went East and—God knows why—never have I seen him since.

That place in the Schiller Building soon seemed nothing at all without him. I had met Robert Spencer, Myron Hunt and Dwight Perkins. Dwight had a loft in his new Steinway Hall building—too large for him. So we formed a group—outer office in common—workrooms screened apart in the loft of Steinway Hall. These young men, newcomers in architectural practice like myself, were my first associates in the so-called profession of architecture. George Dean was another and Hugh Garden. Birch Long was a young and talented "renderer" at this time and we took him to the Steinway loft with us.

Now and then I went with them to talk at women's clubs until they could all speak the language as well as I. But when they undertook to build, what a difference to me! So I decided to let them do the speaking. I would do the building.

About this time came the incipient Arts and Crafts Society at Hull House. There I read the paper, protestant yet affirmative—"The Art and Craft of the Machine." Next day there was an editorial in the *Chicago Tribune* commenting upon the fact that an artist had said the first word for the use of the machine as an artist's tool. Jane Addams herself must have written it, I suspect. She sympathized with me, as did Julia La-throp.

But my novel thesis was overwhelmed by Professors Zueblin and Triggs and the architects and handicraftsmen present that evening. The Society went "handicraft" and was soon defunct. Never have I found support for radical or organic ideas from architects or professors. But there was nevertheless by now a certain cautious emulation on all sides. Soon it was like seeing one's own features distorted in an imperfect mirror. The imitation disturbed, when it did not anger me.

Never having known Sullivan much themselves, at this time these young architects were all getting the gospel modified through me. I should have liked to be allowed to work out the thing I felt in me as architecture with no reflections or refractions from them or libelous compliments until I had it all where I felt it really ought to be. But that was not possible. I was out in the open to stay. Premature though it might be.

To this new Steinway loft came Ward Willets, client number one. I did the streamlined prairie house for him on Sheridan Drive in Highland Park. Others soon followed in this vein which was now really my own.

About this time "Romeo and Juliet," amateur engineering architecture—an idea of structure working out into architectural form—the future in embryo—got itself built. These creations of ours. I see as we look back upon them, or as we look at them and try to re-create them, how we ourselves belong to them because it *was* the engineering architecture of the future in amateur embryo. Here is the tale.

ROMEO AND JULIET

At this time in the Valley were two matriarchal maiden sisters of Mother's. They were my Aunts Nell and Jane.

The buildings for the Lloyd-Jones Sisters' Hillside Home School for boys and girls were designed by amateur me. The first one in which to mother their forty or fifty boys and girls was built in 1887. This school, too, had for its crest, "Truth Against the World." "The Aunts" built the school on the site of Grandfather's old homestead, adding several new buildings. And—the better to guard the development of this beloved school with a high aim, therefore with trouble ahead—its founders made a compact with each other never to marry.

Around about the Hillside Home School farm were the farms of their five patriarchal brothers, my uncles. They always referred to my aunts as "the girls" and with true clan-faithfulness watched over their sisters' educational venture and over them too. Anything "the girls" needed they got, if all the surrounding farms went to rack and ruin. That, at least, was the complaint the wives of some of my uncles used to make. Meantime their brothers were proud of their sisters' school. Boys and girls from a dozen or more states freely called them all "Uncle" and called the Lloyd-Jones sisters Aunt Nell and Aunt Jennie no less than the legitimate nephews and nieces—some thirty or more of whom foregathered there to be educated. Eventually the native nephews and nieces were all "educated" out of the beloved Valley—by way of learning—educated into white-collarites in the big cities.

The school prospered.

When working with architect Silsbee in Chicago I had made the amateurish plans for the very first school buildings; Cramer the local contractor had built them. But inventing new construction to make itself beautiful as architecture was not a Cramer habit.

Now, a big reservoir for a new water system had been scooped out in the white sand-rock of the hilltop above the school. This reservoir finished, the Aunts intended to erect a windmill over it. This was decided upon by a family gathering which the clan usually held to make such decisions concerning the school or important affairs of their own.

Said Aunt Nell, managerial mind of the school: "Why not a pretty windmill tower in keeping with our school buildings instead of an ugly steel tower or, for that matter, the timber ones I have seen? I am going to ask Frank for a design."

"Nonsense, Nell," said preacher-brother Jenkin (he happened to be there on one of his frequent visits). "A steel tower like all the others is good enough. I never ride my horse in this countryside that I don't welcome the sight of one. They are practical and cheap." The other brothers thought so too.

Aunt Jane, emotional, warmly humane mind of the school, disagreed with the brothers. She said, "The hill is visible from all over our several valleys. Something should be there to go with the school buildings. I agree with Nell. Let's ask Frank to send us a design."

The meeting grumbled. But when Nell put her foot down, all usually gave up quietly. She put her foot down now.

So, Uncle James said, "Well, let's see what the boy will do then."

The design came. A perspective sketch of the tower in the trees on the hilltop was included with the structural details. The sisters liked it and thought it becoming to the dignity of the beloved school. To the Uncles it looked expensive and foolish.

Cramer, builder "and good enough architect too, around here," was called in to take the drawings away with him to make an estimate. The family waited in vain for Cramer to come back. So brother James went several towns away to look for Cramer. James came back alone. The brothers got together to consider carefully the facts Uncle James had from Cramer.

"Cramer says wasting time and money to build that tower. Blow down sure as Death and Taxes. Sixty feet high! Fourteen-foot wheel top of that. He says the thing is just a sort of big octagonal wood pipe, 4×4 posts at each corner, boards nailed around to the posts, inside and outside. Then all shingled all over on the outside. The whole thing is just like a barrel, only the staves run around across instead of running up and down. There's a diamond-shaped part cutting into the octagon part, or barrel, to the very center. And the outside half of the diamond makes a 'storm prow.' Frank named it 'storm prow' on the plan. The 'storm prow' . . . looks like a big blade running up to the very top on the sou'west side of the barrel. Up the center of this diamond-shaped part runs a big wood post six inches by six inches—runs up and out of the diamond to carry the big mill-wheel at the top. The boy wants a big heavy stone foundation under the whole thing, eight big strap-bolts built into it, the straps to stick up out of the stone six feet alongside the posts and be bolted to them.

"Cramer laughed. It looked crazy to him. He said we could tell the girls about it ourselves. Frank wants to try some experiment or other."

Anxious family gathering.

AUNT NELL: "Did Cramer positively say he knew Frank's tower would fall down?"

UNCLE JAMES: "Positively."

UNCLE JENKIN: "To suppose such a thing could stand up there sixty feet high to carry a fourteen-foot wheel in the storms we have in this region! Why, Nell, it's nonsense. Trust Cramer. Why build something none of us ever saw the like of in our lives? Not Frank, either, if I know him."

AUNT JANE: "Poor boy, what a pity his tower won't stand up. How can he know it will? I do not for the life of me see. Dear me! How he will be disappointed."

Aunt Nell said nothing, just walked over to the window with her hands behind her back as usual, and looked up at the hilltop. She may have seen the tower there among the trees, the wheel spinning; who knows? All she said was, "I'll telegraph Frank."

To all present this seemed like temporizing with the devil. But there was nothing to do but wait for an answer. The telegram—"CRAMER SAYS WINDMILL TOWER SURE TO FALL. ARE YOU SURE IT WILL STAND" signed AUNT NELL—reached the young architect, by now on his own in Chicago.

Came back the answer: "BUILD IT."

158

Consternation! Into peaceful family relationships came war. Aunt Nell's work was cut out for her. It was clear to them all; she was going to build that foolish tower!

"That boy will be the ruination of his aunts." Conviction settled firmly around there and became a slogan. Cramer came down to argue and expostulate.

But with her back to the wall Aunt Nell said, "Does the boy want to build anything that will fall down any more than we do? He has even more at stake. He says, *'Build it.'* Maybe he knows better than all of us? He would not be so confident unless he had his feet on something in this design."

Said Aunt Jane, "He is never willing to explain fully, but somehow I do believe he knows what he is about, after all."

"Cramer," said Aunt Nell, as she turned around to face the practical builder, "how much will it cost to build this tower just as Frank planned it?"

"Nine hundred and fifty dollars," he said.

"How much would a steel mill cost?"

"Two hundred seventy-five dollars," he said.

"Only six hundred seventy-five dollars for all that difference," was her unexpected reaction. (This was in the country about 1896.) "Of course we are going to build it."

The anxious committee ruefully disbanded.

Dear Aunts Nell and Jane:

Of course you had a hard time with Romeo and Juliet. But you know how troublesome they were centuries ago. The principle they represent still causes mischief in the world because it is so vital. Each is indispensable to the other . . . neither could stand without the other. Romeo, as you will see, will do all the work and Juliet cuddle alongside to support and exalt him. Romeo takes the side of the blast and Juliet will entertain the school children. Let's let it go at that. No symbol should be taken too far. As for the principle involved, it *is* a principle but I've never seen it in this form. No. But I've never seen anything to go against it, either.

Yes, I could explain the way the storm-strains on the harmonious pair will be resolved into one another and be tuned into a pull on the iron straps built deep into the stone foundation. But, after all, for the life of this harmoniously contrasting pair I am chiefly betting on the nails driven into the boards by the hammers of Cramer's *men* to fasten them to the upright corner-posts. We'll see that there are enough nails and long enough. Nails are not engineering but they are "practice." Of course you will build it. I will come out.

Lovingly,

FRANK.

N.B. Romeo and Juliet will stand twenty-five years which is longer than the iron towers stand around there. I am afraid all of my uncles themselves may be gone before "Romeo and Juliet." Let's go.

Cramer, the local builder, "good enough architect too, around there," was sincere in his belief that the thing would fall down. "Sixty-foot post to the spring of the wheel," said he, shaking his head. "And a fourteen-foot wheel," he added—really dejected.

"It beats heck," said he, "the way those two old maids dance around after that boy. He comes up here with his swell duds on, runs around the hills with the school girls and goes home. You wouldn't think he had a care in the world nor anything but something to laugh at."

"Well . . ." He finally stopped grumbling and went to work.

Five gray-bearded uncles religiously kept away from the scene of impending disaster. Two gray-headed, distinguished-looking maiden aunts, between whiles mothering their boys and girls, daily climbed to the hilltop, anxious to see what was going on. Timothy, family friend and excellent old Welsh stone-mason, incorrigible in his quaint misuse of the word "whateverr," had by now got up the stone foundation. Timothy, alone, gave them comfort. He knew well the aunts liked a good word for their nephew.

"The boys [meaning my uncles] don't know what's in the young man's head, whateverr. They'll be looking to him one of these days. . . . Yes, whateverr. Could any wooden tower pull that stone foundation over?" And he built the rods in solider and deeper than they were called for . . . a staunch mason, and man too, that Welshman. Whateverr.

As the frame went up into the air, the workmen were skittish at first. If the wind came up they came down.

But the big windmill wheel was finally shipped way up there in the blue.

The tower swayed in the wind several inches as it should have done but this sway made the men nervous. Some quit for one specious reason or another. It did look very far down to the ground when you were up in the little belvedere—named for Juliet. The tower lifted from the apex of the hill and from up there you looked all the way down the sides of the hill. Vertigo was the consequence of this combined verticality. I came out, once, to make sure all was going all right and the boards were

160

properly nailed to the corner uprights outside and inside. I knew I could count on Timothy for the anchorage.

It was all simple enough. You see, the wooden tower was rooted as the trees are. Unless *uprooted* it could not fall for it would not break, notwithstanding the barrel simile. Try, sometime, yourself to break a barrel!

Romeo and Juliet stood in full view from five farmhouses on five brotherly farms and Aunt Jane could see it from her sitting-room window. Several months after it was finished the first real sou'wester struck—in the night. As promptly as Aunt Jane's and Aunt Nell's, at sun up the anxious faces of five gray-bearded farmer brothers all came to as many farmhouse doors shading their eyes to peer over at the new tower. It was still there. The Aunts promptly took their tower for granted. But the brothers kept on peering. For "what was one storm, after all." A few years later Uncle Thomas, arch-conservative, died.

But year after year this little drama of unfaith—typical of scepticism directed toward the Idea everywhere on earth—went on in the beloved Valley. Storm after storm swept over. But each storm only left all nearer the conviction that the next must be the last. The Uncles would shake their heads doggedly after coming to the door to look at the tower, each storm the tower weathered. Cramer, the builder, died ten years later. The staunch Timothy, stone-mason, followed the builder to the mysterious "whateverr" to which during his long and simple lifetime he had made allusion.

Then Uncle James died. Uncle John, the miller, died some years later. Some twenty-five years after the tower came to stand on the hill both the Lloyd-Jones sisters passed away to rest, their tower still standing. Uncle Philip, arch-sceptic, soon after moved away to the city, an old, old man. Uncle Jenkin died. But Uncle Enos, Sister Anna's younger brother, aged and alone now, never failed true to the habit of that long vigil, to come to the door after a storm and shading his eyes with his hand peer over at the tower to see the damage it had suffered at last. Now he too has moved away to the city where he can no longer see the tower.

Had the tower fallen at any time during that period, unfaith would have found and uttered judgment.

Now nearly forty-four years have gone by since the amateur windmill tower—"Romeo and Juliet"—took its place on the hill in the sun overlooking the beloved Valley. I, the author of its being, hair getting white now as Aunt Nell's was when, before the tower was built, she first walked to the window to see its wheel spinning there among the trees, look over from Taliesin. Seemingly good as ever the wooden tower that was an experiment still, stands in full view. Shall I take it down, faithful servant serving so well, so long? Or shall I let it go until it falls just as I myself must do—though neither tower nor I show any signs of doing so.

The tower is weatherbeaten. My hair is gray. One never knows. But when we fall, there will surely still be those to say, "Well, there it is—down at last! We thought so!"

No. Romeo and Juliet shall live to crash down together.

About the time Romeo and Juliet came to stand on the hill known as "Hillside," I had begun work on the Middle Western prairies: the buildings that came later to be known as "New School of the Middle West."

A contract with the Luxfer Prism Co. of Chicago, I to be consulting engineer for making prism-glass installations in office buildings throughout the country, had enabled me to build the workroom—then I called it a "studio"—next to our little Oak Park dwelling-place.

An old willow tree still stood in the corridor connecting the house with the big workroom. I had succeeded in making the roofs around the tree trunks watertight in a manner that would permit the tree to grow, and the great, sprawling old tree gave us a grateful coolness in the studio in summer. I liked the golden green drooping above the amateurish buildings. If I could have covered the buildings all over with greenery, I would have done so. They were so badly overdone.

Here, in this "studio," I worked away with various boys and girls as helpers and apprentices, to get the houses built that now stood around the prairie and have influenced many of those built in North, Northwest, Southwest and West. And soon, owing to this proximity to the draughting booard, my own children were all running around with thumbtacks in the soles of their shoes.

At last, my work was alongside my home, where it has been ever since. I could work late and tumble into bed. Unable to sleep because of some idea, I could get up, go downstairs to the "studio" by way of the connecting corridor, and work.

As I had regularly gone to and fro between Oak Park and my work with Adler and Sullivan in Chicago, here at hand was the typical American dwelling, the "monogoria" of earlier days, standing about on the Chicago prairie. That dwelling got there somehow and became typical. But by any faith in nature, implicit or explicit, it did not belong there. I had seen that far in the light of the conception of architecture as natural. Ideas had naturally begun to come to me of a more natural house. Each house I built I longed for the chance to build another. And I soon got the chance. I was not the only one sick of hypocrisy and hungry for reality around there, I found.

What was the matter with the kind of house I found on the prairie? Well—let me tell you in more detail.

Just for a beginning, let's say that house *lied* about everything. It had no sense of Unity at all nor any such sense of space as should belong to a free man among a free people in a free country. It was stuck up and stuck on, however it might be done. Wherever it happened to be. To take any one of those so-called "homes" away would have improved the landscape and cleared the atmosphere. It was a box, too, cut full of holes to let in light and air, an especially ugly one to get in and out of. Or else it was a clumsy gabled chunk of roofed masonry similarly treated. Otherwise joinery reigned supreme; you know—"Carpenter and Joiner," it used to read on the signs. Floors were the only part of the house left plain and the housewife covered those with a tangled rug-collection, because otherwise the floors were "bare"—bare, I suppose, only because one could not very well walk on jigsawing or turned spindles or plaster-ornament.

It is not too much to say that as an architect my lot in Oak Park was cast with an inebriate lot of sinners hardened by habit against every human significance except one—and why mention "the one touch of nature that makes the whole world kin"? I will venture to say that the aggregation was the worst the world ever saw—at the lowest esthetic level in all history. Steam heat, plumbing and electric light were coming in as its only redeeming features.

My first feeling therefore had been a yearning for simplicity. A new sense of simplicity as "organic." This had barely begun to take shape in my mind when the Winslow house was planned. But now it began in practice. Organic simplicity might be seen producing significant character in the harmonious order we call nature. Beauty in growing things. None were insignificant.

I loved the prairie by instinct as a great simplicity—the trees, flowers, sky itself, thrilling by contrast.

I saw that a little height on the prairie was enough to look like much more—every detail as to height becoming intensely significant, breadths all falling short. Here was tremendous spaciousness but all sacrificed needlessly. All space was cut up crosswise and cut up lengthwise into the fifty-foot lot—or would you have twenty-five feet less or twenty-five feet more? Salesmanship cut and parceled it out, sold it with no restrictions. In a great, new, free country there was, then, everywhere a characteristic tendency to huddle and in consequence a mean tendency to tip everything in the way of human habitation up edgewise instead of letting it lie comfortably and naturally flat with the ground. Nor has this changed much since automobilization made it stupid as an economic measure and criminal as a social habit. I had an idea that the horizontal planes in buildings, those planes parallel to earth, identify themselves with the ground—make the building belong to the ground. I began putting this idea to work.

Buildings standing around there on the Chicago prairies were all tall and all tight. Chimneys were lean and taller still—sooty fingers threatening the sky. And beside them, sticking up almost as high, were the dormers. Dormers were elaborate devices—cunning little buildings complete in themselves—stuck on the main roof—slopes to let the help poke their heads out of the attic for air. Invariably the damp, sticky clay of the prairie was dug out for a basement under the whole house and the rubble stone-walls of this dank basement always stuck above the ground a foot or so—and blinked through half-windows.

So the universal "cellar" showed itself above ground as a bank of some kind of masonry running around the whole, for the house to sit up on—like a chair. The lean upper house walls of the usual two floors above this stone or brick basement were wood and were set up on top of this masonry chair. Preferably house walls were both sided and shingled, mixed up and down or crosswise, together or with moldings. These overdressed wood house walls had cut in them, or cut out of them to be precise, big holes for the big cat and little holes for the little cat to get in or get out or for ulterior purposes of light and air. These house walls were be-corniced or fancy-bracketed up at the top into the tall,. purposely profusely complicated roof. Dormers plus. The whole roof was ridged and tipped, swanked and gabled to madness before they would allow it to be either watershed or shelter. The whole exterior was bedeviled, that is to say, mixed to puzzle-pieces with corner-boards, panel-boards, window-frames, corner-blocks, plinth-blocks, rosettes, fantails, and jiggerwork in general. This was the only way "they" seemed to have then of putting on style. The wood butchery of scroll-saw and turning lathe were at that moment the honest means to this fashionable and unholy but entirely moral end as things were.

Unless the householder of the period were poor indeed, usually the ingenious corner tower as seen in monogaria, eventuated into a candle-snuffer dome, a spire, an inverted rutabaga, radish or onion. Always elaborate bay-windows and fancy porches rallied around this imaginatively unimaginative corner fetich—ring around a rosie. And all this the builders of the period could do nearly as well in brick as in stone. It was an impartial society. All materials looked pretty much alike to it in that day and do today.

164

Simplicity was as far from this scrap-pile as the pandemonium of the barnyard is far from music. But easy enough for the architect. Oh yes. All he had to do was call, "Boy, take down No. 37, and put a bay-window on it for the lady."

BUILDING THE NEW HOUSE

First thing in building the new house, get rid of the attic, therefore the dormer. Get rid of the useless false heights below it. Next, get rid of the unwholesome basement, yes absolutely—in any house built on the prairie. Instead of lean, brick chimneys bristling up everywhere to hint at Judgment, I could see necessity for one chimney only. A broad generous one, or at most two. These kept low-down on gently sloping roofs or perhaps flat roofs. The big fireplace in the house below became now a place for a real fire. A real fireplace at that time was extraordinary. There were mantels instead. A mantel was a marble frame for a few coals in a grate. Or it was a piece of wooden furniture with tile stuck in it around the grate, the whole set slam up against the plastered, papered wall. Insult to comfort. So the *integral* fireplace became an important part of the building itself in the houses I was allowed to build out there on the prairie.

It comforted me to see the fire burning deep in the solid masonry of the house itself. A feeling that came to stay.

Taking a human being for my scale, I brought the whole house down in height to fit a normal one—ergo, 5′ 8½″ tall, say. This is my own height. Believing in no other scale than the human being I broadened the mass out all I possibly could to bring it down into spaciousness. It has been said that were I three inches taller than 5′ 8½″ all my houses would have been quite different in proportion. Probably.

House walls were now started at the ground on a cement or stone water table that looked like a low platform under the building, and usually was. But the house walls were stopped at the second-story window-sill level to let the bedrooms come through above in a continuous window series below the broad eaves of a gently sloping, overhanging roof. In this new house the wall was beginning to go as an impediment to outside light and air and beauty. Walls had been a great fact about the box in which holes had to be punched. It was still this conception of a wall-building which was with me when I designed the Winslow house. But after that my conception began to change.

My sense of "wall" was no longer the side of a box. It was enclosure of space affording protection against storm or heat only when needed. But it was also to bring the outside world into the house and let the inside of the house go outside. In this sense I was working away at the wall as a wall and bringing it toward the function of a screen, a means of opening up space which, as control of building-materials improved, would finally permit the free use of the whole space without affecting the soundness of the structure.

The climate being what it was, violent in extremes of heat and cold, damp and dry, dark and bright, I gave broad protecting roof-shelter to the whole, getting back to the purpose for which the cornice was originally designed. The underside of roof-projections was flat and usually light in color to create a glow of reflected light that softly brightened the upper rooms. Overhangs had double value: shelter and preservation for the walls of the house, as well as this diffusion of reflected light for the upper story through the "light screens" that took the place of the walls and were now often the windows in long series.

And at this time I saw a house, primarily, as livable interior space under sample shelter. I liked the *sense of shelter* in the look of the building. I still like it.

The house began to associate with the ground and become natural to its prairie site.

And would the young man in Architecture believe that this was all "new" then? Yes—not only new, but destructive heresy—ridiculous eccentricity. All somewhat so today. Stranger still, but then it was *all* so *new* that what prospect I had of ever earning a livelihood by making houses was nearly wrecked. At first, "they" called the houses "dress reform" houses because Society was just then excited about that particular reform. This simplification looked like some kind of reform to the provincials.

What I have just described was on the *outside* of the house. But it was all there, chiefly because of what had happened *inside*.

Dwellings of that period were cut up, advisedly and completely, with the grim determination that should go with any cutting process. The interiors consisted of boxes beside boxes or inside boxes, called *rooms*. All boxes were inside a complicated outside boxing. Each domestic function was properly box to box.

I could see little sense in this inhibition, this cellular sequestration that implied ancestors familiar with penal institutions, except for the privacy of bedrooms on the upper floor. They were perhaps all right as sleeping boxes. So I declared the whole lower floor as one room, cutting off the kitchen as a laboratory, putting the servants' sleeping and living quarters next to the kitchen but semi-detached, on the ground floor. Then I screened various portions of the big room for certain domestic purposes like dining, reading, receiving callers.

There were no plans in existence like these at the time. But my clients were all pushed toward these ideas as helpful to a solution of the vexed servant problem. Scores of unnecessary doors disappeared and no end of partition. Both clients and servants liked the new freedom. The house became more free as space and more livable too. Interior spaciousness began to dawn.

Thus came an end to the cluttered house. Fewer doors; fewer window holes though much greater window area; windows and doors lowered to convenient human heights. These changes once made, the ceilings of the rooms could be brought down over on to the walls by way of the horizontal broad bands of plaster on the walls themselves above the windows and colored the same as the room-ceilings. This would bring ceiling-surface and color down to the very window tops. Ceilings thus expanded by way of the wall band above the windows gave generous overhead even to small rooms. The sense of the whole broadened, made plastic by this means.

Here entered the important new element of Plasticity—as I saw it. I saw it as indispensable element to the successful use of the machine. The windows would sometimes be wrapped around the building corners as inside emphasis of plasticity and to increase the sense of interior space. I fought for outswinging windows because the casement window associated house with the out-of-doors, gave free openings outward. In other words, the so-called casement was not only simple but more human in use and effect. So more natural. If it had not existed I should have invented it. But it was not used at that time in the United States so I lost many clients because I insisted upon it. The client usually wanted the double-hung (the guillotine window) in use then, although it was neither simple nor human. It was only expedient. I used it once, in the Winslow house, and rejected it forever thereafter. Nor at that time did I entirely eliminate the wooden trim. I did make the "trim" plastic, that is to say, light and continuously flowing instead of the prevailing heavy "cut and butt" carpenter work. No longer did trim, so-called, look like carpenter work. The machine could do it all perfectly well as I laid it out, in this search for quiet. This plastic trim enabled poor workmanship to be concealed. There was need of that much trim then to conceal much in the way of craftsmanship because the battle between the

167

machines and the Union had already begun to demoralize workmen.

Machine-resources of this period were so little understood that extensive drawings had to be made merely to show the mill-man what to leave off. Not alone in the trim but in numerous ways too tedious to describe in words, this revolutionary sense of the *plastic* whole began to work more and more intelligently and have fascinating unforeseen consequences. Nearly everyone had endured the house of the period as long as possible, judging by the appreciation of the change. Here was an ideal of organic simplicity put to work, with historical consequences not only in this country but especially in the thought of the civilized world.

SIMPLICITY

Organic Simplicity—in this early constructive effort—I soon found depended upon the sympathy with which such co-ordination as I have described might be effected. Plainness was not necessarily simplicity. That was evident. Crude furniture of the Roycroft-Stickley-Mission style, which came along later, was offensively plain, plain as a barn-door—but was never simple in any true sense. Nor, I found, were merely machine-made things in themselves necessarily simple. "To think," as the Master used to say, "is to deal in simples." And that means with an eye single to the altogether.

This is, I believe, the single secret of simplicity: that we may truly regard nothing at all as simple in itself. I believe that no one thing in itself is ever so, but must achieve simplicity—as an artist should use the term—as a perfectly realized part of some organic whole. Only as a feature or any part becomes harmonious element in the harmonious whole does it arrive at the state of simplicity. Any wild flower is truly simple but double the same wild flower by cultivation and it ceases to be so. The scheme of the original is no longer clear. Clarity of design and perfect significance both are first essentials of the spontaneous born simplicity of the lilies of the field. "They toil not, neither do they spin." Jesus wrote the supreme essay on simplicity in this, "Consider the lilies of the field."

Five lines where three are enough is always stupidity. Nine pounds where three are sufficient is obesity. But to eliminate expressive words in speaking or writing—words that intensify or vivify meaning is not simplicity. Nor is similar elimination in architecture simplicity. It may be, and usually is, stupidity.

In architecture, expressive changes of surface, emphasis of line and especially textures of material or imaginative pattern, may go to make facts more eloquent—forms more significant. Elimination, therefore,

168

may be just as meaningless as elaboration, perhaps more often is so. To know what to leave out and what to put in; just where and just how, ah, *that* is to have been educated in knowledge of simplicity—toward ultimate freedom of expression.

As for objects of art in the house, even in that early day they were bêtes noires of the new simplicity. If well chosen, all right. But only if each were properly digested by the whole. Antique or modern sculpture, paintings, pottery, might well enough become objectives in the architectural scheme. And I accepted them, aimed at them often but assimilated them. Such precious things may often take their places as elements in the design of any house, be gracious and good to live with. But such assimilation is extraordinarily difficult. Better in general to design all as integral features.

I tried to make my clients see that furniture and furnishings that were not built in as integral features of the building should be designed as attributes of whatever furniture *was* built in and should be seen as a minor part of the building itself even if detached or kept aside to be employed only on occasion.

But when the building itself was finished the old furniture they already possessed usually went in with the clients to await the time when the interior might be completed in this sense. Very few of the houses, therefore, were anything but painful to me after the clients brought in their belongings.

Soon I found it difficult, anyway, to make some of the furniture in the abstract. That is, to design it as architecture and make it human at the same time—fit for human use. I have been black and blue in some spot, somewhere, almost all my life from too intimate contact with my own early furniture.

Human beings must group, sit or recline, confound them, and they must dine—but dining is much easier to manage and always a great artistic opportunity. Arrangements for the informality of sitting in comfort singly or in groups still belonging in disarray to the scheme as a whole: *that* is a matter difficult to accomplish. It can be done now and should be done, because only those attributes of human comfort and convenience should be in order which belong to the whole in this modern integrated sense.

Human use and comfort should not be taxed to pay dividends on any designer's idiosyncrasy. Human use and comfort should have intimate possession of every interior—should be felt in every exterior. Decoration is intended to make use more charming and comfort more appropriate, or else a privilege has been abused.

As these ideals worked away from house to house, finally freedom of floor space and elimination of useless heights worked a miracle in the new dwelling place. A sense of appropriate freedom had changed its whole aspect. The whole became different but more fit for human habitation and more natural on its site. It was impossible to imagine a house once built on these principles somewhere else. An entirely new sense of space-values in architecture came home. It now appears these new values came into the architecture of the world. New sense of repose in quiet streamline effects had arrived. The streamline and the plain surface seen as the flat plane had then and there, some thirty-seven years ago, found their way into buildings as we see them in steamships, aeroplanes and motorcars, although they were intimately related to building materials, environment and the human being.

But, more important than all beside, still rising to greater dignity as an idea as it goes on working, was the ideal of plasticity. That ideal now began to emerge as a means to achieve an organic architecture.

PLASTICITY

Plasticity may be seen in the expressive flesh-covering of the skeleton as contrasted with the articulation of the skeleton itself. If form really "followed function"—as the Master declared—here was the direct means of expression of the more spiritual idea that form and function are one: the only true means I could see then or can see now to eliminate the separation and complication of cut-and-butt joinery in favor of the expressive flow of continuous surface. Here, by instinct at first—all ideas germinate—a principle entered into building that has since gone on developing. In my work the idea of plasticity may now be seen as the element of continuity.

In architecture, plasticity is only the modern expression of an ancient thought. But the thought taken into structure and throughout human affairs will re-create in a badly "disjointed," distracted world the entire fabric of human society. This magic word "plastic" was a word Louis Sullivan himself was fond of using in reference to his idea of ornamentation as distinguished from all other or applied ornament. But now, why not the larger application in the structure of the building itself in this sense?

Why a principle working in the part if not living in the whole?

If form really followed function—it did in a material sense by means of this ideal of plasticity, the spiritual concept of *form and function as one*—why not throw away the implications of post or upright and beam or horizontal entirely? Have no beams or columns piling up as "joinery." Nor any cornices. Nor any "features" as *fixtures*. No. Have no appliances of any kind at all, such as pilasters, entablatures and cornices. Nor put into the building any fixtures whatsoever as "fixtures." Eliminate the separations and separate joints. Classic architecture was all fixation-of-the-fixture. Yes, entirely so. Now why not let walls, ceilings, floors become *seen* as component parts of each other, their surfaces flowing into each other. To get continuity in the whole, eliminating all constructed features just as Louis Sullivan had eliminated background in his ornament in favor of an integral sense of the whole. Here the promotion of an idea from the material to the spiritual plane began to have consequences. Conceive now that an entire building might grow up out of conditions as a plant grows up out of soil and yet be free to be itself, to "live its own life according to Man's Nature." Dignified as a tree in the midst of nature but a child of the spirit of man.

I now propose an ideal for the architecture of the Machine Age, for the ideal American building. Let it grow up in that image. The tree.

But I do not mean to suggest imitation of the tree.

Proceeding, then, step by step from generals to particulars, Plasticity as a large means in architecture began to grip me and to work its own will. Fascinated I would watch its sequences, seeing other sequences in those consequences already in evidence: as in the Heurtley, Martin, Heath, Thomas, Tomek, Coonley and dozens of other houses.

The old architecture, so far as its grammar went, for me began, literally, to disappear. As if by magic new architectural effects came to life—effects genuinely new in the whole cycle of architecture owing simply to the working of this spiritual principle. Vistas of inevitable simplicity and ineffable harmonies would open, so beautiful to me that I was not only delighted, but often startled. Yes, sometimes amazed.

I have since concentrated on plasticity as *physical continuity*, using it as a practical working principle within the very nature of the building itself in the effort to accomplish this great thing called architecture. Every true esthetic is an implication of nature, so it was inevitable that this esthetic ideal should be found to enter into the actual building of the building itself as a principle of construction.

But later on I found that in the effort to actually eliminate the post and beam in favor of structural continuity, that is to say, making the two things one thing instead of two separate things, I could get no help at all from regular engineers. By habit, the engineer reduced everything in the field of calculation to the post and the beam resting upon it before he could calculate and tell you where and just how much for either. He had no other data. Walls made one with floors and ceilings, merging together yet reacting upon each other, the engineer had never met. And the engineer has not yet enough scientific formulae to enable him to calculate for continuity. Floor slabs stiffened and extended as cantilevers over centered supports, as a waiter's tray rests upon his upturned fingers, such as I now began to use in order to get planes parallel to the earth to emphasize the third dimension, were new, as I used them, especially in the Imperial Hotel. But the engineer soon mastered the element of continuity in floor slabs, with such formulae as he had. The cantilever thus became a new feature of design in architecture. As used in the Imperial Hotel at Tokio it was the most important of the features of construction that insured the life of that building in the terrific temblor of 1922. So, not only a new esthetic but proving the esthetic as scientifically sound, a great new economic "stability" derived from steel in tension was able now to enter into building construction.

THE NATURE OF MATERIALS

From this early ideal of plasticity another concept came. To be consistent in practice, or indeed if as a principle it was to work out in the field at all, I found that plasticity must have a new sense, as well as a science of materials. The greatest of the materials, steel, glass, ferro- or armored concrete were new. Had they existed in the ancient order we never would have had anything at all like "classic architecture."

And it may interest you, as it astonished me, to learn that there was nothing in the literature of the civilized world on the nature of materials in this sense. So I began to study the nature of materials, learning to *see* them. I now learned to see brick as brick, to see wood as wood, and to see concrete or glass or metal. See each for itself and all as themselves. Strange to say, this required greater concentration of imagination. Each material demanded different handling and had possibilities of use peculiar to its own nature. Appropriate designs for one material would not be appropriate at all for another material. At least, not in the light of this spiritual ideal of simplicity as *organic plasticity*. Of course, as I could now see, there could be no organic architecture where the nature of materials was ignored or misunderstood. How could there be? Perfect correlation is the first principle of growth. Integration, or even the very word "organic" means that nothing is of value except as it is naturally related to the whole in the direction of some living purpose, a true part of entity. My old Master had designed for the old materials all alike; brick, stone, wood, iron wrought or iron cast, or plaster—all were grist for his rich imagination and his sentient ornament.

To him all materials were only one material in which to weave the

172

stuff of his dreams. I still remember being ashamed of the delight I took at first in thus seeing—thanks to him too—so plainly around the beloved Master's own practice. But *acting* upon this new train of ideals brought work sharply up against the tool I could find to get the ideas in practical form: the Machine. What were the tools in use everywhere? Machines—automatic, most of them. Stone- or wood-planers, molding shapers, various lathes and power saws, all in commercialized organized mills. Sheet-metal breakers, gigantic presses, shears, molding and stamping machines in the sheet-metal industry, commercialized in "shops." Foundries and rolling-mills turned out cast-iron and steel in any imaginable shape. The machine as such had not seemed to interest Louis Sullivan. Perhaps he took it for granted. But what a resource, that rolling or drawing or extruding of metal! And more confusion to the old order, concrete-mixers, form-makers, clay-bakers, casters, glass-makers, all in organized trade unions.

The Unions themselves were all units in a more or less highly commercialized union in which craftsmanship had no place except as survival-for-burial. Standardization had already become an inflexible necessity. Standardization was either the enemy or a friend to the architect. He might choose. I felt that as he chose he became master and useful or else became a luxury; eventually a parasite. Although not realized then at all nor yet completely realized by the architect, machine standardization had already taken the life of handicraft in all its expressions. If I was to realize new buildings I should have to have new technique. I should have to so design buildings that they would not only be appropriate to materials but design them so the machine that would *have* to make them could make them surpassingly well. By now, you see, I had really come under the discipline of a great ideal. There is no discipline so severe as the perfect integration of true correlation in any human endeavor. But there is no discipline that yields such rich rewards in work, nor is there any discipline so safe and sure of results. (Why should human relations be excepted?) The straight line, the flat plane were limitations until proved benefits by the Machine. But steel-in-tension was clearly liberation.

After the Winslow house was built in 1893 and Mr. Moore did not want a house so "different" that he would have to go down the back way to his morning train to avoid being laughed at, our bulkheads of caution blindly serving Yesterday—our bankers—at first refused to loan money on the "new" houses. Friends had to be found to finance the early buildings. When the plans were presented for estimates, soon, mill-men would look for the name on them, read the name, roll the drawings up again and hand them back to the contractor with the remark that "they were not hunting for trouble." Contractors, of course, more often failed to read the plans correctly than not. The plans were necessarily radically different simply because so much nonsense had to be left off the building. Numbers of small men went broke trying to carry out their contracts. This made trouble. Fools would come walking in where angels were afraid to tread. We seemed to have the worst of the contracting element in Oak Park to deal with. Clients usually stood by, excited, often interested beyond their means. So when they moved into the house they had to take their old furniture in with them whether they wanted to or not. This was tragedy because the ideal of an organic simplicity, seen as the countenance of perfect integration, abolished all fixtures, rejected all superficial decoration, made all lighting and heating apparatus architectural features of the house and, so far as possible, all furniture was to be designed by the architect as a natural part of the whole building. Hangings, rugs, carpet—all came into the same category. So this particular feature gone wrong often crippled results. Nor was there any planting to be done about the house without co-operating with the architect. This made trouble. No sculpture, no painting unless co-operating with the architect. This made trouble. Decorators hunting a job would visit the owners, learn the name of the architect, lift their hats with exaggerated courtesy and turning on their heels leave with a curt, sarcastic "Good day"—meaning really what the slang "Good night!" meant some time ago. And the owners of the houses were all subjected to vulgar curiosity. Often to sincere admiration. But more often they submitted to the ridicule of that middle-of-the-road egoist, the one-hundred-per-cent American provincial.

Each new building was a new experience. A different choice of materials and a different client would mean a different scheme altogether. Concrete was just then coming into use and Unity Temple at Oak Park became the first concrete monolith in the world. That is, the first total building designed for and completed in the wooden forms into which it was poured as concrete. Even plastered houses were then new. Casement windows were nowhere to be seen except in my houses. So many things were new. Nearly everything, in fact, but the law of gravitation and the personal idiosyncrasy of the client.

THE FIRST PROTESTANT AFFIRMATION

The Larkin Building was the first emphatic protestant in architecture. Yes—it was the first emphatic outstanding protest against the tide of meaningless elaboration sweeping the United States as Uncle Dan Burnham, calling it by a different name, had prophesied it would do.

The United States were being swept into one grand rubbish heap of the acknowledged styles, instead of intelligently and patiently creating a new architecture.

The Larkin Administration Building was a simple cliff of brick hermetically sealed (one of the first "air-conditioned" buildings in the country) to keep the interior space clear of the poisonous gases in the smoke from the New York Central trains that puffed along beside it.

It was built of masonry material—brick and stone; and in terms of the straight line and flat plane the Larkin Administration Building was a genuine expression of power directly applied to purpose, in the same sense that the ocean liner, the plane or the car is so. And it's only fair to say that it has had a profound influence upon European architecture for this reason.

The character and brutal power as well as the opportunity for beauty of our own age were coming clear to me. In fact I saw then as now that they are all one. I saw our own great chance in this sense still going to waste on every side. Rebellious and protestant as I was myself when the Larkin Building came from me, I was conscious also that the only way to succeed, either as rebel or as protestant, was to make architecture genuine and constructive affirmation of the new Order of this Machine Age.

And I worked to get that something into the Larkin Building, interested now also in the principle of *articulation* as related to that order. But not until the contract had been let to Paul Mueller and the plaster-model of the building stood completed on the big detail board at the center of the Oak Park draughting room did I get the articulation I finally wanted. The solution that had hung fire came in a flash. I took the next train to Buffalo to try and get the Larkin Company to see that it was worth thirty thousand dollars more to build the stair towers free of the central block, not only as independent stair towers for communication and escape but also as air intakes for the ventilating system. It would require this sum to individualize and properly articulate these features as I saw them.

Mr. Larkin, a kind and generous man, granted the appropriation and the building as architecture, I felt, was saved.

This entire building was a great fireproof vault, probably the first completely fireproof furnished building. The furniture was all made in steel and magnesite built into place—even the desks and chairs we made with the building. The wastepaper baskets were omitted. I never had a chance to incorporate them later—or design the telephone I had in mind as the office had already arranged for both these items. All else was of or with the building.

Magnesite was a new material to us then, but it was probably the

cement used by the Romans and good in Rome until today. We experimented with it—finally used it—throughout the interior. And I
made many new inventions. The hanging water-closet partition, the
long automatic multiple chair-desk, the wall water-closet, were only
several among them. All were intended to simplify cleaning and make
operation easy. The dignified top-lighted interior created the effect of
one great official family at work in day-lit, clean and airy quarters, day-
lit and officered from a central court. The top-story was a restaurant and
conservatory, the ferns and flowers seen from the court below. The roof
was a recreation ground paved with brick. The new architecture was in
every detail practical or it was only another sentimentality, to further
demoralize the country.

The officers, D. D. Martin, William R. Heath and the employees all
appreciated the building in practice. But it was all too severe for the
fundamentalist English tastes of the Larkin family. They were distracted, too, I imagine by so many *experiments,* some of which, like the
magnesite, delayed the completion of the building. A few minor failures
annoyed them—and made them think the whole might be—merely
queer? They did not really know. They never realized the place their
building took in the thought of the world—for they never hesitated to
make senseless changes in it in after years. To them it was just one of
their factory buildings—to be treated like any other. And I suppose from
any standpoint available to them, that was all it was. In architecture
they were still pallbearers for the remains of Thomas Jefferson and subsequently all built colonial houses for themselves in Buffalo.

Now Unity Temple and the Buffalo dwellings of D. D. Martin and
W. R. Heath came into work at Oak Park.

Several invitations to submit work in competition came along also.
But no matter how promising the program nor how many promises were
made I steadily refused to enter a competition. I have refused ever
since.

The world has gained no building worth having by competition because: (1) The jury itself is necessarily a hand-picked average. Some
constituency must agree upon the jury. (2) Therefore the first thing this
average does as a jury, when picked, is to go through all the designs and
throw out the best ones and the worst ones. This is necessary in order
that the average may average upon something average. (3) Therefore
any architectural competition will be an average upon an average by
averages in behalf of the average. (4) The net result is a building well
behind the times before it is begun.

This might seem democratic if mediocrity is democratic ideal in architecture. No. Competitions are only opportunity for inexperienced youth to air precocious propensity.

Moreover, to further vitiate the competitive objective every architect entering any competition does so to win the prize. So he sensibly aims his efforts at what he conceives to be the common prejudices and predilections of the jury. Invariably the man who does this most accurately wins the competition.

A competition was first thought of for Unity Temple, but the idea was abandoned and the commission was given to me after much hesitation and debate among the committee.

Committee decisions are seldom above mediocre unless the committee is dominated by some strong individual. In this case the committee was so run by Charles E. Roberts—inventor. He was the strong man in this instance or Unity Temple would never have been built.

Let us take Unity Temple to pieces in the thought of its architect and see how it came to be the Unity Temple you see now.

DESIGNING UNITY TEMPLE

Had Doctor Johonnot, the Universalist pastor of Unity Church, been Fra Junipero the style of Unity Temple would have been predetermined—"Mission." Had he been Father Latour it would have been Midi-Romanesque. Yes, and perhaps being what he was, he was entitled to the only tradition he knew—that of the little white New England church, lean spire pointing to heaven—"back East." If sentimentality were sense this might be so.

But the pastor was out of luck. Circumstances brought him to yield himself up in the cause of architecture. And to that cause everyone who undertakes to read what follows is called upon to yield a little.

Our building committee were all good men and true. One of them, Charles E. Roberts, the mechanical engineer and inventor I have mentioned, was himself enlightened in creation. One, enlightened, is leaven enough in any Usonian committee lump. The struggle began. It is always a struggle in architecture for the architect where good men and true are concerned.

First came the philosophy of the building in my own mind.

I said, let us abolish, in the art and craft of architecture, literature in any symbolic form whatsoever. The sense of inner rhythm deep planted in human sensibility lives far above all other considerations in art. Then why the steeple of the little church? Why *point* to heaven?

I told the committee a story. Did they not know the tale of the holy man who, yearning to see God, climbed up and up the highest mountain—climbed to the highest relic of a tree there was on the mountain? There, ragged and worn, he lifted up his eager perspiring face to heaven and called upon God. He heard a voice bidding him get down . . . go back!

Would he really see God's face? Then he should go back, go down there in the valley below where his people were—there only could *he* look upon God's countenance. . . .

Why not, then, build a temple, not to God in that way—more sentimental than sense—but build a temple to man, appropriate to his uses as a meeting-place, in which to study man himself for his God's sake? A modern meeting-house and a good-time place.

The pastor was a liberal. His liberality was thus challenged, his reason was piqued and the curiosity of all was aroused. What would such a building look like? They said they could imagine no such thing.

"That's what you came to me for," I ventured. "I can imagine it and I will help you create it." Promising the building committee something tangible to look at soon—I sent them away.

The first idea was to keep a noble room for worship in mind, and let that sense of the great room shape the whole edifice. Let the room inside be the architecture outside.

What shape? Well, the answer lay in the material. There was only one material to choose—as the church funds were $45,000—to "church" four hundred people in 1906. Concrete was cheap.

Why not make the wooden boxes or forms so the concrete could be cast in them as separate blocks and masses, these grouped about an interior space in some such way as to preserve this sense of the interior space, the great room, in the appearance of the whole building? And the block-masses might be left as themselves with no facing at all? That would be cheap and permanent and not ugly either.

What roof? What had concrete to offer as a cover shelter? The concrete slab—of course. The reinforced slab. Nothing else if the building was to be thoroughbred, meaning built in character out of one material.

Too monumental, all this? Too forthright for my committee, I feared. Would a statement so positive as that final slab over the whole seem irreligious to them? Profane in their eyes? Why? But the flat slab was cheap and direct. It would be nobly simple. The wooden forms or molds in which concrete buildings must at that time be cast were always the chief item of expense, so to repeat the use of a single form as often as possible was necessary. Therefore a building, all four sides alike, looked like the thing. This, reduced to simplest terms, meant a

178

building square in plan. That would make their temple a cube—a noble form in masonry.

The slab, too, belonged to the cube by nature. *"Credo simplicitatem."* That form is most imaginative and happy that is most radiant with the aura or overtone of super-form. Integrity.

Then the Temple itself—still in my mind—began to take shape. The site was noisy, by the Lake Street car-tracks. Therefore it seemed best to keep the building closed on the three front sides and enter it from a court to the rear at the center of the lot. Unity Temple itself, with the thoughts in mind I have just expressed, arrived easily enough, but there was a secular side to Universalist church activities— entertainment often, Sunday school, feasts, and so on.

To embody these with the temple would spoil the simplicity of the room—the noble Room in the service of man for the worship of God. So I finally put the secular space designated as "Unity House," a long free space to the rear of the lot, as a separate building to be subdivided by movable screens for Sunday school or on occasion. It thus became a separate building but harmonious with the Temple—the entrance to both to be the connecting link between them. That was that.

And why not put the pulpit at the entrance side at the rear of the square Temple, and bring the congregation into the room at the sides on a lower level so those entering would be imperceptible to the audience? This would preserve the quiet and the dignity of the room itself. Out of that thought came the depressed foyer or cloister corridor on either side, leading from the main lobby at the center to the stairs in the near and far corners of the room. Those entering the room in this way could see into the big room but not be seen by those already seated within it.

And, important to the pastor, when the congregation rose to disperse, here was opportunity to move forward toward their pastor and by swinging wide doors open beside the pulpit allow the entire block to pass out by him and find themselves directly in the entrance loggia from which they had first come in. They had gone into the depressed entrances at the sides from this same entrance to the big room. But it seemed more respectful to let them go out thus toward the pulpit than turn their backs upon their minister as is usual in most churches.

So this was done.

The room itself—size determined by comfortable seats with legroom for four hundred people—was built with four interior free-standing posts to carry the overhead structure. These concrete posts were hollow and became free-standing ducts to insure economic and uniform distribution of heat. The large supporting posts were so set in plan as to form a double tier of alcoves on four sides of the room. I flooded these side-alcoves with light from above to get a sense of a happy cloudless day into the room. And with this feeling for light the center ceiling between the four great posts became skylight, daylight sifting through between the intersecting concrete beams, filtering through amber glass ceiling lights. Thus managed the light would, rain or shine, have the warmth of sunlight. Artificial lighting took place there at night as well. This scheme of lighting was integral, gave diffusion and kept the room-space clear.

Now for proportion—for the concrete expression of concrete in this natural arrangement—the ideal of an organic whole well in mind. And we have arrived at the question of *style*. For observe, so far, what has actually taken place is only reasoned *arrangement*. The "plan" with an eye to an exterior in the realm of ideas but meantime "felt" in imagination as a whole.

First came the general philosophy of the thing as repeated in the little story to the trustees. All artistic creation has its own philosophy. It is the first condition of creation. However, some would smile and say, "the result of it."

Second there was the general purpose of the whole to consider in each part: a matter of reasoned arrangement. This arrangement must be made with a sense of the yet-unborn-whole in the mind, to be blocked out as appropriate to concrete masses cast in wooden boxes. Holding all this diversity together in a preconceived direction is really no light matter but is the condition of creation. Imagination conceives here the PLAN suitable to the material and the purpose of the whole, seeing the probable possible form clearer all the time.

Imagination reigns supreme, until now the form the whole will naturally take must be seen.

But if all this preliminary planning has been well conceived that question in the main is settled. This matter of style is organic now.

We do not choose the style. No. Style is what is coming now and it will be what we *are* in all this. A thrilling moment in any architect's experience. He is about to see the countenance of something he is invoking with intense concentration. Out of this inner sense of order and love of the beauty of life something is to be born—maybe to live long as a message of hope and be a joy or a curse to his kind. *His* message he feels. None the less will it be "theirs," and rather more. And it is out of love and understanding that any building is born to bless or curse those it is built to serve. Bless them if they will see, understand and aid. Curse them as it will be cursed by them if either they or the architect fail to understand each other. This is the faith and the fear in the architect as he makes ready—to draw his design.

In all artists it is somewhat the same fear and the same faith.

180

Now regard this pure white sheet of paper! It is ready for recording the logic of the plan.

T-square, triangle, scale—seductive invitation lying upon the spotless surface. Temptation!

"Boy! Go tell Black Kelly to make a blaze there in the work-room fireplace! Ask Brown Sadie if it's too late to have Baked Bermudas for supper! Then go ask your Mother—I shall hear her in here—to play something—Bach preferred, or Beethoven if she prefers."

Now comes to brood—to suffer doubt, hesitate yet burn with eagerness. To test bearings—and prove ground already assumed by putting all together in definite scale on paper. Preferably small scale study at first. Then larger. Finally still larger scale detail studies of parts.

An aid to creative effort, the open fire. What a friend to the laboring artist the poetic baked-onion! Real encouragement to him is great music. Yes, and what a poor creature, after all, creation comes singing through. About like catgut and horsehair in the hands of a Sarasate.

Night labor at the draughting board is best for intense creation. It may continue uninterrupted.

Meantime glancing side reflections are passing in the mind— "design is abstraction of nature-elements in purely geometric terms"— that is what we ought to call pure design? . . . This cube—this square—proportion. But—nature-pattern and nature-texture in materials themselves often approach conventionalization, or the abstract, to such a degree as to be superlative means ready to the designer's hand to qualify, stimulate and enrich his own efforts . . . What texture this concrete mass? Why not its own gravel? How to bring the gravel clean on the surface? . . . I knew. Here was reality. Yes, the "fine thing" is always reality. Always reality? . . . Realism, the subgeometric, however, is the abuse of this fine feeling. . . . Keep the straight lines clean and keep all significant of the idea—the flat plane expressive and always clean cut. But let texture come into them to qualify them in sunlight.

Reality is spirit—the essence brooding just behind all aspect. Seize it! And—after all you will see that the pattern of reality *is* supergeometric, casting a spell or a charm over any geometry, and is such a spell in itself.

Yes, so it seems to me as I draw with T-square, triangle and scale. That is what it means to be an artist—to seize this essence brooding everywhere in everything, just behind aspect. These questionings arising each with its own train of thought by the way, as the architect sits at his work.

Suddenly it is morning. To bed for a while.

But returning to the drawing board, here we see penciled upon a sheet of paper, the plan, section and elevation in the main—all except the exterior of Unity House, as the room for secular recreation is to be called. To establish harmony between these buildings of separate function proved difficult, utterly exasperating.

Another series of concentrations—lasting hours at a time for several days. How to keep the noble scale of the temple in the design of the subordinate mass of the secular hall and not falsify the function of that secular mass? The ideal of an organic architecture is often terribly severe discipline for the imagination. I came to know that full well. And, always, some minor concordance takes more time, taxes concentration more than all besides. Any minor element may become a major problem to vex the architect. How many schemes I have thrown away because some one minor feature would not come true to form!

Thirty-four studies were necessary to arrive at this concordance as it is now seen. Unfortunately the studies are lost with thousands of others of many other buildings: the fruit of similar struggles to coordinate and perfect them as organic entities—I wish I had kept them. Unity House looks easy enough now, for it is right enough. But it was not.

Finally, see the sense of the room not only preserved—*it may be seen as the soul of the design.* Instead of being built into the heart of a block of sculptured building material, out of sight, the sacrosanct space for worship is merely screened in . . . does it come through as the living "motif" of the architecture?

Many studies in detail as a matter of course yet remain to be made, in order to determine what further may be left out to protect the design. These studies never seem to end and in this sense no organic building may ever be "finished." The complete goal of the ideal of organic architecture is never reached. Nor need be. What worthwhile ideal is ever reached?

Unity Temple is a complete building on paper, already. There is no "sketch" and there never has been one. There seldom is in a thought-built building.

The hardest of an architect's trials is to show his work for the first time to anyone not entirely competent or perhaps unsympathetic.

Already the architect begins to fear for the fate of his design. If it is to be changed much he prefers to throw it all away and begin all over again. Not much hope in the committee except Mr. Roberts. Why not ask him to see the design and explain it to him first? This is done. He is delighted. He *understands!* He is himself an inventor. And every project in architecture needs this one intimate friend in order to proceed. Mr.

Roberts suggests a model. Without it nothing can be done. So the model is soon made.

All right; let the committee come now. They do come—all curious. Soon confounded—taking the "show me" attitude. At this moment the creative architect is distinctly at a disadvantage as compared with his obsequious brother of the "styles," he who can show his pattern-book, speak glibly of St. Mark's at Venice or Capella Palatine, impress the no less craven clients by brave show of erudite authorities.

The architect with the ideal of an organic architecture at stake can talk only principle and sense. His only appeal is fresh and must be made to the independent thought and judgment of his client such as it is. The client, too, must know how to think a little or follow from generals to particulars. How rare it is for an architect to go into any court where that quality of mind is on the bench! This architect has learned to dread the personal idiosyncrasy—offered him three times out of five—as a substitute for the needed, hoped-for intelligence.

Hoping, we try. We use all our resources, we two—the inventor and I—and we win a third member of the committee at the first meeting. Including the pastor, there are now four only left in doubt. One of the four openly hostile—Mr. Skillin. Dr. Johonnot, the pastor, is himself impressed but cautious—oh very—but tactful. He really has a glimpse of a new world. There is hope, distinctly hope, when he makes four as he soon does and the balance of power is with us. We need three more but the architect's work is done now. The four will get the others. The pastor is convinced. He will work! Doubts and fears are finally put to sleep—all but Mr. Skillin's. Mr. Skillin is sure the room will be dark—sure the acoustics will be bad. Finally the commission to go ahead is formally given over his dissent and warnings. Usually there is a Mr. Skillin on every modern building project in Usonia.

Now, who will build the temple? After weeks of prospecting, no one can be found who wants to try it. Simple enough—yes—that's the trouble. So simple there is nothing at all to gauge it by. Requires too much imagination and initiative to be safe. The only bids available came in double, or more, our utmost limit. No one really wanted to touch it. Contractors are naturally gamblers but they usually bet on a. sure thing—as they see the thing.

Paul Mueller comes to the rescue, reads the scheme like easy print. Will build it for only a little over their appropriation—and does it. He takes it easily along for nearly a year but he does it. Doesn't lose much on it in the end. It is exciting to him to rescue ideas, to participate in creation. And together we overcame difficulty after difficulty in the field, where an architect's education is never finished.

This building, however, is finished and the Sunday for dedication arrives.

I do not want to go. Stay at home.

When the church was opened the phone began to ring. Happy contented voices are heard in congratulation. Finally weary, I take little Francie by the hand to go out into the air to get away from it all. Enough.

But just as my hat goes on my head, another ring, a prosaic voice, Mr. Skillin's: "Take back all I said. . . . Light everywhere—all pleased."

"Hear well?"

"Yes, see and hear fine—see it all now."

"I'm glad."

"Goodbye." At last the doubting member, sincere in praise, a good sport besides.

Francie got tossed in the air. She came down with a squeal of delight.

And that is how it was and is and will be as often as a building is born.

Now, even though you are interested in architecture this story is more or less tedious and partly meaningless to you, as you were fairly warned at the beginning it would be. Without close study of the plans and photographs as it is read it must bore you. I have undertaken here, for once, to indicate the process of building on principle to insure character and achieve style, as near as I can indicate it by taking Unity Temple to pieces. Perhaps I am not the one to try it. It really would be a literary feat and feast were it well done.

A CODE

Concerning the traditional church as a modern building! Religion and art are forms of inner-experience—growing richer and deeper as the race grows older. We will never lose either. But I believe religious experience is outgrowing the church—not outgrowing religion but outgrowing the church as an institution, just as architecture has outgrown the Renaissance and for reasons human, scientific and similar. I cannot see the ancient institutional form of any church building as anything but sentimental survival for burial. The Temple as a forum and good-time place—beautiful and inspiring as such—yes. As a religious edifice raised in the sense of the old ritual? No. I cannot see it at all as living. It is no longer free.

Of course what is most vitally important in all that I have tried to say and explain cannot be explained at all. It need not be, I think. But here in this searching process may be seen the architect's mind at work, as boys in the studio would crowd around and participate in it. You too, perhaps, may see certain wheels go around.

Certain hints coming through between the lines that may help someone who needs help in comprehending what planning a building really means.

But this brief indication of the problem of building out of the man will not clear up the question as to what is style, either. But a little by way of suggestion, maybe.

Man's struggle to illumine creation, especially his own, is another tragedy, that's all.

About this time Mr. and Mrs. Avery Coonley came to the Oak Park workshop to ask me to build a home for them at Riverside, Illinois.

They had gone to see nearly everything they could learn that I had done before they came.

The day they finally came into the Oak Park workshop Mrs. Coonley said they had come because it seemed to them they saw in my houses "the countenance of principle." This was to me a great and sincere compliment. So I put my best into the Coonley house. Looking back upon it, I feel now that that building was the best I could then do in the way of a house.

The story of this dwelling, most successful of my houses from my standpoint, is not included, as descriptions of ideals and the nature of my creative effort in house-building already given apply particularly to this characteristic dwelling.

KUNO FRANCKE

Kuno Francke was Roosevelt exchange-professor in esthetics at Harvard. He came out to the Oak Park workshop from Chicago. He had seen the new type house standing on the prairies, asking the name of the architect each time and again, getting the same name for an answer. Mine.

A German friend, finally, at the professor's request, brought Francke and his charming wife to Oak Park for a short visit. Kuno Francke stayed all day and came back the next day. He, too, as had Mr. Waller and Uncle Dan, wanted me to go to Europe; but he wanted me to go to Germany, stay there and go to work.

"I see that you are doing organically," he said, "what my people are feeling for only superficially. They would reward you. It will be long before your own people will be ready for what you are trying to give them."

I had always loved old Germany—Goethe, Schiller, Nietzsche, Bach—the great architect who happened to choose music for his form—Beethoven and Strauss. And Munich! This beloved company—were they not Germany? And Vienna. Vienna had always appealed to my imagination. Paris? Never!

It would be wonderful to go!

But I had resisted up to this time, only dreaming of Europe.

Earlier, C. R. Ashbee of the London Arts and Crafts movement, while lecturing in America as the representative of the Natural Trust for Places of Historic Interest and Natural Beauty, had come at Jane Addams's instigation, to see me. He had stayed to urge a not dissimilar mission upon me. He had been made to see the future I saw in the United States. Now how to make Kuno Francke see it. . . . I tried the same argument, not so dissimilar to the one I used with Uncle Dan.

"But, where will you be when America gets around to all this?" said the Herr Professor of Esthetics. "Do you expect to live one hundred years longer, at least?"

"Oh, no, but I hope to live long enough to see it coming," I said. "America is growing up fast. This is a free country!" I boasted. And I told him the story of the Chicagoan at the Ashbee banquet who stood Ashbee as long as he could, and then got up on his indignant feet to say that Chicago wasn't much on Culture now, maybe, but when Chicago *did* get after Culture, she'd make Culture hum! We laughed the usual laugh and that was that.

Soon after this inspiring visit came a proposal from Germany—from the very able publisher Wasmuth in Berlin—to publish a complete monograph of my work if I would send over the material. This proposal of the German publisher, was, I think, one net result of Kuno Francke's visit to the Oak Park workshop—though I never really knew.

(I had written the above when word by way of a news-clipping falling on my desk this morning told me Kuno Francke was dead.)

THE CLOSED ROAD

This absorbing, consuming phase of my experience as an architect ended about 1909. I had almost reached my fortieth year. Weary, I was losing grip on my work and even my interest in it. Every day of every week and far into the night of nearly every day, Sunday included, I had "added tired to tired" and added it again and yet again as I had been trained to do by Uncle James on the farm as a boy. Continuously thrilled by the effort but now it seemed to leave me up against a dead wall. I could see no way out. Because I did not know what I wanted I wanted to go away. Why not go to Germany and prepare the material for the Wasmuth Monograph? . . . I looked longingly in that direction.

Afternoons after four o'clock I had been in the habit of riding Kano, my young black horse (named after the Japanese Master), over the prairies north of Oak Park, sometimes letting him run wild as he loved to do, sometimes reining him in and reading from a book usually carried in my pocket, for I've always loved to read out-of-doors—especially Whitman.

Ever since boyhood, horseback riding, swimming, dancing, skating and omnivorous reading. Always music-hungry. Motoring (just that much added or was it deducted?) had come along to interfere with these recreations, a little. The motor car brought a disturbance of all values, subtle or obvious, and it brought disturbance to me.

Nevertheless, changing work to recreation and recreation to work as I might; the intensity of effort; unrelenting concentration; giving up the best in me to an ideal loved better than myself; all this had done something to me that reacted now upon every effort.

Everything, personal or otherwise, bore heavily down upon me. Domesticity most of all. What I wanted I did not know. I loved my children. I loved my home. A true home is the finest ideal of man, and yet—well, to gain freedom I asked for a divorce. It was, advisedly, refused. But these conditions were made: Were I to wait a year, divorce would be granted. The year went by. Legal freedom still refused by Catherine and all concerned in the promise. There remained to me in the circumstances only one choice—to take the situation in hand and work out the best life possible for all concerned. I could not keep my home because, to keep the ideal high, well . . . these three necessities have emerged from struggles precipitated at this time. I will set the three down here, as a means to honest life, instead of intruding the personal details of my own experience:

First: Marriage not mutual is no better, but worse, than any other form of slavery.

Second: Only to the degree that marriage is mutual is it decent. "Love" is not property. To take it so is barbarous. To protect it as such is barbarism.

Third: The child is the pledge of good faith its parents give to the future of the race. There are no illegitimate children. There may be illegitimate parents—legal or illegal. Legal interference has no function whatever in any true Democracy where these three fundamentals are concerned except:

Concerning the three foregoing conclusions:

First: Legal marriage is but a civil contract between a man and woman to share property and together provide for children that may spring from that marriage. So, in this respect legal marriage is subject to the legal interpretations and enforcements of any other contract. But legal marriage should be regarded as no mere license for sexual relation. That relation should not as the law now makes it be the shameless essence of legal marriage in any such respect.

Second: Love, so far as laws can go to protect it, is entitled to the benefit of hands-off and the benefit of the doubt—unless degraded to a matter of commerce. So degraded, it should be subject to the laws that govern any other degraded traffic. Love should be its own protection or its own defeat—if it is to grow strong.

Third: The child being the pledge given to society by love, it is the duty of the State to make and enforce laws that protect the substance of that pledge. The substance of the pledge is that, provided by its parents, every child born shall have good shelter, good food, good treatment and an open door to growth of body and mind. Added to this the child should have whatever in addition the circumstances of its birth may present to it—the most desirable thing of all being love. . . . *This latter can be no concern of the laws.*

What I have tried to set down here was working in great detail in my mind during that miserable year of misunderstanding, overstatement, probation and demoralization. It was working more or less clearly as any man's right to live. The denial of that right not only worked against reconstruction more than anything else but invited, if indeed the deliberate denial did not insist upon, the destruction of my home.

So, turning my clients' plans and draughtsmen over to a man whom I had but just met, a young Chicago architect, Von Holst, and making the best provision I could make for my family for one year, broke with all family connections, though never with such responsibilities as I felt to be mine in that connection, or that I felt I could discharge.

Resolutely, with the same faith I'd had when leaving home and college, I took the train for Chicago: went out into the unknown to test faith in Freedom. Test my faith in life as I had already proved faith in my work. I faced the hazards of change and objective ruin inevitably involved by our society in every inner struggle for freedom, since learning that objective struggle for inner freedom is a far deeper and more serious matter never finished on this earth. Notwithstanding or withstanding, rebellion went its way in exile. A volunteer.

IN EXILE

In ancient Fiesole, far above the romantic city of cities Firenze, in a little cream-white villa on the Via Verdi, the rebel. How many souls seeking release from real or fancied domestic woes have sheltered on the slopes below Fiesole!

I, too, now sought shelter there in companionship with her who, by force of rebellion as by way of love was then implicated with me.

Walking hand in hand together up the hill road from Firenze to the older town, all along the way in the sight and scent of roses, by day. Walking arm in arm up the same old road at night, listening to the nightingale in the deep shadows of the moonlit wood—trying hard to hear the song in the deeps of life. So many Pilgrimages we made to reach the small solid door framed in the solid white blank wall with the massive green door opening toward the narrow Via Verdi itself. Entering, closing the medieval door on the world outside to find a wood fire burning in the small grate. Ester in her white apron, smiling, waiting to surprise Signora and Signore with the incomparable little dinner: the perfect roast fowl, mellow wine, the caramel custard—beyond all roasts or wine or caramels ever made, I remember.

Or out in the high-walled garden that lay alongside the cottage in Florentine sun or in the little garden by the pool arbored under climbing masses of yellow roses. I see the white cloth on the small stone table near the little fountain and beneath the clusters of yellow roses, set for two. There were long walks along the waysides of those undulating hills above, through the poppies, over the hill fields, toward Vallombrosa.

The waterfall there, finding and losing its own sound in the deep silences of that famous pine wood. Breathing deep the odor of great pines—tired out, to sleep at the cloistered little mountain-inn.

Back again walking hand in hand miles through the hot sun and deep dust of the ancient winding road: an old Italian road, along the stream. How old! How thoroughly a Roman road!

Together again tired out, sitting on benches in the galleries of Europe, saturated with plastic beauty, beauty in buildings, beauty in sculpture, beauty in paintings, until no Chiesa however rare and no further beckoning work of human hands could waylay us any more.

Faithful comrade!

A dream? In realization ended? No. Woven, a golden thread in the human pattern of the precious fabric that is Life: her life built into the house of houses. So far as may be known—forever!

AFTERMATH

Characteristic newspaper publicity now pursued me wherever I happened to go. Concerning relentless persecution all I have to say at the moment I will try to set down clearly as three simple corollaries drawn from my own experience at this time of my life. I was pursued and exploited by publicity, together with all those I loved and was trying to respect, while I was making a desperate effort to re-establish a better life for us all upon a fairer, firmer basis for all.

Corollary One: Since all publicity in the United States is privately owned, any exploitation damaging or insulting to any individual in respect to the three fundamentals stated should be seen as demoralizing.

Corollary Two: No publicity exploiting these profoundly personal matters should be marketed for profit. Such publicity should be limited to the purview of the laws unless crime or perversion harmful to all three interests be proved to exist. The burden of proof should be put upon the exploiter and not upon the exploited.

Corollary Three: These three human interests are more important to society than any property interests whatsoever.

How can any social structure deliberately interfering with the three conclusions, or neglecting these three corollaries, hope to endure free?

The passions have all contributed to the progress of life. Sacrifice began as selfishness and even love began as lust. And still so begins. Legislation can be no friend to moral growth except by the "Hands off!" or the "Stand back, please," that allows the individual in the purely private and deeply personal concerns of his own life, to do or die *on his own*. I, too, believe that for any man to have found no lasting relationship in love in this brief life is to suffer great waste. Flogging, ridicule nor censure are needed to make such waste socially exemplar and effective.

Anyone not blinded by fear or eager to play the part of a wrathful Jehovah may see this. But how the laws of our own government are continually used as weapons of blackmail or revenge because the government stays in the sex business as the government went into the liquor business—by way of prohibition and punishment—all this is obvious enough. Naturally, laws will be abused where they interfere with life and try to assume responsibility which they have no business to assume in any decent society. Only where culture is based upon the building of character by freedom-of-choice will we ever have the culture of true Democracy.

Such exaggeration of government must continually resist continual exploitation of itself either as a weapon or a tool in the hands of unscrupulous or passionately vindictive individuals seeking public redress for private and personal wrongs.

Thomas Jefferson, most intelligent founder of our Republic, honestly declared, "That Government is best Government that is least Government."

The sense of all this I am trying in this way to say was fundamentally right. The same faith characterized my forefathers from generation to generation. I suppose that faith carried them as it now carried me through the vortex of reaction, the anguish and waste of breaking up home and the loss of prestige and my work at Oak Park. Work, Life and Love I transferred to the beloved ancestral Valley where my mother foreseeing the plight I would be in had bought the low hill on which Taliesin now stands. She offered it to me as a refuge. Yes, a retreat when I returned from Europe in 1911. I began to build Taliesin to get my back against the wall and fight for all I saw I had to fight.

TALIESIN

Taliesin! Name of a Welsh poet, druid-bard who sang to Wales the glories of fine art. Many legends cling to that beloved reverend name in Wales.

Richard Hovey's charming masque, *Taliesin,* had just made me acquainted with his image of the historic bard. Since all my relatives had Welsh names for their places, why not Taliesin for mine? . . . Literally the Welsh word means "shining brow."

This hill on which Taliesin now stands as "brow" was one of my favorite places when as a boy looking for pasque flowers I went there in March sun while snow still streaked the hillsides. When you are on the low hill-crown you are out in mid-air as though swinging in a plane, the Valley and two others dropping away from you leaving the tree-tops standing below all about you. And "Romeo and Juliet" still stood in plain view over to the Southeast. The Hillside Home School was just over the ridge.

As a boy I had learned to know the ground-plan of the region in every line and feature. For me now its elevation is the modeling of the hills, the weaving and the fabric that clings to them, the look of it all in tender green or covered with snow or in full glow of summer that bursts into the glorious blaze of autumn. I still feel myself as much a part of it as the trees and birds and bees are, and the red barns. Or as the animals are, for that matter.

When family-life in Oak Park that spring of 1909 conspired against the freedom to which I had come to feel every soul was entitled, I had no choice, would I keep my self-respect, but go out a voluntary exile into the uncharted and unknown. Deprived of legal protection, I got my back against the wall in this way. I meant to live if I could an unconventional life. I turned to this hill in the Valley as my Grandfather before me had turned to America—as a hope and haven. But I was forgetful, for the time being, of Grandfather's Isaiah. His smiting and punishment.

Architecture, by now, was quite mine: come to me by actual experience and meant something out of this ground we call America. Architecture was something in league with the stones of the field, in sympathy with "the flower that fadeth and the grass that withereth." It had something of the prayerful consideration for the lilies of the field that was my gentle Grandmother's: something natural to the great Change that was America herself.

Unthinkable to me, at least unbearable, that any house should be put *on* that beloved hill.

I knew well that no house should ever be *on* a hill or *on* anything. It should be *of* the hill. Belonging to it. Hill and house should live together each the happier for the other. That was the way everything found round about was naturally managed except when man did something. When he added his mite he became imitative and ugly. Why? Was there no natural house? I felt I had proved there was. Now I wanted a *natural* house to live in myself. I scanned the hills of the region where the rock came cropping out in strata to suggest buildings. How quiet and strong the rock-ledge masses looked with the dark red cedars and white birches, there, above the green slopes. They were all part of the countenance of southern Wisconsin.

I wished to be part of my beloved southern Wisconsin, too. I did not want to put my small part of it out of countenance. Architecture, after all, I have learned—or before all, I should say—is no less a weaving and a fabric than the trees. As anyone might see, a beech tree is a beech tree. It isn't trying to be an oak. Nor is a pine trying to be a birch, although each makes the other more beautiful when seen together.

The world has had appropriate buildings before—why not appropriate buildings now, more so than ever before? There must be some

At Taliesin just before the tragedy of 1914

Midway Gardens, Chicago, Illinois. 1913–14
"The structure was so solidly built that subsequently, when Prohibition came, it cost so
much to tear down that several contractors
were bankrupted by the attempt."

Imperial Hotel, above and below, Tokio, Japan. 1915–22. (see cable, page 246)

Frank Lloyd Wright with students at Giyu Gakuen, Tokio, Japan

Giyu Gakuen, School of the Free Spirit, Tokio, Japan. 1921

Barnsdall ("Hollyhock") House, Olive Hill, Los Angeles, California. 1916. "The first of the California dwellings and a characteristic California Romanza, embodying the characteristic features of the region for a client who loved them and the theater. She named the house Hollyhock House and asked that the flower be used as a motive in the decoration of the place. The wooden structure of the period and place plastered with concrete and trimmed with cast stone."

Millard House ("La Miniatura") Pasadena, California. 1921 "The first concrete-block house to employ the textile-block system invented by myself several years before."

Frank Lloyd Wright and Olgivanna Lloyd Wright photos taken about the time of their first meeting

Svetlana and "Pal" in the snow, 1924

Olgivanna Lloyd Wright. Spring, 1931

F.Ll.W. and
daughter Iovanna

Iovanna in the garden, Taliesin. Summer, 1930

Iovanna on the hill at Taliesin. 1930

Architect's cabin, "Ocatillo," Arizona

General view of "Ocatillo," the camp on the low mound in the desert, Arizona. 1928

"We start [for New York] from 'Ocatillo' the ephemera in the background"

S. C. Johnson and Son, Inc., Racine, Wisconsin. Administration Building (left) 1936-39, and Research Tower, 1944

kind of house that would belong to that hill, as trees and rock ledges did; as Grandfather and Mother had belonged to it in their sense of it all.

There must be a natural house, not natural as caves and log-cabins were natural, but *native* in spirit and the making, having itself all that architecture had meant whenever it was alive in times past. Nothing at all I had ever seen would do. This country had changed all that old building into something inappropriate. Grandfather and Grandmother were something splendid in themselves that I couldn't imagine living in any period-houses I had ever seen or the ugly new ones around there. Yes, there was a house that hill might marry and live happily with ever after. I fully intended to find it. I even saw for myself what it might be like and began to build it as the brow of that hill.

Still a very young faith undertook to build that house. It was the same faith that plants twigs for orchards, vineslips for vineyards, and small whips to become beneficent shade trees: and it planted them all about!

I saw the hill-crown back of the house as one mass of apple trees in bloom, perfume drifting down the Valley, later the boughs bending to the ground with red and white and yellow spheres that make the apple tree no less beautiful than the orange tree. I saw plum trees, fragrant drifts of snow-white in the spring, loaded in August with blue and red and yellow plums, scattering them over the ground at a shake of the hand. I saw the rows on rows of berry bushes, necklaces of pink and green gooseberries hanging to the under side of the green branches: saw thickly pendent clusters of rubies like tassels in the dark leaves of the currant bushes: remembered the rich odor of black currants and looked forward to them in quantity.

Black cherries? White cherries? Those too.

There were to be strawberry beds, white, scarlet and green over the covering of clean wheat-straw.

I saw abundant asparagus in rows and a stretch of great sumptuous rhubarb that would always be enough. I saw the vineyard now on the south slope of the hill, opulent vines loaded with purple, green and yellow grapes. Boys and girls coming in with baskets filled to overflowing to set about the rooms, like flowers. Melons lying thick in the trailing green on the hill slope. Bees humming over all, storing up honey in the white rows of hives beside the chicken yard.

The herd I would have: gentle Holsteins and a monarch of a bull—a sleek gleaming decoration of the fields and meadows as they moved about, grazing. Sheep grazing too on the upland slopes and hills; the plaintive bleat of little white lambs in spring.

Grunting sows to turn all waste to solid gold.

I saw spirited, well-schooled horses, black horses and chestnut mares with glossy coats and splendid stride, being saddled and led to the mounting-block for rides about the place and along the country lanes I loved—the best of companionship alongside. I saw sturdy teams ploughing in the fields. There would be the changing colors of the slopes, from seeding time to harvest. I saw the scarlet comb of the rooster and his hundreds of hens—their white eggs and the ducks upon the pond. Geese, too, and swans floating upon the water in the shadow of the trees.

I looked forward to peacocks Javanese and white on the low roofs of the buildings or calling from the walls of the courts. From the vegetable gardens I walked into a deep cavern in the hill—modern equivalent of the rootcellar of my Grandfather. I saw its wide sand floor planted with celery, piled high with squash and turnips, potatoes, carrots, onions, parsnips. Cabbages wrapped in paper and hanging from the roof. Apples, pears and grapes stored in wooden crates walled the cellar from floor to roof. And cream! All the cream the boy had been denied. Thick—so lifting it in a spoon it would float like an egg on the fragrant morning cup of coffee or ride on the scarlet strawberries.

Yes, Taliesin should be a garden and a farm behind a real workshop and a good home.

I saw it all; planted it all: laid the foundation of the herd, flocks, stable and fowl as I laid the foundation of the house.

All these items of livelihood came—improved from boyhood.

So began a "shining brow" for the hill; the hill rising unbroken above it to crown the exuberance of life in all these rural riches.

A stone quarry there on another hill a mile away was where the yellow sand-limestone, uncovered, lay in strata like outcropping ledges in facades of the hills. The look of it was what I wanted for such masses as would rise from these native slopes. The teams of neighboring farmers soon began hauling the stone over the hill, doubling the teams to get it to the top. Long cords of this native stone, five hundred or more from first to last, got up there ready to hand, as Father Larson, the old Norse stonemason working in the quarry beyond, blasted and quarried it out in great flakes. The slabs of stone went down for pavements of terraces and courts. Stone was sent along the slopes into great walls. Stone stepped up like ledges on the hill and flung long arms in any direction that brought the house to the ground. The ground! My Grandfather's ground. It was lovingly felt as intimate in all this.

Finally it was not so easy to tell where pavements and walls left off and ground began. Especially on the hill-crown, which became a low-walled garden above the surrounding courts, reached by stone steps walled into the slopes. A clump of fine oaks that grew on the hilltop stood untouched on one side above the court. A great curved stone-walled seat enclosed the space just beneath them, and stone pavement stepped down to a spring or fountain that welled up into a pool at the center of the circle. Each court had its fountain and the winding stream below had a great dam. Another thick stone wall was thrown across it, to make a pond at the very foot of the hill and raise the water in the valley to within sight from Taliesin. The water below the falls thus made was sent by hydraulic ram up to a big stone reservoir built into the higher hill, just behind and above the hilltop garden, to come down again into the fountains and go on down to the vegetable gardens on the slopes below the house.

Taliesin, of course, was to be an architect's workshop and a dwelling as well, for young workers who would come to assist: a farm cottage for the farm help. Around a rear court were to be farm buildings, for Taliesin was to be a complete living unit genuine in point of comfort and beauty, yes, from pig to proprietor. The place was to be self-sustaining if not self-sufficient, with its domain of two hundred acres to be shelter, food, clothes and even entertainment within itself. It had to be its own light-plant, fuelyard, transportation and water system.

Taliesin was to be recreation ground for my children, their children, perhaps many generations more. This modest human programme in terms of rural Wisconsin arranged itself around the hilltop in a series of four varied courts leading one into the other, the courts all together forming a sort of drive along the hillside flanked by low buildings on one side and by flower gardens against the stone walls that retained the hill-crown on the other.

The hill-crown was thus saved and the buildings became a brow for the hill itself. The strata of fundamental stone-work kept reaching around and on into the four courts, and made them. Then stone, stratified, went into the lower house walls and up from the ground itself into the broad chimneys. This native stone prepared the way for the lighter plastered construction of the upper wood-walls. Taliesin was to be an abstract combination of stone and wood as they naturally met in the aspect of the hills around about. The lines of the hills were the lines of the roofs, the slopes of the hills their slopes, the plastered surfaces of the light wood-walls, set back into shade beneath broad eaves, were like the flat stretches of sand in the river below and the same in color, for that is where the material that covered them came from.

Finished wood outside was the color of gray tree-trunks in violet light.

Shingles of the roof surfaces were left to weather silver-gray like the tree branches spreading below them.

The chimneys of the great stone fireplaces rose heavily through all, wherever there was a gathering place within, and there were many such places. They showed great rock-faces over deep openings inside.

Outside were strong, quiet, rectangular rock-masses bespeaking strength and comfort within.

Country masons laid all the stone with the stone-quarry for a pattern and the architect for a teacher. The masons learned to lay the walls in the long, thin, flat ledges natural to the quarry, natural edges out. As often as they laid a stone they would stand back to judge the effect. They were soon as interested as sculptors fashioning a statue; one might imagine they were as they stepped back, head cocked one side, to get the general effect. Having arrived at some conclusion they would step forward and shove the stone more to their liking, seeming never to tire of this discrimination. Many of them were artistic for the first time, and liked it. There were many masons from first to last, all good. Perhaps old Dad Signola, in his youth a Czech, was the best of them until Philip Volk came. Philip worked away five years at the place as it grew from year to year—for it will never be finished. And with not much inharmonious discrepancy, one may see each mason's individuality in his work at Taliesin to this day. I frequently recall the man as I see his work.

At that time, to get this mass of material to the hilltop meant organizing man and horse-power. Trucks came along years later. Main strength and awkwardness, directed by commanding intelligence, got the better of the law of gravitation by the ton as sand, stone, gravel and timber went up into appointed places. Ben Davis was commander of these forces at this time. Ben was a creative cusser. He had to be. To listen to Ben back of all this movement was to take off your hat to a virtuoso. Men have cussed between every word, but Ben split the words and artistically worked in an oath between every syllable. One day Ben with five of his men was moving a big rock that suddenly got away from its edge and fell over flat, catching Ben's big toe. I shuddered for that rock as, hobbling slowly back and forth around it, Ben hissed and glared at it, threatening, eyeing and cussing it. He rose to such heights, plunged to such depths of vengeance as I had never suspected, even in Ben. No Marseillaise nor any damnation in the mouth of a Mosaic prophet ever exceeded Ben at this high spot in his career as a cusser. William Blake says exuberance is beauty. It would be profane perhaps to say that Ben at this moment was sublime. But he was.

And in Spring Green (the names in the region are mostly simple like Black Earth, Blue Mounds, Cross Plains, Lone Rock, Silver Creek) I found a carpenter. William Weston, a natural carpenter. He was a carpenter such as architects like to stand and watch work. I never saw him make a false or unnecessary movement. His hammer, extra light with a handle fashioned by himself, flashed to the right spot every time like the

196

rapier of an expert swordsman. He with his nimble intelligence and swift sure hand was a gift to any architect. That William stayed with and by Taliesin through trials and tribulations the better part of fourteen years. America turns up a good mechanic around in country places every so often. Billy was one of them.

Winter came. A bitter one. The roof was on, plastering done, windows in, men working now inside. Evenings the men grouped around the open fire-places, throwing cord-wood into them to keep warm as the cold wind came up through the floor boards. All came to work from surrounding towns and had to be fed and bedded down on the place somewhere during the week. Saturday nights they went home with money for the week's work in pocket, or its equivalent in groceries and fixings from the village. Their reactions were picturesque. There was Johnnie Vaughn who was, I guess, a genius. I got him because he had gone into some kind of concrete business with another Irishman for a partner, and failed. Johnnie said, "We didn't fail sooner because we didn't have more business." I overheard this lank genius (he was looking after the carpenters) nagging Billy Little, who had been foreman of several jobs in the city for me. Said Johnnie, "I built this place off a shingle." "Huh," said Billy, "that ain't nothin'. I built them places in Oak Park right off'd the air." No one ever got even a little over the rat-like perspicacity of that little Billy Little.

Workmen never have enough drawings or explanations no matter how many they get—but this is the sort of slander an architect needs to hear occasionally.

The workmen took the work as a sort of adventure. It was adventure. In every realm. Especially in the financial realm, I kept working all the while to make the money come. It did. And we kept on inside with plenty of clean soft wood that could be left alone pretty much in plain surfaces. The stone, too, strong and protective inside, spoke for itself in certain piers and walls.

Inside floors, like the outside floors, were stone-paved or if not were laid with wide, dark-streaked cypress boards. The plaster in the walls was mixed with raw sienna in the box, went onto the walls natural, drying out tawny gold. Outside, the plastered walls were the same but grayer with cement. But in the *constitution* of the whole, in the way the walls rose from the plan and spaces were roofed over, was the chief interest of the whole house. The whole was supremely natural. The rooms went up into the roof, tent-like, and were ribanded overhead with marking-strips of waxed, soft wood. The house was set so sun came through the openings into every room sometime during the day. Walls opened everywhere to views as the windows swung out above the tree-tops, the tops of red, white and black oaks and wild cherry trees festooned with wild grape-vines. In spring, the perfume of the blossoms came full through the windows, the birds singing there the while, from sunrise to sunset—all but the several white months of winter.

I wanted a home where icicles by invitation might beautify the eaves. So there were no gutters. And when the snow piled deep on the roofs and lay drifted in the courts, icicles came to hang staccato from the eaves. Prismatic crystal pendants sometimes six feet long, glittered between the landscape and the eyes inside. Taliesin in winter was a frosted palace roofed and walled with snow, hung with iridescent fringes, the plate-glass of the windows shone bright and warm through it all as the light of the huge fire-places lit them from the firesides within, and streams of wood-smoke from a dozen such places went straight up toward the stars.

Furnishings inside were simple and temperate. Thin tan-colored flax rugs covered the floors, later abandoned for the severer simplicity of the stone pavements and wide boards. Doors and windows were hung with modest, brown checkered fabrics. The furniture was home-made of the same wood as the trim, and mostly fitted into the trim. I got a compliment on this from old Dan Davis, a rich and "savin' " Welsh neighbor who saw we had made it ourselves. "Gosh-dang it, Frank," he said. "Ye're savin' too, ain't ye?" Although Mother Williams, another neighbor, who came to work for me, said "Savin'? He's nothin' of the sort. He could'ave got it most as cheap ready-made from that Sears and Roebuck...I know."

A house of the North! The whole low, wide and snug, broad shelter seeking fellowship with surroundings. A house that could open to the breezes of summer, become like an open camp if need be. With spring came music on the roofs, for there were few dead roof-spaces overhead, and the broad eaves so sheltered the windows that they were safely left open to the sweeping, soft airs of the rain. Grateful for care, Taliesin took what grooming it got with gratitude. Repaid it all with interest.

Taliesin's order was such that when all was clean and in place its countenance beamed, wore a happy smile of well-being and welcome for all.

It was intensely *human,* I believe.

Although, thanks to "bigger and better publicity" among those who besieged it Saturdays and Sundays from near and far, came several characteristic ladies whose unusual enterprise got them as far as the upper half of the Dutch door, standing open to the living room itself. They couldn't see me. I was lying on a long walled-seat just inside. They poked in their heads and looked about with Oh's and Ah's. A pause. In the nasal twang of the more aggressive one, "I wonder . . . I wonder, now, if I'd like living in a regular home?"

The studio, lit by a bank of tall windows to the north, really was a group of four studies, one large, three small. And in their midst stood a stone fire-proof vault for treasures. The plans, private papers, and such money as there was, took chances anywhere outside it. But the Taliesin library of Genroku embroidery and antique colored wood-block prints all stayed safely inside. As work and sojourn overseas continued, Chinese pottery and sculpture and Momoyama screens overflowed into the rooms where, in a few years, every single object used for decorative accent became an "antique" of rare quality.

If the eye rested on some ornament it could be sure of worthy entertainment. Hovering over these messengers to Taliesin from other civilizations and thousands of years ago, must have been spirits of peace and good-will? Their figures seemed to shed fraternal sense of kinship from their places in the stone or from the broad ledges where they rested.

Yes. It all actually happened as I have described it. It is all there now.

But the story of Taliesin, after all, is old: old as the human spirit. These ancient figures were traces of that spirit, left behind in the human process as Time went on its way. They now came forward to rest and feel at home, that's all. So it seemed as you looked at them. But they were only the story within the story: ancient comment on the New.

The New lived for itself for their sake, as long ago they had lived, for its sake.

The storms of the north broke over the low-sweeping roofs that now sheltered a life in which hope purposefully lived at earnest work. The lightning in this region, always so crushing and severe, crashed (Isaiah) and Taliesin smiled. Taliesin was a "story" and therefore it and all in it had to run the gauntlet. But steadily it made its way through storm and stress, enduring all threats and slanderous curiosity for more than three years, and smiled—always. No one entering and feeling the repose of its spirit could ever believe in the storm of publicity that kept breaking outside because a kindred spirit—a woman—had taken refuge there for life.

Gradually creative desire and faith came creeping back again. Taliesin was there to come alive and I to settle down to work.

Chicago business offices were now in the Orchestra Hall Building, though the studio-workshop was still at Taliesin. A number of buildings went out from that studio. The neighborhood playhouse of Mrs. Coonley was among them, and the Midway Gardens on the Plaisance near

Chicago University. As the Gardens were a product of the first re-establishment, associated in my mind with the tragedy at Taliesin and because they were so new in so many ways, here is the story of that adventure. An "Arabian Nights" in architecture.

TALE OF THE MIDWAY GARDENS

Some time ago, the fall of 1913, young Ed Waller's head got outside the idea of the Chicago Midway Gardens and he set to work. First on me. One day when I had come into Chicago from the Taliesin studio-workshop, he began on me.

Said Ed: "Frank, in all this black old town there's no place to go but out, nor any place to come but back, that isn't bare and ugly unless it's cheap and nasty. I want to put a garden in this wilderness of smoky dens, car-tracks and saloons."

This sounded like his father whom you have seen in the experience with Uncle Dan in the library of the house at River Forest.

"I believe Chicago would appreciate a beautiful garden resort. Our people would go there, listen to good music, eat and drink. You know, an outdoor garden something like those little parks round Munich where German families go. You have seen them.

"The dance craze is on now, too, and we could have a dancing floor inside somewhere for the young folks. Yes, and a place within the big place outside near the orchestra where highbrows could come and sit to hear a fine concert even if they did want to dine at home.

"The trouble of course is the short season. But we could fix that up by putting a winter-garden on one side for diners, with a big dancing floor in the middle. To make it all surefire as to money we would put in a bar [the 'affliction' had not yet befallen] that would go the year around. We would run the whole thing as a high-class entertainment on a grand scale—Pavlova dancing—Max Bendix's full orchestra playing—you know Max. Music outdoors starting at seven o'clock. Between orchestral numbers there would be a dance-orchestra striking up, back there in the winter-garden, so the girls could get the boys to dance. Special matinees several days a week—'Features' every night. I see people up on balconies, all around over the tops of the buildings: Light, color, music, movement—a gay place!

"Frank, you could make it unique," he went on.

"I know I could," I said, "where can I get the ground?"

"Down on the South Side just off the Midway. The old Sans Souci place. Been on the rocks for years. Stupid old ballyhoo. It's just big enough, I think. About three acres. You'll get paid for your drawings anyway."

All Ed didn't know was where he could get the money. He said "but that is the easiest part of it." He would fix that.

"What do you think of the idea?"

Well, as a boy Aladdin and his wonderful lamp had fascinated me. But by now I knew the enchanting young Arabian was really just a symbol for creative desire, his lamp intended for another symbol—imagination. As I sat listening I was Aladdin. Young Ed? The genii. He knew apparently where all "the slaves of the lamp" could be found. Well, this might all be necromancy but I believed in magic. Had I not rubbed my lamp with what seemed wonderful effect, before? I didn't hesitate.

"When you get back to the office, Ed, send me a survey of the old Sans Souci grounds. Then come back Monday," I said. "You'll see what . . . you'll see."

He came back Monday. The thing had simply shaken itself out of my sleeve. In a remarkably short time there it was on paper—in color. Young Ed gloated over it.

"I knew it," he said. "You could do it and *this is it.*"

Paul Mueller it was whom we both desired as "slave of the lamp." We got Paul-the-builder interested in the scheme. With accustomed energy he started into make the dream reality. His "organization," as he called it, of partners, foremen, workmen skilled and workmen unskilled, all belonged to various departments of the great big Chicago building contractor known as "The Union." Mueller rented slaves from the Union by making the usual terms. But he himself, as usual was really the organization, so far as that went, in getting the Midway Gardens built.

Nor could Young Ed wait for any process very long. He was very young and he—the genii—started all this on the fly, kept it flying.

In another several days old Sans Souci's several acres had begun to boil. The Union was on the job as usual with watchful, jealous eye. Soon all of old Sans Souci there was left in plain sight was a rusty old steel-tower standing up in one corner of the lot. Laborers started to wreck it but the Union simply raised its warning hand. The rickety old tower was iron, therefore consecrate to the steel-workers. Skilled steel-workers only should dare demolish it. This meant a thousand or so wasted, but no time to argue—the Union knew that too. Skilled steel-workers took the thing down.

Mueller, now slave-driver, stood up six feet two inches tall in all this commotion madly shouting through a megaphone to five points of the compass all at the same time, giving directions to seemingly insane activity.

Excavators, steam shovels, wagons, dumping materials and trucks hauling dirt away, barrows, mules, more trucks, concrete mixers, derricks, gin poles, mud, water and men. Cement-bags, sand, brick, beams and timber came piling up into great heaps. Masons, hod-carriers, brick layers, plasterers, carpenters, steel-workers all over the place found the proper thing to do at the proper time because capable foremen were correctly reading the architect's blue-prints in the little board-shanty that had now taken the place of the consecrated iron tower. "Paul F. P. Mueller & Co., Builders" was the legend painted in big black letters across the small edifice.

You know without being told where the blue-prints came from. And Young Ed, genius of all this hubbub—and expected to pay for it— hovered over it all, excited. To date, this was the time of his life.

In Ed's office was Charlie Matthews, a cultivated chap: artistic, music-mad Charlie. He too went off his head over the scheme for the Midway Gardens. Got others into a state of mind to buy stock in the enterprise. And while this frenzied army of workmen were busy—Ed, Charlie and their friends were busy too. Trying to raise money. But, as subsequently appeared, there was only about sixty-five thousand dollars in hand to meet the three hundred and fifty thousand to be paid. No one knew that at the time unless it was Ed. I doubt if even he did. Anyhow, that is about all the real money there ever was with which to build the Midway Gardens.

But all unaware of that fact, the Gardens were well above ground, rapidly moving up toward the blue overhead. Even Chicago weather permitted, entering into the conspiracy, if there really was any conspiracy outside the Union. I knew of none except the conspiracy to get the Midway Gardens done in ninety days, the diners seated, dinner on the tables and the music playing. The date of the opening was fixed for May 1, 1914.

The Midway Gardens were planned as a "summer garden": a system of low masonry terraces enclosed by promenades, loggias and galleries at the sides, these flanked by a Winter Garden. The Winter Garden stood forward on the main street and opposite the great orchestra shell. The Bar, "supporting economic feature," was put on the principal street corner. Ed argued that a bar should be right across a man's path, a manifest temptation. That boy knew a lot about human weaknesses—among other things. This bar, as manifest temptation, was going strong when the nation-wide affliction befell.

At each extreme outer corner of the lot toward the main street were set the two tall welcoming features: flat towers topped by trellises intended to be covered with vines and flowers and ablaze with light to advertise the entrances to both summer and winter gardens. The kitchen, of course, as stomach is to man, was located beneath and at the very center of the building scheme, short tunnels leading direct to the Gardens for quick service, service stairs leading straight up into the winter-garden terraces above it. A waiter could with reasonable ease get direct to all the various terrace levels, balconies and roofs, and the waiters were legion.

"Quick service and hot food," said John Vogelsang. John was to regale the inner man (interior-decorate him) while Max Bendix charmed his ears, the Gardens charmed his eyes, and all together charmed the dollars out of popular pockets into the eager Midway Garden coffers. "Quick service and hot food are the secret of contented diners." John knew. He was a Chicago restaurateur and a success at the time he was talking. So, after getting the kitchen located and appurtenances properly connected up, we made all the kitchen arrangements "according to John."

But the orchestra shell became a bone of contention.

Out of a good deal of experience in such matters with Adler and Sullivan—they designed the Chicago Auditorium and twenty-six other successful opera houses—I had designed the shell, sure it would work out.

Here is where Charlie Matthews's knowledge of music came in, because Charlie having been a director himself was appointed committee of one to see this important feature a success. As anyone knows, acoustics are tricky unless you know them to be simple and scientific. This was little known then. So the first thing Charlie did was to run around the United States interviewing musicians. Each musician wanted it different from the other one and the way I had it. I wouldn't change it. Then Charlie got mad and called in experts. The experts were all agreed that the open sides that I wanted in order to distribute the sound well to the sides of the Gardens were a mistake. Charlie said, "Change it."

I said, "No, Charlie, not just for that. Give me a better reason."

Said Charlie, now unbecomingly heated, "Hell, Frank, do you think you are the only one in the world who knows anything about orchestra shells?"

"No, Charlie," I said, trying to keep my case in court, "but about this particular orchestra shell, utterly yes. I am sure I do."

A little later Ed's voice on the phone—"Say, Mr. Architect, are you sure that shell will be all right?"

"Perfectly sure, Ed."

"Then go ahead and build it. Don't change it for anybody." And I knew "anybody" meant Charlie.

In regard to this shell, you see, I was in the position the Union was in toward the Gardens. Success to the dictator lay in this matter of *time*, for the thing had to be done without delays. All this conflict did make me a little anxious. But had I shown it, all would have been down with the shell, just because it is impossible to build anything more than one way at one time. Had I lost my nerve I should have had to build it six different ways at least at the same time and then, after all, probably tear it down. So I proposed something that made friends with Charlie. The shell was cupped well out above over the orchestra, rising with no complex curves from a wall behind the musicians, a wall about nine feet high. The sides were only partially closed and those open sides being the chief contention, I proposed to make the sides at this point doors that could be swing outward if that proved necessary. If not necessary then they were there as features to carry the programme-numbers and signs in electric lights.

This expedient restored harmony.

The Midway Gardens, meantime, were fast growing up out of chaos. Long, low, level lines and new rectangular masonry forms were taking definite shape. They could be seen now, far enough along to make one wonder what in the world was coming.

At the time the Midway Gardens were designed, 1913, *l'Art Nouveau* was dying in France, where it originated, and gasping wherever else it happened to have caught on, and various experiments in the "abstract" in painting and sculpture were being made in Europe, exciting the esthetic vanguard by insulting the rank and file.

But the straight line, itself an abstraction, and the flat plane for its own sake, had characterized my buildings from the first hour on my own account I had become building-conscious.

Never much interested in "realism," I was already dissatisfied with the realistic element in Art or in any building. Like "Breaking Home Ties" in painting, the Rogers Groups in sculpture, or *Liberty* covers later, the work of the period was flat on its stomach to the "realistic." Or else the buildings were the usual dull vulgar imitations of the old styles—false and imitative. I admired nothing going on in architecture anywhere in the world at the time this design for the Midway Gardens came due to happen.

Clearly I saw my trusty T-square and aspiring triangle as means to the Midway Garden end in view.

I meant to get back to first principles—pure form in everything;

weave a masonry-fabric, a beautiful pattern in genuine materials and good construction; bring painting and sculpture in to heighten and carry all still further into the realm of the Lamp in the same Spirit. A synthesis of all the Arts.

Yes, why not have the whole Gardens as consistently a unit for once in this century as anything in noble music Max Bendix could find to play in them. Why then not go back to the source, bring form alive again in my own way, making a true chime to the tune of imagination, *in Chicago*. Forms could be made into a festival for the eye no less than music made a festival for the ear. I knew. This could all be genuine building, not mere scene painting.

Well, yes, but how about the Chicago audience? Would Chicago be able to see all that if it did happen? Chicago so far behind in judging qualities of either form, sound or color. I believed that was only because Chicago never had a chance to choose the real thing. Notwithstanding "The Fair," the Arts were yet to come to Chicago. A painting still had to be a "picture"; and the more the picture could be mistaken for the real object, the better Chicago liked the work. Sculpture the same way. That too had to look "real" and if it could seem so to the touch, why, that was greatest sculpture. Could Chicago respond to adventure in the realm of the abstract in the sense that I wanted to go into it? Did Chicago know what "abstraction" meant anyway? Perhaps not. Why be silly?

But I didn't argue these points with anyone but myself. I kept still about them. After all, what did these subjective matters signify to others? Fortunately, human beings are really childlike in the best sense when directly appealed to by simple, strong forms and pure, bright color. Chicago was not sophisticated. Chicago was still unspoiled. So probably all this could go straight to the Chicago heart. It would.

Meantime the straight line, square, triangle and circle I had learned to play with in Kindergarten were set to work in this developing sense of abstraction (by now my habit) to characterize the architecture, painting and sculpture of the Midway Gardens. Most places of the kind I had seen at home or abroad were phantasy developed as a cheap, erotic foolishness. A kind of papier-mâché scene painting. In the Midway Gardens there was to be no eroticism: no damned sentimentality either. There was to be permanent structure. The lovely human figure might come into the scheme but come in only to respect the architecture, dominated by a proper sense of the whole. The human figure should be there but humbly, to heighten the whole effect.

The human figure? Well, the sprites of these geometrical forms themselves: they might come into play and share in the general geometric gaiety. How far these ideas would go in flat color I determined when I handed the general schemes for color-decoration to

William Henderson and Jack Norton of the Art Institute, and Jerry Blum of the Orient: schemes for sculpture to young Ianelli whom I brought east for the purpose.

Here in the Midway Gardens painting and sculpture were to be bidden back again to their original places and to their original offices in architecture, where they belonged. The architect, himself, was here again master of them all together. (Making no secret of it, whatever.) But artists are very sensitive beings in their own right. In modern times they have not become accustomed to sitting in the orchestra to play a mere part in an architect's score, so to speak. The incumbent *altogether* means less to them than it did to their ancient progenitors. As an obligation it grinds on them. They lose face when they regard it. But I am glad I got them in anyway. About their own feelings later I am not so sure. I've taken you into confidence in this explanation while these thoughts were taking visible and novel effect in brick and concrete there in the fearless Gardens. The work was going on night and day. Son John helped superintend. I myself sometimes slept at night on a pile of shavings in a corner of the Winter Garden when worn out. John would keep going.

"Look here, Wright," said the exasperated Mueller to me one day. "What's this you got here—this young bull-dog that he is. He follows me around and around. Every little while he sticks his teeth in the seat of my pants and I can't get away from him. Can I pull over everything that goes wrong in this work? Can I? Not if I get these Gardens finished up, already to open on time I can't. Take him off me!"

But that sounded good to me and I didn't take him off. John was in it all up to his ears, and his teeth were serviceable.

We had built a couple of wooden shanties for the modeling of the sculpture. Dicky Bock and Ianelli were working away in them with helpers and a female model. This model was the mysterious object of continuous and extensive male curiosity. Although unable to read, she carried a volume of Ibsen's plays coming and going. Scientifically she had reduced her garments to one piece plus shoes, stockings, gloves in hand and hat so she could "slip on" and "slip off" easily. Her Mona Lisa smile is evident in the figure pieces of the Gardens (thanks to Ianelli).

While sculpture was going on in this shanty painters were working up on wooden scaffolds in the buildings of the Winter Garden. The painter boys got some of their Art Institute pupils to help them, among them an accomplished Catherine Dudley.

One day a plug-ugly stuck his head in the door of the modeling shanty. The Union! Again for about the seventh time on various pretexts.

He said, "Say, what about it? What about that skirt y' got up there doin' paintin'? She ain't no artist, 's she?"

"Sh' is," I said, "and damned clever."

"Aw, come on. Sh' is just one o' them too good lookin' society dames. Say," he went on, lowering his head and sticking out his jaw, "you get that skirt off'n there or these Gardens—maybe . . . they'll *never* open. See? And them three other guys yu' got out there a-paintin' with smocckies on a-smokin'. Don't look like no artist to me neither. Get cards for them, too. See!"

"Artists? Man," I said, "they are and so good, they're teachers at the Art Institute." (I thought that should impress him.) "Go and ask."

"Naw, I ain't askin' nobody. Cards f'r 'em, see? Get 'em."

He glanced at sculptors Bock and Ianelli. The curtains had hastily been drawn across the model.

"What yu got in there behind that curtain?"

'Now look here. You are going pretty strong, aren't you? What business have you got in here, anyway?"

"Business?" he said. "I'll show you what business I got 'n here. Ye're hid'n' men out on me that ought to be 'n the Union. Scabs, see?"

He gave the sculptors a dirty look. "Where's their cards?"

"Don't need cards. They're Artists, too—sculptors. Can't you see they look that way?" (I couldn't resist this.)

'Naw, n' more'n the carvers and modelers we got in the Union. Not's much," he said. "They got to get their cards or this show don' go on."

I called Dicky down from the scaffold where just before this ugly break he had been working away on the model for four big capitals for the great piers of the Winter Garden. I took him aside.

"Dicky, this looks funny to me. The Union is bad enough, God knows, but this fellow's drunk. Got any money in the bank, Dicky?"

"About seven dollars, I guess."

"Fine! Got your checkbook, Dicky?"

"Yes."

I got over to the plug-ugly.

"Look here, rough-boy. How much for these two great Artists?"

"Thirty-five apiece."

"Seventy dollars?"

"Seventy."

"All right. Dick, give the Union a check for seventy dollars."

"Name?"

He got the check, turned, gave another dirty look at the curtains which and when just then parted. Hatted, gloved, volume of Ibsen under arm, Mona Lisa, eyes properly downcast, stepped forward into view.

The ugly grinned. "Yeah! So I see," said he, and laughed himself out of the door.

"My God," said Dicky. "When that thug finds out there's no money back of that check, he'll come back here and murder me—hands up."

"Let's see if he will," I said.

The Union had held up the work a half dozen times on one pretext or another but no issue was ever made of this matter for some reason. The artists *per se*, as such, carried on with no more help from "the Union." I suppose that check cashed by the "delegate" had bounced and inasmuch as he had taken too great a personal interest in it—it was best on the whole to say nothing.

The Gardens, owing to high pressure and night-shifts, were nearly done. The electric needles that I made out of wrought-iron pipe, punctured to let the lamps through thickly at the sides, now stood delicately up into the sky and irradiated the whole place for night work.

Seen from afar, they were good advertisements for the Gardens—but not good enough for John Vogelsang. No, no, not for John. He had secretly started a campaign for a great big electric sign above it all with "MIDWAY GARDENS" blazing in colored lights. I discovered this and fought him. I won for a little while but eventually—sometime after the opening—he did get it up there. The first severe blow to the scheme.

We didn't have money to color the walls as intended, by inlaying scarlet and green flash-glass in the relief patterns made of concrete. We had no money to finish the sky-frames on the four towers of the Winter Garden intended to be garlanded with vines and flowers like the tops of the welcoming features. Nor any to plant the big trees at the corners of the Gardens. I mean that we had nothing at all that even promised money. Even the stage money was all gone now. Gay colored balloons of various sizes in great numbers were to have flown high above the scene, anchored to the electric needles and tower features. They couldn't get these. They wouldn't have cost much, but that little was too much at that time.

Money troubles now. Anxiety. Anger. But still hopes and active promises aplenty.

Mueller stood in the breach with his young partner Seipp, and carried on else the Midway Gardens would never have opened at all. We all had faith that when opened, the Gardens themselves would settle the financial question the first season. They did.

Then, one noon while I was eating a late luncheon in the Winter Gardens, came the terrible news of tragedy at Taliesin that took me away from the Gardens and from all else for a time.

When the Midway Gardens were nearly finished—my son John and

I were sleeping there nightly in a corner on a pile of shavings to keep track of the night work now necessary to finish the Gardens on time—at noon as we were sitting quietly eating our lunch in the newly finished bar, came a long distance call from Spring Green. "Taliesin destroyed by fire." But no word came of ghastly tragedy. I learned of that little by little on my way home on the train that evening. The newspaper headlines glared with it.

Thirty-six hours earlier I had left Taliesin leaving all living, friendly and happy. Now the blow had fallen like a lightning stroke. In less time than it takes to write it, a thin-lipped Barbados Negro, who had been well recommended to me by John Vogelsang himself as an ideal servant, had turned madman, taken the lives of seven and set the house in flames. In thirty minutes the house and all in it had burned to the stone work or to the ground. The living half of Taliesin violently swept down and away in a madman's nightmare of flame and murder.

The working half only remained.

Will Weston saved that.

He had come to grips with the madman, whose strength was superhuman, but slipped away from his grasp and blows. Bleeding from the encounter he ran down the hill to the nearest neighbor, Reider, to give the alarm, made his way back immediately through the cornfields only to find the deadly work finished and the home ablaze. Hardly able to stand, he ran to where the fire hose was kept in a niche of the garden wall, past his young son lying there in the fountain basin—one of the seven dead—got the hose loose, staggered with it to the fire and with the playing hose stood against destruction until they led him away.

The great stone chimneys stood black and tall on the hillside, their fireplaces now black and gaping. They stood there above the Valley against the sky, themselves tragic symbols.

She for whom Taliesin had first taken form and her two children—gone. A talented apprentice, Emil Brodelle; the young son of William Weston the gardener; David Lindblom; a faithful workman, Thomas Brunker—this was the human toll taken by a few moments of madness. The madman was finally discovered after a day or two of frightened search hidden in the fire-pot of the steam boiler, down in the smoking ruins of the house. Still alive though nearly dead, he was taken to the Dodgeville jail. Refusing meantime to utter a word, there he died.

Black despair preceded a primitive burial in the ground of the family chapel. Men from Taliesin dug the grave, deep, near Grandfather's and Grandmother's. Uncle Enos had come to say it would be all right. But I felt that a funeral service could only be mockery. The undertaker's offices—too, the vulgar casket—seemed profane. So I cut her garden down and with the flowers filled the strong, plain box of fresh, white pine to overflowing. My own carpenters made it.

My boy, John, coming to my side now, helped lift the body and we let it down to rest among the flowers that had grown and bloomed for her. The plain box lid was pressed down and fastened home. Then the plain, strong box was lifted on the shoulders of my workmen as they placed it on our little spring-wagon, filled, too, with flowers—waiting, hitched behind faithful Darby and Joan . . . We made the whole a mass of flowers. It helped a little.

Since Taliesin was first built Darby and Joan were the faithful little sorrel team that had so often drawn us along the Valley roads over the hills, in Spring, Summer, Autumn and Winter, almost daily.

Walking alongside the wheels now I drove them along the road to the chapel yard where no bell tolled. No people were waiting. John followed. Ralph and Orrin, two of my young Hillside cousins, were waiting at the chapel gate. Together we lowered the flower-filled and flower-covered pine box to the bottom of the new-made grave. Then I asked them to leave me there alone.

I wanted to fill the grave myself . . .

I remember the August sun was setting on the long familiar range of hills. Dimly, I felt coming far-off shadows of the ages, struggling escape from consciousness, utter themselves . . . Then, slowly, darkness . . . I filled the grave, staying there in the dark. The dark was friendly.

No monument yet marks the spot where she lies buried.

All I had left of the struggle for freedom of the five years past that had swept most of my former life away, had now been swept away.

Why mark the spot where desolation ended and began?

AGAIN

In the little bedroom back of the undestroyed studio-workshop I remained in what was left of Taliesin I.

No one seemed near to me. Nor she who had been struck down.

The gaping black hole left by fire in the beautiful hillside seemed a charred and ugly scar upon my own life—on all life.

This tragedy resulting in the first destruction of Taliesin left me in strange plight. From the moment of return to that devastating scene of horror I had wanted to see no one. I would see no one but the workmen. Work only was bearable.

For the week following there was no one on the hill at night but the watchman and me. He sat on the steps with a gun across his knees. The whole countryside terrified by the tragedy—not knowing what to expect. Before the murderer was discovered groups of neighbors had searched cornfields and woods for the black-man.

Those nights in the little back room were black, filled with strange unreasoning terrors. No moon seemed to shine. No stars in the sky. No familiar frog-song coming from the pond. There was a strange, unnatural silence, while drifts of smoke still rose from the ruin.

Unable to sleep, I would get up numb, take a cold bath to bring myself alive, go out on the hills in the night, not really knowing where. But I would come back again with only a sense of black night and strange fear, no beauty visible any more. Grope how I might—no help from that source. I would find my way back to bed.

Something strange had happened to me. Instead of feeling that she, whose life had joined mine there at Taliesin, was a spirit near, she was utterly gone!

After the first terrible anguish, a black despair seemed to paralyze my imagination in her direction, numbed my sensibilities. The blow was too severe.

I got no relief in any faith nor, yet, any in hope. Except repulsion, I could feel only in terms of rebuilding. I could get relief only by looking toward building—get relief from a kind of continuous nausea, only by work.

That relief by habitual action was all I really had—the only color life kept by my work and music. They had thrown my piano out of the window to save it and, legs broken, it was now blocked up by the studio fireplace. I could sit there and try to play.

But everything else had been swept away or lurked in the strange oppression of some darkened room in which strange shadows lurked and moved.

As I looked back at that time, I saw the black hole in the hillside, the black night over all as I moved about in sinister shadows. Days strangely without light would follow black nights. Totally—she was gone.

No, this is not fanciful word painting. I am trying to tell what happened. Gone into this equivocal blackness near oblivion for several years to come was all sense of her whom I had loved as one not having lived at all.

This was merciful? I believe the equivalent of years passed within my consciousness in the course of days. Time, never very present to me, ceased to exist. As days passed into nights I was numb to all but the automatic steps toward rebuilding the home wantonly destroyed by hateful forces.

The routine of the day's work, three meals a day that were brought to me: all this went on by sheer force of habit. I began to go down. Physically sagged. Boils (I had never had any in my life before) now broke over my back and neck. I lost weight. Finally I got back to my little home at 25 East Cedar Street and lived there alone except for an Irish caretaker, Nellie Breen.

I had never needed glasses, but now I had to have them.

These came between me and my work for the first time.

Nature is merciful as she is cruel. I believe any spiritual faculty as well as physical, overtaxed, becomes numb. The real pain in that realm, too, comes when healing begins. It is thus the spirit seems subject to the same laws as the body.

A horrible loneliness now began to clutch at me, but strange to say I longed for no one I ever loved or that I had ever known. My mother was deeply hurt by my refusal to have her with me. My children—I had welcomed them eagerly always—but I did not want them now. They had been so faithfully kind in my extremity. I shall never forget.

But strange faces were best and I walked among them.

I do not understand this any better now than I did then. Months went by, but they might have been and I believe they were for me an actual lifetime.

Perhaps a new consciousness had to grow as a green shoot will grow from a charred and blackened stump?

Whatever the truth may be, the fact remains—until many years afterward, to turn my thoughts backward to what had transpired in the life Mamah and I had lived together at Taliesin was like trying to see into a dark room in which terror lurked, strange shadows moved—and I would do well to turn away in time.

I could see forward only. I could not see backward. The pain was too great.

It looked for some time as though I might not be able to see at all.

It was this that, like a lash, made me get to work upon myself none too soon. Have I been describing despair? A feeling unknown to me.

Waves of unkind, stupid publicity broke over Taliesin again. The human sacrifices at Taliesin seemed in vain. Its heroism was ridiculed, its love mocked. Its very heart, struck from it at a blow, was profaned by a public sympathy harder to bear even than public curiosity had been.

"Tried and condemned," some said. Well . . . was this trial for heresy too? Was this trial, like Grandfather's, at some judgment seat, to quell a spirit that would not be quelled?

Was this unconventional believer in the good, the true and beautiful seeing it as work, life and love, actually in the midst of all three, thus similarly struck down?

Some months before, sitting on the stone terrace overlooking the valley below, I saw one of the finest cows of the countryside, Taliesin's Holstein Maplecroft, a thoroughbred worth several hundred ordinary cows, standing beneath an oak tree. Two other cows were standing there beside her, comparatively worthless. A lightning flash of flame there below simultaneous with a stunning crash. Two cows walked away from beneath the tree unharmed. It was Maplecroft lay there dead by stroke of lightning. Why peerless Maplecroft?

Why Taliesin?

So many too willing answers to "Why Taliesin?" were publicly made by good men and true. They now had a text upon which to preach. But no preaching was more reasonable than that the "unconventional" gathers enmity of the conventional until, charged beyond the containing point, explosion in some form, obvious or occult, follows. Did this apply to Maplecroft's unconventionality? Hers consisted in being thoroughbred among the "grades." Did the envy or displeasure of ordinary numbers attract destruction to her?

Utter nonsense!

So the rage that grew in me when I felt the inimical weight of human censure concentrated upon me began to fade away until I finally found refuge in the idea that Taliesin should live to show something more for its mortal sacrifices than a charred and terrible ruin on a lonely hillside in the beloved ancestral Valley where great happiness had been.

In action there is release from anguish of mind. Anguish could not leave me until action for *renewal,* so far as might be, began. Again, and at once, all that had been in motion before at the will of the architect, if not the man, was set in motion. Steadily, stone by stone, board by board, Taliesin II began to rise from the ashes of Taliesin I.

Where scenes of horror had identified the structure with ugly memories, I changed it. Where tragedy had been most obvious, an open stone-floored loggia looked up the Valley toward the Lloyd-Jones family Chapel.

A guest unit was added to the west, and a great fireplace. It was for my aged Mother and Aunts. I intended to bring them home to Taliesin.

There was to be no turning back nor any stopping to mourn. What had been beautiful at Taliesin should live as a grateful memory creating the new, and, come who and whatever might to share Taliesin, they would be sure to help in that spirit.

So I believed and resolved.

As one consequence of the ugly publicity given the terrible tragedy

213

hundreds of letters had come to me from all over the country. I tied them up together into a bundle now and burned them. Unread. I went to work. The salt and savor of life had not been lost. That salt and savor will always be the work one does best.

TALIESIN II

More stone, more wood, more work—a more harmonious use of them all. More workmen, more money—sacrifices, not only more creative work on my part but desperate efforts to find and eventually earn the necessary money.

Another Fall, another Winter, another Spring, another Summer and late in 1915, Taliesin II stood in the place of the first Taliesin. A more reposeful and a finer one. Not a chastened Tailiesin. No, up in arms now, declining to take the popular Mosaic-Isaian idea of punishment as worthy the sacrifice demanded and taken at Taliesin. Demanded? By whom? Taken? For what? And the sentimental or superstitious or profane answers from all sides, and from top to bottom, answered nothing.

But something was coming clear, now, through all the brutalizing Taliesin had received. Something—no, not rebellion. Conviction. Purpose now lifted the crown of the head higher. Made the eye see clearer. The tread that faltered for a moment in weakness and confusion becam elastic and more sure as Work came alive again.

Meantime the Gardens—the gardens, though still unfinished, had opened in as brilliant a social event as Chicago ever knew. Not finished yet, no, nor were they ever completely finished. The decoration in the entrance-features remained to be done. The towers of the Winter Garden had no decoration. Certain other things all about. But the atmosphere aimed at, that was there. In a scene unforgettable to all who attended, the architectural scheme and color, form, light and sound had come alive. Thousands of beautifully dressed women and tuxedoed men thronged the scene. And this scene came upon the beholders as a magic spell. All there moved and spoke as if in a dream. They believed it must be one. Yes, Chicago marveled, acclaimed, approved. And Chicago came back and did the same, marveling again and again and again. To many it was all Egyptian. Mayan to some, very Japanese to others. But strange to all, it awakened a sense of mystery and romance in the beholder. Each responded with what he had in him to give, and for the remainder of the season, Chicago, the unregenerate, came to rendezvous with beauty. The coffers of Ed's company began to fill. It looked as though such a success could not be a failure for anyone concerned.

214

I returned from Taliesin and tragedy to Chicago now when this popularity was at its height. Still dazed by tragedy, I was trying to realize this myself. Acoustics proved all anyone could hope for, thanks to a perfect orchestra shell. Charlie Matthews was silent. But the unfinished final touches so significant in any work of art were still lacking. This hurt and marred my sense of the thing. As a success it is usually so.

These were also days of world tragedy. War broke out. Chicago as all the United States was unnaturally excited. The course of normal human life everywhere soon upset. The Gardens opened the following season in financial difficulties, but promising enough if the second season equaled the first. Pavlowa danced. The orchestra superb.

But the official safe was robbed while the creditors were not yet half paid. Dissension came in the management now. Ugly suspicions and threats were rife.

Finally the Edelweiss Brewing Company took advantage of this stupid confusion, virtually chaos, to buy the Gardens for a song. They brought their beer to the Gardens—the beer was good—but they brought no imagination and only beer-garden management. The Gardens never were "beer gardens" in any sense. The Edelweiss did not know that. So the proud Midway Gardens fell into hands beneath their level and languished in consequence. The Edelweiss tried to "hit them up"—hired someone to come in, paint the concrete, stencil the plain surfaces, and add obnoxious features out of balance and nasty. The whole effect was cheapened to suit a hearty bourgeois taste. The scheme that had once been integral was now "decorated" in the meanest and worst of the popular sense of the word. Where there had been form integral with materials and purpose here was raw red, dead white and bad blue *paint*. Another "World's Fair" effect.

And then the affliction befell. The nation went "dry." That was the final blow to the misdirection and insult already befallen the Gardens. Because the country went dry, all the more reason for the sort of thing the Midway Gardens originally represented; the greater the need of gaiety in beauty, beauty in gaiety; the greater the need of some artistic rendezvous for the people of the great city where some stimulating beauty to drink, managed with imagination, could be found.

The Gardens had sunk to the level of the beer-garden—now without beer. No imagination on that level could bring it back into its own. The once distinguished Gardens languished now dreaming of past glory—of possibilities untouched, of a life different from this one of the Chicago gridiron—as sometimes a beautiful woman dreams who has once known honor, position, homage, but—dragged down by inexorable circumstances—knows only shame.

So it went on from this bad to much worse. The place changed hands again, as they say of saloons. These new hands carved it up and over into a dance hall. The Gardens themselves were flooded for a skating rink. The new "They" carried it all to the mob. For this the interiors were bedizened still more. They rouged its cheeks, put carmine on its lips and decked it out in gaudy artificial flowers.

"They" painted the chaste white concrete sculpture in more irrelevant gaudy colors, stenciled more cheap ornament on top of the integral ornament, wrecked the noble line and perfect balance of the whole. All semblance of the original harmony vanished. Yes, a distinguished beautiful woman dragged to the level of the prostitute is now its true parallel. I often thought, "Why will someone in mercy not give them the final blow and tear them down?"

Now, at last, they have been mercifully destroyed to make room for an auto-laundry. I am thankful. The contractor who removed the buildings found them so solidly constructed that he lost more on the contract than it was worth.

RECONSTRUCTION

The German Monograph published by Wasmuth had duly appeared in beautiful format. The work was a success in Germany and Darwin D. Martin helped me to control the sale of the book in America. But the five hundred copies reserved for that purpose went up in smoke when Taliesin burned. Some thirty copies only were saved. The pile in the basement smouldered and smoked for three days after the house had burned to the ground.

Now came relief, a change of scene as—promptly—I was called to build the Imperial Hotel in Tokio, Japan. A commission including the Japanese architect, Yoshitaki, and the intelligent manager of the Imperial Hotel, Aisaku Hayashi. Both had gone around the world to find a model building. Reaching the Middle West they saw the new houses. They were immediately interested in them. Such buildings, though not at all Japanese, they thought would look well in Japan. So they came to the reconstructed Taliesin, Taliesin II, to see me. Taliesin itself impressed them. Said Hayashi-San, "I am taken back to Jimmu Tenno's time." He fell in love with the place as did his gentle wife, Takako-San.

Hayashi's young Takako-San was a beautiful presence at Taliesin at this time, with her exquisite Japanese wardrobe. I regret so few pictures have been preserved for others. Very quiet and reserved in manner, she was very frankly curious about everything, especially our foreign ways. One evening at dinner she said, "Wrieto-San, what means 'goddam'?"

"Goddam?" I wondered where she got that.

"Oh, Takako-San, goddam is a polite word for 'very.' You might say it is a goddam fine evening, or it is goddam fresh butter. Or after dinner you say to your hostess, 'Thank you for your goddam good dinner.' "

"O, O!" she said. ("O" was her invariable English exclamation.) "Oh, I see. Please, Wrieto-San, pass me the goddam fresh butter." And she goddam'd her way through the dinner to a running accompaniment of laughter. Afterward she turned to her host and with perfect naïveté thanked him for the "goddam good dinner."

Was she wiser than she seemed? I was naive enough to wonder if she hadn't known all the time what the laughter meant. Hayashi, whose laughter had joined in, wouldn't enlighten me. I didn't deserve it.

Then and there in the workroom that had escaped destruction I made a preliminary plan according to Hayashi-San's general requirements. The little commission after a week at Taliesin went back to Tokio. Some months later an official invitation came back to come on at once to Tokio. I went as soon as I could. Yes, I was eager to go, for again I wanted to get away from the United States. I still imagined one might get away from himself that way—a little. In spite of all my reasoning power and returning balance I was continually expecting some terrible blow to strike. The sense of impending disaster would hang over me, waking or dreaming. This fitted in well enough with the sense of earthquake, from the actuality of which I should have to defend the new building. But at this time I looked forward to Japan as refuge and rescue. The lands of my dreams—old Japan and old Germany.

AND JAPANESE PRINTS

During my later years at the Oak Park workshop, Japanese prints had intrigued me and taught me much. The elimination of the insignificant, a process of simplification in art in which I was myself already engaged, beginning with my twenty-third year, found much collateral evidence in the print. And ever since I discovered the print Japan had appealed to me as the most romantic, artistic, nature-inspired country on earth. Later I found that Japanese art and architecture really did have organic character. Their art was nearer to the earth and a more indigenous product of native conditions of life and work, therefore more nearly modern as I saw it, than any European civilization alive or dead.

I had realized this during a first visit in pursuit of the Japanese print in 1906. I had gone there to rest after building the Larkin Building and the Martin residence, all but tired out.

A SONG TO HEAVEN

Now again, as the ship's anchor dropped in Yokohama Bay, I was to have earlier feelings deepened, intensified. Imagine, if you have not seen it, a mountainous, abrupt land, the sea everywhere apparently risen too high upon it, so that all gentle slopes to the water's edge are lost. All shore lines abrupt. It is morning. Pure golden skies are seen over far stretches of blue sea dotted in the distance by flocks of white sampan sails—white birds at rest on the blue water.

Imagine, if you can, sloping foothills and mountain sides all antique sculpture, carved, century after century, with curving terraces. The cultivated fields rising tier on tier to still higher terraced vegetable fields, green-dotted. And extending far above the topmost dotted fields, see the very mountain tops themselves corrugated with regular rows of young pine trees pushing diagonally over them. Reforestation, the Imperial Government's share in the pattern, everywhere visible.

Look at the clusters of straw-thatched villages nesting in the nooks of the mountainous land naturally as birds nesting in trees. Or clinging there like the vegetation itself to steep slopes. Turn about, and look at the ruddy-bronze naked bodies of fishermen gleaming red in the sun as they go sculling by. Turn again and see the toilers in the fields, animated spots of true indigo-blue, spots that live in the landscape like the flowers and birds. The birds strangely without song: few of the flowers with any perfume at all but so boldly made, so brilliant and profuse as to seem artificial. I often touched many in flower arrangements to see whether they were real or artificial.

Glance as you go ashore for the first time into the village streets at the swarms of brightly clad, happy children, babies thrust into the bright kimonos on their backs, for the child is the Japanese treasure of treasures. Observe the silhouette of the clothed female figures—young or old—a simple swelling curve from nape of the neck to white cotton-covered heels as all go clogging about with short scraping steps, white feet thrust into tall wooden clogs. These white feet will tell the story of the dwelling ancient Shinto religion built there in that land of the living as a matter of everyday life, and everywhere! The cotton-clad white feet are more significant in the telling of the tale of the Japanese house than anything else could be. Men and women so care for their very young, and their very old, it is said their country is the paradise of old age and of childhood. Old age is a qualification, not a disqualification, in Japan.

218

A proof of civilization, sadly lacking in our own?

All these patient human beings from the very young to the very old seem gladly and humbly resigned to loving one another, respecting one another as they clog along bowing and smiling to one another politely, scraping over damp bare-earth streets the feet made white ,with *tabi,* kept white. These significant *"tabi"* are merely a soft-fitted white-cotton low sock-shoe. When going out, the *tabi* are thrust into the wooden *geta* or clogs waiting at the door. The *geta* are a sort of detachable stilted wooden hoof to be left outside on the dirt or stone pavement of the entry as the "white-feet" leave and step up inside onto spotless *tatami* of the dwelling. The removable sections of firm, padded straw-matting of their house floors are called *tatami.*

So clean are these straw mats of their floors that I have seen women, men too, kneeling on the long side-benches of the railway trains going to and from Tokio—facing the car windows: therefore sitting on their feet in a posture which left the bottoms of their feet nicely put together underneath them but toward you. And, as anyone might see, the very bottoms of their feet were spotless white.

Be clean! Yes—"Be clean" was the soul of Shinto, this ancient religion of Japan the Buddhists found when they came from China. Shinto spoke not of good or a moral man but of a *clean* man. Spoke of clean hands—of a clean heart. And the Shinto religion finally made the Japanese dwelling the cleanest of all clean human things because it is no less *clean* a thing of the spirit. The Japanese have the sense that abhors waste as matter out of place: therefore dirt. Therefore ugliness is dirt. Dirt is ugly. As the centuries went by, every Japanese home whether of the coolie or of the aristocrat has been gradually worked out in this "be clean" spirit. It is as a temple.

Becoming more closely acquainted with things Japanese, I saw the native home in Japan as a supreme study in elimination—not only of dirt but the elimination of the insignificant. So the Japanese house naturally fascinated me and I would spend hours taking it all to pieces and putting it together again. I saw nothing meaningless in the Japanese home and could find very little added in the way of ornament because all *ornament* as we call it, they get out of the way the necessary things are done or by bringing out and polishing the beauty of the simple materials they used in making the building. Again, you see, a kind of cleanliness.

At last I had found one country on earth where simplicity, as natural, is supreme. The floors of these Japanese homes are all made to live on—to sleep on, to kneel and eat from, to kneel upon soft silken mats and meditate upon. On which to play the flute, or to make love.

Nothing is allowed to stand long as a fixture upon the sacred floors of any Japanese home. Everything the family uses is designed to be removed when not in use and be carefully put in its proper place. It is so designed and made. Beautiful to use only when appropriate and use only at the right moment. Even the partitions dividing the floor spaces are made removable for cleaning.

Strangely enough, I found this ancient Japanese dwelling to be a perfect example of the modern standardizing I had myself been working out. The floor mats, removable for cleaning, are all three feet by six feet. The size and shape of all the houses are both determined by these mats. The sliding partitions all occur at the unit lines of the mats. And they all speak of a nine, sixteen or thirty-six mat house, as the case may be.

The simple square, polished wooden posts that support the ceilings and roof all stand at the intersections of the mats. The sliding paper *shoji,* or outside screens that serve in place of windows and enclose the interior room spaces (they are actually the outside walls), all slide back into a recess in the walls. They too are removable. The wind blows clean beneath the floors. The sloping tiled roofs are padded with clay under the heavy curved roof tiles and above the beautiful, low, flat, broad-boarded ceilings to make a cool overhead. The *benjo* or earth-closet is usually made on one side of the garden and set well away from the "devil's corner." And as if to prove that nearly every superstition has a basis of sense, I found that corner to be the one from which the prevailing breezes blow. Semi-detached from the house, the *benjo* is reached under shelter on polished plank floors. Beside it stands always a soft-water cistern, perhaps made of some hollowed-out natural stone or a picturesque garden-feature made or set up out of various natural stones. Or it may be a great bronze bowl brimming with water. A delicate little bamboo dipper lies across the pool of water to be lifted by the little housemaid who will pour clean water over the hands of the master or of his guests as either leaves the *benjo.* Another libation to the Shinto God of Cleanliness. A little confusing at first perhaps to the foreign guest, and no little embarrassment.

The kitchen? Go down several steps to find that, for it is tiled flat with the ground and also goes high up into the rafters for ventilation. It is like a cool, clean, well-ventilated studio. Its simple appointments are of hand-polished concrete or fine hard stone. The kitchen is hung with a collection of copper kettles and lacquer-ware that would drive a Western collector quite off his head, and often has.

The bathroom! This holy of holies is a good-sized detached pavilion, too, again flush with the ground and floored over with stone or tiles so pitched that water thrown from a bucket will drain away. Over the stone floor is a slat-floor of wood on which to stand in bare feet, the water going through freely. The built-in tub is square and deep and wood, made to stand up in. It is always heated from beneath.

As with every native so I have often been soaped and scrubbed before I was allowed to be tubbed. After that only might I step in and cook the germs off me. To any extent I was able to stand up to. Yes, that Shinto bath is a fine and religious thing, but so is everything else about the establishment. And bathing is perpetual. It has been made easy. The Japanese man or woman may loosen only the girdle and the garments all slip off together in one gesture. They put them all on again the same simple easy way. In their costume too, see simplicity, convenience, repose—their bodies as easily kept clean as their houses. Shinto made it and will have it so, the Buddhist notwithstanding. I found it wholly convenient and I wore the native costume whenever in the Japanese inn or dwelling. And much impressed the native inns.

For pleasure in all this human affair you couldn't tell where the garden leaves off and the garden begins. I soon ceased to try, too delighted with the problem to attempt to solve it. There are some things so perfect that nothing justifies such curiosity.

By heaven, here was a house used by those who made it with just that naturalness with which a turtle uses his shell. It is as like the natives as the polished bronze of their skin, the texture of their polished hair or the sly look in their slant and sloe eyes.

Belonging to this domestic establishment, this "domestication of the infinite," everywhere there is to be seen a peculiar concentration on the part of *Ochsan,* the kindly-faced housewife. And even as yet, on the part of her coy daughters O *Kani-san* and O *Hisa-san.* As they all go about their domestic tasks, there must be some religious consecration in their minds to what they do. Or, in their hearts maybe.

"The simplest way with no waste." That is daily Shinto ceremonial in Japan, I found after trying to work it all out that way for my people. You may see this in the most dignified and valued of all Japanese ceremonials—their tea ceremony. All cultured Japanese women, rich or poor, must learn to properly perform the tea ceremony according to cultural rules laid down by the celebrated master-esthete, Rikkyu. He was master too of flower arrangement. I tried to learn it. But this high tea ceremony came simply out of the science or art of most gracefully and economically getting a cup of tea made and reverently serving it to beloved or respected guests. Such reverent concentration as this tea ceremonial carries the idea of "be clean" to such heights—and lengths too—as weary us of the more direct West. We have not the spirit of it nor could we stand it—very long. But in this ceremony the very sense of "be clean" becomes the spiritual attitude that not only abhors waste as

221

matter out of place—therefore dirt—but places disorder of any sort in the same category.

That attitude prolonged, the West finds unbearable. This practical direct application of their ancient Shinto religion would see most of our domestic arrangements tumbled out of the windows into the street, a rich harvest for some junk man. Nevertheless, if Christian houses were ever treated by "Christians" to proper spiritual interpretation such as Japanese interpretation of "Shinto" the resulting integrity of spirit would immediately bankrupt our cherished "pictorial homes." Even if, yes especially *if* such interpretation did not enrich the soul of the West.

How our "good taste" reacts upon and poisons them! By contact with us they have suddenly seen how difficult and unnecessary such painstaking esthetic integrity is. They are seeing now how such discipline as theirs is no longer necessary feature or even part of the temporal authority or power and affluence we exercise. They discover it to be otherwise in the great West they emulate.

Spiritual significance is alive and singing in everything concerning the Japanese house. A veritable song. And it is in perfect unison with their Heaven.

It interested and refreshed me to see the Japanese gratify their desire for fine things—as something naturally added to them. The desire for beauty is no more natural to them than it is to us? But they always have a little recess in even the most humble houses devoted only to appropriate Fine Art entertainment. They call this little treasure-alcove the *Tokonoma*. A single rare painting will be hung for a day in proper season against the quiet-toned plaster walls of the *Tokonoma*. A single cultured flower arrangement in a beautiful vase will be set beside the painting, or *Kakemono*, in this *Tokonoma*. One fine piece of sculpture too, or some abstract form in fine material on a polished lacquer surface, is allowed below that. The three arts are thus brought together by agreeable contrast so that we may see and admire the individual taste of the owner of the house. Never is the trinity without true cultural reference to some poetic significance of the day, occasion or season. Literature, too, would be near by, represented by some poet's profound saying in fine writing framed and hung—usually on the *ranma*—above the interior *shoji*, or sliding paper screens. All these things, however fine, mind you, must be appropriate. And they must be in season or they are not appropriate. They must take the rank of the masterpiece, though, in whatever art.

Truly cultivated people, the Japanese lavish loving care on their beautiful things. To them beautiful things are religious things and their care is a great privilege.

All is in their houses designed for kneeling on soft mats? Of course it is. But the same significant integrity or integrity made significant would work out just as well on one's feet—for us—as it worked for them on their knees. I am trying to work it out for us as I would like to help them do for themselves.

We of the West couldn't live in Japanese houses and we shouldn't. But we *could* live in houses disciplined by an ideal at least as high and fine as this one of theirs—if we went about it for a half century or so. I am sure the West needs this source of inspiration. For once, it can't very well copy. The ethnic eccentricity is too great. The West can copy nearly everything easier than it can copy the Japanese house or Japanese things for domestic uses.

Isn't real barbarism mostly ignorance of principle? Isn't barbarism merely trusting to instinct? Which is just what all our taste does or is with us. Instincts such as ours of the West, demoralized by opulence, are none the less barbaric because they have intellect they don't use, or a past culture they sentimentally abuse. Such demoralization is more dangerous and offensive to life, I should say.

On tortured knees I have tried to learn some of these lessons from the Japanese. I have painfully participated in this "idealized" making of a cup of tea following a Japanese formal dinner, trying to get at some of these secrets if secrets they are. I confess that I have been eventually bored to extinction by the repetition of it all and soon I would avoid the ordeal when I could see an invitation coming. And I freely admit, such discipline is not for us. It is far too severe. Yes, far too severe! We are not yet civilized enough to go that far in idealizing anything in life, not to mention our environment. Or be capable of making our living into ceremonial of any kind except occasionally: for the moment. Our joys and sorrows come and go otherwise. Our recreations mainly—different. And I always become painfully aware of our crudity in the more cultured Japanese environment. Their thumbs fold inward naturally as ours stick up and out. Their legs quietly fold beneath them where ours must stick out and sprawl. It could be said that the culture of our civilization is founded upon the silken leg, the shapely thigh, balanced on the high heel. Theirs is founded upon the graceful arm, the beautifully modeled breast and the expressive hand. The finely molded leg rising from the shapely shoe indicates our heaven. The finely modulated breast and arm and expressive hand indicates theirs. There is a difference.

The truth is the Japanese dwelling is in every bone and fiber of its structure honest and our dwellings are not honest. In its every aspect the Japanese dwelling sincerely means something fine and straightway

223

does it. So it seemed to me as I studied the "song" that we of the West cut ourselves off from the practical way of beautiful life by so many old, sentimental unchristian expedients? Why are we so busy elaborately trying to get earth to heaven instead of seeing this simple Shinto wisdom of sensibly getting heaven decently to earth?

In the morning land I found this simple everyday singing of the human spirit—a "song to heaven" I am calling it—to be the everyday, Shinto-made dwelling place of the Japanese people. I see that song as just as truly a blossom of interior-nature as trees and flowers and bees are blossoms. And I have learned as much for us in our lives from this singing as I could hear or bear. I have seen it on reverent knees beside poor old Baron Kuki—lonely aged diplomat still celebrated for his cuisine and his "collections." Or when some other Japanese gentleman would send for me to come and dine, as so frequently happened, and the solemn tea ceremony as laid down by Rikkyu would inevitably follow the twenty-four or more artistic courses of the formal Japanese dinner.

All this had settled as past experience in my thought of Japan. And the question of modern architecture seemed more involved with Japanese architecture in native-principle than with any other architecture. So in the circumstances—frustration and destruction behind me—I turned hopefully and gratefully toward Japan, once more to live. But as nature and character—both are fate—would have it, I had not come alone as I might have done. And should have done?

Several months after the terrible catastrophe at Taliesin had come a short note expressing sympathy in kindly terms that understood suffering. It came evidently from a developed artist-intelligence. I somehow thought it from some fine-spirited, gray-haired lady-mother who had suffered deeply herself. I spoke of the note to my mother. And, for some reason lonely and spent now, I acknowledged it with a few grateful words. A reply came back asking if the writer might come to see me. She was a sculptress. She said life had crashed for her with much the same sorrow for her as mine. A luckless love affair. She gave me some helpful suggestions as to thought. The philosophy was not so new to me but I had neglected it and needed it now. I wrote, appointing a time at the Orchestra Hall office. She intimated that she preferred to come after office hours.

That was how Miriam Noel appeared in my life.
I was—frankly—astonished. She was the reverse of everything I

had expected. I could not connect her letters with her appearance. But as she sat opposite me at the office desk, when she spoke I understood how she could have written them.

She looked the Parisian by adoption and preference. Brilliant, sophisticated, as might be seen at a glance. She had evidently been very beautiful and was so distinguished by beauty still. A violet pallor. Mass of dark red-brown hair. Clear-seeing eyes with a green light in them. Carriage erect and conscious—figure still youthful. She was richly dressed in the mode, a sealskin cape and cap. On her small hands were several rings. Around her neck she wore a gold chain with a jeweled cross—a monocle, too, was suspended from her neck on a white silken cord. She played with this as she talked. She laid a dainty cigarette case upon the office table. I lit for her the cigarette she took from it—not caring to smoke myself because I did not know how. In her left hand had been a small, black, limp book. She laid this on the desk. It was a copy of *Science and Health* by Mary Baker Eddy. Her latest study in psychology, I thought.

"How do you like me?" she said. A trace of some illness seemed to cling to her in the continuous, slight but perceptible shaking of her head. She looked at me, waiting for some answer to her simple question.

"I've never seen anyone like you," I said honestly.

I learned that her two daughters were married. Her own son a traveling man. She had no one, she said—"nowhere to go and no desires." Her health "had been broken by the tragedy of the luckless love affair which was parallel to mine."

Finally she had been driven from Paris along with other Americans by the recent declaration of war. So she was staying for a time in Chicago with one of her married daughters, Norma. She had heard of me in Paris from the Horace Holleys—had read there of the terrible tragedy. The reading had touched her, and she apologized for being so bold as to write and offer her help. There she was.

Outside the routine of my work I had scarcely spoken to anyone but my mother since the tragedy.

Drowning men—they say so—clutch at straws. Here was no straw but enlightened comradeship, help, more light than I had to see by. Salvation maybe from blackness—blindness. I didn't know. Here began the leading of the blind by the blind.

How do sentimental people ever manage to live on good terms with themselves? By hypocrisy? Often I have asked that question of the most sentimental person I ever knew. Myself. And I am sure the answer is yes. Hypocrisy with oneself—which is the foundation of all hypocrisy toward others.

Now on the way to Tokio the brilliant Miriam alongside.

Arrived in Yokohama Bay for the third time, there stood Fujiyama the venerable, white-hooded, inviolate God of Nippon, against golden sky. After the usual half sea-sickness that always made every hour that would go slowly by on board ship be counted wearily as one hour nearer this landing, the "Empress of China" now rides at anchor in the harbor at dawn. The engines stilled at last—the soft tread of Chinese boys, keeping step with the silence. Remembered beauty of earlier experiences comes rushing to refresh the jaded senses. Two jinrikishas roll off the dock to familiar sights.

We have come here two years after the second crossing to build the Hotel Imperial. High work to be done. Foundation tests already completed, the building is to begin and continue in earnest the better part of four years to come.

Contrary to popular superstition concerning a voluntary, open intimacy between grown-up independent men and women, there is usually a high ideal of life and great self-respect on both sides. There must be. Any sincere attempt to be true to one's self and to each other meets life's demands upon a higher plane of excellence than is ordinary and so a more exacting code of ethics continuously makes demands upon the personal quality and integrity of both the man and the woman. Comradeship makes constant demands that legal marriage may and does dispense with. Especially upon the woman does a voluntary relationship make these increasingly difficult demands. The woman brave enough or foolish enough to go honestly into one has that relationship alone to live by and to live for. Because—it is inevitable—she will owing to environment and circumstances be cut off from society in ways hard enough to bear at first and harder if not impossible to bear as time goes on.

Developed interior life of no mean character is the condition of any success whatever, even temporarily, in any unconventional life a man and a woman may undertake to live openly together.

Still "illegitimate"—that is to say I was still unable to get legitimate freedom from the marriage contract with Catherine. No arguments availing. Therefore any woman foolish enough to be interested in me in the circumstances, if she cared enough for me to live openly with me, would be compelled to take that step into unconventional life or go under cover. Any tragedy after these circumstances is double the similar tragedy in legal marriage, because the relationship is not only utterly defenseless, but is mercilessly assailed, and its failure quite generally welcomed by "good" Society.

Well, I had never in my life learned to hide. If I had learned I should have declined any partnership on those terms with anyone, because unconscious hypocrisy is bad enough. Conscious hypocrisy is a sure and swift corrosion of the soul of any creative artist. No coward ever did creative work, I believed then. I believe it now.

Equivocal conduct hurts those who practice it ten times more than it hurts those it is practiced upon. Secrecy and hypocrisy both do something to the character never to be repaired. And while the hypocrisy of others is hard enough to bear, it is better to *bear* it than to *be* it. It is not the honest living of any life that endangers society, is it? Aren't the *pretended* lives the rotten threads in the social fabric?

I am sure that, while legal marriage in true sense is only for those who do not need it, yet it is so difficult to live long above marriage without the protection it affords and gives that only a coarse character or a very rare virtue can ever hope to survive without the formality.

The management of "The Imperial" allowed me to build a modest place for myself in the new temporary annex. The hotel built this annex from my plans to take care of increase in guests while the "New Imperial" was building. This annex was just finished.

The windows of this little apartment looked out to the south over the Japanese garden and the apartment itself was connected to the hotel for complete service. I had a Japanese boy for my own uses. The fascinating mystery of Tokio was all around us. Tokio is very much like London in many respects. There is so much room in it for surprises. A dingy street outside and palaces immediately within the humble street doors, casual gates and quiet entrance ways.

In my particular nook in Tokio was a small living room with a fireplace—fire always burning—balcony filled with dwarf-trees and flowers, bedroom with balcony and bath, a small dining room where meals were served from the hotel. All were on the main floor of the apartment. But a narrow stair led up from the entrance way to a commodious studio-bedroom built as a penthouse above the roof. I slept there and had set up my drawing board where I could work disturbing no one and tumble into bed when tired out. Into these charming quarters now. For a time a peaceful, mutually helpful relationship. There was a small grand piano—few in Tokio, and our friends were all capable of making good music. There was much good reading, study, rambles through Tokio by night, motor trips sometimes, usually on Sunday, by day. These recreations together with the few friends always faithful in such cases because they understand the situation and respect the characters involved, made up the world we lived in. We knew a good many interesting people and some charming Russians in Tokio, among them the talented Polish Count and Countess Lubiensky, Princess Cheremissinoff, Count and Countess Ablomov, the Ivanoffs, Olga

Krynska, a talented pianist and linguist, and the Japanese Hanis of the wonderful little "School of the Free Spirit." I built a school building suitable to their purpose—one of the rare experiences of my life.

But the clairvoyant Miriam, herself—as I had soon discovered—had for many years been the victim of strange disturbances. Sometimes unnatural exaggerations, mental and emotional. They would spoil life entirely for us for days at a time. I had hunted causes. Yes—I had looked into myself, too, as possible cause.

Nervously she had suffered wreck. Strange disabilities still appeared to cling to her. All would go happily for some days. Then strange perversion of all that. No visible cause. Unnatural exaggeration of emotional nature grew more and more morbid. Mystifying reactions became more violent until something like a terrible struggle between two natures would seem to be going on within her all the time, tearing her to pieces. Then peace for some time and a charming life.

This undertow of strange—often weird—disturbance with happy intervals lasted four years during the construction of the Imperial Hotel. But the outbreaks grew more destructive. Years went by. Drama increased at the expense of good sense and peace. Misery and disquiet not only ran alongside the grueling effort I had to make on the building of the Imperial, but everywhere life itself now went, various galling disturbances would take place.

For me there was always the quest for Japanese prints: the mysterious, wonderful Yedo to explore. The print is more autobiographical than may be imagined. If Japanese prints were to be deducted from my education, I don't know what direction the whole might have taken. The gospel of elimination of the insignificant preached by the print came home to me in architecture as it had come home to the French painters who developed *Cubism* and *Futurism*. Intrinsically the print lies at the bottom of all this so-called *Modernism*. Strangely unnoticed, uncredited. I have often wondered why.

YEDO

Like Ancient Rome, Ancient Yedo was a capital of seven hills, every hill crowned by gay temples, and the highways leading over the hills or to them were hung with long rows of red paper lanterns. Yes, the illuminated sign is ancient! But here, the glowing "advertising" did not repel the eye. The characters, so beautiful in themselves, were ideographs as appropriate to the mind as lantern to the eye.

Teeming, enormous area is fascinating Yedo. A vast city channeled with wide bare-earth streets swarming with humanity their interminable length, beaten down hard by traffic, lined both sides with blue-gray tile-roofed two-story wooden buildings. A great city that is a gigantic village. One of the largest cities in the world. Seven million people already there. Natives in crowds pulling or pushing loaded carts, others peddling, or they go strolling or bargaining along the shopfronts. Queer little horses draw loads so balanced just behind on two great cart-wheels that the loads help push the cart along; strange hump-backed horses are being led through the throngs by their masters. No drivers. Big black bullocks, turquoise headdress wound about their big horns, come laboring slowly along, head down, sullenly drawing enormous loads of logs or merchandise. And sprinkled all through the moving masses of sober-robed people, hand-carts, back-boxes and horses, picturesque strollers and heaving bullocks, innumerable gaily clad children are happily playing. Japanese children seem to always have the right of way in the streets. They are always gaily dressed as flowers in the sun.

Shuttered sedan-chairs, scarlet and gold—the *kago*, blinds drawn, occasionally go by, slung to long black beams carried on the thick shoulders of stout naked-legged coolies, two coolies front, two in the rear. Mystery is everywhere. Maintained—as privacy? Weird figures wander by us seeming from no earthly world. But notwithstanding tremendous activity, brooding quiet is over all as though some enchantment had purposefully wrought unnatural scenes. Yet, everywhere pleasant gaiety gives assurance of intimate human contentment.

Dusk is falling. Softly brilliant globes or cylinders, the red-paper lanterns patterned with strange characters in white or black, begin to glow in the street-vistas of this decorated twilight. And there are rows of soft red lanterns countering on rows along the streets, and always there are more clusters of the beautiful ones and occasionally a simple large one. On every building they hang and move to and fro as the breezes blow. Some hang above the street on bamboo poles. Light, here is something soft to beguile the eyes. Evidently here we see the ancient advertising-medium of a limitless city. The illuminated sign is not only ancient, it is beautiful.

Along all highways and byways the shops; second stories lining the upper sides of the swaming streets are dwelling-places. Sliding paper closure of the openings is usually protected by vertical wooden slats in so many clever geometrical patterns. As evening falls these screens become luminous from within as in daylight they were luminous from without. Charming silhouettes are all the time flickering on them, play to and fro as human figures pass. The plaintive twang of samisen-strings plucked by a broad ivory key blade in the hands of the shop-keeper's daughter—Hirani-san or Nobu-san—maybe, is heard coming into the glowing, unnaturally quiet scene. Yes, it all looks, it does—*just like the prints!*

The lower stories of all buildings lining the labyrinth of earthen highways and byways are shops wide open to the street from side to side. All are ingeniously crammed to overflowing with orderly array of curious or brilliant merchandise. On all seven hills are famous temples and gardens, famous places celebrated by the prints and at this moment—say the year is 1800.

Therefore the quiet but gay life of this ancient modern-capital is aware of Toyonobu, Harunobu, Shunsho and Shigemasa. Utamaro Hokusai and Hiroshige are soon to come to work. Commodore Perry not yet insisted upon international cooperation. No Hollanders have arrived. Will Adams, hardy Englishman stranded there, is the only Westerner to have seen this land of mist, moon, snow, flower—and woman—until we reconstruct it from the prints. This hardy, shipwrecked sailor is there now as much because he wants to be as because the shoguns will not allow him to leave. Through him, only, does this singular culture, developing in complete isolation for three hundred years, learn anything at all of Western ways. By way of the print alone does the West know anything of Japanese ways in ancient Yedo.

Laughter in Yedo—always laughter. Always the sound of the scraping clogs. Always these weird calls and cries of street vendors. Always snatches of weird song and strange animal cries. Japanese music seems to us an animal cry. At night—the mysteries of Silence deepen. Song-like sounds that might be—but are not—made by the wind are everywhere. Nasal twang of *samisen*-strings punctures it all at intervals as the sweet wail of flutes comes to us like lovely colored ribbons of sound from the private family gardens secreted behind the shops. Heard over all is the staccato of running accompaniments to this festival for the eyes, the ceaseless crescendo and diminuendo: measured, scraping sound made by innumerable *geta* in the graveled streets of the thronging city—continuous diapason to obbligato of far-off cries—like strange animals calling to each other. Ripples of soprano laughter and glad voices nearby are reassuring.

But see everywhere warm family affection. True contentment. The night life of Yedo meantime industrious even until midnight—wherever there is light to see by. This strange night-scene is pervaded always by ceaseless quiet movement. Wherever the fascinating red and white paper lanterns glow, deep shadows hover and quiver, for Yedo is not bright at night but subdued like some modern society-woman's red-shaded drawing-room, and the streets are as orderly, mannerly and clean as her carpets.

230

Human figures of this scene are so simply robed! They may be, as simply, unrobed.

This life of Yedo swarms. A perpetual swarming.

Within, behind the shopfronts, all is repose. Kindly, glowing, humane and homely repose. At night, behind all the softly glowing lights of the gently swinging lanterns with their mysterious messages and the lambent flambeaux of open shops there is always this under-growth of dark and mystery. A group of sinister, black-robed, double-sworded figures come by, black hoods on their heads, swords alongside that make all other swords seem innocuous. They pass by us again: gallant strides, reckless swagger. Such side and *style* would make Fifth Avenue gasp. Adventurous *Samurai* abroad! Here come enormous, bulky, brutal figures but with kindly faces. Their long black hair is brushed back high from the forehead. These are the giant strong-men followed by several attendants and the shuffling of adoring crowds. The bulk of several Japanese is in any one of these: they are the *Sumo* or professional wrestlers bred in Tokio for that purpose alone and for many centuries. When famous, the *Sumo*, too, are celebrated by the prints. To inbreed human beings for a special purpose as we breed race horses! Yes, they did it.

See more elegant figures! The *Komuso*, aristocratic street adventur-ers. Faces concealed by huge bell-shaped head-cover-like baskets of woven straw, going about with short-swords stuck in their broad belts.

Tea houses? Everywhere. This one by Tokio-bay is inviting because it is so thickly hung with gay red-paper lanterns, entrances curtained with indigo blue hangings patterned with the huge white *mon* of the keeper's household. Push through the hangings with us and enter to find, looking down at us from the matted floors just beyond the en-trance, smiling pretty Japanese geishas down on their knees bowing low and bowing lower—rising eagerly to take us by the hand and lead us in. Our shoes? Well, we take the things off, step up in stocking feet on to clean, fresh-smelling straw mats. Clean.

Look about you now and see for the first time what simplicity of form and beautiful materials left clean for their own sake can do for a scene of shifting color and quick movement. Clean—clean and silent for soft white-shod feet. How can anything human be so polished and clean?

So we pass by the rooms and glimpse charming sights. Guests too robed in fine silks, fans in hand, heads gleaming with polished black. Ah! you see—in everything inimitable, imperishable style! Black, in it-self a property, is revelation here.

231

Little cages of fireflies hang to the posts, as post by post we pass along the open corridors against the outside dark. Finally all will open along one entire roomside to an enchanted scene: the Japanese garden! *Samisen* notes come from all directions like pervasive insect-notes in a summer field. We hear the tender wail of flutes more distinctly here as though a door had opened; we see moon-lanterns glowing under spreading pine trees as high moonlight streams down over all; soft light of the new moon gleams on the still water, softly glances from the cool splashing of gently falling water over great black stones. Thin silver streams cascade down piles of fantastic rugged rock half hidden in dark masses of green *sonari*. Bright flowers and blooming shrubs massed about the rocks and rugged tree trunks down to the water's very edge.

This seems an ancient countryside, this garden. Or an opal empire. But it may be, yes, *it must be,* very small. How small would be unbelievable! Twenty-five feet square!

We come here from another, noisier, more vulgar world and gratefully kneel on somber silken cushions, subdued, entranced—looking humbly upon this environment of simple perfect art.

A marvelous work of art enters the scene: fashioned upon the head, hand and breast instead of upon the leg and thigh as she would have been fashioned in the West. She softly asks what the most honorable gentleman will be pleased to have her unworthy self bring to him, this most tender of evenings, for his good pleasure? Black heads meantime are moving everywhere within the adjoining rooms. Black gleams over smooth oval powder-whitened faces punctuated by lips of scarlet, scarlet to match the *saki* cups?

Black! the science and art of "black" in everything. Decorous black eyes slyly slant upon you from every direction as the little artful beings move noiselessly about, grace and refinement in every movement. For what, might we ask? Crudely, but with a smile we say simply, *"Gohan."* Leaving all to them. What else to do?

Soon take the clean pine twin-sticks in your fingers, break them apart. The *hashi* are fresh, for use but once, and do your best by the steaming rice as the cover is lifted from the big black lacquered bowls. Rice like that is cooked only in Japan. The pretty maid fills and refills our smaller red lacquer bowls from the large black one. The perfectly done fish on the Nebeshima china on the lacquered trays may please you. Savory fish-soups under cover in the delicately lacquered patterns of the covered golden bowls may not. You are unaccustomed to fish-soup? Curiously designed sweets are laid out on the painted, gaily decorated stands. They are disappointing to us, not sweet enough as we know sweets. Meantime distant drums have been beating beneath the other sounds—beating, as we now become aware, in strange, secretly frustrating rhythms. The ear strives and fails to catch the rhythm—syncopated like nothing so much as raindrops falling from the eaves on hollow metal. Then, tired of eating or the attempt to eat, the little *musme* bring in pretty woven baskets, in each a steaming wet towel wrung dry, and they offer it to us in a separate basket. We refresh our hands and faces. They are gently regarding us the while with shy amusement. The little *musme* break into gales of laughter as we groan and awkwardly stretch our legs to take the strange kinks out of them, or as we fall back to our knees in the attempt to rise after sitting so long on our heels. *Saki* had nothing to do with it but it might have had.

To and fro in the corridors go geisha parties, undulating noiselessly to and fro, *samisen* in hand, faces crimsoned slightly at the temples, foreheads and cheeks whitened all over to the brilliant-scarlet lips. All just as Harunobu, Kiyonaga and Utamaro, Shunsho and Shigemasa faithfully recorded so the world might never lose it. A fine lady plays the *koto,* the *koto's* graceful length laid upon the expanse of matting. She kneels over it and caresses minor chords from it. Then say—as you will—"such gentleness!" "Such good sense in elegant simplicity!" With what disciplined beauty Japan has mingled the uses and purposes of everyday life! Mingled? No. *Made* the necessities of life beautiful. This *is* civilization, you say. Feeling it all too good to be true. There must be some sinister side to the picture, lurking out there in the dark! Maybe! This is the East you know! Skepticism from the West looks warily about. Now we have seen nothing, yet, immoral.

But of course it is. It must be immoral?

Ugliness being a kind of virtue in the West, beauty must be immoral in the East. But *seems* so innocent, naive and charming.

Come now, see the Oriental Courtesan, favorite subject of the prints and basis of much moral reproof.

Immoral in this land of the rising sun? No. Only unmoral.

But can what is naturally sordid be made beautiful? No.

But, well, we climb into sitting posture, knees up to chins, crammed into the romantic Kago, glancing as we pass by into miles of open shopfronts, many of them "news" shops, that is to say, shops full of "prints." We pass peddlers, pilgrims with jangling-staffs, carrying on their backs slender cabinets filled with trays. The trays sometimes filled with exquisite prints of every sort by popular artists of the day, making portraits of popular stage favorites, prints to be sold in public places. These are the animated newsstands of that period. These peddlers were then all the newsboys there were.

We see posted in the shops colored pictures, prints, of gorgeous *Oiran* or Courtesans and their *Komuso,* or little pupils.

"Advertising" was active then as now, but the artist's individuality never suffered on account of it. Why?

Ahead of us looms a great black gate. Directly in front of the gateway a great cherry tree is in bloom; like drifted pink snow in the light of innumerable red and white lanterns. Just inside the gate we come upon the *Oiran* in Yoshiwara procession. The prints prepared us for that. The procession now is prepared for us.

In the center of each group of the elaborate pageant is a gorgeous feminine creature exaggerated by resplendent robes and extravagant head-dress. She is slowly moving with feminine traits deliberately exaggerated, undulating with stately artificiality on white-clad feet thrust into high black-lacquered clogs: face plastered dead-white, lips painted the limit of scarlet. The only animate human thing in the ensemble of gorgeous robes, impassive face and black and gold head-dress is the pair of sly black eyes moving in the white mask to regard you for one brief, seeing moment—mischief in their depths. With measured tread and artificial grace she moves on in slow pomp, surrounded by other creatures as feminine but far less gorgeous. Following just behind this gorgeous *Oiran* come two *Komuso*, plaintive little creatures, wonderfully dressed, made likewise in little: being stately as small editions can be. Such splendors as you can only call barbaric are before you. The procession centering about the barbaric queen, too queenly for any but barbarism, moves slowly to the gate, now softly flecked by the falling petals of the great cherry tree. Other gorgeous *Oiran* are coming, surrounded by similar groups lit by dancing colored lanterns as was she—queen of the Yoshiwara.

The gorgeous procession turns to go back again. Sober-robed men, like gray moths hovering about some glittering flame, follow, fascinated. Such splendor dazzles duller lives. An apparition of heaven.

Individuality marks each *Oiran* and her group, in spite of the severely conventional style that seems imposed upon all.

Here then, as high black-lacquered clogs scrape slowly over the roadway now pink with fallen cherry-flower petals, is the ceremonial glorification of something we of the West never understood, if indeed we are able to understand it.

Here it appears a woman raised to nth power as symbol among men. You will try to understand that these creatures are not "women" but Woman. Woman aggrandized, Institutionalized. Demoralized? No. Only *professionalized* on a plane that here seems to carry premiums in place, grace and preferment. Here a compelling power is made artistic and deliberately cultured. Not yet awakened to "moral" discrimination, so not sinful? Was there pride, think you, in doing surpassingly well this pleasuring of men? Was there conscientious sense of the value of the office—and a real ambition to deserve well of the luxury and opportunity to shine resplendent as the object of man's desire?

Well, judging from the poetic inscriptions on the prints of the period advertising and celebrating the *Oiran*—Yes.

The social power or some more natural power at this stage of Japan's culture placed this premium *"woman"* upon these professional women. In all extravagance. Artists like Utamaro lived and designed popular series of prints wherein woman is made symbol of almost everything. Here in the Yoshiwara the next artist enjoyed and criticized and was enjoyed and criticized. Here in the Yoshiwara of Yedo the literati of the times came to remember to forget. Here the *Samurai* in black masks came seeking release. And romance in the intoxication of a freedom they could never otherwise know made them lay their swords aside.

The social graces and such fine arts of music, poetry, dancing as Japan knew were the higher accompaniment to the conviviality, here on no bestial plane. The "moral" element that could make it bestial was lacking. As it was with the Philosopher and the Hetaira in Athens itself, so probably here in Yedo except that here it was an esthetic rite.

Then all this knew nothing of its own degradation? No.

If we look at it similarly we too may see what beauty it had. If we bring to it eyes confirmed in assumption of the "unclean," then we will see only that.

But in the artist's celebration of this life as we find it illustrated in the now antique Yedo daily journal, prints of the *ukiyoye*, we see proof not of vice but of innocence.

As the prints show it to us we see that love of life and beauty was a poetic theme running like a thread of fine silk through all that Yoshiwara life of the Yedo courtesan. There was raw but elemental romance in it. It could not be so now in the degradation that remains of the institution as it exists in Japan and as it has always been in the West. All would be money now and therefore no romance at all except the fortuitous romance of luck.

We find it so recorded in the most exquisite piece of illustrated magazine making in this world—the graphic journalistic report by Shunsho and Shigemasa called "Beauties of the Little Green Houses," showing, as it does, the elegance of these lives of *filles de joie* of old Japan a century, or more, ago.

So, while conceptions of the great hotel grew, and later the building itself began to rise, Yedo was a presence always in which to search for the invaluable record of that time, in the print: a window through which

I looked upon my own work. A byroad by which I saw it. Yet I must not linger more with the great heart of Japanese life, antique Yedo, but pass to the telling of the building of the New Imperial Hotel of Tokio. Yedo 1915.

BUILDING AGAINST DOOMSDAY (WHY THE GREAT EARTHQUAKE DID NOT DESTROY THE IMPERIAL HOTEL)

From infancy, a sort of subjective contemplation, minds and hearts of Japanese are fixed upon the great calm mountain God of their nation—sacred Fujiyama brooding in majesty and eternal calm over all. They deeply worship as the mountain continually changes moods, combining with sun and moon, clouds and mist, in a vast expression of elemental beauty the like of which in dignity and repose exists nowhere else on earth.

It is not too much to say that the sacred mountain is the God of old Japan; Japan the Ancient Modern.

The dreaded force that made the great mountain continually takes its toll of life from this devoted people, as the enormous weight of the deep sea beside the tenuous island, deepest sea in the world, strains earth-crust, opening fissures in the bottom of the great valley in which it rests and the sea rushes down to internal fires to become gas and steam expanding or exploding internally, causing earth convulsions that betray the life on the green surface. Great wave movements go shuddering through the body of their land, spasmodically changing all overnight in immense areas. Whole villages disappear. New islands appear as others are lost and all on them. Shores are reversed as mountains are laid low and valleys lifted up. Always flames! The terror of it all faces conflagration at the end.

Trained by these disasters of centuries to build lightly on the ground—the wood and paper houses natural to them may be kindled by spark. When fire starts it seldom stops short of several hundred homes. Usually thousands, or complete destruction. So, when the earthquake is violent, fire finishes the terrible work.

The dead not swallowed up are buried, and once more *Shikata-gai-nai* (it cannot be helped) goes patiently on as before. Naturally the earth-waves seem fate and unconquerable. A force useless to combat by strength alone, for it is mightier than any force at man's command. *Shikata-gai-nai!* This stoicism I have seen and lived with four years or more while preparing to meet this awful force by building on ground which the seismograph shows is never for a moment still—preparing to meet the temblor by other means than rigid force.

The foreigner came with the advent of Commodore Perry to share Japanese joys and sorrows. Soon a building was needed to shelter the foreign element of Tokio, the capital of Japan. A social clearing house became necessary as a consequence of the new foreign interest in Japan, because, for one reason, no foreigner could live on the floor. The need steadily increased. At that time the Mikado took it upon himself to meet the need, and asked the Germans to build one of their characteristic national wood and plaster extravaganzas.

That wretched marvel grew obsolete. Need of another, a greater one, imperative. The Imperial household, this time, proposed to share with the capitalists of the Empire, shipowners, cement manufacturers, bankers, tobacco interests, etc. the task of providing the new accommodation, and I, an American, was chosen to do the work.

No foreigner yet invited to Japan had taken off his hat to Japanese traditions. When foreigners came, what they had back home came too, suitable or not, and the politely humble Japanese, duly impressed, took the offering and marveled. They tried to do likewise in their turn. Japanese fine-art traditions are among the noblest and purest in this world, giving Chinese origins due credit. It was my instinct not to insult them. The West has much to learn from the East—and Japan was the gateway to that great East of which I had been dreaming since I had seen my first Japanese prints—and read my first Laotze.

But this terrible natural enemy to all building whatsoever—the temblor!

The terror of the temblor never left me while I planned the building nor while, for more than four years, I worked upon it. Nor is anyone allowed to forget it—sometimes awakened at night by strange sensations as at sea, strangely unearthy and yet rumbling earth-noises. Sudden shocks, subsidence—and swinging. Again shock after shock and upheaval, jolting back and swinging. A sense of the bottom falling from beneath the building, terror of the coming moments as cracking plaster and groaning timbers indicate the whole structure may come crashing and tumbling down. There may be more awful threat to human happiness than earthquake. I do not know what it can be.

The Japanese turn livid, perspiration starts on them, but no other sign unless the violence becomes extreme, then—panic. I studied the temblor. Found it a wave-movement, not of sea but of earth—accompanied by terrific shocks no rigidity coud stand.

Because of the wave movements, deep foundations like long piles would oscillate and rock the structure. Therefore the foundation should be short or shallow. There was sixty to seventy feet of soft mud below the upper depth of eight feet of surface soil on the site. That mud seemed a merciful provision—a good cushion to relieve the terrible shocks. Why not float the building upon it? A battleship floats on salt water. And why not extreme lightness combined with tenuity and flexibility instead of the great weight necessary to the greatest possible rigidity? Why not, then, a building made as the two hands thrust together palms inward, fingers interlocking and yielding to movement—but resilient to return to original position when distortion ceased? A flexure—flexing and reflexing in any direction. Why fight the quake? Why not sympathize with it and outwit it?

That was how the building began to be planned.

The most serious problem was how to get the most carrying power out of that eight feet of cheese-like soil that overlay the liquid mud. During the first year of plan-making, I made borings nine inches in diameter eight feet deep and filled them with concrete. Arranged to test the concrete pins thus made. Got carloads of pig iron and loaded the pins until they would drive into the ground. Kept the test figures of loads and reactions. Took borings all over the site to find soft pockets. Water stood in the holes two feet below the surface, so the concrete had to go in quickly as the borings were completed. Later, tapered piles were driven in to *punch* the holes and pulled out—the concrete thrown directly in as soon as the pile was out of the way.

These data in hand, the foundation plan was made to push these concrete pins two feet on centers each way over the entire areas on which the wall footings were to spread. The strength of the whole depth of eight feet of top soil was thus brought to bear at the surface. That was simple. Here was a compressible soil that might take a squeeze under the broad footings to add to the friction of the pins. Experiments showed the squeeze could safely be added to the friction. This meant a settlement of the building of five inches, the building itself driving the piles that much deeper. This was economy, but dangerous and more complicated.

Finally the building was computed pound by pound and distributed according to test data to "float" below the grade of the ground surface—and it did. With some few slight variations it stayed there.

This foundation saved hundreds of thousands of dollars over the foundations then in use in Tokio. But had the owners of the Imperial superficially known what was contemplated something might have happened to prevent it. Rumor nearly did prevent it. Here, however, was the desired shock-absorber, a cushion, pins and all, to be uniformly loaded and put to work against the day of reckoning.

Now how to make the flexible structure instead of the foolish rigid one? Divide the building into parts. Where the parts were necessarily more than sixty feet long, joint these parts clear through floors, walls,

238

footings and all, and manage the joints in the design. Wherever part met part, through joints also. So far, good sense, and careful calculation.

A construction was needed where floors would not be carried between walls, because subterranean disturbances might move the walls and drop the floors. Why not then carry the floors as a waiter carries his tray on upraised arm and fingers at the center—*balancing* the load? All supports centered under the floor slabs like that instead of resting the slabs on the walls at their edges as is usually the case?

This meant the cantilever, as I had found by now. The cantilever is most romantic, most free, of all principles of construction, and in this case it seemed the most sensible. The waiter's tray supported by his hand at the center is a cantilever slab in principle. And so concrete cantilever slabs continuous across the building from side to side, supported in that way, became the structure of the Imperial Hotel at Tokio.

Roof tiles of Japanese buildings have murdered countless thousands of Japanese in upheavals, so a light hand-worked green copper roof was planned. Why kill more?

The outer walls were spread wide, thick and heavy at the base, growing thinner and lighter toward the top. Whereas Tokio buildings were all top-heavy. The center of gravity was kept low against the swinging movements and the slopes were made an esthetic feature of the design. The outside cover-hangs of the cantilever slabs where they came through the walls were all lightened by ornamental perforations enriching the light and shade of the structure. The stone everywhere under foot in Tokio was a workable light lava weighing as much as green oak. It was considered sacrilege to use this common material for the aristocratic edifice. But finally it was used for the feature material and readily yielded to any sense of form the architect might choose to indicate. And the whole structure was to be set up as a double shell— two shells, an exterior of slim cunning bricks, and an interior one of fluted hollow bricks raised together to a convenient height of four feet or more. These shells were to be poured solid with concrete to bind them together.

The great building thus became a jointed monolith with a mosaic surface of lava and brick. Earthquakes had always torn piping and wiring apart where laid in the structure and had flooded or charged the building. So all piping and wiring was to be laid free of construction in covered concrete trenches in the ground of the basements, independent even of foundations. Mains and all pipes were of lead with wiped joints, the lead bends sweeping from the trenches to be hung free in vertical pipe shafts, from which the curved lead branches were again taken off, curved, to the stacks of bathrooms. Thus any disturbance might flex and rattle but not break the pipes or wiring.

Last but not least there was to be an immense reservoir or pool as an architectural feature of the entrance court—connected to the water system of the hotel and conserving the roof water.

Thus the plans were made so that all architectural features were practical necessities, and the straight line and flat plane were respectfully modified in point of style to a building bowing to the traditions of the people to whom the building would belong. The *nature* of the design too, I wanted to make something their intensive hand methods could do well, because we didn't know what machinery could be used. It was impossible to say how far we could go with that. Probably not very far.

Finally the plans were ready.

No estimates could be had. It was all so unfamiliar, no commercial concern would touch it. Nothing left but to abandon the whole or organize to build it ourselves. The Imperial Hotel and its architect and builder. The language was a barrier. The men and methods strange.

But the foreign architect—with eighteen or twenty architectural students from the Japanese universities, several of whom were taken to Wisconsin during the plan-making period—and one expert foreign builder, Paul Mueller of Chicago, two foreigners, all else native, we organized with the hotel manager, Hayashi-San, as general manager. We had already bought pottery kilns in Shizuoka and made the long slim cunning bricks, of a style and size never made before for the outside shell. They were now ready to use. We had also made the fluted hollow bricks for the inside shell, the first in the Empire. We bought a fine lava-quarry at Oya near Nikko for the feature-material and started a flood of dimension stone moving down to the site in Tokio—a stream that kept piling into the building for four years. The size of the hole left in the ground at Oya was about like the excavations for the Grand Central Terminal.

We had a hundred or more clever stone choppers beating out patterns of the building on the greenish, leopard-spotted lava, for that period. On an average we employed about six hundred men continually for four years. As a large proportion of them came from the surrounding country, they lived round about in the building as we built it. With their numerous families, there they were—cooking, washing, sleeping. And we tried faithfully—sometimes frantically and often profanely—to teach them how to build it, halfway between our way and their way.

We tried the stone-planer with the stone-cutters. It was soon buried beneath the chips that flew from their busy stone-axes. Tried derricks and gin-poles and hoists. They preferred to carry heavy loads and enormous stones up inclined planes on their shoulders. We tried to abolish scaffolding and teach them to lay brick from the inside. Not to be done.

240

They lashed tapering poles together in cunning ways as for centuries and clung with prehensile toes to the framework.

How skillful they were! What craftsmen! How patient and clever. So instead of wasting them by vainly trying to make them come our way—we went with them their way. I modified many original intentions to make the most of what I now saw was naturally theirs. The language grew less an obstruction. But curious mistakes were perpetual. It is true that the Japanese approach to any matter is a spiral. Their instinct for attack in any direction is oblique and volute. But they make up for it in gentleness and cleverness and loyalty. Yes, the loyalty of the retainer to his *Samurai*. They soon educated us and all went pretty well.

The countenance of the building began to emerge from the seemingly hopeless confusion of the enormous area now covered by the building materials of its terraces and courts and hundreds of families. And the workmen grew more and more interested in it. It was no uncommon thing to see groups of them admiring and criticizing too as some finished portion would emerge—criticizing intelligently.

There was a warmth of appreciation and loyalty unknown in the building circles of our country. A fine thing to have experienced.

The curse of the work was the holiday. There were no Sundays, but a couple of holidays every fortnight instead, and it took a day or two to recover from most of them. So the work dragged. And the rainy season! The Japanese say it rains up from the ground as well as down from the sky—in Tokio. We did succeed in abolishing the expensive cover-shed of tight roof and hanging matting sides under which most buildings are built in Japan. We congratulated ourselves until we found they knew their climate better than we did. Had we protected them from the rain and the burning sun the buildings would have been finished about seven months sooner—besides making all more comfortable and so more efficient.

A few more such "successes" would have been enough.

The directors met regularly for a couple of years and began to complain.

Rumors reached them from the English (the English love the Americans in Tokio) and Americans (why are Americans invariably so unpleasant to one another abroad?) to the effect that the architect of their building was mad. In any earthquake the whole thing would tumble apart—and the whole building would sink out of sight in the mud beneath. There was room enough for it in that cushion of mud. Where all had been pleasant enthusiasm, things began to drag. The loyalty of my own office force never for a moment wavered, but manager Hayashi was daily hectored and censured. At this crucial time it became apparent that three and a half million yen more would be necessary to complete and furnish the work. Things looked dark.

By now a small army was working away in the lower stories of the building as it was completed. As soon as one portion was built it became a hive of frantic industry. The copper features and fixtures and roof tiles were all made there; the interior woodwork and furniture—the upholstery and many other things went on in the vast interior spaces as soon as the floor slabs covered them over.

I had brought examples of good furniture from home and took them apart to teach the Japanese workmen how to make them according to the new designs which made them all part of the structure. They were fine craftsmen at this. Rug designs had gone to Pekin. The rugs were being woven there to harmonize with the interior features of the great rooms and the guest rooms. We were about two-thirds of the way over with the building itself. The foreigners had no way of keeping track of costs or finding out much about them in detail. So things had gone on for several years.

The crash came.

The directors were called together.

Baron Okura was chairman of the board—representing besides his own interests, the interest of the Imperial Royal Household, sixty per cent, besides ownership of the ground. There was also Asano-san—a white-haired Samson of the shipping interests—a powerful man with shaggy white brows and piercing eyes. Murai of the tobacco interests—a peacemaker, with pleasant ways always. Wakai, the banker, as broad as he was long, with a beard that reached below the table when he stood up. Kanaka, a half dozen others.

Baron Okura had rather sponsored me from the beginning. He was in trouble now. The meetings had been held in the old hotel building and were pleasant social affairs with refreshments. This one was not. It looked black. A long time, it had been threatening. The Baron, a black-haired youth of eighty—a remarkable man regarded as one of the astute financial powers of the Empire—sat at the head of the table. I sat on his left. On his right sat his cultivated secretary, a Harvard graduate, who was interpreter. It doesn't matter where the others were. They were there and all talking at once. I answered the leading questions without end. The foundations. Always the foundations—and the money. The money!

The Baron was patient and polite—for some time. His lower lip had a trick of sticking out and quivering when he became intense. This personal idiosyncrasy of his was evident now. Suddenly he rose—leaned forward, head thrust forward, angry, hissing, pounding the table with both fists—extraordinary conduct for him.

The crowd went back and down as though blown down by the wind.

There was silence—the Baron still standing looking over toward me. Not knowing what it was all about I instinctively rose. The interpreter rose, too, and said, "The Baron says that if the 'young man' (all things are relative) will himself remain in Japan until the building is finished, he the Baron will himself find the necessary money and they could all go to—" whatever the Japanese word is for the place they could go to.

Although homesick by now and sick besides I reached out my hand to the Baron. The compact was made. The meeting was over. The directors filed out, red and angry to a man, instead of happy to have the responsibility lifted from them.

Was it Pericles who enacted some such rôle as the Baron's when the Parthenon was building? Anyway, the building of the new Imperial went on. Now every director became a spy. The walls had ears. Propaganda increased. My freedom was gone. I worked under greater difficulties than ever. But my little band of Japanese apprentices was loyal and we got ahead until another storm broke.

"Why not," said the directors to the Baron, "eliminate the pool and save 40,000 yen?" The Baron saw sense in this and sent for me. His mind was made up. No arguments took effect. I told him via interpreters that it was the last resource against the quake. In disaster, the city water would be cut off, and the window frames being wood in the 500-foot building front along the side street where wooden buildings stood, fire could gut the structure even though it withstood the quake. I had witnessed five terrible fires in Tokio already—walls of flame nothing in any degree inflammable could withstand.

No matter. The pool must come out. No, I said, it is wrong to take it out, and by such interference he would release me from my agreement and I could and would go home with no further delay. And I left his office. But I did not leave Tokio and the pool went in to play its final part in the great drama of destruction that followed two years later.

Another year and I could go home. The Tokio climate, so moist and humid summer and winter, depressing except in fall and early spring, together with the work and anxiety were wearing me down.

Now came a terrible test that calmed troublesome fears: made the architect's position easier.

The building construction was about finished. The architect's work-room had been moved to the top of the left wing above the promenade entrance. It was nearly noon. The boys in the office, reduced to ten, were there, and workmen were about. Suddenly with no warning a gigantic jolt lifted the whole building, threw the boys down sprawling with their drawing boards. A moment's panic and hell broke loose as the wave motions began. The structure was literally in convulsions. I was knocked down by the rush of workmen and my own boys to save their own lives. It is a mercy there were not more workmen in the roof space beyond, or I should have been trampled out. As I lay there I could clearly see the ground swell pass through the construction above as it heaved and groaned to hideous crushing and grinding noises. Several thunderous crashes sickened me, but later these proved to be the falling of five tall chimneys of the old Imperial, left standing alone by the recent burning of that building.

At the time it seemed as though the banquet hall section, invisible just behind the work-room, had crashed down.

Only one faithful assistant stayed through this terrible ordeal. Endo-San, loyal right-bower—white to the teeth—perspiring. Otherwise the building was utterly deserted. We got up shaking to the knees and went together out onto the roofs. There across the street were crowds of frightened workmen. They had thrown down their tools and run for their lives, even those working in the courts. There they all stood strangely silent, pasty-faced, shaking. A strange silence too was everywhere over the city. Soon fires broke out in a dozen places. Bells rang and pandemonium broke. Women dragging frightened children ran weeping and wailing along the streets below.

We had just passed through the worst quake in fifty-two years. The building was undamaged. A transit put on the foundation levels showed no deviation whatever.

The work had been proved.

Hayashi-San, when reports of the damage to the city and none to the building came in, burst into tears of gratitude. His life had barely been worth living for more than a year, so cruel were the suspicions, so harassing the doubts. The year passed. The building was now so nearly complete there was no longer pressing need for the presence of the architect.

Another wing remained to be finished but it was a duplication of the one already done and furnished. So I could go home with a good conscience. My clients, headed by the Baron, were generous, added substantial proof of appreciation to my fee, and I was "farewelled" first at a champagne luncheon by the Baron and his directors; then at a tea-house entertainment by the building organization itself, all with unique expressions of esteem; finally by the workmen after their no less generous fashion. Witness:

The day of sailing came. To get to my car I had to pass from the rear through the new building to the front. All was deserted and I wondered. Arrived at the entrance courts, there all the workmen were, crowding the spaces, watching and waiting. Already there had been gratifying evidence of appreciation—I thought—but here was the real thing. This could have happened nowhere but in Japan. Here was the spirit I had tried to compliment and respect in my work.

As their architect came out they crowded round, workmen of every rank from sweepers to foremen of "the trades," laughing, weeping, wanting awkwardly to shake hands—foreign fashion. They had learned "aw-right," and mingled it now with "arigato" and "*sayonara* Wrieto-San."

Too much, and "Wrieto-San" broke. They followed the car down along Hibiya way to the station, running, shouting "*Banzai,* Wrieto-San, *banzai!*"

The dock at Yokohama, eighteen miles away, was reached by train, to find that sixty of the foremen had paid their way down from Tokio to shout again and wave good-bye, while they faded from sight as the ship went down the bay. Such people! Where else in all the world would such touching warmth of kindness in faithfulness be probable or even possible?

Two years later—1923—in Los Angeles. News of terrible disaster shouted in the streets. Tokio and Yokohama wiped out! The most terrible temblor of all history!

Appalling details came day after day. Nothing human, it seemed, could have withstood the cataclysm. Too anxious to get any sleep I tried to get news of the fate of the New Imperial, of Shugio, Endo, Hayashi-San, the Baron and the host of friends I had left over there. Finally, the third night and about two in the morning the telephone bell rang. The *Examiner* wished to inform me that the Imperial Hotel was completely destroyed. My heart sank but I laughed, "How did they *know?*" The night editor read the dispatch, a list of Imperial University, Imperial Theater, Imperial Hospital, Imperial this and Imperial that.

"You see," I said, "how easy it is to get the Imperial Hotel mixed with the other Imperials? I am sure if anything is above ground in.Tokio it is that building. If you print this destruction as 'news' you will have to retract."

Their turn to laugh and hang up the receiver. Ten days of uncertainty and conflicting reports, for during most of that time direct communication was cut off. Then a cablegram . . .

WESTERN UNION TELEGRAM

RECEIVED AT MAIN OFFICE 608-610 SOUTH SPRING ST., LOS ANGELES, CAL.

1923 SEP 13 PM 6 00

AA656 27 COLLECT NITE

SPRINGGREEN' WIS 13

FRANK LLOYD WRIGHT C454 99-10 HW

OLIVE HILL STUDIO RESIDENCE B 1645 VERMONT AVE HOLLYWOOD CALIF

FOLLOWING WIRELESS RECEIVED FROM TOKIO TODAY HOTEL STANDS UNDAMAGED

AS MONUMENT OF YOUR GENIUS HUNDREDS OF HOMELESS PROVIDED BY PERFECTLY

MAINTAINED SERVICE CONGRATULATIONS SIGNED' OKURA; IMPEHO "

For once good news was news and the Baron's cablegram flashed around the world to herald the triumph of good sense. Both the great Tokio homes of the Baron were gone. The splendid museum he gave to Tokio and all its contents were destroyed. The building by the American .architect, whose hand he took and whose cause he sponsored, was all he had left in Tokio—nor could love or money buy it now or buy a share of stock in it.

When the letters began to come in and nearly all the friends were found to be safe, the news most gratifying to the architect was the fact that after the first great quake was over, the dead rotting there in unburied heaps, the Japanese in subsequent shocks coming in droves, dragging their children into the courts and onto the terraces of the building, praying for protection by the God that has protected that building; then as the wall of fire, driving a great wail of human misery before it, came sweeping across the city toward the long front of the building, the hotel boys formed a bucket line to the big pool, the water there the only water available anywhere. And then kept the window sashes and frames on that side wet to meet the flames that came leaping across the narrow street.

The last thought for the safety of the New Imperial had taken effect.

Following construction of the Imperial Hotel, I lingered in Los Angeles, aided by son Lloyd working on the new unit-block system I had conceived.

But experience with the Imperial had made all probable experience for some time to come quite tame. When I first came back, I took really little interest in such prospects as would present themselves for solution from time to time. No appetite for less than another "Imperial," I suppose. Or, perhaps, satiated, exhausted by such incessant demands upon my resources as that intimate experience with building represented, I had had enough for a while.

For the better part of four years I had been standing in the thick of creative effort, badgered by increasing domestic infelicity, perplexities and finally the characteristic serious illness that attacks men of the North in that humid Pacific lowland. My aged mother, now eighty years old, hearing that my condition was desperate, in spite of all dissuasion had crossed the Pacific to be near. The fact that she came blew the remnant of my relationship with Miriam Noel back across the Pacific in insane fury.

Luckily the Japanese made much of Mother—old age is a qualification in Japan. So, toward the end of her life, she enjoyed many happy and remarkable experiences, one of them a gratifying appearance at the Emperor's Garden Party where she looked a queen, though looking happier than a queen usually looks.

Shugio, the remarkable connoisseur Emperor Mutsushito had placed in charge of all Japan's foreign art exhibitions, was immensely kind to her, taking her about. All my friends in Tokio came often to the little Imperial place to see her and take her to various "occasions." I think she had no lonely hours in Tokio. Some four months later though, having met with a painful accident while driving to Miyanoshita in my motor car, she got back to America, much the better for her heroism. Cheremissinoff was devoted to her.

A world in itself—a transition world—began to take shape in that transition-building. It was created spontaneously as any ever fashioned by the will of a creator in the Middle Ages. Most all of the plans I had prepared at Taliesin were thrown away and my presence on the work enabled me to make such changes in the work itself as were required or I desired. This comprehensive work had been completed by the hand of one architect. In ancient times such was seldom the case, the work on any great building continuing from the architect of one generation to an architect of the next generation. I could take off my hat to the culture I had learned to revere. Something no foreign architect had ever done before. In a measure I accomplished what I had meant to do.

Again in Hollywood, I was still dreaming of the great edifice not long since completed. I lived over again this romance of one thousand and nine days and nights in Tokio—once upon a time Yedo.

Meantime, during the building of the Imperial the building' of a home for Aline Barnsdall was going forward. She called the house Hollyhock House before it was born. I called it a "California Romanza," this time being frankly on holiday. I met Miss Barnsdall shortly after the tragedy at Taliesin, while I was still in Chicago at the Cedar Street house. Henry Sell brought her to see me in connection with a project for a theater in which she was interested in Los Angeles. Her very large, wide-open eyes gave her a disingenuous expression not connected with the theater and her extremely small hands and feet somehow seemed not connected with such ambition as hers.

Later I made the preliminary studies for the theater she intended to build in Los Angeles. And now coming home from the land of Laotze, Tao, Zen and Bushido, I went to work as I might for the Christians in Hollywood, for a time.

At last there stood Hollyhock House, a silhouette up there on Olive Hill. It had been finally completed with great difficulty, partly owing to my absence in Japan, partly because I had to leave it in amateur hands. Here is the minor strain of Aline Barnsdall's. . . .

HOLLYHOCK HOUSE, HOLLYWOOD

Architecture, the mother art, is a greater art than music, if one art can be fairly said to be greater than another. I believe one can say it only for the sake of argument. Nevertheless I have secretly envied Beethoven, Bach and the other great music-masters. After concentration upon creation, they lifted an ivory baton or perhaps merely gracefully significant hands and soared into execution of their designs with the alert obedience of two score or more kindred, willing hands and minds: the orchestra. That means a thousand fingers trained, quick to perform every nuance of the general effect the master precisely wanted, from instruments whose effects were definitely understood.

Remarkable resource comparatively modern.

Beethoven and Bach are invariably inspiration, even to me, information.

What facility great masters of music were afforded by various forms moving according to mood, from fugue to sonata, from sonata to concerto, or proceeding from them all to the melodic grandeur and completeness of the symphony. I suppose it is well no architect has such facility nor can ever get it. Consequences to the country are bad enough, facility such as it is.

A small boy, long after put to bed I used to lie and listen to my father playing Beethoven—for whose music he had a passion—playing far into the night. To my young mind music spoke a language, stirred me strangely. As I have since learned, music is the language—beyond all words—of the human heart. The symphony, as my father first taught me, *is* an *edifice, of sound.* I now felt Architecture not only might be but ought to be as symphonic in character: the same in mind.

So, when called upon by Aline Barnsdall—her metier the theater—to build a home for her in Hollywood, why not make architecture stand up and show itself on her new ground, Olive Hill, as California Romance? A bit sentimental withal. Miss Barnsdall had pre-named the house for the hill—Hollyhock House—she loved for many reasons, all good ones, and called upon me to render her feeling for her favorite flower as a feature of Architecture.

Unlike many a "patroness of the arts" Miss Barnsdall wanted no ordinary home, for she was no ordinary woman. If she could have denied she was one at all, she might have done so. But the fact claimed and continually got her much to her distress and the confusion of her large aims. If any woman ever hitched her wagon to a star, Aline Barnsdall hitched hers there. So far as her Hollyhock House and the building of the New Theater, that was to follow and carry "Art of the Theatre" a generation to two ahead of itself, were concerned—at the moment—she chose her architect as that bright and particular vehicle.

Now, these words, "poetry," "romance," are red rags, flags or reproachful tags to hopelessly confused house-owners who drift and drift continuing to happen to "period" architects as clients. Romance is—no wonder!—something clients would not bear. Because nearly all good people spoke the language and sought the romantic in good faith, when they became clients drew baleful booby prizes in this lot-lottery of Los Angeles: fell ill of the plague—sentimentality—infected by the systematically "tasteful" architects who mark that region. An exception found his way there, long ago, in Irving Gill. But his antiseptic simplicity did not at all please the fashionable Angelenos.

So, this quest for sentimental bosh in architecture in beloved country has wasted billions of perfectly honest dollars, done spiritual harm, more or less violence, to millions of otherwise pretty good people. Perhaps better to say, as I have said of Taliesin, Hollyhock House was to be a natural house in the changed circumstances and naturally built; native to the region of California as the house in the Middle West had been native Middle West.

Suited to Miss Barnsdall and her purpose, such a house would be sure to be all that "poetry of form" could imply, because any house should be beautiful in California in the way California herself is beautiful. She wanted no ordinary house did Aline Barnsdall.

Yes, our nice word "Romance" is now disreputable because implying escape from life rather than any realization of our own life. Either by inheritance or as evil consequence, it is a loose attempt at illusion, now that is what is the matter with the word. So "Romance" lies loose in the heart, askew in the mind, something fanciful. Unlifelike. Results, at best, exotic. At worst, idiotic. So Romance in the United States becomes a sickly simpering mask for a changed new life. Here "Romance" attempts to escape from the deadly pressure of the facts of life in this Machine Age, and go into a beyond each poor earthworm fashions as he may for himself and—if he happens to be an architect—for others.

In music, *romanza* is only free form or freedom to make one's own. A musician's sense of proportion is all that governs him in the romanza: the mysterious remaining just haunting enough in a whole so organic as to lose all evidence of how it was made. Now translate "sounds and the ear" to "form and the eye," romanza seems reasonable enough in Architecture? In California or anywhere else.

Well, no master of the orchestra, I have to conquer a hard-boiled industrial world stewed in terms of money, and persuade or please idiosyncratic, sometimes aristocratic clients, in order to render romanza or achieve even a modicum of integrity in building. My lot was cast with a hod of mortar, some bricks or a concrete-mixer and steel—a gang of workmen called the Union and the modern Machine. Last, but not least comes the client. These are my *"medium of expression."*

Out here in Hollywood in Hollyhock House now meet Circumstance and Opportunity. So the situation didn't look equivocal to me. Not at all. Nevertheless, these oblique remarks are prompted by trying to remember the circumstances now—many of which I have purposefully tried to forget—of this holiday adventure in American Romanza.

Miss Aline Barnsdall turned this beautiful site, Olive Hill, over to me as a basis on which we were to go to work *together* to build under the serene blue canopy of California.

We went to work—or I did. My client, as I soon found, had ideas and wanted yours but never worked much nor for long at a time, being possessed by incorrigible wanderlust that made me wonder, sometimes, what she wanted a beautiful home for—anywhere. Later, I came to see that *that* was just *why* she wanted one. A restless spirit—disinclined to stay long at any time in any one place as she traveled over the face of the globe, she would drop suggestions as a war-plane drops bombs and sail away into the blue. One never knew where or from where the bombs would drop—but they dropped.

Now, to add to this discomfort, the fates picked me up and were dragging me to and fro over the Pacific. For the larger part of four or five years, to build the Imperial Hotel at Tokio. I would hear from her when wandering about in the maze of the Imperial Hotel in Japan while she was in Hollywood. She would get my telegrams or letters in Spain when I got to Hollywood. I would hear from her in New York while I was in Chicago or San Francisco. Or, hear from her from some remote piney mountain retreat in the Rockies when I was on the Pacific Ocean sea-sick. During the building of Hollyhock House there was no radio, only the telegraph. So Hollyhock House had mostly to be built by telegraph so far as client and architect had anything to do with each other. Yes, until all was too late.

Now, with a radical client like Miss Barnsdall, a site like Olive Hill, a climate like California, an architect head on for freedom, something had to happen even by proxy. So this Romanza of California came out on Olive Hill.

Sublimated mathematics is Music?

Well—mathematics in co-ordinated Form is architecture. I would still streamline the straight line and the flat plane. I had now become accustomed to so using them. But would use them here all together with a third mathematical element clearly defined—*integral ornament* modifying or emphasizing both elements to allow suggestion, and appropriate rhythm to enter. These, I offer as component parts not only of the California Romanza but of Romanza as Architecture.

Would my client be happy with the outcome of all this for a house? Probably not, but happier. Why not? She was neither neo, quasi nor pseudo. She was as near American as any Indian, as developed and traveled in appreciation of the beautiful as any European. As domestic as a shooting star. Conscience troubled me a little. That "voice within" said, "What about the machine crying for recognition as the normal tool of your age?"

Well, my critics, one does weary of duty. Even of privilege—while young. I again told the still-small voice to "go to" for a time. Hollyhock House was to be a holiday for me.

The plans joyfully traveling this fascinating upward road of poetic form delighted Miss Barnsdall. I could scarcely have keyed the romanza too high for her, I found, had I made the romanza a symphony!

My client was in a hurry and I urgently needed in Tokio. If we accomplished more than the preliminary plans in the way of actual building, we would have to amplify sketches into plans as best we could, making added notes and details as we went along as to get the building properly built. This was not unreasonable at the time.

My own son Lloyd introduced the Union in the person of a contractor—Robertson. By all evidence obtainable Robertson should have been competent *Konzertmeister* with the sympathetic aid of my untried amateur superintendent Schindler. But, while Robertson could read the average score, he couldn't read this one, as it turned out. And the superintendent didn't if he could. Rudy Schindler was too smooth a party ever to learn how to be serious, which was one reason why I liked him. But that was bad for the house. Soon I would hear of trouble away across the Pacific.

Robertson said it was all because the plans were so hastily prepared. Only partially true. Every contractor will say that and *always—in any circumstances*—it will be partly true. But he knew the allegation plausible alibi for him because every contractor has seen it, times without number, take effect. The truly unreliable contractor never fails to use it with excellent results, so far as he is concerned, which is mostly all he cares about.

This is all in the day's work. Contractor is seldom contractor for anyone's health but his own and never precisely for that. The drawings were sufficiently complete but—true—details were being constantly added to educate the contractor as and when his feeble grasp fell short.

Now, *the* penalty (one of the many, probably) for being feminine, with extremely small hands and feet, rich, alone and mundane, is to have an entourage of dear "friends." Employees who yearn to justify themselves as *friends,* by undertaking to guard the feminine interest in such manner that they will look faithful until the employer rudely awakens. As employers do. As this one did.

Collectively this insurance-brigade of Miss B's knew about as much about this building as Sodom knew of Sanctity. Unless checked they could only insure defeat. Here enters the eternal triangle at the psychological moment. Architect, Owner, Contractor. All too often the Owner at first sign of trouble with the Architect takes refuge in the Contractor. She did.

My client by now had been angered by certain failings of her architect. They got tangled up with his virtues, among them one difficult to untangle and that one, most offensive at this time, was a distinct failure to regard the mere owner of a work of art in hand like the romanza, as of ultimate importance in the *execution* of the design. There were forthright refusals to allow her to take the life of the work itself by thoughtless changes suggested by these cerebratious guardians of hers without due reference to the architect's opinion—a challenge to combat.

So, building half done—a fortuitous decision. "They" should build the house. Now this is where I should have left Hollyhock House forever. But do you know the feeling of a sentimental architect for his creation? You love your child, don't you? Well, so does he. I couldn't go and leave the upbringing entirely to them.

So, on the eve of sailing for the ninth time on the Pacific to Tokio, I consented to hang on by way of my affable superintendent Schindler and my son Lloyd, plainly seeing that my client as well as I would finally take the consequences of her insurance brigade, eventually the usual conspiracy. Now this on my part was due to utter weariness, or else was utter cowardice: a shame.

It thus might have some moral effect upon the prospects of other architects with self-willed clients, to tell of consequent griefs of the owner's administration when driven to unseemliness and hasty acts by their employer's fiats from long-distance. To speak in detail of the makeshifts the insurance brigade employed, in her behalf of course, "to save money." Makeshifts that usually cost more than the real thing: dramatize, as warning to other architects, some of the architect's own serious mistakes among these his unjust treatment of a naturally resourceful, forceful, now roused and suspicious client.

Enough! Ownership on Olive Hill in Los Angeles took whip-hand of art by way of this insurance brigade, and with the best intentions, with all the justification there was. That justification was myself.

Shades of Beethoven and Bach—Romanza did I say? Rude awakening.

And yet—all too aware of the stubborn facts—a poetic idea was born. It had to conquer this stubborn, suspicious, mean, old world—all its refractory materials in between—to appear at all on that hill. Yes—and this treacherous pack of detractors clambering over the whole hill.

My client's own momentum—Irish and considerable—had wantonly cut the ground from beneath herself and her architect, by making him alien, angered, dazed and puzzled for nothing by all this to and fro.

I am foolishly telling this in detail to show that once started building along any unusual characteristic scheme, no timid owner has other salvation, never had nor ever will have, in the agonizing triangle—this infernal A.I.A. invention of client, architect and contractor. However fearful any owner, it will inevitably appear that the real interests of owner and architect are one and indivisible, were so at all essential points. But the contractor, by no fault of his, sits there as actually the born enemy of both architect and owner: except as his moral worth may rise superior to the very nature of his office. Usually it is necessary from the start to defeat the contractor's experienced and subtle advices to the client. He, the contractor, is by the very nature of the *characteristic* "unusual" building, himself the novice. But he will never openly admit that fact. He fears he would lose his case before he began.

Nevertheless from out this confusion, from this welter of misunderstanding and petty, misapplied heat and fury—enough to have consumed the work out of hand and finally resulting in brutal violence—a shape appeared—inviolate. A strangely beautiful "form" crept inexorably into view. Even the quarreling pack began to see and be impressed. Something held all this shifty diversity of administration together enough to enable a new significance to come out and adorn that hill crown. Was it the marks on paper that this quarreling was all about, these traces of design that, no matter how abused, *would* show itself in spite of friction, waste and slip? Of course—yes.

Somehow, by way of the downright brutality, insolence and persistence of architect and client's desire, though both architect and client were torn to tatters—"Form" got into the building in spite of all folly.

This it is that seems to me the miracle as I saw Hollyhock House in full stature on its hill on my return from Tokio: a miracle to this day.

Even now at this distance, I am sure I exaggerate all this warfare just as any parent, fearful for the well-being of an infant, would exagerate the storm, the danger over. I am underestimating the fine quality of Miss Barnsdall herself, who really desired a beautiful thing in her heart and, capable of loving it, kept coming back to it again and again, fending off her own organization and really seeing beyond the barrage of petty strife in which, owing to her own timidity, she continually involved the work. Well, but what does it all matter now? As you have read between the lines, I was chiefly to blame, myself. Because I flouted my client—unable to understand her as I now see I did not. After all it was her house.

Like it or leave it. There stands Hollyhock House in Hollywood—conceived and desired as California Romanza. No, not so domestic as the popular neo-Spanish of the region. But comfortable to live in well, with true pride in itself. Yes, Hollyhock House is a very proud house.

Aline Barnsdall came back to live in it finally. She stayed in her house longer at a time than ever anywhere before. With son Lloyd to help she planted greenery and color around it, and cared for it. Tried to correct some of the mistakes that grew out of the initial mistakes made in the struggle of client and architect to build it mainly by proxy.

Some of the mistakes neither she nor I could correct. But she took it all now in good part as the sunshine began to build up the green round about it. Loving pines because of the mountain carpets they made, she planted pine-groves behind on the hill and great masses of eucalyptus to enclose the pines. She planted great carpets of brilliant flowers for ground cover beside and in front of the house like the carpets woven in Austria for the inside floors. She brought home a few choice *objets d'art* from Europe to add to others from the Orient builded into the walls of the rooms themselves, and to go with the furniture that was made part of the house-design itself.

It looked for a time as though she would become a valuable Hollywood institution' and do more beautiful things there. Next, perhaps make the dream of her life come true, the New Theater, by now already planned and already to be seen in a new white plaster model I had made.

There on Olive Hill above hillsides furrowed with rows of gray-green olive trees, the daughter of one of America's pioneers had constructed a little principality her very own, more free to live in it than any queen. Nothing like it anywhere in the world. She—the second generation—came, within her consciousness a new sense of home to be handed on to the third generation. To her "Sugar-top." Above all friction, waste and slip, Aline Barnsdall had so far succeeded.

Then, as the little queendom grew in beauty and importance, yes, even as the ideas that built it—on holiday—grew in significance around the world she began to feel alone in the possession of it—became more lonely because of it than she had ever felt without it.

Artists came and admired her and admired it. Hollyhock House became known as a work of fine art in the various ateliers of the continent where she would go every summer. Europeans came and saw in it something of the higher harmony of the spirit of man. The newer protestant felt—perhaps justly, who knows?—that the architect had indulged himself again regardless of the task with the machine to which he had set himself. But this Romanza in California was just another phase of the greatest of arts—Architecture. Call that phase what you will. Call it poetry. Call it what you like if you do not want to call it architecture, as I shall.

In Hollywood, "they" said Aline Barnsdall was a Bolshevik. A "parlor Bolshevik," said some. They rather sneered did some of these little people living by names—those to whom names were ideas and ideas names—at one whose ideas were "proletariat" and hard while living soft herself like a princess in aristocratic seclusion unrivaled by other princesses who lived merely in the traditional and therefore in a more or less hackneyed style. She now lived above commonplace elegance, better, because in a matchless style all her own. So far as that went, she lived in atmosphere rare as poetic. Herself a pioneer, this daughter of the pioneer lived up to integral romance when all about her was ill with pseudo-romantic in terms of neo-Spanish, lingering along as quasi-Italian, stale with Renaissance, dying or dead of English half-timber and Colonial.

Well, no one may say what moved her finally. The motives of human deeds lie deep-buried beneath seemingly irrelevant debris or are so mixed in the tangled threads of feeling in the depths of the heart. She made up her mind to give it all away; the precious hill-top by now sought by every realtor of the realm as a prize. She determined to give it away together with its ideal buildings, to Los Angeles the city.

She did so give it as it stood. Even the faithful Japanese cook, George—he went along, too.

She gave it, most wisely, to be used by the class most needy in these United States, most abjectly mendicant at this time owing to the triumphant march of the Machine. But not, be is said, to the most grateful. She gave it to the artists of California, to be their Art Club home: restricting the gift so that the house should not be touched or altered for fifteen years. By that time, she said, what she felt to be its real riches, its imaginative California Form, would have had its way with them. So far as she herself was concerned, it might then go its way to destruction.

Out there where almost everything is speculation and soon or late for sale, and where—perhaps just because of that—so few of the many having riches have ever given anybody anything culturally worthwhile, the wandering daughter of the oil pioneer bequeathed enjoyment in her home, faith in its beauty regardless of its faults, gave it wearing the Los Angeles realtor's tag of a "million dollars." This she did to help up to the level of life again, if possible, struggling artists, stranded in an era they may never survive. How can they?

Hollyhock House disintegrates, listening to these artists as they chide, complain and admonish. So it admonishes them. Perhaps—as its donor meant it should do—Hollyhock House goes along with their personal issues into fresh life in a new key, looking gratefully toward her whose home it once was. Yes, and whose home it still truly is to a greater extent than ever; because, since without her it never could have been, her spirit is manifest in it, to all.

RETROSPECT

Why should all Usonian houses, so-called, when they are anything but Usonian, be of so-called domestic mold when all Usonian people are not so? Why should Aline Barnsdall live in a house like Mrs. Alderman

Schmutzkopf or even like Mrs. Reggie Plasterbilt's pseudo-Hacienda on the Boulevard-Wilshire. Individuality is the most precious thing in life, after all—isn't it? An honest democracy must believe that it is. And the thing Usonia is going to fight, tooth and nail, to preserve as things are going, if the superficial fashionable standardizing we have seen everywhere on the Los Angeles surface has any meaning beneath the eclectic's latest mode—the passing calling itself the "international style."

Again and again within limited experience the "fashionable" thing is ever the outworn carcass of the early tomorrow. If you would have your house "fashionable" be sure it is on its way out of luck even as it is being built.

In any expression of the human spirit principle is manifest as character and that alone endures. Individuality true property of character. No . . . not one house that possessed genuine character in this sense but stands safe outside the performance of the passing show.

Hollyhock House is such a house.

THE ANGELS

Meantime, Hollyhock House as finished as it would ever be, here I was in Los Angeles looking around me disgusted. There the Angelenos were many and busy as could be with steam-shovels tearing down the hills to get to the top in order to blot out the top with a house in some queasy fashionable "style," some esthetic inanity or other. The eclectic procession of to and fro in the rag-tag and cast-off of all the ages was never going to stop—so it seemed to me. It was Mexico-Spanish just now. Another fair, in San Diego this time, had set up Mexico-Spanish for another run for another cycle of thirty years. The mode was busy making pretty pictures thus—and anywhere at all. Making pretty pictures cheap, getting "art and decoration" in to prettify the little plastered caverns. They made them "comfortable" by piling pillows up and stuffing the interiors with "overstuffed" furniture.

During the several years I had been trying to get substantial work out there in Anglicor no reality could be seen in any building where the house owners or the builders were themselves "art-conscious" or for that matter where they were socially amenable. Every time I thought I had a client, I found the client had nothing except that he really had me.

Desert of shallow effects all curiously alike in their quite serious attempts to be original or "different." But more plain surface was gradually coming in sight—always a relief. But the same old lack of thought seen everywhere. Taste—taste, taste, the usual matter of ignorance—

had moved toward simplicity but little thought or feeling for integrity had entered into this architecture: Flatulent or fraudulent with a cheap opulence. Tawdry Spanish medievalism now rampant, what would such "taste" have for effects tomorrow? Some other inane reaction with the same dreadfully significant insignificance.

WHAT FORM

Soon the gnawing of old hunger for reality. I saw no escape. Not yet had I descended to make believe. Could I go deeper now? I could. I did.

Desire to get some system of building construction as a basis for architecture was my objective—my hope. There never was, *is*, architecture otherwise, so I believe,

What form? Well, let the form come. Forms would come in time if a sensible, feasible system of building-construction would only come first. What about the concrete block? It was cheapest (ugliest) thing in the building world. It lived mostly in the architectural gutter as an imitation of "rock face" stone. Why not see what could be done with that gutter-rat? Steel wedded to it by casting rods inside the joints of the blocks themselves, the loins of the building, the whole brought into broad, practical scheme of general treatment, why would this not be fit for a new phase of our domestic architecture? Be permanent, noble, beautiful. It would be economy.

There should be many phases of architecture all equally modern.

The imagination and experience needed to make such a scheme feasible Architecture was some such plastic medium where steel would enter into inert mass as tensile strength. Concrete was the inert mass and steel would take the tension. Concrete is a plastic material— susceptible to the impress of imagination. I saw a kind of weaving coming out of it. Why not weave a new kind of building? I saw the shell. Shells inlaid with steel. Or steel for warp and masonry units for woof in the weaving. For block-size—say man-handled units weighing 40 to 50 pounds—all such units or blocks for either weaving or shells to be set steel-bound. Floors, ceilings, walls all the same—all to be hollow?

I had used the block in some such textured way in upper walls of the Midway Gardens. If I could eliminate the tooled mortar joint I could make the whole fabric mechanical: do away with skilled labor. I began the experiment on La Miniatura. A home and bookshop for Mrs. Alice Millard, a former client in Illinois.

Lightness and strength! Steel the spider spinning a web within cheap plastic material wedded to it by pouring an inner core of cement after the blocks were set up.

The "shell" as human habitation? Why not? Another phase of architecture organic. The straight line, the flat plane, textured. The sense of interior space coming through, and openings all woven as integral features of the shell. Rich encrustation of the shells visible as mass, the true mass of the architecture. Here ornament would become a legitimate feature of construction.

Decoration should assert the whole to be greater than any part and succeed to the degree that it helps make this good. Genuine mass in this sense will always be modern. A pity were the United States to have only one arrow to its architectural bow, or neglect indigenous riches at any point, anywhere.

I drew my son Lloyd into this fresh effort.

Getting interested again.

ALTER EGO

Meantime some of the young men who had begun architectural careers with me were at work out there—in the midst of the popular falsification as I have described it in this land of the *realtoresque* substitute for the picturesque. What were they all doing to modify popular meanness and qualify imitative Usonia? There were many such—fifty or sixty—young men working in the United States, Europe or Japan as architects by now. All came to me from all parts of the world to enter my work. Not so much as students; I am no teacher. All came as apprentices, beginning with no pay—except their living at Taliesin—or with small pay if more competent to help. As they grew helpful they received a salary in keeping with the work done, or to be done in the office or in the garden, over and above their living. Nucleus of the Taliesin Fellowship.

In the studio at Oak Park, inasmuch as they had to shift for themselves, all received nominal wages—equivalent of board and lodging at the beginning. With the exception of some six or seven I have never had reason to complain of their enthusiasm for their work nor of their loyalty. But, of their loyalty to the cause—yes. After all, were they not taken on, in that cause?

This process of natural selection on their part had advantages. Some disadvantages. Never going out of my way after the material I really needed but always taking those who want to come to me—I do make some sacrifices for sympathetic co-operation, oftentimes not so efficient as should be. Fond of the flattery of young people. (They indulge me and I indulge them.) It is easy for them and for me to do this. But they get the idea that when the master's back is turned, to draw his ideas in his own way, or in theirs, makes those ideas and his way their own. Later on, they must do something to justify them in this "reflection." Soon, consciously or unconsciously, this type of *alter ego* becomes detractor. I am in his way unless good-naturedly I let him trade on me. Or in me.

But the individuality of my work has not swerved from first to last. It grows steadily on its own center line. The system—(or lack of it—I have never had an "office" in the conventional manner)—has become fixed and works well enough—but only because I stay with it directly in every detail. When I go away there is usually trouble and sometimes unpremeditated treachery. No. There was never organization in the sense that the usual architect's office knows organization. Nor any great need of it so long as I stood actually at the center of the effort. Where I am, there my office is: my office me. Therein is great difference between my own and current practice. A severe and exacting limitation as well as the freedom I intended.

THE NOVICE

Always hard to turn a boy down! An instance:

Sunday morning at the Oak Park studio. Working late the night before I was called: a boy in the studio to see me. Got up, went down. There, standing by the big detail table center of the draughting room, stood a small boy, face covered with adolescent pimples, blushing furiously. "Wanted to be an architect"—liked my buildings, believed he "would like to build that kind."

Name?

Frank Byrne—young Irish lad.

Where working?

Montgomery Ward's.

What doing?

Wrapping packages.

Getting how much?

Ten dollars a week.

Good preparation for architecture, I observed. Common school only? Studied at home?

A little.

Rather sudden, isn't it—getting into architecture right off the reel like this?

Yes—he thought so, too.

What did he think he could do for me to earn ten dollars a week—knowing nothing about draughting?

Well, he could be office-boy—sweep the floors, wash the

windows—anything. But, I said, we have already several boys doing that. His face fell.

There was something touching, and fine too, in this straightforward break in the direction of his ambition, that appealed to me. Such breaks always do. It looked as though there might be something in this boy. He stood there, pale now. I didn't need him. I didn't want him, but there he was. He was—young, unspoiled—how know what might be in him?

All right, lad, I said—come in.

This boy stayed four years: turned out better than many who had years the start of him in every way. He was my first Catholic. "Catholic" helped him when he got out on his own.

This episode might stand as typical, although many apprentices were nominal architects and many, college graduates. A number of cultivated European architects joined the work at Taliesin. But all on the same basis, whatever their qualifications. Apprentices—when they qualified—would stay from two to ten years.

The same formula was impressed upon all: they were not to imagine they were coming to school. They were coming in to make themselves as useful to me as they could. I was an architect at work. They would see work going on under their eyes and would be taken into the work as far as they could go. Their living was assured meantime but they would get much or little else from their experience, as they were able. It was all up to them. The discussions in the studio—pro and con—schemes and sketches for buildings in general and more often in detail were made by myself in the midst of the studio-group, each man or boy taking over finally, as he could, whatever I assigned him to do. Some would soon drop out—unable to stand the great freedom— abusing it. Some would take it and go away with what they could pick up to sell it as their own. Others would thrive on freedom. A fine loyalty characterized all but very few as they were with me in full freedom of their own choice—entirely on their own.

Well, how about them? What have they accomplished?

The architectural world into which they emerged was being wholly commercialized by the A.I.A. and fashionably if not fatuously inclined now toward the "great" styles. The profession of architecture itself— because it had no basis of principle—is further demoralized by the functioneer professing the practical, nevertheless exploiting "taste." I have had occasion to reproach some of my young men for what seemed to me selling out—going too easily with this current of commercial degeneration. The usual answer was "Mr. Wright, we have to live."

"Why?" I have said.

I don't see why anyone "has" to live, at any rate not live as a parasite at expense to the thing he loves! Why not try something where a living might be had honestly, had fairly to all concerned?

Some identified themselves with other architectural movements: "So hard to stand alone." Others became competitors, the "also-ran" no less. There had been nothing much in my work they didn't have access to meantime.

Too well I know the weight of opposition all of them encountered. Inclined to sympathize with them. Much easier for them now, though many must be ground up (buried perhaps) before it will be easy enough. Many of "my boys" are giving a good account of themselves, Middle-West, North-West, South-West and West, even across the Seas. But current life mocks most effort forward, breaks it to fragments. To save only a few for future reference as life goes on its way is all we have a right to expect?

Nevertheless, principle is defense and refuge from chaos. Otherwise utter defeat.

This digression because several young men were at this time doing good work in California on their own—while the work on La Miniatura was going forward. The block experiments had been made. I was ready to start the first one. Its owner named it La Miniatura—the first block house. Since we are in work now here is the story of

LA MINIATURA, FIRST-BORN
USONIAN OF CALIFORNIA

La Miniatura happened in that region as the cactus grows. But what folk from the Middle-Western prairies did when, inclined to quit and the prosperous came loose and rolled down there into that far corner to bask in eternal sunshine, was wholly different.

Near by that arid, sunlit strand is still unspoiled desert. You may see what a poetic thing this land was before this homely midwest invasion. Curious tan-gold foothills rise from tattooed sand-stretches to join slopes spotted as the leopard-skin with grease-bush. This foreground spreads to distances so vast—human scale is utterly lost. All features recede, turn blue, become bluer still to merge their blue mountain shapes, snow-capped, with the azure of the skies. The one harmonious imported note man has introduced into these vast perspectives, aside from the long, low plastered wall, is the eucalyptus tree. Tall, tattered ladies, these trees stand with careless feminine grace in charming abandon appropriate to perpetual sunshine, adding beauty to the olive-green and ivory-white of an exotic symphony in silvered gold and rose-purple. Water comes, but it comes as a deluge once a year to surprise the roofs, sweep the sands into ripples and roll boulders along in the gashes, washes combed by sudden streams in the desert. Then—all sun-baked as before.

No, not all, for man has caught and held the fugitive flood behind great concrete walls in the hills while he allows it to trickle down by meter to vineyards, orchards and groves. And—yes—to neat, shaven lawns two by twice. Little "lots" just like those back home in the Middle West. Funny and fixed little features—homes—stare above the lawns wearing as many different but curiously unvaried expressions of the same fixed face just as there are the same "different" people looking out of the windows at each other.

Newcomers from the fertile midwestern prairies came to make sunshine their home. But at first the home did not know how to bask any more than they themselves did. Shirt sleeves might be their limit but their homes had not shirt sleeves nor anything at all easy-going about them. No indeed, those homes of theirs were still as hard and self-assertive as the flat sticks they took to make them out of: defiant as ever they were in the mud and snows back there midwest at zero. These Yankeefied houses, for that is what they were, looked even more hard in perpetual sunshine where all need of their practical offensive defenses had disappeared entirely.

Now, when the sunshiners turned to the planting of their places out there the result was not much better. They could easily grow in that sunshine all kinds of strange plants and trees. They did so, as a neat, curious little collection all nicely set out together on the neatly shaved lawns of their little town-lots. The porch and the parlor had come along with the pie and ice-water, the rocking chair, the chewing gum with the appropriate name—Wrigley.

Long before—however—Fra Junipero and Father La Tour had been there and began to have incidental influence now; for it gradually appeared that the Italo-Spanish buildings of the early missionaries' own "back home" had just happened to be more in keeping with California.

This Southern type of building had already given shelter from a sun that could blister the indiscreet in Spain or Mexico just as it was now able to do in Southern California. So it came to pass that the old Catholic Missions as buildings lived long enough to transform a little and somewhat characterize the details of the Middle-Westerner's home in California—although the *actual* mission was at first rejected as being far from midwestern spiritual conviction.

Finally now the midwestern émigré fell to copying Fra Junipero's buildings, his furniture, his gardens and style. Fell to buying his antiques. But though the invading Middle West had fallen for all that, it still clung *in toto* to its hard straw hat, English coat, trousers and boots and other customs in general. As a concession to climate, however, the Middle-Westerner himself occasionally did put on a shirt with a soft collar and forgot his hat. But when "dressed" he had not one iota budged. He looked in his Fra surroundings as the Fra himself or a silken Spaniard would have looked in little midwestern parlors. Only for the Fra it would be plus—for the sunshiner it was forever minus.

Mexican Spain, by way of California despised Mexico, gradually moved up into the midst of this invasion. Plain, white-plastered walls—so far so good—of little pictorial caverns gleam or stare at you through the foliage in oases kept green by great mountain reservoirs. A new glint of freshness, a plainness that is a refreshing foil for exotic foliage. There are cool *patios* there too, patios for the Joneses and the Smiths. Luxurious haciendas for the richer Robinsons. Arched loggias and vine-covered pergolas all run about on the loose. Rude Spanish-tiled roofs stain the sunshine dull pink. Adzed beams or rude construction real or imitated is there, covered by gay stretched awnings. They put awnings over the windows in the thick plastered walls.

Thus California has retraced the first steps of an earlier invasion by priests who came there from a climate more like California climate than that of the Middle West. But the Californians of today—born Iowan, Wisconsiner, Ohioan—have yet nothing to say for themselves in all this except superficially acquired taste for Spanish antiques to go with the missionary houses. Nevertheless, the town-lot on the gridiron; modern bathroom; the incorporation of the porch and kitchenette with the cozy breakfast-nook; all these prize possessions of his own "back-home" are now features of "mission style." Such is progress? To have and to hold all you can hold, while merely seeming to *be*. But California, given to drink, smothers the whole concatination in eucalyptus, takes into mimosa arms as she gently kisses all with roses. Thus buried are the mistakes of the picturizing architect whose art and decoration have entirely taken the place out there of architecture.

Here, then, at some length is the pictorial background against which La Miniatura, Alice Millard's little studio-house, is to stand: the flourishing sentimental "taste" into which it was born a stranger.

All true building in this Usonian land of the brave and home of the free, is a soul-trying crusade. I assure you it is, just as Fra Junipero Serra's mission that failed was that kind of crusade. But his building thus succeeded was not high adventure because he only brought it with him from "back home" because and solely—he had none other to bring.

Not so La Miniatura. This little building scientifically and afresh began to search for what was missing in all this servile background.

What was missing? Nothing less than a distinctly genuine expression of California life in terms of modern industry and American opportunity. That was all.

Few out there seem to miss anything of the sort but La Miniatura desired to justly call itself *architecture,* be able to look itself in the face. Mrs. George Madison Millard from those same midwestern prairies near Chicago was heroine of this story: slender, energetic—fighting for the best of everything for everyone, be it said, she knew it, too, when she saw it. Got it if she could.

The Millards had lived in a modern wooden dwelling I built for them fifteen years earlier at Highland Park near Chicago. Proud now I was to have a client survive the first house and ask me to build a second. Out of one hundred and seventy-two buildings this made only the eleventh time it had happened to me.

So, gratefully, I determined she should have the best I had in portfolio. That meant (to begin with) something belonging to the ground on which it stood. Her house should be a sensible matter—entirely interpretation of her needs in book-collecting for book-collectors. Alice, artistic herself, with her frank blue-eyed smile beneath her unruly gray hair, didn't fully know that she was to be lightly but inexorably grasped by the architectural fates and used for high exemplar. She probably suspected it though. Now I don't yet know why houses have so much grief concealed in them if they try to *be* anything at all and try to live as themselves. But they do. In this like people I suppose. Gradually I unfolded to her the scheme of the textile block-slab house gradually forming in my mind since I got home from Japan. She wasn't frightened by the idea. Not at all.

We would take that despised outcast of the building industry—the concrete block—out from serfdom now underfoot in the gutter—find a hitherto unsuspected soul in it—make it live as a thing of beauty—textured like trees. Yes, the building would be made of concrete blocks, but as a kind of tree itself standing there at home among the other trees in its own native land.

All we would have to do would be to educate the concrete blocks, refine them and knit all together with steel in the joints and so construct the joints that they could be poured full of concrete by any boy after they were set up by common labor and a steel-strand laid in the interior joints. Walls would thus become thin but solid reinforced slabs, receptive to any desire for pattern imaginable. Yes, common labor could do it all.

We would make the walls double, of course, one wall facing inside and the other facing outside, thus getting continuous hollow spaces between, so the house would be cool in summer, warm in winter. Dry always. Inside, the textured blocks—or the plain ones—would make a fine background for old pictures, fine books and tapestries. Outside—well, in that clear sunshine, even the eucalyptus tree would love it for what it was. Instead of a fire-trap for her precious book-collections and antiques she would have a house fireproof. I talked this idea over with her, and the more she listened to me the more she liked it. So I made tentative plans. Provided the whole has "an old-world atmosphere" said Alice Millard, I will like it. I said it would have and better.

I forgot to mention that Alice had just ten thousand dollars to put into the house—might get two thousand more, probably not. Bankers were Yesterday, out there too, hostile to ideas as everywhere: greater the idea the greater this bank-phobia. So the whole scheme must be excessively modest. For instance, Alice Millard wanted only an unusually large living-room with a great fireplace, a beautiful balcony over it from which her own sleeping room might open. That bedroom should be roomy too, with dressing room, a balcony in that too and a bath, of course. One for the balcony would be nice to have.

Then there must be a good-sized guest-room that might be an office when not in use otherwise, and two baths of course. And dining room, not so small either (little parties) with pantry, kitchen, servants' bedroom, store-rooms and baths. Making three baths. My client's tastes were good. She did not want cheap woods. She did not want, of all things, cheap hardware. She abominated poor workmanship and knew it when she saw it. She never failed to see it. There was to be nothing shoddy about that house. And a garage was to be thrown in as integral feature of the whole just for good measure. She would be glad to have all this permanent, fireproof, and have it as beautiful as it was going to be for $10,000.00 (The first sum mentioned).

So one day after the plans were ready she came enthusiastically to say: "I've just found the man to build our 'thoroughbred' house. I've been talking with him and went with him to see a house he's just finished for a friend of mine. It cost her less than he said it would. He gave her lots of little extras and never charged for them at all. He was so good and efficient they scarcely needed an architect at all. Let's go and see the house."

Here the other leg of the triangle showed its foot once more—its toes at least already in the door with an ingratiating smile. But I could not refuse to go to see his house—yet. So we went.

That house was not badly done, a lot for the money, almost half as much as Alice Millard wanted. I talked with the contractor, and she even went so far as to say, by now, she wouldn't have anyone else build her house anyway.

"I feel," said she, "we can trust him 'utterly.'"

Now, she had been just as uncompromising as that about her architect. So I understood her regard for her new-found friend the contractor. But here was already familiar and pretty slippery ground to go on.

"How do you like him?" said she, brightly but (as I could see) anxiously.

"Well," I said, "a woman's intuition is valuable even in these matters. He does seem intelligent. He has had a good deal of independent experience. He likes this block-slab idea and volunteers to take the contract without any profit—for the sake of experience. So he says. Therefore he *is* a volunteer. Since you won't have anyone else build for you anyway, why . . . I am inclined to take him at face-value."

She sighed with relief.

She now felt quite safe. I had no good reason to oppose her ultimatum. But—I wish I had felt as safe as she. In honesty I should add to this that I knew of no one else, not in that region at the time, anyway. Who could, or would, make such sacrifices for her? Some material supply-men recommended the man highly. I called them up. That was how we got the god-father to the new idea.

Here the familiar villain, invented by the A.I.A., the contractor, enters the piece disguised as a philanthropist. Alice Millard's ultimatum was my flimsy excuse. But I knew just how staunch her faith could be—dreaded any attempt to change it. Had she not disregarded warnings of all friends. A lone woman has hundreds, and she consented to the loss of some life-long friendships in order to embark with me in this innocent challenge to their ways and what they approved as means. Well, he began well. They all do.

You see I explain this in detail to show how every idea, even as with the Barnsdall Romanza, enters to encounter life as does a new-born child, pretty much as things happen to be—to take all when and where it may come. The idea then begins to grow up, to work like yeast in these haphazard conditions and it may survive, become important, or dwindle and die as the child may. It is at every moment squarely up to the author of its being to defend it. He has to save its life—continually. He has a chance only if all cards are on the table!

But, here's for confession—let's see how good for the soul it is in this whole affair.

Let's call this builder-fellow the god-father of our idea. I could add appropriate adjectives to the word god and to the word father. But after a while, you do it. Alice Millard trusted this gift of the gods for she felt she needed him. I am ashamed to say this, because she could have trusted me instead. Out there where, as I soon learned, no one ever thinks of trusting anyone or anything, yet she trusted *him*. Because everything and everyone is too much on the surface, or too recent, or too something-or-other, this was rash.

At the time I didn't know this characteristic of the place.

But I've hardly ever trusted anyone myself since, nor has Alice Millard—scarcely even me, although she wouldn't admit it to me—and denied it to everyone else.

As you may see by now, the gray gray architect and client were by nature incorrigibly young: firmly believing in Santa Claus. Both encouraged by Mrs. Millard's Pasadena builder to believe they could accomplish their mission for around eleven thousand some odd dollars. That was the contractor's romantic, affectionate estimate. Unhesitating, he signed a contract.

Why should he not sign a contract? Or indeed sign anything at all?

Meantime we had rejected the treeless lot originally purchased, as my eyes had fallen upon a ravishing ravine near by, in which stood two beautiful eucalyptus trees. The ravine was reached from the rear by Circle Drive. Aristocratic Lester Avenue, heedless, passed across the front.

No one would ever want to build down in a ravine out there, I believed. They all got out onto the top of everything or anything to build and preferably in the middle of the top. It was a habit. I considered it a bad habit but because of this idiot-syncrasy of the region we could get this ravine lot very cheap. We got it half price—and better than the best at full price.

We would head the ravine at the rear on Circle Drive with the house, thus retaining the ravine as at the front toward Lester Avenue, a sunken garden. The house would rise tall out of these ravine gardens between the two eucalyptus trees. Balconies and a terrace or two would lead down into the ravine from front of the house. Neighbors either side liked this idea, as we left the entire front of the lot next their home open.

We began to build. The builder grew in Mrs. Millard's estimation until well over life-size. He settled down full in the saddle. I could not fail to see this with some alarm and no little chagrin. No it is not pleasant for an architect to see his client clinging to a contractor as insurance against what might prove to be too single-minded devotion to an idea on the part of her architect. Her friends had already got that far with her? Or perhaps it was her nature. I don't know. She would not have admitted this unfaith, I do know, so I admit it for her here with wrinkles at the corners of my eyes. The architect not infrequently in this region—for some peculiar reason, perhaps it is the climate—has to endure this rivalry for the confidence and esteem of his client. I had learned this from others before. But what is this "something" about a contractor or builder that inspires confidence in the client—especially if the client be a woman? Of course, it is easy for her to believe that he is, before all, *practical*. It is easy for her to believe that *he* is the man who really builds the building, in spite of the architect. He knows clapboards and shingles and so he must know concrete blocks, etc., etc. Always, to the woman client, the appeal of the practical man is irresistible. Woman is far more objective than man anyway. She is more susceptible to the obvious and every time. Nature made her that way.

So, still smiling, though I will say I secretly resented this rivalry, I cheerfully did nothing about it. Let me admit, if less cheerfully, that I *could* have done nothing about it anyway, had I wanted to. So I helped along, as best I might, every day on the ground myself. I made more studies and details until finally we finished the flasks and boxes in which to make the blocks; got the right mixture of sand, gravel and cement carefully chosen; and so varied it that the blocks would not all be the same color. Our builder picked up some relations of his in Los Angeles to make them. We needed no skilled labor yet and so more of the builder's relatives came to set the blocks, carrying them up ladders on their shoulders to their scheduled places in the walls. You see, the model house had to be clumsily home-made as it might be, for the price was very low. A good deal would have to be put up with on that account. Otherwise everything went along according to design—smoothly enough. By now, that house represented about as much studious labor over a drawing board and attention to getting construction as was required by the Cathedral of St. John the Divine in New York City, for instance. Certainly more trouble to me than the architect had with the Woolworth Building.

Inventive effort was all thrown in, of course. It always is where the architect is concerned.

But never mind! The house was to me, by now, far more than a mere house. Yes—Mrs. George Madison Millard's friends were quite right. Her architect had gone so deep into his idea that concentration upon it was no longer innocent. No, it was now amounting to a passion. The blocks began to take the sun and creep up between the two eucalypti as though one with them. I, the Weaver, dreaming of effects. Came visions of a new architecture for a new life—true life of romantic, beautiful California—of the coming reaction upon this hitherto unawakened people. Other buildings sprang full-born into my mind from this humble beginning. They arose in bewildering variety and peerless beauty. Gradually all complications, all needless expense of the treacherous, wasteful, wicked building system of a whole country, all went by the board. Any humble cottage might now live as architecture with integrity known only to former ages. The machine should be no longer the bar to beauty in our own. At last, here I was grasping the near-end of a great means to finer order. Standardization *was* the soul of the machine, and here I was the Weaver taking it as a principle, knitting a great future for it. Yes, crocheting with it a free masonry fabric capable of stunning variety, great in architectural beauty. And, well, I might as well admit it—I quite forgot this little building belonged to Alice Millard at all. Palladio? Bramante? Sansovino? Sculptors—all! Now here was I, Frank Lloyd Wright, the Weaver. What might not now grow out of this little commonplace circumstance?

This "Weaver" concentrated on other studies and drawings to carry the idea further. Yes, argued the Weaver—is anyone smiling?—have not all great ideas in art had an origin as humble as this? Or more so? At last: a real building-method beginning in this little house; here at last was a weaving in building that could go on forever and not go wrong for anyone: by nature, a prohibition of affectation, sham or senseless extravagance: integrity in architecture in the realm prostitute to the expedient! Mechanical means to infinite variety no longer an impractical dream! Thus I—already too far beyond poor little La Miniatura!

To come back again rudely to my story, how lucky to have found the intelligence in a client to go through initial steps with me—go along with comprehension and faith complete in her contractor—some faith in me yet, no matter what anybody said. For that is what she had, although I seem to take it lightly in this tale—I appreciated Alice Millard.

Thus the home got well above the second story level and Alice to Europe for the summer. She paid her builder herself before she left, without a word to me. No vouchers asked. She wrote me she had done this. Under the circumstances now existing between us all, to ask for vouchers from him would have been to look a gift-horse in the teeth. . . . This payment, unauthorized, was the final blow to my self-esteem. But I was above hurt—or beneath it—by now!

I drove over daily to carry on, but day after day found no builder. I chafed, complained, drove to and fro to find him. Finding him I got promises. Finally Mrs. Millard's builder came to me for more money, explaining that if he got it he could forge ahead. I gave him some money myself. He didn't forge ahead. Mrs. Millard did, when she came back with renewed enthusiasm for the whole thing, and found so little done. The idea had grown on her, too. Doubt now crept into our triangle. I investigated her builder—well, *our* builder by now and—well let's have the matter over with—even if no one ever trusts me to build a house again: I found him building a new house for himself way off somewhere. Tile floors throughout. New furniture. Grand piano. Strange! We investigated some more, found everything absolutely all right because everything was in his wife's name!

Here we were about half through: money two-thirds gone. Some of it, maybe, gone into tile floors? New furniture? Grand piano? Why harrow the details? The builder now quit, angered by my own angry ungrateful attitude toward him in this whole matter. Mrs. Millard was now left in deep water with her inventive architect! I must say her architect made me especially tired myself at this juncture just as he is making you tired right now, and very much for the same reasons. Now I believed her friends were justified in their opposition to him. With me they could now all enjoy their "I told you so."

Now here is where my client rose and made herself the true heroine of this piece.

She said, "We are going to finish that building if it takes every cent I've got in the world or can get to do it. I see that it's going to be beautiful—and while it's not going to be so well-built as I hoped—I know something worthwhile is coming out of that block-pile there in the yard." That was that. And better than I deserved.

Somewhere, sometime, a prospective client asked me how much I could build a ten-thousand-dollar house for. I said I didn't know exactly but I supposed it could be built for about what it would be worth, with something fine thrown in for good measure that money couldn't pay for. That home cost $18,000.00. The owner admitted it was worth it. It looked as though Alice Millard's $11,500.00 studio-house would beat this now. I knew she couldn't stand it so I wrote home to see if my credit could be strained to go into it with her to what extent. By submitting to a collection of financial humiliations it could be. I felt that I deserved to be fined enough money to finish that house, and so I fined myself with the six thousand available. Saying nothing about that at the moment, we will go ahead.

We were now adrift among Monyana men all in demand in this busy place so well over-sold and so badly under-built. I knew no one but the Hollyhock House crowd and they wouldn't do. They had already done. There were heart-rending trials of faith and friendship as one slippery human agency after another was seized from among the flotsam and jetsam of Monyana-land and put to work. I knew my client was avoiding her best friends. It is the least one can do when in trouble.

I knew Alice Millard's heart was breaking. But she stood up to everything with her usual cheery brave smile. With never-failing energy she again kept bringing in new builders. She could find them when no one else could. But they kept fading away until I found one who promised well. This man of mine put the final work into place no better than the rest. All told, I should say he was even worse.

Here we were now, facing deficits and duns, ridicule, threats, liens, insults. More liens. Finally lawsuits, or anything else they had around there. Let me tell you that region is particularly rich in all such active ingredients. Lucky I had that six thousand ready.

A lawsuit was brought by our trusty builder himself. I never knew such gall or just what the lusty contractor fellow wanted or expected to get until the judge fined him $500 and costs. For his effrontery—I believe—and fired him. That cleared the matter up for us a little though I still believe he brought the suit just because he couldn't refrain from trading a little further upon the beautiful credulity he had found in us both. It really was *very* beautiful!

Well, anyhow the little studio-house was there, battered up a little, patched somewhat, but believe it or not—not badly built after all. Alice Millard had some grief over it—her standards were high and Monyana men not so good because really, they don't get much pay. But she had joy in the building now. She fought a good fight.

Both having taken so much trouble with it from first to last, we had a fool's pride in it. Of course. How with the added terrace walls, balconies and other things it could ever have been built even for the sum it had now cost, we couldn't see—though we knew some of the money had been—well, perhaps not wasted, but . . . who knows?

We rested. Enjoyed installing the old books and other old things, especially appropriate antiques, its tasteful owner with her usual discrimination had picked up in Italy. We sat at the tea-table in the afternoon, a blazing fire in the now charming fireplace. The interior was all either of us had dreamed, it had "an old world atmosphere." And if you didn't go looking too hard for nicked edges or something like that where the Monyana men had run into one another with the blocks or fallen down with one, it wasn't so badly built. Its owner with her taste for luxury—fine materials and workmanship etc.—though, would stop in the midst of enjoying the general result—to point to a manifest mechanical defect as though shot through the heart. Nevertheless, we enjoyed a triumph—a satisfaction that goes far, this seeing of one's desires established on earth by means of what had been, less than ten months before, only an idea.

The undesirable ravine became a lively little garden, a pool reflecting the beauty of the block mass and texture among the trees.

The mass and texture of the little home made the two eucalyptus trees more beautiful as they, in turn, made the house more so.

272

The appropriate but expensive garden terraces, balconies and roof garden that came to join the original inexpensive programme of interior rooms made the whole so naturally a part of that ravine that no one could even think of that building anywhere else or regret what additional features cost. A miracle had come to pass. The old ravine got for half price—was one that was used to take away street water. It had been converted before our very eyes through all confusion and treachery into a living home with charm. Oh, yes—it had charm! There was a quality living, holding all together through friction, waste and slip that so blessed the result. Such *is* an Idea!

La Miniatura. New-born entity where before was but a sunken ravine.

The Gods will allow no creative effort of man's to go untested. The Japanese themselves believe them jealous, purposely leaving some glaring fault in a conspicuous place to placate them. The Monyana men had done this in many places but we had not done so. Just for that came an unusual cloudburst concentrating on that ravine, it seemed. In every fair-weather region like this it is always the unexpected that happens. No one in fifty years ever saw the culvert that now took the street water away below the basement of the house overflow. But the heavens opened wide, poured water down until it got to the level of the pretty concrete dining-room floor, determined to float the house if the thing could be done. The flood must have mistaken the house for another Ark, but this time, failing utterly to move it, left a contemptuous trace of mud on the lower terraces, put out the fires in the sub-basement, burying the gas heaters beneath solid mud. And went away. Mrs. George Madison Millard's spirit, faith and pride went out with the fires. She wept.

But soon we got this little matter fixed up by aid of the city of Pasadena. Even this was not to be enough to add to what had already been. Depths of misery were yet to be plumbed.

Cyrano de Bergerac, high-adventurer, after a lifetime of triumphs as idealist was inadvertently knocked on the head by a flower-pot. The pot fell from a window ledge above him as, rapier in scabbard, he passed below. I've always believed there was only a common red-geranium in that pot.

Well, La Miniatura's hard-fought all-but-won idealism was now to share a like fate. Yes—let no one imagine that because this region is perpetual sunshine the roof is more negligible a feature of house-happiness than back there in rain, snow and ice. The sun bakes the roof for eleven months, two weeks and five days, shrinking it to a shrivel. Then, giving the roof no warning whatever to get back to normal if it could, the clouds burst. Unsuspecting roof surfaces are deluged by a three-inch downpour.

I knew this. I know there are more leaking roofs in Southern California than in all the rest of the world put together. I knew that the citizens come to look upon water thus, singularly ungrateful. I knew that water is all that enables them to have their being out there, but let any of it through on them from above, unexpectedly, and they go mad: a kind of phobia. I knew all this, had seriously taken precautions in the details of this little house to avoid such scenes as result from negligible roofs. This is the truth.

The details were perfect, proved so to everyone's dissatisfaction. But what of it? What defense when any roof chooses to leak? It subsequently was found that our builder had lied to me about the flashing under and within the coping walls—that's all. I had cautioned him concerning this before leaving, when called away to Lake Tahoe. But not until I had safely escaped to Taliesin did La Miniatura decide to leak. I knew nothing of it. Saying nothing to me, not wishing to hurt my feelings, I imagine, Mrs. Millard deliberately invited somebody if not anybody and everybody in to talk it all over and try to fix up that roof. Easy to fix, for there would be no rain for another year. You may feel that by confessing in this manner I am making light of a bad matter. But really I am doing penance here. Maybe I am only making a bad matter worse. However that may be, Mrs. George Madison Millard's spirit, though dampened, was not one made to be broken even by this last trial. Enough of left-handed confession. I finally fixed the roof. When I found out about it!

Yes, the strength of Alice Millard's determination, the real courage of her faith in La Miniatura, lived to laugh at that trial too. Yes, we two laugh about it all now. But not then.

Not, sometimes, when I think what La Miniatura would have gained for the future of our Architecture and my own petty fortunes had the gods not been jealous and given the local A.I.A., Mrs. Millard's private secretaries, her too many vigilant and confidential advisers, the local realtors, aspiring inferior desecrators, convincing contractors, roofers, loafers, lawyers, plumbers, tourists, butchers, grocers, rooters and servants—all working for her in the "I told you so" brigade—this last fatal chance to assassinate it. It leaked! I curse still. These eager publicists had all the while been roosting à la flower-pot—to get the satisfaction of this final knockout. We ourselves survived the untoward circumstance—yes, because the house was mainly all right all the time. But not so for them, because La Miniatura had insulted them all by what it aspired to be. "They" had no wish for it to *survive* anything at all. Not if they could help it.

Well—Cyrano is dead. La Miniatura is not dead. Still too young to die. La Miniatura, first-born Californiain in architecture, takes place in the esteem and affectionate admiration of our continental judges in architecture across the sea—at least. The process that built it is now in use "over there," as here. The humble concrete-block gives to architects another simple means to establish indigenous tradition instead of buying apples from abroad. Thus, it appears in this perhaps too light recital of serious woes that no creative impulse as genuine idea ever does or ever can choose its hour or its means or control its ends, once started. The Idea starts and if really one soon shows itself so much bigger than the puppets it plays with that they take, miserably or thankfully as may in them be, whatever they happen to get and go their way. If meantime they get ungratefully troublesome they may get into court, be fined $500 and costs by the judge, and "fired." But inevitably as the sun shall also rise, after some reaction, a few bad days, there will come to the seeker for integrity something beyond fashion, beyond price, beyond all neighborly cavil.

I believe that reward is the only atonement one can make for the privilege of being able to build a house at all.

La Miniatura stands in Pasadena against the blue sky between loving eucalyptus companions in spite of all friction, waste and slip, triumphant as Idea. Friction, waste and slip did not destroy it—cannot now. Alice Millard lives in it. She says she would have no other house she has ever seen. She fought for it and won—whoever may think or say she lost. It is her home in more than ordinary sense: the reward anyone has a right to enjoy in any sincere high adventure in building.

Seeking simplicity as sought in La Miniatura, you will never fail to find beauty—though contractors betray, workmen botch, all your friends backslide, bankers balk and dread jaws of heaven open wide to hitherto unsuspected deluge—even if all the gods, but one, be jealous.

As for me—probably living too long as a hermit—reading mostly in the book of Nature's creation—I may have these things out of drawing—because I would rather have built this little house than St. Peter's in Rome.

THE BLOCK

Months before La Miniatura was finished, many improvements and changes were made in block technique. Other block houses began to grow up in that equivocal region, even as the first was being completed. The Storer House was one. The Freeman House was another. And then the Little Dipper, kindergarten for Aline Barnsdall, which she destroyed halfway through. And she employed my superintendent of Hollyhock House, himself—by the way, he was all ready—to turn it into a garden terrace.

The little palace, the Ennis House was fifth of the block-shell group. I had drawn my son Lloyd into this effort and after completing the plans and details for this latter house I entrusted it all to Lloyd to build—and I, too soon, went back to Taliesin.

Some one hundred and seventy-nine buildings, as this is written— both large and small—had been built from my own hand by now and are known as this work of mine. About seventy more, the best ones, had life only on paper. The most interesting and vital stories might belong to these children of imagination were they ever to encounter the field. Say, the Lake Tahoe Project, the Doheny Ranch Project, San Marcos in the Desert, St. Mark's Tower and others.

Such stories of actual buildings as are included here are intended to be typical in some way of the characteristic ills that mean success or failure and of certain phases of the whole group of buildings, although the building of many was untroubled and a delight to all concerned— about three out of five were so I should say.

Many another building, as I see, might have served here the better purpose: say the Winslow House at River Forest; the Hillside Home School buildings; the first "Dampfer House"—that is to say the Robie House down by Chicago University, now belonging to the Congregational Church. Especially the Coonley House at Riverside. The Martin House at Buffalo. The little "School of the Free Spirit" in Tokio. The interesting Fukuhara Country House at Hakone—it parted in two during the great earthquake—the great living-room at the front following the rock-cliff on which it had stood, down the mountainside some thousands of feet into the valley below—all being in the bedrooms behind it, no one harmed. The establishment of the Bitter Root Community in Montana—and many others. Success might be thus emphasized. Instead I have spoken of failure, of a kind.

It would be worthwhile to tell the story of the house for Henry Allen at Wichita, Kansas. Henry was as colorful a client as all out-doors. And of the new home I did not build for William Allen White because Will had an animal fear of being turned out of the old one.

I would like to tell of the home at Peoria for Francis Little, himself an intelligent builder and manager of civic gas plants for John R. Walsh. Mr. Little retired and sold the Peoria house to Bob Clarke. And— amusing to me—tell of the second and especially of the third beautiful home I built for him on the shore of Lake Minnetonka, Minnesota. I liked the house much and the Littles more, but it has never been published. I could tell the amusing story of how I got the Hotel and Bank block to build at Mason City, Iowa. And tell of the Aeroplane House, Submarine, the Coach-and-Four, the Polar-star and of Perihelion. The Dana House at Springfield—dear old Mother Lawrence, salt-risen bread, blackberry preserves and the way we kept faith with the old homestead. Tell, especially of the lifelong interest and loyalty of Darwin D. Martin and the building of several houses for him—under fire from Mrs. Martin—who finally joined us. Of the help of the inventive Charles E. Roberts at Oak .Park.

So many come trooping to mind, as children troop into school at the ringing of the bell after recess. And I can say truthfully enough if not modestly, that not one building great or small but was the working out of some single-minded far-reaching idea, the practical demonstration of many principles at work and for that reason as of record, not one has yet been lost to the record. Although many have been torn down to make way for changes in the city they have not been lost. A number of dwellings have "changed hands"—as the advertisement used to read—because of the rapidly shifting changes in the lives of the people for whom they were built—inevitable in a young and rapidly changing country. Two were bought back again by the same people who had built them and sold them, because they said they could not feel at home in any other. Especially I should like to tell the story of "the house that was never built." It was, of course, the best house I ever built.

Kaleidoscopic! These gratifications of social-shifts demanded and taken by the restless to and fro of our artificial, hectic, economic life in the United States. What European would understand it? The people of these United States live under it, are familiar with it but do not understand it themselves.

But there have been stories enough. In choosing the tales of Hollyhock House and La Miniatura I have willfully taken those experiences in which I was most at disadvantage owing to the vicious triangle, or by way of Time, Place and Circumstance, or by way of my own fault—intending, as I have said, to show how all creative effort in the direction of any ideal is continually at the mercy of human nature—the trivial idiosyncrasy characteristic in the circumstances, and the vicious building system of our country. But I should retract. Where creative effort is involved there are no trivial circumstances. The most trivial of them may ruin the whole issue. Yes, eternal vigilance is the only condition of creation as well as Freedom in our architecture in Usonia.

Certainly it is only fair to include one's mistakes and errors of judgment—any characteristic failings that at any time had relation to results as a whole, in this presentation of architecture as essentially human stuff.

L'ENVOI

During the two years passed in the beautiful Southwest, building conditions there had seemed to me a shallow sea of cheap expedients. Nearly every effort I made out there was afloat on the surface and in some way for sale. I felt that were I to stay longer I too would be knocked down cheap to the highest bidder—if any. Desire for depth, for the quality that is genuine, seemed to be all far away in the future. Everybody and everything was getting by with something to sell, selling themselves. Always selling, eventually sold.

So coming back to Taliesin once more I continued work on the preliminary plans for a cantilever glass office building. I had begun it in Los Angeles—plan-making now to go forward for Mr. A. M. Johnson, President of the National Life Insurance Company of Chicago. He had offered to grubstake me with $20,000.00 to prospect in his behalf with this structural idea for a skyscraper as I had already laid it before him the year before.

Cantilever construction was one of the principal features that brought the Imperial safely through the great quake, and Mr. Johnson was interested to see how this cantilever principle, so successful there, could be adapted to modern skyscraper requirements. How would it all work out in a great office building for the site he owned on Water-Tower Square, Chicago?

Ideas attracted this insurance man. He kept saying, "Now, Mr. Wright, remember!"—with his characteristic chuckle—"I want a virgin. I want a virgin."

The studies were finally in presentable order. I took them in to him and he took them to his house and put them in his own bedroom. The glass of one of the drawings, the color perspective, one day being broken by the houseman, he put the drawing in his car, took it over to the framer, waited until it was fixed and brought it back home himself. He wanted no one to see the design but himself. Intensely interested in ideas, I believe, though not himself the kind of man inclined to build much, he seemed rather of the type called conservative who, tempted, will sneak up behind an idea, pinch it in the behind and turn and run. There is this type of man bred by our capitalistic system, not the captain, nor the broker or the banker but a better sort not quite contented with the commplace, not quite courageous enough to take risks. I have met many such men.

BUSINESS MYSTIC

I believe that a good part of this is obliquity due to the fact that an idea so soon attracts a man of that kind—all the agencies he is connected with or definitely knows react for him. The engineers shake their heads, rental experts will shake theirs, banks hang out the "busy" sign. Architects will stand together, ridicule the idea—until the businessman who had a moment of illumination and some desire for initiative, by sheer weight of the circumstances in which he has himself taken root, is pushed back—where he belongs, I suppose—is quite lost. He may be our chief asset in time. He is far ahead of the conservative that battens and fattens on capitalistic enterprise of true captains—turning the vision of real men into the perquisites of the parasite. To this latter type of conservative nothing much happens, either way. He is the middle-of-the-road egotist. The middle of the road is the place for him. As it is the place for "everybody" he will have plenty of company there. He feeds upon "company" such as it is.

Here was Mr. A. M. Johnson, Chicago National Life Insurance, paying a round sum to me to see how an idea would work out in his behalf?

A. M. Johnson was a strange mixture of the fanatic and mystic; Shylock and the humanist. Withal he was extraordinarily intelligent. His back had been broken in a railway accident but by sheer strength of intelligent will, he had survived. A slight stoop stayed in the way of his walk. We took a trip together into Death Valley, where he and Death Valley Scotty had made a place in which to live. He drove his own car, a Dodge, and as I rode beside him Nature staged a show for us all the way.

He was a convert to Billy Sunday, a revivalist famous for his religious activities, or rather his activities in religious matters. So he was fundamentalist, controversialist of no mean order. Religiously we were at the poles apart, but he grubstaked me in search of an idea, just the same.

No pigeonholes in nature, human or otherwise, in which to put a man. A singular man, Mr. Johnson's singular trait was his singular friendship for Scotty. Scotty was suspected of having murderous connection with gold mines on some location known only to him. But I suspect A. M. Johnson was Scotty's gold mine. The demonstration made by the Imperial Hotel had interested him. He wanted to know why the same construction wouldn't apply to a skyscraper, Water-Tower Plaza, Chicago.

THE GLASS SKYSCRAPER

A lot of approximately 300 × 100 facing 300 feet long to the south.

Sheet-copper and glass the mediums I chose for the thin pendent wall-screens to be carried by the outer edges of cantilever floor slabs. To avoid the prejudice I saw in my client's hard mind against excessive glass surface, I decided to make the exterior area of this project about ¾ of copper and ¼ of glass. Sheet metal—copper—would therefore characterize this building more than the glass.

At work upon this scheme—metal and glass house—the metal and glass service station, brother to the car and the plane, seemed near at hand. For the Machine Age should have a great many types: at least as many types as there are materials and methods of construction: genuine. Why not? But now, what form? I had not gone very far into skyscraper steel-construction before.

So the A. M. Johnson plans for this insurance building were fresh opportunity to devise a more practical solution of the skyscraper problem. The advantages offered by modern materials and methods add up mostly heavily in their own favor where they can go farthest—either up and down or crosswise. So standardization here might come completely into its own because standardization is in the nature of both the sheet-metal process and of reinforced concrete.

Exterior walls as such may disappear—instead see suspended, standardized sheet-copper screens only slightly engaged with the edges of the floors. The walls themselves cease to exist as either weight or thickness. Windows in this fabrication are a matter of units in the screen fabric, opening singly or in groups at the will of the occupant. Outside glass of the building may be cleaned from the inside with neither bother nor risk. The vertical mullions (copper shells filled with non-conducting mastic) are large and strong enough only to carry from floor to floor. Mullions themselves project much or little as more or less light is wanted. If much projection, the shadows are enriched. Less projection dispels shadows and brightens the interior. These projecting mullions, really vertical blades of copper, act in the sun like the blades of a blind.

Unit of two feet both ways is small because of Mr. Johnson's fear of too much glass. In this instance the unit is emphasized on every alternate vertical with additional emphasis laid on every fifth unit to enlarge the metal areas and create a larger rhythm. There is no emphasis needed on the horizontal units. They would catch water or dust. The edge of the various floors are beveled to the same section used between the windows where engaged with the wall screen. So these appear in the screen as one of the horizontal divisions occurring naturally on the two-foot unit-lines. The floors themselves however do appear at intervals in the recessions of the screen: this in order to bring the concrete structure itself into relief, seen in relation to the screen as well as in connection with it, thus weaving the two elements of structure together.

The outer building-surfaces become opalescent, iridescent copper-bound glass. To avoid all interference with fabrication of the light-giving exterior-screen, the supporting pylons were set back from the lot line, the floors carried by them becoming thus cantilever-slabs. The extent of the cantilever is determined by the use for which the building is designed—in this case twelve feet. These pylons are continuous through all floors and in this instance are exposed at the top. The pylons enlarge to carry electrical, plumbing and heating conduits branching from the shafts, not in the floor slabs at all but all in piping designed into visible fixtures extending beneath each ceiling to where the outlets are needed in the office arrangement. All electrical or plumbing appliances may thus be disconnected and re-located at short notice, no waste at all in time or material, free of the building in vertical shafts.

Fabricated upon a perfect unit system, the interior-partitions are all to be made up in sections, complete with doors ready to set in place. Designed to match the general style of the outer wall-screen. These changeable interior partition units thus fabricated may be stored ready to use and any changes to suit tenants made overnight with no waste of time and material. Mr. Johnson was an experienced landlord. These simples appealed to him. Again it was the kind of standardization in building that gave us the motor car, the aeroplane and ship.

The increase of glass area over the usual modern skyscraper fenestration was only about ten per cent (the margin could be increased or diminished by expanding or contracting the copper members in which the glass is set), so the expense of heating was not materially increased. Inasmuch as the copper mullions were to be filled with insulating material and the window-openings all tight (mechanical units in a mechanical screen), this excess of glass was compensated. The radiators cast as a railing set in front of the lower glass unit of this outer screen-wall were free enough to make cleaning easy. The walls of the first two stories, or more, were of unobstructed glass suspended from floors above. Dreams of the shop-keeper in this connection fully realized.

Connecting stairways necessary between floors are here arranged as a practical fire-escape forming the central feature, as may be seen at the front and rear of each section of the whole mass, and though cut off by fire-proof doors at each floor the continuous stairway thus made discharges upon the sidewalk below without obstruction.

The construction of such a building as this would be at least one-third lighter than anything in the way of a tall building yet built—and three times stronger in any disturbance: construction balanced as the body on the legs, walls hanging as the arms from the shoulders, the whole heavy only where weight insures stability.

Of chief value as I see it is the fact that the scheme as a whole eliminates the masonry that now vexes all such buildings. This scheme takes away from field construction all such elements from the architectural exterior or interior. Architecture in this scheme is become a complete shop-fabrication. The most complicated part of the building, prefabricated, assembled in the field.

The mere physical concrete construction of pylons and floors is non-involved. The fabric, indestructible, is made entirely independent of anything hitherto complicating it and mixed up with it in our country as "architecture." As practiced at present the skyscraper is expensively involved but entirely irrelevant as "architecture." Here entirely relevant but uninvolved.

Piping and conduits of all appurtenance systems may be cut in the shop, labor in the field reduced to assembling only. No fitting. Screwing up the joints all that is necessary in either heating, lighting or plumbing.

Thus, literally, we have a shop-made building in all but the interior supporting posts and floors, which may be reinforced concrete or concrete-masked steel cast in place in the field. In this design, architecture was frankly, profitably taken from the field to the factory. A building is here, standardized as any mechanical thing whatsoever might be from a penny-whistle to a piano. It is dignified, imaginative, practical. The economic advantages are enormous and obvious.

There is no unsalable floor space in this building.

No "features" inside or outside manufactured merely "for architectural effect."

To gratify our landlord, his lot area now salable to the very lot-line itself and on every floor, where ordinances do not interfere and demand that they be reduced in area as the building soars.

Architecture here in evidence is a light, trim, practical commercial. A fabric—every inch and pound is in service. Beautiful. But best to say nothing about that to Mr. Johnson. I said very little about it.

The aim in this fabrication employing the cantilever system of construction was to achieve scientific utility by means of the Machine. To accomplish—first of all—standardization not only serving as the basis for keeping the life of the building true as architecture but enabling me to project the whole, as an expression of valuable principle into a genuine living architecture of the present day. American Architecture.

Work began on this study the winter of 1920, main features of it having been in mind ever since the building of the Imperial in 1917. I had the good fortune to explain the scheme in detail and show the developed preliminary drawings to Lieber Meister Louis H. Sullivan shortly before he died. Gratefully I remember—and proudly too—he said: "I had faith that it would come. It is a work of great art. I knew what I was talking about all these years—you see? I could never have done this building myself, but I believe that, but for me, you could never have done it."

I know I should never have reached it, but for what he was and what he himself did. This design is dedicated to him.

During this period while building the Imperial Hotel and the block-buildings in Los Angeles, life of legal necessity—divorce still denied me—remained unconventional. Voluntarily in exile. Taliesin meantime had become refuge to the unfortunate Miriam Noel. She who had gone with me to Japan.

But life when resumed at Taliesin II had now much changed: No longer carefree walks over friendly hills, nor swimming in the river below. No horseback riding along the country lanes, no coasting and skating or happy sleighing in winter. No freedom, no singing. Involuntarily, all intention otherwise, life seemed paralyzed by subtle indirection. Taliesin so it seemed—had encountered disintegration from within.

Only caretakers and one faithful apprentice, William Smith, stayed. Restlessly, during these years following, Taliesin had languished, called in vain.

Dust had settled on the heads of ancient gods at rest upon the broad ledges. But Taliesin had been calling me all these years and I was looking forward to the time when it should come alive again for me and all those I loved. Now I had come back from Japan. I had married Miriam several months before, marriage that resulted in ruin. Instead of improving as I had hoped, our relationship became worse.

With marriage she seemed to lose what interest she had in life at Taliesin and become more than ever restless; vindictive. Finally under circumstances altogether baffling—she left "to live a life of her own." To oppose her now in the slightest degree meant violence. But I did not really wish to oppose her.

She went first to Chicago. But even now I would not give up hope or effort to make good a human relationship gone so far wrong. Suffering and sacrifice had already entered both sides. Unfamiliar moral cowardice kept me from acknowledging defeat, although by nature and equipment unfitted for the task I had undertaken. But the circumstances becoming more than ever violent, even dangerous, I consulted Dr. William Hixon, a famous psychiatrist of Chicago now at Geneva. A tardy consultation. Long dreaded, it had been deferred.

Convinced by his observation that the struggle of the past six years had been hopeless from the beginning and that Mariam had all along been a danger not only to herself but especially to anyone with whom she might live in close association, I agreed to end the relationship, modifying only somewhat the terms dictated by herself. She had returned to Los Angeles. Dr. Hixon said that the only hope for a longer freedom for her lay in letting her "have her head." To oppose her would only be to burn her up more quickly.

So final arrangements for divorce were made by Judge James Hill. I stayed on at Taliesin.

Young people had come from all over the world attracted by Taliesin's fame abroad to share its spirit; to learn I suppose what message the indigenous United States had for Europe. Evenings, after good work done, the piano, violin and cello spoke there the religion of Bach, Beethoven and Handel. William Blake, Samuel Butler, Walt Whitman and Shelley often presided. Carl Sandburg, Edna Millay and Ring Lardner, too, had something to say or sing. Life in the Wisconsin hills revived for the little cosmopolitan group eager to know this "America," for Taliesin was at work quietly Americanizing Europe while American architects Europeanized America.

But peace even for these seekers from afar was not to last. There were but eleven months of growing good-will. The living things of art and beauty belonging now to the place as the eye to the face, become like Taliesin's own flesh, became a loneliness. A sorrow. Occasionally a living thought would go over them as they stood dignified but neglected. Taliesin dreamed, meditated, worked and slept.

Primeval fireplaces sent streams of light and warmth into the house itself, but it no longer seemed to know how to live. Dissension and discord had shamed the peace, outraged lifting walls and friendly ceilings.

ISAIAH

When about a year after separation from Miriam, one evening at twilight as the lightning of an approaching storm was playing and wind rising, I came down from the evening meal alone in the little detached dining room on the hill-top to the dwelling on the court below to find smoke pouring from my bedroom. Again—there it was—Fire!

Fire fanned by that rising storm meant a desperate fight. I realized all but two besides myself had gone from the place for the evening. Mell, the driver, Kameki, a Japanese apprentice.

I called for water. Water came to the constant cry of "Water!" for two hours. I thought I had put the fire out when an ominous crackling above the bedroom ceiling indicated fire had got into the dead spaces beneath the roof. I sent out alarm again. Again the people of the countryside came and turned to fight flames at Taliesin.

The rising wind blew the flames—raging now beneath the roof surfaces—out above the roof in a dozen places. "Let us save what we can of the things inside," they cried.

"No, fight the fire. Fight! Fight I tell you! Save Taliesin or let all go!" I shouted, like some dogged, foolish captain on the bridge of a sinking vessel doomed to all eyes but his.

More water was the cry as more men came over the hills to fight the now roaring sea of devastation. Whipped by the big wind, great clouds of smoke and sparks drove straight down the lengths of Taliesin courts. The place seemed doomed—even to me. How cruel the wind may be, cruel as fire itself.

But I was up on the smoking roofs, feet burned, lungs seared, hair and eyebrows gone, thunder rolling as the lightning flashed over the lurid scene, the hill-top long since profaned by crowds of spectators standing silent there. I stood up there—and fought. Isaiah?

I could not give up the fight to Isaiah. Now came the fight to save the workrooms. But everyone else had given it up. Taliesin, so they said, was gone.

Destruction reached to the workrooms—the studio—began to take hold of them too—water gone, human energy gone. Men were lying about the roofs to recover strength and breath to keep on fighting flames.

Suddenly a tremendous pealing roll of thunder. The storm broke with a violent change of wind that rolled the great mass of flame up the valley. It recoiled upon itself but once as the rain fell hissing into the roaring furnace. The clouds of smoke and sparks as by a miracle were swept the opposite way. It was as though some gigantic unseen hand had awed the spectators. Super-human Providence perhaps—the thought in their minds was—who knows?

In that terrible twenty minutes, the living half of Taliesin gone. Again!

The heat had been so intense that plate glass windows lay, crystal pools in ashes on hot stone pavements.

Smoldering or crumbled in ashes were priceless works of art— blossoms-of-the-human-soul in all ages—we merely call them works of art. They lay there broken, or vanished utterly.

Another savage blow had struck at Taliesin.

Now left to me out of most of my earnings since Taliesin was destroyed, all I could show for my work and wanderings in the Orient for years past were the leather trousers, burned socks and shirt in which I now stood defeated. But what the workshop contained—was intact.

But Taliesin lived wherever I stood! A figure crept foward to me from out the shadows to say this, and I believed what Olgivanna said.

Lightning had struck again. Is human carelessness and fallibility the wrath of God? Again searching causes I wondered. Everything of a personal nature I had in the world, beside my work, was gone. But . . . this time reason to be thankful—no lives lost except those images whose souls belonged and could now return to the souls that made them—the precious works of art that were destroyed—my reward for four years work in Japan.

I had not protected them. Yes I . . . a poor trustee for posterity. I thought now "they should live on in me." The thought with which I consoled myself. I would prove their life by mine in what I did. I said so to the suppliant figure standing on the hill-top in the intense dark now following the fierce brilliant blaze and went my way.

That lurid crowd! During terrible destruction the crowd stood there on the hill-top, faces lurid—lit by the flames. Some few sympathetic. Others half sympathizing were convinced of inevitable doom. Some were already sneering at the fool who imagined Taliesin could come back after all that had happened there before. Others stood there stolidly chewing tobacco—entertained?

Were they the "force" that had struck again? Were they really "Isaiah"?

Well—counseled by the living—there was I, alive in their midst, at least. Was I the key to a Taliesin nobler than the one lost if I could make it? I had faith that I could build another Taliesin! Taliesin III.

A few days later, clearing away still smoking ruin to reconstruct, I picked from the debris partly calcined marble heads of the Tang Dynasty, fragments of the black basalt of a splendid Wei-stone, soft-clay Sung sculpture and gorgeous Ming pottery that had turned to the color of bronze by the intensity of the fire. All sacrificial offerings to— whatever gods may be, I put the fragments aside to weave them into the masonry fabric of Taliesin III. Already in mind Taliesin III was to stand in place of Taliesin II. I went to work again to build again better than before. I had learned from building the other two.

So, again after confusion, destruction, desolation, I at work again in the workshop at Taliesin, out in the fields—walking, swimming in the river, driving over the hills, skating in winter. Appetite for creation was still lagging—a little. But coming rapidly alive once more. Hunger for the creative life was not far away—salvation was near by.

REUNION

Just before destruction of Taliesin I, Lieber Meister and I had come together again.

Things had not been going well with him since the separation from Dankmar Adler shortly after that triumphant disaster the Columbian "Fair." The Guarantee Building, Buffalo, had just come into the office as I left. It was the last building build under the Adler and Sullivan partnership.

To go back many years into history: owing to the nature of such creative work as theirs Adler and Sullivan, Architects, had made no money. Their work cost them as much, often more, than they received for it, although they were paid as well as any first-class architects—probably better than most. The depression following the Columbian Fair hit Adler and Sullivan hard. At this psychological moment Crane of the Crane Company came along as tempter. He offered Dankmar Adler $25,000 a year to sell Crane Elevators. In a fit of despondency the Big Chief accepted. Some money had to be earned by someone.

Sullivan, left alone, was resentful.

Their clientele had been, mostly, Adler's, as Sullivan now found out. Louis Sullivan soon faced the fact that he was where he must take what was left to him from the Adler connection and start to build up a practice for himself. Only one Adler and Sullivan client stayed with the now lonely Sullivan: Meyer, of Schlesinger and Meyer, who employed him to design the new retail store building on State Street.

Meantime, I got the story, a curious mishap had befallen Crane's new lion. He went to New York to sell Crane Elevators for the new Siegel Cooper Building in Chicago. The opposing bidder, Sprague Electric, simply pulled out a report Adler the architect had made concerning their elevator for the Auditorium Building some years previous. It gave the Electric everything—yes, including the Siegel Cooper work. Mr. Adler came home. Some words from Crane. The lion was unused to being talked to in that tone of voice, especially from one who had hitherto come to him for justice or for favors. The result of the interview was a check from Crane to Adler for a year's salary and a contract canceled.

We all now hoped to see the two partners together again. But no, the Master was resentful still and the Big Chief had had enough.

About this time Mr. Adler at the Union League Club called me. I went to talk things over with him. As yet I had not communicated with

Lieber Meister since leaving. The old Chief seemed morose. He had been greatly worried by the risks he had taken to please his clients in certain features of the Auditorium; addition to the height of the tower to please Sullivan; addition of the banquet hall over the trusses spanning the Auditorium to please Ferdinand Peck *et al.* Movement not yet stopped. The tower settling, taking down adjoining portions of the building.

I noticed a great change in him. He spoke bitterly of Sullivan, who had published the Guarantee Building with Adler's name deleted from the plans.

"But for me, Wright, there would have been no Guarantee Building!"

"Yes," I said. "But I am sure the omission was not Mr. Sullivan's. Probably the publisher's. Why don't you make sure?"

"I'm sure enough," he said.

I tried him out concerning his former partner. I told him there was such general disappointment over the separation—believed they needed each other—and if ever two men did, they did—had done such great work together—the depression couldn't last. Many other private pleas for resuming the old relationship.

"No, Wright," thrusting out his bearded chin in characteristic fashion, "I am going to keep my office in my hat so far as I can—there's nothing in the big office with big rent and a big salary list. I'll do the few buildings I can do, and instead of earning $50,000, keeping $1000—I'll earn, by myself, $5000 and keep $2000."

Looking at me sharply under his honest, shaggy eyebrows: "Take this from me, you do the same, Wright." He added, "No architect on that individual basis ever needs a partner."

I saw something that had lived between the two men who so needed each other already burned out.

We walked over to the several small rooms he had taken on the Wabash Avenue side of the Auditorium—while Sullivan was still carrying on up in the tower. It seemed a heart-breaking situation. But I still believed they would come together. I said so when I left. Worry and disappointment had already done something to the grand old Chief. This was no way of life for him.

In a short time he was dead.

Some seven years later Lieber Meister and I met again. I saw instantly that he too had gone from bad to far worse. The Auditorium management had refused finally to carry him further in the splendid tower offices, and offered him two rooms below, near those Adler had occupied on the Wabash Avenue front. He accepted them, but later even these were closed to the Master. On that occasion he had called me over long-distance. Luckily I was able to reinstate him. But habits engendered by his early life in Paris had made havoc with him. He had "gone off," as they say, and frightfully.

Much softened though, and deepened too, I thought. He gently called me "Frank." I loved the way the word came from him. Before that it had always been "Wright."

His courage was not gone. No, that would never go. His eyes burned as brightly as ever. The old gleam of humor would come them and go. But his carriage was not the same: the body was disintegrating.

I remember sitting on his desk noticing that it was uselessly littered with his papers. There were photographs of the small bank-building he had been doing. These showed only remnants of the great genius that flashed upon him in the Wainwright Building as in the old days in the tower. He was leaning heavily now on George Elmslie, who was still with him at the time these buildings were done. George the faithful.

But at least Lieber Meister was safe in an armchair by a fireside. He had been made life-member of the Cliff-Dwellers. A few cronies stood by. One of the great virtues of that social organization that it did this for him. I had corresponded with him while in Japan, and from Los Angeles. Whenever I got to Chicago I took a room at the Congress for him, next mine. He was now staying at the old Hotel Warner way down on Cottage Grove Avenue, an old haunt of his with little else to recommend it. He had taken great pride in the performance of the Imperial Hotel, wrote two articles concerning it for the *Architectural Record*. "At last, Frank," he said, "something they can't take away from you." (I wonder why he thought "they" couldn't take it away from me? "They" could take anything away from anybody, it not by hook, then by crook.)

Several architects in Chicago befriended him, were kind to him. Gates of the American, T. C. Lucas, Hottinger, and others of the Northwestern Terra Cotta Company especially so. But he was no more tolerant of his contemporaries in architecture now than ever before. Less so.

For many years he had been compelled to see great opportunities for work he could do so much better as to make comparison absurd— going to inferior young men, going just because personal habits had given provincial prejudice a chance to "view with alarm" or dislike, though the matters involved were no concern of theirs nor directly connected with his efficiency as an architect. Prejudice, provincial, quotidian, was his implacable enemy. A genius? Well, that term damned him as it was intended to do. It will write off any man from the commercial scene we live in.

Finance. Tiptoe to safety when that word comes through from the common man!

His efficiency was actually impaired by himself. Increasingly he sought refuge from loneliness—frustration—yes, where and as so many of his gifted brothers have been driven to do since time was. Betrayal too.

Had opportunity really opened, even this late in his life, he might have been saved for years of remarkable usefulness. But popular prejudice encouraged by professional jealousy built a wall of ignorance around him so high that the wall blinded his countrymen and he was wasted. At times his despondency overcame his native pride and natural buoyancy. Even his high courage would give way to fear—for his livelihood. Then all would come clear again. For only a little while.

Caustic when he chose, the old Master. When in a bitter mood, a dozen or so of his hard-boiled contemporaries would come tumbling from their perches on high, top side down, inside out. His blade could cut: flash as it cut.

Writing the *Autobiography of an Idea* at this time, he would occasionally read chapters to me. He always loved to write. Now completely shut off from his natural medium of expression, he turned more and more to writing. Soon "the book" meant much to him I saw.

He had visited Taliesin some years before. But it proved rather a strenuous experience for him—the result a bad cold. Two years later, his breath was shorter still and after several cups of the strong coffee he loved too much, his breath so short he would take my arm to walk—even slowly.

Sinking. I continued to see him oftener than every week if I could.

Weeks passed and a telephone call came to Taliesin from the Warner. I went to Chicago and found the place up in arms against him. He had fallen very sick. Violent spells came over him more and more often. I made peace with the manager—after raising Cain over the condition I found in his room. The manager was really devoted to Sullivan as he said he was, but now at his wit's end. We finally got a nurse who would stay. His devoted comrade, the little henna-haired milliner who understood him and could do almost anything with him, was herself in the hospital at the time.

He begged, "Don't leave me, Frank. Stay."

I stayed. He seemed to be himself again toward morning. We talked about the forthcoming *Autobiography of an Idea*. He hoped there might be some income in it—for him.

He had everything to make him comfortable, so after he had fallen asleep, I went back to Taliesin again with a promise from the nurse to call me if I was needed.

In town a few days later, I went to see him again.

Seemed better. There—at last—the first bound copy of his *Autobiography*. It had just come in, lying on the table by his bed. He wanted to get up. I helped him, put my overcoat round his shoulders as he sat on the bed with his feet covered up on the floor. He looked over at the book.

"There it is, Frank."

I was sitting by him, arm around him to keep him warm and steady him. I could feel every vertebra in his backbone as I rubbed my hand up and down his spine to comfort him and feel his heart pounding. This heart, his physician said, twice its natural size owing to coffee and bromide was bulging through his ribs.

"Frank, give me the book! First copy to you. A pencil!" He tried to raise his arm to take the pencil; couldn't lift it. Gave it up with an attempt at a smile.

I have never read the book. All I know of it are the chapters he read to me himself. I could not read it. My copy was lost in the fire at Taliesin.

Yes, courage still there. He cursed a little—gently enough. Eyes were deeper in their sockets, but still burning bright. He joked about the end he now saw and again cursed—under his breath. For the first time he would admit to himself the end. But to me he looked as though he were better, notwithstanding that helpless arm. But—bad sign—he seemed indifferent: didn't want to talk about it at all, either way. Life had been hard on him. Such friends as he had could do little to make up for the deep tragedy of his frustration as an architect. In solitude only a year or so before he had made the beautiful drawings for the *System of Architectural Ornament,* his hand shaking as with palsy until he began to draw, then firm as could be. These drawings then made show little falling off either in style or execution from his best at any time. Ornament was his inextinguishable gift to the last. I had passed through many situations with him that looked worse than this one. So I put him back to bed again—covered him up—sat there by him on the edge of the bed. He fell asleep. Another crisis had apparently passed. He seemed to sleep well, breathe deeply enough and once more easily. The nurse stepped out for a moment. An imperative call came from Taliesin. I left a note for the nurse to call me immediately if there was any change in him for the worse.

At Taliesin I listened anxiously for the telephone. No call coming, I felt reassured.

But the day after I learned of his death from the newspapers and a long-distance call from Max Dunning. He had died after I left.

Several architects, warm-hearted little Max one of them, Andy Rebori another, happened to come to see him and had taken charge. I was not sent for.

The Master had nothing in the world he could call his own but the new clothes it had been a pleasure of my life to see him in—these and a daguerreotype of his lovely mother, himself and his brother, aged about nine, seen standing on either side of her.

Knowing he was dying he had given this prized possession to the nurse to give to "Frank."

I should have liked to keep the warm muffler he had worn about his neck. What use? *He* was gone!

Nor did anyone think to advise me concerning any of the funeral arrangements. His friends planned an ordinary funeral at Graceland, at which Wallace Rice, his crony at the Cliff Dwellers, spoke and I attended. Later they designed a monument for him . . .a slat of his ornament designed for his grave in his own vein! "They" caused this to be designed by George Elmslie, young understudy brought over to Sullivan from Silsbee's because the Master wanted me to train someone to take my place in case anything should happen to me. George had taken my place when I left, and stayed with the Lieber Meister ten years or more. But to me, who had understood and loved him, this idea of a monument to the great Master was simply ironic. There was nothing to be done about it worth doing. It was their own best thought for the man. No monument is ever more than a monument to those who erect it. Is it?

By the Eternal: these monuments! Will we never make an end of such banality or such profanity?

What great man ever lived whose memory has not been so traduced, made ridiculous or unwittingly insulted by the monument "they" erected to themselves in his name when he was dead! Thomas Jefferson, Abraham Lincoln to mind. Monuments! They are made by those who, voluntarily or not, never did anything but betray the thing the great man loved most, those who were "charitable" when he was in need; officious when he died. Hell hold them all!

I wrote something in the fullness of my heart, at the time published somewhere. I forget where. This is it:

THE MASTER'S WORK

The New and the Old and the Old in the New ever is Principle.

Principle is all and single the reality my master Louis Sullivan ever really loved. It gave to the man stature and to his work great significance.

His loyalty to principle was the more remarkable as vision when all around him poisonous cultural mists hung low to obscure or blight any bright hope of finer beauty in the culture of this world.

The buildings he has left with us for a brief time are the least of him. In the heart of him he was of infinite value to his country, the country that wasted him. His countrymen wasted him not because they would: but because they could not know him.

Work, great or small—as human expression—must be studed in relation to the time in which it insisted upon its virtues and got itself to human view.

So it will be with the work he has left to us.

Remember, you who may, the contemporaries of the first great building, our Chicago Auditorium.

They were the hectic Pullman Building, W. W. Boyington's "Board of Trade," the hideous Union Station and many other survivors in the idiom of that insensate period.

Outside the initial impetus of John Edelman in his early days, H. H. Richardson, the great emotional revivalist of art Romanesque, was one whose influence the Master felt. John Root, another fertile rival who knew less than the Master but felt almost as much, sometimes shot very straight indeed. They were his only peers. They were feeling their way. But he was feeling *and* thinking his way, to the New.

Dankmar Adler, master of the plan and master of men, was his faithful partner.

The Auditorium Building is largely what it is, physically, owing to Dankmar Adler's good judgment and restraining influence. But it was Louis Sullivan who made it sing.

The Getty Tomb in Graceland Cemetery was entirely his own, a piece of sculpture, a great poem, addressed to human sensibilities as such.

But—when he brought the drawing board with the motive for the Wainwright Building outlined in profile and scheme upon it, threw it down on my table, I was perfectly aware of what had happened.

This was the great Louis Sullivan moment. His greatest effort. The skyscraper as a new thing beneath the sun, an entity imperfect, but with virtue, individuality, beauty all its own—*the tall building* was born. Until Louis Sullivan showed the way, tall buildings never had unity, never were "tall." They were built up in layers, fighting tallness instead of gracefully (and honestly) accepting it. What unity those false masses had now piling up toward New York and Chicago sky is due to the master-mind first perceiving the tall building height triumphant.

The Wainwright Building prophesied and opened the way for the *tall* office building we now point to with pride. To this day, the Wainwright remains the master key to the skyscraper so far as the skyscraper is a matter of architecture.

Only the interior of the Chicago Auditorium, pictorial Transportation Building for what it was worth, the Getty Tomb, the Wainwright Building are necessary to show the great reach of creative activity that was Louis Sullivan's. Other buildings he did, but all more or less on these stems. Some were grafted from them. Some were grown from them. But all were relatively inferior in point of the quality finally associated with the primitive strength of the thing that got itself done (or born) regardless and stark to the idea.

The capacity for love—ardent, true, poetic—was great in Louis Sullivan. His system of ornament in itself, alone, would prove this. In this his work was esoteric. Is it the less precious for that?

Do you realize that here in his system of ornament is no body of culture evolving through centuries of time but a scheme and "style" of plastic expression which an individual working away in the poetry-crushing environment of a more cruel materialism than any seen since the days of the brutal Romans had made out of himself. In this he was an individual evoking the goddess that whole civilizations strove in vain for centuries to win; wooed her with this charming interior smile all on his own, in one lifetime all too brief.

Regarding this achievement we may say that the time will come when every man may have that precious quality called style for his very own.

Then where on earth I ask you are the others?

Ah, that supreme erotic adventure of the mind that was his love of fascinating ornament!

Genius the Master had, or rather, genius had him. Genius possessed him: reveled in him. And he squandered it.

The effect of any genius is seldom seen in its own time. Nor can the full effects of genius ever traced or seen. Human affairs are flowing. What we call life is plastic, in everything a becoming and is so in spite of all efforts to fix it with names, all endeavors to make it static to man's will. As a pebble cast into the ocean sets up reactions lost in distance and time, so does a man's genius go on infinitely. Forever, for genius *is* and expression of Principle. Therefore in no way does genius ever run counter to genius nor could.

We may be sure that the intuitions and expressions of such a nature as his in the work to which he put his hand no less than the suggestion he was himself to kindred or aspiring natures, is more conservative of the future Architecture of our country than all the work of all the schools of all our time combined with all the salesmanship of all the functioneers on earth.

Not long ago, weary, in a despondent moment, he said—"It would be harder now to do radical work and more difficult to get radical work accepted now than it ever was.

"The people have stopped thinking!

"The inevitable drift toward mediocrity, taking the name of Democracy in vain, has set in. I see it so."

No, my Master, believe me it is not so. There is never an inevitable contrary to nature, and nature is love of Life. The torch flung to your master-hand from the depths of antiquity, from the heart of this human world—kept alight and held aloft for twenty years at least by you—shall not go out! Ever it has been flung from hand to hand and never yet— since time began for man—has it gone out.

TALIESIN III

My mother gone now only eighty-three years of age.

My Master, gone before his time.

Three beloved homes gone. The first—cottage and studio at Oak Park—stood for nine years. The second, Taliesin, withstood five. The third, Taliesin II, eleven years. Taliesin III?

Now the fourth home built by my own hands: new home built out of a battered and punished but still sentimental self in the same quest—life!

Help as ever came from the deeps of life. Understanding and ready for any sacrifice came Olgivanna. A woman is, for man, the best of faithful friends if only man will let her be one. This idea of the virtue of personal life had come with Taliesin II. Conviction, now.

That idea? Simply said, "Any man had a right to three things if he is honest with all three." Had I been, could I be, honest with them all?

Honest with the man's own life, the man's work, the man's love?

The only answer lies in the retrospect. But to work again. Another spring of co-ordinate effort more in love with life than ever before. Another summer came and autumn. Another winter and, early 1925 came one more chance to live and work in peace in another, yet the same, Taliesin.

Now—Taliesin III, none the less proudly, if ruefully, took place where the ashes of Taliesin I and Taliesin II, together with the life lived in each, fallen in ruins.

The limestone piers, walls and fireplaces of Taliesin II turned red and crumbled by fire, but I saved many stones not destroyed thus, dyed by fire; built them together with the fragments of great sculpture I had raked from the ashes, into the new walls adding a storied richness to them unknown before. Whereas the previous buildings had all grown by addition, all now could be spontaneously born.

So, taught by the building of Taliesin I and II, I made forty sheets of pencil studies for the building of Taliesin III. Still in debt for the second, but no discretion whatever could detain me now from beginning work on the third.

Waves of publicity, this time neither ribald nor unkind, had broken over the ruins. After all, even newspaper folk are kind when they really understand. The frustration of the life of the seven years past had ended in the destruction of everything frustrated life had touched. I sought comfort in that thought as one fine thing after another I had loved and learned would rise out of its ashes and reproach me with shameful sense of loss.

Again, more and better building materials: more and, by this time, better trained workmen. More intelligent planning and execution on my part, and difficulties in ways and means. I myself had more patience, deeper anxiety: more humility yet the same faith. Moving forward.

Taliesin's radiant brow marked now by both shame and sorrow should come forth, shine again with serenity unknown before. This third trial, granted by Life itself, helped build the walls: make them more noble than before. Real comradeship at last!

Many years of sorrow, trial and defeat, Taliesin III refreshed by gift of a little new soul, long desired to bring back to Taliesin something it had not found, or, finding, had lost.

Taliesin III built by and for Olgivanna, Iovanna and Svetlana.

No doubt Isaiah stood there in the storms that muttered, rolled and broke again and again over our low-spreading shelter. Lightning often played and crashed above us but the happy friendliness sheltered there was ready for any sacrifice if only Taliesin might come to Life. Give more proof of quality.

Mosaic Isaiah, eyes aslant where the beautiful would show or the lovely dare lift its head, curly locks or black abundant tresses—waiting there behind the hills to strike, should life at Taliesin rise from its ashes a third time?

If the angry prophet struck twice he could strike again.

Human obliquity still going hand in hand with bigger and better publicity conspired with the ruthless prophet; self-appointed agent of an angry Jehovah, to do "righteous" work? This time do it not by death and fire but by madness. Taliesin the gentler prophet of the Celts, of a more merciful God tempted to lift an arm to strike back in self-defense, suffered in silence and waited.

296

Again hue and cry of "punishment" reached the official doors. Some moved by it. Knowing only the hue and cry they added blows to give richness to the hue, adding injury to the insult of the cry until the sovereign insult in the gift of its own people—who should have protected it and many who would protect it had "Isaiah" not blinded them too—was now put upon Taliesin. Taliesin raged, wanted to strike back. Again held his arm. Strike at what?

Like Isaiah—at little children and women, torn in the streets and bleeding?

Taliesin turned to work. Work is true defense even against Isaiah. At least life was no longer betrayed *within* sheltering walls. However it might be beset from *without* by any wrathful prophet whatsoever.

This stand stood firm while newspapermen, editors, reporters, cameramen, publishers, lawyers, petty officials, federal, state, county, local officials, lawyers in Washington, lawyers in Minneapolis, lawyers in Chicago, lawyers in Milwaukee, lawyers in Madison, lawyers in Baraboo and Dodgeville, in Spring Green, newspapermen everywhere, judges, commissioners, prosecuting attorneys, process-servers, sheriffs, jailers, justices of the peace, federal immigration officers, police officers, Washington officials, senators and congressmen, governors—anything "authority" had—did their worst. That is, their best. This rolled over Taliesin once more.

Finally all ended by interference of my friends and clients to save Taliesin from wreck and myself too for more work there. Work? Again a saving clause.

To you Isaiah, vengeful prophet of an antique wrath, I say Taliesin is a nobler prophet, I am not afraid of him. Ancient Druid Bard he sang, forever sings, of merciful beauty. Wherever beauty Taliesin sings in praise of "the flower that fadeth, the grass that withereth." Taliesin loves and trusts—Man. But men not too much.

Standing where and how Isaiah, the great Jew, may stand in this third and nobler construction in the name of Taliesin—Taliesin Celt declares not only an architecture on this soil for a conscious United States of America but declares and for the same reason—the right of every aspiring man, so long as the man shall be as honest as he knows how to be with all three, his own life, his work and his own love.

But, leave the abstract figure I have employed. To be homeless without work when life and work have become synonymous terms, powerless to protect either; to see home, work and loved-ones at the mercy of exploitation by irresponsible fury, bigger and better publicity, is to go to the bottom of the vulgar pit any man may dig for himself by his own acts. My trial now was to see the weakness and helpless exaggeration of a hostile woman incited to destroy herself and all that had touched her or been touched by her thus to make holiday copy for those who neither cared for her nor really for anything she cared for except "copy."

"News" is usually bad tidings. Tidings not bad . . . they must be made bad, to make news.

Trials by heartless, vulgar imposition in the wake of self-inflicted failure are always harder to bear, I believe, than those failures we cannot trace to our own fault. For three years past I had self-inflicted failure to bear as secrets became open sores by way of scandal that finally reached the depths of humiliation and falsification. But never have I been allowed to bear failure alone. So I remember and record and leave the rest to life. Sensational distortion and exaggeration will here meet quiet fact for the first time. That perhaps is the main purpose of this somewhat premature autobiography, every word of which, at least, is true.

Within this extraordinary public excitement, a poor sense of the dignity and human-value of our public institutions got to Olgivanna, figure that crept forward out of dark shadows cast by lurid flames destroying Taliesin II.

Ashamed, sorry that she should be compelled to see this obnoxious phase of American life, first I tried to explain all these gratuitous performances of a public character making up this charivari. I said we had been betrayed, forced into seeming disrespect of established order, and tried to take the blame upon myself. As I should. Olgivanna took it all suffering—but without resentment. We stood our ground.

Born in Montenegro of people not unlike my own Welsh forbears, her upbringing had much in common with my own. At the age of nine she had gone to her married sister at Batum in the Caucasus, in order to have the advantages of education in Russia. Her father was Chief Justice of Montenegro for nearly twenty years. During the latter years of his life he was blind. He never saw the little daughter who used to lead him by the hand through the streets of Cettinje. He was still Chief Justice for many years while blind. Her mother was the daughter of "Vojevoda" Marco Milanoff—Balkan general to whom popular credit went for preserving Montenegro's independence. For Montenegro, like Wales and the country of the Basques, was a mountainous little country whose people were never conquered.

Olgivanna herself had grown up in a patriarchal family with a mind and will of her own.

When we first met I considered myself free in the circumstances, as did she. Though she never had met Miriam Noel, she knew as much about the circumstances of my life as I did. We both knew that only the final signature remained to be fixed to the divorce that settled complete separation from Miriam Noel, a separation in effect for more than one year before I met Olgivanna. That signature *was* added soon. But these facts were not in the news. The term "Montenegrin dancer" was invented by the fancy of the more imaginative reporters. They wrote their stories on that, implied character according to their limitations and usual devices with whatever slant seemed to suit the sheet that paid for their work.

I play the piano, but that doesn't make me a pianist? Olgivanna dances, but only as a feature of the training at the Gurdjieff Institute at Fontainebleau. This institution, too, came in for a measure of low implication in order to complete the picture, desired or not, as the case might be.

Unexpectedly, thus, came public charivari to add to the two just past.

I managed to get Olgivanna to Hollis, safe with her brother, Vladimir. I like Vladimir, and his wife. Love and protection around her—a great change from the humiliation and misery of the past fortnight. Her people insisted on my coming to stay at Hollis. I would go back to town with Vladimir in the morning, roam the streets of New York alone. I didn't care to see anyone at the time for fear of revealing our whereabouts to newspapers in pursuit of news.

I began to write: tried to write some impressions of the big city. "In Bondage" was one. "The Usonian City" another; later began this work.

Olgivanna did not improve as she should. The weather, cold and disagreeable, the situation severe. After Christmas I began to wonder where we could go, and hit on Puerto Rico. A long shot. But warm at least. Puerto Rico was now a possession of the United States of America. We would need no difficult passports. As a matter of fact, anywhere we went in the United States now we were likely to splash more muddy water over the public dam now represented by the "press."

Incognito, we took the boat for what remained of Atlantis: put up at a pleasant inn—the Coamo—far down the island. Coamo had natural hot-sulphur springs piped into enormous old Spanish stone baths in which we could go for a swim. At night we went under mosquito nets, but had to make constant war on the pests. Days and nights were sultry, oppressive until we would drive up into the mountains. The air there was delightful. These old mountain roads of Spanish Puerto Rico are remarkably beautiful.

The primavera there in bloom, enormous white tree trunks, white limbs loaded with brilliant scarlet blooms lying in great high drifts on the roads—roads piled with falling scarlet splendor.

We put our young daughter, Iovanna, in a basket in front of the tonneau from the cross ribs of the top of the open car. She was comfortable swinging there as we explored the island.

Lunch put up at the Coamo, we would go over the island every day. Slight showers would fall frequently but soon clear away.

Puerto Rico is beautiful but Puerto Ricans are pitiful. They seem small, fine-featured remains of a highly civilized race. Gentle, apathetic. Poor beyond belief. "Americanos" had already bought up the sugar-plantations. Most of them in the hands of capital from the States. Wages? Seventy cents a day, no raise in sight. It would affect the price of sugar.

Evident poverty of the place spoiled the beautiful place for Olgivanna, touched by the sight of so many ill-fed, mournful-eyed children and frail-looking women with sorrowful faces.

So poor were the Puerto Ricans! We remember a man coming down from miles away to Coamo on a peaked little horse, carrying a small chicken covered with a big red handkerchief, to sell this one chicken to the hotel to get a little money. Such sights were everywhere.

So, after two months we said goodbye to the beautiful islands with the romantic history—why not fragment of Atlantis?—returned to Washington where the first signs of Spring were beginning to appear.

Iovanna had her airing every morning in sunshine at the foot of our native Capitol. The faithful Alma never left the baby out of her sight, nor did the mother leave either out of her sight.

By this time Olgivanna was a shadow. The kind proprietor of the hotel, solicitous, asked if there was not something especial he might prepare for her. She ate so little.

These peregrinations had to cease. Anxieties too great. We needed home. Braving all persecution, we turned to Taliesin to take the consequences. Anything was better, and safer, than this equivocal, dangerous migration from place to place—a nightmare.

In this connection, I remember the time when and the circumstances by which I was soon thereafter forced to leave Taliesin because legally I had lost it. My bank, by formal process, asked me out. The drain of the two fires and lost collections at Taliesin, consequent years of forced inaction, wasteful legality, so many lawyers—had left me finally at the mercy of rented money and its machine process. That process is interesting because it shows how, when legal machinery goes wrong, it is like machinery better or worse than the automation. Or, it is

300

like any other cherished man-toy—strapped to the animals on the farm.

Some time before finality came, I had against my will taken my lawyer's bad advice to take Olgivanna and Iovanna and Svetlana from Taliesin and go away again—this time go and entirely lose ourselves for three months at least. Leave him, the lawyer, to work out the situation now so complicated through the advantages taken, on every side—of my own indiscretion in going away.

"Go away," said Levi Bancroft, "and I'll have your situation straightened out in three months. Publicity will then quiet down. There will be no further excuse for such performances as are being staged by Miriam Noel and the sensational press to which she appeals.

"So long as there is any chance she will perform for them and you will be good for headlines and 'stories.' They may get 'the authorities' stirred up," said Levi. "The minor official of our country is owned by the newspapers because he gets or loses his office pretty much as they are with him or against him. More often he gets it that way than any other. Newspapers, to get a story, will put officials in some position or other where they will have to act to arrest you. Olgivanna, too.

"Think it over," said Levi.

He went on: "They are working on the cupidity and weakness of an irresponsible woman with nothing to lose except her insane appetite for publicity and a fancied revenge. They will stop at nothing. She can't: there is nothing there to stop with.

"She overturned her arrangements with you after she had agreed to them and signed them because they made her see she had a good chance to put you where you would have to give her everything you had left in the world.

"Now if you don't give it to her she thinks, and probably is so advised by her lawyers, that she can take it anyway. It isn't and won't be their fault if you have a cent to your name or any place to lay your head."

I listened, knowing it all to be too true. I had seen something of publicity and a fancied revenge. They will stop at nothing. She can't: which Miriam Noel had been exploited in the press by her lawyers. I had every reason to believe such exploitation would continue.

When I now walked out of the Dane County Court rather than blacken the character of two women—I found there I would have to do this in order to get a divorce—I left this woman who was posing as the "outraged wife" free to attach and confiscate by way of contingent-fee lawyers everything I owned. I now owed the Bank of Wisconsin a round sum of forty-three thousand dollars—owing to the building of Taliesin III, the loss a second time of the collections I had made in China and Japan, and the plans upset in work by previous and present storms of publicity preventing me from earning anything.

In the circumstances Judge Hill and Levi Bancroft, both my lawyers now, said, "Go to the bank. President Hopkins is your friend. He will be glad to help you in order to protect himself.

"For a loan give the bank a blanket mortgage on everything you have. Don't leave out anything. Cover your plans, collections, drawing instruments, your tools in the studio and on the farm. Write it all in. Do this until we can get time to turn around against this 'legal' enterprise."

"A man who has a lawyer but takes his own advice has a fool for a client." Judge Evan Evans handed that to me.

Jim, and they don't make them any better than Judge Jim Hill, took me to the bank and explained the situation.

"All right," said the bank, "we'll help."

Jim had to catch his train and left me alone in the president's office at the Bank of Wisconsin.

I waited an hour at the bank for elaborate papers to be drawn by the bank's attorney. "Here," said the bank, "sign here." I did. A check for fifteen hundred dollars was handed to me, and I had nothing else in the world except by sufferance, or on honor of this bank.

This was now the situation at Taliesin.

Levi touched upon that too. "The bank will look after things for you while you are gone.

"Everything is in their hands and they'll do that to protect themselves."

"But I have a feeling, Levi, that if I turn my back on this fight and hide or run away as you suggest, I'll lose what I have been fighting for. It isn't my conviction nor my style. I don't know how to carry on along those lines. I already regret what I did with the bank."

I pleaded: "Why not let me stand up to this business and fight it out? Use *me*. I am all right—ethically if not morally—much as it may look the other way. You know it. Now, why not allow me the courage of *my* convictions—and to stand by?"

Said Levi, "You forget, Frank. There is your child. There is where they have you. And Olgivanna can't stand any more of this. She is under a terrible strain."

"I know," I said. "But so long as we are all together, that can't matter so much as it would if we were separated."

"Well," impatiently, "you'll all to be together—the way I suggest. Think it over."

I did. And I refused.

But Levi wouldn't give up. Olgivanna herself thought it wise to go. By appeals on behalf of Olgivanna and the child—Levi won his point.

One had to respect his forceful sincerity. As a lawyer, he was right enough. His uprightness has never been questioned.

My little family and I were to set out in the Cadillac for somewhere. Why not go to Minneapolis? Minnetonka was beautiful. Our friends the Thayers were there. It was September. But not what Levi wanted. He was thinking of Canada, I guess. But I knew if Olgivanna left the country in the circumstances I would have a hard time getting her back again.

I wasn't going that far. Together we might stand—divided we would surely fall.

So we drove up the Mississippi along the river and over it at La-Crosse into Minneapolis.

We didn't know at the time that we had by doing so given the Federals a chance to declare a federal crime. Had we known enough to get out and walk across the line we should have committed no crime. That is the way laws work.

We found a charming cottage at Minnetonka owned by a Mrs. Simpson. I persuaded her that she needed a vacation and she let us take the house as it stood for three months—the time Levi had specified. She let her accounts stand as they were in her name. We to be her guests in her absence.

We were to be the Richardsons or something. We kept forgetting to remember who we were.

We stowed the handsome Cadillac with the patent leather Victoria-top away in the Simpson garage and took to Cleaver's sailboat on the lake and went walking in the countryside. We were now in hiding for the first time in my life. The Thayers in on the secret. Soon their friends, the Devines.

I had already begun this book and at Olgivanna's earnest solicitation was working away on the first two volumes in Mrs. Simpson's cottage. Maude Devine came in afternoons to do the typing.

Well, we learned from the newspapers before long that we were "fugitives from justice." A nice legal phrase for reporters, with possible sensational consequences.

The father of Svetlana, it seems, from whom Olgivanna had been divorced, now making common cause with the lawyer of the persecution—was taken to Taliesin a few days after we had left. Finding us gone and his little daughter Svetlana, too, he was taken by the mutual lawyer to the county seat of Baraboo to swear out a warrant of arrest for the "abduction" of his daughter. The devices of the law are devious resources but they are more useful to the unscrupulous than to the conscientious. Not for nothing are lawyers smart. But we knew no better than to keep on hiding. So cautious, we really believed we were incognito. It was hard for me to take any of this business as more than hocus-pocus, knowing what was at the bottom of it all. Back of it all, too. So we went on living. I kept on working at this book. Son John came down to get instructions about clearing up certain details of work at Taliesin and we settled down. To what? We didn't know.

You see?
I had made a fatal error.
Flight had given color to low accusations: given courage, too, to insane persecution.
Implications fed to the public by the press gained life-like color by our disappearance.

Six weeks went by. The lawyer son of Mrs. Simpson came down from Minneapolis on some pretext or other. To look for his fishing tackle? In his mother's attic he said it was. I saw him sizing us up intently—but dismissed him from my mind. Olgivanna saw him too and worried. "Never mind," I said. "He is his mother's son. She is a lady."

We had just dined. The baby put to bed. Svetlana asleep in her bed out on the porch. Maude Devine was typing away at the book. Fire burned in the grate, all warm and cozy on a late September evening. About half-past-nine came a rude knock on the door of the living room toward the street. I went to the door and opened it. A dozen or more rough-looking characters—led by Miriam Noel's lawyer—now mutual with Svetlana's father—accompanied by members of the press, several of whom I had seen somewhere before. They shouldered their way into the room and surrounded us.

"You are all under arrest," said the heavy-handed one, the bigger sheriff. There were three of them, each of a different size and type and town.

Olgivanna shows her quality in any emergency.

She got up and asked them to kindly step out into the next room. I opened the glass door and they all did exactly as they were bid—a little ashamed. They could still watch through the glass door, however, and so were content.

They recovered after finding themselves there, and the heavy-faced lawyer employed by Miriam Noel said loudly with a swagger, "Well, here they are . . . at last: now, where's the kid?"

He opened the door to the bedroom and went in. I went in after him and saw him jerk the blanket from the sleeping infant. He laughed. "Yeah! here it is!"

The sheriffs each took an arm, all I had, and said, "No violence. Take it easy. Take it easy . . ."

To the sheriffs' credit be it said, they immediately moved that plug-ugly out.

Olgivanna now opened the door and came in. "Don't, we must make the best of it, Frank." And I saw that I was only making scene for more copy. The usual circus had arrived.

"Please take it quietly," she said.

So I did.

Of course it was a newspaper "frame-up" by the "lawyers." A reward had been offered and the Simpson "mother's son" found his information profitable. Cameras had already been set up around the house to illustrate the story as we came out the door.

The horror of such impotence as mine! I pleaded with the valiant sheriff to take me and leave the mother and children where they were with a guard over them until morning. The trap had been sprung on purpose late—after ten o'clock—and having pretended to call up his superior at Minneapolis (it would have spoiled the newspaper story to leave them behind that way) he came back to say that it was impossible to get him.

But he agreed to leave my little family in custody where they were. I went out in the face of puffing flashlights, got into his car and was driven down to the sheriff at the county jail in Minneapolis. His name was Brown.

Brown was a man of some parts in the Hennepin County community. A sheriff, but serving as a patriot without pay to clean up the Baptist belt and make it moral or something. A reporter volunteered the information that he had got himself into the newspapers a few days before, handcuffed to two thugs—to show "the people" how serviceable a sheriff they had.

He knew of us only as he had read newspaper reports of the case and scented more favorable publicity.

Well—I argued the great Brown down: but I pleaded in vain. At length and with reason I pleaded with this sacrificial honor-man to leave the nursing mother and the two children at the cottage until morning . . . I would go to jail willingly if he would be considerate of them.

"I give you my word, Mr. Wright, I couldn't do that. No. Not even for my own brother. No. I am an officer sworn in to uphold the law."

There was a cast-iron sense of duty for you. They had said of him that he would accept no salary either.

"Not for your own mother either, I suppose," I said . . . again at wit's end. "Well . . . then, will you let me call my little family and tell them what to expect, and what to do in the circumstances. I want to call them long-distance," I said.

"No need," he said, "they are here. In any case you are not allowed outside communication. You are under arrest." Ignoring the sheriff's promise, my family had been brought along to jail in the car following the one that brought me.

The crowd was busy now doing their daily stuff. In the next room they were word-painting the noble "volunteer" sheriff as a hero. This was his reward for playing up to their game.

Coming to me now was the sovereign insult a free country has to offer one of her own sons.

Olgivanna!—The two children! If only I were alone!

But my sin had been done two by two. And that can never be paid for one by one, even in a free country such as ours. Not while noble sheriffs volunteer anyway.

So I went up the elevator with my distinguished republican jailer, the impeccable Brown. Brown turned me in.

Legality searched me, took away my money all but small change: entered my family pedigree in the jail record of Hennepin County: with businesslike hospitality, representing Minneapolis whose dishonored guest I now was, Brown, getting a little dubious by now I thought, said "Good night"—uneasily.

A warden took me down a long corridor along brutal heavy animal cages built tier on tier within a great empty space arched over by a high trussed roof. The clang of the gates he opened and shut as he went reverberated behind us in space. He clanged our way to the far end where the "better element" of jaildom, the high-swindlers and bootleggers were kept. All quiet. Asleep. He opened the little door of a cell a little longer than I am tall, a little narrower than I am long, a soiled mattress on one side and a dirty toilet-seat at one end: the government allotment of squalor for manhood on such terms as had fallen to my lot.

I went in.

The warden said "Good night" and locked the iron door.

My country! To one of your own free sons this "Good night"?

The ponderous door of the animal cage slammed shut, automatically shot its heavy steel bolt. My sensation one of suffocation.

But I reached up and took hard hold of the cold iron bars to keep my mind clear. Tried to hold on to my sense of humor. It was all that could save me now.

Then I turned and used up the three steps in one direction—there the filthy water closet. Nausea. Again dreadful suffocation.

306

Scarcely able to breathe, I sat down on the mattress. Saw it stained. Was it blood? Whose and how?

I looked above. The polished steel ceiling I could reach up and touch.

Where was Olgivanna? Where were the children? I had begged for information but prisoners although convicted of nothing are not allowed to communicate.

"Let me send a note to their mother?"

Said Brown, "Against the rules."

This was the machine-made Brown. Brown the volunteer, driver by rote and routine or . . . wreck this machine. A jail.

Intelligence? All on the outside.

Humanity? Outside.

Life, love, work, honor? Destroyed?

Cut down? Cut off!

Dung and dishonor!

Man's cruelty to man!

The blackest mark in human life? Man's deep distrust of his fellow man! The deepest chasm dug by himself across the course of his own future.

I say every citizen, good or bad, as a feature of his education should be condemned to spend two nights in one of his own jails.

Let the good, the obedient, the wary-wise sense the endless repeat of the monotonous "forever" they call a jail and keep to defend their own goodness, obedience and wisdom.

Impotent, I cursed. Again and again on my feet to measure my length against the bars. Head far enough back I could breathe.

Footsteps along the corridor.

The warden-watch reaching the end of his beat—outside my cell.

He glanced in. He was just in time. I found myself. And I found "they" had overlooked a piece of paper in my pocket. Strangely, a broken stump of pencil, overlooked, lay on the mattress. I said, "Wait a second?" Scribbled a note.

"Take this to her. They brought her in here with me. Will you?" And wrapping a fifty-cent piece in the paper, poked it through the bars to him. He put his finger to his lips, nodded his head as he pushed back the silver and took the note. He went away.

Next time around.

"Did she get it?"

"Sure," he said. "She's all right. The Missus is looking after her and the kids."

This fellow's sense of duty was remiss. He broke the devil's rules in hell.

A little light came through. I could breathe now. It would be morning sometime. It always was. My sense of humor was on its way back. What remained of the night I sat up on the one clean corner of the mattress or pacing the few steps to and fro—to rest—paced in my stocking feet so as not to wake my good neighbors.

At daylight a distant clanging. It came toward me with an increasing roar until the tumult seemed to rock the very jail and it must fall of its own insane weight. The door to the cell suddenly flew open with a reverberating clang following all the others by electrical release. The clanging tumult died in echoes.

The narrow paved passage connecting my cage with the other cages was open there in front. I could now go out into that. A tin cup of Brown's chicory appeared at a little door set in the bars—a piece of Brown's bread beside it. I tasted his liquid and swallowed a bit of his bread. Without choking.

After a while my next-door comrade came in to say Hello. He had the morning paper that gets to the cells too.

There were our pictures.

"Say," he said, "you got a swell girl. She sure stands by you."

"Sure she does."

"Well," he said, "it's something not be in here for nothing. You got something to tie to."

"Trouble is she's tied up here too."

"Aw, they won't do nothing to her though. They'll let 'em go all right."

"Will they?" I said. "I wonder why? The sheriff said he couldn't do anything for his own mother in the circumstances."

"Yeah!"

"What are you in here for?" I asked.

"Me? Sellin' a little likker. Second time. Say, I got a swell girl myself," he went on. "Do you know what she done?"

"No, what?"

"You see that place out there where visitors come to see us fellows?"

I looked and saw a broad space with a shower on one side where an inmate might go, stand up and converse through a screen wire with someone standing in the outer space. You could have pushed a pencil through the screen but that is about as big as anything that would go through.

"You see, she hears that I'm in, from the papers. She comes up out there and they calls me. Then I goes out to see her. She watches the warden go away. 'Stand up close, Jimmy,' she says. I stands up close. Say! She unbuttons her dress and what do you think she's got in there between 'em? Guess?"

"I couldn't."

"A quart, by God! A quart!"

"The warden goes by and she waits. Then she slips me three straws out of her pocket. 'Go to it, Jimmy,' she says, 'Go to it. It'll do you good, besides helpin' you.' And I slips them straws into the stuff and takes it all. Say! Can you beat that?"

"No," I said, "I don't believe anybody could beat that."

I stepped out into the gangway to walk a little but ran into another prisoner. There was room for only one in the width of the corridor.

"Hello," said this one. "You look funny in here."

"Yes, I feel funny," I said.

"I read the papers about you and her this morning. Say, I had a bigger spread in the paper than that when they got me in here." He pulled out a greasy old clipping and proudly showed it to me.

"I'm third in for the bogus bail racket. Trial coming up soon, see. But, I got a good lawyer. Nash! Best in the state. He'll see me through, all right."

"Nash is his name?"

"Nash," he said.

"How can I see him? They won't let me call anyone."

"I'm going out to see him today and I'll tell him to come in and call you out to see him."

That is how I got another lawyer to add to the collection.

Nash was a good lawyer, too.

He soon found out I was in jail for no reason that anybody knew except a telegram from some bailiff in Sauk County, Wisconsin; that a warrant had been sworn out for my arrest there. This telegram had reached Brown. Confirmation was lacking. Who sent it? We were all in jail on suspicion, so far as the beneficent Brown was concerned. Not so the newspapers. I was taken out by Brown to be interviewed by them that morning. We were eventually formally released in another public court scene, the authorities at Baraboo, Wisconsin, when appealed to, refused to prosecute.

The "case," such as it was and whatever it was, was dropped. The thing had been set for late enough at night so that no correction or relief was possible without going to jail. All for "copy." Such is the ingenuity of lawyers working with reporters and justice.

The Law in the hands of any professional blackmailer is a mean instrument of revenge or extortion. Many angles, all fertile "points." We were not yet free to go. No, not yet. The Federal authorities had meanwhile been seen. We were to be held there in jail pending appearance before an armchair Federal, famous in the Northern Baptist Belt for "moral" tendencies. He had grown to the chair with comparative affluence. I forget his name.

We now went before this august limb of the Federal law on the charge of having violated that malign instrument of revenge diverted from its original purpose to serve just such purposes as this: the Mann Act. Mr. Mann and his wife used to sit across the aisle from me at my uncle's church: All Souls. His law was dead letter so far as public sentiment went. But for ulterior purposes a law just the same. Instead of walking, we had ridden across the State line.

So, accompanied by the press-gallery cameras, we went through the streets to the Federal hearing together with the American public invited by the announcement in the enterprising press. I had successfully shielded my little family from both press and camera until this episode. For twelve months I had beaten the reporters at their own game at every turn, although my little daughter had to go out of the Union Station three days old at her mother's breast to get away from them. I had saved Olgivanna from a single interview. Now it all ended in this triumph for hoi-polloi, ragtag and bobtail.

Bail was fixed at fifteen thousand dollars for us both. A separate count was lodged against each by Lafayette French, a resourceful, politically ambitious young press-concious attorney with a flair for salacious detail, as appeared at the investigation.

Bigger and Better publicity always the objective.

Our case now seemed serious. Far too serious for our friends. They began to protest. It seemed serious enough to us all by this time. Nothing could keep my sister Jane from rushing from Philadelphia to Minneapolis to reassure herself concerning us. Maginel called attorney Nash from New York for such reassurance as he could give. We were released on bail after this second public appearance—the public again invited—after another night in jail for us all on account of this new ruse.

This second night in Hennepin County Jail was not so bad as the first. I had not been allowed to see Olgivanna except in court. The children not at all. But I now knew from her that they were well, and though ready to drop, she was facing it all like the thoroughbred she was. Tomorrow we would all be together again? Meantime after the new "case" was lodged and before my new attorney, Nash, could get to Olgivanna, a Federal officer had insinuated himself to get her story. She had no more sense of wrongdoing than had I. She told him everything. Puerto Rico included. All of which he duly recorded—with the matron's kind assistance of supplying missing details. No detail was omitted, questions asked in terms Olgivanna did not at all understand. The Federal game seems to be a game of points—or at simplest a game of hide and seek.

Thus the confession was complete. We were now involved with Immigration Acts.

Nash raged against this exploit of the Federals. But Federals, too, are resourceful. I guess they have to be to get enough points to live on.

Our Puerto Rico sojourn for two months after the birth of Iovanna, to try and get peace and restore Olgivanna's health, seemed could be made another violation of the complex immigration-laws. Puerto Rico was the United States but was so without grace of legal technicality as such. It was still a foreign country. So, by the morbid virtue of technicality, "they" said we had "entered the country for immoral purposes." So the Federals could do with us as they pleased. We had made it all as simple for them as that. The law is an implement only. Technique is the Federals.

Going back to jail I found Brown had sent in a clean mattress. The water closet was cleaned. I lay on the clean mattress that second night getting the sense of jail prisoners had told me they got—a sense of protection. At least nothing can happen to you in jail. After the evening feeding of the animals through the trap-doors in the bars, some of them in the upper animal cages began to sing—one or two taking turns leading—fine manly bass or baritone voices. Other caged animals in the lower tiers picked up the familiar songs: joined in. Tremendous! They sang familiar song after song. Some popular, some were religious. Were there hundreds of sinners singing? Reverberation, I suppose. Twenty-five or thirty, maybe more, a hundred at times? They kept on singing up to nine o'clock. Everyone then must be silent. A splendid sense of unity in their misery.

They made me feel ashamed of my shame because, after all, I was there for a passing moment while they were there for years, maybe for life.

The little chap, cage second to me, in for bogus bailing, had gone out to his trial this day. Late I heard him come in. He was whistling a popular tune softly. I rapped a little on the bars to let him know I wasn't sleeping.

"How now?" I whispered.

"Twenty years," he hissed back and went on whistling. Soon he was asleep. I heard him snore. Callous? Or was this fortitude?

Next morning I saw him in the corridor.

"Nash will get it cut," he said.

He gave me the details of his game. These illegal details were as complicated as the legal details to which we were subjected, and almost as ingenious. A crook has technique too. This fellow had professional pride in a scientific piece of work. Initial direction gone wrong, that's all, gone wrong for such curious, haphazard reasons. He had turned left instead of right.

After court opening at ten o'clock, my turn came to go up and be dismissed. I asked Brown for permission to set up porkchops and mashed potatoes to the singers of the night before and all their listeners.

"Sorry," said Brown, "against the rules."

The boys themselves bade me good luck. Their jailers all shook hands with me warmly; they had done their best for me. Even so had Brown. But a man no bigger than his job has no right to have a job where humanities are concerned even though he makes himself a gift to the job.

Days afterward I was sitting in Cleaver Thayer's car near the railway station waiting for Cleaver. A Ford suddenly stopped by the curb opposite.

A man got out, grinning, rushed across the street holding out his hand to me: "Hello, Mr. Wright, Hello! Say—my wife's in the car over there. I want her to meet you. Can I bring her over?"

It took a second or two to recognize the warden. His uniform changed him—or was it the other way around?

"No," I said. "Let her stay where she is. I'll come over with you to meet her."

She was pleased to meet me. He had a nice girl, too.

After all was over it took some time longer to get permission to leave the State. Some other kink in the endless coils of law in which we were now entangled. I forgot what kink or what coil of what law but the State was Minnesota.

The Thayers and Devines had been most kind. Cleaver went bail for me and put me up at his club. Both families at the jail early to see Olgivanna, took the children for an airing. I don't know how they ever got them out. Brown must have been having his photograph taken—so his back turned. Cleaver fine all the time, coined a phrase that pleased him enormously. "From Who's Who to the Hoosegow."

Another flood of news-print had gone over the big dam.

312

While marking time in Minneapolis awaiting the swell young Prosecuting Attorney's permission to leave the State a demand came from the bank to "pay up."

A little surprised I wrote the bank reminding them of circumstances of their mortgage. No reply to this. The circumstances were unfit for record or publication, so it seems. Only another technicality out of line with other technicalities, that's all. The classification is minute and the differentiation arbitrary but the consequences often amazing. Maybe my situation, in view of this Federal action, looked bad to the bank. The bank soon threatened foreclosure, insisted upon the immediate sale of the print collection I had placed in New York in Mitchell Kennerly's hands to be, sometime, sold! It was a bad time to sell. The bank insisted on sale. A block of rare prints, therefore, worth several hundred thousand, disastrously sold for $42,000. Kennerly took a "commission" of thirty-five per cent, which didn't help much. I understood it would be only fifteen, at most. When you fall into the ruck you went down the line while you lasted or there was anything on you to get away from you.

During the months that followed the Minneapolis debacle in the "Northern Baptist Belt," we were in New York. Sister Maginel took us in. Some respite now because my little sister and her home are charming. She did everything in her power—and she is resourceful—to mitigate the desperation of our circumstances. We were together—to fight it all. But the resources of ultra-legal publicity-persecution were by no means exhausted. A deportation story got into the papers. "They" were now after Olgivanna. She was formally arrested by immigration officials at the door to my sister's home and I gave a Liberty Bond—the last one—posted for bail.

The latest aggression added to our other woes, a cup too full. My sense of humor began to fade. The immigration service notoriously cruel, almost never kind, is a merciless machine with minor officials for cogs.

So a bank is a machine. My bank, now stirred to action by all this impending disaster, pressed harder and harder for money. I had nothing to give the bank because everything I had was in its hands. The bankers knew this. Under pressure of these desperate circumstances I conceived the idea of incorporating myself—selling myself to such friends and clients as would "buy me" in order to raise the money to rid Taliesin and such collections as remained in the bank of the claims of the pressing bank itself. This would allow me to go to work again unmolested. The proceeds of the work would then be safe from suits sure to be brought by the "persecution" were I able to earn anything at all.

With this scheme in mind, soon subscribed to by the bank itself, we returned to Taliesin. But owing to that blanket mortgage we were liable to eviction at the bank's pleasure unless we paid up completely.

Now began incorporation of what looked like a lost cause.

Darwin D. Martin liked the corporation idea. He subscribed—heavily—and his lawyer drew up the first papers. I took them to others. My client, Mrs. Avery Coonley, subscribed. My best friend, Dr. Ferdinand Schevill, Joe Urban, my sister Jane, too, among numbers of other friends who could ill afford to subscribe. Finally seventy-five thousand dollars were subscribed. Alexander Woollcott helped at this crucial time in more ways than one. Charlie McArthur did what he could—to keep a smile on my face. Phil La Follette now stepped in, sympathetic.

"Frank, you have had bad legal advice."

"Phil, I have. I have taken it far worse than the advice itself. Suppose you help?"

"All right," Phil said, "but not to take the case directly. Leave Jim (Judge Hill) where he is. I'll do what I can from the side lines."

He went to see Ferdinand Schevill and Mr. Martin to see if they would stand by me. Response satisfactory. Things quieted down. The figure-head of all the persecution, the outraged wife, was now in Hollywood without funds. Her lawyers too were without funds, the press suffering time-lag. The story was dragging for them all. Something had to be done to revive it—or they had all failed.

Frank Lloyd Wright incorporated, if now executed as originally designed, would keep them all out of funds. No news either until prepared to treat fairly and reasonably the circumstances. A drive along this line would have been effective. The various creditors pressing for settlement were proposing fair terms.

But Phil reversed the plan for procedure. He began negotiations for divorce. To get this we must go into court with "clean hands" as the choice phrase runs in legal circles. To do this he advocated the voluntary deportation of Olgivanna. And eventually handed a thousand dollars of corporation money to me for the purpose.

Phil took Levi's ground: "District Attorney Knudson (of our home county) could not long stand against popular prejudice moved by the press." Phil said he knew district attorneys well. But attorneys do not seem to know each other very well. Too frequently surprise each other.

"But," I said, "Knudson has stood up pretty straight for what he sees as right. I don't believe they can stampede him. Let me go see him myself."

"Keep away from him," said Phil. "You will only compromise him

314

and tie his hands if you go near him."

This looked reasonable to me.

"Frank, there is only one way. Send Olgivanna and the children away for a year, or with her defective passport the government is going to send her anyway. There is no way that feature of your case can be fixed up. Go to work and make some money meantime. Then you can go over like a man and get them back. A year after you get your divorce you can live a regular life, no compromise."

"Phil, how long to get the divorce on your revised plan?" I asked.

"Don't know. Say six months."

"A year and six months for Olgivanna and the children with no home at all? And little if any money? No, Phil," I said. "Your plan is no good."

But again Phil and his partner Rogers put me into the sweat box.

"You are unfair to Olgivanna because they'll arrest you both, sure: then what? One of the provincial juries around here? What chance would you have?"

Said Phil, "You're thinking more of yourself than of the woman, Frank. You might stand this but she can't. You are vain and selfish in all this. Take care of her now as you should have done so long ago. Send her away. Your courage is commendable but your cause is hopelessly illegal!"

This high moral tone offended me.

Did not seem to me like his father's son.

I said, "You may be 'legal,' Phil, but neither human nor wise. Your idea of 'taking care' of Olgivanna would put an end to her and Iovanna. Yes, of course I am selfish. Apparently in selfishness I started all this. I might as well keep on that way. I'll take our chances standing together where we are, at our own home: fight this thing out—and we will take what comes."

More pressure. My legal advisers brought in friends who were contributing money to untangle our affairs and give us protection. The advice I was now getting was really theirs too. This was cited. Well, I gave in—took the money and I, the embarrassed parent, went home to my little family to break the news.

"Get ready, Olgivanna," I said. "We're going straight to Washington."

I thought I'd try my own hand as a last chance. So I took Olgivanna to Washington headquarters. Laid the cards all on the table—told the unvarnished truth of the case as it stood, supported by affidavits from Judge Hill and Svetlana's father which I already had.

Of course Olgivanna, by all moral standards, was my wife: the mother of a desired child born in our home in our own country. Daughter, Svetlana, was the child of a naturalized father. We had all been deliberately by enemies legally tangled up in a coil of legal rope and legally trapped for a "story." The truth was continually ignored in order that we might continually be exploited for more "story." The law was also being used merely as a cat's paw to pull chestnuts out of the fire for an irresponsible woman urged to unseemliness and indiscretion by a free-for-all press—not an unfamiliar form of persecution to the department at Washington as I found when I listened to them there.

Well, Superior officialdom is not minor officialism. At last I had reached intelligent responsibility.

"Could we have a respite to straighten out?"

"How long?"

Six months."

We could.

I wired Phil no need to carry out the plan.

Coming home.

Indignant letter from him. I had broken an agreement with him. "On no account come back to Taliesin."

But we came. There was nowhere else to go and no money to go there with. "Clean hands" or no "clean hands." Home.

Without funds, her so-called attorneys now pressing for settlement and already confiscating her many "things," Miriam Noel came into court for separate maintenance and eventually sold the divorce she had already agreed to and signed two years and some months before for exactly the price she had agreed to then, but plus the ruination she had planned and wrought by the false, sentimental appeal of "outraged wife."

But Wisconsin divorce, desirable as it then seemed, was divorce with a curse on it. Wisconsin law forbade re-marriage within one year after divorce, though divorce was—in the language of the judge— "absolute."

I had thought this divorce was to end our trials. I had heard the word "absolute" from Judge Hoffman's own lips.

But it seems the curtain had only been rung up by divorce. Legality now wiped out personality, character, courage, common-sense. We were playing a legal game of tag—of legal hide and legal seek. If I was caught in any "immoral situation"—in other words at home with my own little family—during the year to follow, "absolute" divorce was null and void. So Phil informed me.

Lawyers know only legal aspects. For this it is that they are lawyers.

My friend Clarence Darrow had given me some good advice—

316

long before. He said, "Your case is no legal case, Frank. What you need is the advice of some wise man of the world who will be your friend and will see you through. *Keep away from lawyers.*"

No doubt Phil was all right and his advice sound, as life ran popularly or regularly with him. But as Clarence had said, the case never was a legal one, except in certain superficial aspects of the whole affair. But I said to him, "Phil, how unethical your 'moral' can be."

Well . . . no sooner was the money divorce-settlement paid over to the aggressors than the "outraged wife" aided by a group of reporters were besieging the truly upright and independent young Knudson, District Attorney of our county. The "case" so far as the press was concerned was still more public game now. More cheap drama. Scene after scene. Staged by the resourceful press as news. The "outraged wife" was still played to the absurd limit by them all. She snatched a revolver from the District Attorney's desk and, telling the gang of reporters to "come on," she started for Taliesin to attack divorce "absolute"!

We were at Taliesin, now standing our ground. At the same time trying to work. Strange to say, several building projects were at hand.

But the course of incorporation changed. This was not what the subscribers had anticipated. The bank was not satisfied. My clients were not satisfied. If my friends could pay $75,000 to end a clear case of persecution with no better effect than was now visible, they could be made to pay up all down the line . . . professional legality was such a success and has many diverse angles, all legal-forms.

The prosecution thought if only they would go after me hard enough now why should anybody wait longer for money? The bank itself refused to stand by its subscription to stock in the new corporation. Several other subscribers, none too warm, learning of this cancellation and that my sole property consisted of a divorce that left me more than ever at the mercy of unscrupulous exploitation—cancelled several subscritions too.

What corporate money had been paid had gone to Miriam Noel and—mostly—her lawyers.

Creditors stiffened up. The situation was out of hand so far as the man in it was concerned. He was written off and the case no longer a matter of live and let live, but of legal quibbles. Each and every one of which involved and demoralized life; added cost to cost to keep a vicious game going.

Afternoon during our absence, the bank president drove out to Taliesin and hired our help to remain there in the bank's employ. They were all told we were going away as I learned this from a faithful young apprentice, John Davis, who had heard it from some of the help, thought I ought to know it.

Next day, by way of my bank, we received a long legal notice to the effect that as the premises were being used for immoral purposes—the mortgage was outraged. The mortgagee objecting, we were asked to leave.

I called Phil at once.

"Well?" he said. "I don't see what *we* can do about it."

"Do you mean to say I shall have to take this, too, lying down?"

"I don't see what we can do about it, Frank!"

So we got to Chicago to see what *I* could do.

Nothing.

We went adrift.

The day before I had received a telegram from my young apprentice—my friend and client Warren McArthur's son—Albert McArthur: "Can you come out to Phoenix?" to build the Biltmore Hotel. It seemed providential. You see, the corporation was an unfinished fragment—helpless now, in these or any other circumstances.

We had the coveted divorce but not "clean hands." So we were homeless and about penniless. We got to Arizona. Went to work with Albert on the new Arizona Biltmore Hotel. The bank entered into legal possession of Taliesin as a whip to enforce collection of the sum due them, now augmented by attorney's fees, court proceedings, foreclosure suits, interest on interest. Interest on a $25,000 mortgage given them as general security for current loans and held by them seven years, this charged into the sums due them—when judgment was entered. Forty-three thousand dollars had become fifty-seven or fifty-eight thousand.

Yes. Legality supreme!

Strange how legally right a man may be and utterly wrong outside all equity! Legal makes right? So it seemed.

What went on thereafter was in my friend and client Darwin D. Martin's hands. Phil La Follette worked with the bank, at Mr. Martin's request, to effect a fair settlement. Law and Money now at deadlock. Meantime, to whip my friends into line over my shoulders, the bank went through the business of auctioning Taliesin equipment, furnishings and collections. The bank had thrown Taliesin into the street. Whereupon many saw it who otherwise would never have seen it. But the bank changed its mind when a few bids came in.

Then Money tried to sell the whole place, whole, but no one wanted to buy it. For several reasons. Some of them humane as I afterward learned.

Finally in September, a compromise effected, a telegram came from Phoenix, from Mr. and Mrs. Martin, reached us at La Jolla—"Taliesin open for your return." After all the harrowing circumstances of nearly four years past. The words set us all madly rejoicing. The same real friend and client, Darwin D. Martin for whom I had been building a summer home on Lake Erie when we agreed to leave for parts unknown. I sent John to Mr. Martin to finish up the work. "No," said Mr. Martin, "there can be no substitute for Frank Lloyd Wright. We will wait till he is out of trouble."

I could help him now, a little. The bank accepted substantially what had been offered due in settlement before I had been forced to leave Taliesin and the legal machinery began to pile up waste costs in ruinous hungry legalities.

The bank vacated the premises, which it had used during the summer as a rendezvous as it pleased, to the detriment of the place. We now free to return. That was the main thing. A settlement, too, had been meantime made with the creditors. Darwin D. Martin and Ferdinand Schevill were the substantial means by which this settlement was finally effected.

Many stories of this incorporation of myself appeared. The idea gained credence that my financial troubles were over. That I could now work with no financial harassments or restrictions. The reports had me taken over and managed by Capital so that my usefulness might be indefinitely extended. Later the original corporation was somewhat extended by Harold McCormick and Mr. George Parker. Charlie Morgan came forward as a volunteer, and interested a few others. But I wouldn't have liked the sound of this immunity on such terms even if it were true.

As a matter of fact a few staunch friends, Mr. Darwin D. Martin at their head, had invested what money they could, and some of them at sacrifice to themselves, to save me for any future usefulness at Taliesin, merely using "incorporation" as a legitimate means to protect me by owning Taliesin and my earning-capacity. They owned all the corporation's preferred stock: I owned the common stock, which could have no value until the preferred stock was paid up.

The corporation was paid up, non-assessable, had no capital whatever, nor any means of getting any, except as my earning-capacity could produce it. Unless I could carry on from this point there was no point whatever in corporation. I and mine would starve. The stockholders of course would then lose their money.

Now appeared a singular reaction. I could get no life insurance

anywhere. Sound and acceptable in every physical requirement, but—
"too much publicity."

Before the final return to Taliesin was effected, one more act in the
cheap drama of "legality"—divertissement. We were discovered by the
persecution in our little cottage on the beach at La Jolla, California. In
our absence the "outraged wife" from whom I had had "absolute" divorce for not yet quite one year, invaded the premises. Smashed up the
interior, appropriated what she liked.

She then went into court at San Diego in the now practiced rôle of
"outraged wife," "absolute" divorce notwithstanding, swore out a warrant for "immorality" on the part of her "husband."

Another hectic story went broadcast. By present arrangement of
"absolute" divorce I was legally financing various legal strangleholds, as
public entertainment! Private aggressions invented to entertain readers
of the daily papers.

Instead of allowing me to use my reputation as an architect in order
to earn a living, publishers were capitalizing it by headlines for news to
profit themselves.

The fact that I had made a wide reputation as an architect was all
but ruining me in the circumstances. Were I obscure, a nonentity, I
should have been left in peace. So, after all, I was being plucked solely
because of what I had myself built up by painstaking labor with success
during a stormy twenty-two years.

Shortly after legal marriage to Olgivanna took place quietly at Santa
Fe following the year of probation which had followed "absolute divorce," this sort of crazy exploitation ended with a final move by the
persecution—at Milwaukee.

Miriam Noel, now on her way to Paris, reached Milwaukee encouraged to start suit to keep the trust fund now established in her behalf up
to level. My earning capacity having been cut off by her, the trust fund
established by me in her behalf had been drawn by monthly payments
to her as agreed upon, to a balance of eleven thousand dollars. This suit
started, she fell seriously ill. Her malady of long standing was aggra-
vated by an operation in a Milwaukee hospital. She became unmanage-
able. A long-distance call from a friend she made in Milwaukee told me
this. I confirmed it.

Several months later, having been removed in a state of coma to a
private sanitarium, she died without regaining consciousness.

Her several children, married daughters and unmarried sons, were
near her at the last, but their mother was buried with no assistance
from them.

What was left of a remarkably vital high-spirited woman, for fifteen

Mrs. Wright at Taliesin, 1945

Iovanna and her father
viewing an obstruction,
Taliesin, 1930

F.Ll.W. on "Johnny Walker," 1956

Jacobs House, Westmoreland, Wisconsin. 1936
"The house of moderate cost is not only America's major problem but the problem most difficult for her major architects . . . Withal, this Usonian dwelling seems a thing loving the ground with the new sense of space, light and freedom—to which our U.S.A. is entitled." Cost in 1936: $5500. including architect's fee

B.

C.

Kaufmann House ("Fallingwater"), Bear Run, Pa. 1937. "A solid high rock-ledge rising beside a waterfall . . . The natural thing seemed to be to cantilever the house from that rock-bank over the falling water. The first house in my experience built of reinforced concrete—the form took the grammar of that construction."

Taliesin West, Scottsdale, Arizona. 1938. Living room

Taliesin West. Entrance. Drafting room at right

Price Tower, office
and apartment
building for H. C.
Price Co., Bartles-
ville, Oklahoma.
1952–56

Solomon R. Guggenheim Museum, New York City. 1943–1959. "One great space on a continuous floor . . . an atmosphere of the unbroken wave—no meeting of the eye with angular or abrupt changes of form. All is as one and as near indestructible as it is possible to make a building." (Opposite page, above) Frank Lloyd Wright at the Guggenheim Museum during the early days of construction.

Lloyd Lewis House, Libertyville,
Illinois. 1940. Living room

Meeting House for the First Unitarian Society, Madison, Wisconsin. 1947. "The Unitarianism of my fore-fathers found expression in a building by one of the offspring. The idea, 'unitarian,' was unity . . . I tried to build a building here that expressed that over-all sense of unity . . . The roof is triangular and out of this—triangulation—(aspiration) you get this sense of reverence without recourse to the steeple."

years psychopathic, had been going up in flame, seldom knowing real rest unless by some artificial means. She was at last beyond reach of legal exploitation.

Finally Mercy to herself and all who had ever cared for her.

At no time did any newspaper dare print the truth concerning her mental state. For one thing, it would be actionable to use the word. In the next place it would have spoiled the entire setup for publicity.

Her own children refused to touch anything hers, the Milwaukee friend and a Milwaukee lawyer became the unfortunate Miriam Noel's "Estate."

RETROSPECT

This literal recitation of fact as disgraceful to my country as to myself was written many years ago and resentment plainly shows in the recital. None would show now were I to write the record of persecution aroused by my own indiscretion. But the facts were so grossly misrepresented and so destructive then that I did not refrain from recording the truth then as it should have been clear at the time: bad enough, but I have never felt uneasy with truth. True-speaking, there can be no resentment.

Now, I know that recounting facts does not constitute truth. Truth lies deeper. It is something we feel but seldom touch with our facts. So I am no better off to have got the facts on the record. Then I thought I would be.

All is left in this book as it was for what it might be worth. It is worth less than nothing to me—I don't see how it is going to help anyone else unless in danger of being in my case and the fix I was in at that time is a warning.

I hope no one, not even my worst friends or my best enemies, needs it. No, not even the man who hadn't an enemy in the world but whose friends did not like him.

But this is our Civilization.

Where is our Culture?

This will only be found in our work.

BOOK FOUR □ FREEDOM

HYMN

AUTUMN

Nature is now visible song.

Scarlet sumach runs like forest fire along The Valley hills.

The Future lies perfected in the seeds of bright fruits still hanging from naked boughs to tempt the present.

Acorns drop from the oaken bough to be eagerly sought in the mould beneath and carried far away. And bright berries, devoured by birds and beasts, are gone to new life in new ground. By appeasing Hunger and Desire—the Species makes sure of the Future?

Another life by way of infinite veins and arteries has added stature to the trees, given consequence to shrubs and flowers. The grass still green.

Flaming creeper wreathes the singing bough as leaves take on the hues of bloom, growth's greatest moment—until now.

Gentle touches of coming frost bring natural response to inner rhythm. Work done, the trees and shrubs, the flowers, return precious sap to the root.

To sleep.

In the little family chapel, "truth against the world" there under the mass of dark green firs planted by Uncle Thomas—the old Welsh family stands up. To sing.

Again hear "step by step since time began we see the steady gain of Man."

The grey old heads; the not so young; the not so old. The young and the very young. All together the false, falsetto, and the flat lift that brave assurance to the boards of the chapel ceiling: an ancient challenge ever new, going out through open windows to fade away in the many-colored hills beyond.

The boy, too, sings. Human exaltation. Fervor all about him floods the masses of gold and purple plundered from the roadsides to wreathe the pulpit with the gold and purple cloth and to match the purple berries of the woodbine pulled from trees twining the branches of scarlet sumach gathered from the hills.

White antimony from the pastures shines through them all like stars.

The family slowly sits down, and the grey heads, those not so grey, those not so young furtively wipe away their tears.

This boy wonders why they always weep? And they weep most when everything is best!

The book . . . lies open on the purple cloth, gilded edges flashing gold.

The white-haired preacher for today—the boy's Aunt Jane—now rises behind The Book.

Her text: "The time of Grace has come." Gratitude!

"Freely we have received

Freely then, let us give.

Grace? The gift of freedom to the strong soul.

The time of grace has come: yes, the time of grace to others.

Living up to life—Man loves Beauty.

So, it is that Beauty loves Man."

"Beauty loves Man" sinks into this boy-mind.

Tenderness for all life suffuses this thought, with happy feeling.

Freedom?

No.

Faith.

FREEDOM

FREEDOM TO WORK AGAIN

Taliesin 1927. The load of debt mounted, beyond any fair reckoning, but familiar creative urge gathered energy. Once more debt and urge still seem to go on together. Objectives once dimly felt, gropingly sought, are coming pretty clear. Confusion and distress of disgraceful turmoil have ended? Sanity? The normal? Both are true basis of human freedom. Taliesin has been stripped to join destitution at Hillside: Plundered by "the Bank," abused by curiosity, Hillside Home School buildings were defaced. All but destroyed. The water in through the decayed and broken roofs. The entire place there is rapidly becoming a ruin. Taliesin itself is unkempt. Bank-rented fields are grown with weeds. Buildings, in this climate so destructive to buildings, badly need repair. But the next move, even the next meal, is becoming a problem to be solved somehow. There is less than no money.

But the economic sky is clearing a little. Familiar signs of the better thing in a better way are gradually bringing hope back to life at Taliesin. There is more definite encouragement from Europe. I should be grateful for this at this time as I am.

But the last actual work on plans was done at Taliesin 1923–24, nearly seven years ago. Hungry for work, some further work on the cantilever glass and metal skyscraper for Mr. Johnson of the National Insurance Company; a study for the automobile objective for Gordon Strong; these seemed to have ended my active period of work.

Several young couples recently come from Zurich, Vienna and Tokio to work with me—Werner and Sylva Moser, Zurich; Richard and Dione Neutra, Vienna; Kameki and Nobu Tsuchiura, all talented. Faithful William Smith, young major from Ottawa, in his ninth year at stormy Taliesin—all that life had gone to other fields, there was no one working with me now but at last I was free to work.

Denied work, what Freedom have you?

WORK AND HONORS

At this time, to join the earlier publications of earlier work by Wasmuth, Berlin in 1910, Holland contributed by way of the fine art publication *Wendingen,* edited by Wijdeveld, a splendid volume devoted entirely to my work. I had never expected anything like it, nor had I known anything about this publication. I suspect no architect ever had greater tribute. *Wendingen,* a Dutch-English-German fine art publication, organ of a group of some nineteen architects, sculptors and painters of Holland and Belgium, was edited by the distinguished architect H. Th. Wijdeveld. In Holland they said that but for my work the modern architecture of Holland would not have existed. So Wijdeveld easily found support for this work. There are now many publications if that work were to end now. Four in German, two in Japanese, two in French, one in Czech, etc. None yet in my own country, however. Honorary membership in Academie Royale d'Anvers, ancient Flemish academic institution of the fine arts beginning as far back as Rembrandt and Frans Hals, gave me another surprise. Honorary membership too in the German Royal Akademie, first recognition of modern architecture by the Reich. These and other appreciations from European contemporaries reached me at this time when for several years I had walked the streets of American cities, an exile with the now all too familiar worm's-eye view of society.

After four years of exile from Taliesin—and from Architecture, much the same thing—I began work on more definite plans for Mr. Johnson's cantilever office building, the standardized gas-station, San Marcos in the Desert, and especially upon St. Mark's Tower. Meantime the box appeared in the offing. The box offering itself as new had named itself "the international style."

Now the ideal of an organic architecture, gone abroad, had come back thus deformed. Up above the ground on stilts it names itself a style? As though any universal "style" were not more than ever offensive, now and of course, undemocratic.

But a certain eclecticism—emulation by the perennial novice is seen along the much too obvious, extremely meager lines of this new candidate offering itself for a "style." Emulation, too, begins to show itself. Architects, born propagandists, begin to push this offshoot or left branch of modern architecture by characteristic propaganda, advertisement *à la mode.* Little cliques form outside the original, all of them trading upon the narrow margin of "originality," meanwhile carefully concealing actual origins. Each in turn, or out of it, pushing each other aside while alike as two peas in a pod. All denying the pod and especially denying the vine on which the pod containing these peas grew. Small matter. But poor Usonia! Because of ubiquitous managed publicity she is prone to this sort of thing beyond all other lands. But why? Why have these United States of America never allowed themselves to learn something of architecture? As for my own place in my own work, at this particular moment of bogus-renaissance, along came exodus.

ARIZONA

While still in exile, anxiously waiting first at Phoenix then at La Jolla for the legal *yakamashii* to finally clear away from Taliesin so we might go back to work, the unit-block system I first used in Hollywood, 1920, had built another building: the Arizona Biltmore, a million-dollar fashionable resort-hotel, Phoenix, Arizona.

This project was promoted by Charles and Warren McArthur and their brother Albert, who was one of my boys in the old Oak Park Workshop. Albert was accordingly commissioned to build this building. Like rich men's sons, did not much like work. At this psychological moment of my exile and unemployment his brothers appealed to me to help him establish the block system as construction of this project. Wanderer, now, myself, although no longer "fugitive from justice," I gladly turned into quarters at Phoenix and worked some nine months during a characteristic Phoenix summer (118° in the shade) to help Albert establish the thing wanted. I was to remain incognito and behind the scenes, glad to do so. The building was finally built, but meanwhile encountered the inevitable opposition to the unusual in design and new in construction; Albert was totally unable to stem the co-lateral tides of suggested changes which experts and engineers proposed in my building technique. Soon the system was robbed of any economic value whatever. When they had left off their expert services the unique block system was standing as a novel and beautiful outside only for a most expensive and unintelligent engineer's beam and wall construction; whereas great structural economy was first and foremost an integral feature of the system itself. It was now, except the attractive cottages, a beautiful extravagance. Had it been naturally allowed to work with its own integrity, several hundred thousand dollars would have been saved in the cost of the building. But the cost of the building seemed nothing in the circumstances which were in every way now equivocal.

Having no authority myself beyond bullying Albert, making unofficial threats and suggestions behind the scenes, I was powerless to prevent this tragic waste or the addition of a fourth story to the building although I conducted many tests to prove our case and all were more

329

than merely successful. But such figures as the engineers could use could not be used in this case. In the building of the hotel cottages later, however, the details of the original scheme were better followed with somewhat better results, of course. There should have been more of these and no fourth story.

But the tale of this building—the Arizona Biltmore—Albert should himself tell someday. It would be a valuable warning to young architects and maybe a reward. I don't know. But he is too near to it yet, too personally involved in meum and tuum, to tell it straight, even to himself probably, for another twenty years at least.

Meanwhile, during this debacle we had the salvage of reunion at Phoenix with the McArthurs—old friends of my family—the mother and her three sons all living in a group of charming homes near the Country-club, built by Albert. Mother McArthur's hospitality made our exile much more bearable. If Phoenix had not had the McArthurs, it would certainly have had no Arizona Biltmore.

While working in behind the scenes thus with Albert, 1927, I met Dr. Alexander Chandler of Chandler, Arizona. He came over one day from the little town named "Chandler," to see me. His own town was on the mesa near the Mormon town of Mesa, about twenty-two miles east of Phoenix. Already in building that decent little town named for himself, and in other serviceable ways, he had built himself into the region. It had taken him forty years to do it, but it was done to good purpose. He was widely known as a man of superior taste, judgment and character. A handsome man.

A dream of Dr. Chandler's it seems was an undefiled-by-irrigation desert resort for wintering certain jaded eastern millionaires who preferred dry desert to green, wet fields. He wanted to build this characteristic resort on a tract of several thousand acres in great stretches of pure mountain desert. The site was over there in the Salt Range ten miles from his still successful San Marcos, an aristocratic hotel in his little town. So, learning I was in the neighborhood, he came over to invite my little family to come with him and stay awhile to talk it all over at the pleasant, aristocratic Hotel San Marcos.

Dr. Chandler had certain definite ideas concerning this new desert resort. They were good ideas, or better, I thought. He said he had waited ten years before planning the building because he knew of no one who could give him what he wanted, unless now I could. And as he said this he smiled his beautiful smile. There is only one smile more beautiful than his and that is his wife's.

So, together we went to see the spot, his inimitable black driver Harris at the wheel. Harris, too, is an artist . . . portraits. Only one Harris! But sometimes he takes a severe cold and says he finds it necessary to stay in bed next morning as late as ten o'clock to be rid of it.

Well, there could be nothing more inspiring to an architect on this earth than that spot of pure Arizona desert he took me out to see. So I believe. At last here was the time, the place, and in Dr. Chandler, the man. He looked like the man always necessary to characterize a thoroughbred undertaking in building, or anything else. Immediately I liked him and in spite of tragic failure still do. I went to work *for* him and *with* him, making the first sketches for the building while living by the seaside at La Jolla. We were there still in exile but anxiously awaiting at any moment now the promised opportunity to return to Taliesin. I showed him the drawings on my way back there in October. The design pleased him. He proposed to begin to build during winter, 1929.

We had got back to Taliesin. 1927. I was at work on this project for some two months, when a telegram came from the Doctor suggesting we all come out and make the plans for the new resort right there.

Joyful news. A swift "comeback" at last? $40,000 fee in that commission. We were, at the moment, housebound at Taliesin in a blizzard, twenty-two degrees below zero and blowing hard. Nevertheless, ignoring mentor La Follette—Phil—secretary now of F.L.W., incorporated, we broke away and went out into a blowing snowstorm on the way to Arizona. A real blizzard. The household and workshop at Taliesin were quickly closed and the trek by automobile to Arizona began, fifteen of us in all because I had gathered some boys together to work on this and a few other prospects.

I meant to embody in this desert resort all I had learned worthwhile about a natural architecture. First to be considerably better than any such hotel I knew about. The building to grow up out of the desert by way of desert materials, naturally as the Saguaro grew. The Saguaro the motif that inspired its style and details. I had played with it a little in the plans for the Biltmore. Creation so long denied—after nearly seven years of waste and turmoil here a great opportunity came: an ideal site unspoiled, the man promoting it well up to the thing he wanted done. Something like this is the rarest good fortune in any architect's life. If the United States is ever to have creative architecture, more such opportunities are needed by her creative architects.

Held off so long from action, I could scarcely wait to begin. I could not get the project off my mind. The sketches were successful. Important too, I had pretty well mastered block technique by this time—good desert technique. With a man like Dr. Chandler to work for and this mastery I felt certain of success.

So in early January, 1927, we all finally arrived at Chandler after extraordinary risks, only to find that suitable quarters in which to live and work would cost us several thousand dollars if we took them for the rest of the Winter, Spring and Summer. And they said we couldn't live there in Summer. Too hot. I already knew the heat though I had always wanted to camp in that region. Why not camp now? Why not spend the inevitable "several thousand" on a comfortable camp spacious enough to use not only in which to plan the building but from which it might be officered during construction later? I took this idea to Dr. Chandler and said that if he would give me a site somewhere we would build the camp ourselves. He reached for his hat, led the way to the little gray Ford coupe which he drives around the mesa at an average of fifty miles an hour and we went over toward the Salt Range.

Ten miles away we came upon a low, spreading, rocky mound rising from the great desert floor—well away from everywhere, but within view of the site of the new resort.

"How would this do?" said he.

(Ground where I came from was hard to come by.)

"This—do you mean it—can we have this to build on?" I said.

He nodded.

"What more could anyone ask?" I said.

"But," he suggested, "let us go a little further over toward the hotel site, you might like that better."

"Oh, no—I'll take this as it is, right here."

It was all too good, but true.

Lumber began to arrive that afternoon. Native 1 × 10″ redwood boards and 2 × 4's (unluckily undersized and very green) and two-inch battens.

I sat down in a cold, vacant office upstairs in the little town offices to make the plans. The shivering boys stood around me watching, handing me the tools. We set up the drawing boards on boxes. It was cold. They said in Chandler "unusual" weather, but whenever I had been there it was always "unusual" weather: "the coldest or warmest or wettest or dryest in thirty or fifty years." The scheme was soon ready. Next morning we started in to build the first camp. In fact we ate breakfast at the campsite as the frost came out of the air and a great red sun-disc rose over a sublime spectacle of desert mountain ranges and gorgeous sunrise sky.

We made such progress that day that one of my boys, Donald Walker, slept that night outside on a pile of lumber, rolled up in blankets. But by next night we had set up the first "box-bottom" of the tent tops and put cots in it for three more boys. Next day there was room for all to sleep except my little family of three and myself. Reluctantly we went back to Mesa to sleep in the hotel. But we came back for early breakfast to that wonderful dining-room sixty miles wide, as long and tall as the universe. We were shivering, oh, yes. But we were all singing happy in that clear cold sunrise. A great prospect!

We had a sweeping view all around us of this vast battleground of titanic natural forces, called Arizona. It will make *the* playground for these United States someday. But too soon yet. The 100 per cent American would spoil it now, *à la Hopi* or Mexicano-Hispano, or perhaps even "the latest"—the boxment *à la mode*.

Out here in the great spaces obvious symmetry would claim too much, I find, the too obvious wearies the eye too soon, stultifies imagination. Obvious symmetry usually closes the episode before it begins. So for me I felt there could be no obvious symmetry in any building in this great desert, none especially in this new camp. No, there would be nothing but occult symmetry in the new "San Marcos in the Desert."

The sound constitution of Entity is pregnant with graceful reflexes. Seek those reflexes, my young architect! Now by way of our work-camp came fresh adventure in the realm of Architecture. We called the desert camp: "OCATILLO."

Victor Hugo wrote: "The desert is where God is and Man is not." Arizona desert. But the Arizonan living in these desert towns has got himself a carpenter-built midwestern cottage, or sometimes, more fortunate so he thinks, a mid-Mediterranean or Mexicano palazzo, or a mud-walled patio. Believe it or not, he has already built a few skyscrapers in towns on the mesa. He would build more if he could and a better place for them than crowded into cities.

But the Hopi-Yankee house is Phoenix favorite just now. In all this weird, colorful, wide-sweeping terrain nothing is quite so deciduous as Arizona buildings, unless it is the crows lighting on the fences of the irrigated fields only to fly away.

To see unspoiled native character insulted like this! Arizona character seems to cry out for a space-loving architecture of its own. The straight line and flat plane, sun-lit, must come here—of all places—but they should become the dotted line, the broad, low, extended plane textured because in all this astounding desert there is not one hard undotted line to be seen. The great nature-masonry rising from the great mesa floor is all the noble architecture Arizona has to show at present. But it is inspiration. A pattern of what appropriate Arizona architecture might well be lies there hidden in these mesas and the Saguaro. The Saguaro, perfect example of reinforced building construction. Its interior vertical rods hold it rigidly upright maintaining its great fluted columnar mass for centuries. A truer skyscraper than our functioneers have yet built.

These remarkable desert growths show scientific building economy in the patterns of their construction. The stalks especially teach any architect or engineer who is modest and intelligent enough to apply for lessons. In these desert constructions he may not only see the reinforcing-rod scientifically employed as in the flesh of the saguaro but he may see the perfect lattice or in the reed and welded tubular construction of the stalk of the cholla, or staghorn, see it too in the cellular build-up of the water-barrel, Bignana. Even the flesh of the prickly pear is worth studying for scientific structure. In most cases of cacti Nature employs cell to cell or continuous tubular or often plastic construction. By means of plasticity Nature makes continuity everywhere strongly effective without having to reduce the scheme to post and girder construction before she can figure it out. She has this great advantage in her architectural adventure over our very best engineers. Engineers are quite often almost as silly as architects. Plasticity is the new problem now ready to be met in building construction. As for me I have seen that experts *can* be "wrong for more than fifty years."

Yes, Desert is rock-bound earth, rock-trimmed earth or earth-trimmed rock prostrate to the sun. All life there below the crystal is tenacious sun-life and all life there dies a sun-death. Evidence is everywhere. Sometimes ghastly I admit.

For our purpose we needed fifteen cabins in all. Since all will be temporary we will call them ephemera. And you will soon see them like a group of gigantic butterflies with scarlet wing spots, conforming gracefully to the crown of the outcropping of black splintered rock gently uprising from the desert floor. This mound where Dr. Chandler first took me. A human gaiety in the Desert is under way. But here in this wonderland an architect and his helpers are actually working away to build a simple inexpensive camp. A camp we shall call it: human inhabitant of unmitigated wilderness of quotidian change—unchangeably changing Change.

To keep out varmints the little box-board cabins themselves are to be connected by a low staggered box-board wall with a horizontal zig-zag—(for the same reason Thomas Jefferson worm-walled his four-inch brick walls). It will be self-supporting and complete the enclosure just referred to as the "compound." Necessary openings in the light canvas-topped shell buildings we will close with canvas-covered wood frames. Flaps hinged with rubber belting. No glazed doors or windows. Glass is not for this type of desert camp if indeed much glass belongs in the Desert at all.

Now, when all these white canvas flaps—wings like sails, are spread, the buildings—butterfly simile good—will look something like ships coming down the mesa, rigged like ships well balanced in the circumstances.

Oh yes, the group *will* look like some new kind of desert fleet. We painted the horizontal boards with cold-water paint, continuing the board walls around the varied buildings connecting all the cabins about the mound. I chose dry rose as the color to match the light on the desert floor. The one-two triangle used in planning the camp is made by the mountain ranges themselves around about the site. And the magical one-two triangle is the cross-section of the talus at their bases. This triangle is reflected in the general forms of all cabins as well as the general plan. We will paint the canvas eccentric one-two triangles in the gables scarlet. The one-two triangles of the ocatillo bloom itself are scarlet. This red triangular form in the whole plan and treatment is why we called the camp "Ocatillo": "Candle flame."

Presently I found that the white luminous canvas overhead and canvas flaps used instead of window glass afforded such agreeable diffusion of light within, was so enjoyable and sympathetic to the desert, that I now felt more than ever oppresed by the thought of the opaque solid overhead of the much too heavy midwestern houses.

The dust columns of the desert devils would come whirling along like a dancing dervish and go in drifting spirals rising high in the air. Occasionally a devil would cross the camp and it would shudder in its grasp like a ship—but hold fast. No damage at all.

I believe we pay too slight attention to making slight buildings beautiful or beautiful buildings slight. Lightness and strength may now become synonymous terms.

Usually we spend much too much to make buildings "last," as we say. Unqualified to build, we are still too busy making caves for cave-dweller survivals. Heavy, heavy hangs over thy head.

"Ocatillo"!—little desert camp—you are "ephemera." Nevertheless you shall drop a seed or two yourself in course of time—on ground now needlessly barren.

Meantime my draughtsmen—at this moment Heinrich Klumb, Donald Walker, Vladimir Heifetz, Cy Tomlins and brave George Kastner—he was still ill and so was good Canadian Catholic Frank Sullivan—Will Weston and I—we all made the camp between ourselves: put it together with nails, screws, rubber belting for hinges; rigged up the flaps with ship cord, all designed as carefully, probably more carefully than any permanent building. Not as carefully as a ship nor so well executed, of course, but done as well as we knew how with such technique and endurance as we had. Good enough, for all was to pass away in a season—or two?

As a matter of fact it did pass to the Indians in less time than that. The Indians carted it all away during the winter after we had turned our backs upon it, and characteristic disaster, the panic, befell the U.S.A. No, not prohibition. I mean the Fall of 1929 when Architecture and architects ceased to function throughout the U.S.A.

UBIQUITY

Yes, Navajo Indians carried it all away. But, I have learned not to grieve long now that some work of mine has met its end; *has had short life,* as we say, even though it happens that a better one cannot take its place: consoled by the thought that today any building *design* may have far-reaching effect on the record, and because our social machine—publicity—so easily gives it, as an idea of form, to the mind's eye of all the world. For an instance, "Ocatillo" with no help or suggestion from me was published in German, Dutch and French magazines two months after it was finished. It has since appeared in magazines all over the world. Thank the Machine Age for that: for universal ubiquity. Or curse it as the case may be, of course.

But dissemination and consequent prevalence of an Idea in some graphic thought-form certainly is one of the better—or maybe worst—things the machine has done for us in our time.

When *organic* architecture really finds its way to American practice we shall have no such senseless destruction of life as we see going on around us now. Could striving for such establishments as we now have end, life would become more abundant for all: much better in quality for everyone. These foolish little differences without real difference but to which we so pridefully cling continually lead to tedious repetition of insignificant resemblances. We seem so afraid of any true differences. How afraid we are of any genuine "difference"! I have every reason to know.

This is the evil of such philosophy as we know in educated "thinking" today; it never does nor ever can go to seed that can grow anything at all fresh *from our own soil. Indigenous* growth is the essential province of all true Culture. It is so today as it was yesterday, or there will be no tomorrow for us! So rather than ponderous permanent blunders in expensive materials, until we learn more of good appropriate building, why not "ephemera" as preliminary study, say? America was given

336

permanent building materials to work with—much too soon. Say a century.

RETROSPECT

The little camp finished, we love it. The canvas overhead—the windows and doors of Ocatillo *are* like ship-sails when open and may shut against dust or open part way to deflect desert breezes into the interiors. Screened openings for cross ventilation are everywhere at the floor levels, a discovery I made in seeking coolness, to be used during the heat of the day; closed at night. The long sides of the canvas slopes lie easily with the lines of the landscape, the slopes stretching themselves wide open toward the sun in order to aid a little in warming the interiors in Winter. These long canvas roof-sides are to have additional cover of canvas, air blowing between the two sheets of textiles if the camp is ever occupied in Summer. We can add this cover later if we stay on in Summer.

Gratifying it is to look and see as we look how well we fit into this strange, linear, well-armed, creeping cover of the abstract land. Peculiar *growth* almost as abstract. The inexorable grasp of growing vegetation upon the earth itself is more terrifying to me as a principle at work than what we call death. Growth is everywhere more terrible and terrifying than all other evidence of inexorable force put together.

There seems no mortal escape, especially not in death, from this inexorable earth-principle of growth-change—or is it sun-principle—of growth in death or death in growth. This creative creature of the great sun-architecture?

What of the subsidence we see now changing the streamlines of these endless ranges of mountains coming by erosion gently down to the mesa. Going abruptly up into the sky from the plains only to come back to the mesa. In this geologic era, catastrophic upheaval has found comparative repose by way of these sculptors, Wind and Water. To these vast, quiet, ponderable masses made by fire and laid by Water— both are architects—now comes the sculptor—Wind. Wind and Water ceaselessly eroding, endlessly working to quiet and harmonize all traces of violence until a glorious unison is again bathed in the atmosphere of a light that is eternal.

Finally to "justify" Ocatillo, our wild adventure, it cost not so much more than the rent and keep asked for equivalent accommodations in Chandler or in Phoenix for the one season we were to stay, the same number of persons provided for. The cost was about two hundred dollars per occupant. But the labor was mostly our own. We are the better for that—because we have met the Desert, loved it, lived with it and made the Desert ours.

SAN MARCOS IN THE DESERT

Our little spontaneous camp was finished about January 19th, 1928. Something of lively human significance had come to the Desert. Under the suffused glow of the translucent canvas overhead we worked away on Dr. Chandler's resort for jaded millionaires such as might still be able to see beauty and seek solitude in quiet comradeship with surroundings. We were going to call it San Marcos in the Desert and we worked on it until the middle of the following June. Often we worked at night by gasoline lights until we put in a Kohler plant and had all the electric light we wanted.

We worked out this desert "resort" as a great block-system, a series of intercommunicating terraces facing to the sun of the south. There were three of these terraces, each room with its own small pool and little garden, one long terrace range of them rising above the other back against the mountainside: A mono-material building, latest expression of the block-shell system started in La Miniatura and carried over to the Arizona Biltmore. The block system in this case is genuine reinforced masonry, within and without. The block-shell here will be integral with structure. It is the structure itself dedicated in form to the Saguaro.

The deep "wash" or ravine, a deep gorge between the two great hills back of the terraces, we used to conceal the road leading to the main entrance of the building. This entrance placed well back under the building in the gorge itself. An organ tower for evening vespers, block-shell design, rose like a giant group of saguaro from this gorge to emphasize entrance: intended also to give voice to the whole. Echo-organs are to be planted in the hills—Dr. Chandler's idea—for open air concerts in the desert at sunset.

The dining room? It is a top-lit glass and copper arbor topping the central mass and so connected to the hill slopes on either side by the terrace tops of the upper stories of the wings that adjacent dwellers in the mountain cottages—to be built later as part of the whole—may reach it comfortably on foot along the top terrace.

The plan is of a far-flung, long-drawn-out building. Owing to the placing of the levels of the sun-lit terraces, each room, each bathroom, each closet, each corridor even, has direct sunlight. Every portion of the building to be lived in is free to the sun and also to magnificent views. The whole has the warm southern exposure every winter resort covets.

338

The whole structure would approximate what we may honestly call permanent. Say three hundred years at least. Three hundred spacious rooms with bath, all appurtenance systems being more than adequate and virtually indestructible too with beautiful lobbies, dining rooms, etc., etc.—for luxurious living.

Now, observe if you will that every horizontal line in San Marcos in the Desert is a dotted line. Every flat plane is grosgrained, patterned like the Saguaro itself. The entire building is in pattern an abstraction of this mountain region itself and cactus life is set up in permanent pattern of masonry shells. The whole building made more cactus than any cactus can be in itself. Do you know what I mean? But none the less, rather more a human habitation to live in as long maybe as the mountain behind it lasts.

Human habitation here comes decently in with due reverence where God is. Man comes in as himself something of a God. And that is just what Architecture can do for him—not only show him appreciative of Arizona's character but qualify him in human habitation to become a native part of Arizona itself for so long as any building ever endured. Arizona desert itself was architectural inspiration and was actually the architect's workshop in this endeavor so the feeling of the whole building in all its parts now designedly belongs to the terrain. This is what I mean by indigenous organic architecture. San Marcos in the Desert proves it is not only possible but that it is here.

So, of course, it was all too good to happen. Sometimes I think it was just a dream. But here are the completed plans: you may see the carefully studied details. Responsible estimates were complete: the contract was signed by Paul Mueller the good builder, awaiting the Doctor's signature—complete for 480,000 dollars, 1929.

Then at that moment as Dr. Chandler took the train to complete the arrangements for coming to build came the crash of 1929. Where was Dr. Chandler? Now instead of a $40,000.00 fee, I found myself with a deficit of $19,000.00 to add to the mounting mountain of debt at Taliesin. $2500.00 was all there was to set against the whole, so the good Doctor said. Knowing his situation I accepted it and never asked him for more.

Never mind. Something had started that was not stopping thus. Later you will see consequences as this record proceeds.

By this time May heat was becoming the heat that made the Desert desert and keeps it desert. The Winter season now passed, dormant desert life was coming alive. Nine rattlesnakes were found in the compound. All living there now must have a care. Nevertheless we planned, worked and drove about the region in a free sun-life of the wide spaces for several weeks more and watched our step.

For the homeward drive to Taliesin North we acquired a used Packard sport Phaeton wide open to the sky. Camp broken, contents stored against return the following Winter, the big Packard stands by the gate to the compound to begin the drive overland to Taliesin . . . the full extent of the 1929 breakdown and its effect upon our enterprise not yet more evident than beginning to be known at Chandler. There was still some hope.

Olgivanna and I sat in front to take turns driving; Svetlana and Iovanna snug in the tonneau behind the rear windshield we had installed. We waved goodbye to the gay little camp and drove off to pick up Dr. Chandler who was going with us as far as Holbrook. We wanted to investigate a new natural cement found in that region, as perhaps an ideal material for our block-building. This material—a magnesite, I believe—was found in drifts on the mesa floor. It was white, set quickly and hard. Waterproof. We had left a plaster-model made of the actual block units proposed for use in building San Marcos in the Desert, standing white and brilliant in the center of the camp compound on the crown of the hill. That was as far as the structure ever got on the ground itself.

Chicago was finally reached by way of long Western-midwestern highways, towns and commonplaces. This long overland drive so full of incident and interest further west monotonously continued on the way to New York City. I was to consult with Reverend William Norman Guthrie, brilliant Rector of St. Marks on the Bouwerie, and his vestry, concerning the tall apartment building to be built in the little park at Tenth Street and Second Avenue for revenue to support the church. We found our Eastern cities and towns very like Western and Midwestern cities and towns. General lack of resourceful individuality, except that in the East there was less new construction. The village carpenter of New England had spread and spread until he had "styled" them all. I could not escape the feeling while in the East that the young men had all left home and taken the East out West with them, never to return. Eastern towns and villages all seemed waiting for their "young" to come back again to help do something about the ugly smugness of it all. Will they never come? We drove through the new Holland Tunnel into urban scenes of indescribable traffic confusion. The erstwhile village streets of New York City were in unusual uproar and turmoil of reconstruction— new subways, taller buildings all soon to be gripped and paralyzed in the now rapidly spreading panic. The little Iovanna had heard of the Empire State skyscraper as ultimate. As we emerged from the Holland Tunnel and caught a glimpse of it her face fell. "Daddy," said she, "they

could have made it higher—couldn't they? . . . Then why didn't they?"
You see that is really all "height" can really "amount to."

SIGNIFICANT INSIGNIFICANCE

Seen here in New York is the same architectural insignificance due to
the national blind-spot found all along the way from coast to coast except bigger and better insignificance. The insignificance we had seen
all along the line had some rights. None here. Here in the greatest metropolis of the U.S.A., in ambitious but fatal variety, is the same deadly
monotony where the building is concerned. Man-eating skyscrapers, all
tall but seeking false monumental mass for 1929 riveted steel skeletons,
nineteenth-century architecture. Not twentieth. This utter contradiction
of structure and idea is what is most destructive everywhere in New
York. Chicago architects long before had discovered the possibility of
using iron and steel to make a stone and brick building stand up so it
could go on up making masonry faces at admiring throngs all the way,
piling story on story. Of course, the tenuous open steel frame of these
tall buildings is, in character, the reverse of feudal masonry mass into
which it eventuates in New York. Lightness, openness and tenuous
strength combined should be its building characteristics. These ought
never to be associated with heavy stone or concrete as the building code
still insists it shall be, but with light insulated covering metals with
glass insertion—this instead of heavy walls: the whole be so designed
and the fabric so insulated as to emphasize the pattern of the structure
itself and not belie the way it was actually built. An old, old story now,
this pet American falsehood. Masonry materials do not only belie such
steel structures but the practice is really a threat to the life of the structure itself by adding enormous useless weight to the fabrication of the
whole. That very human equation, the factor of safety—really it is as
Dankmar Adler used to say "the factor of ignorance"—scientifically
never was put to work behind all this crowded mass of pier buildings,
crenelated tops and feudal masonry walls. The vaunted "sky-line" was
haphazard anyhow. Its vaunted "picturesque" a make-up of senseless
feudal-masses standing there on steel stilts to mask (and belie) the real
appearance of the purpose and character of the building itself: betray
the real significance of this new man-unit in this old-style city: a kind of
bastardizing of great opportunity. The engineering was here mere
functioneering, architects merely putting architecture on the outside.
Looking behind these false masonry masses . . . what, really, was it all?
The urbanite lost, that's all—helplessly drifting toward extinction by the
domination of the machine and its unearned increment over the
humanities.

AN ANGRY PROPHECY AND
A PREACHMENT: THE CITY

Is our great city triumph of the herd instinct over such sanity, such sanity as humanity may know? Or is it only ignorant hangover from the infancy of the race, to be outgrown as the performances of humanity grow—modern? Civilization has seemed to need and feature the city meantime or I suppose it wouldn't be with us now? No doubt the city *has* expressed what the civilization that built it most cherished. So the city may truly be said to have served civilization if not now.

But history records that the civilizations that built the greatest cities invariably died with them. Did the civilizations themselves die *of* them? I think they did.

Urban accelerations—history records this fact—always preceded such decay and we are seeing just such acceleration in our own American cities, today.

So in the streets and avenues of this great city of New York, acceleration due to the car and skyscraper—itself one of the accelerators—is singularly dangerous. Increasingly dangerous to any life the city may have left over even though its very own interests fail to see it as a danger until circumstances be left to take hold of the situation by force. They are beginning to do so.

RENT

As I believe in Freedom as ideal, so I believe that the American city as we know it today is not only to die but dying of acceleration. In this intensified urban-activity seeming to the thoughtless like success, we are only seeing characteristic acceleration going before ultimate dissolution. This ceaseless to and fro in the gainful occupation of this army of white collarites: is it an activity of parasites upon and in the various forms of artificial "rent"? Money itself now being most lucrative form of rent. RENT is become the fetish of an artificial economic domination that now really owns and operates the great city at a loss. The city is itself now money-coming-alive as something in itself to go on ceaselessly working to make all work useless and make war a continuous commonplace to keep gold the "Standard."

Yet there is hope that our American civilization may not only survive its great cities but eventually profit by them because the death of these cities—now conceivable—will be the greatest service the machine has ultimately to render the human being. If by means of his machine

342

man ever does conquer his own machinery. What beneficent significance to him otherwise has the machine? Cities are already outgrown as
overgrown. Any great city cannot feed upon itself now. Its present carcass is past such redemption. But, should the machine conquer man,
will man remain to repeat urban history? Will he perish with his city as
all other urban civilizations have so perished? The City, like all minions
of the machine, is grown up only in man's image. But when it is minus
the living impetus that is man, the city is only man becoming or already
become—the machine. Even now the city is only the baleful shadow of
the sentient man that once did need a city and who built it and maintained it because he did need it. That ancient city, once a necessity, and
proof of some greatness in him is now dying or dead of his own excess.
Humanity must find a means to go beyond it to a Freedom undreamed
of before. Humanity has already found the means in the machine itself.

What built the cities that have invariably died? Primarily necessity.
That necessity gone, now only a dogged tradition, sentimental habit
cannot keep any great city alive for a great length of time. Necessity
built the city on the basis of "leg-work or the horse and buggy; wood
and coal consumption; and food distribution, when the necessity for
communication was to be had only by personal contacts."

No effective mobilization of the individual making one mile as one
block nor any electrified means of intercommunication then existed.
Various physical contacts in that earlier day needed a certain congestion
to facilitate and stimulate life. Life does not need that congestion in that
way or for that purpose. The ancient city naturally grew and existed as
the great aid and abettor of human intercourse and culture. A city became the immediate source of wealth and power by way of such human
intercourse as was essential to social, industrial and financial growth of
mankind. Only by congregating thus in aggregations, the more vast the
aggregation the better, could the fruits of human living then best be
had. In that day the real life of the city lay in the stress of individual ties,
the contacts of super-individuals countering upon other individualities.
The electric spark of curiosity and surprise was alive in the streets, in
public meetings. In the home it was found only occasionally as people
congregated there. All was excitingly gregarious and gregarious in order
to be exciting.

Government, the city had as now. Fashions and fads also. But the
salt and savor of individual wit, taste and character then made the city a
festival of life; a true carnival as compared with any drab overrun city of
our day. Even Paris. But this original human concentration is not to be
so quickly changed as the conditions of its existence would warrant because human-habit changes slowly as water wears away a stone.
Perhaps less rapidly. So it would seem.

So our Architecture, fundamentally, were it a living architecture would reflect this livelier human condition were it here today. But this modern common denominator, the Machine, had not then arrived in the ancient city. Now? The common denominator has not only arrived but come down by, with and where the man is imprisoned and growing helpless just because of the machine. So at the moment new machine powers are rendering so many of the old powers impotent if not entirely obsolete. It is only natural then that sudden release of all these new scientific machine factors and forces should at first be fearfully and self-ishly held back to hold habits. And to ulterior purposes bred by fear and greed. What so timid as a million dollars? Several millions.

But machine-prophecy grows and shows, as nothing else shows, that we are to deal with the fact and principle of machinery in its most dangerous form right here among us in the city—and now. The social results of machine-uses show the cultural sentimentality in human af-fairs trying to break these new forces down to old habits is impotent to deal with our new "daemon"—the mechanistic element. But, architec-ture must soon deal with it or our new devil will finally deal with us in our posterity not only as common-denominator but as dominator ex-traordinary under some other name.

To deny inherent power of growth and virtue to our new common-denominator the machine which, were man in his senses, might soon be the common-emancipator—would this be absurd? But the eventual city that this new common-denominator will build with our common Machine will be so greatly different from the ancient city or from any city of today that we will probably fail to recognize its coming as the city at all! At any rate it will not be, I think, a graveyard for individuality nor obliterate the man. Any city of *futurism* to be valid will be only more individual than in ages ago. Not less so.

To put a new outside upon any existing city is impossible. The car-cass of the city is far too old, too far gone. It is too *fundamentally* wrong for the future we now foresee to make much use of it as it is.

Hopelessly, helplessly, inorganic it lies there where the great new forces molding modern life are most concerned. Those forces are mak-ing concentrations not only useless but deadly, by force of circum-stances being driven inward, meantime relentlessly preparing to explode. Reactions that should by organic change drive the city some-where into somewhat other and else are everywhere at work upon it. The new city will be nowhere, yet everywhere. Broadacre City?

THE HUMAN-ELEMENT in equation in our modern life is not yet recog-nizing or not acknowledging an equivalent. But humanity may already be seen drifting—or pushed—going blindly. But *going* just the same and in several different directions, but to accept and to await the inevitable.

Congestion of super-concentrations was no great evil until electric power, electric intercommunication, individual mobilization and ubiquitous "publicity" became common factors, common denominators, true decentralizing agents for human life. Add to these "decentralizers" the airship when it lays away its wings and becomes a self-contained mechanized unit. Add many other things kept under cover by our heavy, still hardy capitalistic hands, all in safekeeping for the moment.

If we accept these molding modern agencies that science has made ready to confer upon us, the form of everything changes, as time runs, for better or for worse. Everything but human nature changes—whether we will it so or will against it. Though "Nature her custom holds," here and elsewhere we do change, none the less and notwithstanding. But how slowly for the better.

Consequences of organic inevitable changes unperceived at first begin to appear all about us now—waiting for recognition.

Freedom of human-reach and movement, therefore expansion of the human horizon as a sphere of action, is enormously widened by the new services rendered by the Machine. Horizontality has received immense impetus, impulse that will soon make human activity immeasurable; therefore unendurable on any present terms or scale of spacing now established or practiced.

The pain of additional human city-pressure is senselessly caused if we take a clear view of our coming of age in this new era. This amazing Twentieth Century of ours—why not inhabit it?

But here we are, apparently helpless to face this issue, though witnessing fatal internal collision between mechanistic factors. We neglect their significance and thoughtlessly find release, new pride in cowardly human tendencies in many emergencies. We do not know whether to run or stay right there where we are. We do both with animal fear exaggerated by human sentimentality. But mostly we pig-pile in consequence—to feel safe?

Eventually it is fear of freedom—under economic pressure, the skyscraper was born. Invention, for twenty years, looking for salvation to the engineer. The elevator, has been trying to thus hold the profits of super-concentration. But the skyscraper is now seen as a landlord's ruse to have and hold thoughtless super-imposition. In our skyscraping boxes we see not only a commercial expedient but one that enabled landlords to exploit the herd and to the limit of egotism. By ordinance and official order, as usual, it is done and maintained.

Thus the greater human freedom, ability to spread out on the new space terms of our new country without personal inconvenience (and this is the most valuable gift brought by undreamed-of powers of electrical intercommunication, automobile, the telephone, the airship, radio, television and the press). By twist of the capitalist wrist the skyscraper represented, for the moment, every great city perversion from the man himself to the exploitation of some form of profit or lucky realty. As the realtor's super-concentrations boomed, 1929 reaction was inevitable.

Let us readily admit the thrill for the thoughtless in such magnitude lengthwise or up and down acceleration and super-concentration in supremacy directly due to unwise exaggeration. But no one just now, as socio-economic temperatures run high, seems to want to know whether the acceleration is healthy excitement of normal growth or really the fever of disease. Few seem to care much about whether such acceleration means human progress or only some form of commercial exploitation, likely to be and make this Machine Age the swiftest but the shortest-lived civilization in all history. The architect, however, does care. He must. It is largely up to him.

TIME

This iteration and reiteration of an idea is probably wearing upon my reader now when the story of the Idea has hardly begun. I feel the matter so important that at the risk of turning *An Autobiography* into propaganda I go on with it.

Forces themselves seem blinded to it as if blinded by it. Reading between the lines, history will show that human beings, unaccustomed to thought as organic therefore helplessly involved, also remain time-blind. Over long stretches of time. But—a saving clause! Today along with these new revolutionary factors, there come new means of communication amounting to the realization of a new human faculty that may wipe out Time. An ubiquitous publicity often succeeds in now getting done in a month what formerly took a decade. Yet, we are Time-bound in all forms of our life and thought today. What took a century in human affairs not long ago now takes but about ten years. Emancipation or destruction may lie just ahead.

Ten years, in our twentieth century, is an epoch. Thirty years, an "age"!

So Time-reactions to any human activity or problem—notwithstanding ownership of this Machine as agency as of all other popular agencies—in less than one lifetime show either the wisdom or folly of such perversion of life-ownership even now. Humanity may yet call for correction before the affair has gone too far. Since we are prone to publicity, publicizing needed organic influences may help avert organic disasters that overtook earlier civilizations. It may also precipitate disaster.

TRAFFIC

The "traffic-problem" already forces economic attention to tyrannical building in cities to feed the elevator.

Although economic attention seems our best attention, yet the traffic problem—a time-problem where time is said to be money—is yet wholly unsolved. But the calls for solution are increasing. There is, of course, no solution. The metropolis started all wrong on the ground for any organic development there now. The gridiron originally laid out by the village for horse and buggy, now grown to the metropolis, is a basic cause for economic waste. Constant danger we call the traffic problem is now high blood pressure in the veins and arteries of the village gridiron and daily becomes more intolerable.

Pretended means of relief by experts eagerly employed by space-makers for rent—the expedient, the nineteenth-century skyscraper—renders this distress only more acute. The same means of relief carried only somewhat further along the line and "relief" by experts will soon have killed the patient—the city. Witness the splitting-up of Los Angeles and Chicago into several "centers," each again already splitting up into several more. You may already see the wise decentralization of the big department stores and mail-order houses. Migration of factories in spaciousness has already begun. The financial center and prostitution alone hold place by the sheer main strength and awkwardness of authority. Nevertheless the population of the big cities decreases steadily and few are now solvent.

In face of all realistic evidence we still view such prophecy as the cubistic city of *"futurisme."* "La ville radieuse" for instance. The tyranny of the skyscraper finds there a sophisticated philosophy fortifying itself as "ideal" by proposing to get new cities built—*on the sites of the old ones!* Standardization up on stilts again seen as Salvation! Enormous exaggerations of avenues of traffic are suggested but making all intercommunication utterly impractical because the actual nature of circumstances is surely making such exaggeration entirely unnecessary—out of human scale altogether.

Made plainer by this kind of "drawing-board" architecture, we see how humanity involved in any machine-made city of this machine-made future of a machine-manipulated humanity is to be "dealt with" by machine-made esthetics in order to hold and render such human benefits as electricity, the automobile, the telephone, the airship and the radio into a systematic herd-exploitation of mankind instead of rendering mankind more free, serviceable and happy.

WHY BUILD POVERTY AS AN INSTITUTION INTO OUR NATION?

Along with such uptown confusion worse confounded as this modernistic myopia, there now goes the vexing problem of the tenement on the gridiron. This would-be beneficent—by government—"housing of the poor." Yes, the poor are not only to be with us always, but the poor are to be recognized and multiplied per se as such. And so be multiplied officially. Too, they are to be built in by insurance companies as official fixtures of the cities of our great free United States of America. Yes . . . the "poor" are to be so poor as to be accepted, confirmed and especially provided for as inevitable factors therein. As seen in any Federal plan, catastrophe is to be made organic. The poor are to be *built in!*

Yes, the slums of today are to be made into the slums of tomorrow. As the sinners of yesterday are the saints of today.

That the poor will benefit by increased sanitation may be granted at a glance. But, not only are the living quarters of the poor to be more germ-proof, but life itself where individual choice is concerned is to be rendered antiseptic. If we trust our eyes.

Or the skyscraper is to be let down sidewise or the ground flat-plane tipped up edgewise as traps to crucify, not liberate, humanity.

Poor? The poor man's life is to become just as the rich man's—find No. 36722, block 99, shelf 17, entrance K, West, with a few twists and turns thrown in to distract attention from the ugly facts. "Poor" the man gets a bathtub and a flower-box, a patch of lawn, but what Freedom to say and believe what he says, were he to say his soul is his own?

Surface and mass in more than one sense are his life and so, his architecture thus *extinguished,* the poor man has already *distinguished* his landlord: therefore why should the poor man complain? Has the poor man not still his labor for his pains? And what has the rich man else for his, I ask you? Ask him.

Yes, there is, the poor man! No longer in a rubbish heap. No.

In the United States of America he is where Government is not through with him until he is a mechanized unit in a commercial system paying more rent with public help for his new blessings. But so far as he himself goes there, he is a form of "rent" himself. Still a cog for rent and to rent. Forever? Still the poor man's life is but two by twice. He has been cleaned up but toned down. He has been further plucked of indi-

348

viduality and tucked in if not marketed. The unsightly "slum" has thus been whitewashed and fumigated of its bums. It will be recognized in future as, still, the slum for another kind of bum.

Nor can the poor—thus made decent surface-and-mass in the great institution of poverty individually (or collectively for that matter) choose anything esthetically alive to live with. At least not if neighbors and landlords can see that he hasn't. But the "social" objective is attained . . . the dirty rags of the poor have been temporarily covered from sight by a clean smock at public expense.

Yes, the poor man in this hard governmental picture, exhibit B, is cog 3,000,000,128 in the new model for the standardized city, is it "la ville radieuse"? The poor man it seems has no other choice. Because his choice is either more or less sentimental or senseless? But observe the simple aspect of housing the poor. How easy it all is!

This, by government or by order, is the "Ne Plus Ultra" for the poor man or the "E Pluribus Unum" of such social progress as the Machine Age has forced upon us where authority takes architecture in charge by order.

Modernistic dreams of the new city where and when no real need exists for any such city at all are painful because so utterly impartial. These new "ideals" in architecture distinguish no one, nor perceive anything except certain routine economies and the rent-paying rituals sacred to a businessman's investment. Routine economies are to be shared with other ubiquitous-numericals (they are still the common-denominator), sharing them with the nominators of the system, the system being officially perfected as still, Ideal! Well, the economies are shared fifty-fifty? Half to the initial nominator—the Federal Banking System. Fair enough—or—who can say what fairness is in so equivocal a time as ours?

Division of these economic benefits within range of this authorized standardization of the man must be either left out or left entirely to the generosity of the initial nominators, the same as always before. We have learned to *speak* of democracy, only?

Yet, what would you, Mr. Architect! Humanity is here orderly. Decent on the surface again—rank and file—in the great war behind all wars is the great "to-have and to-hold." The common denominator in this scheme is here gratuitously officered, standardized like any army, marched not only to and fro, but up and down no less. Six or sixteen stories? The common denominator (plain citizen) on such terms would be no more able to work without the initial nominator (capitalist) than the Machine would be able to work without the human touch. No, the growing ranks of the accepted poor themselves, the government pawns. In theory and in fact they have become the machine itself.

349

"The Noble Duke of York, he had ten thousand men," they all go six floors up, and up sixteen floors again. None may know just why they go, so narrowly up, up, up, to come so narrowly down, down, down—instead of freely going in and out and comfortably round about among the beautiful things to which their lives are related in horizontal lines on top of green earth. Why not spend the money on transporting them to grass—as herders do?

The modern system of devising life on what we may call skyscraper terms (skyscraper laid down flatwise and occupants not much better off) is the intention to reduce all but our mechanistic supervisors and devisors who may live in penthouses above or on top floors—those who may secure the privileges of the upper stories, to the ranks of the poor? Themselves the poor in spirit in consequence?

Free country, democratic in the sense that our forefathers intended ours to be free, means *individual* freedom for each man on his own ground? And it means that for all, rich or poor alike, the true basis of opportunity. Or else Democracy is only another expedient to enslave man to the Machine and in a foolish way try to make him like one. Why not then and now, the means comes to hand, let his line of action be *horizontally* extended: Free. Give him the flat plane expanded parallel to green earth, gripping all social structure comfortably to the ground! Or a true capitalist system, apex in the air, broad base on the ground. This awakening sense of interior space due the free man in the building and as in the ways of life to match it must break through to sunlight, sky and air, or we will have a communist factory hand instead of a democratic citizen of free initiative, a land of opportunity for that free worker. As for the cavicular present idea of building? Ancient, it is vanishing with the walls now seen standing as feudal-masonry. When that wall vanishes only, will the machine be as the consequence the natural conqueror of drudgery and imposing demoralization of earth, fit to use for the extension of the spirit of man in a new civilization.

WHAT FREEDOM

Freedom? Yes, when the margin of human leisure and culture of every man who works may widen if he will with his work. And when therefore every man works with joy and self-respect in his soul. The machine thus comprehended and controlled would succeed for the man himself and widen the margin of leisure increasingly to be spent in a field, on the streams or in the public or private domain or in the wood: the wild so easily reached on great architectural roads—a feature of our architecture.

Spaciousness for all in Usonia. The great highway becoming, and rapidly, the horizontal line of a new Freedom extending from ocean to ocean, tying woods, streams, mountains and plains, great and small, all together, tapping outflow from the overcrowded urban fields for the better building by men of men in a better way. Human occupation of Earth thus expanded will add intrinsic beauty to feature to the truly noble nature-environment into which our nation has been born. Only then will we be justified in bringing children into the world. They will become the United States (our Usonia) of tomorrow: each pair of little expectant feet born to its own acre? What right, else, has intelligent parenthood to exercise its function as a cultured civilization?

If our enormous machine-power were humanely used it would enable all that was ever desirable in any city to go at any time now to a greater natural beauty and enjoy the freer life we could honestly call *Democratic*. True culture must grow up with the ground. I believe that only when Machine increment, placed there where it belongs, enabling human life to be fruitful because Man is *with* his own ground and not merely a parasite either upon it or away from it—only then will indigenous culture come to us as a Nation.

The better personal element has already withdrawn from what is now extreme urban, leaving it to the business of the port of call or leave. Better elements are already so far withdrawn from the city that gang-rule is harder to break. The City infested by evil as a wharf is infested by rats.

When we become thus frankly utilitarian and bucolic instead of alcoholic we can go with the new reality to the order that is beauty, the simplicity of its expression to which our machine facilities, in proper as well as competent hands, entitle us.

I see such organic change soon defeating static "establishment." Already it shows us Centralization giving way to decentralization and we must take hand in re-integration or be the shortest-lived civilization in all history.

THE ROAD ALWAYS BETTER THAN THE INN

Meantime these States afford increasingly traveled great road-systems. Splendid highways becoming ours. Telephone and power poles that everywhere mar these highways and the countryside were long ago obsolete only to be removed when the investment in them lags. The old pig-tight, horse-high, bull-strong fence is no longer much needed as modern farming goes. Electrical fencing already makes it unnecessary. These great road-systems, hastening movement toward the city at first, are facilitating reaction now. The countryside steadily rising in importance as a consequence.

Railroads, once dominant metallic lines of communication strung in competing lines conquering the country, are gradually less useful except for the long haul overland. These private railroads will soon be turned into great natural concrete arteries for mobile uninterrupted traffic on several levels. Clumsy heavy coaches dragged roaring along on hard rails are soon obsolete. The present heavy railway, no matter how amended, is too cumbersome and slow for requirements of modern mobilization, will pass with the passing of the city.

As new and greater road and air systems are added year by year they are more splendidly built and safely operated. I foresee that roads by earth and air will soon be architcture too. As they well may be great architecture.

Leading toward the city, at first to gratify a hindered or frustrated social and civil life, our great Usonian roads work the normal way, leading in the right direction, away from senseless congestion and sordid competition to new life, greater integrity. Freedom of the country when man with machine leverage by his own hand takes it over.

LAND

Thanks to provisions of early Government, great natural and National Parks are becoming everywhere available for recreation. One-eighth of all America is government-owned.

Millions of individual building sites, large and small, now easy of access are available owing to our great continually developing road-systems. These sites may be seen everywhere neglected. Why where there are so many billions of acres of idle land now easily reached by cheap transportation should land longer be parceled out by realtors to needy families in strips 25 feet or even 100 feet wide be commonplace land division, and the slum be extended next door to itself? The survival of feudal thinking comes to its end. Routine establishment striving to preserve traditions of the ancient city to perpetuate social and economic crimes practiced by might upon the serf is less fashionable. Yes, an acre to the individual should be democratic minimum in our nation if this machine of ours is ever to be a social success.

What is standing in the way of coming liberation? Nothing. Only Habit, Greed and Fear.

352

It is only necessary to realign standardized efficiency of the machine in this new direction, confine the concentration of its operation only wherever it may belong, and manage the distribution of benefits at large not merely as speculative profits but insist upon a basis of decentralization. We are learning that machine-benefits are human-benefits or they are bitter fruit. Much bitter fruit already hangs in the city tree alongside the good, or rotted. Only a small part of our enormous machine increment is where under decentralization it naturally belongs. Circumstances are inexorably taking it first to the regional field on the way to country fields. By evolution? Certainly—by bloodshed maybe.

THE GAS STATION

One more advance agent of reintegration, an already visible item in decentralization of the City, may be seen in any and every roadside service station happening to be well located along the highways.

The roadside service station may be—in embryo—a future-city service-distribution. Each station may grow into a well-designed convenient neighborhood distribution center naturally developing as meeting place, restaurant, restroom, motel or whatever else will be needed as decentralization proceeds and integration succeeds. Already, hundreds of thousands occupy the best places in town or, more significantly, well outside towns.

Eventually we will have a thousand new small city-equivalents at work. Proper integration of these would help overcome the super-centralization now trying to stand against Freedom.

Added to many such minor sections destined to someday become beautiful countryside features will be larger traffic stations at main intersections. There may be really neighborhood centers where there will be more specialized commerce and such special entertainments as are not yet available by every man's own fireside, increasingly few because soon there will be little not reaching any man where he lives, coming by space-annihilating devices such as broadcasting, television and incessant publication. Of course. The cultural quality of these new means is steadily advancing in spite of the old commercial tides of advertising now swamping them. The huckster in the parlor and bedroom. The neighborhood garage is an "eating" or sleeping place—the auto camp or "motel" will largely supplant the hotel as a luxury feature. These roadside units are increasing in numbers, in scope and scale as well as in range and desirability.

Perfect distribution, then like the ubiquitous publicity that serves or destroys, is a common capacity of the machine probably never to be completely realized above rapacity. Nor ever be even approximately realized in such "centralization" as the back-and-forth haul to the big city. This affair of mobilization for distribution to auto-mobilization to air transport, once it really begins to operate, will soon evolutionize present arbitrary, wasteful transportation arrangements.

The now hated chain-merchandising linked to chain-servicing, decentralized and reintegrated in countryside markets, may give more direct and perfect machinery for all kinds of distribution of stores in connection with the traffic-station than could be had by expensive, outdated, back-and-forth haul.

THE MOTOR CAR MUCH MORE
AND MORE TO THE FORE

Complete mobilization of our American people is one natural asset of the machine fast approaching. Opportunity is coming for the homeward-bound individual to pick up by the wayside anything in the way of supplies he may require, just as the stranger may find there entertainment and satisfactory lodging. In these United States great highways are becoming arteries of the integration of otherwise decentralized great cities, the city of the future: Broadacre City?

Common wayside interests, plus entertainment centers, will, because of the motor car, soon be commonplace. As the importance of Freedom appears to the human mind the need of it increases in the human heart. So no doubt a new sense of quality in all these expressions will appear. The luxurious motor-bus traveling over superb road systems is making travel and intercommunication not only universally available but highly interesting. The aeroplane remodeled some day as a self-contained mechanical unit will pick up and continue this surface traffic as super-traffic in air and routed anywhere on earth. Then, not until then, the airport will further develop as integral feature beside the highways, infinitely extending space-arteries and the possibilities of modern life extension.

Even as now, were the truck lanes beside the railroads, a day's motor journey becomes something to be enjoyed in itself—enlivened, serviced and perfectly accommodated *en route*. No need to get tangled up in spasmodic stop-and-go traffic in some wasteful stop-and-go trip to town nor to any "great" city as center for everything whatever except to "view the ruins." These common highway journeys may soon become the delightful modern circumstance, every-varying adventure within reach of everyone. Already as Cervantes said, the Road is better than the Inn.

DISTRIBUTION

Cities today are voracious mouths. And New York the greatest mouth in the world: terrific drains on national transport. But with generally perfect economic distribution of food completed within the immediate area of the countryside, a vital element that helped to build the city to its present extent has left it forever to spread out in direct relation to the soil from which the produce to feed it came. Local products find short haul to direct consumption. Expensive long hauls to the city and then haul back again is a wasteful feature of present urban centralization. Freshness has to be sacrificed. The same applies to the human item concerned.

Soon within easy distance of any man's dwelling anywhere everything needed in the category of foodstuffs, factorialized or cultural products which the city itself can now supply. So many the city never dreamed of. The centralized city of the past may become only a depot of some kind. One will be found at the ports or where vast supplies of natural material are located for manufacture. But wherever it is, it is certain that it will be only a degraded mechanistic servant of man himself. He will have escaped to find all his city ever offered him, plus Freedom. Privacy the city never had and is now busy trying to teach him he does not want. He will have gone to seek and find a manlike freedom for himself and his own that any free democracy ought to mean to him today: Beauty of life is man's birthright where men are really free. This on individual terms when the country he lives in is in fact a truly great Free country in this expanded extended sense of Space.

APPEASEMENT

Then with this appropriate ideal of democratic freedom, how to alleviate, how to mitigate meantime the horror of life held helpless or caught unaware in the machinery we call city? How easiest and soonest assist the social unit to escape the growing paralysis of individual independence characterizing the "educated" machine-made moron? Paralysis of the emotional nature is necessary to the ultimate triumph of the machine over man—serves only to quicken man's ultimate subjection to the entrenched machine "Capital." It is interesting to observe that we have no United States equivalent of the English Cockney to stand out against the universal standardizing practiced upon his equivalent in our nation.

To stand up against such standardizing is the A.I.A.'s real job as I see it. I wish I could have clearly seen it, instead of only feeling it many years ago when I walked out of the University of Wisconsin—to take the open road.

Measured over our great Usonian areas, the living human-interest today should be persistently uneducated, inspired to try along this fresh contact of free-individuality with growing faith in self and the freedom of work in, and for, sunlight and air in breadth and beauty of the new spacing. The new scale, with and of new ground. That I am sure is the greater *human* interest in our Democracy such as and where it is. That should now characterize our free land even though it might be necessary to close the universities, museums and especially the art institutes now to get it into effect. Were I a Rockefeller—Ford—or Du Pont, I mean as rich, I would buy up our leading universities—close them for ten years and hang out the sign—closed by the beneficence of one Frank Lloyd Wright.

THE TRAVESTY "TASTE"

Taste? Still a matter of ignorance. But for the purposes of this hour together, let us not regard this all too characteristic recession by way of "educated" taste, our fashionables, eclecticisms, too seriously. Let it be as it is, travesty, now tragedy, and proceed to pick up the latest architectural issue in sight. Miss Flat-top has, innocently, perhaps hopefully been calling it a bad name, "modernistic." Let us stop a moment to think . . . and reason a while together concerning her infatuation.

Such licentious waste of ourselves as we have called "taste" in getting ourselves built into America does become, at long last, more vitally important than the stricture—Education. No eclectic affair, nor any eclecticism whatever, can see our national life struggle. Coming along toward us so fast in this twentieth century is "out of the ground into the light," the true way of cultural growth. Not groping or fancifully two-stepping by way of more artificial background into complete outer shambles. We, the architects, have had quite enough of background seen as our foreground. Now clearly see background as background and we advance.

Sheldon Cheney somewhere said, truly, in his book *New World Architecture*, I think he said, "we are, as a nation, standing at the beginning of a world slope in this obscured human interest called architecture." Well . . . we, as a people, can descend culturally no lower than we are, so however steep or slow that upward slope may be for us, it can only be upward toward the time when it will be just as natural for things to be genuine and grow beautiful as it is nowadays for things to be false and remain ugly. Great art has always been inseparably connected with

356

the full bloom of a country's life? Wherever art has declined—that is to say, got itself as as antique, anybody's antique, into the hands of the connoisseur or "the dealer," either coming or going—the whole country never grows, or, having grown must soon degenerate. I do not believe we are a people—as has been said—"passing from barbarism to degeneracy never having known a civilization." We are too ignorant and new for anything to happen to us on the high plane of degeneracy.

No, we are an ethically confused but still morally strong and simple-hearted people, a people that will yet instinctively bring forth a strong and healthy art when ethics and a true philosophy take hold. Let us, therefore, at the moment console ourselves with the thought that we cannot yet degenerate. We cannot degenerate because in art, generation itself is something American culture has not yet known. This affair we choose to call taste may pall and change—as it does continually. But thank whatever Gods may be it is not high enough as a quality to degenerate.

THE OLD ORDER

The United States of America while still very young in years is grown old at a tragic rate. But unfortunately for the new architectural opportunities trying to emerge as natural, or native, we are too old—because all that such pseudo-classic architects as we have had to copy from as architecture was never more in the original than a kind of antique sculpture. That is to say, all these ancient buildings we owe to pseudo-classic traditions were at one time some great block-mass of building material, "sculpted," that is to say, fashioned from the outside into taste-conceived and desired or necessary "features." They were therefore exterior in Idea and relatively exterior in every sense. Always there was an "outside" as an outside. And the "inside" was there merely as an inside. Outside and inside were usually quite separate, wholly independent of each other. Holes were cut into the block-mass at intervals for a little light and some air; the deeper the hole looked to be, that is to say, the thicker the sides of the hole were—the architects called these sides the "reveal"—the better. Great attention was paid to a rather pretentious hole to get inside by, or to get out by . . . so, pseudo-classic buildings resembled more or less trimmed-up masonry fortifications. Often the originals were actual fortifications. Quite necessary to be fortified in those days.

Yes, the houses and public buildings had to be fortifications, for civilization itself was first and foremost fortified: that is to say, it was frankly founded upon force. So, usually, so-called classical and even feudal dwellings were little masonry caverns. If more pretentious, they were, at best, great caves.

Thus viewed in the perspective of this new ideal of lightness and strength conquering space, we must conceive this old architecture a sculptured block of building material as hollowed out within. Or we cannot imagine anyone living in it at all. All life then was living in the heart of a hollowed-out masonry block if the grammar of building in that time had any meaning.

Yes, that is the essential sense of the esthetic whole in all that we call "classic" architecture.

Now this ancient, honorable enough at the time, idea of a building, that is to say, masonry-mass as such, ornamented outside and ornamented inside, is now a serious setback for any plastic architecture in our civilization that would look toward freedom to form a sound ethical basis in the proper use of entirely new materials by entirely new methods. Indeed, the survival of this "classic" ideal, be it modified as "Colonial" or what have you in the circumstances, is mostly what interferes with any hope we have for a fruitful pattern for living a free democratic life in our great country as of today.

THE SYMBOL OF AUTHORITY

The dome, this hangover of the ancient and feudal (still pagan) ideal of building received its final illumination, therefore its ruination, in the 500-year-long decadence of the European Renaissance. Michelangelo, great sculptor that he was, crashed the crumbling ruin when in Rome he finally hurled the Pantheon on top of the Parthenon. The result of the great Italian's impulsive indiscretion was named St. Peter's. The world agreed that it was a day, celebrating the great act ever since in the sincerest form of flattery possible. Specialists in it ourselves, as we well know that supreme flattery is *imitation.*

Now, Buonarroti, being a sculptor, naturally set about making the grandest statue (call it a building) that he could conceive coming out of the Italian Renaissance of his day. This great new church dome of his, St. Peter's, was empty of meaning, had no significance at all except as the Pope's mitre has it, or had it. But although this upstart dome was violating all the principles of good construction, it nevertheless seemed to be just the sort of thing temporal *authority* had been looking for as a showy symbol. A label. And the unnatural dome up on stilts became the symbol of great authority, holy or unholy. A ponderous anachronism has become accepted officially to characterize and idealize authority in all civilized countries both great and small.

Before Michelangelo turned architect, domes had their haunches, that is to say, the thrust of the dome (the dome is an arch), well down within the building walls themselves. St. Sophia is a noble example of true doming, but built when the Roman empire was oriental. The Orientals first knew the beauty and value of a real dome: see the Persian doming.

But a great sculptor now divorced his dome from the mere matter of reality. So he got it up higher than all other domes. He got it way up above the building, up into the blue sky resting the great arch on high stilts. Call the stilts columns. Ah, that was better! So much more sensational. So grand! But history records cracks opening in the base of the dome before finished. The massive masonry arch—again remember a dome is an arch—was pushing out on all sides, with nothing but air to push against. Thus the dome itself and the stilts upon which the great arched mass rested became an awful threat to human life there below. A desperate call went out to the blacksmiths of Rome. A grand chain demanded—links the thickness of your leg. And desperate was the hurry at the forge to keep the great sculptor's monumental grandeur way up there long enough to do its deadly work upon the imaginations of subsequent generations of by no means stupid men, and the dome became equivocal symbol of authority throughout the world.

Well, the blacksmith's chain finally fastened round the haunches of the great dome that had been impulsively lifted so high out of its natural thrust (but nevertheless lifted to immortality?) by our hero, the great sculptor. As an architect, I can imagine the relief with which the sculptor crawled back to bed when the obliging and competent blacksmiths had made all secure, and slept for thirty-six hours on end without once turning over.

This ponderous anachronism thereafter proceeded to project other continental domes, a family, one of them our own national Capitol. The dome went downward to the domes of our various state capitols—some forty-eight of them? And then to the lesser domes of the county court-houses. From them it went on down to the little domes of minor city halls. There the accepted symbol, saved by the blacksmith, grandly stands. Seen everywhere in this great new country dedicated to·Freedom, it proclaims our debt to a great artist's indiscretion. And see it, too, as democracy's greatest heritage from the rebirth of architecture in Italy, called Renaissance. Native grando-mania took that form. That's all. It might have taken any other form, but it happened to take the Michelangelo dome.

Sir Christopher Wren on behalf of England had previously borrowed the sculptor's dome—before we got hold of it—but wisely and beforehand this time, Sir Christopher borrowed the chain for St. Paul's from the Florentine blacksmiths. Amusing record: canny Sir Christopher said his masonry dome would have stood without the chain! All the same he did not try it. His caution showed him more a man of sense than his remark showed him competent as an architect.

Worshipping at the false shrine of that false dome, Usonia's architects more shrewd, even, than Sir Christopher, our grand masonry domes are all blacksmith now. They are cast-iron curved plates or shells imitating the sculptor's masonry, all nicely bolted together at the seams! A hollow shell imitating the arch, ribs and all.

The blacksmith has arrived but the architect has gone out. Certainly so far as domes go. Whether the poor architect has gone for a recess or never to return, who can say? We may now honestly say that unless he comes back converted to the kinetic energy of this age and a true master of the blacksmith's iron work too, seeing it clearly as no imitation arch whatsoever but seeing it as good and true iron work in some form, there soon will be little use for him to come back. Here as anyone may see, out of a great sculptor's sense of grandeur in an art not quite his own arises a tyranny that might well make the tyrannical skyscraper—our own St. Peter's of the present hour—sway on its socket, sick with envy.

How dangerous imitation is! Always. How tragic to allow authority ever to usurp the functions of validity. That once done, what Freedom? Take warning, you American architects.

Paying thus our equivocal respect to the now ubiquitous stilted dome—no longer a dome but complicated cast-iron work imitating the unnatural masonry of St. Peter's—is only by way of emphasis of the fact that all ancient architecture of monumental character, the duomo, the temple, the palazo, even the minister was mostly all sculp, sculpturesque, sculptorial or sculptoretto. I must also insist that all artificiality, commonplace grando-mania as such, was and will always be carried to excess. Hyper-artificiality invariably becomes—either in the individual, the parlor, the classroom or building—really a form of senility or mere child's play. Depending on the circumstances and the architect.

How ridiculous, then, when not dangerous or positively vicious, this extravagant senility that would obliterate the living by sentimentalizing over the dead! Erecting the monuments to the dead-and-gone instead of erecting memorials for use of the here-and-living.

THE ENEMY

Well, our country is now where choice has to be made between such spiritual senility made official, called academic, or true progress. President Hoover, lining up with much other official timber going over the same dam, officially recommended this senility to the French at their 1939 exposition in Paris. Showing the folly of automatically constituting a pretty good executive, an authority on Fine Art. Political or established Authority, in my lifetime I have observed is, and always soon, the enemy of all validity in the life of the spirit.

To sum up: Because then the only established order, this ancient sculptorial sculptoretto was at least moral. But the old order has become betrayal, immoral because of the hyper-artificiality called Renaissance or "rebirth." Eventually this rebirth came to us in virulent form and was seen everywhere in our great capitols as current eclecticism. The ancient order is now economic crime. Soon, I hope, a public nuisance. But worse than all beside, it has become the provincial grando-mania of the cultural lag.

YOUTH

Hope is not dead! This minority report is yet as it always will be the life of any true Democracy. Our architecture has arrived as that vital minority report. As architecture today taking shape in the noble realm of Ideas to make our machine power and undemocratic millions really beneficent, there is one great new integrity—the sense of the within as reality—and behind this dawning sense of reality there are five more limitless new resources to make it ours and one more.

The first resource is this sense of the within—Space—as Reality.

The second new resource is a super-material—Glass. Glass is air in air to keep air out or keep it in.

The third new resource is a new standard means of spanning spaces by way of strands of steel cast in concrete. Tenuity. The spider spinning.

The fourth new resource is the newly awakened sense of Materials: their nature understood and revealed in building.

The fifth new resource is Pattern as Natural—Integral ornament. A spiritual element no less real than the first four resources.

All together are modern in the best sense and may be used to create a new grasp on art of building we now call organic. All are a demanding new significance in architecture and making architecture again natural to our way of life in this twentieth century. But all five resources are not only now basic to Modern Architecture in this century; they are no less a great lesson to be learned by Modern Life itself, because what Life is, Architecture now is in this true sense.

Because of infinite new riches in materials, because of our infinite new power in work, notwithstanding our present educational culture-lag and social distraction, a deepening sense of life sees all these new resources at hand at this moment as *modern* and sees them as the stuff of which our culture is to be made.

This being the fourth Book, you are in work with me and shall have another "Talk." I have had to give a great many during these idle years to so many thousands of people all over the United States. Should they seem too much like lectures here, just skip them because I know they were intended for the young man in architecture. After all, you know, an architect is writing this autobiography and you have no right to forget that fact.

A PHILOSOPHY IN THE NATURE OF MATERIALS

Our vast resources in America are yet new, new only because architecture is old. "Rebirth" (perennial Renaissance) has, after five centuries of decline, culminated in the imitation of imitations as seen by our Mrs. Plasterbuilt, Mrs. Gablemore and especially now by Miss Flat-top. In general, and especially officially, our architecture is at long last completely significant of insignificance. We do not longer have an architecture. At least no buildings with artistic integrity. We have only economic crimes in its name. Our greatest buildings are not qualified as great art, my dear Mrs. Davies, although you do admire Washington above all.

If you will be patient for a little while—a scientist, Einstein, asked for three days to explain the far less pressing and practical matter of "Relativity"—we will take each of the five new resources in order, as with the five fingers of the hand. All are new integrities to be used if we will use them to make living easier and better today for us all.

The first great integrity is deeper, more intimate sense of reality in building than was ever pagan—that is to say, than was ever "Classic." More human than any building realized in the Christian Middle Ages, although the thought that may ennoble it now has been living in civilization for more than twenty centuries. Innate in the simplicities of Jesus as it was organic five hundred years earlier in the natural philosophy, Tao (The Way) of the Chinese philosopher, Laotze. But not only is the new architecture sound philosophy. It is true poetry.

Said Ong Giao Ki, Chinese sage, "Poetry is the sound of the heart."

Well, like poetry, this sense of architecture is the sound of the "within." We might call that "within," the heart.

Architecture now becomes integral, the expression of ever new-old reality: it lies in the livable interior space of the room itself. In integral architecture the *room-space itself must come through*. The *room* must

362

be seen as architecture, or we have no twentieth-century architecture. We have no longer an outside merely as outside. No longer an outside and an inside as two separate things. Now the outside may come inside, and the inside may, and does, go outside. They are *of* each other. Form and function become one in design and execution if the *nature* of materials and method and purpose are all in unison.

This interior-space concept, the first broad integrity is first great resource—true basis for general significance of form. Add to this for the sake of clarity that (although the general integration is implied by the first integrity) it is in the nature of any organic building to grow from within on its site: come out of the ground an organism into the light— the ground itself held always as a component part of the building itself. We have then primarily the new ideal of building as Organic. A building dignified as a tree in the midst of Nature.

This new architectural Ideal is, as well, an adequate ideal for the general culture. There can be no separation between our architecture and our culture. Architecture is still as always basic to Culture we lack. Nor any separation of either from our happiness. Nor any separation from our work.

Thus in this rise of organic-integration you see the means to end the petty agglomerations miscalled civilization. By way of this old yet new and deeper sense of reality we may really have organic civilization. In this sense we now recognize and may declare by way of plan and building—the *natural*. Faith in the *natural* is the faith we now need to grow up on in this coming age of our confused, backward twentieth century. But instead of "organic" we might well say "natural" building. Or we might say integral building: intrinsic building.

Now consider the second of the five new resources: glass. This second resource, new, a "super-material" only because it holds such amazing means to modernize life for awakened sensibilities. It amounts to a new qualification of life itself. If known in ancient times glass would then and there have abolished the ancient architecture we know, and completely. This super-material GLASS as we use it is a miracle: air in air to keep air out or keep it in. Light itself in light, to diffuse or reflect, or refract Light itself.

By means of glass, the first great integrity finds prime means of realization. Open reaches of the ground may enter the building and the building interior may reach out and associate with these vistas of the ground. Ground and building thus become more and more obvious as directly related to each other in openness and intimacy, not only as environment but also as good pattern for good life lived in the building. Realizing the benefits to human life of the far-reaching implications and effects of the first great integrity: let us call it the interior-space concept. This interior realization is possible and desirable in all the vast variety of characteristic buildings needed by civilized life in our complex age to-day.

By means of the miracle, glass, something of the freedom of our arboreal ancestors living in their trees becomes a more likely precedent for freedom in twentieth-century life than the cave.

Savage animals "holing in" for protection were characteristic of life based upon the might of feudal times or based upon the so-called classical in architecture, both in turn based upon labor of the chattel slave. In a free century, were we ourselves free, organic thought in building might come out into the light without animal fear; come entirely away from pagan ideals of Form we dote upon and teach as "Classic." Or what Freedom have we in America?

Perhaps more important than all beside it is that by way of glass the sunlit space as a reality becomes most useful servant of a higher order of the human Spirit. It is first aid to the sense of cleanliness of line, form and idea when directly related to free living in fresh air and sunlight. It is this freshness that is coming in the new architecture with the integral character of extended vistas gained by marrying buildings with ground levels, or blending them with slopes and gardens. This new sense of earth as a great human *good* we will call the move forward in building our new homes and great public buildings. Works of great Art.

I am certain we will desire the sun, spaciousness and integrity of means-to-ends more and more, year by year as we become aware of the possibilities I have outlined. The more we desire the sun, the more we will desire the freedom of the good ground and the sooner we will learn to understand it. The more we value *integrity,* the more securely we will find and keep a worthwhile civilization to set against prevalent abuse and ruin by education.

Habitual congestion will no longer encourage and reward the "space-makers for rent." The "space-maker for rent" will himself be "for rent" or let us hope "vacant." Give him ten years or "life."

These new space-values enter now into our ideas of life. All appropriate to the new Ideal that is our own, this Ideal we call Democracy.

GLASS

A resource to liberate and implement this new sense of interior-space as reality is a new qualification. We call it glass: qualify us not only to escape from prettified cavern of our present domestic life as also from the caves of our past, but competent to actually awaken in us desires for such far-reaching simplicities of form in life as we may see in the clear countenance of Nature. Good building must be seen as the nature of good construction, but a higher development of this "seeing" will be construction seen as nature-pattern. *That* seeing, only, is inspired architecture. Organic architecture.

This dawning sense of the *Within* as *reality* when it is clearly seen as *Nature* will by way of glass, steel and concrete make the garden be the building as much as the building will be the garden: the sun and sky as treasured a feature of daily indoor life as the ground itself.

Even now see walls vanishing. The cave for human dwelling purposes is disappearing.

Walls themselves because of glass become windows and windows as we used to know them as holes in walls will be seldom seen. Ceilings will often become as window-walls. The textile may soon be fit to be used as a beautiful overhead for space; textiles an attribute of genuine architecture instead of mere decoration by way of hangings and upholstery. Modern integral floor heating, gravity-heat, will follow integral lighting and standardized unitary sanitation. All these make it reasonable and good economy to abolish building as either hyper-boxment or super-borough.

Haven't senseless elaboration of the box and false mass become sufficiently oppressive to our intelligence? Yet, senseless elaboration and false mass were tyrannical as "conspicuous waste" and the attempted new "classic" in all of our nineteenth-century architecture either public or private! Wherever the American architect, as scholar, went he "succeeded" to that extent. But the twentieth-century Architecture is yet to be recognized.

CONTINUITY: ANOTHER REALITY

As third resource, now the resource essential to modern architecture destined to cut down this outrageous mass-waste and lying-mass, is the principle of *continuity*. I have called it tenuity. Steel is its prophet and master. You must come with me for a moment into so-called engineering. This an unavoidable strain upon your kind attention. Unfortunately, gentle reader, you cannot understand architecture as *modern* unless you do come, and—paradox—you can't come if you are too well educated as an engineer or as an architect yourself either. Your common sense is needed more than your erudition but is in your way.

However, to begin argument: classic architecture knew only the post as an *upright*. Call it a column. Knew only the beam as a *horizon-*

tal. Call it a beam. The beam resting upon the upright, or column, was to them structure throughout. Two things, you see, one set on top of another in various materials. Put there in various ways. Ancient, and nineteenth-century buildings science too, even building *à la mode*, consists as it consisted in simply reducing the various stresses of all materials and their uses to these two things: Post and Beam. Really, construction used to be just sticking up something in wood, steel or stone and putting something else in wood or stone (maybe iron) on top of it: simple super-imposition, you see? You should know that is all "Classic" architecture ever was. Still is some such form of direct super-imposition. The arch is a little less so, but even that must be a load so "figured" by the structural engineer if you ask him to "figure."

Now the Greeks developed this simple act of super-imposition pretty far by way of their innate tasteful refinement in search for the elegant solution. The Greeks were true estheticians. Roman builders too, when they forgot the Greeks and brought the beam over as a curve by way of the arch, did something new but with consequences still of the same sort. Observe, all architectural features made by such "Classic" agglomeration were killed for us by cold steel. And though millions of classic corpses yet encumber good American ground unburied, they are ready now for burial by youth in Architecture!

Of course this primitive post-and-beam construction will be still valid, but both support and supported may now by means of inserted and welded steel strands or especially woven filaments of steel and modern concrete casting be plaited and united as one physical body: ceilings and walls made one with floors, reinforcing each other by making them continue into one another. This "Continuity" is made possible by the tenuity of steel.

So the new order wherever steel or plastics enter construction says: weld these two things, post and beam (wall and ceiling) together by means of steel strands buried and stressed within the mass material itself, the steel strands electric-welded where steel meets steel within the mass. In other words, the upright and horizontal may now be made to work together as one. A new world of form opens inevitably with the appearance of the cantilever.

Where the beam leaves off and the post begins is no longer important nor need it be seen at all because it no longer *is* actual. Steel in tension enables support to slide into supported, or the supported to grow into the support somewhat as a tree-branch glides out of its tree-trunk. Therefrom arises the new series of interior physical reactions I am calling "Continuity." As natural consequence the new esthetic or appearance we call *Plasticity* (and plasticity is peculiarly "modern") is no longer a mere appearance. Plasticity is actually the normal *countenance*,

366

the *true esthetic expression* of genuine structural reality. Interwoven steel strands may so lie in so many desired directions in any extended member of structure that extensions may all be economical of material and much lighter, be safer than ever before. In the branch of the tree you may see the cantilever. The cantilever is simplest of the important phases of this third new structural resource demanding new expression. It has yet had little attention in modern architecture. It can do remarkable things to liberate space as twentieth-century Architecture.

But Plasticity was modest new countenance in our American architecture at least thirty-five years ago and in my own words and work. But then denied such simple means as welding and the cold-drawn mesh. Already all the separate identities of post and beam in architecture were eliminated. Steel in tension entered by way of mesh and welding to arrive at actual, total plasticity if and when desired by the architect. To prove the philosophy of organic architecture, form and function were one. This now enters architecture as the *esthetic* countenance of *physical reality* of the third dimension.

To further illustrate this magic simplifier "plasticity": see it as *flexibility* similar to that of your own hand. What makes your hand expressive? Flowing continuous line and continuous surfaces used continually flexible as mobile, part of the articulate articulated structure of the hand as a whole. The line is seen as "hand" line. The varying planes seen as "hand" surface. Strip the hand to the separate structural identities of joined bones (post and beam) and plasticity as the flesh expression of the hand. We would be then getting back to the joinings, breaks, jolts and joints of ancient, or "Classic," architecture: thing to thing; feature to feature. But plasticity is the reverse of that ancient agglomeration and is the ideal means behind these simplified free new effects of straight line and flat plane architecture we call organic.

I have just said that plasticity in this sense for thirty-five years or more has been the recognized esthetic ideal for such simplification as was required by the machine to do organic work. It is now true of my own work in our era.

A significant outline and expressive surface, plasticity (physical continuity) is a useful means to form the supreme physical-body of an organic, or integral, American Architecture.

Of course, it is just as easy to cheat by simplicity as it is to cheat with "classical" structure. So, unluckily, here again is the "modernistic" architectural picture-maker's deadly facility for imitation at ease and again too happy with fresh opportunity to "fake effects." Probably another Renaissance is here imminent and soon again Classical.

Architecture is now integral architecture only when Plasticity is a genuine expression of actual construction just as the articulate line and surface of the hand is articulate of the structure of the hand. Arriving at steel, I first used Continuity as actual stabilizing principle in concrete slab construction also and in the concrete ferro-block system I devised in Los Angeles. See La Miniatura.

In the cantilever or as horizontal continuity this new economy by means of steel-tenuity is what saved the Imperial Hotel from destruction during the great earthquake of 1922. It did not appear in the grammar of the building for various reasons, chiefly because the building was to look somewhat as though it belonged to Tokio, Japan.

Later, in the new design for St. Mark's Tower, New York City, this new working structural principle as method economized material, labor, and liberated or liberalized space in a mass developed sense. It gave to the structure significant outlines of remarkable stability and instead of false masonry-mass significant open outlines came out. Abstract pattern of the structure as a complete structural-integrity of Form and Idea may be seen fused as in any tree but nothing evident as imitating a tree.

Continuity invariably realizes remarkable economy of labor and building materials as well as space. Unfortunately there is yet little or no data to use as tabulation. Tests will have to be made continually for many years to make the record available to slide-rule experts.

In the ancient order there was little thought of economy of materials. The more massive the whole structure looked, the better it looked to the ancients. But seen in the light of these new economic interior forces conserved by the tensile strength of strands of steel in this Machine Age, the old order was sick with weight as the Buonarroti dome. Weak . . . because there could be no co-interrelation between the two elements of support and supported to reinforce each other as a whole under stress of weight or elemental disturbance by gravity.

So *tenuity,* this tremendous new resource—a quality of steel—is this quality of *pull* in a building (you may see it ushering in a new era in John Roebling's Brooklyn Bridge). This element was definitely lacking in all ancient architecture. Steel had not been born.

The tenuous strand or slab as a common strength had yet to come. Here today this element of continuity may cut structural substance nearly in two. It may cut the one half in two again by elimination of needless features, such elimination being entirely due to the simplifications I have been calling "plasticity."

By utilizing mass production in the factory, some idea of the remarkable new economics possible to modern architecture may be seen approaching those realized in any well-built machine. If such standardization can be humanized, made flexible in design, and the economies brought to the home owner, the greatest service will be rendered to our modern way of life. It may be really born—this Democracy I mean.

Involved as a matter of design is this mass production, the involute, all but involuntary reactions to which I have referred: the ipso facto building code and fact that the building engineer as now trained knows so little about them. However, the engineer is learning to calculate by model-making and model-testing in some instances—notably Professor Beggs at Princeton University.

The codes so far as I can see will have to die on the vine with the men who made them.

MATERIALS FOR THEIR OWN SAKE

As the first integrity and the two first new resources appeared out of interior nature in the kind of building I call Architecture—so now—naturally interior to the true nature of good building comes the fourth resource. This is found by recognizing the nature of materials used in construction.

Fascinating different properties, as many as there are different materials that may be used in building, will continually, and naturally, qualify and change all architectural forms whatsoever as design and purpose change.

A stone building will no more *be* nor will it *look* like a masonry or steel building. A pottery, or terra-cotta building, will not nor should it look like a stone building. A wood building will look like none other, for it will glorify the stick. A steel and glass building could not possibly look like anything but itself. It will glorify steel and glass. So on and on all the way down the long list of available riches in materials: Stone, Wood, Concrete, Metals, Glass, Textiles, Pulp and Plastics: riches so great to our hand today that no comparison with Ancient Architecture is at all sensible or anything but obstruction in Modern Architecture.

In this particular, as you may see, architecture going back to learn from the natural source of all natural things—Nature.

In order to get Organic Architecture born, intelligent architects will be forced to turn their backs on the antique rubbish heaps with which Classic eclecticism has encumbered our practice of Architecture. So far as architecture has gone in my own thought it is first of all a character and quality of *mind* that may enter also into human conduct with social implications that might, at first, confound or astound you. But the only basis for any fear of them lies in the fact that they are all sanely and thoroughly *constructive*. Truth is a double-edged sword and can cut both ways, but why cowardice?

Instinctively all forms of pretense fear and hate reality.

THE HYPOCRITE MUST ALWAYS HATE THE RADICAL because radical is of the root. The radical is a root man always alert to why and how, where and when.

This potent fourth new resource—the Nature of Materials—gets at the common center of relation to the work it is required to do. The architect must again begin at the very beginning. Proceeding according to Nature now he sensibly goes through with whatever material may be in hand for his purpose according to the methods and sensibilities of a man of this Machine Age. When I say Nature, I mean inherent interior *structure* seen and unseen by the architect as complete design. Good design is in itself, always, intrinsic *nature-pattern*. This profound interior sense of materials that enters our new world as Architecture now. It is this fifth new resource that must captivate and hold the mind of the modern architect to creative work. The fifth will give life to his imagination if it has not been already killed by school of one sort or another.

Inevitable implication! New Machine Age resource requires that all buildings do *not* resemble each other. But new ideals do *not* require that all buildings be of steel, concrete or glass. Often that might be idiotic waste.

Nor do the resources even *imply* that mass is no longer a beautiful attribute of masonry materials genuinely used. We are entitled to a vast variety of form in our complex age so long as the form be genuine— serves Architecture as Architecture serves life.

But in this land of ours, richest on earth in old and new materials, architects must exercise well-trained imagination to see in each material, either natural or compounded plastics, their own *inherent style* for the purpose in hand. All materials may have beautiful consequence. Their beauty much or entirely depending upon how well they are used by the Architect.

In modern building we have the Stick. Stone. Steel. Pottery. Concrete. Glass. Yes, Pulp, too, as well as Plastics. And since this dawning sense of the "within" is the new reality, these will all give "*motif*" to any real building made from them. The materials of which the building is built will go far to determine its appropriate mass, outline and, especially, proportion. *Character* is criterion in the form of any and every building or industrial product we can call Architecture in the light of this new ideal of the new order we call Organic.

NEW INTEGRITY

Strange! At this late date, it is modern architecture that wants life to learn to see life as life, because architecture must learn to see brick as brick, see steel as steel, see glass as glass. So modern thought urges all of life to demand that a bank look like a bank (bad thought though a bank might become) and not depend upon false columns for credit. All of life to demand that an office building look like an office building, even if it should resemble the cross section of a bee-hive. Life itself should insist in self-defense that a hotel look and conduct itself like a place of residence and not like some office building. Life should declare, too, that the railroad station look like a railroad station and not try so hard to look like an ancient temple or some monarchic palazzo. And while we are on this subject, why not a place for opera that would look something like a place for opera—if we must have opera—and not look so much like a gilded, crimsoned bagnio. Life declares that a filling station should stick to its work as a filling station: look the part becomingly. Why try to look like some Colonial diminutive or remain just a pump on the street. Although "just a pump" on the street is better than imitation Colonial. Good Life demands that the school be as generously spaced and a thought-built good-time place for happy children: a building no more than one story high—with some light overhead, the school building should regard the children as a garden in sun. Life itself demands of Modern Architecture that the house of a man who knows what home is should have his own home his own way if we have any man left after F.H.A. or A.I.A. are done trying to put them, all of them it can, into the case of a man who builds a home only as a house. Our Government forces the home-maker into the real-estate business if he wants a home at all. He builds to sell.

Well, after all, this line of thought was all new—uncommon common sense in architecture in Chicago some thirty years ago. It began to grow up in my own work as it is continuing to grow up more widely in the work of the world. But, insulting as it may seem to say so, nor is it merely arrogant to say that the actual thinking in that connection is still only a little less strange today than it was then. Although the appearances do rapidly increase, the interior nature of the Idea is still to come through.

ORNAMENT INTEGRAL AT LAST!

This fifth resource, so old yet now demanding fresh significance. Here now we arrive at integral ornament—the nature-pattern in the expression of actual construction. Confessed as the spiritual demand for true significance, comes this subjective element in modern architecture: an element so hard to understand that modern architects themselves seem to understand it least of all and most of them turn against it with such fury as is born only of impotence or ignorance.

True that this vast, intensely human significance is really no matter at all for any but the most imaginative mind, a nature not without some development in artistry and *gift* of a sense of the appropriate. Certainly we must go higher in the realm of imagination when we presume to enter here because we go into the nature of Poetry.

Now, very many write good prose who cannot write poetry at all. And although staccato is the present fashion, just as "functionalist" happens to be the present style in writing—poetic will never be undesirable. But who condones prosaic poetry? None. Least of all those fatuously condemned to write it.

So I say this new resource and demand for new significance and integrity is ornament *integral to building as itself poetry.* Rash use of a dangerous word. The word "Poetry" *is* a dangerous word where a practical man is concerned with building.

Heretofore, I have used the word "pattern" instead of the word ornament to avoid confusion or to escape passing prejudice. But here ornament is now in place. Ornament meaning not only *surface qualified by human imagination* but imagination giving *natural pattern* to structure. Perhaps this phrase says it all without further explanation. Integral ornament is new in the architecture of the world, at least insofar not only as imagination qualifying a surface—a valuable resource—but as a greater means than that: *imagination giving natural pattern to structure itself.* Here we have new significance, integral indeed! Long ago this significance was lost to the scholarly Beaux Arts trained architect. A man of taste. He, too soon, became content with symbols and appliqué.

Evidently then, this expression of structure as pattern true to the nature of the building and the materials out of which it is made, may be taken much further than physical need alone would dictate? "If you have a loaf of bread break the loaf in two and give the half for some flowers of the Narcissus for the bread feeds the body indeed but the flowers feed the soul."

As music to the ear, painting to the eye, so architectural ornament is to the senses.

It is by this last and poetic resource that we may give greater structural entity and greater human significance to the whole building than could ever be done otherwise. This statement is heresy, this left-wing moment.

Again in this connection let us refer to Ong's Chinese observation, "Poetry is the sound of the heart." So, in the same uncommon sense integral ornament is the developed sense of the building as a whole, or the manifest *abstract pattern of structure itself*. Interpreted. Integral ornament is simply *structure-pattern made visibly articulate* and seen in the building as it is seen articulate in the structure of the trees or a lily of the fields. It is the expression of inner rhythm of Form. Are we talking about Style? Pretty nearly. At any rate, we are talking about the qualities that make *essential architecture* as distinguished from any mere act of building whatsoever.

What I am here calling integral-ornament is founded upon the same organic simplicities as Beethoven's Eroica or his Fifth Symphony, that amazing revolution in tumult and splendor of sound built on four tones based upon a rhythm a child could play on the piano with one finger. Supreme imagination reared the four repeated tones, simple rhythms, into a great symphonic structure, a great poem that is probably the noblest thought-built edifice in our world. Architecture is like music in this capacity for symphony.

But concerning this higher development of building to more completely express its life principle as significant and beautiful, let us say at once by way of warning: it is better to die by the wayside of left-wing Orriaphobia than it is to build any more merely ornamented buildings, as such; or to see right-wing architects die any more ignoble deaths of *Ornamentia*. All period and pseudo-classic buildings whatever (although their authors do not seem to know it), most protestant buildings which, they call internationalist, are really ornamental in definitely objectionable sense. A plain flat surface cut to shape for its own sake, however large or plain the shape, is, the moment it is sophisticatedly placed, no less ornamental than egg-and-dart. All such buildings are objectionable because, like buildings of the old classical order, they are wholly ignorant of the *nature* of the *first* integrity. Both ignore the five resources and both neglect the nature of machines at work on materials. Incidentally, and as a matter of course, both misjudge the nature of time, place and the modern life of man where poetry is concerned.

Here in this leftish emulation is only the "istic," ignoring fundamental principle merely to get the "look" of something that *looks* "new." The province of the "ite."

In most so-called modernistic building we have no true approach to organic architecture: we have again merely a new, superficial esthetic trading upon organic architecture because such education as most architects possess qualifies them for only some kind of eclecticism past, passing or to pass as a fashion.

Nevertheless, I say, if we can't have buildings with integrity we would better have more imitation machines for buildings until we can have a truly sentient architecture. "The machine for living in" is sterile, but therefore safer, I believe, than the festering mass of ancient styles or imitation organic.

GREAT POWER

Far greater power than slavery, even intellectual slavery as in the schools of the Greeks, is back of these four demands—plus one—for machine-age integrity of significance. Stupendous and stupefying power. That power is the immense compelling leverage of the machine itself. But as set up in all its powers the machine will confirm these new implicities and complicities of organic architecture at every point, but destroy them soon if not checked by a new more ethical, integral simplicity of heart.

The proper use of these new resources demands that we use them all together for mankind if we are to realize the finer significances of life—free. The finer significance, prophesied if not realized, by the sovereignty of the individual. It *is* reasonable to believe that life in our country will be lived in full enjoyment of this new freedom of the extended horizontal line because the horizontal line now becomes the great architectural highway: the life of the ground. The flat plane becomes the regional field. Integral-pattern becomes "the sound of the Usonian heart." The cover-graph of this book I have called "Freedom" uses the great highway and the regional field of decentralization as significant pattern.

I see this extended horizontal line as the true earth-line of human life, indicative of freedom.

The broad expanded plane is infinitely extended. In that lies such freedom for man on this earth as he may call his, now or ever.

USONIAN

This new sense of Architecture as integral-pattern of intrinsic type and kind may awaken the United States to fresh beauty, and the Usonian horizon of the individual be immeasurably extended by more enlightened uses of this great lever, the machine. But only if it gets into creative hands loyal to humanity.

By way of these five new means—all "Architecture"—this monster power, if re-awakened now and quickened by the creative artist, must gradually come into new uses. Instead of crucifying all integrity by stupid quantity eclecticisms, monotony in variety, and utterly wasting the life of the spirit by the academic sham capitalized and sold under by and to our own academic authorities and "captains of industry," American life may know the salt and savor of good work and true creation. Our culture-lag inherited with our various nationalities, especially that one washed up on our Eastern shores, overcome in time.

The "captains" both of the cap-and-gown variety and the shop and counting house can only see machines as engines of wealth founded upon convenient economic business systems of quantity-exploitation: the only means to wealth they know. But the captains themselves, I observe, when sufficiently enriched, become culture curious, turn traitor to their own machine-born increment and waste it all in bigger and better imitations of the already sufficiently devastating antique. Ask Sir Joseph Duveen! He was not knighted by the English for nothing. Do the people need further proof of the system's sterility than that Knighthood? Then look for what it means in these recurring wars settling nothing except the necessity for more and greater wars—territorial or industrial. Empire, both the apotheosis of War.

WHO LOOKS AND SEES

I must believe that notwithstanding all shallow newspaper hokum, our people are weary of this commercialized life of "taste." I believe they see more clearly through current respectable academic lies. The American in the street looks and sees the aeroplane fly overhead, emancipated from make-believe, free to be itself, be true to itself. He looks and sees the steamship ride the seas, triumphant as the superb thing it is, for what it is. Sees the motor car becoming more the machine it should be, daily less like a horse and buggy or a ferry-boat, gradually acquiring freedom to be itself for what it is. In all modern mobilizations or utensils whatsoever in architecture, awakening, he may see this age of the machine more freely declaring for Freedom to express the simple facts of structure for more and better life. Malformations of material and the misuse of tools and utensils grow less.

So I believe that in the new uses of these new and valid economic standards in organic architecture here enumerated you may see and measure cure for the causes of oncoming urban decay. And urban decay may be a real service rendered twentieth-century mankind by what we are here calling "Machine."

Well, up to and including the nineteenth century, mechanical forces *did* place a premium upon centralization. None the less, twentieth-century mobilizations—electrifications in multiple forms—*are* advance agents of decentralization, fresh integration.

It is not so difficult now to see that man has only to get this monster, the Machine, into focus—into service of trained imagination and get machine-increment where it belongs—into the hands of his better self—and the big city is a survival only for burial. The natural consequence of our grand mechanical success today is truly only a form of human excess. A finer ideal of machine-age luxury as primarily human is coming out of, or coming along with, our modern architecture. This will live to bury the corpse of every great overgrown village in America. Someday.

Meantime journeyman, beggarman, thief and merchant-chief—beware! This group of ideas is set forth here as one great demand for finer integrity of life, and we must repudiate any symbol it may itself create as likely to relapse into imitations as minds are now educated in our popular colleges: institutions now enemies of creative thought and work.

Nor can this new sense of reality look to any ready-made abstraction—Ancient Greek, Hindu, Chinese, English—as authority. This thought must look all full in the eye for the impostor any such authority must finally become by way of current, now standardized, philosophies. Whatsoever.

I must and do believe that this new demand for life as organic—therefore life as itself a noble kind of architecture as architecture is life—must read first lessons afresh in the great book of creation, of Nature itself, despising with the fervor of youth all that lives either ashamed or afraid to live an honest life *as itself:* proud to live for what it is or may become because of *its own virtue.*

Common integrity of life will then carry these four and one more significances as a single great integrity to full expression as the great Usonian Life, the universal life of our own true democracy.

America! There is no need to be afraid. "We may disregard the laws, but if we are for NATURE . . . we are never lawless." I believe George Meredith was right.

JOURNEYMAN PREACHER

The circumstances at Taliesin made it necessary to go on more talking tours North, South, East—West. I became a sort of addition to the long line of preachers to which I congenitally belong on both sides of my ancestral house.

Young men, young women in many communities of our country themselves the great fact in the various lectures I gave upon this same subject to which you have just been subjected here. These young men and women were the circumstance that encouraged me to openly assume the hateful unpopular guise of the itinerant preacher. They paid thousands of dollars to hear me talk to them, eager to help extend exhibitions of my work to various places here at home, as it had already gone abroad. I recounted some of the experiences of the congenital preacher, somewhere in me, here, to show how the on-coming generation in our country is keen and coming clear, with a fresh strong voice, where the present generation has been stultified by the sentimentalities of our Victorian past. You will soon believe that at least the coming generation is trying to learn to differentiate between sentiment and sentimentality, between the Curious and the Beautiful. Not so easy in these times of double-barrelled reaction, high-powered commercial radio and press, cinema salesmanship and graphic propaganda for all other and else.

So from what I have myself seen, I say to you with confidence that the next generation now in high-school will overturn the falsity in which as Art and Philosophy it was reared—and themselves with their feet on the road to Freedom in Usonia give a fairer break to fine-sentiment, so it be honest, than the generation before them of which they will eventually become expositors. That future generation will have its meed of action. It cannot be denied.

ANOTHER MODERN INSTANCE

One evening came the New York Town Hall meeting. A meeting called to protest against the non-employment of myself by the Chicago Fair authorities and the A.I.A.

Embarrassing anti-climax!

I had given plenty of good reasons already for such non-employment. I was only too ready to give more. Surely it was better to have one architect out of employment in such parlous times than the eight or ten already employed on the Fair? Were I to come in they would go out because I could not work with them and would not work against them.

Another group entirely would have come in with me if ever I came in at all. They all knew that too.

But this Town Hall meeting was prefaced with a dinner at the Crillon to which a congenial exponent of the Fair, good old Ray Hood, had invited me. He came over to shake hands before whatever it was that was coming at the Town Hall later. I didn't know what was coming. Nor did Ray, so it turned out.

No, I didn't know what was coming. I guess, by the way Ray looked when he came, he didn't care what came either.

The hall was packed. Alec Woollcott in the chair. I have seen Alec bubble with wit in his lair by the river, scintillate with the mutual admiration society at the Algonquin. But that night Alec was effervescence itself. At least living in New York City does keen the rapier and polish the thrust, if he is a fair example.

At once the meeting took on an air of laughing gaiety. But that changed when Lewis Mumford got up to speak. With the essential manliness and nobility seen in the man as seen in his work he made no attempt to be apologetic or conciliatory. He was earnest and seriously wrote down the matter of the Fair where modern architecture was concerned more clearly and effectively than I had done the evening before.

As for me, still embarrassed, caught off guard in all this, I hastily decided to pay my respects to the Fair by building, building a fair while the crowd listened, build a fair or two of my own quite for myself and by myself—three in fact—and of diverse character.

It seemed to me in a flash this would be constructive criticism worth something to architecture, entertaining to me at least, and fun for them—maybe—meantime. As for the rest, it was dead issue so far as I was concerned. I knew it to be hopeless.

Because the only real interest I had in the Fair since first hearing of it, or any hope of it whatever, was to prevent any such catastrophe to our culture as occurred in 1893. Pro or con.

I did hate to see the careful, devoted sacrifice of so many faithful years in building up a great cause again played up, and—as now impending—probably played on by the clever pictorializing of the current salesmanship I knew would be snatching the great cause of organic architecture to feather the architectural offices of a few New York and Chicago plan-factories. However much I might like or be flattered by the factotums of those factories, I could see no more than that coming out of the circumstances with Ray Hood at the helm.

So placed in an embarrassing, awkward position by this meeting because it would seem that I was present and spoke because I myself

378

resented being left out of the Fair. Whereas the truth was I resented only their quick turnover to my work and the pretentious scene-painting I knew coming of it as unworthy the modern Architecture I had myself given to them years past. Was it only for this exploit?

Standing there to speak, given no previous thought to the matter, several contrasting ideas of a fair that would be worthy modern architecture because square with our new resources came into my mind. These ideas not unnaturally, as I was simply talking and thinking out of my everyday self, developed as I talked easily enough.

The ideas were spontaneous.

THREE PROGRESS FAIRS IN ONE

Scheme One:

As skyscraperism characterizes the thought of the group characterizing the Fair—and they had themselves idealized the Fair in so many words, as "like New York seen from one of its own high buildings . . ."

Why not, then, the Fair itself the apotheosis of the skyscraper? A mile high!

Build a great skyscraper in which the Empire State Building might stand free in a central interior court-space devoted to all the resources of the modern elevator.

Instead of the old stage-props of previous fairs, the same old miles of picture-buildings faked in cheap materials, wrapped around a lagoon, a fountain or theatrical waterfall in the middle—to be all eventually butchered to make a Roman holiday—let there be, for once, a genuine modern *construction* to remain as a great memorial.

If elevators could handle the population of New York, they could handle the crowds at the Fair. Why not handle the crowds directly from several expansive tiers of mechanized parking spaces as great terraces from which the true skyscraper itself would directly rise? The construction should be merely the steel core itself designed as integral pattern in the structural framing. Then concrete slabs for floors projecting as cantilever balconies from floor to floor—garden floors intervening as restaurants, etc., etc.

Instead of glass for enclosure—some of our many light, transparent glass substitutes might be used. Multitudinous area thus created could be let to the various exhibtors. The entire feature of the top stories could be garden observatories, pleasure places. Vast auditoriums might join at the base to the skyscraper and handle great aggregations of people on the ground. This tower construction of steel might rise from the triple-decked parking terraces, one corner of the terraces projecting and extending into the lake two ways at right angles to make piers and harbors for all water-craft. Beneath the lake nearby where the reflections of the tower would fall, powerful jets of the lake itself rising by way of inserted power pumps to great height. All to be illuminated by modern light-projecting apparatus, projecting toward the tower and projecting from it. The lake thus at contingent points becoming a series of great fountains irradiated by light.

The Lake Front Park itself would thus become merely landscape adjunct to and parking for the great modern structure which might easily, and modestly, rise five hundred and twenty-eight stories. The total construction say five thousand two hundred and eighty feet above the lake level—or about a mile high.

The clouds might naturally or artificially drift across its summit. Or effects be created by aeroplanes laying down colored ribbons of smoke to drift across it.

Such construction—the fake architecture of the New York functioneer obsolete—construction much like aeroplanes today would be no impossible feat, financially or structurally. In fact, entirely within reach as safe and reasonable. Practical—say cost a hundred million.

And it could stay thus, a feature of the Chicago Lake Front, beautiful as the Eiffel Tower never was. The Eiffel Tower would reach only well up one fiftieth the way.

Every floor would be a practical resource for future affairs of every sort. The business of the city itself might move into it with all its multifold minor branches. Still there would be room enough left for a mighty, continuous, never-ending industrial fair that would embrace the products of the entire civilized world in Chicago and be permanent.

Something accomplished worthy of a Century of Progress? Beacons from the top would reach adjoining states: radio from the antennae lifting from the tower crown would be in touch with all the world.

But if not thus skyscraper-minded and preferring to roam instead of lifted up by the hundreds on high . . . then . . .

Scheme Two:

A weaving characteristic of this age of steel in tension. Accept from John Roebling his pioneer work—message of the Brooklyn Bridge.

Build noble pylons—since the Fair commissioners seemed to like the word "pylon"—on the Lake Front five hundred feet apart each way until enough park, including threading waterways, had been covered to accomodate all exhibitors on the park level and in one balcony level surrounding the great enclosed area. This plastic-slung canopy to be anchored by steel cables to the outer series of appropriate pylons. Weave, in the main and minor and intermediate cables, a network that would support transparent fabrications such as we have as modern glass substitutes in our day. Thus make an architectural canopy more beautiful and more vast than any ever seen. The canopy could rise five hundred feet at the pylons to fall to one hundred feet above the park between them. The fabric should fall as a screen at the sides to close the space against weather. Rain water, falling, would wash the roof surfaces clean or they could be flushed from the pylon tops as fountains, the water dropping through openings at the low points of the canopy into fountain-basins, features of the system of lagoons that would wind and thread their way through the greenery of the park beneath the canopy.

All trees, foliage and waterways could be combined for the beholder by moving walkways reaching the individual plots allotted to the individual exhibitors. Little footwork. Each individual exhibitor thus free to set up his own show and ballyhoo it how he pleased.

The old fair-spirit, exciting as of old—but thus made free to excite the sophisticated modern ego once more by great spans and wondrous spinning of the spider—steel in tension.

Well, this type of construction with appropriate illumination and hydro-electric effects should cost less in standardization thus extended and made beautiful than the pettifogging, picture-making, privatistic individual buildings of so many architects all only interfering with exhibits and exhibitions in order to say exactly the same old nothing. Yes, and say it in the same old way. Tagged—only publicity-tagged—as "new." And, at least, the great "pylons" might remain always as lighting features of the Lake Front Park. Whereas the privatistic buildings faked in synthetic cardboard and painted would all have to be thrown away.

Or if more romantically inclined? Then why not—

Scheme Three:

There on the Lake Front is the Chicago harbor already enclosed against the turbulence of Lake Michigan.

Why not use that lake surface for a genuine holiday? A gay festival for the eyes. Why not a vast Pontoon Fair.

Make sealed, lightly reinforced metal cylinders, air exhausted from these like those of the catamaran; use them for floating foundation. Fabricate light thin tubes, some large and others not so large: some slender and each in any desired length. Fabricate them in pulp in order to be very light, soaked and stiffened by waterproofing or in transparent synthetics. Use these "reeds" in rhythmic verticality, grouping them to get support for light roof-webbing. Again use the steel strand anchorage to the metal drums to get and hold the webbing for roof cover. Large pontoons for tall buildings, long buildings. Square for Square buildings. All to be connected by interesting floating bridges. Floating gardens too could be connected to the buildings—the whole ground plan of assembled floating units to be connected together by characteristic linking units, themselves attractive features, so that while all were joined, yet all might gently undulate with no harm to any unit, securely anchored to the lake bottom.

Then introduce transparent colored glass tubing amid the plain pulp tubing. Why not illuminate the glass and have, for once, the airy verticality as a sheer legitimate modern fabrication, only aimed at as "similar to the charm of New York" seen there only at night in the rain?

This parti-colored opaque and transparent building-verticality would be doubled by direct reflections trembling in the water of the Lake.

The Lake itself could be thrown up by force-pumps to great heights and in enormous quantity, effects costing nothing but power. The Fair, a whole world of illuminated illumination, irradiating and irradiated light—an iridescent fair or a fair of iridescent, opalescent "reeds" in prismatic light.

The great whole would be a picturesque pleasurable "float" and not expensive.

Modern pageantry, this?

Genuine as in itself. Appropriate space could be easily created for any specific purpose, adapted to suit each commercial purpose: all these varied units would be linked together as a continuous, varied, brilliant modern circumstance of good planning.

Then, after the Fair was over, certain appropriate units could be detached and floated to an anchorage in the lagoons of the varied parks and waterways of the Lake Front Park or other parks to serve as restaurants or good-time places or as concessions rented from the city.

I said that if there are these three ideas genuine and practical as Modern Architecture, they could be sure there were, as easily, hundreds to choose from.

Well, I had done my best to get out of a trying situation. An appeal to Imagination! Of course I can hear the eclectic group saying they had thought of all these schemes themselves and rejected them as impractical. To reject them so would be their judgment and, no doubt, their necessity, too.

MILWAUKEE INSTANCE

The several exhibitions of my work around the world were now over. Material itself safely back at Taliesin, always a great relief. Perishable stuff. Charlotte Partridge, curator of the Layton Art Gallery, center of Milwaukee's culture in Art, asked me to send an exhibition and give a lecture. She volunteered to raise the necessary fee would I come.

The last place I could imagine interested in anything modern (or spiritual), Wisconsin's own great Milwaukee.

I agreed. Miss Partridge therefore seems to have had her private troubles getting necessary funds. But exhibition went forward. I was busy directing the boys busy setting it up when Miss Partridge introduced a tall, fair young person "doing the show" for the *Milwaukee Journal*. I thought she was much too good-looking to know much about architecture, the blind spot of the nation. I went on working. She, persistent, followed me about as I worked at this and that, asking questions meanwhile. I answered between moments here and there. Finally: "Mr. Wright, would you mind telling me what you think of our new nine-million-dollar courthouse?"

Now, this new courthouse was a usual steel structure inside but surrounded by three stories of solid stone punctured occasionally by windows, all according to architects' Classic-for-Courthouses. Above that, a tall stone classic order ran all around. Surmounting the whole "Classic" mass was a heavy stone cornice. A steel building inside, stone building outside is bound to have consequences. I did not know at the time who the architect was.

"Well," I said, unaware of her intention—she looked innocent— "your new courthouse will set Milwaukee back fifty years from any cultural standpoint," went on working, not thinking I was talking for "publication."

"Oh, I'm so glad to hear you say that!" dancing up and down with glee.

Then from her, conscientiously: "Would you mind if I put that in print?" This request was so considerate that, touched, I stopped, thought a minute. What did it matter? True at least. "No, go ahead." The interview ended and I thought no more about it.

Got home late that evening. Next morning, early, a long distance call from Milwaukee. The *News*. "The *Journal* was out with a statement [always statement] headline quoting you: 'New courthouse sets Milwaukee back fifty years from any standpoint of culture.' How about it?"

"All right," I said, "make it a hundred. I've been thinking it over."

So the fight was on. The pottage began to boil. Other newspapers called wanting confirmation. They got it. Then came the usual follow-up interviews with Milwaukee's "leading" architects by these journals. Reporter comment upon this, "All afraid to express an opinion, not caring to incur shafts of radical architect's wit." This pleased me. One of their number, Tullgren, said, "Wright always was twenty years ahead of his time." The inference being, "and so why worry." Albert Randolph Ross, I soon found out, was winner of the competition for the new courthouse. He himself, interviewed now by the *Journal*, explained why his design was "Classical" instead of Modern.

Here is Randolph Ross:

"Mr. Hoover, talking in Washington recently on the occasion of appropriations for public works, said it was a good thing to carry on the traditions established by Washington.

"When I went into the competition I doubted whether to design a building in the modern and experimental trend for a great public courthouse. I made modern sketches, but in my opinion they fell flat for this purpose. They were not typical and expressive of public work. So I turned to that type established by our forefathers."

Turning to a defense of the courthouse design, Mr. Ross said, "It was chosen unanimously by three of the country's most brilliant architects as the plan that completely met the requirements of beauty, plan and utility.

"I have no quarrel with trends in modern architecture. I take a fling at it myself. I even considered it for the courthouse. But it simply won't do for public buildings. It violates the dictates of a definite style built up through one hundred and fifty years of our history.

"No. A departure into modernism would not be suitable for a courthouse. We must be trained slowly to things violently new. The public's money cannot rightly be used to force experiments down its throat.

"This esthetic side of the new courthouse counts only ten per cent. All that is needed in a building is a design that will arrest light in such a way as to give it a pleasing effect. That has been accomplished. The plan of the courts, offices and corridors and the building's utility are most vitally to be considered."

This point of view of one of America's casual eclectics is here completely expressed. But if the esthetic design of the courthouse is an affair separate from the courthouse estimated by Ross at "ten per cent," why spend fifty per cent on an extravagant, showy, useless stone envelope so far removed from date?

Reply to Ross:

Milwaukee—go look at Chicago's county building, twenty years ago the last word in pseudo-classic, chosen the same way. Today that build-

384

ing is manifest to all as a ponderous anachronism, a cultural crime. A lie and a foolish extravagance.

I say that the Milwaukee county building is today just the same criminal waste of the people's money, modified only by Ross's superior "taste." Within a few years this crime will be manifest to all Milwaukee citizens. The thought of the world is growing more sensible.

Architect Ross says he is "unwilling to spend the hard-earned millions of Milwaukee's money on any experiment." This may sound good to Milwaukee. If so, it is one of the things that is the matter with Milwaukee and that eventually will leave her a permanent backwater in civilization.

Architect Ross says he is not willing to "experiment." No. But as an architect he *is* willing to "bet" nine millions of the people's money on a narrow margin of the unsure "taste" of a transitory period. His "taste," so he says, is no risk? Why?

Why should the future have any more respect for a Milwaukee-lie than for the Chicago-lie? And there was some excuse for the Chicago-lie. The age had not awakened to engineering architecture. For the Milwaukee-lie there is no such excuse. The world has waked up in the last forty years.

Were Architect Ross utterly blind to the progress of the last decade in his own profession the world over, he might still consider honest engineering architecture as "experiment."

Notwithstanding all conservative opinion, the Milwaukee county building will stand as a late "experiment" in an experiment in sentimental falsehood, foredoomed to failure by unscientific construction.

Since *experiment* the courthouse must thus be, Mr. Ross, why not *experiment* with sanity and truth in construction?

"Our forefathers" notwithstanding, monumental stone mass disappeared as truth when steel in tension, clear glass and ferro-concrete became the actual body of the Machine Age. To combine stone and steel, even in the name of the "forefathers," is dangerous, Architect Ross. Young men in architecture all over these United States see this fact today. That means, every man who thinks will see it soon. Steel and stone do not expand the same.

Why bet on or "experiment" with pure sentimentality according to your own taste, Architect Ross?

Why not *know* consequences?

So much public talk of consequences infuriated official city-fathers. They got together, argued the question as to whether or not I should be called before them to explain the disparaging remarks. A vote was taken. The vote stood ten to ten. The opposition claiming I was a notoriety-seeker and to call me down publicly would only add fuel to my flame. So I was not called after all.

The press had a good time adding headlines to the editorials.

ANOTHER LITTLE STORY

Children and students were pouring into the exhibition. Miss Partridge said nothing; the controversy had attracted much interest among the young people of Milwaukee.

Milwaukee architects, few exceptions, kept away. To be seen going into that show was too much for most of them. Merely to gratify curiosity? And not much curiosity.

But a lecture was yet to come. For some reason I had to postpone it for several days. Friday of the week following the Wednesday the exhibit opened I got to Milwaukee about four o'clock to speak that evening.

Charlie Morgan and I were at the Pfister Hotel . . . a bath and getting dressed for a little dinner Miss Partridge was giving . . . A knock at the door. Loud!

Charlie opened it. A life-size Milwaukee sheriff stepped in with a warrant for my arrest.

What charge?

A judgment entered against me to pay seven thousand dollars to the deceased Miriam Noel. Brought by her estate!

The payments due her by contract were all made during her lifetime from a trust fund deposited in a Madison bank for the purpose at the time of divorce. There was eleven thousand dollars still left in the fund when she died. The balance of this fund reverted to me at her death, so the charge was only my failure to pay myself this seven thousand dollars, to bring the trust fund up again to its original standard for no purpose whatever except—what?

Why Milwaukee? Of course. It worked. It served the city's "legal" purpose. The attorney of the "estate" (whoever and whatever the "estate" unless myself?) had sworn to the document, so I was taken into custody, entered in the record at the county jail (not finger-printed this time) and motored over to the "Justice" before whom I was to be tried, of course photographed all along the way as I went. Prearranged cameramen stood around all posted where they could do the worst good.

Angry enough, I understood the foolish situation, so I put the best possible face on the whole affair. Keeping my head up.

"Justice" asked questions. Got answers. Lawyers having gratified the curiosity of the assembled press, then urged the "court" that I be kept in custody over night. (The lecture in mind.)

But the "court" thought this might be carrying things rather too far, I imagine, for he denied the motion. Cold feet at the last moment, he set me free. So the "plan" only partially succeeded. The evening papers of course were on the street with fresh headlines opening old sores as Charlie and I got back to the hotel late for the public lecture.

Well, Miss Partridge had been reproached by certain Milwaukee architects for bringing a disgrace upon the city. Having me there, she didn't seem to care. She is something of a captain herself.

It was now seven-thirty. Time for the little dinner? We got there. Charlie more raging than I. We dined pleasantly nevertheless, reaching the lecture hall only a little late. I think none of us knew just what might happen next. And I remembered Olgivanna's reluctance to have me go to Milwaukee at all: her plea to cancel the lecture engagement and stay away.

But the place was overflowing, one of the courthouse commissioners appeared in the audience. There was a general feeling, they said, that when I talked I would modify the remark concerning the nine-million-dollar courthouse.

Instead of the "arrest" putting a damper on my spirits that evening, the dinner and kindness of all concerned, even the complimentary sheriff himself, who apologized, more decent than his superiors, restored me for as enthustiastic and appreciative an audience as I've ever had anywhere. They heard me through.

Then I stepped down to give them all the half hour I knew they expected.

Many questions came and were answered.

The commissioner got to his feet: "Mr. Wright, we had hoped you would modify your remarks concerning our new courthouse, or at least explain them. Will you do this?"

"I will," I said and proceeded to say:

"Milwaukee's new nine-million-dollar courthouse belongs to the nineteenth not the twentieth century. A great stone mass over steel such as the building is can be memorial to Milwaukee only as a backwater in civilization. The courthouse can only advertise to posterity that Milwaukee was neither scholar nor gentleman. No scholar because Milwaukee was ignorant of the current of advanced thought abroad in the world at the time. No gentleman because regardless of her duty to others as well as herself.

"A steel building inside and a stone building outside is an anachronism inviting destruction. It will come apart," I said, and turned to leave the hall.

Strangely enough, the commissioner seemed pleased. The audience was no less so.

The commissioner, on his feet again, said, "Well then, why not tell us just what kind of a courthouse we should have had, were we 'scholars and gentlemen.' "

Turning back again, I gave them a modern building as I saw it, as it came to me.

"The solid preparation of solid masses of terraced stone or concrete. Rising upon this 'stylobate' an iridescent light-enmeshing fabric of steel and glass. All luminous within and brilliant without. The structure light, strong, free in space, economical of materials. Free in thought, an expression of our own new opportunity in our own time." I carried it on into some detail and delivered the whole to them where they sat for about five million dollars. More than enough to build it—I was sure.

Thus unethical, I made it so obvious that the audience broke into applause, including the commissioner and his party. Milwaukee was a closed episode so far as Ross's courthouse was concerned.

So I wrote a note to Ross saying I hoped and believed no harm had been done to him in the post-mortem. I had really meant none. I felt called upon to at last openly champion the cause to which I had already given everything as an architect.

Unfortunately I soon began to find that behind every pseudo-classic plate-glass window, however small the window, there is some fine, well-meaning individual to be hit by a brick thrown by anyone. It was the "Cause" with me however, in this as ever. Not the man. Ross, I think, was intelligent enough to know this. Never before had I thrown a brick directly at any architect's "classic" performance. But it now seemed high time to make a public issue. The modern hat was in the pseudo-classic ring in Milwaukee.

My note to Ross received a gracious "no harm."

But saying, guardedly, that he envied the future its coming freedom.

The lawyer for the "estate" dismissed his fake suit with profuse and servile apologies, offering to pay all costs. He volunteered the interesting information in the presence of Jim Hill, my own lawyer, that he hadn't wanted to do the thing but no less than five leading Milwaukee citizens had insisted upon his "going through with it." So he did.

Interesting to follow this up? I had the means. But like all persecution by publicity, of what use? More publicity? Yes, only more publicity: always the final weapon where publicity is not wanted. Where it is wanted, well, it is for them to sell it or no publicity.

This is fair enough?

CONSEQUENCES

Several years later, articles appeared in the Milwaukee papers—"cracks opening in stone walls of county building . . . Expensive repairs necessary." The press called again. But I had no taste for "I told you so." I would say nothing.

HONORABLE INTERVAL

Letter from Holland saying the exhibition opened at Amsterdam in the State Museum by our American Ambassador, Swenson. He tried to say something about the show but could talk only of America and the flag. The president of the Architects' Society then got up and made the speech for him that he might have made if he had known at all what the exhibition was all about, or why it was over there at all. A cablegram from Dutch colleagues congratulating me, many kind words upon my "consistency in a great Cause."

That word consistency! It is seldom the word for the imaginative man in action, is it?

I was inclined to deny the allegation for conscience's sake.

I sincerely believe I have not been very "consistent." Off on holiday too often. But direction has never changed nor development hindered. I've always returned refreshed for the work in hand—having learned much more from every "aside" than from the "line" itself.

Is that consistency? Well, then I should plead guilty to the soft impeachment and I will plead.

The exhibition goes over to the German *Akademie der Künste* at Berlin; erstwhile "Royal" Academy. The first time I believe the "Reich" has honored modern architecture? From there it went to Frankfurt, then to Stuttgart, finally to Belgium. It came home to Taliesin again in October so that it might go to work in our own country where I believe it is most needed, even if not so much wanted. A country once so hectic an eclectic. Forever eclectified? The years go by meantime.

Again solicited by the New School for Social Research under Dr. Johnson—director—and many others, I went as journeyman preacher to a week of preaching in New York City to earn the only fees anywhere in sight at that time in my life. I could talk about it if I was not asked to do it. This began to look like recognition at home? Or was I only losing my grip on the future—by thus gaining on the present?

MORE

From the excellent state university at Eugene, Oregon, came a hand-lettered appeal for an exhibition of my work signed by all the young architectural students and their shepherd, Walter Wilcox. Walter is one of the best shepherds. That it came at this time touched me. Though so far away I managed with help to get there with the European exhibition. Then on to Seattle. Success. Two lectures I had given in Denver following the six at Princeton. The Princeton six were built by the Princeton Press into the published book, *Modern Architecture*. Five more lectures were given in New York City, a pleasant one in Philadelphia at the Contemporary Club—charming dinner to a small group by courteous Paul Cret. Two more lectures and exhibitions again at Madison, Wisconsin. Two at Minneapolis—I hope Sheriff Brown came. He would have felt at home in the enormous fashionable throng overflowing the Art Museum and barricading the museum grounds with motor cars until I got myself in with great difficulty. Two lectures and an exhibit at Chicago Art Institute, published by the Institute. Many of these meetings, so crowded by the young sons and daughters of my fellow men and women, affected me strangely: "at home" in Chicago and Wisconsin especially, where warm welcome in places of long association aroused the sleeping sentiment in me, though not to the point of modifying my ideals to accept sentimentality as such. But dangerously near demoralization just the same. What did this awakening appreciation mean, I wondered. A little uneasy.

Overheard: "The man is still an iconoclast!" Often whispered indignation. Gossip: he must be lonely, etc., etc.: perhaps any or all surmises usual in the circumstances. But I used to wish they would dub me "radical," and let me go home to stay. A good honest word, that word "radical"? It means of the *root*. And how know life unless through knowledge of the "root"? But "radical" on the academic tongue usually spells "red!" because as I have said, the hypocrite instinctively hates the radical especially in the United States. But if so, was I no longer radical, or perhaps I was "slowing up" and were they overtaking me?

Well, everywhere I found the halls overflowing. Everywhere I went I found youth eagerly questioning. Enthusiastic. Modernity naturally seems to have captured the imaginations of Usonian youth. I hope the new integrity will possess the young American heart, making indigenous culture on more liberal terms than the substitute which the schools have accepted and are offering so far. The far more fundamental concept of natural law as organic is necessary at first. Under fire of intent and intelligent questionings by youth, I began to feel myself a "youth," to take free and deeper breaths: began to feel less alone in my work and world.

What effect this would have upon me I did not know.

ECHO

At Chicago, I remember an echo of my earlier youth. One afternoon in the gallery at the Art Institute where the exhibition stood, a tall, graying, but still handsome woman came toward me smiling. A moment's hesitation. And then I recognized Catherine. I had not seen her in fifteen years. These years seemed to have dealt with her gently and she looked—frankly—young and happy—as she said she was. She was married again—now Mrs. Ben E. Page. We went about the exhibition together noticing many a work that had grown up out of the "other half" of the Oak Park establishment where her children had run about with my thumb-tacks in the bottoms of their shoes. However ill-advised Catherine's attitude toward me had been, she had never been other than loyal to anyone she ever loved.

AUTOBIOGRAPHY

Trying to be honestly autobiographical in writing these pages, telling only what is true, I see why all autobiography is written between the lines. It must be so.

No matter how skilled the writer or spontaneous he may be, the implication outdoes his ability or undoes his intention. The law of change is at work as he writes and the circumstance flows from beneath the fixation at the point of his pen into endless other forms and significances—except as a single facet may catch the gleam of the reader's intelligence and he writes truth in between the lines for himself.

Autobiography is impossible except as such implication. For the life of me, I cannot see why I recounted so many episodes that were far inferior to those I delight to remember and tell now. I do not know why I have not written of many features and incidents of my life so much more deeply intimate, so much more suggestive even in architectural thought. Certainly more picturesque. They come crowding into mind at odd moments. Press upon my heart for utterance too late, and go away again.

Even those I have tried to utter here go away, unsatisfied if not dissatisfied.

Does this fluid nature of life and work, I wonder, really allow nothing to be wholly held? Is nothing to be arrested and directed in human experience—so far as the essential quality, the *life* in it goes— except by the greatest of art? Is the writer helpless as the surgeon is helpless with his anatomical study of the corpse on his dissecting table to put his hand even for a moment upon what was the life of that corpse?

To me, it seems so more and more.

The sufferings of growth itself, as growth, even without the agonies of the sentimentality that vainly tries to hold life by "institution" and "establishment," trying to extend the fleeting hour until the simple inevitable becomes high tragedy to the soul. Are not these sufferings our punishment for violation of the first simple law of Freedom? What is that law except the law of organic change natural to whatever changes? Does not all live in change?

As I remember, the best of life is a becoming. So I record the lines and leave the rest to go the way of all life.

MEMORIES

I remember the third week after I left my first home in Oak Park, the misery that came over me in a little café somewhere in Paris on the Boulevard St. Michel. Caring neither to eat or drink I was listening to the orchestra. It was the end of a rainy day in a long depressing rainy season, the Seine most of the time over its banks. Late at night in a café or cabaret, the cellist picked up his bow and began to play Simonetti's madrigale. Lloyd had played on his cello the simple old Italian tune often. I would play with him, on the piano. But the familiar strains now gave me one of those moments of interior anguish when I would have given all I had lived to be able to begin reliving the old strains again. The remembered music drove me out of the café into the dim streets of Paris with such longing and sorrow as a man seldom knows, I hope. It was not repentance. It was despair that I could not achieve what I had undertaken as Ideal. I wandered about not knowing where I was going or how long, finding myself at daylight facing a glaring signboard—still, somehow, somewhere near where I had started out on the Boulevard St. Michel.

I REMEMBER:

When all was well with the new life at Taliesin, during my first two years of life there, whenever I would go to Chicago to keep track of my work I would take time somehow to go out to Oak Park: go there after dark, not wishing to be seen. Go to reassure myself that all was going well there too—with the children at the little home on Forest Avenue.

I would see light streaming from half-open windows and hear happy voices.

Or perhaps they were playing the piano or cello. The violin.

Perhaps singing and playing.

Perhaps calling to each other. Oh, yes. I might have known it. All cozy enough.

I would turn away to town again. Relieved.

I REMEMBER:

Llewellyn coming down to stay with me when I came down to town occasionally as he did at the Congress Hotel, bringing his mandolin to play for me. It gave me pleasure to see him fold each garment neatly and put it carefully by on a chair when he went to bed. And I would tuck him in. My "deserted" child.

He is a young lawyer in Washington now . . . well, fate would . . . etc.

I REMEMBER:

The little suppers with Catherine and Frances at Hironymous's Tip-Top Inn atop the old Pullman Building about that same time. These young ladies . . . my "deserted" daughters. So much "young ladies" now they were that I was suspected by new acquaintances of mine of dereliction from the straight and narrow path of the devoted though conventional lover by unconventional attentions to gay young things.

I remember too . . . but this volume must reach timely if unseemly end, or if not timely, at least some kind of seemly end.

So, "I will now remember" to forget most of what I should have written to make writing at all the full, expressive record I want it to be.

As with the stories of adventure in building I left out those I should have liked best to write, so these pages lack the faces, names and places, the times and circumstance that would be most revealing, really more significant than any I have recalled. But mutability, is it not the charm of life, alive?

Live up to life, bravely, sensitively, conscientiously or even philosophically, how we may, this fleeting and becoming defies fixation the more we do so live it.

Therefore who can put his own life into his own hands? Or put it into the words of his own mouth? Then how to put it into the pen on this paper?

Unlucky he who could, however lucky we might be if he did.

TALIESIN III

Taliesin! Three times built, twice destroyed, and yet a place of greatest repose. When I am away, like some rubber band stretched out but ready to snap back immediately the pull is relaxed or released, I get back to it happy to be there again.

At sunrise late last September I stood again with bare feet on the virgin sod of the Taliesin hill-crown. Looking off to the South I saw the now big dark-green clump of fir-trees Uncle Thomas had planted there fifty years ago to keep the little family chapel company and shade the Lloyd-Jones picnics on a Sunday.

A little farther to the left—East—above the farm that used to be Uncle James's, rises the range of hills I sometimes walked along at night, a barefoot boy in search of Peace, Beauty, Satisfaction, Rest. Over to the right, a little West, are the faraway hills where I went to look for the cows: where I believed the surplus of the fervent hymns sung there used to go. Below and between are the many-colored rolling, ripening fields where Uncle James used to call to the young dreamer, "Come back, Frank, come back!"

Over the nearby ridge, wasting away, lies a reproach and a sorrow to me—what is left of Aunt Nell's and Aunt Jane's Hillside Home· School. Deserted and decaying now.

"Romeo and Juliet," the windmill tower, still stands bravely at work on the hill-crown just above the old home-school. Again a new wheel needed, the third to be wrenched from its moorings by severe northwest storms. But the tower still stands. Uncles, aunts, nephews and nieces—all gone elsewhere—or forever gone beyond. Occasionally, as in that boyhood time, come moments of other where . . . inner abstraction of the spirit. But now I hear no one calling, "Frank! Come back! Come back, Frank!" Of that past there is only the free, long retrospect of Time, Place and Otherwhere to come drifting back through the present: retrospect now many times strung around the earth—probably to go stringing around again. Who knows?

Many but not so many dreams of the future? Moments of anguish? Oh, yes—of course—there are many; but no moments of regret. Day by day I enjoy more the eternity that is now. Realizing at last that eternity *is* now, and eternity only divides yesterday from tomorrow as an artificial affair of Time.

It is now as though the mind itself at times were some kind of recording film in endless reel, to go on perfecting and projecting effects endlessly as the moment changes, seldom if ever the same. But the same scene and scheme may show itself from infinitely varying angles as the point of view varies, if informing principle, the *impulse* living in it all, stays in place. Else the impotence of confusion, or chaos of madness, vain imprisonment in the dead or dying Past.

No—the several years since Taliesin first steeled itself and settled down to work and its ideals have been free, but of course not carefree. Sad memories not excluded—they have been happy years. Short. Hope never really dies. Because of those troubled years, life is richer than ever before, though with "hard times" as we like to say—we must say it—lying all around us. Coming nearer every day to Taliesin, the menace of its mounting load of debt due to tragic circumstance.

HOME AGAIN

Olgivanna, Svetlana, Iovanna and I, we were up at sunrise this late September morning walking in the thick blue-grass, bare feet in the thick white rime of frosty dew. The rime so cold that every few steps we would have to stop to warm our feet in the hollow backs of our knees.

Tall red-top, grass on the hill beyond the garden, gleaming in the slanting rays of morning sun, the tall grass everywhere, hung with a gossamer covering of spider webs of amazing size: now a jewelled, sunlit brilliance. Delicate patterns were sparkling with the clinging dewdrops, myriads that turned each separate strand of all the marvelous webs into a miracle of light: a kind of construction that might well inspire this age, because it's beauty we might realize in steel and glass buildings. We could if we would.

My German Shepherd, Kavé, always leaping, nosing, nipping and biting at our bare heels, we reached the melon-patch on the hillside below the reservoir.Once there, we gathered ripe melons, cool with the frosted morning dew. I broke them across my knees and we ate our fill of the rosy, watery sweetness, crushing our mouths handfuls of the pink flesh decorated with black seeds. So many melons were lying all about that we ate only the hearts and threw the rest aside for the birds.

Fruit seeds were invented for birds and animals, to spread the species by tempted appetites, for us too this morning.

Faithful Kavé always shepherds us, sleeping by my bedside at night. Or sometimes by his mistress. If he is shut out, his howls and protests are not to be borne. He gets in somehow and lies down there to waken us in the morning by brushing a cold nose to our faces or giving a warm tongue to the cheek at precisely a few moments before the breakfast bell regularly rings from the tower on the hill. Then we get up, go into the big living room with its expanse of waxed cypress wide-board floor, turn on some favorite dance music and have the morning frolic we calling setting-up exercises, but really they are more like danc-ing. Olgivanna learned some of them at the Institute at Fontainebleau and taught them to us.

Winter nights—all frosty white or deep snow—icicles hanging from the eaves outside—we love to build great blazing fires in the big stone fireplaces, closing the inside shutters of the whole house, and lie there story-telling, arguing or reading until we fall asleep. Sometimes we take turns reading aloud, Iovanna's fairy-tales always coming first. Carl Sandburg's "White Horse Girl and Blue Wind Boy" is her favorite at the moment, ours too. I read it to Olgivanna on our first trip to New York—in a lower berth together.

So, you may see, Taliesin scenes are homely scenes. These latter years—Iovanna is nearly six years old now—have been a succession of changing hours made up of changing moments each with its own lovely picture to be treasured among all pictures. Curly heads and loving dark eyes, lithe supple bodies, eager minds living life, all make beautiful pic-tures. And all make constant demands.

But though life is home at Taliesin, it is never monotonous. Taliesin days are one continuous series of changing play and work changes, hard to say usually which is which, but emergency is always. Always emergency. The landscape itself changes outside the windows as the sea changes, only these valley changes are more variably immutable than the sea.

No fixed habits yet. Not even good ones. Unless it is that breakfast bell. We avoid habits as I did when, a young man, I made up my mind that they killed imagination. So I have always avoided them, feeling habituation the enemy of imaginative well-being in any creative work.

Good company comes our way but rarely. But sometimes it finds its way to us as far away as we are. We are still pretty far away. We do not often regret it.

Free now, here we are, for the time. Winter living in quiet seclusion at work and play all over the house and workshop. We see no difference between our work and play. Usually if the weather is severe seven or eight of the great stone fireplaces at Taliesin are burning holes in the forest. Some of them burn oak. Most times at evening. Our fireplaces have established a pretty good market for cordwood in the neighborhood, although the fireplaces are really for good measure since the whole place is heated by steam and lighted by our own hydro-electric plant by the waterfall below. A pull on a switch-cord by the bedside lights the grounds about the house. I am a little ashamed of this precaution, because that is what it is.

We love the snow at Taliesin. And icicles yards long, a hanging fringe from the eaves all around the house.

In summer our range of activity widens somewhat, takes in the farm and gardens, the horses, our walks over wooded hills, rolling fields and country roads. We still plunder, as I did when a boy, the roadsides, choice branches of bloom or berries to "arrange" in the house or studio. There below and beyond is the broad, sand-barred Wisconsin River's changing flow in the broad bottomland—for walking and swimming. Our entire resources are constantly taxed. "Something is always happening in the country," as Wilhelm Bernhard—a draughtsman—used to say.

So we dream and plan great things. Good music is essential to life at Taliesin. A grand piano stands by the living room fireplace, a cello resting against its hollow side, a violin on the ledge beside it. There are several recorders there also. A harp is to come. Olgivanna plays Bach, Beethoven, old Russian music. I let the piano play itself a few moments sometimes while the feeling lasts, knowing nothing. Sometimes something comes out. I can never play any of the things, such as they are, a second time. Olgivanna says she likes to hear me play. Hers is a gentle encouraging soul and she would not hurt even such outrageous pride as mine.

Svetlana too plays now, and the young Iovanna plays with perfect style all the while: finger movements perfect. But the notes she selects are not even often well-suited to each other. No matter, Iovanna plays too. So we all play.

My little five-year-old daughter Iovanna and I among constant inventions have invented a game. An architect's daughter, she has many kinds and sizes of building blocks, among them all a set of well-made cubes about an inch square painted pure bright colors, red, yellow, blue, green, black and white. Some of the cubes are divided on the diagonal into contrasting colors. Well, whoever deals, deals seven blocks to each and two diagonals. Iovanna's turn to play. She chooses a color-block—not fair to start with a diagonal—and places it square on the waxed board floor. Then I select a color-block and put it, say, touching hers at the corner. Her turn. She studies a little, head one side, finally putting down a block in whatever way she chooses, but however put down it will now make a decided change in the geometric figure. Her imagination begins to stress the judgment to decide the next play.

Instead of extending the figure on the floor, she may now put a block on top of the one already "played" by me. She does so. The figure on the floor begins to look more and more interesting as the "third dimension" enters and the block masses creep up into the air. The group begins to be a construction. I may follow up and down, or I go crosswise with whatever color-block I may have. But whatever I do, I will change the whole effect just as she will when her turn comes to play—change the figure—make a pattern.

Sometimes she sees she has spoiled the figure with her "turn" and asks to change it.

Always she may.

The fourteen blocks in place, we take in the result, critical or enthusiastic.

Sometimes these little form-and-color exercises in block-pattern make a good thesis in "Modern Art." Fact is, I intend them so.

Not too late, Taliesin life at this time is one continuous round of movement, usually happy rhythms ending in sound sleep for all . . . only to begin again with play and laughter at sunrise, settling down after breakfast into serious work that is play too—for we love the work we do, even when we are all "adding tired to tired" and adding it again.

Usually we are together all the time. Everywhere we go, whether in work or in play. Iovanna does nearly everything we do as well as she can. Her half-bushel of gold-brown curls pile up on her head. They lie in ringlets there and look at you like eyes. Her name was made from her maternal Grandfather's—Ivan, or John, and her paternal Grandmother's, Anna. Literally John Anna, Johanna or Iovanna, to go with Olgivanna, properly Olga Ivanovna. And the name of the charmingly disposed little daughter before we met, Svetlana. The name means—in Russian— "light."

Iovanna's original stories often astonish us.

Buddha, whom she sees all about in various forms, intrigues her imagination. She romances with Buddha. But recently she has become interested in another great personality. Here is something concerning that new interest Olgivanna wrote down, word for word, changing nothing.

I am calling it Ave Maria. But as I have already assured you, I am not in the least sentimental.

AVE MARIA

"Go to bed now, Iovanna, you have run around enough. Come, time to go to sleep," I said to my little daughter Iovanna.

"Wait, Mother. I must go and tell God 'goodnight.'"

As I heard this for the first time, I was surprised. I followed her into the living room and she stood there in the middle of the room and said clearly, right into space, "Goodnight, God."

We went back to the bedroom, I tucked her in bed.

"Stay with me, Mother, sit down, Mother, I would like to see God. Will you buy me some flying-wings at Marshall Field's, so I can fly up into the sky to see him?"

"But God is not in the sky only. Remember what your Father told you in the church in New York, God is in your heart?"

"Yes, Mother, I know, only I think my heart is too little for God. You see it is too little? When it gets cold, he gets cold in my heart and he goes up in the sky to build a big fire there to keep warm."

"But your heart, Iovanna, is a fire. Your heart is love, it is like a flame, it keeps God warm."

"Oh, no, Mother, I told you it is too little for God. He is big and my heart is just little, just like—well, you see just like a little grain of seed."

"But think of all the hearts there are in the world: children's hearts and grown-up people's hearts, all together they make a great big fire for God to keep him warm."

"Oh, but he needs food, or he will get very hungry. We must give him something to eat. He is very kind you know. We must take care of him."

"He does not eat. He lives on love. He is never hungry if he has enough love."

"But, Mother, we should send him something just the same. We should make a big bouquet of flowers for him. You know he loves flowers. And he loves shells, too. You see, all the shells of the sea come to him. They bring him food and everything he needs. I want to send him something."

"Send him your love by being good, minding your Mother and Father. You should also work if you want to please God."

"Oh, I am working. I swept the sitting room, I brushed Svetlana's dress for her, I rubbed Auntie Maginel's poor neck. I work very hard. Do you have to mind God too, Mother?"

"Certainly."

"And does Father, too?"

"Yes, of course he does."

"Would God punish you if you and Father were not good?"

"God never punishes, we punish ourselves."

"But would God punish *me* if I were not good?"

"No, but I would have to punish you if I could not make you good by being nice to you. I don't like to do it, but I have to do it so God can be warm in your heart. He is very cold and sad when you are not good."

"Is he warm right now?"

"Very."

"Mother, I wish I could see him."

It became very quiet in the room. In another moment Iovanna was asleep.

And so these several books within a book.

All of them to the Anna who is my mother.

To the Ivan (John) whose daughter

Olga Ivanovna, called Olgivanna, is

Mother to Iovanna—little "John Anna" . . . the last of the generation calling me Father. Svetlana included . . .

and to Olgivanna herself.

Because, but for her this book were never written.

POSTLUDE

Here on this low hill in THE VALLEY there is Freedom to make life and work really synonymous terms. In retrospect is a vast panorama of good life. Human experience a colorful tapestry shot through with threads of gold as light gleams whenever truth is touched and love rose worthy of noble selfhood or life higher because of death.

Or where living faith justified defeat and defeated doubt.

Sincerely sought, well-loved, we see that Principle—is it the very quality of life itself—vaguely felt by me as a boy left out in that early lesson preached by Uncle John's familiar feet in the snow up the slope of the valley field?

The order of Change limitless and profound we have experienced.

As natural order I have sought the Nature of this order, trying to see it as Principle. I have long seen it as Reality. Perhaps as Heraclitus said—the only reality we may ever know?

Insofar as change comes by natural growth, we need fear no change. Though we may fail to see it, change is beneficent. No menace.

Inevitable and good, organic change is no mere chance. To any natural order or true culture founded upon reality, Change would be friendly. Age becoming a desirable, a great qualification. Where age is not so, then what sort of civilization have we?

Our lives here on earth should be blessed, not antagonized, by this true attribute of all natural growth ... Change ... death—but a change—only a crisis of growth.

Many violent breaks in my field of work I have already encountered, studying as normal this element not in the reckoning. I am reconciled now to respect. Armed, but not to establish. Armed to foresee and forefend the flow that is human life wherever I can see it or feel it to flow true.

Romance to me is become Reality in this fateful, flowing sense of life and work.

I have been seeking life Ideal as I have been seeking ideal building, just as at the beginning of *An Autobiography* I sought naked weed rising above blue arabesque, sunshot on spotless white—unaware of Uncle John's "straight is the way."

Thus life has been, as it must be, changing test of Eternal Principle.

Leading Life-adventure now in architecture is this keen new romance of Time, Place and Man I have called modern, flowing on together, going out from my hand into the making of a beneficently changing world: a world so instituted—as institution still must be—as capable of change without the constitutional disorder we now so dread, or fear of fatal disaster as a kind of unease or disease.

Freedom is the title of this fourth book, but there is no such thing as Freedom in itself. Freedom has not been attained on earth by mortals, least of all by the one who professed to have discovered it, the Buddha himself.

Freedom is from within—an achievement sought and found in work—in love—in faith.

Mere escape is not Freedom! Even at large the only freedom we have a right to ask is the freedom to seek—to be—to believe—to love the beautiful, free to conceive it, perceive it, feel and courageously find it.

The only Freedom for men.
Freedom enough in this—Our Country.

BOOK FIVE □ FORM

SHAM   NOR TO FAVOUR FORSWORN WEAR MASK CREST OR THORN MY WORK AS BEFITTETH A MAN
SHAM   NOR FOR FAME E'ER MAN MADE SHEATH THE NAKED WHITE BLADE MY ACT AS BECOMETH A MAN

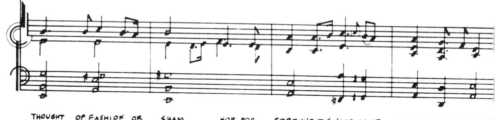

THOUGHT OF FASHION OR   SHAM   NOR FOR   FORTUNE THE JADE SERVE   VILE GODS OF TRADE
SLAVE OF FASHION OR   SHAM   OF MY   FREEDOM PROUD HERS TO SHRIVE GUARD OR SHROU

MAN   MY   LIFE   AYE! WHATEVER BETIDETH THE   MAN

WORDS   FRANK LLOYD WRIGHT 1896
MUSIC   OLGIVANNA LLOYD WRIGHT
                    TALIESIN 1933

I'LL LIVE AS I'LL WORK AS I AM!   NO   WORK IN FASHION FOR
I'LL THINK AS I'LL ACT AS I AM!   NO   DEED IN FASHION FOR

WORK THAT BEFITTETH THE MAN   2. I'LL   WORK AS I'LL THINK AS I AM!   NO
ACTS THAT BECOMETH THE MAN   4. I'LL   ACT AS I'LL DIE AS I AM!   NO

HT AS BESEEMETH A MAN MY THOUGHT THOUGHT THAT BESEEMETH THE MAN   I'LL
   AS BETIDETH THE   MAN

FORM

WORK-SONG

We have battle hymns, war songs, anthems, and we do have some fine Negro labor-chanties. But we have no work-song of our own that is a thing of the militant work-spirit in our country in our own time.

These T-square and triangle verses, a kind of disturbing fife-and-drum corps drumming down the street—straight-line pattern—were spontaneously written early in my work life—I think I was twenty-seven—and should have preceded Book Three—WORK. They were omitted because the song then seemed, still does, to be shouting "damn." Why not? It takes an ego shouting "damn" to withstand emasculation by such imitative erudition as ours and the education in place of cultivation any true ego, upright, is sure to receive at our very best hands. So, here, to you is the reckless, militant work-song. Not as literature whatsoever, but for worse work.

Olgivanna set the lines to music and the song is now sung upon occasion in the Taliesin Fellowship by our a capella choir.

The only time these curious verses came out of hiding was long ago, when, urged by well-meaning friends, I sent them on under the title of THE DRUM to Richard Watson Gilder, editor of *The Century*. The Work-Song came back with a polite "The rhythms of the drum, Mr. Wright, can hardly be translated into Poetry."

Our very best literary measurements, especially scholastic appraisals, seem to disdain Life.

All such become a lifeless asset, or upset where cultural growth is earnestly sought or deeply enough desired.

Outside of currents or conventional tides of what constitutes Architecture, Art or Literature, who knows Poetry; the soul of it all?
. . . Listen to the drum-beat!

The quest begun by a child in his ancestors' beloved Valley, young feet woolen-warm in fresh-fallen snow; both aching arms full of the structure-pattern of a multitude of lives already given, "useless" dried weeds, the early search for FORM, here continues. Self-seeking search? Yes, of course, with what freedom I could win—or take.

Well ... after the first four books FAMILY—FELLOWSHIP—WORK—FREEDOM are done, like the "Freshman at the Party" I now look back. Ten years later, wistful now as ever, I imagine what I might have truly said to go deeper and come off with more Spirit. Perhaps even make a better book for you to read. I realize with some chagrin—but not ashamed—that I have written no autobiography at all. What I have set down is more an anti-Broadway Creed. I do not regret the "anti" nor the "Creed" because both are needed badly and *An Autobiography* has been with me an act of faith in what lies deeper than any Creed. Every word I have written is fact—at least truth—and Truth as I see it. But facts no more make Truth than boards, bricks and mortar make Architecture. Only Imagination using facts honestly as mere structural material can so imbue fact with Spirit as to make truth—another life, the life of Man—take fresh inspiring Form. The work of Art.

So this fifth book is the continued search for FORM—Truth.

THE CHARACTER OF FORM AS NATURAL

Among so many disheartening discoveries stands the all-heartening truth (something at least to "tie to") that true FORM, like true poetry, is always organic in character, is really nature-pattern; inspiring. In nature-abstraction, therefore, lies the difficulty as well as the simple centerline of the honest ego's search for—truth of—integral FORM. And since all FORM is a matter of structure, it must be a matter of government—discipline—as well as a creative matter of architecture; a matter of the framework of a free society—the constitution of an amazing new civilization.

Proved by my own experience, I too can say with Lieber Meister that "every problem carries within itself its own solution," a solution to be reached only by the intense inner concentration of a sincere devotion to Truth. I can say this out of a lively personal adventure in realizations that give true scheme, scheme line and color to all life, and, so far as Architecture goes, life to what otherwise would remain mere unrelated fact. Dust, even if stardust. But I must confess that the exception that proves the rule is to me most important.

As a matter of fact, any good architect by nature is a physicist, and as a matter of reality, he must be a philosopher and a physician. So the new spiritual physiognomy of old-world philosophy is still at work on the pages of this haunted fifth book of *An Autobiography*. Here you find outlines of a true social pattern hidden by the realisms which may enrich but which also obscure Reality.

What we are seeking together must be found between the lines?

An Oklahoma editor claiming to be a cousin of mine (great printer but no great editor) once blazed at me in disgust and anger, "Hell, Frank, if you don't like the system on which this country's run, why don't you get out of it? Go somewhere else! Goddammit."

"Not to please you, Richard, nor any of our relatives," said I. "If I see something wrong with my country, am I going to stay right here doing my damnedest to set upside-down right-side up? I am."

Now, as a matter of course, to get my own conscience or yours on straight, or for *you* to get yours or mine to work, we may trouble each other's cousins, sisters and our aunts—annoy a good many people, such as people are. And as we are. But if to you and to me Democracy really means anything at all it must mean just that kind of trouble with cousins and even our sisters: our uncles and our aunts. Not to mention our own parents and especially our dearest friends. Trouble thrown in, maybe, with the Police: as things are. But, millions of consciences like yours and mine, likewise uneasy, struggling against what seems unnecessarily stupid, are essential to the life of any honest country wherein Democracy may be, after all, only that "state of unhappy consciousness" Hegel said it was.

But no, Dick. I have a better right to stay right here dissatisfied out loud than you have to stay down there in Oklahoma satisfied out louder. Just because you happen to own a newspaper or something, Richard, doesn't qualify you.

If this country of ours (it *is* one of God's many good countries, either won—self-baptized in their own name by their own blood—inherited, stolen or bought, isn't it?) were incurably lame, halt or blind, the Cousin Richards of these States might be all right. To criticize would then be only cruel. But I don't think this country is *incurably* lame, halt or blind. At least, the people in it are not while I belong here and love belonging as well as I do: loving the country not so much for what it is—no, but more for what it meant to be and for what a good many of us still hope it is going to be. I know, with good enough reason, there are many loving it just the way I love it: a love that means eventually, if not soon, true democratic FORM not only for our buildings, but for the lives we live in them, and even the cultivation of the ground on which they stand. That means organism.

Meantime, in any sound—that is to say *honest*—Democracy, Peace or War, true discretion, from now forward, consists in the resolve to speak out, *act* the living Truth where it concerns us *as we understand it* and squarely face the consequences of so acting and speaking, gentle Richard or Richard ungentle. If we do make general practice of such wise honesty, then sure I am that there are enough of us sufficiently developed to find the social, economic (and therefore the organic—*truly architectural*) FORM normal to the Declaration of Independence and the culture of Freedom we profess. That Freedom now is the new Integrity not alone in this Nation but in all the world. We will call it, hereinafter, the new Reality. Now all is search for true FORM.

Are we in great danger of entirely running out of ideas concerning the very simple but startling idea of the freedom we once professed, just because we who ran away from the "old country" and came over here for safety are scared out of our native wits, waving not our own flag but an empty "ism"?

Patriotism—your specialty, my cousin, has been written down as the last refuge of the scoundrel.

I admit that my people the Lloyd-Joneses were all handsome folk. But my mother and my maiden aunts, Aunt Nell and Aunt Jane, and my Uncle James were, I think, handsomest of the ten children of Grandfather and Grandmother—Lloyd-Jones. The five brothers, shaggy-maned, bearded, patriarchal, were handsome. Four of the five: James, Enos, John and Jenkin, happening into Madison one fine day were driving along in an open rig on University Avenue, where flocks of students come and go (two of the uncles were University regents), when someone shouted from the sidewalk—"Where are the other eight?" They were all like that.

The neighboring uncles of the Valley all called their Lloyd-Jones teacher-sisters "the girls" and their school boys and girls all called them Aunt Nell and Aunt Jenny. The two sisters were disciples of John Dewey by way of Francis Parker under whom the sisters once taught school. They were nearing seventy. Their school becoming harder than ever for them to manage and support. Added to the naturally unprofitable nature of their enterprise, the unfortunate, tragic death of their brother James (my favorite uncle) had thrown them into acute financial distress. Bankruptcy threatened the Hillside Home School where for twenty-seven years "the Aunts" had mothered some forty to sixty boys and girls aged seven to seventeen—preparing them for college by keeping a staff of thirteen teachers in residence besides themselves. They had done a pioneer work in home-school co-education. The Hillside

Home School was perhaps the first—certainly one of the first—co-educational home schools in our country: probably in the world. Mary Ellen Chase has drawn their portraits with a sympathetic hand in her book *The Goodly Fellowship*.

Meantime "the Aunts" tried manager after manager. Some of the managers were their own nephews or nieces. Some they brought in from educational enterprises in the cities. But none were ever able to do very much, and there were good reasons. My beloved Aunts themselves were those good reasons—they refused to grow old. Their plant had grown old though, and they were deeply in debt without realizing how deep or just why. But, in fact, they were themselves as mentally alert and potent was ever. They simply could not reconcile themselves to be directed by others or see any of their prerogatives go into untried, probably less competent, hands. I myself never thought of them as "old." They really had no age. These two maiden sisters of five brothers and three sisters, aunts of some forty nephews and nieces, born in the Valley, were really foster-mothers of hundreds of other women's children. But their very strength became their weakness. Their famous brother Jenkin, great Chicago preacher, had been a strength to them and he tried to help them now. It was the same with them even where he was concerned. They would take neither domination nor advice, and while he could have found money for them if control went with the money, he could not get control himself nor deliver control. So they got no financial aid at this crucial time. Some blamed me for this.

As it was with Uncle Jenkin Lloyd-Jones, so it was with their own alumni who might have been expected to come to their assistance. I don't know why some of them didn't come to the rescue of their faithful old teacher-mothers. But none did come. I believe a few thousand dollars did come in from several such sources. But they needed some fifty thousand. Finally things at the School came to such a pass that Aunt Nell quite lost her mind with worry. She would wander up and down the room wherever she might happen to be, talking to herself, wringing her hands—moaning. Aunt Jane, still quick and sympathetic, would try to comfort her when these fits of despair darkened her mind. Sister Anna (my mother)—a great help to them always—was especially helpful now. There seemed no way out; no one else to help. So I did. To "pay up" and give them a little rest—rest they so much needed but which no one, least of all myself, believed they knew how to take. They wanted to turn everything over to me, asking me to promise that their work would continue. I promised to continue it in my own way, someday.

411

That promise comforted them and, borrowing forty thousand dollars, I paid their debts.

They had put their best into the advanced ideas of co-education on liberal principles which they now represented. I had found money for them before when the 1902 buildings were built. One of my clients, Mrs. Susan Lawrence Dana, gave them the little Art and Science buildings, next the School building and full equipment. Complete. She loaned the Aunts twenty-seven thousand dollars more to help complete the main School building. Another client, Charles E. Roberts, gave nineteen thousand dollars to help the subsequent pinch. I think there were other helping hands at that time but I don't know whose.

This, partly, was why they had turned to me now when all else had failed. Though loved no one else helped—probably because they thought I would.

About the time the new buildings were built—1902—there was some family feeling (and saying) that they would ruin the Aunts. But all the Aunts ever put into them from first to last was less than a third their cost plus the considerable work volunteered by myself and the Jones family. The new buildings were their pride and joy—probably the greatest they had known.

I did think of finding some schoolmaster to carry on but could not imagine anyone in their place. There could be no one they could bear to see in that capacity nor could I.

Neither Aunt long survived after giving up active participation in the life of their own beloved School.

Aunt Jane, gallant fiery disposition hers—in contrast to the cool, more managerial disposition of Aunt Nell—about this time had not been so very well. I think she suffered the loss of the School most, for "loss" they both regarded it when only a promise took the place of the reality they had both so loved. Occasionally, when weather permitted, Aunt Jane liked to go back to sleep in her own room over the hill at the School. She was found there, dead, one morning when we all least expected anything of the kind.

Aunt Nell contracted smallpox while young. Her hair turned snow-white when she was twenty-six, but her health, subsequently, had always been good—her outdoor activity kept it so. She now lingered along for another year or two, finally losing control of the fine clear mind she had, always—becoming, because of her indomitable will which had had its way, not at all easy to manage. But finally, she too found release. She died in the boys' cottage of the School where the

412

Aunts had mothered seven small boys aged seven to nine. There was where she preferred to be and refused to be taken anywhere else.

Now a strange thing concerning their "property"—property quite generally believed to be the plant of the Hillside Home School. It appeared that the individualities expressed by the glowing personalities of Aunt Nell and Aunt Jane had been pretty much all there was of the Hillside Home School except the idealistic buildings I had built for them, 1902–3, into which went some of the enthusiasm and faith they had put into their own work. The physical side of their work was otherwise slight. The several other buildings were so ugly as to be worthless and only waiting to be torn down. Out of an old metal bedstead and clean fresh bedclothes, a print on the wall, a piece of rag carpet, an improvised stand, a wash-bowl and a nicked pitcher skillfully combined with a vase of flowers and a bowl of fruit, the lovely view through the windows and the living presence of the Lloyd-Jones Sisters, a miracle to go with the shining waxed boards of the floor had come to pass.

Now with Aunt Nell and Aunt Jane gone, their "property" vanished into the surrounding hills—all except their ancestral ground and the buildings standing upon it to which their spirit had given better than ordinary concrete form. But even these buildings, now being ruined, were suited only to their own school work and, placed where they were, of no great value unless they could be used as farm buildings, which they could not be. The old octagonal barn in bad repair had been badly placed, as had the dormitory and servants' building—all carpenter-built buildings (no design) and were in such a state of disrepair that, all things considered, it seemed best to tear them down, as they spoiled the buildings that did express their spirit. All of the active Hillside Home School "plant" other than the 140 acres of farm land (worth about eighty dollars an acre without buildings) had little or no value. There were almost no Lloyd-Jones Sisters "assets" so called. Were all gathered into a heap they would hardly bring one thousand dollars.

What a lesson in the enlivening, characterizing, saving power of human individuality the old Hillside Home School! The only thing in which faith should ever be placed, the only faithful human "asset." Things grow old to vanish like that? But such individuality as theirs—once achieved—perhaps by way of the use of "things"—is beyond reach of age. Or, better to say is developed and strengthened by age—until age itself should bring the most desirable of all qualifications to life.

These great women possessed such individuality and to such a degree that where they were, there was consequential order out of insignificance—the usefulness of even the inferior object, atmosphere, warmth and light out of little or nothing material.

413

Hillside Home School! High-hearted in service of a great ideal—such service as seldom seen—became toward the end of its life a kind of eleemosynary institution which "the Aunts" were supporting. Parents bereaved or who had separated would send their children to the Aunts. The Aunts would become attached to the children. Dues paid for a little while, then as various disasters would befall the parents, payments would cease but the Aunts would keep the children on and on. This in so many various forms was the story until at the end the too many teachers were unpaid and faithful old employees had not asked for pay in years; uncollectible bills had mounted to the impossible. A ledger of accounts which came along with other "assets" after their death shows bills due and receivable of some forty thousand dollars. Not one cent collectible.

POST-MORTEM

For years (and even now) after the Aunts passed on (typical experience)—some old farmer I did not know would step out into the road ahead of me and say, "Frank, I never ast no pay for the forty cords o' wood I hauled 'the girls' back there Febuary nineteen-fifteen."

"Well," I would say, "why didn't you ask, and why have you said nothing about it to them nor to me until now?"

"Oh," he would say, "I knowed they was hard up then and I didn't need the money bad. But it's differ'nt now. Yes, *sir*, it's differ'nt."

Trying to read the man, I said, "But your bill is outlawed now."

"Oh, sure," he'd say. "Outlawed sure, but you're their nephew, Frank. You're willin' to pay me *somethin'* on the old account, ain't ye?"

"Of course," I'd say, "how much do you say?"

"Oh, pay me half—sixty dollars and I'll call her square."

"But I haven't got sixty dollars right now."

"Oh . . . ain't ye?" he would say. "All right then. I'll jest as soon come 'round sometime when I'm down thet a way and pick it up. I knowed you wouldn't let your old Aunts down, Frank," said he.

And he would get the money when I got it. Such bills were outlawed, of course, but, worse, some were undoubtedly false. I used my own judgment. Grew to be less and less easy to convince. Paid some, told the others to go. What else to do?

PERSPECTIVE

To anyone looking back over the life and work of these two dear great maiden-aunts of mine, their work, of great consequence to us all, is still living. I see it so cruelly set and hard beset by the circumstances of their provincial environment, which is of course still our own environment at Taliesin. Age became disqualification when their great life-work was endangered. They were wasted as though animals in a market. Their wisdom and rich experience went for naught in their circumstances. Just as in the provinces the age of a horse determines his value, or a cow her desirability, the chickens their egg-laying and edibility, so the deadly farm provincial American mind carries this over to human life. Instead of growing old gracefully, with the distinction and genuine honor we see it attaining in wiser civilizations (the Oriental, for instance), if we look about us we will see all that finer quality of living being thrown away. Cancelled by this characteristic animalistic view of age. Age driven to conceal its venerability under devices of the cosmetician—the plastic surgeon—devices of dress. Age tries so pitiably hard to "look" young because it *is* young and in most precious ways stronger than ever. But when traces of use are regarded as mere wear and tear, they do become ugly indeed. A "lived in" face should be no disqualification either in the countryside or on hard pavements of urban centers. But, owing to the way life is spent thereafter, the young have their fling and they are flung, flung upon the scrap-heap of the Old, while their innate youth persists and the best time of life still ahead: instead of the fruiting of the tree comes dreary waste. Our people are doing this thing to themselves, a damning count against all Western Civilization, especially ours.

If Age brings no great reward to itself and others in a society, something is radically wrong with the individual or the society. Perhaps both. I remember well a great woman friend of my mother—Mrs. Lydia Avery Coonley-Ward, herself an example of what I heard her say—"If a woman is not attractive at twenty it isn't her fault, but if she isn't at fifty, it certainly is."

A PROMISE

I have made many promises in my life, always intending to keep them. I believe I never made one I didn't intend to keep. But my corner of hell—all the hell there is right now—is paved with those promises that turned out to be only intentions. Time and circumstances destroy promises as distance dims one's view. But one promise would not let me go.

Love for my Mother and my Aunts, admiration for their grand gray heads and dignity of their beautiful personalities which age had brought them were now bound up in that promise as though they lived on *in* the promise I had made to see their educational work go on at beloved Hillside, site of their own pioneer homestead. That filial promise would keep along with me wherever I went. If I settled down, it settled down with me. In course of time it became a subjective urge as well as objective. If I lived I was sure to keep the promise whether I wanted to or not. I became an "Instrument of Fate."

Whatever reason might dictate I would keep that promise in good time. Since I was what I was, I would keep it in my own way. I had no idea in what way; procrastinating as always. This time for years. I had faith in myself or whatever it is that keeps the promises we make.

I believe now, *from within,* that whatever I deeply enough desired I should have, if and because, it first had me.

No longer necessary to bend my mind in that direction. Something had taken root there that would simply turn circumstances and events in that direction in good time. Deeply enough desired it would be there.

ANNO DOMINI 1929

This now historic, economic, nationwide failure of the attempt by Production to control Consumption, termed a "depression," is here. Economic breakdown is so complete at this time that no workman's hammer is ringing in our great state of Wisconsin. Native workmen of my own countryside, laborers, carpenters and masons of Iowa County as in the next Dane County and the next Sauk County are all but starving, many at the poor farm, while I watch the shingle roofs of the 1902–3 Hillside Home School buildings falling in for lack of some labor such as theirs. All of them—too—(laborers included) idle—rotting away. Roof water is coming in on most of the fine interiors. Waxed sand-finish walls of the rooms are, like some provincial privy, completely scribbled over with proper names of passing vandals, desecrated by this ever devastating passerby whose better name is Curiosity. Should what is still left of these buildings I so proudly built in 1902 for those gallant pioneers, Aunts Nell and Jane, go through one more winter in this agonizing condition, then no use attempting to repair them. The matchless flesh-colored, sand-stone walls built under my direction by twinkling-eyed, bewhiskered Timothy, the old Welsh stone-mason ("and whatever-r-r") would be left standing alone. There was no money even to pay long outstanding money-debts caused by a tragic worm's-eye view of society. There was now hardly carfare to get to the big city in

416

order to find work there, should there be any work to do. Where might work come from? None could say. Except as we could raise it ourselves, there was no food. My friends were losing what money they had or had already lost it. How did I know? They knew how they knew I knew!

The incorporation of Frank Lloyd Wright Architect has proved a failure.

No architect in these United States of America, if he has no ground of his own and if he cannot go to work on some farm, has anything to do now unless he is "related" to someone who happens to be sitting pretty, and (because the more cautious were hit hardest) sitting pretty meant, merely, lucky. Barely subsisting from day to day, the architects in our great country that had tried so hard to control Consumption by Production were still in "pursuit of happiness" but, living on "savings" or money bought by insurance, got by marriage, or inheritance. Or more than likely, got by borrowing something somehow from someone while Production was impatiently waiting to be consumed or trying to force Consumption. Not only my own "earnings" (merely what "they" call them) are gone now but any credit I may ever have had gone because of them. But we were only sharing now in all this the fate of the far more provident: mortgages, etc. Judgments, private chagrin, humiliation private and public, disgrace—all nation-wide—pursue not only us but the Nation. Blackmail and slander of all kinds accumulate in the foreground of our glum national picture.

A motley horde of outstretched hands comes frequently to Taliesin's door there in the beautiful Valley! Comes knocking in all too familiar guises: legal "repossessions," press interviews, duns, more repossessions, duns, more threats. Private blackmail, private and public "adverse examinations" by shyster lawyers, long-distance telephone duns. Duns by friends, duns by relatives, duns by employees. All desperate. No money—and at last, sabotage. Threats: some more threats, finally assassination. These all stand outside our door of Taliesin, lit by sinister flares of the ulterior motive. Casual self-righteous "saviors" heap the sordid measure of tragic defeat to running over with well-meant (and too well-known) advice.

Worse than all, like Festus Jones, I myself, not having much conscience anyway, find what little I have is pretty guilty!

I know my trouble, too, is that I yearn to be on good terms with myself and have never yet succeeded in getting rid of this deep-seated, inherited, ancestral plague—this tragic desire to stand well with my kind—to win the esteem and affection of my fellows. And to heap the cup, I have always been ready and willing—still am—to do without the Necessaries of Life if only I may have the Luxuries. This has seemed the only way to do "the things that are more excellent" while the Criterion—Money—secretly calls the turn for good and bad alike. The capitalist System now in ruins.

FLIGHT OF THE SOUL

Many times before, in desperate circumstances (perhaps because of them) came an IDEA. I, too, can get a bad idea—but not this time. The now subjective promise came to its object as the idea? No buildings to build at the harrowing moment but, capitalizing thirty-five years of past experience, why not build the builders of buildings against the time when buildings might again be built? Using what we had to work with, Olgivanna and I put our heads together as our hearts were.

Congenital Education, dormant family influence, now again up and out—at last! To make a promise good? Yes, and supply a lacking feature in Architecture.

Numbers of young men were always coming from around the world to work with me at Taliesin. Several at Taliesin now. After talking the "idea" over, pro and con, we, a son of Wisconsin Welsh pioneers and a daughter of Montenegrin dignitaries, aimed to be educators, composed and sent out during the summer of 1932 the following circular letter to a small list of friends and universities. Here is that circular letter:

AN EXTENSION OF THE WORK IN ARCHITECTURE AT
TALIESIN TO INCLUDE APPRENTICES IN RESIDENCE

Frank Lloyd Wright together with a number of competent assistants in residence at Taliesin will there lead the work of a new Fellowship of Apprentices to be now established in Architecture.

Three resident associates: a sculptor, a painter and a musician, eventually chosen for the work to be done, are contemplated. An inner-group of seven honor-apprentices having the status of senior apprentices or university professors and three technical advisors trained in industry will also assist.

Leaders in thought, artists and philosophers from many countries may come to occasionally share for a time in our activities, perhaps temporarily reside.

We believe that a rational attempt to integrate Art and Industry should coordinate both with the everyday life we live here in America. Any such rational attempt must be *essential architecture* growing up by social, industrial, and economic processes natural to our way of life—learning by doing.

Not only must this framework and background of future Democracy be developed as itself a kind of organic architecture, but the very qualities most basic and worthwhile in Philosophy, Sculpture, Painting, Music and the Industrial Crafts are also fundamentally Architecture. Principles underlying life and

418

the arts are the same. So it is the Architecture of Life itself that must be the fundamental and therefore first concern of any true culture anywhere if the world is to be made safe for Science. A way of Life.

No alliance between "Art" and Commercial Industry is ever enough because no mere "alliance," however useful, can be Creative. Appropriate forms must be developed from within and they must be forms having worthwhile relation to our actual industry. Necessary original work will be done best where the workers will have not only spontaneous recourse to modern shop and working conditions but have at the same time, as workers, benefit of inspirational leadership and the fellowship of genuinely creative architects. Constant working contacts with the nature of structure and materials, the ground, and of nature-growth itself are the only reliable texts to be used in this connection. Only as these are actual forms of daily experience directly related to the inspirations of leadership in daily life and work are they the texts we must now use to begin again at the beginning to raise architects.

What little creative impulse survives in the confusion of this machine age might thus have some chance to live uncontaminated by old human expressions already dead or dying. The Big City is no longer a place for more than the exterior applications of some cliché or sterile formula, where life is concerned. Therefore the TALIESIN FELLOWSHIP chooses to live and work in the country. The FELLOWSHIP establishment is located on a farm forty miles west of Madison, on State Highway 23 in beautiful Southern Wisconsin. Near the Wisconsin River, four miles from the nearest village.

THE WORK IN ARCHITECTURE first done at Oak Park and in Chicago, later at Taliesin, has proved itself during the past thirty years: gone far enough in the world-current of contemporary change so that good work may be done in full cooperation with our more advanced producers and manufacturers: those who sincerely desire to improve the nature of their product. American industry need no longer depend for artistic excellence upon the copying of imitations nor need ever do so again if our country will learn to utilize resources such as our resources at Taliesin.

As the TALIESIN FELLOWSHIP therefore, we now propose to extend apprenticeship from the several draughtsmen to whom it has been limited now to include seventy* apprentices working as described under leadership.

Each apprentice will work not only under the inspiration of direct architectural leadership, toward machine-craft art in this machine age. But all will work together in a common daily effort to create new forms needed by machine work and modern processes if we are to have any culture of our own worth having. A number (a hundred or more) of such young workers in Architecture have already come to Taliesin from various parts of the world. Others may now be immersed in the many-sided activities of a growing Fellowship of apprentices, all engaged in actual projects. Activities, we hope, will be gradually extended to include collateral Arts. Living in direct personal contact with the construction of modern concepts and with the currents of thought in the world now demanding new Form, we believe young architects, artists and craftsmen may here find

* Note: *changed to twenty-three.*

means to build up spiritual force and technique that will guarantee a life work in *the essential architecture of all art* and eventually be enabled to practice them as the natural fulfillment of an experience and training belonging—by doing—peculiarly to our own time and country.

SO WE BEGIN this working Fellowship as a kind of daily work-life, as actual experience. Apprentices work on buildings or in crafts which have a free individual basis: direct *work-experience* made healthy and fruitful by seeing Idea as work and work as Idea take effect, actually, in the hand of the young apprentice under the inspiration of competent leadership.

OUR HOME LIFE SIMPLE. Meals in common. Fixed hours for work, recreation and sleep. Each worker will have his or her room for study and rest. Suitable toilet accomodations will be made convenient to rooms. Entertainment too will be a feature of our life at work. Plays, music evenings; cinema and conferences to which musicians, literary men, artists, and scientists will sometimes be invited and (occasionally) the public. The beautiful region itself is never failing source of inspiration and recreation for all concerned. Daily life will be planned to benefit by its beauty as well as its comfort.

Fellowship work in manifold branches of building will come directly under the influence of organic philosophy: an organic architecture for organic life. At Taliesin this life will be lived with such sense of the Future as may belong to the present.

Actual study of Architecture *as a kind of practice by experience* will in this broad sense be taken into detailed studies of building design and principles of construction. Eventually biology, typography, ceramics, woodcraft, and textiles will be taken into consideration. These practical studies go hand in hand with characteristic model-making and soon will go on to practical experiments in the crafts made by such apprentices as go into the workshops which we hope to build.

Apprenticeship not *Scholarship* is to be the actual condition and should be the attitude of mind of members of the Fellowship. Fair division of labor required in maintaining all branches of work will fall to the share of each member, each serving the other. Especial predilections, even idiosyncrasies, although respected, will not be encouraged. There will be no age limit for apprentices but the qualifications of each will be decided finally by Mr. Wright after a three-month's trial in Fellowship work. The right to reject any applicant at any time is reserved—either before or after being formally received into the Fellowship. The Fellowship is not on trial. The apprentice is.

TALIESIN THUS AIMS to develop a well-correlated human being: since correlation between hand and the mind's eye in action is most lacking in modern education.

A Democratic establishment a primary requirement: each member will be asked to engage in all the daily work of necessary Fellowship maintenance.

LABORATORIES AND MACHINE SHOPS are not yet built but, eventually, will be built next to the daughting room.

Studios and galleries already built or being built. The first experimental units ready are those of architectural construction and design, the philosophy of architecture, typographical design, the printing of a publication *TALIESIN—*

organ of the Fellowship; also molding and casting adapted to modern systems of construction in glass, concrete and metal. Woodworking by modern machinery. A collateral study of philosophy and the practice of sculpture, painting, drama and rhythm. These units are to be followed by actual glass-making, pottery, weaving, modern reproduction processes in any form we may be able to establish. We believe that business men in industry will find it worthwhile to cooperate with us in setting up these crafts. Experimental building construction will be continually going on.

A personal testimonial, only, will be given each worker at the end of his or her apprenticeship. Each will have a holiday of six weeks each year, arranged as the work may permit.

THE FELLOWSHIP IS NOT YET THE "FOUNDATION" IT HOPES TO BE but is an independent cultural enterprise and the sustaining revenue of the Fellowship for the next years must come mainly from apprenceship fees and maintenance work, four hours each day, of the apprentices. Added to this may be Architect's fees, compensation from industries for services rendered or to be rendered; the sale of complete art objects; a publication to be printed by the Fellowship and the possible but not probable contribution of money or equipment from "Friends of the Fellowship," a group organized among those who believe in our work and are able and willing to add scope to our usefulness.

Undoubtedly, prosperity of the Fellowship must depend upon the *quality* of its membership but more upon the *spirit* of cooperation felt and practiced by the members and myself in the work we do. Only the apprentices themselves can make the apprenticeship useful to a master or a master make apprenticeship valuable to them. Therefore no apprentice will be accepted without trial: the right to terminate any Fellowship without notice, reserved.

EACH WILL BE REQUIRED TO PAY THE FIXED FEE for initiation—as stated on the application blank herewith. As a necessary feature of their training, each will be required to contribute his or her share of work each day on the grounds, new buildings or the farm, for the privilege of participation in the experimental work going on there and in shops, and such production of art objects as practical exemplars for industry and building as may be for exhibition and sale. An account will also be kept of the money had from such sales. At the end of each year a fair dividend will be paid to each member which may eventually reduce or abolish the tuition fee.*

FARM AND GARDENS will be so managed to employ the help of the apprenticeship that a portion of the living of members may come from their own labor on the ground, thus enabling apprentice fees to remain as low as possible.

No sooner was this ambitious scheme proposed than we abandoned it. After sending out the circular we decided we would do better to stick to what we already had than to go too far institutional or "educational." I had certain qualifications; Olgivanna had others to add to mine. So we

* Note: The original fee was six hundred and fifty dollars for a full year, but, next year, for cause, changed to eleven hundred dollars.

put our heads, as well as our hearts, together, simplified it all to come within our immediate capacities, so we thought, and wisely cut down possible membership to twenty-three. But the foregoing text—text by no means simple enough—was nevertheless sent out. It had the effect we hoped for and intended. Twenty-three young men and women brought twenty-three times six hundred and fifty dollars—one year each—to work it out at Taliesin. And a fair cross-section of Young America assembled there October 1, 1932, eager to go to work—ill-prepared for anything except academic study of some sort. Least of all for the Freedom Taliesin had to offer.

TO THE ENEMY—THE CLICHÉ

Since we had now started something, supplementing the foregoing statement, the following letter replying to a *Manifesto* issued at that time by the Beaux Arts of the United States was directed to the heads of the "Beaux Arts" schools. The letter was mailed with a request to post the letter where students might see it, should the institution be so inclined. In some cases it was so posted.

The reader understands quite well by now that the servile Beaux Arts societies in these United States would be anathema to any ideal of indigenous USONIAN culture such as we proposed.

If this dull lack of indigenous culture ("pattern") in the fabric of our weaving is not wrong then should we be content with no pattern at all? Better off sterile? None will say so. As the matter stands we cannot afford to lose one single strand native or natural to our growth as a free nation or allow one fresh attempt to build it be destroyed by the old patterns of prejudice we jealously drag along. This cultural lag has completely stultified instead of inspired the to and fro of mere artifice that we call Standardization. If we do allow cultural back-drag to be our "Art" much longer, there can be no life of the Spirit left in our weaving of a civilization. We can never have inspiring culture of our own that can lift these inevitable routine standardizations above the belt, because Civilization is truly this matter of inspired and inspiring pattern in the social fabric.

Civilization is this affair of Pattern. Culture is the Architecture, Art and Religion that is its fruit.

A witty Frenchman has said of us: "The United States of America is the only nation to plunge from barbarism to degeneracy with no culture in between."

422

Here is the reply to innuendo "by circular" of the *Manifesto* of U.S.A. Beaux Arts: the Circular is on record threatening the students interested in modern architecture—if persisting in their addiction to the work of myself, of Le Corbusier and Gropius—they would be "pushed back to Classicism."

TO STUDENTS OF THE BEAUX ARTS INSTITUTE OF DESIGN: ALL DEPARTMENTS

A notice to you, taking my name in vain (together with the names of two other modern architects whom I respect, Gropius and Le Corbusier), has been sent to me.*

If this circular is proper evidence of the quality of inspiration to which your young architects are now subject this may be the time for them to help themselves. Reading between the lines of this lively circular which contains a threat, I see that the Beaux Arts establishment in America realizes that neither old practices nor the old doctrines can be made to apply longer, except by force.

But as this circular bears witness, the Beaux Arts is now ready to speak the language of the new thought in architecture. Must then the Beaux Arts leadership deny or betray modern architects before it can "come over" to modern architecture as gracefully as it thinks becoming to its dignity? Or else, say (it does so in this circular) it won't come over to modern architecture at all and "all the students will be pushed back to classicism"?

Are you, as students, reliably informed concerning what constitutes modern architecture? You are officially told that "it is not going to become a style based upon Wright, Gropius and Le Corbusier."

It *is* true that much that passes for modern architecture is not organic because it is already contaminated by American Beaux Arts standards of imitation. To unfortunate young architects so contaminated I am a friendly enemy. But architecture as "modern" has a future only because these modern architects, whatever their faults (from whom I am sorry to say the circular in question derives only language), are what they are, and because they have done what they have done.

Yet it is because of their work that the Beaux Arts is now ready to modify its programme or "push you all back into classicism"!

Admit that the principles and practice of *organic* architecture are yet insufficiently familiar to some of these modern architects against whom you are officially warned. But they will be the principles you will be moved by and that you will master if you do not betray your country to the "Beaux Arts" as it will betray you now and everywhere if it can do so by assuming a virtue it cannot have. Unfortunately the Beaux Arts training in architecture has been all the Academic training Young America has had a chance to get.

But today no man able to think for himself believes in such pseudo "training." No training like it can aid any young man to grow into a creative architect.

Note: See Notice to Students and Correspondents—Architectural Department—School Year 1931–32, April 20, 1932.

These very principles of an organic architecture (modern architecture) which the Beaux Arts "views with alarm" and from which it derives the unfamiliar language it tries to use in this circular—"the meaning of materials," etc., etc., would blow their method and practice away were they or their students able to grasp the real meaning of that language.

When "in all history" has "the meaning of materials" or anything deeper than fine composition been found in these academic circles until the men whose work you are now officially told "modern architecture is not going to resemble" came along? The simplest knowledge of simples, "the meaning of materials," my thesis in particular, would utterly destroy these native "Beaux Arts" establishments. It has already gone far toward doing so because of utter ignorance in the practice of the very nature of materials and the uses of modern methods and that misunderstanding of modern architecture which is a sublime American Beaux Arts characteristic! "Composition?" *That* only is the shrine of all Beaux Arts training.

Well, "Composition" is dead! We now integrate.

The silhouette of masonry mass over steel only lives as a false gesture. But organic architecture, inspiration creative, still lives as the Magna Charta of our Liberties. Yet you are told your work must not resemble this organic architecture!

So it is a natural inevitable that hypocrisy should flower in the realm of architecture as result of this system of scholastic imitation not only fostered, but now *featured* by the institution calling itself the "American Beaux Arts"! The result must be—no fruit. Nothing creative. No integrity.

But, should fault be found with an ostrich because it persists in sticking its head in the sand or because no ostrich is a lion? Where, I ask you, young man in architecture—are you going to learn the truth that "intelligent mass," "consideration of the three-dimensional block of the building" are not *fundamentals:* learn that all are properties of good design no longer applying, fundamentally, to truth in architecture? These effects are not principles but qualities—more *by-products* of good design than good design. Cart before the horse is no longer "fundamental."

So if you *are* to be "pushed back to Classicism" (the threat contained by circular) therefore condemned to these old reactions referred to falsely as "the fundamentals of good design," it is because apparently principles make modern architecture objectionable to the Beaux Arts; make it so chiefly because it has become a threat to Beaux Arts self-preservation. The accompanying plan explains what I mean by fresh opportunity. Taliesin has already established a living, worldwide Tradition and has good reason to know that Youth is everywhere hungry for this New Reality. Everywhere Youth is rocking an old academic craft no longer seaworthy. Even in the dock for repairs, the "classic" of "American Beaux Arts" can no longer be made safe for sincere youth. Nothing modern architecture has to give the sincere student can reach him by way of superficial eclecticism as now captains and sails that clumsy old caravel.

The Beaux Arts, however reformed, cannot afford to forget that it must never learn.

Taliesin, January, 1932.

424

Training for the Architecture of Democracy will always be beginning at the beginning with the young or else breaking through all training with its naturals in training to Nature's principles: the source of inspiration.

The Taliesin hat thus, without equivocation, "in the ring," some twenty-three young men and women responded. Although Taliesin itself rambles over a good many acres of hillside and valley, we had to makeshift to house the twenty-three—even temporarily. We could manage to feed them with outside hired help. But we had to go to work *with* them and forty outside workmen to get them all becomingly sheltered, bedded down and provided with adequate places to be planned, in which to work together as promised. I felt in duty bound to use what money they paid (in usual installments, of course) for that purpose only. And this use, notwithstanding the circumstances of importunate debt—debt well armed, as always, with lawyers, advance agents of bolted doors and barred windows, or even worse, the still small voice of Conscience that is my misfortune—steadily carried on. I suspect numbers of our young people borrowed money to come to Taliesin.

Dankmar Adler once said to me that he got his start in life because he owed money to the right people. He borrowed money to pay for his education as an architect; being unable at the time to pay it back to the people who loaned it to him (he said), they felt that the only way to ever get it back was to give him a job—a building to build. So he got his first jobs. I pass this along (in confidence) to posterity for what it may be worth to the young man in Architecture.

As the plan for the Taliesin Fellowship unfolded itself, I had hoped that apprentices—like the fingers on my hands—would increase not only my own interest and enthusiasm for my work as an architect, but would also widen my capacity to apply it in the field in their interest.

The first came true. But the second, as yet, is temporarily frustrated hope. We somewhat overshot the mark. But I have not yet given up hope. We are steadily improving, and support by creative work is increasing.

We had designed a heading (one, Hillside roofs in snow; one, Taliesin roofs in snow) and started a weekly column beneath it, one in Editor Evjue's Madison paper *The Capital Times,* one in the *State Journal.* The articles, beginning 1932 and signed by the apprentices, and sometimes by me, ran for several years. Although apprentices themselves usually wrote the articles (architects, I thought, had need to be especially articulate), occasionally Olgivanna and I took hand. Here follows one of mine. The articles, many of them, are hard to come by now.

425

WHAT IS THE MATTER WITH HUMAN NATURE?

A young apprentice for a year—now an architect, young friend of mine—writes concerning the Taliesin Fellowship: "Your idea is good and your work should succeed, but you are asking too much of Human Nature. I wish you had attempted something in which you had a greater chance of success."

Alden Dow

To my solicitous young friend:

I admit Taliesin *is* preaching an unpopular gospel: preaching, by practice, the gospel of Work, and Work has been pretty well knocked out of American youth by way of inflated "Education." It is going to be no easy matter as I can see, to put the joy back into work that alone can make work creative and lift it above drudgery by substituting Culture for "education."

There have already been many youths here at Taliesin who applied themselves to a college curriculum four to six years and had come out with the usual "degree." Some of them honor men. They could sufficiently concentrate to arrive at that. But they know, as I do, that this is less, much less, than half the right thing in creative Art.

In Architecture "less than half" means that most college-grown men today are rather less then half–men. They are sometimes interesting, often informed, controversially conversationalistic, pettily egotistic, but usually creatively impotent. Skilled labor involving their physical resources is beyond them. They imagine it beneath them but, really, it is beyond them. To use tools well, especially a shovel, a hoe, or an axe requires at least as much Science and more Manhood than swinging a golf club on a golf ball correctly, rooting or kicking at a football game.

To stay with a good piece of work in the field or on a building requires more stamina than football because football is showing off and field work in building is a kind of skilled sacrifice to nothing immediate but something stored up far into the Future. The man who plants a tree knows something of this deeply satisfying aspect of work. If the Taliesin experiment in apprenticeship fails, it will fail because our modern youth have been left high and dry above the capacity to surrender to work in its rich, manifold forms. And because the individual, as educated youth, where physical nature is concerned with his head, is unable to be and continue to be a good workman—per se, as such. That is to say, where his head and hands should be together.

So I look with increasing distrust (alarm too) on the coddled, addled product parents turn adrift upon society by way of the colleges. Yes, by hundreds of thousands, these teen-agers and half-baked novitiates in the study of the universal congregate, all looking for dignity, worth and wealth outside the only source from which either can spring for them: the creative energy of their whole interior manhood, projected with enjoyment into useful creative employment in work wherein physical force must be so related to mind that none can say where the one begins and the other ends. Beauty of life in life the aim.

I have the same feeling of repulsion for the one-sided development of, say, a sedentary teacher or artist I would have for some man with enormous muscular right arm hanging from an undernourished, undeveloped body. I should consider that arm a spiritual deformity as well as a physical monstrosity because inorganic in the sense of an organic architecture. "Specialties" are usually developed at such expense to the health and soundness of the whole man or unit. They offend even more now since I have been leading youth into action by way of the plan—the axe, the saw, the plane, the hammer and the scythe, the shovel and the hoe, and the building. The stone chisel, the paint brush, as well as just cooking and washing up. The use of the T-square and triangle on the drawing board as imaginative resource—means more.

But no more mere drawing-board architects at Taliesin! Not if I can help it. Nor, can I help it, any more one-sided specialists who can't and won't take work as though their daily bread did not depend upon a modicum of sweat on the brow and joy in their own decent skill. The sedentary materialist has had his not sufficiently brief hour in Capitalism. For fifty years, at least, the academic pigeon-hole has had its fill of peripatetic young professors conditioned to materialism, and here we are as we now are, a nation of employees of some employee of an employee asking life for security! We do not know who our Employer is. Increasingly few have the heart or the brains to inquire. Of what use to know now?

What "Educated" youth is worth employing as a creative workman on his own stark merit? Lack of correlation and stamina is what is the matter with his imaginative resources. Here in work at Taliesin we are seeking to find and build up in the young lad that joy and stamina in work which will enable him to take hold of life afresh and *anywhere!* Were the world of men and things destroyed as it stands, he could take hold and make a better one in every way. If the weakness and indolent habits of sedentary American professional and college life are incurable—well then, America hasn't much chance: Taliesin can't succeed. But young men are here already *enjoying* work, enough to prove that essential manhood is still potential in the *insurgent* at least. But at Taliesin we have our Ups and Downs. Our Ins and Outs.

These several sketches as background-sets—for our stage props?—must serve to give you some idea of what the Taliesin Fellowship is all about, what we meant to meet as best we could. Also give you the attitude of the Fellowship itself at this time.

For weeks we had driven together up and down the ramifying valleys of our matchless countryside looking for lumber and other materials to work with. We needed, desperately, lumber, stone, lime and laborers of all sorts. At first, as you see in the lines (and between them), we had very little or no money at all to pay for these coveted desirables. The search lasted for years and still goes on. Finally, materials lacking—having failed to secure most of the essential materials, I got forty workmen together from the highways and neighboring small towns—laid my partnership scheme before them in the following proposition—anxious and still wondering where I could get the materials to work with—I succeeded and they did come to work. I proposed to dissipate what money the apprentices brought in by putting most of it each week into the pockets of the all but starving workmen, sheltering them in comfort, feeding them well, and paying them installments on work they did. Willingly they signed the following agreement. I suppose in the circumstances they would have signed anything. Most of them were a hungry lot and in despair.

—SPECIMEN NOTICE*

All workmen, as party of the first part, and Frank Lloyd Wright, as party of the second part representing the Taliesin Fellowship, agree to work in partnership as follows: suitable board and lodgings to be provided by the Fellowship and one-third of the wages as agreed upon in each individual contract signed by each workman will be paid in cash weekly. The balances are all to be paid when the buildings now under construction are completed—ready for occupancy and therefore increased apprenticeship fees can be obtained.

(Signed) _____

Frank Lloyd Wright

Each workman was asked to sign the following contract:

INDIVIDUAL CONTRACT†

Charles Curtis, party of the first part, and Frank Lloyd Wright, party of the second part representing the Taliesin Fellowship, hereby agree to work in partnership as follows:

Charles Curtis is to go to work as mason on the buildings as planned for the Fellowship by Frank Lloyd Wright, and work as directed by him from the date hereof until October 15th, 1932, for the sum of four dollars ($4.00) per working day—to be paid as follows: twenty-five dollars ($25.00) a month and board as work progresses. Balance due to be paid Charles Curtis October 15, 1932, by Frank Lloyd Wright out of funds of the Fellowship.

While Charles Curtis is with the Fellowship it is agreed that satisfactory board and room shall be provided by the Fellowship.

(Signed) _____   (Signed) _____

Frank Lloyd Wright   Charles Curtis

*Note: Posted on the walls of Dining Room, October 1, 1932.

†Specimen.

428

In some cases, Karl Jensen, Fellowship secretary at the time, neglected to get some of the men on the dotted line, but when they were taken in on the work they were all told and knew well enough what the terms were upon which they were working. The general notice, lettered in black and red on a white placard, was posted in the Dining Room and in the buildings where they worked.

The workmen were appreciative, grateful. So I believed. Be that as it may, I soon had forty of them for partners and put all to work saving the Hillside Home School buildings from utter ruin. Other workmen (some were continually tramping by), some were at the poor-farms learning of our setup, asked us to take them on. Some came from as far away as San Francisco and New York City. That man-power of ours was a motley of urban, rural, married, unmarried, young and old, good, bad and indifferent America: now blasted dregs of the economic system, fairly good workmen some of them.

We fixed up the old laundry building at Hillside with a wood range and managed running water, hot and cold. We made long board tables, covered them with white oil cloth, and put hard benches beside them. Fixed up the old place until it seemed inviting, homey, and began to feed our men comfortably. Workmen are captious where food is concerned, but we fed them so well that, believe it or not, they really admitted it. There was very little drinking on the premises. Some few of the men went to town for that and would come back and fight. But we could always start a backfire. In a little room near their dining room, we—now the Fellowship—set aside a dining room for ourselves. We had our noonday meal together every day (pretty well cooked farm produce), met to consider things in general, using the white plastered walls for illustrating details. Problems were plenty. Always pressing. General activity was soon gratifying and exciting. The men glad to get to work after long enforced idleness—and near starvation.

To keep them all going on in right order with proper direction was a problem we solved afresh each night about four in the morning and worked out on the drawing boards next day. During that wakeful early morning hour, which I have known ever since, I can remember creative work, an hour devoted to prospect, retrospect and perspective when all is still and I rested, and know I can turn over and rest several hours more: then things come clearest. At that time the unsolved problems seemed to work themselves out with comparatively little assistance from me.

We had man-power. About forty men—grateful to be at work with some little money in their empty pockets and a prospect of more as their work added up to completed buildings.

429

The moral?
What conclusion?

MATERIALS VERSUS CASH: LUMBER AND LIME

We were where we had to have more lumber and lime or stop work altogether. Standing around in the woods of our county were many piles of sawed oak, chiefly marketed for railroad ties. I coveted them all as I coveted gravel, sand and cement. Surrounding farmers had cut the timber on their own wooded hillsides keeping the lumber for barn-building. I tried to buy some of these lumber piles, pay part down, part on credit. But nothing doing. The hard financial going all around had made everyone, especially farmers, doubly suspicious, especially so of the spender of so much money with no visible means of support so far as they could see. For many weary patient weeks I met the same answer to all propositions and petitions. "No—we must have cash." "Cash is what we need most of anything. Pay right now, or else!" Of course they did need "cash" desperately. Cash was more than ever King now. But I finally learned that Herb Schoenman (ten children), decent neighboring farmer, had four hundred acres of virgin oak timber standing just over the ridge from Taliesin. I drove over to see Herb, offered him a fair price and terms for his four hundred acres of timber, on the stump. Herb accepted. (Yes—he was paid.) Then I found a good sawyer on the other side of the river who agreed to saw the logs at the regular price if we cut them and brought them in. I found another farmer (a good fellow out on parole for stealing his neighbor's chickens) who would cut the trees for a price and his old father and two young sons (really nice boys) would haul them in, so he said, if we would help in the logging with our cater-pillar tractor and some of our Fellowship boys.

So back to first principles: materials for us to work with were in sight!

Forthwith, we went headlong into logging. The Hillside Home School now became a logging camp. Soon, after overcoming innumerable difficulties of a time-consuming, painful but picturesque character, green-oak timber was going up into the walls and trusses of our coveted buildings. Sap still running from the boards. Green twigs still on the logs when we sawed them into boards, scantling and beams according to Henry Klumb's lumber lists. None too evenly sawed timber either. But never mind.

We had lumber. Seventy thousand or more board-feet.

It was our own.

Our boys—yes, girls too—seemed to enjoy the hard work as well as the painful though picturesque experiences. Those experiences were consequential too: in unexpected but perfectly natural ways—profitable.

We had incurred a debt of several thousand dollars besides our own labor and spent what money we had. But we now had something to build our superstructure with. Rather hard to manage green oak but we would have taken anything that could not positively crawl off the building lot. You should have seen those inexperienced boys tackle that heavy logging job! No worldly-wise, pavement-sore urbanite parents could ever believe their boys capable of such hard continuous physical punishment as their boys took and liked it! I mean the boys.

Lumber-yard lumber was still way beyond us. Prices were still, though way down, far too high for us. About double what we paid for the green oak. Lumber, like telephone and telegraph service and other "System" items, had not dropped one cent during the "depression" nor were any concessions made if headquarters knew what was going on. They were all holding the fort: which means keeping up prices. Meantime work on the buildings continued. Workmen no longer hungry nor grumbling. They were satisfied with what money we paid them. The framework was now there in the rough and they could all see the buildings coming.

AGAIN THE LEGAL EPISODE

After some months more, we ran out of lumber and into a characteristic snag. Again I went about the country, covetous—seeking another piece of timber to cut.

Finally, I located some logs just out. Young Richardson, another farmer some miles away, had dropped about twenty thousand feet of red oak to the ground and the logs were lying there on the slippery hillside to be hauled. We bought and paid for them! I borrowed that money from an apprentice, Alden Dow.

But unfortunately we were soon on our way to Arizona. The Fellowship is an outdoor-work affair. We need to be outdoors on buildings as much of the time as possible. Inasmuch as it costs thirty-five hundred dollars to heat all of Taliesin and Hillside, we went out to Phoenix, Arizona, and on into the desert to build a camp of our own to work with and work in. We called it Taliesin West for a winter resort.

Meantime Tom King, local attorney-banker, had accepted a collection item against me of several hundred dollars for a disputed account with an eastern publishing house. This house was receiver-holder of Payson (*Disappearing City*) from whom I had bought back the copyright and "remainder" of that book. I disputed the account because I had returned the "remainder" when I found the books unbound. Nevertheless the long arm of the law, learning of the logs (the "long arm"—the banker—owned the local lumberyard too), this neighboring banker-lawyer accordingly "attached" them. We, who merely bought and paid for them, first learned of the act upon our return from Arizona the following Spring when we went to haul our logs. The Law and taxes never sleep. Money is at stake. Often they make very little noise on the way to execution. Tom King, lawyer-banker (and the bank's lawyer), had posted a sign on the fence near the family chapel yard conforming to legal requirements (so he said), but a notice which none of us ever saw, nor could see because we were two thousand miles away.

This was a hard blow—unexpected—another kind of legal boot with a hard heel, an underhanded, hustling sort. But visiting the scene we found a few thousand feet the Law had left behind. (Overlooked.)

We ruefully hauled the remaining logs. But no use.

CATASTROPHE

Before we could get the logs into boards came the national CATASTROPHE! Government Relief!

Labor in the U.S.A. went on "RELIEF." No need now to work.

On account of "relief" we, the Taliesin Fellowship (in partnership with labor), had no more use for building materials for several years to come. Our labor had been "bid in" to rest—"relieved" by Government under Franklin D. Roosevelt.

I mention this entirely "legal" interference with our plans and specifications as the final blow, characteristic of the very many ultra-legal, but entirely unjust interferences from first to last, partly because, though all were desperate for "money," none could be had by labor, none at all unless by *gift*? Tedious to remember most of the circumstances to say nothing of narration. But just the same, though dashed, our work on the buildings did partly keep on for a time. We had a few good workmen left.

The buildings kept on growing up a little. Taliesin boys themselves were begging to be able to carry on—becoming capable.

But the workmen were no longer satisfied.

All had gained weight except Will Schwanke, the foreman carpenter. Will was faithful and worried.

Will Schwanke was foreman of carpenter construction, Spring Green carpenter. He was lean because he was faithful, perhaps. Will

432

was not half dominant enough though, for that tough gang. I had to step in, continually. His wife, who told Will all about himself frequently, strongly objected to us also. She kept "telling him off." Jarred him frequently, but Will stayed faithfully by us on the carpentry just as Charlie Curtis, the seventy-nine-year-old Cornish mason from Mineral Point (whose wife took it from *him*), stayed with us on the masonry.

Both staunch men stayed for the duration.

Both were fine characters. A good influence on the boys, good instruction too. Stone walls as fine (almost as fine) as Timothy's, which are the finest in the world, were nobly standing there now ready for the framing.

"I don't want you to pay me much, Mr. Wright," said Charlie. "I am a contributor to the Fellowship because I think it's a grand idea."

The boys made a lot of the old mason, while he made good masons out of a lot of them. We all liked Charlie.

John Commons, grand old man of the University of Wisconsin, came to see us discouraged, about beaten down. He declared he was all in—an old man at seventy-two he said, and well did look as though he hadn't long to last. But we all went to work on him, gathered 'round him and made much of him. I took him out to see Charlie working on a new stone fireplace in my bedroom. "John," I said, "this is Charlie Curtis. He is eighty-one years old and a grander mason than ever, if such a mason now lives."

Well, John Commons looked as though he had seen a ghost.

His jaw dropped. But the lesson went home—eighty-one!

He began to "come back" as the saying is. After a week or two with us he went home.

His friends, Governor Kohler among them and Louis Hanks, the banker, wanted to know what we had done to John.

"Oh, nothing," I said, "we just put him on good terms with himself, that's all." That was six years ago and John is still going strong down in Florida now.

Charlie Curtis was kind and tolerant to all the amateurs except one rather elaborate traveling philosopher from the Colonial belt who came hitch-hiking in, enthusiastic. All the screws needed for correlation were loose in him. But he had a polished mind and brilliant cerebration to expound. He *would* keep on expounding. I put him on as helper for Charlie, chipping stone and carrying mortar. One day, after a week of surplus theory and excess lack of correlation, Charlie put his hand up to my ear and said, "For God's sake, Mr. Wright, take 'im away. Take 'im away before I kill 'im. I can't stand 'im no more." I took him away and kept him in general circulation for the duration.

Charlie Curtis often used to say to the lads, "You've got to get the feel o' the rock in your 'ands, m'boys. It hain't no use 'til y'do! No use 't all to build a wall."

We had "stripped" the ledges and again opened the old quarry from which the beautiful stone for the Hillside buildings was taken. This quarrying was a mighty experience for the inexpert—we were all amateurs but, Charlie Curtis helping, we did it. Soon we had plenty of stone which we had quarried ourselves, hauled, and piled about the buildings. Our fellows were getting into splendid action. Blocks of flesh colored sandstone, cords upon cords of it out of the ground, two miles away and enough there build a city.

So our buildings kept on growing up by way of more and more long stone walls. We now had four local masons and a group of our own boys working under Charlie.

LIME

But now lime or stop. The prideful Cord now getting tired, started traveling again. Finally I found some lime freshly burned but it was way up north in the state. However, they agreed to deliver it to us at a low price partly on credit. But weird stories were beginning to travel concerning our credit. They travel fast (and fixed) by "The System." So, on the way to deliver the lime, stopping at the local lumber yard in Spring Green, the up-state dealer was told by the local Spring Green dealer that if he sold us any lime at all he (the local man) would have him declared unfair by the "Association" (the Association, like the T & T and the lumber companies, hadn't relaxed a bit during the breakdown) and if he did so, no lumber yard in the state would buy any more lime from him. The lime-burner came to us with the story instead of the lime— apologetic, of course, very. He really believed in us. He was willing to help us but was actually up against it as he said.

He said, "You buy lime but once. The lumber dealers keep on buying lime." So he said he could not afford to go against them and sell lime to us—this in panic-time.

What to do? Conspiracy in restraint of trade? Undoubtedly. But what of it? We were out on a limb because the whole nation was now a conspiracy in restraint of action.

The men were soon entirely out of lime. We couldn't afford to buy cement. The lumber yards were full of cement—but for us to keep our workmen going, deliveries were only for cash-down. The cement dealers, like the lumber dealers, all knew their way out of the scraps they were in: stick together. Keep prices up. We came up against this fine fellow-feeling of theirs for their fellow-creatures on more than this one typical occasion. It was organized.

Things were pretty tightly interlocked, I can tell you. There was little or nothing lying around loose in our county or those next to it. And rarely was there an "independent" to be found. Independents were soon "brought around." Independence cost too much—this independence was only Ideal.

The principal materials were all under "production-control" and credit associations.

Strictly up against it again, under pressure, I remembered that lime for the original Hillside Home School buildings—old Timothy had used it back in 1902—had all been burned in the hills not more than several miles away. The old kiln might be there yet! August Cupps owned the place now. So we went up over the hills to see August. "Sure," said he. "Sure," said tall awkward August, sorghum-maker. "Sure, go ahead, fix up the old kiln. I'll sell you wood to fire it at three-fifty a cord. Cut it myself." There was yet lots of wood on the hill-slopes nearby, and still plenty of limestone near the old kiln. So up went the boys to bring the old wrecked lime-kiln back to life again and themselves learn how to burn lime. A bunch of greensters, but I got an old-time lime-burner from Black Earth to instruct them. We fixed up the broken grates with old ones from the old buildings at Hillside—patched up the tumbled walls, stripped a section of the old stone quarry and filled the patched-up restoration of the kiln with good raw lime rock; piled cords and cords of wood alongside in long ranks to feed the roaring fires. Our boys took their food up to eat beside the kiln and would also take turns sleeping there by the kilnside on the ground under blankets, getting up every two hours all night long to keep the old kiln burning.

We got good lime . . . hundreds of bushels of it. We could have gone into the lime business, and thought seriously of doing so. We were A-1 producers of an essential building material.

We burned many full kilns of lime from first to last and we all loved it. It was picturesque!

Somehow we grew strong by it. All of us. That old kiln there on the hillside in the woods was a sight at night—lighting up the countryside for miles around.

We watched that light in the sky from Taliesin itself. When the iron door would open to engulf more cordwood, the boys, stripped to a loincloth, looked like stokers in the hold of a battleship. That old kiln *was* a battleship. Back to the primitive again to beat the tieup—the "bottleneck"—the rap.

We had good lime.

It was our own. We made it.

SHOPPING FOR THE FELLOWSHIP

The old Auburn Cord (four thousand two hundred pounds in itself) became degraded to a beast of burden. But a handsome thing it was when not put out of sight by provender and put nearly out of commission by our weekly trips to the wholesale grocers in the neighboring towns of this Iowa County and the next, to get provender for about thirty-five, Dane County, and the next, Sauk County. The car had taken several foreign prizes for body design and it was the nearest thing to a well-designed car I had ever seen outside Europe. And right here comes the feeling that the Cord should be heroic in this autobiography somewhere.

On the edge of entering the national Money breakdown when several large commissions loomed in the foreground, I gave up the Packard for the Cord, taking it on installment-plan contract that ran us ragged for years. But it (the Cord) seemed to have the right principle—front-wheel drive pulling instead of pushing along, and certainly it looked becoming to my houses—the best design from my "streamline" standpoint ever put on the market. I had myself driven myself (my own hands on the wheel) some five different top makes of car (beginning with the Stoddard-Dayton roadster in 1910) the equivalent in miles of some seven times around the earth—and, believe it or not, with never an accident—not even a smashed fender. But let me say I did not drive in Japan. I had four or five different drivers during that sojourn—they are a special class and how—high silk stockings (ladies'), patent-leather shoes, knickers and a military cap. They high-saluted as they passed each other. Owing to narrow tortuous high-on-a-bank roads of Tokio countryside, their proficiency was similar to that of a slack-wire performer in a circus. The passenger felt that way.

INCIDENT

Due to a compound fracture of the wrist got while cranking the heavy Knox roadster in Oak Park—I owned one (after the Stoddard-Dayton)—I kept a driver there for a time. He was very careful of my broken member—but eventually stole the car. He turned out to be one of a gang of auto thieves. The police finally got the car in a St. Louis barn as they were putting a coat of green paint over its beautiful gun-metal finish.

But I never cared for the Knox. At high speed it would settle down and shake itself almost to pieces in a perfect frenzy (the garage-doctors call this a shimmy). And they couldn't show it how not to.

I think I got almost as much enjoyment (1922, '23, '24) out of the long, low, black, specially built Cadillac as out of the Cord. Patent-leather Victoria hood over the rear seat, windshield between first and back seat, no footboards, sides built down. I drove it in L. A. when I returned from Japan. That Cadillac thus had mostly the look of the later foreign built cars—streamlined—very compact. Wherever we parked, the crowd would gather to see the "foreign" car—trying to guess the make.

But the Cord was a prideful car—innovation along right lines—and for one thing—changed the whole field of body design for the better.

Headed for Chicago one fine morning, very early, between Madison and Evansville, a florist's covered truck ahead. I, about to pass, honking hard, when, no warning at all, sudden the truck turned left and turned sharply directly in front of me! I jammed on the brakes, but the low nose of the Cord caught the already careening flower-wagon full on the side—nosed it over and over again and again and again as a hog might nose a truffle. Over and over went the Madison florist, three times, well on the way to the fourth turnover before the cover of his truck finally collapsed in a heap—the head of the Madison florist coming up through the debris—cursing loud and cursing plenty.

Never were swear-words so sweet to my ear. The man not even hurt!

He recognized me with a "G-- d---- it, Mr. Wright!!!! G-- D----!! Jesus Christ, why don't you look where you're going!!!" He got disentangled from the collapsed top, got up just a little wobbly, and galloped off to the nearby roadside station to call up—whom do you suppose? The press! He was asking them to send a photographer out to get the wreck. A left turn into traffic rarely gets damages, especially as we were three to testify to the fact that the florist had given no warning whatever; and had he perjured himself to the contrary, why he was only one. Our journey was interrupted, but the Cord not badly hurt.

They picked up what had been the Madison florist's truck and threw it away.

Where were we? ... going shopping, now going in the Cord to German's Wholesale Warehouse at Richland Center, thirty miles away. (I was born in Richland Center.) We did all the shopping in person because long sojourn in Japan had cultivated my bargaining instincts, and technique. Usually we got good measure and good prices wherever possible. After selection we would start loading—sacks of flour on the fenders—crates of fruit on the bumper. Rump and back seats piled high with everything a grocer keeps, and a green-grocer as well. And when we would finally lash the load to the Cord the springs were on the bumpers. If we ever hit anything with that load we never could have been distinguished from the groceries, unless by color.

Reaching home, unloading began: the Taliesin storeroom filled up a little for a week maybe, and then again we went. Sometimes west or east, north or south. We traded with the neighboring wholesalers for years—until added to my practice in Japan buying prints was so vast an experience to now aid in the lore of provender-buying that I would have made a bet with you that I could buy anything you had to sell for one-quarter less than any sum you had secretly made up your mind was the very least you would ever take for it.

Sometimes there was "remaindering" to go on. There was where we would shine and the Fellowship would be fed that particular bargain—say, dried apricots, pink salmon or roadside melons or you can think of something—until that particular "success" was out—which really means in or gone.

Our rapid-fire gatling-gun buying pleased the storekeepers. Pointing with my stick I would indicate what we wanted with little or no hesitation, and we would be loaded and off on our way, yes, loaded down (almost out) while another customer was buying a crate or two of something or other. They used to say of me in the old family days at Oak Park that I was a "good provider." But I was a grand "good provider" now.

I have always liked to "provide"—especially luxuries, and spread them about in a decorative fashion on the tables. The apple-barrel-with-the-head-knocked-out of my boyhood days I suppose. The bushels of roasted peanuts set around in big bowls; grapes lavished in big bunches in glass semi-globes; all kinds of nuts—rare fruits like persimmons—figs—grapefruits—strawberries—from the South. Pomegranates—avocados, etc., etc., etc. We were especially fond of small fruits and raised them.

I judge a hotel by two things—do they have fresh fruit, and are the toilet accommodations clean? Many a time we have walked away both in Europe and America after the invariable preliminary inspection proved unsatisfactory.

Herb (Jacobs of Usonian House number one) told me of the Elam Mills, an old brick building down on Halsted Street, Chicago, where the best cereals are ground in good old ways. Corn, wheat and oats. That delicious taste of corn, wheat and oats! That mill ground keeps all the life-giving features, vitamins, I suppose. Good stuff to maintain young bodies in mental vigor, and good complexion. Add, from our Guernsey herd good milk, plenty, our own fresh eggs, fresh fruit in and out of season, a glass of good wine on holiday occasions, and our own inimitable Wisconsin cheese—what have you? Well, that is about what we have to eat at the Taliesin Fellowship.

438

Only now we aim to raise most of it ourselves.

The Cord is gone.

Our boys haul the provender into the root cellar at Taliesin and pile it up. We "put down" this year (1942) one thousand quarts of tomatoes, besides many hundreds each of green beans, peas and vegetables. But that isn't much in the circumstances.

That underground reservoir of food can take several carloads and ask for more.

Were my mouth multiplied by sixty wide and sixty high you might easily drive two trucks in it. The Taliesin Fellowship is sixty wide.

A tunnel leads to the root cellar in the hill. At the arched door in the masonry wall you switch on the light—and the sight that meets the eye is a treasure-filled cave, not unlike Aladdin's. To the left are Olgivanna's wine casks: wild grape wine, elderberry wine, chokecherry, rhubarb, dandelion, potato wines, beet, tomato, tame grape, wild grape, plum brandy, cider, chokecherry mead. See the apples. Cider, vinegar. Rows on rows of jams, fruits, marmalades, jellies, sauces, pickles, vegetables. Sauerkraut! To the right, on sand, are piles of potatoes, squash, beets, carrots, cabbage, onions, parsnips and rutabagas. Melons in season. Hanging from the ceiling are dried herbs from the herb garden and cabbages wrapped in paper.

If a barbed-wire entanglement were put around Taliesin for the winter we would all come out the next spring with double chins.

So these first years of Fellowship went rapidly by for young and old. A few young fellows hitch-hiked across the continent—from as far away as the country was wide—to join if they could. We were compelled, for lack of means and room, to refuse hundreds. Had I enough money to keep them at work and feed them we could have filled the Valley with hopeful young workers. Might have started Broadacre City right then and there, ourselves. They kept on coming in from all sides though we have never proselytized for apprentices as we never have for clients. But the sad fact is, those we were compelled to refuse were often the most desirable ones. Skilled workers they were, often.

THE STORY OF TALIESIN AND "RELIEF": THE OFFICIOUS SAMARITAN

And then one day when we were looking forward to getting into our buildings the blow fell—not prohibition this time, but "RELIEF." The Administration of our government suddenly placed some forty or more of our workmen in a position where they could figure out that by doing

439

nothing at all they could have a few dollars more in pocket from the government than they were getting from us. We had been keeping about seven families in Iowa County out of the poorhouse and about as many more in neighboring Dane County. All our men had good quarters in which to sleep. They had good food, the best, and plenty of it. They were pleased and satisfied. But now the men—several or more at a time—would decide to quit; more and more would come in to me and say, "We are going to take advantage of Relief." I had no argument to advance because the only inducement I could make would be to outbid the Administration and I couldn't. Many men probably would prefer to get their money without working anyway. Thus this matter of Money still stood with us.

Just to make this affair of money worse, of now being able to eat without working, an I.W.W. or two from New York City (I had a couple of them in on the work) got a dozen or more of the worst ones among the local men to join up in repudiating the partnership agreement, demanding that I pay up all the balances *right now.* Someone in Madison had told Mike Lazar, the lather, about an old dead-letter law on the Wisconsin statute books to the effect that no wage laborer had a legal right to make any contract whatsoever for his labor. The worker was thus so classified that legally he was nobody but a slave to be paid in full at least every two weeks, or he and his employer, too, would go to jail. He had no right to himself. The workmen got together on this, shamefacedly at first, but the get-together soon gained headway. The men formed in queues outside my study door and then several at a time would come in to my corner of the studio to ask for "pay," reckoning the sum due them on the overall contingent wage agreement, but those sums were stipulated as wages only if they stayed on until the time came when I could get the buildings into use. *Now* this unexpected demand struck in addition to the board, room and weekly cash payments we had agreed upon and that I had managed to pay them so far when they could do a little better by living on the U.S.A. and doing no work at all.

Of course, I had already given these men all the money I had. There was no source from which I could then get more. There was no relief for me or mine. The agreement I made with them stated that I could get the sums stipulated only when I got use of the buildings. And unless I could get those buildings we started to build together for the apprentices, I could get no money to pay the balance of their stipulated wages. The buildings were only about half-done. But all the money I had already paid for labor and materials (some forty-five thousand dollars) was tied up in unfinished buildings as useless to me as to them.

The buildings now stopped growing altogether. Instead of getting suitable places in which to work in three years, it was to take seven, until we learned to build them ourselves for ourselves.

RELIEF

Karl Jensen was Fellowship secretary at the time, and Henry Klumb was my right bower. They would be with me at these trying times as I sat over there in my little corner of the old studio by the big stone fireplace. The gang (gangsterism was what they were in now) had formed this habit of lining up outside, and kept on day after day, for months, coming in to me for money they were really only entitled to when they had kept their word as men and performed their part of the partnership agreement as workmen.

Well, I thought of making a test case of the foolish slave-law—one of those "three laws passed to cure one flaw." But it so appeared, after appealing to the State Industrial Commission (which, I suspected, suspected me of exploiting labor), that under this law the state had made the laborer a slave, and that any attempt to make an agreement with him only laid us both liable to jail. The law was just as they had been told. Although most of the men had gone on government relief at the time, that did not stop them from tearing the agreement down and pressing for money. This they proceeded to do. This feature of money due them where relief was concerned was not "legal." I might have informed the authorities of the money coming to them in the circumstances, but I felt ashamed to knock the men out of anything they could get when they had so damned little. I have always rather shied at any appeal to "authority" anyway. No good ever came of the policeman where I am concerned. So foolishly I made promises. We kept the promises just as well as we could, all the while looking and hoping for miracles.

The miracle would be "work"—buildings to build.

There was no building. Little money was coming in to go into so many hands, and so some of the men began to get ugly. But they would go away with a little. During many ensuing weeks there were outrageous scenes. One, Jones, a troublesome ringleader, attacked me in the studio one late afternoon—got his hands well on toward my throat when Henry jumped at him, yelling so loud with anger that Jones was scared into "taking his hands off Mr. Wright." Human nature in the raw was not unfamiliar to me. But I had not yet learned *to make no promises to anyone:* the mistake I had now made.

Karl was like a secret-service man, prolific in subterfuges and stallings—untiring and resourceful. But Karl was scared—really. In

Karl's mind probably was an incident that took place in an obscure street in Madison where Jimmie had driven me in the Cord to get some tools for Fellowship work. Blackhand letters had kept coming from "a nice character" every now and then—after he saw us, as he soon did, carrying on our buildings under the Fellowship banner while he—a pre-Fellowship creditor—was not yet fully paid. Evidently he felt himself entitled to desperate measures. So one hangover from pre-Fellowship days, but now a situation, was an attack upon me in the street by an angry farmer—Indian blood in him.

A COARSE INCIDENT

Business transacted, I was about to get back in the Cord when someone came up behind me, struck me violently several times on the back of the head. Partly stunned, I turned toward the Indian farmer, saw Jimmie some distance away on the sidewalk struggling violently, his arms pinned behind by the farmer's son brought along for the purpose. A planned, well-timed assault. I took this in at a glance; as I caught other blows in the face I turned toward the assassin. Instinct warned me not to strike the man. So I clinched with him and he went down into the gutter on his back. I held him down there until he said he had enough. But, in the split second when getting off him I stepped back to let him up, he kicked backward and up at me with his heavy boot, caught me on the bridge of the nose with his boot heel. I pinned him down again. Blood spurted all over him. This time I had both knees on his chest, his head still in the mud in the gutter. While holding him down there I deliberately aimed the torrent of blood with a broken nose full in his face. His own nose, his mouth too, clotted with blood, he gagged and gasped for breath. Jimmie, meantime frantic, was unable to break away and come to the rescue. The nice character was cursing and appealing to the several astonished bystanders . . . "God damn it, men, take him off," he shrieked. "Take the man off me, for Christ's sake! He's killing me!" But I had not struck him. I was careful not to. I was only holding him down there in his own gutter in his own mud, painting him a gorgeous red until his features were clotted with my own blood. I let him up and he disappeared in the astonished crowd, which must have thought a murder was being committed.

I didn't know but that I was disfigured for life. Jimmie now free to drive, I got in the car. "Jimmie," I said, "my nose is broken. Drive me to the Clinic."

Everything I had on was saturated in front with what the doctor assured me was remarkably young blood, and it must have been so, for

442

the break mended with astonishing rapidity, the perfectly good nose showing no trace. That boot was a symbol.

So was the nose.

Never mind, dearest . . . I know what the moral is with both!

This adventure with "ideas plus work" as against "money plus authority" was thus ushered in. When I got home, bandaged, wholly unknown to me, my boys (four of them) went out after their man, got into his house in town to find him there on the other side of the dining table, holding his wife in front of him for protection. Later he got a kitchen knife in his hand and the ugly fellow threatened them from behind his wife, she and the daughter meanwhile screaming imprecations and calling for the police. Of course, the police came and arrested the boys and the assassin. All were in the county jail when I heard of their well-meant sympathetic "uprising" and got there to take a look at them behind bars. There were they, a nice-looking lot of boys, but a nice case for the District Attorney. Before I could get the young lads released, they spent a couple of nights in the county jail. But the nice character himself stayed in for quite some time to await trial. The case was finally settled in court, the nice character leaving the state. The boys were paying a fine of several hundred dollars. On the "installment plan," of course with "official" help.

The Taliesin Fellowship had got off to a very bad start. Indeed? Or did it?

DEFENSE

There were subsequent approaches now, to a similar thing until somebody from Brooklyn suggested that I employ a bodyguard or, at least, carry a weapon. Both suggestions were ignored by me because I believe any man is safer unguarded and unarmed in almost any emergency.

The time that perfidious unemployed gang spent standing around trying to get money out of me in such equivocal circumstances would have paid them much more in work—time times over—had they stayed with me than the money they got on relief or declared I now owed them. But there was no work for them to do if they would work, except that which I offered them. Were they enjoying this act, sitting pretty and being paid for sitting while they shook me down? A situation?

But I kept on faithfully handing out to them whatever I could get—collected dues, or fees from the boys, if any, sums I might still borrow somewhere, somehow (it is amazing how gullible my friends were) or something I might sell, but still on and in came the gang.

Frequently I was without a cent in my pocket. But I was used to that. And I grew to believe that if I parted with my last cent more would come. More—a little—always did come. I got rid of that gang finally, one by one, though not until blackhand letters had been in my mail for a year or two. Anonymous always. For many years afterward, some of the men would turn up asking for forgotten unpaid balances. But I must say that a few were really decent, a half-dozen or more, and one of the tragedies of the situation thus created by my effort to put ideas-plus-work against money-plus-authority was that the more decent the men were, the longer they had to wait for money in such circumstances. Of course, ethically these men were not entitled to be paid. Morally, I don't know. I knew there could be no more building until we could do it ourselves.

We had boys now who could handle carpenter's tools, do good masonry, plastering. Painting was easy. They learned to weld and use woodworking, as well as road-building and farm machinery.

Just at this high moment in our mundane affairs the Employer's Mutual Insurance of Madison moved in on us: stepped up for money for past-due protection for these men which the men hadn't needed. Well, enough is enough. Let's not labor the details but say that from the advent of "RELIEF" and its innumerable consequences we hung fire on construction, except for what the boys themselves could do, for nearly five years. Then my work in Architecture began to come back, and I could add my fees as an architect to apprenticeship tuitions, pay for the materials we needed, keep some expert workmen and go ahead to salvage what we had already done or lost. Even this now in a state of decay. But altogether thirty-five thousand dollars a year plus tuitions would not keep us going for materials, Fellowship upkeep. I found I had got into something only a multi-millionaire should have attempted. But, of course, none such would have attempted anything of the kind. That I kept up in the circumstances, not murdered, only still further "disgraced" as they say (ungraced would be nearer), was a surprise even to myself as well as my friends.

"I don't know whether you are a saint or a fool," said my lawyer. I said, "Is there a great difference?" As I've looked around me I never could see that there was. Much.

But I had made a promise worth keeping plus a promise to myself and now to youth. When I remember my promise to my grand old Aunts—Nell and Jane—and my Mother, I often wish they, and the Lloyd-Joneses, might look in now upon what we have accomplished these ten years past, and say—fool or saint! But who cares to be either one or the other even in the fond eyes of one's own family?

I know something better, but who wants to know what it is?

So this fifth book of *An Autobiography* is determined to be no work of art, but actually the sorry tale of a congenital urge which found itself anew in this rash determination to make architects while making architecture: the consequent "sweat, blood and tears" (and laughter) connected with that structural phase of our national revolution: a rebellious banditry itself which, instead of being merely punishable by death, is cruelly subject only to the severest social penalties and economic sacrifices our fearsome body-politic, now staggering under its overload of government can devise or inflict by Ignorance, by Neglect or by Law. Laws put above man.

Thomas Jefferson! Where are you? Is the muddy wave of an "ism" closing over your gracious head? Did you foresee Depression?

But we are almost reconciled to punishment. Why should this insolent adventure of ours in education not be punishable?

Established order must yield to growth iota by iota, but usually only over its dead body. And then it will yield only when well underground or undermined it falls by its own excess by duress. Lucky if after yielding, not frightened back and forth again and again. But at Taliesin we manage somehow to live on and keep on working appreciatively in the direction and actual service of a great Ideal, no less in these ten years past than single-mindedly for a lifetime in architecture.

However, we have been compelled to work for the construction of an indigenous Architecture as revolutionaries in a far too uncommon War (I say, the right kind of war if war must be): earning another half million to go with the million dollars already "earned" and lost in my lifetime. Yet, never really having any money. No . . . throughout these forty-five years an out-and-out culture-bootlegger, forced by the nature of our now national tumbled house to work and live under the banner of a bandit: that is only to say, the banner of the Radical!

Why is the Radical never solvent as banking goes in a "Free" Country? All the time and overtime, the honest counter-revolutionist where the social system under which we live is concerned for its way of life . . . is chiefly concerned for what it calls its own safety! Its "safety," does it say? Well, it too is "out on a limb." But good God! Should I say that what it deems and calls "safety" may be seen as ultimate destruction unless in common with our enemies we lose what we try so foolishly hard to win and hold on to . . . not yet understanding that no world-revolution can be won as any nation's war unless it is *a volunteer people's war*. And then? We wouldn't like the security we would win.

Walt Whitman to the rescue! Dear old Walt, we need you now more than ever: your salt and savor in this dish of humble-pie we are called to eat in shame and defeat, win or lose! Your robust soul might save us even now for the proper use of ourselves.

War! We have taken the wrong way. We must wait for you on a closed road somewhere—sometime.

If you, reader, are sympathetic you may see, between these lines at least, how the Taliesin Fellowship could only come into being and get into open service of its Ideal as a threat to such smug "safety" as the current agents (broadcasters of our current "morale") advocate. I say the Taliesin Fellowship could have come into actual social service only as a special kind of social bootleggery. Yes, unhappily, not being "regular," our Fellowship has had to be called bad names, thievery in some kind. At any rate, an Indigenous Architect, Native Architecture, and the Taliesin boys could have come to be in no legitimate way under the despotic Money criterion of present-day Usonian life where it is being educated. We will see.

STARS AND BARS

And thus it comes to be in a new free country such as ours ought to be—our country has become a kind of hard-up "tour-de-force" (speaking English far too fluently but none too plainly) that any Ideal above the belt or below the Bank is illegitimate as things go. Only Money can justify Work or pay for it or should ever talk sense above a whisper . . . if at all. Like the Administration-extraordinary of all this blood-letting money-getting fracas, I have had, so far as the Ideal is concerned, somehow to get into unrepayable money-debt myself for everything related to me if directly related to this Cultural Ideal which we call the Taliesin Fellowship. Even the warm pioneer family-life so enjoyed by the Joneses as children in this beloved Valley by the broad sand-barred Wisconsin River—life so warm that it warms me still—eventually had to go broke—go away; go by way of the bad choice of its own numerous offspring, some forty of my cousins, to scatter in faraway cities to seek the cash-and-carry yeshood of the white collarite. So the "hired-man"—the common man—working for the humanly glowing, noble family life of that pioneer day now owns most of the original family farmsteads: "owns" (and so exploits regardless) the ground which my people broke and loved so greatly in the wise breaking, conserving the wooded hills and the tilth of the soil. Yes . . . my people, the Welsh pioneers lived and died for this, their Valley—for the Common Man?

Not so. Even the architectural forms I myself may discover honestly and try to practice around the world are themselves revolutionary, are gaining strength to the rescue.

Are they, too, a kind of banditry? They must be so because if we find a better way to build a better building and actually build it that way, we change and probably destroy existing values everywhere. Even overnight. Therefore in modern times let us say the Taliesin Fellowship *is* on the modern social level of ancient Robin Hood with his medieval band of freebooters?

But we don't cut the throats of our neighbors or rape their women. Nor do we ever disturb the overflowing hen roosts much as the boys— loving eggs—would like to do. But we are true to ourselves so must do no violence except to their most "sacred" feelings. Continually insult hallowed "tastes" and do outrage upon the established property rights and "beliefs" of worthy creatures of social habit. We do this, whenever we build a new building, furnish it and plant the grounds. Outrage upon the educational system of our country (ahead of motor cars, kitchen gadgetry, engines of war and munitions) by the way, our greatest mass-production is not that great establishment, endangered, too, by this attitude when we go seriously—that is to say, naturally—to work in search of the radical results of the Ideal? So this search of ours for Democratic FORM is necessarily revolutionary. But a Revolution utterly essential to the life of this our country. If the Republic is ever going to grow up to be *itself*, a true self-supporting Democracy is only itself when independent of foreign exchange, safe from Money in the role of arch-commodity of the Spirit and we go revolutionary as essential: what is the proper name for that?

Since the Taliesin Fellowship is here (we celebrated our 520th Sunday evening—October, 1942—all together in the living room at Taliesin every Sunday) and has actually come to be a cultural entity (lasting ten years to that moment), it follows that even if what we have done is a miracle, it is the more illegitimate. Inasmuch as I am but a halfhearted believer in miracles anyway except as they are the uttermost commonplaces of Nature, I must admit us as illegitimate: myself Usonia's illegal but natural, therefore inevitable son. Prodigal? Yes. But not contrite. Not yet: the revolutionary Evolutionist is never exactly penitent.

To look back is almost more than can be borne. Overwhelming pity rises for the defeated ones, those great braves ones who aspired and are dead, those who expired in enforced isolation, desolation, defeat and despair.

ETTA

Well—our boys were getting a new view of things and I back to boyhood. They were no longer strangers to the Reality I wanted young architects to meet—omitted from their college education. Taliesin by now is itself a kind of kiln—burning not cord wood but labor, materials and food. Year in and year out, re-building kept on growing. New roofs were going on. Tile roofs: a story in itself . . . and standing there in the half-light of this, to you, confusing picture is a graying, gay, gray-eyed little woman—daughter of old Mr. Parsons—a fine old citizen of Dodgeville, up over there on the ridge seventeen miles away: Etta.

Olgivanna and I and the young Iovanna, tired of tough breaks and tough steaks, used to drive up to the Parsons meat market. Father Parsons would go back into his box, take down his best and cut off a rib roast for us. It would be "best we ever ate."

Etta was helping her father. She would wrap the parcel up, hand it to us with a salty remark and the friendly smile of which only Etta knew the secret. The neighbors were all fascinated by or fearsome of Etta's native wit. She was kind but she was shrewd. She knew them all right down through—and they knew she knew. She was a staunch "La Follette man." But her ideas were her own and she missed nothing of what went on. "I see Phil is getting around again speaking to the farmers. He was over at the 'Point' yesterday," she said. "It was a hot day so when he warmed up too, he threw his coat away, tore his collar off. Then he rumpled up his hair, and went after them." Her gay, light-hearted laughter would let you know what she thought of the act that Phil had put on. Mother Parsons (the family mother lived back of and on a level with the shop)—she would look in through the door between the shop and the living room—a gentle soul with the same captivating sweet smile as Etta's, to ask us how we were. Somehow we were always all right. Sometimes we would go back and sit down by her windowsill full of plants and flowers, have a slice of bologna sausage and a cracker and tea, or a cup of coffee and a cookie she had made.

Mr. Parsons died. Etta and her husband, Hocking, carried on the shop—selling meats, groceries, a few plants in season. And seeds. They were pretty well off. But soon Etta lost Hocking. We went to his church funeral. They were greatly respected so the whole town attended—all feeling deeply for Etta, now a widow in black; her mother in black too.

The Parsons shop went on just the same. Etta now behind the block in white butcher's apron, sometimes cleaver in her small hand with the plain gold wedding ring on her finger, mother still sitting by

Broadacre City. 1934 "Typical view of Broadacres countryside. Patterns of cultivation mingling with good buildings. Helicopter seen in foreground and, beyond, automatic overpass enabling continuous, uninterrupted traffic four ways."

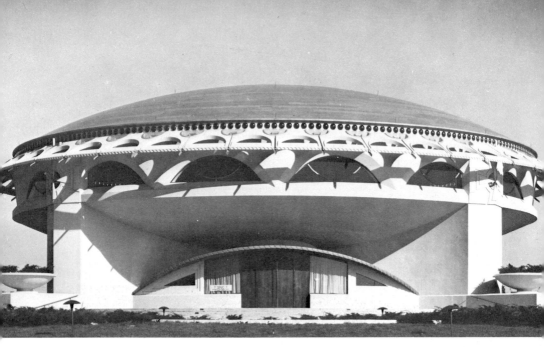

Greek Orthodox Church, Milwaukee, Wisconsin. 1956

Beth Sholom Synagogue, Elkins Park, near Philadelphia, Pennsylvania. 1954–59

Marin County Civic Center, Marin County, California. 1957–70

Grady Gammage Memorial Auditorium. Arizona State University, Tempe, Arizona. 1959–64

Pfeiffer House, Taliesin West, Scottsdale, Arizona (designed 1938) constructed 1971

Feldman House, Berkeley, California (designed 1938) constructed 1975–76

Lovness Guest House, Stillwater, Minnesota (designed 1958) constructed 1976

Frank Lloyd Wright, Taliesin, Wisconsin

". . . freedom and opportunity to be yourselves . . . At your best . . . you have good foliage and eventually blossoms, then you bear fruit." — F.Ll.W.

the door looking in occasionally. They didn't butcher any more. Their meat in by truck from "the System."

Our need of groceries and meats grew and grew—and we thought it might do Etta some good to have our trade, but things turned out the other way around. For years we drove seventeen miles to Dodgeville to trade with Etta, leaving everything pretty much to her. We gave her a few hundred dollars now and then, and she never sent us a bill—except, as she would say—"You are in about three hundred now." We would pay up. She gave us pretty near wholesale prices—"Good idea you've got down there. Want to see it go through—think I'll come down and strike you for a job just as soon as you've eaten us out of house and home here." And she would gaily laugh that one off.

"Any time, Etta. Come on and 'run' us. The places is yours that way, anytime you want it. Come take it!"

Things were going fair and well enough until Government-Relief came. Some of our Dodgeville workmen spent the money we paid them with Etta. From first to last a good deal of Fellowship money went into her till—still no bills. We didn't ask for them either.

"How many boys and girls have you got down there now?" she would say, as the groceries heaped up on the Cord and hid it from sight (I carried out the provender and stacked it).

"Oh, about twenty-five—say."

"My," said Etta, "they must eat an awful lot, don't they?"

"They do—why? Are we buying an awful lot for twenty-five?"

"How many workmen now?" she would ask.

"Oh, about thirty now, I guess."

"Which eat the most?"

"Why . . . I don't know. I guess the young apprentices do," I said.

"I'll bet you're right," she said. "I'm going to bring mother down and see 'em at it myself." She did come several times, watching everything with an amused half-smile as though she had indulged them in food—herself. We got good advice from Etta. She would say, "Good work you're doing down there—but your bill's running high."

"How much?"

"Oh, about fifteen hundred," said Etta. And then panic. We would get after some money right away and turn in all we could. A stern chase is always a long chase, but we were getting even when Relief befell. Then we went behind. We were beginning to see that "the good idea down there" was a good deal of a money affair, after all. Etta didn't seem to care much. The men who got money to spend at her shop didn't get it from us now but they got it just the same from the government and gave it to her. She had a fair share of this town trade. We were in a fix though, and Etta knew it. We expected the worst—that Etta would have to cut us off. Etta was warned by friends. "Nope," she'd say, "I know they haven't got it now, but they'll get it some day—some way, I'll bet. Good work they're doing—smart people. But not too smart." And she would gaily laugh that one off.

She would never tell us any more what our balance was but our best thought on the painful subject would have been about three thousand at one time. That was the stock Etta took in the Taliesin Fellowship—the good idea she liked.

Etta is a good business woman and has plenty of good ideas herself. She is there, business as usual, to prove it, after our patronage.

She went into partnership with the good idea. Will Etta ever be paid in full, do you think? I'll bet she will. What do you bet?

THE LIGHTER SIDE

In the living room at Taliesin, continuing at Taliesin West in Arizona, our Fellowship gatherings on Saturday and Sunday evenings began—October, 1932. These Fellowship gatherings for supper and a concert, or a reading and perhaps pertinent discussion (probably sometimes a little of them together), as I have said, have been going on for many years. As for me, I have never failed to enjoy one of them. They were always happy, always fresh—not only composed of perfectly good material, good music, good food, enthusiastic young people, good company, but something rare and fine was in the air of these homely events by way of environment. Atmosphere. No one felt, or looked, commonplace. The Taliesin Sunday evenings (Middle West or West) are made by music for music and enter into the spirit of the occasion as if the Fellowship was made for music. Eye music and ear music do go together to make a happy meeting for the mind. This happy union charms the soul: happy meeting is rather rare as independent intelligence is rare. We lived it.

Olgivanna felt that the Fellowship—looking like the wrath of God during the week—should wash itself behind the ears, put on raiment for Sunday evenings and try to find its measure in its manners. Most of it had both. In the right place too. The girls all put on becoming evening clothes, did look, and were, charming. I hardly knew some of them. Clothes do make a great difference—one of the justifications for our work as designers. On Sunday still I scarcely recognized some of my own Fellows of the workday week. There was something vital and happy radiating from all on these happy occasions when everybody served everybody else as though he were somebody too—and willingly took the part in the entertainment he had been rehearsing. Partly, of course, because they were where they all wanted most to be, were all volunteers—doing what they most loved to do: *very much at home.* I am sure none will ever forget their share in Fellowship life on these eventful but simple occasions. While the Fellowships change with time and circumstances—these events keep their character and charm, nevertheless.

Many of our Taliesin young people came because they had read something I had written or seen my work, probably both, and dreamed of someday working with me. They had come somehow from all over the United States with money begged, borrowed or received as a gift. Many foreign countries were gratefully giving their best to Taliesin. Most of our boys and girls were individuals by nature with an esthetic sense rejecting commonplace elegance. That rejection by Taliesin itself would be the natural attraction for them. Artificiality that passed current for Art had no place in Taliesin's instincts nor in theirs. To a man, the boys were naturally averse to the dull convention, either social or esthetic. Girls likewise. Alexander Meiklejohn—himself the advance experiment at my old University (Wisconsin), on several occasions guest at Taliesin, said to me one such evening, "Yours is the most alive group of young men and women I've seen together since I became an educator."

ESPECIALLY DESIGNED

Sunday Evening Occasions at Taliesin take place in the homestead living room, the third living room to stand in the same space. The most desirable work of art in modern times is a beautiful living room? Or let's say a beatiful room to live in. If perpetually designing were perpetual motion the world would have in Taliesin that much-sought-for illusion for the millennium. The Spirit of Design was pervasive, presided really, at these Sunday evening Taliesin events. The Saturday evening rehearsal in theater and these Sunday night occasions in living room were natural Fellowship festivity. But discipline at Taliesin in doing anything anywhere lies in the fact that all throughout must be especially designed. In none can anything go that is not especially designed to be perfectly natural to itself at Taliesin as sheep, crows and butterflies are to themselves out of doors. I want to insist that no discipline from the exterior is so severe a strain or as fruitful as this discipline from within.

Discipline applies to our boys and girls when they take their turn providing the customary house decorations in appropriate scale or getting "especially designed" effects with native wild things or familiar tree branches and garden flowers, effects invariably original and charming in seasonal arrangements, fresh in touch and idea with each individual taking charge. Seeds of good design fell all about the place as naturally as apples fall from trees or thistledown drifts from the thistle crown. "Design" especially in festivity—why not especially—was like air because of what was around about, like the thistle crown, to fill and excite the mind. Every move in any direction is an opportunity to become a developed designer. A designer in embryo was simply to be a natural member of the Taliesin Fellowship. Every member from the first to the last one was in active service to Organic Design in some form or another.

From the very first in our life and work we have had these pleasant distinguished weekend companies—although guests are seldom invited because we were not really ready, we felt, but they were welcome just the same and plenty came. Soon after the first years of professionals playing high quartets, we got our own trio and quartet going into rehearsals. Soloists were plentiful among us from the first. Professionals from the various orchestras had come to join us for the summer but we soon got tired of playing second, ourselves being merely entertained. We found, also and soon, that the musical activity of the Fellowship languished when the professionals did come. There were many reasons for this. So now, as I had desired from the first day of the Fellowship, we have our own a capella choir singing Palestrina, Bach, Negro spirituals, folksongs and other good music: already a repertoire of some seventy-five songs. We have an instrumental quartet, a trio and many soloists. Svetlana has cultivated the old-fashioned recorder too. Recorders now form a choir, and we mingle harp, piano, strings, recorders and voices. A really good Bechstein concert grand piano takes the corner of the Living Room, and one is on the floor of the Playhouse. A harpsichord is in the blue loggia joining the group. Iovanna's harp stands alongside. A César Franck cantata last Sunday evening brought out our present resources. The young people have lately gone all-out for folk dancing Friday evenings.

You should see our collection of grand pianos. We have eleven appropriately and usefully placed about the buildings, not to mention the harpsichord.

About twenty-five years ago I sat playing the piano in my own way (no notes, no pattern) letting the piano play itself for my own amazement. Carl (Sandburg) listening. For mischief suddenly I stopped, wheeled around toward him with one mischievous impulse I like to practice on my friends and that often ruins me. I said, "Carl, if my mother hadn't decided for me that I was to be an architect, I should have been a very great musician: perhaps another Beethoven! Since the mind required for greatness in either art is the same, I should have ranked with Beethoven, I am sure." I turned back to go on playing. But Carl didn't forget the episode and tells the story to this day to illustrate my colossal egotism. I suspect Carl uses the word egotism when he relates the episode as I have heard from others. Supercilious, yes. Egotism, no, not yet.

BEETHOVEN

In Beethoven's music I sense the great master mind, conscious fully of the qualitites of heartful soaring imagination that are godlike in a man. The striving for entity, oneness in diversity, depth in design, repose in the final expression of the whole—all these essentials are there in common pattern between architect and musician. So I am going to a delightful, inspiring school of architecture when I listen to Beethoven's music—music not even yet "classic"—soul language to be classified because of soul-depth and breadth of emotional range. Beethoven's music is in itself the greatest proof of divine harmony alive in the human spirit I know. As trees and flowering or fluttering things under the changing lights of a sun beclouded pervade all the out of doors, so Beethoven pervades the universe of the soul.

When I was a small child I would often lie awake listening to the strains of the Beethoven Sonatas—perhaps the Pathétique—Father playing it on the Steinway square downstairs in the Baptist minister's study at Weymouth, Massachusetts. It takes me back to boyhood again when I hear it now. The other sonatas were as familiar then as the symphonies and later quartets are now. When I build I often hear this music and, yes, when Beethoven made music I am sure he sometimes saw buildings, like mine in character? Whatever form they may have taken then—buildings.

I am sure there is kinship there. But my medium, architecture, is even more abstract—so the kindred spirit who understands the building is even more rare than in music. There is a similarity of vision in creation between Music and Architecture. Only the nature and uses of the materials differ. The musician's facility is greater than the architect's can ever be. The idiosyncrasy of the client does not exist for the great composer. Utilitarian needs play but small part in his effort. The rules and regulations imposed by the laws of physics upon the performances of the architect are not present to any great extent in the scheme of things submitted to the musician. But both must meet and overcome the same prejudice—the same cultural lag. The limitations human stupidity puts upon insight and appreciation—these are the same in both lives.

But I keep on saying that an artist's limitations are his best friends to keep up my courage, knowing it to be true.

So perhaps the more severely limited art when success does crown creative effort is the greater and more abiding achievement—if for no other reason than that the one is the Abode while the other is the Song. Both are best when the song dwells and the abode sings: as both may when creative power and the passion of love makes both glow from within.

Mastery is no mystery. Simple principles of Nature apply with peculiar emphasis and force to all a true master does: a scheme in keeping always with the nature of materials (instruments), materials used in such a way as to reveal the beauty in tone and texture they possess. The strings were his, par excellence, but percussion, brass and woodwind—he knew them all so well that he never gives one away nor asks of the one what belongs to the other; continually enriching each with all and all with the character of each. But what gives *consequence* to mastery *is* a mystery. Inspiration is not definable.

Planned progressions, thematic evolution, the never-ending variety in differentiation of pattern, integral ornament always belonging naturally enough to the simplest statement of the prime idea upon which structure is based: Beethoven's rhythms are like that—integral like those of Nature!

And likewise the work of the inspired Architect.

Organic character once achieved in the work of Art, that work is forever. Like sun, moon and stars, great trees, flowers and grass, it *is* and stays on while and wherever man is alive and hungry for beauty.

Other musicians have this mastery, and greatly, but none I understand so well, none so rich in the abstract idiom of Nature as he—whose portrait Meredith drew in the sentence: "The hand of the wind was in his hair; he seemed to hear with his eyes."

I am humble and grateful in his presence. "Who understands my music is safe from this world's hurt," he said.

ANOTHER "I REMEMBER"

I remember John Fiske (great historian) coming to the little brown house by the lake, coming there to dine and play or sing with Father, Mother afterward remarking upon the great man's voracious appetite (as famous as his histories). I see his thick lips nesting in the great brown beard, eyes hidden from sight by the light glancing off his enormous spectacles. After dinner the great historian sang and even I could see how he loved to sing. In fact, Father (who played his accompaniments, of course) said that he was utterly proof against any compliment or blandishments where his powers as an historian were concerned but let anyone be so indiscreet as to praise his singing, even a little, and he was singing in their ears thereafter. So it is with me. I love to sit in on chamber music rehearsals of Fellowship talent and criticize—knowing as much of the particular composition probably as John Fiske knew of the art of singing—but dreadfully pleased to have my criticism—regardless of the composer's notations (and perhaps sometimes his intention)—heeded.

Such are joys of the amateur, and far from innocent they are. I am sure Franklin Roosevelt got much the same reaction where his supreme command of the American Army and Navy was concerned—with consequences.

UPKEEP OF THE CARCASS

Fellowship food under Olgivanna's inspiration and guidance was excellent and, after proper training, well served to the Fellowship and our guests by the Fellowship itself. Olgivanna started this. She said, one summer day, early in the second year of the Fellowship, "Frank, let's have no paid help. They don't belong here, you know. They vulgarize everything. There is no reason why these young men and women themselves can't learn to cook and serve their own meals gracefully without hiring outside help. Our boys and girls do their own rooms anyway and many of them do their own laundry. Do let me try! I want to see what I can do. You will see they will feel all the more at home, more a part of all this activity they are in here with us, if they take their share of the household routine upon themselves and serve each other. We can make good cooks."

Skeptical at first, I was afraid of the time consumed and the interruption it would be to our other labors. And I didn't believe in trusting our own good health and well-being to that great extent to amateurs. But I soon found she was right. We fared well indeed. Better than ever before. But it took a lot out of her from first to last. Nevertheless she made the plan work. And while there were plenty of individual breakdowns and many failures, she did succeed in making the Fellowship see the light in it all and soon learn to discount the hardships: the garbage, perpetual dishwashing, though enjoying the cookery.

Many unexpected reactions appeared. For instance, the nearer to the habitual wage-earner class a boy or girl was, the more rebellious he or she felt when doing what seemed to him "menial" labor. Just as those

Fellows we would sometimes take into the Fellowship without fee, allowing them to work their way along with us, would be the least cooperative, most of them instinctively "keeping shop" with us: being there only to "get" what they could, they gave least and left soonest.

But Taliesin kept on growing. Our buildings were safely under roof. The boys had not only "the feel o' the rock in their 'ands" but the look of a board among boards, and what the stick was good for in building, as they went from drawing board to the actual sticks and stones and boards. Learned for themselves what tools can do, with them and for them.

We now put a scheme of rotation into operation in our work in the fields, on the buildings and in the draughting rooms. I named a head man for the fortnight ahead, one who was free to choose his first aid or right bower. First aid became leader next. He named the leader to follow him who in his turn chose his own aid. After consultation with me the leader each day laid out work for the others. The work of the following day was thus planned the evening before. Something resembling this way of directing Fellowship life was now applied to the housework as well as office and field.

MUTUAL SERVICE

Olgivanna tells of this: It takes years for the young people who join us in this work to throw off the old concept of academic conduct at school. At first some may be unhappy because they are not all the time at the draughting board, they miss the class lecturing and want formal instruction. They are suddenly dropped into a world of *interior* discipline, without a rule written down. Discipline which turns them to their own resources and makes them act with a sense of their own conscience. Our concept that all work is important is new. There is no menial labor here. There is no backyard. Taliesin is all front yard. The field work as important responsibility as work in the draughting room, in the garden or the kitchen or the dining rooms. This seems difficult for Young America to accept. One of our young men could not see the work in the kitchen as anything but menial to be done by a servant. When he was told he didn't have to do it his conscience troubled him because all the others were doing that work. They began to tease him about it—'til he felt foolish in making an exception of work which he was beginning to see was part of the whole. Later he became one of the best in making beautiful decorations in the dining room when in turn it came into his charge and the tables were arranged in new original ways, and he be-

456

came a good cook. After the work in the kitchen he would sit and make drawings for the new arrangements he felt we needed. He would suggest new systems in serving, which would eliminate waste motion. He was just as interested in that work as in any other. His knowledge of the working of a kitchen and dining room on whatever scale is instilled into his very being—a knowledge earned and gained by him by way of actual experience—not by way of a superficial inadequate theory by instruction.

Thus participation in our maintenance had a strengthening and unifying effect on the individual group. Taliesin became their real home. One part of the group is headed by one with experience in planting the garden in the Spring. Every morning all of the young people work in the garden for an hour or two. Afterwards the seniors go directly to the draughting room, some go planting trees (there have been thousands planted about Taliesin), some may go checking and fixing an electric fence, hauling gravel, grading roads. They learn how to handle themselves by contact with stone by building the walls, laying the floors, putting up piers. They learn work with wood, metals and textiles. They arrange their own rooms, rebuilding the interiors according to plans made by them which they submit to their master for approval. The large draughting room is like an abstract forest with light pouring from the ceiling in between the interweaving of the oak trusses. The atmosphere there is one of intense quiet concentration—which sometimes under pressure keeps the young people voluntarily working on drawings until the late hours of the night. Yet the draughting room responds to lively relaxation when tea is brought in at four o'clock and everyone gathers about the great fireplace, or in the stone-circle outside or on the hill: talking, discussing Fellowship problems, or getting engaged in dynamic politico-social discussions. Tea is prepared in weekly rotation by young women of the Fellowship. Most intriguing recipes are tried. Those the group particularly enjoys are put into the Taliesin Cook Book, which is already a rich collection of Taliesin favorites owing to participation of our foreign apprentices.

It is great fun to plan meals with our young people. For instance, as to what meat we shall use this week—shall we butcher the calf or the pig, the goat-kid, geese or chickens? We would wander together through our old cook books, some of them fifty years old: American, Russian, Yugoslav, Polish, of all nations really, and find new delicacies, always learning new exciting ways and always succeeding in getting interesting meals prepared. When the wine-making season comes, we all go in automobiles, station wagons, trucks—taking picnic lunches with us—to gather wild grapes, chokecherries, blackberries, elderberries. Permeated with warm autumn sun, we return home. The following weeks we crush and prepare our grapes and berries for wine. We gather our apples and the golden season of apple cider sets in. Large crocks are filled with cider and tin cups hung by them stand in the court for the boys to drink while the cider press keeps on working, making more for the hard cider we will drink next spring and the vinegar we need. Etc. Etc. Etc.

About this time the plans for the annual Hallow'en masked ball are being made. A committee of entertainment is appointed. Small secret group-meetings are held and all Taliesin is sensitive to a mysterious mood that pervades everything. The party will be full of surprises—original and exciting—since each one of the young people is talented and designs with spontaneous quick imagination astonishing effects.

Many of our young people, as I have said, are musicians and keep on working in music. They have programs to prepare for every Saturday and Sunday evening. Chamber orchestra has been in existence for five years, playing Bach, Vivaldi and Beethoven, Brahms and Haydn trios, quartets, sometimes quintets. The choir of eighteen young voices sings Palestrina and beautiful old English and American songs. On Saturday night come to the Playhouse. Buffet supper is served, then listen to chamber music and solo. Sometimes a short play, impromptu, is put on the stage. Then see moving pictures which come to us from all countries of the world. Sunday noon we often go picnicking, exploring new places, going back to our favorite ones—of which there are inexhaustible variety in our region of southern Wisconsin.

This rewarding social-life of Saturday and Sunday ends the Taliesin week and begins the next. All dress in their best clothes, and where we entertain our weekend guests, many famous artists may be seen among them. Frequently they entertain us, and taking their turn, sing or play, speak or read to us. These gatherings usually break up in small groups engaged in quiet discussions gradually dispersing one by one. Quiet descends upon life at Taliesin and the graceful figure of Buddha on his stone-pier on the hill stands serene—unperturbed in warm human movement thus projected into Space.

REHEARSALS

Meantime Fellowship life goes on in the Taliesin studios, designing, drawing. Always details of details for the buildings steadily growing up at Hillside in spite of RELIEF and all other obstruction. Our own boys learning to *build* our own buildings first. Designs were perpetually made by the apprentices for the fittings and furnishings of their own rooms to be executed by themselves (if a boy's room were changed he threw out what his predecessor did and started "fresh"). Perspective renderings; abstractions of plant life; studies from nature, and the nature of materials especially. All the while our hands were in the mud of which the bricks were made. The boys saw designs they made take shape in the actual work of their hands and stand there before us in actual materials. But what was more important, our boys had to live with their errors or successes in building themselves into their own rooms or see the mistakes corrected. We do not learn so much by our successes as we learn by failures—our own and others'. Especially if we see the failures properly corrected.

To see a failure changed to a success—there is proper Education?

We tried to include photography too. Without much success, although several of the boys have recently shown remarkable ability in that resource. We didn't have enough money. As for music: at the beginning we tried several professional musicians—composers—to get that side of our work going, but it was too soon for that—we were much too engrossed in construction. Just for that perhaps, we didn't go very far or very fast with that. However, the intimate little Saturday evening rehearsal dinners in the Playhouse, and the Sunday evening events, music and supper in the Living Room, went on to give relaxation its place.

INSTANCES OF THE CASUAL

Sophie Breslau, for instance (she said with a laugh, "A thousand-dollar package where singing was concerned"), coming out from Madison, bringing Ima Roubleff, her accompanist, standing up in the Living Room singing gloriously and happily there until three o'clock in the morning. There were many others from time to time as features of our entertainment.

All music lovers, or else mad about music, which is not quite the same thing, many such informal occasions were thus stolen—another kind of "bootleggery," you see?

A. I. A.

The most extraordinary instance of casual evaporation by translation I ever knew occurred when Mies van der Rohe was to be inducted as

Pilot into the chair of Architecture at Chicago's Armour Institute.

Mies and I fond of each other. He has known me all of his architectural life. I believe him a sincere man as well as an architect. He asked me to come to introduce him at a big dinner given by the A.I.A. in honor of the occasion of his being inducted into his job at Armour. The dinner took place in the ballroom of the Palmer House. I sat near the center of the platform table at which were ranged various A.I.A. architects and other dignitaries. My turn to speak, after listening to Emerson and other professional speakers reading from notes, and another lot of other bores intending eulogy of "the talented German," now their guest, taking over the helm of Armour . . . but saying nothing except that modern architecture had come from abroad.

It was all most empirical labored lip-service. So when I rose to speak I put an arm across Mies's shoulders (he sat next to me), and simply said, "Ladies and gentlemen, *I* give you Mies van der Rohe. But for me there would have been no Mies—certainly none here tonight. I admire him as an architect, respect and love him as a man. Armour Institute, *I* give you my Mies van der Rohe. You treat him well and love him as I do, he will reward you." And, sickened by the giveaway, I stepped down and walked out of the room.

When Mies's turn came to speak, he read in German, as he knows little or no English—a twenty-minute paper he had prepared. He went into the origin of his discipleship and reverence for me frankly and to the point. He told how much he was indebted to me. He was proud to stand there and say it. The German architect paid a considered tribute to an American architect, affectionate, such as is rare in the history of the architect's world at least.

The interpreter (he was Woltersdorf of the A.I.A.), after Mies had paused before going on with the rest of his speech, "Mr. Mies van der Rohe says he is sorry Mr. Wright left so soon." Unless you understood German, that is what you got from Mies van der Rohe's twenty minutes so far as he went at the crowded dinner in his honor.

My friend, Ferdinand Schevill—Chair of History, University of Chicago, who was present—told me this. Mies came expecting to find America Frank-Lloyd-Wright-conscious, only to find the support unpopular with the A.I.A.

The many boys and girls of Taliesin, hundreds from first to last, all behaved themselves with self-respect. So far as Olgivanna and I could see, with circumspection (none too far, of course). The first several years, however, there were some exceptions to the latter. But during all ten years of Fellowship-in-residence we have yet to look back and complain of an insolent act, or any unwillingness to carry on as requested—or very much shirking. While free cooperation was a hard lesson to be learned, we had only a few slackers, some with native disabilities, some dazed—not knowing what it was all about, but few real incompetents. Perhaps a dozen that I can remember. Naturally such would not last very long in our atmosphere and activity anyway. This loyal Spirit of the Fellowship in face of such handicaps of accommodation and equipment as ours was truly remarkable. We all look back upon the circumstance with no little gratification.

Our first years we had much altered and reconditioned the old buildings. We were trying to complete a large one—our Draughting Room, flanked by sixteen small apprentice rooms, eight on either side. The old buildings had a new lease on life—all protected under good tile roofs. The tile roofs that are a separate story I don't want to forget.

FELLOWSHIP MARRIAGES

The current of Fellowship life flows on.

Davy and Kay decided to marry. There was nothing we could do about that, except help celebrate. Theirs would make the sixth marriage in the cause—or is it the course?—of nature since the Fellowship began. First there were Rudolph and Betty, then Vernon and Margaret. Quite an interim, then the tragedy—Wes and our own Svetlana—that turned out well. Then came Hulda and Blaine, followed by Cornelia and Peter. Now it was Davy and Kay. We conceded to all appropriate wedding parties and probably there were six happy honeymoons.

There would be other weddings—the one certainty in co-education? Another couple already in sight: My God, is propinquity necessarily fatal? Or are Olgivanna and I too good an example to set before young bachelor girls and boys?

Now came the question of the weather—we who live in the country become completely weatherized if we are not weatherwise. We have learned that to run from it, hoping to escape from "bad" weather (of course, we mean bad for us), is to run into worse. I have learned that everywhere in the world the weather is unusual and unless one learns to "land on one foot," so to speak, concerning it, nothing ever happens as planned. So we planned the wedding weatherwise. The weather turned out to be fine. So did the wedding part of the wedding later.

Davy and Kay were both favorites. Davy, a talented manly chap;

Kay, a natural-born charmer. (Let that be sufficient introduction.) Olgivanna laid things out. Inspired, she planned another Taliesin fair-weather wedding in the little old family chapel. (Truth Against the World.) It was Spring, and we threw open windows and doors. The birds flew clear through the chapel without stopping, and the boys went out in the big truck, as they liked to go, after wayside decorations. The old chapel walls under the high wooden ceiling of the interior which I had put there myself when a boy, became a festive bower of sun-splashed branching, aromatic green with masses of spring flowers arranged around the pulpit where the bridal couple would stand for the simple ceremony. Auctioning the virgin in the Roman slave mart still looked down on it all from the wall behind the pulpit; and a family heirloom, our old Steinway square piano (Father rapping my fingers into proper position every time I see it) stood beside the pulpit where the golden Bible lay there shown as centerpiece: Olgivanna set slender stacks and groups of tall white candles (Greek Orthodox childhood—she loves candles) here and there in the foliage to burn in the shadows; they seemed religious, nevertheless they were a good decoration too (even in religion isn't that always a primary motif?); Iovanna's golden harp brought in from home was placed to the rear for pervasive incidental music. She played Debussy softly while the ceremony was taking place.

The cooks for the week were standing back there in the rear room, ready in tall white caps and white jackets, eager to carve the feast. They had baked the traditional ring into the wedding cake. Olgivanna's best wine was bottled from her big cellar casks for this especial occasion. The milieu and menu were quite festive enough, too beautiful, I should say, even for the wedding of some Russian Lady-of-the-Royal-Bedchamber.

Then, as had Kay and Davy (Davy's little sister alongside to carry the bride's bouquet), we all got dressed up. The wedding party, including Olgivanna and myself, climbed into the old Hillside carryall to be driven in state by the old farm-team over the hills to the place where the wedding bells had been ringing for at least half an hour, the old Lloyd-Jones Chapel. The bride's headdress got pretty well jolted on the way over because the tattered canopy of that old rig had been wreathed with wild grapevines, as a substitute for covering, and they kept coming down and mixing in with us. Thus embowered, beflowered and bedizened, too, we, the happy Taliesin wedding party, reached the chapel gates (Truth Against the World) without further incident. Very like the other gay weddings, although, to me, each seemed nicer than the last.

The ceremony went off with a few tears from the next of kin, but mostly there were smiles all around. The feast so attractively spread, itself a superlative decoration, we soon reduced to a mere remnant of its

462

former self as healths were drunk in our homely wine. Then (indiscretion) the boys—Edgar in the lead as usual—in the role of local devil, rushed the old chapel organ out into the chapel yard, set it down in the grassy space between the graves and the road. Shaded by the gigantic cottonwood that grew by the gate, the youngsters danced old-fashioned square dances with the bride and groom. Our Fellowship talent took turns playing the dance tunes on the chapel organ. Some friendly village folk attended, standing there against the dark evergreens to watch the gaiety, and also some of the old family group were there by another group of evergreens not seeming too happy, and I soon had reason to know they publicly disapproved of this gay use of the sacred chapel, family churchyard shrine. I noticed their expressions and they were not good. A gathering storm?

Davy and Kay disappeared in a plane after a little of this—soon a small aeroplane zoomed overhead and there they were above and off on wings, for a wedding journey the modern way. The bride's bouquet had been thrown to Gene. Upstretched hands waved to get it and happiness to the bride and groom as they sailed away over the hills.

Another Taliesin man and wife.

Thereupon followed a family scene in the chapel yard. The storm broke. Bitter reproaches were lavished upon Olgivanna and myself, the guilty promoters of this violation of sacred family tradition (which I had thought I fairly well understood—and represented too). But no, such callous disregard of family dignity! Besides (and this was true) the chapel wasn't mine anyway. It belonged to the Lloyd-Jones family.

Something well worth keeping had thus, in a self-righteous moment, been ruthlessly spoiled. Well . . . the organ was hurried back as it had been hurried out, and put into its accustomed place none the worse for the dance tunes. The music and the harp were gathered in with the remnants of the guilty feast. The tall candles (a little shorter now) were blown out and all came away from the beautifully decorated Lloyd-Jones Chapel—depressed.

Where happy Fellowship had been in high spirits a few moments before, chagrin in our hearts.

Hatred had struck at Joy. The Taliesin Fellowship hurried away.

Evening shadows, no longer blue but long and lengthening, had about crossed the Valley to the opposite hills. The slender marble obelisk in the chapel yard gleamed tall and white against the chapel evergreen: Ein Mam, the simple legend on one side; Ein Tad on another. This simple monument marked the graves of my old Welsh Lloyd-Jones grandparents. Around this central obelisk were the surrounding headstones marking the graves of their five pioneer sons and five daughters. Further away but surrounding them were graves of their grandchildren. About all the pioneer life of the beloved Hillside Valley. They—the Lloyd-Jones family—were all there safely, according to clan tradition, gathered in around the family shrine: the ancestral white marble obelisk.

I sometimes sat there under the trees to wonder and remember, partly because Taliesin's tragedy had sent its share of graves among those of this charmed old pioneer family circle. There now.

Sun had set. The afterglow was dimming in the sky as I sat there on the grass again to wonder and remember. I remembered my dear aged mother dropping to her knees, reverently pressing her lips to the cold white marble monument to Ein Mam and Ein Tad, as I was taking her by on my arm to stand beside the open grave then waiting for her preacher brother Jenkin: another faithful daughter soon to join the ancestral group. And I remembered standing there alone, just over there underneath abounding evergreen trees, beside another open grave, at this same fading time of day; a new grave I filled to the brink with flowers and and, joined by two nephews waiting at the chapel gate, filled the grave with solid earth—covering the earthmound with fresh evergreen branches. Both grass-covered mounds now, still waiting for their headstones.

ALLEGORY THAT FAILED TO CONVINCE EVEN THE AUTHOR

Read aloud in the family sitting room: Olgivanna and Iovanna listening. Title of this Allegory is *"Truth Against the World."* I began to read:

> I sat, disconsolate on a low grass-covered mound in the chapel yard, wondered, pondered, and remembered as twilight deepened to dusk and darkened under the evergreens—the sacred chapel-evergreens. They were softly sighing, stirring to and fro in the gentle breeze. As I carelessly listened, did I hear—I thought I heard . . . is it possible? A quite human sigh, then the whisper of my name. Listening now intently, I heard nothing more. Still I listened, wondering . . . still remembering. Silence for a time. Then the gentle human seeming whispering of intelligible words began, extending all around me. Intent, I peered into the dusk, pale blue wraiths were slowly wreathing upward, spiraling out of the family graves like pale blue mist rising all around me, but wreathing slowly; wraiths taking on familiar human shapes. A moment more of the gentle sighing and then the whispering of the spiraling pallid shapes began again, the wraiths now quite blue flames swaying with the breezes to and fro, to and fro as the breezes rose and fell. The ghostly company all seeming to gather there on their own headstones.

464

OLGIVANNA: *Oh, Frank dear, oh, this is too much! This Thornton Wilder graveyard thing. He got away with it but you simply can't.*

Listen . . .

> Nearby a shade arose in shimmering silver, head bent forward, hands folded in her lap. A whispered name—again—my own! The ghostly family conclave rising now, one and all and standing there together in one group, swayed gently to and fro, and as gently nodded and whispered together in the dusk. I leaned, looked and listened for the secrets of the dead.

OLGIVANNA: *Frank, you simply can't put this sentimentality into print. They'll say of you as they did of Turgenev's later and so sentimental work, "Age is breaking in on him."*

Listen . . .

> Again familiar—my name, and the wraiths grew more luminous as the dark deepened and their whispered words grew more distinct, there on the edge of the dark. In wonder—I whispered, "Mother . . . why are you here like this . . . my mother . . . surely *you* are a spirit in heaven!

OLVIGANNA: *Terrible! Terrible! Oh, Frank, how can you be so foolish! Trite—you convince no one, not even yourself as I can see.*

Listen . . .

> A pause . . . "A spirit in heaven, yes, my son: but spirits in heaven cast blue shadows here on the green earth as the golden sun casts the blue shadows of the green trees. Our shades may rise and go on earth whenever the breezes blow if they but blow gently." Family shades gently swaying now with the breeze nodded assent. Again soft whispering together as before.

OLGIVANNA: *Pah! Frank, you are gone, gone, gone. This must never get into print, that's all.*

Listen . . .

> The breezes for a moment grew stronger, and I listened to all the family in chorus. They were whispering a song—"If they still love us, we may rise. When breezes gently blow earthly shades arise. Arise and go, go to those who love us." In bewilderment I looked around curious and amazed, listening, still wondering, as the family shades, these flickering ghostly flames in lambent blue resting on their gravestones were gently swaying, nodding assent. Silence for a time, but gently as ever, timed with the breeze in the trees, the gentle swaying to and fro, to and fro, went on.

The nearest spiral flame, the one shimmering silver, now whispered, "When gentle breezes fan your cheek or stir your hair, my son, it may be our gentle touch, the caress of those whom you love but have lost on earth, those who still love you in heaven . . . their touch upon your head."

OLGIVANNA: *Oh! Oh! Oh! this spiritualistic thing! Frank, how can you?*

As the dusk deepened to dark the breezes were dying down. Again silence. . . .

(Now sweet-sixteen) IOVANNA: *Why, Daddy, this is something I might have written, but not you. It's not like you at all. Please don't.*

But an author is desperately determined.
Listen, World . . .

The evergreens were now hard to see, but still gently stirring breezes, faintly sighing as before—but the sighing and whispering grew more indistinct . . . I heard "When you live deepest, then we come. . . ." The shades slowly bent their heads and were swaying assent.

Oh, Daddy—Daddy! That swaying business—it's just awful. AWFUL! can't you see?

Listen . . .

The silver shade now gently lifted the semblance of my mother's beloved venerable head, eyes hidden deep in shadow as, more faintly, scarcely audible, now that the breeze was dying, whispered . . . "You know what your beloved want you to know, my son, if you turn to look again at the symbol on the chapel gate."

For heaven's sake, Frank! Do wake up! This is the end. I won't listen to another word. How awful!

Nearly done.
Listen . . .

The breeze barely stirring now the mass of somber evergreens, the swaying shades spiraling downward to their own graves, each swaying gently as they grew to resemble the so long beloved family ones, so now as slowly, surely sinking, wreathing away . . . vanishing as dew vanishes from the grass into nightly mist. Utterly, all was still.

A lurid howl from Baby Brandoch, hitherto peacefully playing on the floor. SVETLANA *rushes to pick him up: Gosh, Daddy Frank, what are you up to? If it's all like the little I overhead—well, I just don't see how*

Mother and Iovanna stand it.

Listen, all of you! The idea at least is good . . .

> Now dark, the wind so dreaded by ghostly shades, rising as the moon arose. I got up and went out by the way I came in. Wondering still and remembering I looked back at the chapel gate. There it was in stone . . . the symbol "Truth Against the World," the revered, ancient Druid symbol old Timothy had carved there on the gatepost for the Lloyd-Joneses, those whose "shades" had just wreathed upward for a ghostly gathering of the whispering clan and gone away. Had they come to give their verdict?
>
> Strange . . . a new meaning . . . why had I not seen it so before? . . . the downward rays of the sun were Joy! Joy set against and dispelling the mean hatreds that were all the sorrows of this world.
>
> That then was what the old Druids knew? Was that what the family ghosts flickering in lambent blue there above their graves in the graveyard had been trying to whisper to me?
>
> "The truth to set against the woes of this world is Joy!"
>
> Joy it is that elevates and transfigures Life.

OLGIVANNA *in despair: Pah! And you think you have discovered something? Why, the old Greeks all knew that. Everybody knows it. And here you are just picking it up! Oh, Frank, my dear, throw it away and forget it. Just stick to Architecture. You are safe there.*

But of course, my girls were right. They always are! So we laughed and I threw the thing away. My innocent little excursion into "writing" was one more blasted hope.

THE MORAL

And I here admit that like all truth, this one—the ancient Druid symbol /|\ Truth Against the World, which the Lloyd-Jones family adopted as its own is dangerous because so few of us ever learn here on earth to know the difference between Joy and Pleasure. I now know the dead know. When will the Living learn?

Sentimentality is decayed sentiment, although if I had the skill to make the Allegory stand, sentimentality might have persuaded the more foolish among you otherwise. Selfhood is not selfishness, though it is often hard for any but a Lloyd-Jones to know when the one is eating up the other. No, Joy is not pleasure, and the abuse of the good is so often taken for the good itself, that symbols are no longer good themselves either.

That is truth?

And what can American wagery know of Joy when working so desperately hard and overtime in order to live for pleasure?

FOUR SEASONS IN FOUR VERSES

Somewhat akin to the unconvincing Allegory, here is an early study in aspirates: sibilant verses to be whispered. My mother came over when she read "the study" and said gravely, "My boy, when a young man starts versifying it is a sign." She didn't say a sign of deterioration, but I knew.

This early abstraction and design in the fashioning of a verse to render the movement of the subject—the Breeze—into its own rhythm, starting slowly, enlivening and dying down, belongs to the same period as the Work Song. Both, as you see, are experiments in straight-line or streamlined design that really belong on the drawing board because both are abstract-pattern in line and color. Unfamiliar at least, and unlikely in words, although Edgar Allan Poe seemed often to come pretty close. Emphasize the aspirates a little.

> Slender grows the tender mesh of silken threads and films of
> green,
> Sunbeams glimmer through between the leaves in nestling
> sheen,
> Genly wavering and fluttering like butterflies a-wing,
> As in melody the rainment of the spring . . .
> Stirs and is still.
>
> Languid vapors veil in torpid heat the deep of azure,
> Lazy insects drone in drowsy bloom and glow of verdure,
> Faintly uttering the gutturals of Summer's lush o'errun,
> As in sultry ease the ripe of Summer's sun . . .
> Stirs and is still.
>
> Gleaming crystal overarches seas of gilded leaves,
> Flaming vine entwines the glowing oak, and deftly weaves
> Rustling radiance in fashioning of iridescence fair,
> As with transient heat the rhythmic Autumn air . . .
> Stirs and is still.
>
> The frozen earth in starry night lies waiting tense and proud,
> Glistening moonbeams shadow askance her glittering shroud,
> Frail with frost the breath of life wreathes and rises to a
> shrine,
> As the dying breeze, adream in Wintry pine . . .
> Stirs and is still.

Enough:

Meantime the buildings grew. They were worth what they cost us all from first to last. And there were many compensations down the line. Tough as the going mostly was, continual accomplishment. Both inside and outside, this thing we wanted most, a suitable, characteristic place in which to work and play, grew. Integrity, beauty and usefulness, kept on growing up on the hillside at "Hillside" as though it belonged there. It did belong there. We saw new ideas familiar on paper becoming useful and beautiful features of life and important effects that stood on the ground and would live long for others by the virtue of young architects.

We worked, we sang, we played, all with the enthusiasm of youth undiminished. Love's creative labor well spent.

OUR GOODTIME PLAYHOUSE OUT OF THE OLD GYMNASIUM

For one thing, we got our little recreation room—a happy thing—(call it The Playhouse for lack of a better name) with the Bechstein concert grand below, and above in the balcony a fine cinema (35-mm. equipment). Operation began shortly after "Relief" had thus laid *us* on *our* back in the gutter. That playroom was fun—on the installment plan, too—three years to pay for the piano, seven to pay for the equipment, etc., etc., etc.

Originally we cut up the old Hillside Home School gymnasium and rearranged it into a bright nightspot in Fellowship life. Then we changed it and cut it open more. Then we changed it some more by deepening it. Ever since we have continued changing it here and there and lavishing upon it all our scheming skill to make the great oak-roofed and oak-walled room a lovely, likely place to be expectant: sympathetic to sound as a viol.

For our events we combed the available supply of the best foreign films in the world as well as our native products.

What I myself have received from that source alone would justify the Playhouse.

I may as well confess right here that it appears to be, after all has been done and said, it is my own culture that the Taliesin Fellowship has undertaken—much more so than I have undertaken that of incidental Fellowships . . .

An amazing additional wealth of experience and broad range of travel is stored up in the already much-traveled traveler, as the result of those films. It would be impossible to travel about the world and see for one's self as deeply or richly the life of the strange parts of the world as the cinema in the hands of great writers and good directors working with the historic resources of the various great nations that have gathered and now present it.

From Austria and Germany thirty-three splendid features; from China, three; from Czechoslovakia, one; England, forty-four; France, fifty-nine; Ireland, two; Japan, three; Mexico, three; Norway, one; Russia, seventy-two; Sweden, two; Spain, two; and the United States, forty-four. To date a total of two hundred and sixty-nine top films of the world.

Our stage curtains were the first craft-work of the Taliesin Fellowship—rectilinear, brilliant, colored felt abstractions (I made the design), colored felt cuttings applied to a neutral coarse cotton fabric. We bled the silver screen (the screen is about eight by ten feet). The screen is luminous white instead of beaded silver.

We let the sound-track play through on a red felt band about one foot wide, up and down on the left side of the picture. Straight-line sound patterns were there in light to harmonize the moving picture with our characteristic type of design.

We indulged in some interesting experiments in sound—reflexes ending up with the loud-speakers beneath the stage pointing toward the rear wall of the recess in which the screen stood. Sound to permeate the house instead of hitting hard on the ear. From this back board wall, the sound—now a reflex—spread to the audience. Integral sound. Many guests having seen the films elsewhere which they now happened to see in our playhouse, would say they enjoyed them as though they were seeing them for the first time, discovering more in them than they had ever thought was there.

Incorporated in the Playhouse:

1. Reflex seating arrangement instead of seating on centerline with eyes directly front.
2. The stage, part of the audience room.
3. Bled screen for cinema.
4. The sound track playing through beside the picture on a red band. A straight-line decoration in light, harmonizing the picture with the house.
5. Electric lighting without glass.
6. Sound magnifiers beneath stage floor—directed against rear wood wall of stage—sound thus becoming part of the room instead of directed at the ear.
7. A dais for quartet, one for the piano, and seating for choir, arranged and related sympathetically to the stage at one side—instead of pit in front of the stage.
8. A real "Foyer"—a fireplace in the Playhouse itself. The use of

470

architectural screens to reproportion the room and provide service for feasts and cloakroom space.

9. The top of the seat-ranks a broad ledge on which colorful table service is arranged for ear-and-eye feasts. Good interior decoration.

The whole construction in native oak aside from the supporting walls is stained dark, with a brilliant play of polychrome against the dark throughout.

Our special act: "Snatching victory from the jaws of defeat."

SNATCHING VICTORY FROM THE JAWS OF DEFEAT

We had quite a time getting seated in this Playhouse of ours. After looking about a good deal, being refused often, we finally decided on some movable metal chairs manufactured in Elgin, Illinois. About eight hundred dollars for about the one hundred chairs needed. We accepted the terms offered. But nothing happened. The Company, after agreeing to deliver, refused, demanding the never-yet-forgotten "cash." Cash! We had waited some weeks in blissful ignorance of this demand—setting our opening date to correspond with promised delivery. But the characteristic blow fell. So, what to do? Eight hundred wasn't much, but we couldn't spare eighty dollars at the time. We might have expected it by now; it had blocked us ad libitum—ad nauseam. Strangely hope does spring eternal in the Taliesin breast—we still believed in Santa Claus. Though in the claws of the System, we have never yet learned how to lose hope.

Thus driven to pay for the trifle which was not trifling, in order to open on time we again sat down at our drawing boards to see what we could do with green oak boards, $1'' \times 9''$, a keg of nails, and a few screws. We evolved a system of bench seating, more appropriate than the coveted Elgin metal product: far more interesting in character. Rough green lumber was all we had, but we fitted it all together into a new idea of seating—where seating an audience was concerned. The girls cut up cotton bed-pads and tripled them to pad the seats and backs of the benches which had a broad top rail to hold supper service. We found some cheap red denim (ten cents) to cover the cushions, sewed colored cords to the covers, and tied them on to the seats and bench backs. And we had seating.

Pretty hard, but not impossible if the play was really very good. Most always it was better than good.

The Playhouse was becoming charming entertainment in itself—entertainment that could never fail. The magic of something new and interesting appeared among us again "to snatch victory from the jaws of defeat."

I had wanted a theater of my own ever since, as a boy, I read of Wilhelm Meister's puppet-theater in the attic of the house Goethe designed for him. Now here it was—far beyond Wilhelm Meister's or any Goethe himself could have designed. This surely counted us *one*?

Every time unexpectedly cut off from a source of "cash-and-carry" supply, we had come up smiling, really better off for the rebuff because the demand upon our own resourceful inspiration gave us problems to solve and we solved them—plus. Of course middlemen were still hanging by their eyebrows from sky-hooks. Their bosses were taking no chances—those still in business.

Nevertheless we found generous cooperation enough so that we are not yet convinced that no one wants to go into partnership with us. We thought we were a good thing at a time when all was dead or dying. We are surer than ever now, now that the dead and dying are actually here all around us.

REST FOR THE WICKED

We kept on trying to get and give cooperation whenever need to ask accommodation appeared, as it did, constantly. But always the risks seemed too great to those who could help us on our way if they would. So far as they went or could see, our Cause was way beyond their mark. We never could "pay." Seriously, why should the System want to compromise itself by helping us anyway? What interest to the "make" of the middleman were we, or was anything for the common man whatever, if there was no cash profit in "the deal"? They had to live: so they said. So discounts were naturally not only few but very suspicious.

Help was spaced far apart on centers in those equivocal, trying days. We might say that in the early days help was in reverse.

At this point I may as well confess that I was certain financial help from some source *would* appear when we really got something going to show the nature of the cultural effort to which we were now wholly committed. But we never got to the point where I was ready to show what we had done and ask anyone for financial help. We are not there yet. So all the friendly help we've had has been small and haphazard. You might say, accidental, but none the less appreciated on that account. The more welcome, I should say. I should like to tell the stories of several such. Some day I will write them.

I am no longer so sanguine where financial help is concerned. This effort of ours is far too individual to attract it. No nameplates of donors nor much glory in substantial giving to us I guess. We must make ourselves or break. Only the Institution can get named help. We don't want to be the usual Institution. Neither are we "all dressed up and no place to go."

We are not much dressed up at all but we look well. Well indeed.

In many desirable ways we would like to be dressed up and yet, in many respects our self-respecting poverty stands as itself by itself for the thing it *is*—the open countenance of devotion to Principle: something out of our own soil belonging to our own time and place naturally.

It is crude as the bark on a tree at some points—at others past belief beautiful.

But the tree itself is there—under the bark the branches are springing, the green leaves will spread to the light—as the whole endeavor grows slowly, painfully but happily and proudly according to the true principles within it.

We believe that we have planted a fruit tree and our cultivation will bring the tree to bearing.

Unfortunately there is no source of inspiration our country won't copy. In this substitution of experienced example and exemplar we call master and apprentice, we have met certain characteristic traits of character, liabilities as well as assets, and while we believe we are fundamentally democratic, we are as anti-"cash-and-carry" as we are anti-war.

Here are some of our principal liabilities and, in general they would be those of a true democracy: for instance:

When building Edgar Kaufmann's house at Bear Run, Pa., I had one of my enthusiastic, faithful boys, Bob, "Little Sunshine" we called him, on the usual apprentice arrangement made with every client. At an early stage of the proceedings, "Take him away," said E. J. in despair. "His blunders cost me money. Take him away!"

"No, E. J.," I said, "not yet. Be patient. He may be, and he is, costing us both a little money, but not much. You gave me a thousand dollars to help make the models of Broadacre City. Well, it's only fair for you to pay your small share of the education of these young fellows— America's future architects. It is fair, if for no other reason than just because they are giving you and me, where your opus is concerned, something no money can buy: an alive and enthusiastic interest in our work and eager cooperation that goes with it too, as well as they can— none of them are fools. I know it is an intangible I am talking about. I know. Your building will come out right-side-up in the end, and you'll have something in the way of experience as well as a building that money could never pay for. I assure you that the building won't have cost you as much either as it would have cost you were the whole thing 'regular' according to your best knowledge."

"All right," said E. J., but unconvinced (he is a good business man as well as a good fellow too). "We'll see." And now, to tell the truth to E. J. (and the same goes to all our clients in this struggle for superior character and integrity in building), the experienced professional would be just as much or more at sea in the way of doing things where our work is concerned. And the experienced professional would be much harder to inform and convince of error in his trying of the new way than my amateurs. He would make mistakes, too, and he would stick to them to save his face, where one of my boys would say, "Sure, how stupid of me—I see it all now." The boys did add a lively human interest all down the line, on every house built. For better and some for worse. Sometimes prospective clients, coming to see the work on a new building and being shown about by the boy, would like him so much they would ask to give their work to the boy!

A bad system was then in force allowing a Fellow to do work with his name on the plans but all designs and details to be submitted to me for approval. The same fee, ten per cent, to be charged; divided one-third to apprentice, one-third to cover the cost of plans made by the Fellowship, and one-third left in the Fellowship for it to grow up on. This was a mistake from every standpoint as I will explain later. While authentic originals are available, why devote the resources of Fellowship to warmed-up or warmed-over amateur productions, especially as they seemed to destroy Fellowship rather than build it up? More on this subject.

It is only fair to say that on the buildings I have built with the Fellowship alongside (there are some thirty-five or -six or -seven such buildings now), from the very first I have found quicker comprehension and more intelligent faithful cooperation, counting in all the aggravating dropping of stitches from first to last, than I ever got out of "experienced" professionals at any time. This would not apply were we doing the standard thing done by the popular *regular* architects for which the channels are all cut. I well know that. But once we do go afield from the beaten track, not for novelty—never—but for the necessarily different because it *is the better thing*, we (my clients and myself) are better off (time limit aside) with the honest amateur than we could ever be with the conventional "expert" in the rut. The expert is usually a man who has stopped thinking and so is perfectly able to be utterly wrong for at least the rest of his lifetime. He has made up his mind, not upon principle, but upon expedients in practice. So usually is quite likely to be, himself, a rule of thumb already out of date where we are concerned. Our difficulty is to find true skill of any kind.

As a matter of fact, during the rational pioneering of these past forty-five years, I have developed a technique of my own—still flexible—therefore still growing with each new experience, which means each new building we build. Not only is it not probable that "the practical man of experience" would be likely to grasp and apply it: he *wouldn't* do it if he could. But in all frankness, let me say he couldn't do it without more study than he can afford to give it, and, by the way, that study means more failures. Failures which would be more numerous, more difficult to remedy and as much more costly as he was certain of his "experience." Saving his face would be more costly to my clients, therefore, than the quickly corrected blunders of my amateurs under me. But I realize that my proximity to the work done is more than ever essential. Not likely soon to change except as I have in time trained enough good builders myself. The Fellowship should now have several such, and will soon have more like Harold Turner and Ben Wiltscheck. We have a score of boys, though, who could already build one of our houses and build it well if backed by proper supervision.

But the time when we can thus build our own buildings, milling our own materials, is yet far away.

We are looking forward to the time, however—fifteen more years?

But no more drawing-board architects if I can help it, nor contractors trying to build buildings they know nothing about no matter how many others they may have built.

To bear me out in all this, about all my clients have testified to the joy and satisfaction they get from their own particular building, believing theirs to be the best I have built, as indeed it is for them. Their experience with the sincere try for the organic in character—honest experiment in their behalf—has often opened a new world to and for them. Were it not likely to be misleading—looking like boasting, or a plug–- should like to introduce here several hundred letters from many, even from most all clients, testifying to that fact. My clients are a cross-section of the distinctly better type of American—I should say Usonian, to be specific—most of them with esthetic sense of their own, many of them traveled, artistic, accomplished, and most of them cultivated. They have sometimes learned about us when abroad.

We seldom get the wealthy provincial. The wealthy provincial doesn't dare trust his own judgment of cultural cause and effect. If he has been abroad, his education such as it is, usually confirms his eclecticism. He is the country's characteristic cultural coward.

The houses we build are usually enjoyed by people who are rich in other things than money. It sometimes seems as though the appreciation of our work is inversely proportioned to the financial standing of the person involved, although this is changing.

But sometimes when Usonian houses are very far away and my proximity to the work there is not possible, after work is "practically complete," we have had to go back to the opus as a body of workmen ourselves to straighten out mistakes, meantime perhaps bettering the original, correcting faulty workmanship and materials in order to save the owner harm and generally re-establish what was originally intended but perhaps in this or that particular instance, maybe by the owner's interference, unhappily lost in execution. We do this, and we ought to have and will soon have a Fellowship follow-up group organized to help furnish and use the house after it is done, in the style intended, with the ease, grace and distinction which the new forms make possible. We are sometimes already doing this.

Our Fellowship method grows steadily more effective as we go along, until I am assured by my clients, comparing their own costs with the known costs of neighboring buildings, that one of our operations will result in more actual space accommodation and greater material advantages in every way than the more "regular" houses, much more easily had, that abound around them. What style and distinction our buildings possess is therefore "thrown in." "No charge." But it is only fair to say that it *is* more difficult to find ways and means to get our houses built.

The distinction of our buildings (the countenance of principle will stand out in any house-crowd) is inevitable: it marks them and makes them. Should they fail at any point—temporarily leak or show defects and especially should they exceed expected costs—immediately they become a common mark for the envious skeptic. Most of the skeptics are architects. Or neighbors and friends who live in fashionable homes.

We are yet, thanks to our lucky star, unfashionable.

Our faults are those, not of a common system but of an independently growing thing: a challenge to Fashion and sham. But our faults are corrected much more easily than the faults stock-and-shop would be sure to perpetrate. Because every problem carries within itself its own solution, and, because we make the buildings what they are, thoroughbred, we are perfectly competent to cure evils and rectify errors as they arise. We have the secrets conferred by our experience with the type of building we originate.

476

Any experiment we make is not on our part a seeking for novelty or notoriety—but sincere and intelligent experiment made in the client's own interest. Cure and correction are a matter of pride with us because, in a peculiarly intimate sense, every building we build is not only the client's own, but also *our* own. We must and will see that that building becomes what we intended it to be or we would soon be ashamed to look ourselves in the face. And since the building is always a public mark, the building must be maintained as intended even if we go down in our pocket to help. Sometimes a matter of enough money of our own to be able to do this. But we get the money eventually. No client who has stood by us has yet been let down. Only fair also to say that most all of them have not let us down either. Many of them have taken a lot that seemed at the time beside the mark in order to get what they were certain was coming, glad to stand by the principles we practice, principles in which they as firmly and faithfully believe as we.

Their investment in their building is dated some years ahead (say, ten to twenty) and increases in value with time because our buildings cannot go out of fashion. They are not and never will be dated because they are not of or in a Fashion.

TALIESIN WEST: DESERT CONQUEST

Taliesin West in the mountains above Phoenix is a look over the rim of the world. As a name for our far-western desert camp, we arrived at it after many more romantic names were set up and knocked down. The circumstances were so picturesque that names ran wild—so we settled sensibly to the one we already had, adding "West."

To live indoors with the Fellowship during a Northern winter would be hard on the Fellowship and more so on us. We are an outdoor outfit; besides it costs about thirty-five hundred dollars for fuel to heat our buildings at Taliesin, so to move Southwest. The educational trek across continent begins November. Each trek an event of the first magnitude. This Fellowship annual hegira with sleeping bags and camping-outfit, big covered truck, cars and trailers for forty, *was* an event even in Fellowship life. To conquer the desert we had first to conquer the intervening two thousand miles between East and West in cold weather. The first several years we stayed at Dr. Chandler's hacienda at Chandler, Arizona. Very happy there, too, but eager to build for ourselves.

We were growing in proficiency and able to do our own—now.

A major rule in the Fellowship always "do something while resting." So we preferred to build something while on vacation. I was earning something again, as an architect, and we could get materials. But first we had to settle on a site. By this time that vast desert region, Silence and Beauty, was as familiar to us as our part of Wisconsin. There was plenty of room and plenty of superb land, high or low—open or sequestered. Every Sunday, for a season, we swept here and there on picnics. With sleeping bags we went to and fro like "possessed" from one beautiful place to another. Finally I learned of a site twenty-six miles from Phoenix and across the desert of vast Paradise Valley. On up to a great mesa in the mountains. On the mesa just below McDowell Peak we stopped, turned and looked around. The top of the world from Maricopa Hill.

Magnificent—behind words to describe! Mystic desert vegetation, but what a hard road. It was the only trail crossing the great wash of Paradise Valley, the broad wash to the Verde River was this miserable Hell that trail across the desert was in wet weather. There was a rainy season too about January until later it got to be raining all the time.

But roads can be improved. The site could not be. After tedious search we found this land could be bought from Stephen Pool at the Government Land Office. Pool said he was keeping it for some fellow (he said "fool") who would fall in love with it and "do something with it." I said, "Here is your fool—how much?" we got about eight hundred acres together finally, part purchase, part lease, and next year began to "do something with it." We made the plans and were all ready to build—an architect's camp.

We knew about what thirty apprentices, alongside our little family, would need—one of the things was "room" for action. Why not Style?

There was vast room so we took it and didn't have to ask anything or anybody to move out or over. Plans were inspired by the character and beauty of that wonderful site. Just imagine what it would be like on top of the world looking over the universe at sunrise or at sunset with clear sky in daylight between. Sunlight and pure air bathing all the worlds of creation in all the color ever was—all the shapes and outlines ever devised—neither let nor hindrance to imagination—all beyond reach of the finite mind. Well, that was to be our place on the mesa. Our buildings had to fit in a new world to us and cleared the slate of the pastoral loveliness of our place in Southern Wisconsin. Instead came an esthetic, even ascetic, idealization of space, of breadth and height and of strange firm forms and a sweep that was a spiritual cathartic for Time if indeed Time continued to exist in such circumstances.·

Imagination of the mind of man is an awesome thing. Sight comes and goes in it as from an original source, illuminating life with involuntary light as flashes of lightning light up landscape.

478

So the Desert seems vast but the seeming is nothing compared to the iridescent-effervescent reality.

For the design of our buildings certain forms already abounded. These were simple characteristic silhouettes to go by, tremendous drifts and heaps of sunburned desert rocks were nearby to be used. We got it all together with the landscape—"where God is all and man is naught"—as a more permanent extension of our original. "Ocatilla," the first canvas-topped desert camp in the world of Architecture. By youthful enthusiasm posterity was to ponder the real thing.

Superlatives are exhausting and usually a bore—but we lived, moved and had our being in superlatives for years. Never bored.

From first to last, thousands of cords of stone, carloads of cement, carloads of redwood, acres of stout white canvas doubled over wood frames four feet by eight feet. For overhead balconies, terraces and extended decks. We devised a light canvas-covered redwood framework resting upon this massive stone masonry belonging to the mountain slopes all around. On a fair day when these white tops and side flaps were flung open the desert air and the birds flew clear through. There was a belfry and there was a big bell. There were gardens. One a great prow running out onto the Mesa overlooking the world, wide desert below, a triangular pool nesting in it—another garden sequestered for quiet, another plunge-pool, water raining down from the wall around it was at a corner of the garden room garden.

There were play-courts for the boys, rooms for them, and pleasant guest-quarters on a wide upper deck overlooking the terrace and the Mesa.

"Warning," said the local wise-men, "No water on that side of the valley—waste of money to try." But I was unable to believe God made a valley with water on only one side of it.

So we tried and got a wonderful well at 486 feet—85 degrees when it emerged at the surface in the pool. All went forward pretty much as usual, but upon the most marvelous site on earth—utterly different in character from Taliesin I.

The Arizona camp is something one can't describe, just doesn't care to talk much about. Something sacred in respect to excellence.

How our boys loved the work! Talk about hardening up a soldier. Why, those lads could make any mere soldier look like a walking stick! They weren't killing anything either, except a rattlesnake, tarantula or scorpion now and then, as the season grew warmer.

No, we weren't killing anything: we were just getting something born, that's all, as excited about the birth as the soldier is in his V's when they come through. If my observation counts, more so.

Our reward came soon.

Olgivanna said the whole opus looked like something we had not been building but excavating.

Our new desert camp belonged to the Arizona desert as though it had stood there during creation. And also built into Taliesin West is the best in strong young lives of about thirty-five young men and women during their winter seasons for about seven years. Some local labor went in too, but not much. The constant supervision of an architect—myself, Olgivanna inspiring and working with us all, working as hard as I—all living a full life, almost too full, meanwhile.

Difficulty for us in that the place had to be lived in while being built.

Rainy season we were sometimes marooned for days at a time. In hot dry weather the "desert devils" would swirl sand all over us. When it was dry we could see whole thunderstorms hanging below over the valley, see the winds rushing clouds toward us, and we would get the camp ready as though we were at its mercy, as though we were a ship at sea. At times, too, on the way driving the Dodge to and from Phoenix for supplies, sitting in the car, Olgivanna by my side, my feet were on the brakes under water up to my knees.

The Masselinks, Gene's parents, coming to visit their son, were lost in the desert water-waste overnight, the flood up to everybody's knees. We could not get to them until afternoon the next day. The son in a forced attempted rescue was almost carried away by the rushing flood.

Frequently visitors trying to see us were nearly drowned in the desert, on the way.

Hardships toward the latter end of the great desert experiment were almost more than flesh and blood could bear. Living in the midst of a rushing building operation for seven years began to wear us down.

Otherwise our Fellowship life went on much the same at Taliesin West as Taliesin East—except that the conspiracy of Time and Money was a little more against us in Arizona because no garden or farm.

However once you get desert in your blood—look on the map of Arizona Highways for Taliesin West and drive up if you can take it.

N.B. I've forgotten to speak of our desert playhouse: a solid stone, about 40′ 0″ square "kiva," solid inside and out, with sunken fireplace and outside hangar for our cinema to peep in through the rear stone wall. Arrangements for feasting and music were coming. A triumph of imagination by way of simple form and limited space in the heart of a great square masonry block.

DEMOCRATIC BACK-DRAG

I have said this could not be peculiar to us but would simply be those common to Democracy. Walt Whitman, asked for the cure for evils of Democracy, declared "more Democracy." And so it is here.

I. THE SERVANT MIND

The servant mind is a menace to us for the same reason it is a menace to American Democracy. It is, I guess, a natural inheritance of the melting pot. Comes from the lower ranks of society and permeates the upper ranks to eventually destroy them—the drag on the struggle for independence of innate servility: the congenital curse put upon true or innate aristocracy, placed there by feudal servility. The servant mind is so inbred as not likely to be cast off except as it is unbred by patient culture.

For instance: a well-to-do country gentleman visited by a friend. The gentleman's valet met the guest, showed him to his room, meantime complaining of his master. In small invidious ways he deprecated him until the exasperated friend, a true friend, said: "Well, Michel, if you don't like the way your master treats you, why don't you leave him? Go somewhere else . . ."

"Oh," said the valet, "it's all right—I gets even. I spits in his coffee every morning."

Now there are as many variations and modifications of that spit in the cup of coffee as there are valets, masters, people and circumstances. But there is a general example of what I mean by "the servant mind."

Of course, since freedom of Fellowship is impossible except on terms of self-respect and equality—some form of kick-back or treachery is the inevitable consequence of the servant mind, should it get into our midst, which is more and more the wrong place.

II. THE INFERIORITY COMPLEX

Not far removed from the servant mind, probably descended from it or descending to it in some way, is this troublesome inferiority complex. Even more dangerous to Fellowship than the servant mind because it is harder to diagnose and deal with. It is something that will make a young fellow ashamed to pick up a walking stick dropped by an elderly man, or a companion, for fear of seeming servile; something in the boy that makes him bad-mannered and awkward in fear of his own inherent servility. The fear makes him look as he is—cheap. That same thing prevents him from ever earning the title gentleman, and stands in the way of his ever becoming a truly manly man. We have observed it sometimes in the Fellowship in the more feminine types of young men. But the girls are not entirely exempt. In them it may stem from their attempt to throw off domination by the male.

Of course only a man who believes in himself can ever render loyalty to an Idea or be faithful to the Master of one, or to one who is Master of the Idea.

In true apprenticeship interchange must be between the two, which puts them into a trust with one another.

So the inferiority complex is dangerous to us because it cannot safely be put upon a footing of equality in comradeship nor, because it cannot trust itself, its loyalty to masterhood or to mastership is not be trusted.

Always a questionable troublesome type.

Judas was probably a better sort of the type who sought to save his Master from himself, seeing his Master as he (Judas) saw himself. The consequences of discipleship where this complex is concerned are always humiliating.

The Inferiority Complex shows itself most in unbecoming self-assertion—trying too hard to make itself believe what it wants to believe or have others believe: that it is not inferior. It is the opposite of modesty, protests too much always because it so much wants too much, fears itself too little. Nothing more damaging to Fellowship can be imagined or harder to root out, because, for one thing, it is a hangover of the umbilical cord. For another, it is the same inevitable subjective association of ideas that goes back to an aristocracy not natural. False.

Dr. Spivey (hero of Florida Southern College, Lakeland) once said that the boys who came to work their way through college were usually the malcontents, eventually the troublemakers. Instead of gratitude for the privilege extended to them, they themselves were suspicious that they were not in the same category as the paying students, and fancied slights, soon or late, developed resentment.

Our Fellowship also finds that the less a boy or girl actually has had in life before coming in to the Fellowship, the more super-sensitive to fancied slights or resemblance to servitude he is.

But there is something deeper there, undermining good fellowship, that tries to set up artificial barriers in order to "even up" the score? Something not openly acknowledged even to itself. Perhaps the same thing happens that happens when an article is "marked down" for sale. What we get cheap we seldom value much.

III. THE UMBILICAL CORD

The grown-up child today seldom casts it off entirely—especially the regenerate favored son. Usually it is sentimental, the tie-back to tastes or prejudices of the former generation: the "hold-back" to the parent who wants to see the child grow up, but suspects and dreads the consequences of necessary enlightenment. Father, a "conservative," fears for the son who is becoming a radical. Mother instinctively hovers over her young, perhaps in the position of a hen who has hatched out a duck. Or Father is the cock who has fathered a feather. The umbilical cord drags after the offspring or coils about the neck, preventing, so far as it may be, free action of the free spirit of the child. Because, if affectionate and dutiful, the child is sentimental where Mother and oftentimes Father are concerned. The Cord hurts and drags the boy or girl back if going too far or too fast ahead. So no asset to Fellowship. The cure for it is tragic. When the Spirit-parent encounters the carnal or flesh-and-blood parent, there is usually uneasy feeling on the part of the usual parent that parental authority is getting a bad break or being betrayed, his offspring led astray. Usually that parent feels that the child's own individuality is being sacrificed but does not believe that if so it is to his natural parents not to his spiritual ones. Certainly the only place a young mind could be led when the umbilical cord remains around the neck is "*astray.*" But why led? Why not inspired?

IV. PIN-FEATHER EGO

Worthless cargo always. But Fellowship falls heir to it not so much in the refugees from Education as those who come to Taliesin after four, five or six years of fairly successful college-life. These "degree" men, even more than those who break with college and come with a habituated mind and a tightly strung nervous system. Premature (which is immature) criticism characteristic. On a moment's notice, categorical wisdom! The callow premise and the categorical thesis. Always stock-and-shop points of view. Mental disjecta membra on every subject ever catalogued. Damage thus done to Youth by the classroom authorities Incalculable. This type is the ultimate Expert in embryo.

The embryo is living what life it has on information but is never really able to learn because short-circuited.

Young men living this vicarious life of the vicar devotee are individuals who try to escape the herd by herding. Intense but futile.

Mere association of ideas is what we call wishful thinking and too easy for most of us. We too easily make ourselves believe what we want to believe. The young man educated far beyond his capacity, it is possible to erect a complete synthetic tower and live there in it life long if his experience still stands long enough to allow him to get into the tower. But in certain circumstances in Usonian Urbania such intellectualism does stand out. I have seen it so stand, as potato sprouts do on potatoes in a dark cellar. This vicarious character is a prematurity and eventually an utter emasculation of soul where the manly ego should be. The result of Education, it is destined, as designed, to die on the vine: "designed mis-education." But meantime occasionally it has been a Fellowship stumbling block. Time, often months, sometimes years, must be given the victim in which to relax before he becomes sufficiently receptive either to perceive or acknowledge the mastery he meantime subconsciously emulates. Nothing can be put into hands so self-conscious with nervous tension as shuts so tight. When the hands open, palms upward, voluntarily held out together in the dignity of true appreciation, then is the time to give without fear of wasting the giver and the gift.

V. THE EVER WOMANLY

Woman always wins and she should win over the woman.

The Eternal Feminine is a Fellowship problem of no mean dimensions: the one never solved and may never be so long as we hold to our co-educational ideal. This is woman's day in civilization, her day, and her hour is her life in America. When left to her choice in our country she dresses her figure to emulate the style of the male, as her sons grow more and more to resemble the silhouettes of her own figure. Figures of the sons of their mothers and daughters of their fathers are thus growing more and more to resemble each other. Also they trade characteristics with disconcerting frequency.

Woman is steadily winning in the Fellowship.

She can turn a Fellowship into a nursery or a hospital, half trying.

To what extent co-education, under ideals like ours today under her rights can be trusted as desirable, we have no mind, except that we at Taliesin are not for the average woman. Certainly married companionship should be no bar to Fellowship were the average woman less possessed and possessive. But she is the natural cup to be filled—to which her man is to bring not only himself, but the makings of a future for their children. She is seldom cultured to be honestly idealistic in herself. She remains pragmatic because of her biological character in nature. She is concerned, if subjectively, soon objectively, for the little shovelful of coals that will enable her to start a little hell of her own at the very earliest possible moment. She is cooperative only until she gets her man. Thereafter she is only waiting to establish herself and wherever her man can bring to her, *hers*.

Now if there is an average woman she is a wise provision of nature for the preservation of the species. We—the Fellowship—cannot and should not quarrel with her, but we must, for the time being, learn how to go around her. The average-man may still be servant of an Ideal, but his inspiration comes frequently from his love for a woman minded otherwise, and so long as she sees him turning toward her, all is well. But she has to have a place for this. "He" must make a place especially for her, so either we must include in our plans separate households, independent for the purpose of raising children—which we are considering—or accept only such womanhood as has evolved the satisfactions of the artist, the philosopher, in short the Idealist who does not sacrifice but rather intensifies womanliness. Such women are rare, but we hope to have them. But how are we to recognize them before it is too late?

VI. THE CASH-AND-CARRY SYSTEM

Democracy badly needs a new Success Ideal. The present one is a form of slow paralysis. Not only does democracy need a new one but must have it soon or democracy perishes. Cashandcarry "Success" knows quantity but no quality nor can admit or permit of any mastership but Money. Money must be in the very nature of things as things are, be proof of Success such as our System is in our System. So most American universities inculcate and prepare for that venal sort of Success. Inevitably our American colleges and universities are enlarged Trade Schools—all qualifying the youth of the nation to cog in somewhere in the commercialized machine, and *earn money*. We, not yet so constituted, find that many youths must go back into the wagery of Cashandcarrydom to pay back money borrowed to be educated. So the wires get crossed. It is unfortunate for us that the trader-instinct—shopkeeping—lies in ambush everywhere: price tags already fixed on humanity as they are fixed upon any other commodity. But so it is. We of the Fellowship can scarcely hope entirely to escape the mark-up and the mark-down continually being made by American institutions. The result of this idiocy is what I am calling the Cashandcarry mentality we live by. That mentality is a routine, commercialized, middle-of-the-road substitute for a mind. You can move anybody in it around for a little more money than he has been getting.

It is more than merely difficult to set up, and almost impossible to maintain, a way of life for young men and women otherwise on the basis of their own individuality.

Such life as ours in the Fellowship *is* in unfair competition with that surrounding mentality. We (the one) must come and go to the many to a certain extent. That is inevitable.

Due to this opposing philosophy of our surroundings we suffer most.

Just as Democracy always suffers most and is lost in war. So our Cashandcarry nation needs every man wage-slave, dignify it how we may, just as the nation in war needs every man a conscript soldier. Because, in its false economy wherein production seeks control of consumption, it must be so. Commander-in-Chief of the Cashandcarry would have to be the banker as the case stands now. Commercial, professional propaganda, using the proper names, could make either defeat out of victory or victory out of defeat in any commercial circumstances if the props could be kept up long enough. That faith in production and continuous increase by unrelenting advertising is the touching faith of the average-man of our day in Peace. It is of course the same in War. Is that what this depression really means?

The most dangerous characteristic of The System however, from any cultural standpoint, is the short-cut to burial for the inherited inferiority complexes which the System breeds.

Money can do it to humanity as we see.

So our Fellowship is looked upon by the casual Cashandcarry with suspicion. "You are just a kind of Art Colony—ah!" Or: "You are a kind of country club for art students, ain't you?"; or, well, there are dozens of the common-man's choice of ideas of what we are. "Fellowship" sounds to them like some religious sect or other. Anyhow, no good can come of "getting off the beaten track." "The machine can't go there." "Stick to the boulevard, my boy!" "Main traveled roads are best, as everybody knows." "I have no patience with this conceited assumption of the try for something different." "The affair insulting *our* intelligence." "Who the hell are these people anyway?" "And what *is* their assumption?" "If what we got ain't good enough for them, all right. Who cares a damn about them. Let them get outa the country," etc., etc., ad libitum, ad nauseum.

If Cashandcarry mentality (wage-slave) gets into our Fellowship, it would probably soon be found mixed up in some kind of secret exploitation inside or outside of the Fellowship. The Cashandcarry mind is constantly worried by "What am I getting out of this anyway?" "Will it pay?"

"Never mind what I am giving to it: let them get what they can out of me."

486

So the natural fundamental of the profit system is ever present. It gets us down when we get it. But we don't get it now if we can see it first. Often we can't. It is only under pressure that it appears what it really is.

Suggested motto for the Cashandcarry: "Let us then be up and doing"—for *me!*

Running along with this mundane membrane Money, there is another parallel invention: Time. Time is a kind of policeman. Time, the policeman. But a policeman susidized by money. Time is money. Is money then time? Culture—ain't that what they put around the Flowers?

VII. THE BROADWAY CREED

Belittlement is in business now.

Confusion of the best with the worst is a vocation.

Concerning the wisecrack: we have always a supply in the Fellowship. We laugh at his cracks and in good turn we take a crack at him. He comes most frequently from the large urban centers of the East, but he comes also from Kansas, Dakota, California, or Minnesota. He is American. The Nation dotes on him.

The Broadway Creed has covered the country pretty much until it has Hollywood on its other end; pretty much commonplace all the way between: especially wherever the upper region of the pantaloons is promoted . . . and that is the box-office! Box-office? The particular cynicism of our era is a kind of smart smut which the breed of the creed instinctively uses to besmirch the common faith of the common man's enjoyment of himself.

Faith of any kind is a mark for the creed's experts, especially any surviving faith in the virtue of human nature. Selfishly bred, children of pleasure herding on hard, crowded pavements in congested urban areas, these are the patrons of the breed. The worm's-eye or low-down view suited to Cashandcarry mentality.

More important, the Broadwayman's Creed is the solace and the line of defense for the common-man inferiority complex.

In spite of Immigration laws, the complex grows up among us as the natural product of our melting pot.

As Carlyle said of Democracy, so say of the Broadway Creed, "A disease. Let us have it so we may have done with it and get on to rule by the bravest and the best." Nevertheless, human conduct may eventually grow to be a little wiser for the Broadwayites' side-walk happy-worm's-eye view. But a sense of the ridiculous assuming the airs and graces of humor, which is really what it is, has robbed us of too much native salt and savor. A Winchell is unwholesome Broadway substitute for a wholesome Will Rogers.

Among us all today there is enough punctilio to be punctured. Enough stuffed shirts to thump and hypocrisy enough to play up, infested as the country is with the flood of commercial exploits as erotically idiotically extolling their own "cheap" good piece of business by so doing.

The ratlike perspicacity of the breed raised on the Creed is not worth much where good work is to be done. How much?

Well, among so many examples, there's Mickey Mouse. He's amusing at least and not guilty.

Amusement is the indispensable Urbania. And while the laugh provoked by cruel ridicule and the vulgar funnies is not the same as the laugh provoked by the salt and savor of true humor, even that cheap laugh is worth something to our plight. The Creed may thus deserve its turn. The breed does own the Box Office. Its Box Office, social position; its laugh a cheap laugh. A laugh is our best medicine—that and a good physic.

Well . . . perhaps both save the day for some purpose for which neither was really intended and without which neither body nor spirit would survive.

This search for FORM must reject the Broadway Creed entire, because its laugh is not only a cheap laugh, but septic, as sterile as a belch. Inorganic, therefore it cannot reproduce, and the future dies with it, if not of it.

CONSCIENCE

Alter Ego is the distorted mirror (concave or convex as the case may be) in which mastership may see its own reflection. The alter ego may be a form of flattery but it is more often caricature to be borne for the good of some cause.

The young, if innocent, are hardly conscious of being guilty of alter-egoism, but the more sophisticated ones who do know they are guilty soon grow a hatred of the original of their borrowed image. The pictures they make and in time the alter ego himself thus becomes the instinctive detractor of his exploited original. His trouble is that the original is there behind his closed cupboard door, a threat to his own sense of himself every time and as he himself performs. He would like to escape and to destroy his original in the short cut.

Murder is his only self defense.

So the Disciple is a legitimate form of Alter Ego. Jesus had twelve, such as they were, and they were pretty much as they always are. But, occasionally, even the great inspired poet Jesus got up high in the high mountains to be rid of his disciples for a time. Nevertheless, I think the Alter Ego justified as a necessity. He is an asset to Fellowship but only so long as his alter-egoship is an open door or window through which you may see him looking out upon a natural world otherwise dark to him, the outside of a world wherein his alter-egoship might gradually grow independent by way of the sincerity of his devotion to his master; his devotion becoming the door or window through which he sees what his master sees—eventually gaining direction at least: perhaps being saved years of wasted effort by the light that shines from his exemplar, who under certain conditions is himself that door and window. Then is alter ego justified. The only is he an honest asset to Fellowship. His apprenticeship stepping stone to his own independence; even if his aim continues lymphatic, it continues to be collateral. It is usually unfair to accuse an alter ego of plagiarism. He "*steals*" nothing. He gives himself to his master simple-mindedly with no reservation, while his own sense of himself in whatever is to be done by him is forming within him. I have found that those in the Fellowship who had least Individually worried most about it. Those who had it most were seldom concerned. It would take care of itself naturally without offense or defense. Emulation is what we expect and rightfully desire.

Emulation and imitation are enemies.

The Alter Ego seldom directly "copies." His original source of inspiration although inherent in the masterpiece is the expression of that in which he participated. If a good disciple he is himself worthy as an implication of his master. Maybe for life. But most disciples are a weariness to future mastership. Before very long it is seen that he has not been inspired, so is parasitic, is only using his master as a shield for his own inconstancy, or vain exploitation.

To enter sincerely into the spirit of a master, standing loyally by his side in his work, proud to acknowledge it, is, so it has always seemed to me, the greatest privilege any novice apprentice or disciple may ever have.

Education has nothing so precious to offer to youth as conscientious emulation.

Usonia needs thousands of Taliesins, not one only.

But to go too far with the letter in any implications of great work is to insult both the master and the apprentice himself.

Men of achievement in Arts and Sciences should continue their activities by placing themselves where their experience may serve the oncoming tide of life. But how far should the Alter Ego go with his apprenticeship? The answer is that all depends upon circumstances and the individual Creative Conscience. With that Conscience developed both novice and master are safe and happy in each other. Time is of no essence in the matter. Apprenticeship may go on five—ten—years profitably to both, perhaps for life. It all depends. The sincere search for FORM can use the honest alter ego for life and the alter ego, if sound, use the master for life. Both can go along. They will both be there when inspired FORM becomes fact.

Creative Conscience then lies deep in the heart of the artist, as in manhood. The arbiter of the fashioner of FORM, it demands the whole truth or suffers defeat. It gives the whole truth.

Marvelous to stew, like fruit, in one's own juice and then set one's self back to simmer for a while before final judgment.

FELLOWSHIP ASSETS—GOOD CORRELATION!

    I. AN HONEST EGO IN A HEALTHY BODY
    II. AN EYE TO SEE NATURE
    III. A HEART TO FEEL NATURE
    IV. COURAGE TO FOLLOW NATURE
    V. THE SENSE OF PROPORTION (HUMOR)
    VI. APPRECIATION OF WORK AS IDEA AND IDEA AS WORK
    VII. FERTILITY OF IMAGINATION
    VIII. CAPACITY FOR FAITH AND REBELLION
    IX. DISREGARD FOR COMMONPLACE (INORGANIC) ELEGANCE
    X. INSTINCTIVE COOPERATION

These human attributes of Taliesin Fellowship when inspired by love will eventually evoke THE CREATIVE CONSCIENCE where otherwise it might have slumbered for life.

THE FIRST-PERSON SINGULAR

The only thing a man has that ought never to be taken away from his is himself. But he can never afford to be selfish. In Selfhood the more of himself he gives the more he will have to give. The less he gives the less he will have to give.

As I already said: I find that young men who had most individuality were troubled least about it. To be too much concerned with your own is a pretty sure sign that there is little there to be concerned with. A sound man does not think or speak much of his health nor willingly speaks of what he thinks most deeply. So until a man knows the difference between individuality and personality he may confound them in any issue where either is at stake. Usually what he is worrying about is his personality. Individuality is the essential innate character of the man: his fate. His personality is merely the way he looks, walks, speaks, his form, features and habits. Idiosyncrasies are mainly matters of mere personality. None of these personal things constitute the man's Individuality. Individuality lies deeper and is of the soul, probably looking out at you from the eyes of the one you are looking at, looking from under the roof of his mind quite all unconscious of person or fact—inspired by love.

We don't often labor the first-person singular. We let it pretty much alone, as it likes to be if genuine. We have allowed none to get in here without enough of it to be respected. Bored, however, with the intellectual disguise which is the abuse of the thing—mistaking mere egotistic curiosity for a thirst for knowledge but seldom able to draw the line between the curious and the beautiful: the first-person singular is the man. He grows best and becomes strongest and most fruitful when it is not too aware of itself, not encouraged to pull itself up by the roots every now and then to see how it is growing—so often nothing really takes roots.

Walt Whitman said he loved the companionship of animals—they were not worried, or worry others, on account of their souls.

I like Emerson, walking out under the elms: "The great elm-trees looked down upon him and said, 'Why so hot, my little man, why so hot?' "

Why indeed!

ALDEBARAN

Among the very first college graduates (engineering) to come in to Fellowship was a tall dark-eyed young fellow who early turned up at Taliesin. Son of an Evansville editor. *Who's Who* says the editor was the man who drove the Ku Klux Klan out of Indiana. He did, practically single-handed. The lad was a fountain of energetic loyalty to the ideas for which Taliesin stood. He soon took a leading hand in whatever went on. Mind alert, his character independent and generous. He was young—about twenty.

Svetlana, our charming adopted daughter (came to Taliesin with Olgivanna) now sixteen. Soon it appeared that Svetlana liked to ride the truck Wes drove. A general sympathy amounting to a conspiracy grew up behind these young people in the Fellowship. Everybody except Olgivanna and myself aware of a budding romance. Not we. When we did wake up—there were some accusations and unkind words. Too soon! Both too young! The budding romance which looked like a kind of treachery then went underground, but partisans for the young couple formed to fight their battle for them. No use. We wouldn't have any of it. So after a while the principals and their partisans struck out for parts unknown. We had been so fond of them both we couldn't see the thing as other than the treachery of ungrateful irresponsible children.

We didn't hear from them for a year or more. But we greatly missed them and the inevitable reconciliation took place after they had been married—Svetlana studying music in Chicago, Wes building buildings in Evansville. Were we happy to have them back—giving good accounts of themselves? We were. Perhaps the break was a good thing all around. Certainly both were much improved by this break on their own. And we were a good deal the wiser. So I guess we improved too.

Wes's father soon died, and Wes inherited a small income and widowed mother. Taliesin had a son-in-law as well as a devoted cooperator.

There was a picturesque group of hills to the West—next door. A farm on the river next Taliesin, a farm of about three hundred fifty acres. Wes coveted it and I egged him on to buy it. He seemed the kind of lad who could use ground. I wanted to see Taliesin expand—expecting someday to see its collaterals owning as much of the countryside as together we could well use in order to protect the landscape development I planned.

Our son-in-law bought the ground—named it Aldebaran (the follower), and Taliesin soon after jumped to the control of about one thousand acres with about three miles of waterfront. The naming of the place shows the spirit of the lad: a genuine apprentice. His ambitions were not cheap: individuality strong. He didn't need to worry about that. He was glad and proud to stand by and contribute his strength to Taliesin and Taliesin appreciated him, believed in him as much as he believed in Taliesin. Here was apprenticeship in flower. Wes planned his house on that nearby hill—a well-conceived house for his young wife, who gave him a young son they named Brandoch, a name which puts it up to the boy to be at least a hero.

Taliesin had a daughter, a son and a grandson. Taliesin has other faithful competent sons—an asset to Fellowship, but none with more strength, energy and loyalty than the young man Olgivanna and I drove away years ago on the unkind assumption that he was stealing a daughter. Well, Svetlana, the daughter, is now somebody in her own right.

Here in the Wisconsin Hills, Aldebaran is Taliesin's first real extension—collateral human growth. But inside Taliesin Wes is a young leader and the charming lively Svetlana—both have a large share in cultivating the life of the Fellowship. Svetlana has an innate sense of music. Wes is so interested in farming that I can scarcely get Architecture out of him or into him any more. But it is there and makes, I guess, a Taliesin showpiece.

Wes (then ten years at Taliesin) is a right bower, example of What-Taliesin-Can-Do-for-a-Young-Apprentice (his wife thrown in) and, what a young apprentice can do for Taliesin.

THE STORY OF HIBBARD THE JOHNSON WHO DID SO MUCH FOR HIS OLD HOME TOWN—WAX OFFICIATING

Hibbard (alias Hib), attractive young son of a great waxmaker, who was also the son of a waxmaker. Hib's father, so they say around about Racine, Wisconsin, (his old home town), was famous for his "hunches." Not only did Hib inherit the ancestral factories but the ancestral facilities. He has hunches and this now world-famous modern office building to house the administration of the ancestral wax-manufacturing company was one of Hib's hunches. Hib's remarkable house too, now standing broad, wide and handsome out in the prairie countryside near by, was . . . but of that, later. Hib's hunches made him, for one thing, the only Racine boy to do anything really worthwhile to culture that industrial area: the big successful wealthy Wisconsin Factory owners by Lake Michigan where millionaires originate and from which they always go somewhere else for fun, to spend their money for culture, if any. Along with Hib's family inheritances a valuable lieutenant-general, John Ramsey by name, manager by nature. No manufacturer, so I believe, ever had a better manager or a better man than Jack. Jack, like Hibbard, had seen and participated in the education manufactured at Wisconsin U., but both refused to bite off more standard erudition than either could well digest. Hib's brother-in-law, Jack Louis by name, was head of a prosperous advertising firm in nearby Chicago, guiding the publicity side of S. C. Johnson Wax by radio. "Johnson's Wax" gave Fibber McGee and Molly a long ride, eventually greatly to the benefit of the wax-polish industry, and no doubt—Fibber and Molly Mcgee.

Well, this particular hunch of Hib's so had it that the prosperity of his overcrowded and solidly prosperous concern should enable the company to do something worthwhile for the daily lives of its numerous office employees, young and old. So the limit in convenience and beauty in a building for this purpose his intelligence could find and the best in quality the Johnson Wax money could ever pay for, was none too good for Hib now.

When the sky at Taliesin was dark, the days there gloomy, as I have described them, Hib and Jack were the ones who came out to Taliesin one day to see about that new building. They came, you might say, like messengers riding on white steeds trumpeting glad tidings. Jack Louis had been willing, but skeptical; Architecture was not Radio. But, some time before, a group of art directors from Chicago had visited Taliesin—egged on by good friend Bill Kittredge, and Willis Jones came along. Willis, a discerning and greatly appreciative young art director, was working for Jack Louis at the time, making designs for his Chicago advertising company. After this visit, of his own volition Willis got after the Johnson folk and also a talented young architect, Howard Raftery, put up a sacrificial fight for Taliesin. As a result, this now official visit. Gratifying annunciation occurred sometime in July, 1936. The occasion was pleasant all around. Next day came a note from Hib enclosing a retainer (ten thousand dollars) testifying to his appreciation of what he saw on that occasion. The pie thus opened, the birds began to sing, sing again below the home at Taliesin; dry grass on the hillside waxed green; the hollyhocks went gaily into a second blooming. The orchard decided to come in with a heavy crop of big red harvest apples and the whole landscape seemed to have more color; Iovanna rode more fiercely through the Valley; and both Olgivanna's responsibilities and mine were doubled—with smiles. Work was incessant. Taliesin galvanized into fresh activity. A good commission!

Well . . . pretty fine sketches for the administration building, best I could do, just about as the building stands there now in its utterly unworthy environment, went forward. Returning home after that momentous visit, the abandonment of plans resembling a fancy crematorium which some local architect had contributed was enacted and Hib gave over the coveted commission to the architect Jones and Raftery had persistently advocated—an architect held back outside the current of building for some seven years. Here and thus his feet were put back on the road to an activity. Almost "struck out" by the very long chain of untoward circumstances hereinbefore related. I could now look back upon that visit—July 20, 1936—with a deep and pleasant satisfaction, never ceasing to be glad that I have for friends the two men who came to see me that day.

What a release of pent-up creative energy—the making of those plans! Ideas came tumbling up and out onto paper to be thrown back in heaps—for careful scrutiny and selection. But, at once, I knew the

494

scheme I wanted to try. I had it in mind when I drew the newspaper plant at Salem, Oregon, for Editor George Putnam, which he had been unable to build. A great simplicity and grace—organic.

Owing to a high ideal of simplicity, organic, this building was bound to be an exacting piece of work. For quite some time I conducted myself like a pregnant mother, I imagine.

And there were enough headaches to go all around on all sides: the "union" strong in Racine, the building codes wrong in Wisconsin. Also, in addition to the law of gravitation, here was the terrific time-lag for Innovation to overcome. But no cultural lag! None. Both Hib and Jack were at the head of the procession from start to finish. "They" say I am "hard to get along with" (meaning, really, hard to *go* along with), but I was never too much for these boys. The opus added unto itself a vast domiculated carport, a small hemicycle for the entertainment and instruction of employees got up over the entrance and then came squash courts, garages, etc., etc. All these, and more, came knocking for admission. We started with a paltry $250,000 in the "rock pile." Before we started, it jumped to $350,000—and as time went on landed in a pile nearer $550,000. But we had more to show for that pile than anybody who ever built a similar industrial administration building of the first rank. The entire thing thoroughly fireproof, air-conditioned, floor-heated (gravity heat), and, including appropriate furnishings designed by the architect, was built for about seventy-eight cents per cubic foot. And observe—although a building is not radio, it was the psychological world-moment for the more serious sort of thing we now did. Hib knew that in his "hunch" and took the gaff with only a stab at his architect now and then. Just for luck I suppose. Consequences were already coming.

But no stabs in the back.

Jack kicked around a little—managerially. But why not ?Some kicking was a necessary feature owing to the great simplicity of that building.

Also, to preserve the great simplicity, I made some 132 trips by motor car from Taliesin to Racine (a distance of 165 miles) to superintend the structure in detail and over a period of two years in all weathers, just to get it built the way I thought it should be built—carrying on until, toward the end, pneumonia had me down just to interrupt proceedings. More patience had to be added to infinite patiences in order that the great simplicity required up to that time stood. Perhaps only Ben, the Wiltscheck, our builder, can quite realize how much was required. Ben was no contractor's contractor. Educated at Penn in architecture and failing to satisfy himself with his own designs, he went out to build buildings for me. Ben was "au fait." He went about everywhere in Racine society on equal terms with employers. But more to the point, he was a careful builder—well aware of the great importance of keeping the architect right there on the job. Not one move would Ben make until the detailed drawings of the original drawings were detailed some more. So far as I know, for once in a way the Builder did not try to destroy the Architect. There was real cooperation, confidence in each other's ability all around, and all the time. Without that circumstance no such building as that modern thoroughbred could ever have been built at all. It was, and altogether is, such a Simplicity as never found in stock. It was in no sense and nowhere—shop but creative.

When the "Johnson Building" was opened the world seemed to have been waiting for the event—because it was there outside trying to get in to see it. When finally it did get in, reams of newspaper copy began to pour from the press, and such talk!

Everyone who saw the building tried to describe it. "It is like a woman swimming naked in a stream. It is cool, gliding, musical in movement and in manner. The inside of an office building like a woman swimming naked in a stream? Yes, that's right." (Leading feature article: *Life Magazine,* May, 1938.)

Bill Connolley, competent "man on the job" for the advertising of the S. C. Johnson Co., calculated that (with no help from him at all) two or more millions of dollars could not have bought the front pages in newspapers and top-notch magazines the building had attracted to itself—gratis.

The movie "shorts" took it up and carried on.

Radio came running. Meanwhile streams of visitors from all over the world went on and continue to go on to this hour.

Why? Because something universal in the air, that's why. High time to give our hungry American public something truly "streamlined," so swift, so sure of itself and clean for its purpose, clean as a hound's tooth—that *anybody* could see the virtue of this thing called Modern. Many liked it because it was not "modernistic," but seemed to them like the original from which all the "streamlining" they had ever seen might have come in the first place. As a matter of fact, the word "streamlined" had been first applied to buildings by the architect of this one.

INCIDENTAL

The Wisconsin Industrial Commission vexed us when we asked for a permit—wouldn't say yes and didn't say no to the plans. But I've learned since from contacts with other building commissions in other states (let's say Missouri for one) how sensible and considerate that Wisconsin Commission under Mr. Wrabetz et al. was. This partly, I believe, because Hib himself stood up at the board meeting beside me and squarely told the commission that he wanted that building that way and he was damn well prepared to stand back of it to the hilt—no limit. Finally, if we would agree to make tests as the building proceeded, should the commission require them, we were told to go ahead. We did make several important tests. We made them with such startling and gratifying success that new precedents for reinforced concrete construction were established. The Industrial Commission raised no further objection.

The Tokio Building Commission (1914) asked for a permit to build the Imperial Hotel (proved earthquake-proof), the Japanese authorities enacted a scene somewhat similar. They couldn't say yes and didn't say no because they had never seen anything like the scheme proposed, but said—"Go ahead: we will watch you with the hope that from you, world-famous architect [deferential bows both sides] we may have something. So we will follow carefully. Please proceed." We did. And they did follow. Very carefully, indeed, let me say.

So there was never an official permit to build the Imperial Hotel earthquake-proof. It was all a gigantic experiment on behalf of Japan by the *Kenchiku ho* of the Imperial Household—myself. Experiment not yet understood nor fully granted success by my own people, except with a grudge. The Japanese, however, were pleased with the results.

After all, it was their affair? The A.I.A. sending a committee to Japan to study the results of the quake. Read the published report. No mention of the Imperial Hotel.

And there never was more than a conditional permit to build the unique Administration Building of Johnson's Wax; nor ever a permit to build the original textile block houses in California, nor the later board-and-brick Usonian Houses in seventeen different states. No. Nor—but we are talking about the building that Hib's "hunch" set up life-size in his own home town, Racine, and partly for the edification, amazement of the home town itself. But too much so.

BEAUTIFUL BUSINESS

Organic architecture, this great building is as inspiring a place to work in as any cathedral ever was in which to worship. Meant to be a socio-architectural interpretation of modern business at its top and best level.

Laid out upon a horizontal unit system twenty feet on centers both ways, rising into the air on a vertical unit system of three and a half inches: one especially large brick course. Glass was not used as bricks in this structure. Bricks were bricks. The building itself became—by way of long glass tubing laid like bricks—crystal where crystal either transparent or translucent was felt to most appropriate. In order to make the structure monolithic the exterior enclosing wall-material appeared inside wherever it was sensible.

Main feature of construction was simple repetition of slender hollow monolithic dendriform shafts or *stems*—the stems standing tip-toe on small brass shoes bedded at the floor level.

The structure throughout light and plastic—an open glass-filled rift up there where the cornice might have been in classic-times. Reinforcing was mostly cold-drawn steel mesh—welded innovation.

The entire steel-reinforced structure stands there earthquake-proof, fireproof, sound-proof and vermin-proof today. Amost fool-proof but alas, no. Simplicity is never fool-proof nor is it ever for fools.

This building by way of a natural use of steel in tension, appears to lift and float in light and air; "miraculously light dendriforms" standing up against the sky take on integral character as plastic units of a plastic building construction, *emphasizing* space instead of standing up in the way as mere inserts for support-destroying space.

The main clerical work-force was correlated in this one vast room, 228 by 228 feet. This great room, air-conditioned. Besides the top lighting and rift for light at the cornice level, the room is daylit also by rifts in the brick walls. The heating system of the main floor of the building is entirely beneath the floor slab. The structure is hermetically sealed and air-conditioned in addition to this gravity heat. Gravity heat—the system I brought from Japan, 1919.

The building complete, destined to stand in unimpressive surroundings and bounded by three ordinary village streets, we settled upon the main entrance as interior to the building and the lot; thus the motor car was provided for as a modern indispensable with new hospitality. Ample parking facilities are under cover of this great domiculated spread of carport at the center of the building.

The main building itself in which the dendriform shafts are floated is set back from the street on three sides; a colorful band of planting dividing the main brick walls from the sidewalks, enlivening the dreary environment. Above, the carport, tile-paved, was to have become a playground for the workers.

The hemicycle—a cinema seating 250 for daytime lectures or entertainment, wired complete for sound, is placed at mezzanine level at the middle of the floor arrangement. An enclosed glass-roofed bridge spans and connects the officers' quarters in the penthouse to a tall wood-lined squash court rising high above the garage. President Herbert Johnson's private office, an office for his stenographer and a private chemical laboratory ride at the apex of this penthouse; the officers, Jack Ramsey at their head, are built in on the same level (roof level) in each of the wings extending from it.

Below this penthouse arrangement of officers who, by way of the open court under the glass ceiling, have a view of the big workroom on the ground level, are the several hundred office workers sitting at especially devised desks on chairs that belong to the desks. Sub-heads of various departments function just above them in a low gallery, mezzanine to the big room where direct vision and prompt connection with the workers in the big room itself is had directly at convenient points by spiral iron stairways.

The few enclosures within the big workroom are low glass walls, screened by Aeroshades. Thus the plastic sense of the whole, most stimulating, is well preserved in various parts even to the uttermost detail.

The main toilet accommodations are located conveniently, directly beneath the working staff, directly reached by means of small circular iron stairs located at appropriate intervals for convenient access.

The entire building operation, by way of cost-plus arrangements, was in the architect's hands, ably managed by Ben Wiltscheck, supervised by myself, superintended by the Taliesin Fellowship, mainly by Wesley Peters and Edgar Tafel.

To enumerate in detail or even catalogue the innovations to be found in this one building would require more time and patient attention on your part, and mine too, than either of us cares to give it. So let's say here that it is technically, and in the entire realm of the scientific art of Architecture, one of the world's remarkably successful structures. I like it. They like it. Let it go at that.

For once, again an up-to-the-minute thoroughbred, daughter of the Larkin Building—1906—was born—1938—on provincial American soil. A great modern building completely furnished, planted complete in perfect keeping with the original idea of this more feminine building as a whole, was its sire, the masculine Larkin Building of Buffalo.

This legitimate offspring is now here to be seen. But, you can only see as much of the harmonious whole as your inner vision permits.

That will be however much your sense of innate rhythm in building construction enables you to perceive. It takes a developed "someone" to see the Johnson Administration Building altogether. That is, to see it *all*. But most folks see enough to delight them. Or make them resentful. To see *in* is not the same as to look *at*.

Hib's hunch not only worked in building but built up advertising returns—and also began to work in terms of increased work and employee morale. Work and morale increased one-tenth to a third during the first year the building was in use, Jack Ramsey said. The officials, all except the old timers, loved the place as much as the help did, and some of both of them said they hated to leave it to go home. Jack Ramsey himself (who had a fine new happy home) was one of these. But there were many others. Hib must have felt something that way himself . . . because just as I had got out of bed with pneumonia, the idea of building a house of his own, to match it, grew up in his mind. One day he had taken me out to see the tract of prairie (a small lake running its length) that he owned by the big lake (Michigan), and had for years been keeping as a kind of wild-fowl preserve. Some days after we had walked and talked about a house on that site I had explained a zoned house to him, Hib brought me a little sketch plan he had himself penciled of the general outlines of a house zoned pretty much as his stands out there now on the prairie.

Just before I had come down with devastating fever, Hib had been dining with us and, after dinner, I was demonstrating with a Victrola the essential lack of modern cacophony as compared with Music—jumping up and down meantime to change the records. "Man," he said, "don't you know you waste a lot of energy that way when you might be resting?"

Shortly after this, an agent of the Capehart, by name Cushing, came out with instructions from Hib to measure the house for a complete three-station installation of that remarkable record-changing, playing instrument. A super-fine record-player with a radio attachment just as Scott's a super-fine radio with a record-playing attachment. Hib put in the most complete installation ever seen. More complete than his own. He was like that sometimes—another "hunch."

HUNCHES

I respect "hunches" of others, that is, should they correspond with mine! This one—the little sketch made with T square and triangle—did. Soon that new "zoned" house for the young bride Hib was to bring to it was designed, and under way. He had mumbled something to me in a vague sort of way about "cost," but I knew he didn't mean *me* to be too much interested in that: *his* affair—after all. So I laid the house out on a scale befitting a young industrial prince of the Johnson line, who life-long had had about everything he wanted. Now I intended he should want something finer than he had ever seen to want. What else than a house such as the home I could build for him could he buy with money or time that would yield him such returns? This house I wanted to build for him should be, definitely, his "capital" not only safe during his lifetime, but go on as true capital into the lives of his children and their children—a joy meantime and a distinction: proof of quality. What more genuine capital to make of "capital"? There were some arguments about that point. Some feeling about it later. Not much though, because Hib is, after all, pretty much right and well off so far as money goes.

Two youngsters—a charming girl and a nice boy were his own, result of a former marriage and now his newly promised bride had two boys of her own—hence the children's wing for four. Next the high Wigwam (the living room) under the mass of wild grape vinery, shooting out from the center four independent wings. One wing (a luxurious mezzanine), continuous balcony toward the great lake, for Prince Hib and princess, on the ground floor one wing for four children—another wing on the ground for workspace and help, another on the ground for guests and motor cars.

We called the house "Wingspread" because spread its wings it would. We set a cast bronze door plate into the wide stone slab of the doorsill with abstract wings upon it in low relief to signify the name: wings in more than one sense.

This structure is another of the "prairie-type" common to earlier years. A type proving itself good for a home in the climate around the Great Lakes, popularly known as brick veneer. Outside upper members are wide cypress plank, roofs tiled, floors concrete; four-foot-square concrete unit system slab tiles laid over floor heating, here as in the Administration Building.

Thus "Wingspread," unique prairie house nearby Racine became another zoning experiment, began in the articulation of the Coonley House at Riverside, built 1909, wherein Living Room, Dining Room,

Kitchen, Family Sleeping Rooms, Guest Rooms, were separate units grouped together and connected by appropriate means.

This building is orientated so that sunlight falls in all rooms and the ground plan shows a completely logical expression of the Zoned House. (The first design for such a house was printed in the Taliesin Monograph, December, 1934.)

At the center of the four "zones" forming a cross, stands the spacious wigwam of a Living Room; a tall central brick chimney-stack with five fireplaces on four sides divides this room vertically into four spaces for the various domestic functions: Entrance, Family Living, Library and Dining Room. Extending from this lofty central wigwam are four wings. This lies, very much at home, quiet and integral with the prairie landscape. In this case, especially, green growth will eventually claim its own; wild grapevines swinging pendent from the generously spreading trellises over all the living room windows; extensive collateral gardens in bloom, extending about the wings—great adjoining masses of evergreens on two sides and one taller dense dark mass set on a low mound in the middle of the entrance court—the single associate of this spreading dwelling on the prairie is Lake Michigan and lies well off ahead but within the middle distance, is seen over the wild-fowl pool which stretches away in that direction from just below the main terrace of the house. Charming foreground.

But this house, while resembling the Coonley House at Riverside, Illinois, is more bold, masculine and direct in form and treatment. Better executed in more permanent materials. This building has a heavy footing course of Kasota sandstone resting on rock ballast laid deep in broad trenches, has the best brickwork I have seen. Materials of construction and workmanship throughout are everywhere substantial. Especially the woodwork and furniture by Gillen of Milwaukee show unusual craftsmanship. Hib's house is architecturally furnished throughout in fairly good keeping with the quiet character established by the building.

Here, because Hib rubbed his lamp and parted from a little more "capital," another prairie house in 1938 came out of the blue to join the earlier ones of 1901–10 built in times when building costs were less than half.

Unhappily the young bride never lived to enter the home. Out of the blue (the house three-fourths finished) one day an old workman on the house told me that a white dove we had seen frequenting the belvedere of the building—and in which both Hib and I were interested—had flown away and disappeared. The workman shook his head. A bad omen said he. "The young mistress will never live in this house," and she too, as we soon learned, had passed away.

502

Hib's interest in our building went way down. It took good persuasion to get him interested in ever going on with the house again, although it was three-fourths done at the time this blow fell. I, friend now as well as architect, did my best to represent to him what I thought his young wife would wish were she living. I felt sure she would want to see him finish what he had so happily begun with her; now more than ever he needed refuge such as that house would be for his children (fast growing up); he owed it, if not to himself, if not to her, then to Racine not to leave an empty shell of a house desecrating in desperation instead of nobly memorializing the wife he had lost. After a while I guess he began to see it something like that. Because we began work on it again. We completed the house in every particular as planned for a wife and four children. Hib seemed to sigh with relief upon seeing actually realized the home they had both worked on with me and of which he had fondly dreamed. The house, not yet a home, had begun to justify the hopes from the first invested in it. It turned out a veritable thing of the Spirit: a true consort of the prairie. The "last of the prairie houses" it shall be, so I said and thought—though I don't know why there should ever be a last one.

SEEING IS BELIEVING

Should you ever see the house, observe this fact . . . the house did something remarkable to that site. The site was not at all stimulating before the house went up—but like developer poured over a negative, when you view the environment framed by the Architecture of the house from within, somehow, like magic—charm appears in the landscape and will be there wherever you look. The site seems to come alive.

Hib saw this. He felt it did express, in a finer sense, human feeling for the young wife lost than anything else he could have done. Soon Hib began to wake up really and actually live in that house. That house, more than anything else, I believe, brought Hib back again. But he might be unwilling to say so. He is not sentimental. Oh no.

HERESY

A test is usually heresy. Ever since I can remember trying to build at all, tests have been going on under my supervision or in my experience. A test of some kind always either in sight or just around the corner, or just evaporating results and another necessary. The supreme test, I suppose, was the earthquake's grasp of the Imperial Hotel. Leading up to that final test were foundation tests with borings and pig-iron leadings; slab tests; cantilever tests; tests of the value of continuity in heavy concrete beams; tests of stair-flights extending from floor slabs like extended arms. Not to mention plumbing tests, wiring tests. Test by test we arrived at the ultimate: the Imperial's stable flexibility.

Large or small, nearly every structure I have built required some test. Or many. Foundation tests. Floor-heating tests; novel wall-construction tests; tests of new details of fenestration. Fireplace construction to be tested; roof construction in new materials to be tried out. Experiment following experiment. Frequently one test would require others. One experiment would lead to the next until the building process extending back over a period of forty-five years resembles the continuous test to which life itself subjects the serious architect himself.

Is it true that Nature never puts an idea of Form into practice, plants a new type of species, that she doesn't plant its natural enemy beside it? Nature has her equilibrium to maintain. She is continually maintaining her sense of proportion in all things. So when we make tests we are really trying to discover her status quo (for so it is), or, shall we say, the laws of proportion inherent in her own designs. Her equilibrium is a seldom unknown quantity. It probably amounts to God and we cannot reach God on the stepladder we call Science. And probably a very short and rickety one. But lightness and strength in erection, volume and weight at the ground levels, certain obvious limited patterns, we may see make sense before our eyes. There are many variations—hence the tests.

The serious architect comes closer to certain secrets of nature in his practice if he is master of organic FORM than most artists and even scientists. Although in any final analysis we are all in the same category—all making tests according to primary calculation or better than calculation—inspiration. Testing an inspiration? Mere expert in building-construction would declare it absurd.

That "absurdity" has characterized my life.

An architect is either on the winning side grasping the laws of nature or on the losing side, the side of dead data, the idée fixe, the Code.

Book data, the result of some testing limited at the time by this and that circumstance. Most important of such data as we know serves only for a time, the length of time determined by how flexible the mind of the man and the formula were when "datum" was fixed.

Organic flexibility is the only chance a mind or a datum has for survival.

Heraclitus was right: all is in a state of becoming.

So Codes are the short mental limitations of men, short of vision,

504

short of imagination, short of courage and eventually short of common sense.

Compel the bureaucrats (those "blessed by a little brief authority") to throw the codes out every five years and enact new ones. Meanwhile (as it has already been done in England) a referendum should be set up as a Court of Appeals with better mental equipment than can be expected of the administrators of fixed codes. Referendum qualified to listen to ideas and give sanction to likely experiments—proper safeguards provided—in order that the data for the best ideas for the next five years may be at least a matter of record.

The bureaucrat is a short-time man, however long his legs or term may be. His life of the mind is only fit for a bureau. Undersize in most respects. Being a limb, as some member of an Authority, he worships Authority and since Authority is all the strength he has he cherishes what little he has with all his strength.

Truth, justice, advancement—these are not his concern or his problem.

In fact these become his enemies. He does not feel safe with any one of them, not to mention several, of these vital concerns of humanity in one lump.

Tradition—the formula—in that the bureaucrat is invested with whatever power he has. Anything irregular inverts him. So he is one of the grains of sand in the sandbags that ballast the flying ship of Progress. That is good enough for him. He asks—"but that little here below." So in vain to submit tests to a bureau or a Crat. Both are in the position of the black crow who declared, after the other crow had tried hard to convince him that he could sing, "No, no good. No, I don't like it. No. Youse is wastin' your time—'cause I wouldn't like it, even if it was good!"

Fatal weakness of Democracy you are—the bureaucrat. The weakness of Democracy does not lie in gangsterism, political chicanery or civil disobedience or anything like them. It lies in this dumb sheeplike submission to Authority, "this drinking of the vanity of office." Especially in this taking sanctuary by the bureaucrat. That is why Democracy sets Authority under Authority which is set under another Authority that can go to court and have the lower Authority reversed. But how long? O Lord, how long to get any error reversed after it has thus been built in?

The Wisconsin Building Commission, Wrabetz et al., is a superior building commission as commissions go, but enforcing an old code which they revise from time to time, by calling in for the purpose those architects who abide by the Code and do not make trouble for the commission by experiments. Thus the "body of the politic" is safeguarded?

Now, in the case of the Johnson Administration Building, I referred to a board meeting wherein Hib and I appeared to ask the commission to give us permission to proceed on a test basis . . . one of those tests, not because it is more important than a dozen others but because it is recent, is recounted here.

The Code allowed a maximum height of seven feet for a concrete column nine inches in diameter no matter how constructed. Concrete is concrete, n'est-ce pas?

To go to the height of the dendriform shaft twenty-four feet high, spreading into a ceiling as was now contemplated, three feet in diameter would thus have to be the senseless size at the base—for a spacing of the shafts on 24'0" centers—because two thousand five hundred pounds was code-limit on concrete. There would still be space to sit around in the building but little visibility. Hence the scene in the board room described in the story of that building.

My dendriform shaft was predicated on cold-drawn steel-mesh reinforcement, steel integument embedded in the outer high-grade concrete flesh of the shaft—the circular membrane of steel thus becoming one with the flesh of concrete. The resultant strength was far and away beyond anything the usual rod-reinforcing, on which the code had been framed, could allow. Also by agitating the concrete while pouring, it was quite easy to raise the code-limit on concrete from twenty-five hundred pounds to an actual twelve thousand at least.

A field test was decided upon and declared open: no objection to publicity. Having the expensive steel forms already made (we were that sure of success), we set up an exact duplicate dendriform out on the site in plain view, steadied it by slight diagonal wood braces and with a steam shovel we started dumping weighed gravel and cement bags on the extended flat floor on top of the shaft. By the time the load appeared in sight not only the commission but the town and neighboring press were observers. I sat with several apprentices looking on—woolen shawl on my shoulders (it was cold) but was soon walking around with Hib watching for the first telltales of failure. The crane kept swinging and dumping, swinging and dumping, until the sun went down. We were still there waiting for collapse. Long ago any requirement by the commission had been passed and doubled. Still the heap up there on top kept growing.

The sight became incredible. The police had now taken charge and roped the populace from the vicinity of that heroic slender stem, standing up there a graceful thing on tiptoe, standing straight and true, until at least sixty tons instead of the twelve required were on top of a shaft

506

nine inches in diameter at the tip on the ground, and the concrete was only eight days old. Slight cracks were now discernible in the upper part of the shaft where it splayed into the spreading top. No more load could be put on without sliding off, so I gave the word to break it down. I wanted to see where failure would come first, although it was pretty evident where. A lateral push against the shaft brought the enormous overload tumbling to the ground causing a tremor felt to the surrounding streets. The shaft, still unbroken, lay on the ground. The spreading head had broken off at the shaft. The commissioner, saying nothing, disappeared.

Later their silence gave consent.

We went on with the building scheme trembling in the balance, but in the balance only up to twelve thousand pounds. The code was satisfied at that figure of twelve thousand. Yes, silence gave consent. We proceeded.

Other tests. An amusing one wherein the circular metal elevator and its enclosure was challenged. Could anyone get the car released from the outside? None of us could. But a clever operator appeared from the bureau, who, having had much practice in picking elevator locks by a means no layman could have thought of, did finally succeed in starting it. So we lined the car with a transparent substitute for glass the hand could not go through.

Such is the Expert and his Bible—his good old Building Code.

No doubt the Code as a check for the jerry-builder has saved some lives where jerry-builders are the quarry. But it didn't save the new capitol wing at Madison where code sizes were as prescribed but superintendence so faulty that I had my first lesson in building collapse while, in a former chapter, you have seen me hanging to the iron fence looking in on Catastrophe.

THE CHURCH OF THE FUTURE

Here's to good old Reverend Dr. Burris Jenkins of Kansas City, Missouri, and his young right bower in the parish, Joe Cleveland, both wholeheartedly trying to do the right thing by the Future . . . but hampered by three good Kansas City lawyers working with a zealous (not to say jealous) building commission composed of one good "old foundation man" and one ex-architect (his clerk), all strictly of Yesterday.

So far as these building-committee lawyers were concerned, they never cared much for that sort of building anyway. But this church-of-the-future business was all right enough, if Dr. Burris wanted it, though everything must be strictly legal . . . as it is in the lawyer haven.

Church plans were hurriedly made because all anxious to get a start. Money insufficient for needs but everybody, even the lawyers, thought likely to be easier after we got going. So we tried to get going in a hurry in order to get the necessary money. The building scheme had to be simple—a thousand seats at least, Sunday School rooms, a separate chapel, offices for the church officers, kitchens and a clubroom or two. Such a program as would have cost about five hundred thousand dollars under ordinary conditions. We had to get the congregation inside and fairly comfortable, if possible, for one hundred and fifty thousand at most ... $25,000 was what we had. The scheme was therefore the simplest thing we could devise. Incredibly simple. Economical. And, if I do say so myself, a good scheme. The plans called for a light *tenuous* steel frame, flexible in shape—a hex—*resting for the sake of flexibility on rock ballast foundations.* The same foundations as used in the Johnson building at Racine and other buildings I have built. The light steel skeleton walls were to be covered each side by heavy paper strung with steel wires (Steeltex) securely wired to the skeleton and then the cement-gun process, so successful on the West Coast and used in K. C. itself to waterproof old brick buildings, was to be used to put a thin but sufficient shell over the insulating paper. The paper shells were 2¼" apart, the shell held by the wires to the paper like plastering on a lathed wall. This was to go on both inside and outside. Probably, I thought (and still think), the most advanced and desirable cheap building construction yet devised for any climate. Provided the Gunite is good. There was little or no detail involved except the open framework of two shallow sloping roofs over the two chancels. All surfaces plain. All corners slightly rounded to aid the Gunite process. The structure depended upon its shape, graceful simplicity and lightness of treatment for esthetic effect. The estimates came in finally, but only after no one in K. C. had confidence enough in the church and its architect, or faith in the novel technique, to bid.

I turned to Ben Wiltscheck in the emergency, and in the midst of a church turmoil such as conflicting interests and ideas can set up on a building built by lawyers and a building commission enforcing antique codes, Ben took on the main structure at about one hundred thirty-five thousand dollars, but leaving the chapel, the parking terraces and the block of Sunday School rooms to be built at a cost of about twenty-five thousand more. We all felt sure that the twenty-five thousand would come in on top of the other forty thousand we needed, when the character of our effort was recognized.

We went after a building permit. Snag one. The newly elected commissioner himself said he was an old foundation man and I couldn't put anything like that foundation over on him.

508

"Never heard of naked pounded rock for foundations," he said. Nothing but ready mixed concrete imagined in Kansas City he said.

Said I, "Look at the railroads of the country. Their heavy loads (moving too) have been on rock ballast for a hundred years."

Said he, "Nothing to do with Kansas City foundations; peculiar conditions in K. C. ground; cracks open in dry weather and walls settle."

"But the thick rock ballast would be just the equalizer for a thing like that, wouldn't crack nor could it harmfully settle."

"Oh, no! No! Not here in Kansas City. Nothing but concrete underground here. Only concrete. Nothing but concrete footings can go underground in Kansas City." This, unalterable, was a serious knockdown blow because there is a certain lateral come-and-go possible to the light superstructure in a hexagram when the light steel fabricated structure rests on coarse broken stone; in this case, particularly, a necessary flexibility lost if the frame were fixed to solid concrete at the bottom of the hex. There is a contraction and expansion going on in all solid footings that is not present in rock-ballast. I protested and tried again and again with all I had, but the legal disbelievers insisted that "all should be perfectly legal." "Regular," said they.

Well . . . the time to assert the rights of an owner to his own building had arrived. The essential scheme should have been rejected or accepted by all and sundry, right then and there, building committee fired. A new start made.

But Dr. Jenkins, Joe, and I wanted to save the thing and trusted to our ability to subsequently "snatch victory from the jaws of defeat." So I proposed, "Allow us to go ahead and we will make any tests you require." The lawyers hesitated, hemmed and hawed, deliberated and visited the commissioner, looked wise and looked for compromise. They found the compromise by employing a local engineer (recommended by the commissioner himself) to design solid concrete foundations. I don't live in Kansas City and heard of it only from some reporter who dug up the story.

Some seventeen thousand dollars up on building costs.

Again—right then and there— should have stopped the building where it was on account of this treachery and withdrawn from any connection whatever. The building was, henceforth, in the hands of the enemy. The fundamental condition of success of a rational experiment in behalf of the church was gone. The flexible hex-frame could not contract and expand in its own way, so cracks were sure to appear in the envelope. But I too am an optimist. I hated to "abandon the child," hoping to find something if they did appear as expected, that would serve—perhaps another coat of Gunite after the first winter was over. It is always possible to build up the thickness of the shell indefinitely with that process.

But no—the worst was far from over. Snag now after snag was set up. The building was soon no longer mine except in shape—the shape which had already lost some of its meaning. "The good foundation man," the inside K. C. engineer, began stiffening up the frame. Making the frame rigid where I wanted it to be and remain flexible.

Some fifteen thousand dollars more up on the building costs for rigidity not wanted.

Now Ben Wiltscheck had a contract and had to build the building. Ben also thought that by making these concessions he could get by and save the thing somehow at the end in spite of legal interference. But the lawyers intended to win the case not the contractor.

So we made tests but were warned there must be no publicity. The commissioner suspected because "the engineer" challenged the strength of the balcony. On the conditions he made, that there should be "no publicity," we made the tests with loads prescribed. There was no visible deflection anywhere. The structure was safe.

Well, the new floor-construction next came under suspicion. Still specifying "no publicity," the commissioner observed that test. Twice the required load and no deflection whatever!

These proofs seemed to shake "Authority." Thoroughly mad now.

Of course, there was no way of testing the footings the building needed, except the buildings standing for generations.

But behind Ben now was no Church and no Architect. There was only the good old foundation man, his clerk, their stand-in, the local engineer (the blind leading the blind) and three lawyers. The lawyers knew their law. Masters of the profession, they were sure they could take care of anything when the time came, especially any contract they themselves made. They knew how to make them, they said.

Now Kansas City is just about as near Taliesin as New York City, so far as accessibility goes. Had I been able to go down and live on the job, the wrecking crew might have been checked even then, if there had been a building committee less lawyer and more rational—faithful to the idea we started with. So I offered to go down if that could be set up. Dr. Burris Jenkins had himself fallen ill. He was a sick man. Joe Cleveland, succeeding to the chief ministry, did all he could and did (eventually) do so much that he resigned, which was probably the same thing as being fired.

Dr. Burris himself, now somewhat better, was told to "keep out" and leave the "whole Goddamn affair" to the lawyers. He did. Worn out, I guess. The usual game was being played. It looked as bad for Ben as it had been looking for me. Worse.

510

The Church of the Future was now a row between K.C. lawyers and the K.C. building commission, their K.C. experts that the lawyers had called in over Wiltscheck's head, and Ben Wiltscheck himself. There had been no reference by them to me in the matter now since the essential foundation scheme was wrecked and the frame "strengthened," "made safe," as the K.C. engineer said. I don't know what superiority over Wisconsin-licensed engineers (we had two of the very best beside myself) the Missouri engineer (unlicensed) could have except that he was down there in Kansas City himself.

I have always known that lawyers make the poorest building-experts on earth. They are narrow-minded specialists, dealers in, for and with the strictures of law. And they are poor sports because they are men of specified opinions.

If only we could have had several forthright American business men on the committee to back up the novel experiment in housing a deserving congregation for much less than half the usual cost of the ordinary thing, with comfort, beauty and distinction, success would have been ours. It may be yet.

But meantime . . . well . . . Joe Cleveland, elevated to the ministry by Dr. Burris Jenkins, himself ill, out of a job. I'll never get another building to build in Kansas City, which is less than no matter at all. But Ben is out about twenty thousand he could ill afford to lose, and just because he stuck his head out too far. I am now "ex-architect." Kansas City, Missouri, just missed something that might have been a jewel in the town; it will now resemble a busted pearl in a swine's snout, until finally after all the messing around is over, we do go down there our-selves to take what will be left of the whited sepulchre and make it what it was intended to be before it went all-out *legal.*

The lawyers meantime are busy. They have their hands full of the sort of thing that makes lawyers what lawyers are. But some lawyers I know are pretty decent fellows at that. Out of court.

There must be something, too, about "this here Missouri" that makes its Kansas City what it is today—Yesterday . . .no place at all for the Church of the Future.

BREAKFAST AT TALIESIN

To get away from failure . . .

There may be other breaks for a fast, but none so far as I know, like a Taliesin breakfast, say, on any one of Taliesin's seven terraces, the one where the view is best or the sun is right, or the one where the wind is not disagreeable, or where all are right together. Light early supper, early to bed the night before, are the conditions on which breakfast is happy digestion willing and happy to break-fast. Push the button of the Capehart as you pass? Haydn pouring from the built-in speaker over the hill garden this early morning. But, fresh as dew themselves, breezes blow the scent of sloping clover fields our way, birds in the tree-tops below are singing as though delirious with joy, perhaps nothing at all is best. Yes, it is. Let's sit down (ourselves fresh) in comfort to a wide well-spread tastefully set low table, ample cloth of Chinese linen fancifully colored and great big napkins to match; big enough to tuck into the neckband and spread all over whatever it is you wear for breakfast. This morning Alec (Woollcott) wears dark-blue silk pyjamas, belted coat to match, large white polka-dots the size of a dime sprinkled all over his person.

The table decorations this morning? By Herbert. Are unusually good, even for him, in a big shallow glass platter brimming with clear water: anemones nestling in a big branch of fern brake held up by a curious yellow moss-covered stone set in the water.

Horizontal ribbons of the white mist into which the overhead morning sun has already resolved the dew are lifting, going up to ride as clouds in the blue while the shadows are still wide and long.

Alec is not talking, just looking.

Cowbells tinkle, gently coming up from the meadow running up the valley below by the flowing stream. White peacocks gather nearby on the roofs and Yoo-hoo-oo!

Olgivanna, picturesque in a big hat tied on her head with strings under her chin, to shut out the sun shining in everybody else's eyes, presides over all. Iovanna fluffs out, already dressed for school, coming on the breeze, and sits down opposite. Because both of them like Alec, Svetlana, wearing bright slacks, bright ribbons perched in splendid dark blowing hair, and big Wes come in for this occasion.

Me? Oh, I have on raw linen. Loose wide-sleeved jacket buttoned at the wrist, wide baggy trousers tied close around the ankles. Carl (Sandburg) once visited me while working on his *Lincoln*. I dressed him up in a spare velveteen suit in similar style. Lloyd Lewis there got a good "shot" of us in this artistic, semi-elegant négligée. For years Carl has been trying to buy that picture from Lloyd for fear someone will see it! Well, that is what I have on.

Everybody wishes everybody an affectionate "good morning" as we finally draw up to the table.

First, we all look around the room and listen to the birds, then look again and keep listening.

Fresh strawberry leaves laid over them, here come heaps of noble Taliesin strawberries in a big old Chinese Celadon bowl. The stains of

512

the strawberries are lovely on its cool pale-green surface. Just picked the berries in the garden down there just below, dew still on them. Devonshire cream, perhaps, if you will?

Then real Scotch oatmeal (Elam's)—four hours in a double boiler—with Guernsey cream? Fresh eggs with *baked* bacon—the eggs still warm from the nest. Will you have yours, white or dark, in the original package?.We raise all this ourselves on the farm.

Here comes William with a wide old Celadon platter of asparagus, freshly cut—he has just the moment before gathered the asparagus. You cannot fail to observe how the color of asparagus agrees with Celadon. Beside each place see a tall glass of our fresh Guernsey milk—the herd tinkling below there on the green meadow. Cold? No? All right then, hot. Comb honey? Our own: Hans a good bee man. As honey is passed somebody tells the story of Wilde's important urban lady who asked for some more of "that extremely delicious honey" with the remark, "Do you know! Were I, too, to live in the country, I, too, should keep a bee!"

As Alec looks at me more in sorrow than in anger for this quote, I feel suitably reproved.

Jams and preserves of many novel sorts—Olgivanna now presses them upon us. She made them herself. What color! What flavor! We are served on the terrace this morning by Kenn, William and Kay of the Fellowship.

Naturally, steaming hot coffee is right there keeping hot on the service table. And crisp original-Graham toast (toasted one side only, please) comes, the toaster tended by Olgivanna.

Well, after the awful break concerning the English lady's bee has somewhat evaporated, we all sit back and just enjoy being there forgiving each other everything. Eating meanwhile with appetite . . .everybody all right? Good.

Our fast completely broken, breakfast means just what it says.

There is no "Let us then be up and doing" for us this morning. We are going riding . . .

As he begins to do the talking, Alec continues to sit with his hand on the handle of a special coffee pot we have set beside him (no, the pot is not Celadon nor is it distinguished), pouring out a fresh cup, now and then. (I could hardly get a word in edgewise for three or four days, even had I wanted to do so. No one does when Alec will.) I always prefer to listen to him. He is charming us one and all by the play of his wit—waving a fly away now and then as though he were enjoying waving a flag.

Alec is not like "The Man Who Came to Dinner" when he comes to breakfast, I can tell you. I look at his fine square face, firm shapely chin—distinguished mature man of a becoming age, whatever it is or ever will be ... something very fine in Alec's face due, I believe, to innate kindness of heart: a really warm heart-beat. Generosity possessed by few men I've met. We watch him now, seeing that steaming coffee-bowl carrying excess cargo to his liver between scintillating sallies. We are enjoying the real conversation of a friend among friends, Alec making marvelous things out of commonplaces as other less gifted people make marvelous things commonplace. We sit there oblivious of Time until time for lunch?

I have misgivings about Alec—such "goings-on" with coffee? No physical weakling myself, perhaps because I had my first cup when I was fifty-five, I can't drink one without some slight exhilaration for an hour or two afterward. So I remonstrate with Alec a little. No effect whatever—used to it.

Lieber Meister used to come down to breakfast with me at the Congress—ask for coffee—pound the table for coffee, his hand shaking, morose until he got coffee. Then, soon pleasant, expansive mentally as a blooming rose. Different, certainly, but good too, when in his coffee.

I've never seen a match, though, for Alec! He makes me feel as though I had just come down from way-back yonder on a load of poles ... damn him! You know?

No. "The Man Who Came to Dinner" can't compare with The Man Who Came to Breakfast. The Breakfast Man a wit, colorful cynic, man of the world but a bitter smart Alec. The man who came to breakfast is a true friend, lover of fine things, an esthetic enthusiast, one who well knows why he loves them—a man of rare discrimination as well as the master of a wit seldom at wit's end. One of the kindest, most generous men I know is Alec. And I know many kind and gentle men. Put that beside *The Man Who Came to Dinner,* which you've probably seen. Alec in it?

If you get Alec straight he will be both breakfast and dinner and probably as many more tiffins in between as there are occasions. No chameleon either. He just takes circumstances as a diamond takes light—that's all. And flashes the distinguished kindly man who came to breakfast. One and all. I speak for the Fellowship too—we like Alec.

Olgivanna put into his hands as he departed a simple little glass Madonna made in Holland, because he admired it much: a chef d'oeuvre a little taller than an overcoat pocket is deep. Because I don't know why Alec should have a Madonna or what he might do with one I tried to be a little jealous and failed. Somehow you can't do that to Alec.

514

AND NOW BACK TO USONIAN HOUSE I

The house of moderate cost is not only America's major architectural problem but the problem most difficult, if not improbable of solution, for her major architects. As for me, I would rather solve it with satisfaction to myself (and Usonia) than build anything I can think of at the moment except the modern theater now needed by the legitimate drama unless the stage is to be done to death by "the movies." In our country the chief obstacle to any real solution of the moderate-cost house problem lies in the fact that our people do not really know how to live— would not know the house when they saw it. They imagine their idiosyncrasies to be their "tastes," their prejudices to be their predilections, and their ignorance to be virtue—where any *beauty* of living is concerned.

To be more specific, a small house on the side street or village might have charm if it didn't ape the big house on the Avenue, just as the Usonian village itself might have a great charm if it didn't ape the big town. Likewise, Marybud on the old farm, a jewel hanging from the tip of her pretty nose on a cold, cold day, might be charming in clothes befitting her state and work, but is only silly in the Sears-Roebuck funery that imitates the clothes of her city sisters who imitate Hollywood stars: lipstick, rouge, high heels, silk stockings, bell skirt, cockeyed hat and all. Exactly that kind of "monkeyfied" business is the obstacle to architectural achievement of a good house in our U.S.A. This provincial "culture-lag" in favor of the leg which does not allow the person or thought to be simple and naturally itself. It is the real obstacle to a genuine Usonian culture.

I am now certain that any approach to the new house needed by indigenous culture—why worry about the other kind of house?—is fundamentally different. That house must be a pattern for more simplified and, at the same time, more gracious living: necessarily new, but suitable to living conditions as they might so well be in this country we live in today.

Need of a house of moderate cost must sometime face not only this ignorance but the realtor. Why not face it all now? The expedient houses built by the million, which journals propagate, and government builds, do no such thing—the realtor got there first.

To me such conditions are really stupid makeshifts, putting on some style or other, really having none—no integrity. Style *is* always important but *a* style is not. There all the difference lies when we work *with* style and not for *a* style.

Forty-five years I have insisted on that point.

Notwithstanding all efforts to improve, the American "small house" problem is still a pressing, needy, hungry, confused, faked and faking issue. But where is a better thing to come from while Authority has pitched into perpetuating the old stupidities? I do not believe the needed house can come from current education, or from big business. It isn't coming by way of smart advertising experts either. Or professional streamliners. It is only super-common-sense that can take us along the road to the better thing in building, the general average American into a beauty of his own. God help us all.

What would be really sensible in this matter of the modest dwelling for our time and place? Let's see how far the Herbert Jacobs house at Madison, Wisconsin, is a sensible house for the Jacobses. It wouldn't do for any but the Jacobses, of course. This house for a young journalist, his wife and small daughter, is now under roof. Cost: fifty-five hundred dollars, including architect's fee of say, five hundred fifty. Contract let to P. B. Grove.

To give the small Jacobs family benefit of the advantages of the era in which they live, simplifications take place. Mr. and Mrs. H. Jacobs must themselves see life in somewhat clarified terms. What essentials in their case—a typical case? It is not only necessary to get rid of all unnecessary complications in construction, necessary to use work in the mill to good advantage, necessary to eliminate, so far as possible, field labor which is increasingly expensive: it is necessary to consolidate and simplify the three appurtenance systems—heating, lighting and sanitation. At least this must be our economy if we are to achieve the sense of spaciousness and vista we desire in order to liberate people living in the house. Ideal to complete the building in one operation as it goes along. Inside and outside complete in one operation. The house finished inside as it is completed outside. No complicated roofs. A one-process house.

Every time a hip, valley or dormer window is allowed to ruffle a roof the life of the building is threatened.

The way windows are used is naturally a most useful resource to achieve the new characteristic sense of space. All this fenestration can be made ready at the factory and set up as the walls go. But there is no longer need to speak of doors and windows. These walls are largely a system of fenestration having its own part in the building scheme—the system being as much part of the design as eyes are of the face.

Now what can be eliminated? These:

1. Visible roofs are expensive and unnecessary, though desirable.

2. A garage no longer necessary as cars are made. A carport will do, with liberal overhead shelter, walls on two sides. Detroit still had the livery-stable mind. It believed the car must be stabled so—no longer.

3. The old-fashioned basement, except for a fuel and heater space, always a plague spot. A steam-warmed concrete mat four inches thick laid directly on the gravel or broken stone filling, the walls set upon the same, is better.

4. Interior "trim" no longer necessary.

5. No radiators, no light fixtures. We will heat the house the "hypocaust" way, gravity heat, make the wiring system itself the light fixtures, light upon and down the rooms. Light will thus be indirect, except for a few outlets for floor lamps.

6. Furniture, pictures and bric-a-brac unnecessary because walls can be made to include them or *be* them.

7. No painting at all. Wood best preserves itself. A coating of clear resinous oil would be enough. Only the floor mat of concrete squares needs waxing.

8. No plastering in the building.

9. No gutters, no downspouts.

To assist on general planning: what must or may we use in our new construction? In this case five materials: wood, brick, cement, paper, glass. To simplify fabrication we must use our horizontal-unit system in construction: also use a vertical-unit system which will be the width of the boards and battenbands themselves, interlocking with the brick courses. Although it is getting to be a luxury material, the walls will be board-walls the same inside as outside—these thicknesses of boards with paper placed between them, the boards fastened together with screws. These slab-walls made of boards—a kind of plywood construction throughout on large scale can be high in insulating value, vermin-proof and practically fireproof. These walls like the fenestration may be prefabricated, with any degree of insulation we can afford, and raised into place, or they may be made at the mill and shipped to the site in sections. The roof can be built first on props and these walls shoved into place under them.

The appurtenance systems, to avoid cutting and complications, must be an organic part of construction but independent of the walls. Yes, we must have polished plate glass. It is one of the things we have at hand to gratify the designer of the truly modern house and bless its occupants.

Roof framing in this instance is beamed overhead by laminating three 2 x 4's in depth, easily making the three offsets seen outside in the eaves of the roof; enabling the roof span of 2 x 12's to be sufficiently pitched without the expense of "building up" the pitches. The middle offset may be left open at the eaves and fitted with flaps used to ventilate the roof spaces in summer. Then these 2 x 4's sheathed and insulated, covered with a good asphalt roof, are the top of the house. Shelter gratifying to the sense of shelter because of the generous eaves.

517

All this in hand—no, in mind, we plan the disposition of the rooms.

What essential now? Say we have a corner lot—an acre or two—with a south and east exposure? We will have good gardens. The house planned to wrap around two sides of this garden.

1. As big a living room, as much vista and garden coming in as we can afford, with a big fireplace in it, open bookshelves, dining table in the alcove, benches and living-room tables built in. Quiet rug on the floor, in color if possible.

2. Convenient cooking and dining space adjacent to if not a part of the living room. This space may be set away from the outside walls within the living area to make work easy. This is the new thought concerning a kitchen—to take it away from outside walls and let it turn up into overhead space within the chimney, thus connection to dining space is made immediate without unpleasant features and so no outside wall space lost to the principal rooms. A natural current of air is thus set up toward the kitchen as toward a chimney, no cooking odors escaping back into the house. There are steps leading down from this space to a small cellar below for heater, fuel and laundry, although no basement at all is necessary if the plan should be so made. The bathroom is usually next so that plumbing features of heating kitchen and bath may be economically combined.

3. In this case (two bedrooms and a workshop which may become a future bedroom) the single bathroom for the sake of privacy is not immediately connected to any single bedroom. Bathrooms opening directly into a bedroom occupied by more than one person or two bedrooms opening into a single bathroom have been badly overdone, sure of unpleasant consequences. We will have as much garden and space in all these space appropriations as our money allows after we have simplified construction by way of the techniques we have tried out in so many cases.

A modest house is this Usonian house. A dwelling place that has no feeling at all for "the grand" except as the house extends itself in the flat parallel to the ground, a companion to the horizon. Floor-heated, that kind of extension on the ground can hardly go too far for comfort, beauty of proportion, provided it does not cost too much in upkeep. As a matter of course a home like this is an architect's creation. It is not a builder's nor an amateur's affair. Both run too fast. There is considerable risk in exposing the scheme to imitation or even emulation.

This because a house of this type could not be well built and achieve beauty of design except as an architect conceives and oversees execution of the building.

The building would fail of proper effect unless the furnishing and planting were all done by advice of the architect—or especially under his prescription.

Briefly these few descriptive paragraphs, no floor plan, may help to indicate how stuffy and stifling the little colonial hot-boxes, hallowed by government or not, are where free Usonian family life should be concerned. You might easily put two of the colonials, each costing more, into the living space of this organic one and not go much outside the walls. Here is a moderate-cost brick-and-wood house that by our own new schoolology has been greatly extended both in scale and comfort: a single house well suited to prefabrication too, because the factory can go to the house instead of the house going to the factory.

Imagine how the costs would come down were the technique a familiar matter to the contractor, or if many houses were to be executed at one time—according to number built and location.

A freedom of movement, a privacy too, is afforded by the general Usonian arrangement unknown to the current "boxment." Let us say nothing about beauty while beauty is the ambiguous term concerning this idiosyncrasy of taste in the provinces of which our big cities are the largest offenders.

But I think a cultured American, say Usonian, housewife looks well in it. The now inevitable car will be apart from it but eventually belong.

Where does the garden leave off and the house begin? Where the garden begins and the house leaves off—that's all.

Withal, this Usonian dwelling seems a thing loving the human-being on his own ground with new sense of space, light and freedom—to which our U.S.A. has entitled him—legally. Why not now spiritually?

USONIAN HOUSE II

We have built some twenty-seven of them now in seventeen different Usonian states. Building costs in general in the U.S.A. rising and rising still. We find that seventeen thousand dollars is about the sum needed to buy what the first Jacobses bought for fifty-five hundred. The Usonian house would have cost from seventy-five hundred up to ten, twelve, and in certain programs fifteen, sixteen and on up to twenty thousand dollars. We have built several extended in every way that cost double that sum.

Houses cost, I should say, several times more to build than when we started to build them, 1938. But this holds true—any comparison with the "regular" houses around them shows that they are for the money more physically for the sums they cost than the "regulars." Their freedom, distinction and individuality are not a feature of that cost except as it does by elimination put the expenditure where it liberates the occupant in a new spaciousness. A new freedom but yet little understood by the professions.

It is true, however, that no man can have the liberation one of these houses affords, liberal outside views on three sides becoming a part of the interior, without incurring extra fuel for heating—say twenty per cent more. Double windows cut this down—but also cost money and we don't like them.

GRAVITY HEAT

Concerning floor heating. Heated air rises naturally. Therefore we call it gravity heat because the pipes filled with steam or hot water are all in a rock ballast bed beneath the concrete floor itself—we call the ballast with concrete top, *the floor mat*. If the floor is the second floor about ground it is usually made of two-inch-square wood strips spaced one inch apart. The heating pipes are in that case set between the floor joists.

Gravity heat came to America in this way: In Japan to commence building the Imperial Hotel, winter of 1914, we were invited to dine with Baron Okura, chief of my patrons representing the Mikado. It is desperately uncomfortable in Tokio in winter—damp clammy cold that almost never amounts to freezing or even frost—but harder to keep warm there than anywhere I have been, unless Italy. The universal heat is from the *hibachi*—a round vessel sitting on the floor filled with white ashes, several sticks of charcoal thrust down into the ashes all but a few inches. This projecting charcoal is lighted and glows—incandescent. Everyone sits around the *hibachi,* every now and then stretching out the hand over it for a moment—closing the hand as though grasping at something. The result unsatisfactory. To us. I marveled at Japanese fortitude until I caught sight of the typical underwear—heavy "Long John" woolens, long sleeves, long legs, which they wear beneath the series of padded flowing kimono. But as they are acclimated and toughened to this native condition they suffer far less than we do.

Well, although we knew we should shiver, we accepted the Baron's invitation to dine—he had a number of houses scattered around the Empire. As expected, the dining room was so cold that I couldn't eat—only pretending to eat and for some nineteen or twenty courses. After dinner the Baron led the way below to the "Korean room." So it was called. This room was about twelve by twenty-four, ceiling seven or eight feet, I should say. A red felt drugget covered the floor. Walls were severely plain, a soft pale yellow in color. We knelt there for conversation and Turkish coffee on yellow zabatons.

A Miracle. The *climate* had changed. Changed? No, but it wasn't the coffee or *saki*. It was Spring, that's all. We were cozy, warm and happy again—kneeling there on the floor mats. An indescribable warmth: no heating visible nor was it felt as such directly. It was really a matter *not of heating at all* but an affair of *climate*. Organic heat!

A Japanese graduate of Harvard interpreted what the Baron now explained. The Korean room meant a room heated under the floor. The heat of a fire outside one corner of the floor was drawn back and forth underneath the floor in tile ducts, the floor forming the top of the flues (or ducts), made by the partitions, the smoke and surplus heat going up and out of a tall chimney at the opposite corner to the corner where the fire was burning.

The indescribable comfort of being warmed from below was a discovery—sitting warm, feet warm.

Immediately I arranged for electric heating elements beneath bathrooms in the Imperial Hotel—dropping the ceiling of the bathroom to create a space beneath the bathroom floor above, each in which to generate heat. The tile floor and built-in tile baths were thus always warm. It was pleasant to go in one's bare feet into the bathroom. This experiment was a success. All ugly electric heat fixtures (dangerous too in a bathroom) were eliminated. I've always hated radiators. Here was the opportunity to digest all that paraphernalia within the building—creating not a heated interior but creating climate—healthful, dustless, serene. Also, the presence of heat thus integral and beneath makes lower temperatures desirable. Sixty degrees seems for normal human beings sufficient. But neighbors coming in from super-heated houses would feel cool at first. A natural climate is generated instead of an artificial forced condition—the natural condition as a matter of course much more healthful.

Determined to try it out at home at the first opportunity, that opportunity seemed to be the Nakoma Country Club, but that Indianesque affair on Lake Wingra near Madison stayed in the form of a beautiful plan because—well, just because.

Then the Johnson Administration Building came. Gravity heat just the thing for that and we proceeded with installation. All professional heating contractors except one objecting (Westerlin and Campbell), scoffed, refusing to have anything to do with the idea. But as chance had it, the little Jacobs House turned up meantime and was completed before that greater venture got into operation.

So the Jacobs House was the first to go into effect. Great excitement and curiosity on the part of "the profession." Crane Company officials came, brushed by Catherine Jacobs when she opened the door, dove beneath the rugs, put their hands on the concrete in places remote from the heater, got up and looked at one another as though they had seen a ghost. From them, "My God! It works." Where were radiators now?

As usual with innovations, articles on "radiant heat" began to appear in testimonial journals. Several "I thought of it first" appeared, but it was in no sense "radiant heat" or panel-heating or any of the things they called it that I was now interested in. It was simply *gravity heat*—heat coming up from beneath as heat rises naturally.

Some thirty or more Usonian buildings now have floor heating. We have had to learn to proportion the heat correctly for varying climates and conditions. We have accumulated some data that is useful and put the thermostat outside.

There is no other "ideal heat." Not even the heat of the sun.

THE UNKIND FIREPLACE

Lloyd (Lewis) is not only my own dear friend but a client after my own heart. Lloyd is one of my warmest and most faithfully insulting and insulted critics. Long ago when I was down and getting a worm's-eye view of society, Lloyd was a rising young "publicity man." I engaged him to *keep me out* of the newspapers. He lasted a little less than three months. Then I paid him off and fired him for cause. The thing couldn't be done. He blamed me. But why blame me for my own fault?

Now came his turn. He employed me to build his house. He was a hard client. But not hard enough.

Having been there myself, often, I knew it was so damp and hot out there on the prairie by the Des Plaines River where he wanted to build that I set Lloyd well up off the ground to keep him high and dry in Spring, Fall and Summer; his domicile winnowed by the wind. Beneath! Thereby I exposed him in Winter not unnecessarily, but somewhat expansively and expensively. For the good of his health? Yes. But more for the good of the life he would live in his house.

That type of house I believe ideal for a prairie site on low, damp land of that type. But no such proceeding could be called cheap because of the extra floor level.

So, up there off the ground, the beautiful river landscape coming in through three sides of the wide spreading house and the woods showing beneath, it was hard to keep Lloyd warm in Winter. Kathryn, his wife, didn't cool off so readily as Lloyd did, but the sixty-five degrees we set for normal in a floor-heated Usonian house just didn't jibe by about twenty degrees with the *Daily News* office where Lloyd worked as editor. And there was something the matter with the boiler pump there which we went down to fix or else the house would have risen to seventy-five. I am glad of an excuse to go to Lloyd's home anyway. I went and got it fixed but he would have been better off at sixty-five.

With usual bravado, pretending to make light of the thing, I thought of various ways of keeping the writer of the life of Sherman warm. I thought of wiring him to an electric pad inside his vest, allowing lots of lead wire so he could get around. But he waved the idea aside with contempt as a passing of the "buck." No patience at all, so we dropped the idea. Then I suggested we appeal to Secretary Knox to turn down the heat at the *Daily News* from eighty-five gradually to sixty-five so he could become acclimated. But Lloyd said the cold-blooded *Daily-News*-men couldn't get their stuff out at that temperature. Anyway he didn't want to be cultivated; he said he *was* cultivated. So we dropped that one too.

There was nothing left for me to do, since I had made the house part of the landscape and the landscape all around it came in on three sides (and underneath as well) but put on some double windows at Lloyd's expense just like the other folks in hiding around there do. In those fashionable woods it was humiliating to get down thus into that clandestine society but we just had to go through with it. After all it was for Lloyd and Kathryn.

In the same spirit of bravado still, knowing that it is not at all in my own interest, I now refer to the unkindest ordeal of all. The innocent very simple little fireplace I built for Lloyd to sit by when he writes just refuses to draw . . . too simple, I guess, to function. We have built some three-thousand-odd fireplaces that do draw and a few that didn't know how, at first, but that do know how now. This particular one, though, Lloyd's own, doesn't know how. We haven't given up. It will learn.

Meantime, the curious neighbors coming and going park their cars in the vicinity to watch and see if there is any smoke coming out of that part of the chimney top yet.

But was his own house doing it to Lloyd or was Lloyd doing it to the house?

Well, there is is . . . my beloved most intimate friend, the Historian, Critic, Sports Editor, sitting there by that damn little fireplace I designed especially for him (brick) now so obtrusive you can hear the midget miles off by way of a sort of clinical or morbid interest in the telephone on the part of the neighbors. Those who had undergone operations of their own kept calling up to know if the fireplace "drew" yet.

There it is. One out of three thousand, to speak truth, that did not draw.

I know what: should we fail to teach that fireplace its place and it still refuses to draw, we can put a little fan, a kind of secret agent, up there in the chimney with a switch down nearby where Lloyd sits so when he has enough fire he can turn it off and when he doesn't want smoke he can turn it on. In the whole galaxy (or is it phalanx?) of three thousand fireplaces that little one (it is a sidekick of the successful big one) will thus be Lloyd's!

We'll let you know how everything turns out. You needn't telephone.

If we don't, the neighbors will—anyhow you'll read about it in the papers.

Although, if it turns out well they will have lost interest in it and dropped the whole affair.

Lloyd's house made a gardener of his wife—Kathryn—and a farmer-without-a-barn out of Lloyd. You should see that boy around the place in those coveralls! He raises pigs. You should see the way he looks.

There is a lot of the best in both of them built into their house because I knew and loved them so well, well enough to put it there. And they earned it and deserved the best I could do. They were up to it too. They loved the house and made it a home.

Nevertheless the tragedy that befell so many of my clients happened to the Lloyd Lewises. They just liked to stay in their house and didn't care to go out anywhere unless they had to go—became stay-at-homes.

Many of their friends, like the Alfred MacArthurs, for instance, just pretended to like the house because they like Lloyd. But I know some of their neighbors didn't. But those who didn't were living in period houses dated way back there when and furnished "way back" to match.

In fact, the new dwelling made quite a stir in the society of that squeamish, highly stylish neck of the flat woods where Old Mexico, Norway, Ancient Sweden and Camden-village Gothic were in hiding behind trees and to no good purpose, believe me.

Lloyd and Kathryn also furnished their exciting but very quiet Usonian House "to match" and in such good Usonian style that even I like to go back to enjoy it myself. So does Marc (Connelly). So does Alec (Woollcott). First time he saw it Alec wrote a nice little letter to me about the house which was fine. And generous again.

Hoping Alec won't object, if Lloyd doesn't, here is the little note which I cherish. I'll share it with you. He was in Chicago.

DEAR FRANK:

I hear you will be returning to Spring Green tomorrow so I am leaving promptly for Rochester, New York, but not before making a second visit to Libertyville to see that exhilarating house you have built for Lloyd Lewis. I was there last Sunday and went to confirm, by a second visit, the impression it made upon me. On the strength of that house alone I think I could go forth and preach afresh the gospel of Frank Lloyd Wright.

I see now more fully than ever before what effect the right house can have upon the person inside it. I told Lloyd that this one makes even a group of *his* friends look distinguished.

Lloyd, whom I admire and enjoy, never did anything so wise in his life. Just to be in that house uplifts the heart and refreshes the spirit. Most houses confine their occupants. Now I understand, where before I only dimly apprehended, that such a house as this can liberate the person who lives in it.

God bless you.

A. WOOLLCOTT

April 15, 1941

THE STAMPEDE

Refusing to be stampeded by the wave of urbanism which swept the U.S.A., affecting such of our architects as Harvey Corbett, Lamb, Van Allen, Ray Hood, Bel Geddes, etc., to name but a few: in fact, *all* of our commercial A.I.A. architects, both great and small; I seemed pretty much alone. I could see little more in *la ville radieuse,* a greater New York by Hugh Ferris, or the exploitations of Bel Geddes et al., exploitation of what was already exploitation. The taller congestion of Chicago, the more-up-in-the-air San Francisco, etc., etc., were stupidities that, when they did not alarm, bored me. Higher and higher up and up went the rat-race for skyscraper distinction—big business. Skyscraperism by way of the urban man-eaters came, by way of false civic pride, popular science monthlies, T-square and triangle architects, a startling nightmare of a future in which man himself as a feature became a speck of no spiritual significance whatever, except as he had brought to an apex his own abnegation to this splendiferous, hard-as-nails design for his own tomb.

This skyscraperist tomb for our civilization was due to our big-business vanity played upon by the false pride of Science in itself. Or, should I say, the pride of false science in our day and hour?

The skyscraper was the needed hallmark for modern commercial, stupendous *Success*! Certain civic ambitions *were* served by it. Really, at bottom, it was a mere unethical exploit by the landlord to hold the profits of super-concentration: socially a menace and in the crowd architecturally, false. The blind perverted mechanization of the period. Realtorific faith and fatalistic promotion are the danger and the curse of this mechanistic triumph of the American skyscraper in the overcrowded city.

My faith went the other way.

I could see the very tall building in the country. Broadacre City, as agrarian ideal as well as urban, was eventually the answer I found to this spectacular folly of prevalent commercialized vainglory. But the "man-eaters" had captured the imagination of business men and to such an extent that nearly every city of the country had its skyscraper in the worst possible spot. It was *on* the street but not *for* the street. Why the skyscraper so readily found so many false prophets among our American architects, if their work could be seen standing up and out free on the Western prairies, under circumstances that made them independent all right, but as headstones in the cemeteries of those overcrowded places, is a question I could answer if really worthwhile.

Notwithstanding all considerations, ethical, esthetic, economic, the skyscraper, an achievement in itself, was only serving as the banner of American commercial ambition: the success that was running the nation ragged, down and out, Anno Domini 1929. America's cow, so to speak, was, by this ruse, taken indoors, spoon-fed in a stanchion behind glass walls for advertising purposes chiefly. The cow was steadily declining in health and productivity in consequence? Well, all this when the national cow from any standpoint of real wealth or health should have been turned out to grass.

ON TAKING EFFECTS FOR CAUSES

Forty-five years I have seen, intimately, the origin and growth of the modern movement in Architecture in which the work I have done myself has been a major factor. Now that I am principal witness to its inception and subsequent development (the inception and development of that movement which is now called "Modern" architecture for lack of a better name—everything built today is modern), I am still seeing History made, able to compare the making as seen by very best critics with facts with which I am myself familiar. What I have seen makes me more than ever suspicious of the Historian. This applies, too, to any Historian of himself. Yes, I am sometimes suspicious of myself. Three

Scotch highballs would lay me liable to suspicion.

I have seen my own original work, as an original impulse spread worldwide, take general form on the surface of the globe: increase here at home and especially abroad, but take outward form only—a superficial resemblance . . . sans spirit.

Contributed new forms continually—hundreds—only to see them merely exploited, even put forward wrong end to, and if not exactly upside-down—then certainly inside-out. Since 1910 I have seen the European reaction to work I have myself done and know full well its contemporary effects on other architects at home. I have seen the direct and creditable obvious implications of that work often credited to others as their own original impulse, although I have never seen the obvious implications of the work of others credited to me.

Critical views of what were mere effects I have seen persistently, often wilfully, mistaken for causes, and vice versa. So equivocal and confusing were they in their inevitably posterior view of the origins concerned that I usually read critical reviews of my own work in relation to the work of my contemporaries with grim appreciation and appropriate profanity. Since I cannot read them backward, most reviews are so far out of focus (designedly or not), so badly out of drawing, as to put effects forward as causes and set causes back into the category of mere effects.

Such, I see, as the History of the so-called Modern Movement in Architecture, "a badgered, managed miseducation" in general. Instead of growing more simple with time, the causes of mere Effects multiply and obscure actual Causes. They are seldom discussed: comparisons multiply, analysis is rare.

The gift of seeing a cause rise from its source, take its natural direction and begin to be—in contemporaneous life—maintaining a just proportion in the seeing and the being: well, it is simply not characteristic in Architecture. Now or ever.

Perhaps origins are entitled to the seclusion denied by such confusion?

A nice provision of Nature?

Thus the subsequences of artificiality are soon universally looked back upon as of primary consequences and there is no remedy in truth.

Our "higher education" is too much a cheap conceit hoping to thrive on consolidated Information but never really able to learn, inferiority mistaking patriotism for Honor—sacrifice for Duty—money-punctilio for Character and a hectic noisy self-assertion for a good time.

No wonder this great provincial museum of a nation has such faith in managed publicity!

Perhaps there is something in the English tongue that makes it the efficient prevaricator, a natural equivocal perverter of Truth. Yet how could things have been very different in earlier times? How can we be sure that all History is not made in the same way: effects mistaken for causes, causes mistaken for effects?

The long arm of coincidence plays strange tricks on the average Critic. I have seen appearances too often be the only basis for utterly false rationalizations after the fact: all entirely beside the mark. No more than a pleasant fiction or an interesting speculation will make "good reacting." Amusing as well as exasperating.

A long list would only open profitless controversy because the Critic, per se as such, is no respecter of an original source of information, and certainly, even were he a competent judge, no detector of an original source of inspiration. The thing is all too simple for him on any such basis. There is not room enough there for his own misinformation. History "à la mode," I suspect, is mostly the personal view, a sort of mirage in a distorted mirror: the mind of the Historian. In our day true proportion in true perspective does not exist with our temper or pace *or* the effects we aim to produce. "Speed," as Meredith says, "is a kind of voracity." Voracity is by nature none too particular. That for one thing. But, for another, out of our academic pigeon-holes we are swamped by the departmental mind: a mind that sees in parts only and patches the parts together to make a case for its own sake, for himself and, unfortunately, for the future.

Any sincere search for truth of FORM is meantime betrayed to this inimical, and worse, *confusion* from Generation to Generation. The inferior mind learns by comparisons, the superior mind by analyses.

We need something safe to build on, of course. That something is none other than the *Truth*. But the real seeker for Truth always gets back to simples—and with rectitude, amplitude and impartiality lets the shallow surf of erudite self-assertion break upon itself and roll back where it came from.

Bred to greatness and splendor by Art and Science, Architecture has cosmic destinies as yet undreamed of . . . by the critics: these Horatios in their philosophy.

FRIENDS OF OUR FELLOWSHIP

Did I say that the Taliesin Fellowship had received very little outside help from anyone? I should take that back if I did so say. In pre-Fellowship days, to be sure, but there probably would have been no

Fellowship at all, but for the occupant of the Chair of History at Chicago University—by name, Ferdinand W. Schevill. You have been told of the incorporation of Frank Lloyd Wright: how seven of my friends and clients between them contributed some seventy thousand dollars to defend and get me back to work again, keep me working at Taliesin. They were Dr. Ferdinand Schevill, Harold McCormick, Mrs. Avery Coonley, Darwin D. Martin, the principal subscribers. Ben E. Page, Mrs. Jane Porter, and George Parker of Parker-pen contributed also.

Dr. Ferdinand was president of the corporation (much against his will, I suspect), an enterprise wherein all of the thousands were lost in the national collapse of 1929–30 except the objective for which the money was originally intended and subscribed; and that had a narrow escape. What preserved our cultural endeavor is problematical.

The purpose of incorporation as has been paid was getting me back to work again where, protected, I could keep at work and work out.

Ferdinand won't like this—but most of the corporation subscribers were "rich," while he had only a good revenue from his historical textbooks and his salary as Historian. Only recently I learned that he had not only subscribed his original quota, seventy-five hundred dollars, but had secretly put up five thousand more in the name of a friend who afterward became secretary of the corporation; and, moreover, to show you what use such a man has for money, Ferdinand was a heavy subscriber to Sherwood Anderson's publishing venture—no more profitable than ours was to Ferdinand, I venture to say. Poor Sherwood! Ferdinand loved him more than he loved me, because Sherwood was so much more lovable.

I think it all goes to show that money is no estimate or stricture in the hands of a man like Ferdinand, the intellectual recluse. For he now lives and writes—retired—in a nice little home Woltersdorf built for him in the woods near Michigan City, Indiana, not far from the Carl Sandburgs. Carl took a national hero to pieces, put him together again, and got rich. The true Carl was born to be a poet. He is a glorious failure, not a Success. "Success" would be very unbecoming to the best Carl.

The fact that my upheaval didn't allow me to build that house for Ferdinand hurts me more, I guess, than Ferdinand helped me—because I would gladly have given the price of his subscription to have built it for him. But at that time I was far away, the going uncertain; Dr. Ferdinand was in a hurry and . . . well . . . you will probably have your own idea as to why he didn't want to take the trouble to go through a building operation with me absent. The circumstances I admit were not propitious. But do you know what? I believe Ferdinand didn't try to overcome the obstacles so that I might pay back to him in kind that much because he is so essentially modest and retiring. He really wanted a commonplace house? If I had built his house he might have been rooted out at all hours of the day by tourists and young students of architecture; he would have been exemplar, a showpiece. Having no mind to charge fifty cents for the privilege of viewing his abode, he chose obscurity and that went with A.I.A. president Woltersdorf.

I am therefore jealous of Woltersdorf—and obscurity.

Obscurity is so much easier to live up to—probably the richer thing.

Had I followed my own shy, youthful bent, I might have been allowed to build a house for my best friend and live in one in obscurity—myself.

They say the woman always pays . . . Nonsense!

It is the poor man who allowed himself to be famous who pays—and pays—and fails to collect.

THE MERRY WIVES OF TALIESIN

While alone at Taliesin after coming back from Japan, I had three wives, Sylva, Dione and Nobu, looking in on me, keeping up my spirits. But they were not really mine. They were the wives respectively of Werner (Moser), Richard (Neutra) and Kameki (Tsuchiura)— apprentices from Zurich, Vienna and Tokio. But I can't imagine what I would have done without these wives at that time. On the rocks economically, publicly, emotionally.

We had concerts in the Living Room at Taliesin III. Evenings as we used to do in the Living Room of Taliesin II. Werner (Werner played the violin) and Sylva had a fine little boy, Lorenz. I loved to have him around. I liked to hold Lorenz sometimes. A beautiful boy. Richard and Dione had a small son, too (named for me before leaving Vienna); Kameki and Nobu were only just married. Together with Major Will (Smith)) they were all my immediate family. A happy one because all good to what was left of me at that bad time. The boys kept my mind on my work; the girls kept kind attentions and flowers all through the house. While they did make me feel less lonely, they only made me feel all the more need of "the woman in my life" during these several pre-Olgivanna years. The Sylva-Werner baby boy especially made me long for a little soft one of my own at Taliesin. After all, what was Taliesin without a young princess? I guess the happiness of these young couples pushed me gently over the precipice of divorce and marriage to really live again completely.

The young women were three differing individualities. Their young husbands were talented fellows, but not to be compared to their wives. Sylva was a true-hearted beauty; Dione was a genius, good to look at, played her cello and sang while playing, doing both with style: her own! And like most Europeans she played the best music. Nobu was like a black-headed, sloe-eyed petite Japanese doll—when exquisitely dressed in her native costumes. Kameki was extremely competent, blinking intelligently behind his glasses. I look back upon that period of life at Taliesin as a quiet prelude before the storm. The outside storm broke when Olgivanna appeared upon the scene, which she did some time before they had all left Taliesin, two of them going home (terms were up), and one to the West Coast to "get jobs."

Werner came to me with a letter from his distinguished father, Herr Professor Moser of Zurich, then one of the leading architects of Europe (Herr Professor Otto Wagner gone), asking me to take his son Werner as a pupil. I was happy to have the great architect's son. Kameki came by way of the Imperial Hotel to study with me. Richard had been knocking on my door from Vienna for admittance to Taliesin for several years, until at last, coming over anyway and finding me gone, he camped down with Holabird and Root a few months to wait until I came back. All are building reputations for themselves in, respectively, Switzerland, Japan and California.

Autobiographers publish a good many letters, I believe. So here is one I received from Herr Professor Moser's now distinguished son, Werner, himself author of many important, interesting buildings in Switzerland.

DEAR MR. WRIGHT:
Since we have this terrible totalitarian war in Europe there is much uncertainty, much dissatisfaction and opportunism in our European architecture. There is great need for a constructive, clear, direct mind. You can demonstrate in your life-long work one continuous line of architectural development, of course expressed in a big variety of applications of the one principle. Your work is a consolation today for every sensible architect, and an encouragement not to resign, because it shows to us the deeply rooted belief in everything which is positive today and the possibility to express it beautifully with the characteristic elements of this time.

(It is bad English but I hope you know what I mean.) I had a great pleasure to follow your new ideas from the recent publications in preparing a lecture about your work. There were many young students and a really spontaneous interest in all your achievements. It was a good thing, in comparing it to your designs, to show up the weaknesses in Swiss architecture. The lack of thoroughness, of coordination and imagination, and so on!

Of course, you never can replace an ingenious mind, you can only try to follow his basic idea! Sylva and I had many thoughts for you since we saw Olgivanna and you three years ago in Paris. I remember well your critical call referring to my designs: "Werner, you need a good spanking!"

We would enjoy strongly to hear how you and your inner-Wright family are going through these times!

In your work we feel the never-tiring youth, which is over-shadowing everything done by the younger generation, in respect to inspiration and courage.

You certainly know how precarious the situation in Switzerland is. We are trying very hard to keep independence.

I would like to forward pictures of my works to get a severe critic from you! I hear of your big exhibition in New York and regret very much not to be able to see it. It is about time to have an exhibition like that in Switzerland!

Sylva and the three children are very well, we are for a few days in the winter sports to do skiing. Lorenz is almost my size and wants to be an architect. He will be through school in a few years and I should like him to be some day apprentice to you.

Very many thanks and sincere wishes for 1941 to Mrs. Wright and you from all the Mosers, especially from your Werner.

LULU BETT

Zona (Gale) once told me, "I think the wisest thing you have ever done in your lifetime is to stay in the country."

I pondered this. She might have implied so many things.

While Sylva, Dione and Nobu were all the wives I had at Taliesin, I occasionally drove them in the Black Cadillac up the river to Portage to see Zona—in spite of the columnar village-palazzo she lived in. The old-colonial box (of course, she didn't build it) stood emptily forward on the street leaving a great lawn to the rear—a few nice trees there—running to Wisconsin River bank—the same sand-barred river that flows below the windows of Taliesin. Zona knew all my people. My Mother and my Aunts much admired her. While in Japan I read her *Miss Lulu Bett*. Straightway I made up my mind to know Zona Gale better when I got home; if not, to know the reason why. I had met her one day at Taliesin with Charlotte Perkins Gilman.

We used to come to her house with arms full of wild flowers—golden-rod, wild asters, bittersweet—gathered on the way up the river. Once or twice we were loudly invited to throw them all out. The violent reactions by Father Gale. Hay fever!

Sometimes I used to take Nobu and Kameki along in Japanese costume (Japanese umbrella too), pose them on the lawn by the river—making pictures for Zona. Zona and her friend (one day she might be the Lulu who wrote the play *Sun-up* or some other literary celebrity—

they were always around) would get a little supper together for us.

Of course, I hated her environment as utterly unworthy of her (an exquisite thing was Wisconsin's Zona Gale). I hadn't met Olgivanna then and I thought Taliesin would be a much more appropriate place for the author of *Lulu Bett*. But I had been spoiled, or something. Perhaps I had always expected women to make love to me. I just didn't know how to make love to Zona.

Being kind by nature—a little sorry for me I think—she was always glad to see us, asking me to come again. She said she valued her Regency at the University of Wisconsin too much ever to be seen with me in public. (There were other reasons I guess, because it wasn't so very long before she married the local banker.) For any woman to be seen with me in public at that time *was* pretty dangerous for the woman (not to mention dangerous to me). So I loved the Zona who wrote *Lulu Bett* privately—at home. After I knew her a little better I told her that I didn't believe she ever wrote the book, she was herself so unlike Lulu Bett. But no one could quarrel with Zona. She was too complete and lovely in herself. She was like something exquisitely carved out of ivory, most of the time.

I wonder, though, what she meant when se said, "the *wisest* thing you have ever done," because it was no *wisdom* of mine that kept *me* in the country. No, it was something constitutional. My mother so deeply loved life in the Valley that I am sure I nursed at the Valley's breast when I nursed at hers.

Love of terrestrial beauty grew on me so as I grew up that the longer I live now the more beautiful this countryside becomes. A walk over our country hills when the shadows are lengthening is to look and drink a poignant draught—look and drink again. I wonder if anything there can be in "Heaven" is so lovely. If not, how tragic Death! Death or no death, I see our countryside as a promise never to be broken—a heritage from all the heaven my people knew or cared to know.

THE AMERICAN CITIZEN

Olgivanna was Montenegrin—educated in the Russian Caucasus and at Fontainebleau, France. Here now in the midst of this small trilogy of reminiscences, where, when and how she appeared in my life, between the Three Merry Wives of Taliesin and Lulu Bett, is Olgivanna. Fate the dealer dealt her to me at this particular moment. Since Fate so decided this for me and this is, in a way, a kind of loose-leaf autobiography, I do not have either the hardihood to fly in the face of Fate and change the place of her appearance nor can I leave her out. These eighteen years she has been a vivid living presence, next my heart and she in the hollow of my arm, a joy and inspiration.

But she is here now under the casual title "The American Citizen," which, though a triumph of understatement, is true and a most becoming title for Olgivanna.

Were I to keep on "growing up" I had now reached a "jumping-off" place. At least a critical stage in the growth of that thing which is me. Things had gone pretty low so far as I was concerned: something long past due. What was it? Was it Olgivanna? Time and Olgivanna prove it was.

When I met her thus at the parting of the ways, a mad genius-of-the-pig-bristles painter, Jerry Blum, was alongside me. A better than good, much-traveled, diamond-in-the-rough painter, Jerry was rather terrifying. His parents spoiled him with too much easy money so he traveled and traveled. There was an artist fury in him now damned by trouble with his wife Lucile. Myself, lower down in my own estimation than I had ever been in my life, was staying at the Congress for a night or so occasionally, and Jerry of auld-lang-syne (the Midway Gardens) would happen in and all unsuspecting "Les Misérables" strolled over a block or two to see a Sunday matinee of the Russian ballet. Our tickets landed us down near the stage in two balcony-box seats, by the rail. A third seat in the box was empty: apparently the only unoccupied one in the big overcrowded house. Karsavina was the dancer. Her performance had just begun when an usher quietly showed a dark, slender gentlewoman to the one empty seat in the house near me. Unobtrusive, the stranger, but lovely. I secretly—so I thought—observed her aristocratic bearing, no hat, her smooth dark hair parted in the middle and back down over her ears, light small colored shawl over shoulders, little or no makeup, very simply dressed. French, I thought—very French . . . and yet perhaps Russian? Whatever her nationality I instantly liked her and wondered who she was, where from and why here. Losing all interest in the stage, although I can perfectly see Karsavina poised on one toe as she stood when the gentle stranger entered the box and my life for good.

Jerry too more intent on the dark, slender lady with the graceful movements who sat beside us than on Karsavina, moved a little closer to her—but evidently frightened the gentle stranger for she moved a little further toward me. I looked over the rail to see where he would land if I dropped him bodily out of the box, but he would hurt too many people down below. The fool—he addressed a remark to me intended for her, foolishly complimenting Karsavina, so I gave him one also intended for the gentle stranger.

"No, Jerry," I said. "No, Karsavina won't do. She's dead and all those people down there are dead the same way." And waving toward the audience below, "The dead dancing to the dead."

A quick comprehending glance from the young woman with the sensitive feminine brow and dark eyes . . . was she a Russian princess?

The glance went home: a strange elation stole over me. Suddenly in my unhappy state of heart, lonely for one thing, something cleared up—what had been the matter with me came to look me in the face—it was, simply, too much passion without poetry. Starved . . . for poetry . . . that was it . . . the best in me for years and years had been wasted—starved! This strange chance meeting was poetry to a man hungry for poetry.

We didn't notice Jerry after that until the intermission. Something long since out of drawing had come to life in me. The intermission came and evidently this painter-man Jerry intended to find out who the lady was. "Pardon me, Madam, we have met somewhere before?"—the familiar old approach. She seemed unconvinced and unimpressed. Jerry persisted, "In New York, at Waldo Frank's perhaps?" The lady gave me a startled look. A long shot. Jerry's. Yes, it so happened that the gentle stranger did know Waldo Frank's wife, Margaret Naumburg. That clever knight of the bristles picked out a few more names she duly recognized and Jerry had opened the way to introduce me: "My friend; he is Frank Lloyd Wright, the famous architect. You may have heard of him?" She hadn't, but she looked at me as though she had seen me before and was pleased to see me again. So much so that for a moment I thought she had. I thought I must have met her—somewhere? But no, no one like her—that I could remember—and yet—where? There was something . . . coming clear.

She spoke in a low musical voice. In a sentence or two she criticized Karsavina from our point of view, showing unusual familiarity with dancing and dancers. No longer quite so strange, Emissary of Fate, have mercy on my soul, from the other side of the known world. She bowed her head to my invitation to tea at the nearby Congress. She accepted with perfect ease without artificial hesitation.

Yes, I was in love with her.

It was all simple as that. When Nature by the hand of Fate has arranged her drama all else is beside the mark. All is as it should be and still is—thirty-two years later.

Over tea cups obvious conversation ranged the gamut of Philosophy and Art. The implications were colorful overtones, deep undertones. She held her own in either: and "her own" was a famous architect. Manifestly well educated, she was unusually well trained in self-possession, more than anyone I had ever met. And, incidentally (not so important), I learned what you already know, that Olgivanna—that was her name—was born to an official family in Cettinje, Montenegro, educated by her sister in Batum, Russia, had just arrived from Paris with her seven-year-old little daughter, Svetlana. They had come to Chicago to confer on business matters with her husband, from whom she had separated, intending to return to Paris as soon as possible. You already know, too, the attractive name Olgivanna was made by her friends out of Olga Ivanovna as it had been in Batum—Russian for Olga, daughter of John, Ivan. The nickname Olgivanna was a respectful form of address not unlike our Mrs. or Miss.

Olgivanna had come to America with the Gurdjieff Institute for the harmonious development of man. I had already heard about his work. Asiatic savant, he had brought his group to New York the summer before and performed remarkable studies in human correlation at Carnegie Hall. She herself had been in the group and I now learned from her more of that remarkable training. The Institute took unrhythmical neurotic human beings in all the social stratas, took them apart, and put them together again better correlated, happier, more alive and useful to themselves and others. I am putting here what Olgivanna said with her own inimitable accent into my own words. It seems that Ouspensky, Orage, Lady Rothermere, Katherine Mansfield and many others were Gurdjieff disciples. Olgivanna, Jean Zartsman, Lili Galounian, the De-Hartmans and the Schoenvalls were all star leaders in the teachings Gurdjieff had promulgated and was still preaching—nearer Dalcroze it seemed to me than any other well-known system. But more profound. Fascinating revelation as she described it. She seemed to approve and like what I had to say about it all. Between us across the tea table went more from each to each than I will even attempt to describe. Not in words, although the words were good. I am no novelist. Meredith could do it. But I should be dissatisfied with what he did and so would Olgivanna, I believe.

Jerry kept on gushing as though he was interesting her. Even more than her acquaintance with philosophy I admired the more than ladylike art, art is the word, with which Olgivanna let Jerry slide off without hurting his feelings too much. Jerry was a good talker though, and discussion at the table had been stimulating, so let's forgive his trespass. After a half hour Olgivanna arose to go (arose is the word), to go to her child, she said. But I couldn't bear the thought of letting her go—I was afraid I should lose her. She hesitated, but only for a moment when I said, "Olgivanna, please leave your address so we may call on you? I want to learn more. I can't think we should let our remarkable meeting end here." But I was eager to "teach" as well as eager to learn as anyone could see. Jerry took the address because he, being a painter, had a pencil. I, being an architect, never have one.

Olgivanna—what a winning name I thought—was gone. When she went the light went off. But I knew well enough that nothing could stop us from seeing each other again, nothing either for her or for me. I went East for a week, but sent her a little note from the train. I dropped back into that aching void.

Soon as I got back I called Jerry to come over and stay with me, knowing that he would have been to see her. Poor Jerry was all broken up over Affair-Lucile. I had to listen to that first.

"Yes, Jerry, but have you seen Olgivanna?"

The unhappy painter-wretch had been to the address Olgivanna had given. "But," he said, "Olgivanna only wanted to talk about you and that is that."

I felt grateful to Jerry for being bored that way, and much that pleased me more he imparted with a few characteristic curses— marking his unkind fate.

I wrote another note asking when I might come. Time fixed, I went to take Olgivanna to the theater. Neither of us can remember, nor care to, what the play was. She had several faithful North Side friends, music-makers some of them, and some on whom we began to impose.

Some several days later I invited Olgivanna to Taliesin to have her meet Sylva, Dione and Nobu, and their clever husbands. Olgivanna and the European "Merry Wives" had much in common. Next afternoon she left. My 1924 household, knowing full well what had happened to me, all agreed that Taliesin was the place for Olgivanna. None so sure as I. Her divorce was in court—granted. So was mine, ready and waiting for signature—so why wait? Two fountains of arrested energy didn't wait. Waiting was not in either nature. Never was. Never has been. Isn't now.

Although we didn't know how much would have been saved had we "waited," it probably would have made no difference anyway.

We had each other for better or worse, let whatever might come.

Olgivanna was mine. The night we were off to New York in her berth I read her to sleep with Carl's fairy tale of "The White Horse Girl and the Blue Wind Boy." I guess he so intended it. I had just discovered the *Rootabaga Stories* and they so delighted me that I wrote Carl a little letter in gratitude.

But the story of the plight that followed this brave flight into new life—passion with poetry now—you have already read in the fourth book of *An Autobiography*. What you have not read is how well the chance meeting dealt by the hand of Fate turned out for us and for everyone else who had any right to be at all interested in how it turned out. For more than three decades, the perfect mistress, Olgivanna, and I have lived and worked in luck and out of luck at Taliesin, in any case constantly together. This in sickness and in health. Mostly health. No fair-weather friend was Olgivanna. There was great work to be done now as well as a full life to be lived. But one that would have destroyed any human being less well trained for struggle for the better thing; less inspired by natural gifts, mutual love and understanding.

Just to be with her uplifts my heart and strengthens my spirit when the going gets hard and no less so when the going is good.

We were married, yes, certainly, but we didn't need to be except for greater convenience, wouldn't know it unless you insisted on the point. I found that the girl qualified by years of hard, patient trying to understand, inspired by ideas quite similar to my own, was qualified to be a vivid inspiration, a real mate.

Whatever we undertook, she never shirked.

Strangely enough—or is it so strange—she, whose parents were Montenegrin dignitaries, had pictures of her Montenegrin forebears, looked just like my Welsh ancestors. We might have been of one family although we ourselves resembled each other only in spirit.

John Commons (a good part of Wisconsin U.) told us there was nothing to wonder about in that resemblance because the Montenegrins, the Basques and the Welsh were all a related mountain people. Her severe bringing-up was so similar to mine that we liked not only the same fundamentals, but what went with them in much the same way. There was just enough difference in the non-essentials to make whatever she did interesting to me. She would take a case of any kind in the Fellowship, straighten it with a grasp and effectiveness that could not be matched. Olgivanna could paint or sculpt, cook or dance, play and sing. Svetlana is like her in that respect. It isn't mere versatility: there is a driving fire in it all.

Olgivanna's little daughter's name is Svetlana. After some legal difficulties which you have read about already, she came to live at Taliesin with her mother where she is now married to the stalwart Wes.

As for the little "soft one" that I wanted to complete beloved Taliesin in the Valley—Iovanna? Why, she is already' a lovely plus-seventeen, tall and swift as her mother, a young lady now with beautiful masses of brown hair, hair such as mine at her age. She looks at you something like me, but enough like her mother to make the resemblance to me of not too much consequence.

Now, this isn't much of a story. It is all too close to home to write about. But too long a time elapsed before Olgivanna and I finally found each other. Pretty late? Olgivanna often says, "Oh, why didn't we meet before all the Past had a chance to be the Present?" Well . . . after all, that is probably a little ungrateful because Olgivanna wouldn't have liked me until I had been battered into shape by the many untoward circumstances of outraged previous experience, passion properly starved for poetry, and the harm done by too much damage, by too much flattery, somewhat undone. If she hadn't been properly starved too, probably I wouldn't have such faith in Olgivanna as I have now—with that serious noble look in her face of which I am proud, the graying hair drifting back from her temples proves my point.

Brave. The heart of a lioness.

No, I think we were planned behind the stars—just right. I don't even wish I were younger because we both seem to add up to just about the right age for us, and I admire due maturity much more than youth. I would prefer to die to going through my own "youth" again.

When "inducted" to citizenship, standing up straight in court to answer the question asked by the old judge, she answered all the questions correctly in a firm clear voice, except one. She made one mistake. "Mrs. Wright," said the judge, "what form of government do we live under?"

Unhesitating she said, "A democracy, sir."

The judge bent his head, smiling a little, while poking with his pencil at the blotter on his desk. "No," said the judge. "No, Mrs. Wright, we *are* a Republic."

The American Citizen . . . Olgivanovna Lloyd Wright.

TO POET CARL THE SANDBURG

DEAR CARL:

I read your fairy tails now nearly every night before I go to bed. They fill a long-felt want—Poetry.

I'll soon know them by heart.

Have you sent the book to Lord Dunsany? It would make him feel sorry he was born a Lord and so had to fool around with Gods and Goddesses.

I've tried so long to play the guitar with my mittens on that Henry Hagglyhoagly is mine—and O Man! the beauty of the White Horse Girl and the Blue Wind Boy! And the fairies dancing on the wind-swept corn! And the Wedding Procession of the Brown Stick and the Rag Doll! And the Skyscraper that Decided to have a Child!

And all the children that will be born into the Middle West during the next hundred years are peeping at you now, Carl—between little pink fingers—smiling, knowing in their hearts they have found a friend . . . such as Hans Christian Andersen used to be and still is.

Lucky Spink and Skabootch—to have a daddy—"fire-born" who understands blue. Blue is happy imagination. Something that wakes and sings no matter how much it hurts—or is it always singing?

Yes, Carl, only the Fire-born understand blue. You are the kind of artist for me. Stick this little posy in your hatband for a day. I fling it to you from where, as always, the tracks leave the ground for the sky and I'll be waiting for you at this station in the Rootabaga Country to bring Spink and Skabootch to play with their Uncle:

FRANK

Taliesin

And then Carl, the genius, had to ride to riches by way of counting the hairs on the head and fingering the buttons on the vest of our most beloved national hero: that great leader who truly believed the Union could only live if half of it was destroyed in the name of Freedom by the other half: the agrarians on the wrong track, slavery, wiped out by the industrialists on the wrong track, machine-production trying to control consumption.

Lincoln, the great fanatic who invented conscription-in-a-Democracy and by way of white-slavery drove black-slavery into the body-politic, instead of banishing it—enthroning the money-power and the machine to wave the stars and stripes over a wrecked and devastated half of our country, where a Culture might have taken root that would have cured its own evils from within if any real understanding and help had come from the North.

The dying Napoleon said: "What amazes me more than anything else? The impotence of force to organize anything."

War itself is denial of Civilization, its very nature a failure.

540

INVITED

BRAZIL—RIO DE JANEIRO

October, 1930

Invitation from Brazil came via the Pan American Union to go to Rio de Janeiro to serve on an international jury as member representing North America, to judge the accumulation of competitive drawings in the worldwide competition for a memorial to Columbus. Herbert Kelsey (Kelsey built the Pan American building in Washington) was engineering the affair. The program included wives and we thought the excursion might be beneficial—although Olgivanna and I were both bad sailors. Perhaps this time in quiet southern seas we might do better.

All right. We packed, caught the boat as she was casting off the pier: the Grace Line—United States-built boat.

Kelsey was already in Rio.

Diplomats were on board, and Saarinen, Finnish architect, who for some reason was representing Europe, coming from America. The two great continents, Europe and North America, would see something of each other then by way of Wisconsin and Finland. I had always resented Saarinen a little, regarding him as our most accomplished eclectic—a little jealous, too, of the easy berth, bestowed on a foreigner by the hand of American riches, while I had to wait, work and scrape the hard way for mine so many years. Yes—I know, this seems small. But our provincials still feel that our culture, 160 years old, comes from abroad if at all. The import is looked upon in the provinces, especially at Detroit, with great favor. I suppose they think we can't have much at home that should be looked up to as Culture.

But it is only, of course, because they wouldn't know how to look where.

Saarinen, the Finnish cosmopolite with the Norse accent, spoiled all that mild ill feeling of mine when we went together to South America. We became friends—no basis for disagreement whatsoever. I wouldn't agree with Saarinen and he couldn't disagree with me if he would.

Which reminds me: some time ago we met at a railway restaurant in Chicago—he was on the way to a church he was building in Columbus and I on my way to one I was building in Kansas City. He had a million dollars to do his (usual luck). I had one hundred and fifty thousand dollars (maybe) to encompass the same thing (my usual luck). He asked me if I had seen his design. I had, in a newspaper. "What do you think of it??" he asked.

"Well, Eliel," I said, "when I saw it I thought what a great architect—I am!"

We laughed and he slapped me on the wrist. Well, that's Eliel Saarinen and that, I am afraid, is me. Saarinen was born and will die—a Finn.

By way of Wales and the British, I was born native . . . and I still refuse to die.

Speaking of Saarinen always brings to mind the power behind the throne at Cranbrook, the sculptor Carl Milles.

Carl *is* a sculptor—probably now the greatest.

In the hall of his house he has the whole wonderful Barberini collection of Greek sculpture. He bought it outright on the installment plan and brought it home from Rome.

Carl will give it all to Taliesin.

Cranbrook cannot have it.

I wish this simple statment of the disposition of the wonderful Barberini collection were true.

On the way to South America! . . . The old half-freighter pushed up to the great pier at Rio in early morning—wonderful harbor at sunrise! There were a lot of boys (students, I thought) climbing on board. They surrounded us. Only one (and a half, say) spoke English, which astonished me.

They were a delegation from some seven hundred or more students of the Brazil Belles Artes, out on what they called (borrowing from us) a "strike." The institution was modeled by and on the French Beaux Arts of course. Latins for the Latins. The Beaux Arts professors of the Belles Artes had ruled me out altogether by banning my books and forbidding magazines on modern architecture in their library, together with all of my kind.

The youths were a delegation sent by the student body to ask me for help.

Would I help?

I would.

"Look out," said Saarinen. "This is a revolutionary country—first thing you know sssκκκ [he drew his finger across his throat]—and it will be all over with you."

"Never mind," I said. "Come. Get in and help." He stood on the sidelines, however; while I was soon in over my head with those tempestuous boys.

My head still on my shoulders, I met Herbert Moses, editor of *El Globo,* Rio's leading newspaper, and soon learned how to make a speech in a foreign tongue. Moses was not only remarkably intelligent, but also (an experienced editor) remarkably articulate. I filled him up with the point of view. He was enthusiastic and eager to do the work.

First meeting with the Belles Artes enemy was in the old hall of the Belles Artes. The Beaux Arts dignitaries, myself, and the handsome president of the University of Brazil presiding. I sat next to the president. "How do," he said. I did a little better, but it was in my own language. I knew less Portuguese than he knew English. He knew no more English than that "how do." And only one and a half boys we had already seen out of the seven hundred at Belles Artes spoke English! Many read it, though.

El Globo spoke English like a Yankee.

Our ambassador, Morgan, a genial competent one, was always there on every occasion and sometimes he spoke.

We, and the dignitaries, were ranged at a long elevated "bench" such as judges use in our courtrooms. The boys were massed down there below the parapet that divided us.

The meeting began with Latinesque formalities. The president offered a welcome, a professor or two chimed in. My turn—but without waiting for me to speak, bedlam broke.

When they let go a little I got *El Globo* by the arm and, standing that way, would tell him in a sentence or two what I wanted to say. Having been rehearsed, he would put it over to the young rebels with such effect that they would go wild.

Of course Latins love to go wild.

I gave them all I could—pleaded their cause as the future of Brazil. If Brazil was to have a future. How could she deny her youth the advanced thought of the world whether or not her elders disagreed with that thought and—well, my reader knows by this time what I would say. I stopped; Moses (*El Globo*) stopped . . . and then the mass of youngsters charged the judges' bench, pushed their dignitaries aside, *El Globo* and the ambassador too, picked me up and carried me away from·them down to the street, called a taxi, and sent me off to the Copacabana with all of the boys on board who could stick there.

There was now meeting after meeting.

The affair "Columbus" took a back seat although we finally did judge that show, and there were great dinners and celebrations, galore. I wrote the opinion and the other judges politely concurred—not looking for argument. What was the use anyway? A young Englishman got the prize. Deserved it. The whole mass of entries, with a half-dozen exceptions, was a bad form of grandomania and wonderful draughtsmanship. Like most competitions it was all in vain. What can a competition be except an averaging upon averages by the average? The first thing the jury itself (a picked average usually) does is to go through and throw out all the worst ones and the best ones. Then the jury, itself and average, averages upon some average design as it could only do. But this time I wouldn't have it that way.

Well, the Belles Artes "strike" began to turn the heat on the Belles Artes. I don't remember where or how many times I spoke, or how many newspaper articles I wrote for *El Globo* and *El Manha*, leading newspapers of Brazil.

The boys would come after me and I would go, and Herbert Moses would "interpret"—if that is what he did. He became fiery eloquent—I suspect he frequently put more into his interpretations than I had put into him. I met the "modern" professors the boys wanted. They were good architects, excellent men. The authorities were negligent or else indulgent because they didn't arrest me, but finally they did arrest one of the coveted professors who spoke alongside me—Araujo.

Saarinen said my turn was coming next.

He enjoyed the whole affair in a way peculiar to the Finns . . . I guess.

They have a National Academy in Brazil, medal dispensary something like the National Académie Française. This Academy tendered me an honorary meeting and subsequently honorary membership.

The Architects' Society of Brazil gave a dinner, with wives. I was in the very thick of the stuggle then, and I took the occasion to plead the cause of the boys until I brought tears to their eyes to go with the seven different kinds of wine—my own eyes near tears without wine. They tendered me honorary membership in their National Society. Yes, I accepted conditionally: on condition that they help the boys at Belles Artes.

Finally they agreed with congratulatory speeches.

Ah—the Rio de Janeirians are a fiery, gallant folk. I never thought I would ever like the Latins so much as I like them. Olgivanna and I hardly touched the ground during our stay. We went place to place with a grand set of fellows and their handsome wives. We weekended at Petropolis, bathed on the beach before the Copacabana, rode in the suburbs and along the marvelous Rio waterfront dominated by curious mountain silhouettes.

Kelsey must have hated me for it all—because what had it to do with the competition for the Columbus Memorial? He attended to that himself, made a good job of his knitting and didn't dock me for time off.

A famous French landscaper was there at the time with plans for the replanting of the Versailleslike gardens of the waterfront. The Rio de

Janeirians brought the architect and the plans to exhibit both to me . . . for criticism.

I didn't feel competent or willing.

The new *Atlantique* came to harbor one day during our six weeks' stay and the great city turned out en masse to meet her at the pier. Our ambassador had a stalwart bodyguard who fought a clear-way through the crowd so we might follow the ambassador up the gangplank, get on board and see what I thought was France's greatest contribution to modern architecture.

Truly, the elegance and beautiful craftsmanship of the interior of that great ship were stunning. I sat and marveled.

The Rio de Janeirians have but one social fault. They are committed, heart and soul, therefore so are you, to photography. Everywhere we went in public or in private at unexpected moments, at table in the garden, there was the puff, puff—and startling flash—of flash bulbs. Ambassador Morgan was usually with us. Our ambassador popular in Rio. They couldn't have a function public or private without "El Ambassador."

After the dinner-in-honor at which everybody was photographed, and photographed everybody else, the architects took me over to be especially photographed again by their famous star portrait-photoist. The photographs were good and I had to sign them all for all the architects of Brazil.

Time came to go away. Things had been tremendous. Students now came to say they wanted to do something for us. They said they had been "out" so long that (like me) they had no money left. Some of them wanted to bring flowers to Olgivanna but they would not afford to buy them.

"Might they not then come to the Copacabana and serenade us that evening?" They could. They did—hundreds of them . . . a unique experience, not to be forgotten.

They rushed the piano out to the middle of the ballroom floor. Some of the boys improvised instruments and costumes, native songs and dances, till three in the morning while we looked on seated in a balcony. I wish some American movie magnate could have filmed that show for our country. But down there I couldn't say *American* movie magnate without giving them either offense or to think that I meant one of *their* own. The Rio de Janeirians always resented any reference to ourselves as *the* Americans. So I said Usonia when I talked about our country to them. They liked the term. They had never heard it before but thought it appropriate.

Well, we got home safely after a long journey in perfect weather on an old United States steamer (why do we build them half-freight, half-passenger, I wonder?). Probably subs have sunk it. Anyway, we were happy to get home.

Taliesin was again a beautiful dream realized. There is nothing like homecomings for happy realization.

A fortnight after we were settled again, a cablegram from Ambassador Morgan said that the boys had what they wanted. Organic architecture had won a temporary victory.

The students of the Belles Artes free to grow up to serve the future of Brazil!

We brought such a mass of photographs, newspaper pictures and clippings that Henry sat down and compiled an album, thirteen inches square and two inches thick, which you may see at Taliesin to this day.

THE TALIESIN SNIFF

Independently of wide-open windows seldom shut, letting in varying smells of the four seasons, Taliesin is pervaded by its own very special smell. The visitor on coming in for the first time will sniff and remark upon it, ask what the fragrance is. That fragrance is partly oak fires in. open fireplaces and the masses of dried antimony from the hillsides now on Taliesin shelves. Odor of the long white drifts of wild-plum bloom on nearby hillsides drifts in—crabapple and hawthorn in the meadows send their scent on, over the treetops. Later the sweet breath of clover fields rides in to the rooms on the morning and evening breezes. Soon the scent of new-mown hay pervades the place. So our windows, like the doors, are seldom closed in Spring and Summer. In Autumn, when they are closed, mingling with the odor of freshly burned oak, is the smell of bowls of apples and unshelled shag-bark hickory nuts and prince of all perfumes, the sumach. But for Winter, there inside the rooms is the newly gathered, everlasting, cream-white antimony. Gentle pervading odor is to the sense of smell what the flavor of slippery elm is to the young boy's sense of taste. Oak fires then start in the seventeen ever-present stone fireplaces to go out seldom until the following Spring. Not unless fuel gives out.

A few of our collection of fireplaces smoke just a little, just enough to contribute a trace of the burning oak. When the evenings are chill in Autumn or Winter, and Taliesin is covered with its thick protecting blanket of snow, thin white wood-smoke going straight up toward the evening star is good to see.

So it is in Winter especially that Taliesin is most itself. Smells best at least—and most home.

The Taliesin smell, then, is compounded of the acrid odor of oak-wood fires, overlaid and softened by the odor of great bundles of ever-lasting (antimony) gathered from fields in Autumn. Great masses of the decorative creamy white herb-blossoms stand about on tables and ledges in big old Chinese jars. This is the authentic recipe for "the Taliesin sniff."

A WAR FABLE—AGGRESSIVE FOREIGN POLICY

There was once a nice Johnnie on his way to school with a lot of other little Johnnies, Tommies and Jennies all around him. Johnnie saw a curious thing he hadn't noticed before—a hornet's nest hanging in the bushes. Not knowing much about hornets, he got a stick and poked the nest—whereupon the hornets swarmed out, stung all the little children except Johnnie, who went bravely on to school. At school, in the midst of the boo-hooing and wailing, Johnnie told his tale. The teacher said, "Why, Johnnie, you are a *hero*! I didn't know hornets were so dreadful." So Johnnie, the hero, sat up front and all the children went out in-structed to destroy all the hornets everywhere to make the woods safe for such as Johnnie.

TOKIO—JAPAN

Invited to Japan to build the new Imperial Hotel, the Teikoku at Tokio—during that four years' residence, and a preliminary visit in 1906, I learned some little something of a culture that I had studied and worshipped from afar. Owing so much to Old Japan, it would be absurd for me to leave her culture to the mercy of the "patriotic," destructive, "white-eyed" ignoramus who will write and rate her now. Typical trash in this dedication of a new book published by Macmillan: "Dedicated to the gentle, self-effacing and long-suffering mothers of the cruellest, most arrogant and treacherous sons who walk the earth—to the women of Japan, who will as always, reap the richest harvest of suffering as their reward."

Well—there you have it—about the general, generous size of the average Western comprehension of the Orient.

Extraordinary nonsense that for so many centuries "these arrogant sons" should have sired this paragon of virtue and she should in turn have mothered "the most treacherous sons on earth"? But no common sense nor. any sense of decency stays with our traveling provincials

547

when they undertake either to underwrite or destroy Japan. The basis for any sense of proportion whatever is still lacking.

Kipling said, among other things with a grain of truth in the saying, "East is East, West is West, and never the twain shall meet."

I am sure they should not meet, not yet because, except for a few culture-hunters (and exploiters?) like myself, the West has no tolerant comprehension whatever to give to the East—from first to last. And the East has conceived a thorough, grossly exaggerated contempt for the culture, honor and character of the West. Both China and Japan have preserved a great deal of their native sense of beauty and artistry. True, too, the Japanese have from their first knowledge of us regarded us as vulgar barbarians. From their standpoint I suppose we are.

The Commodore (Dewey) who fired the shot that compelled Japan to "open up" was no violet.

That rude awakening of Nippon—the Land of the Rising Sun—from the peaceful pursuit of culture for several hundred years, during which time her Art and Craft rose to high-water mark in all the culture of the world, was a terrible shock to the Sons of Heaven.

"What is the secret of this strange power of these vulgarians? They have neither character, manners nor brains," said the Nipponese wisemen. And they sent their elder statesman, Count Ito, journeying around the world to find out. He was absent some two years, staying longest in Germany. Japan's Number One statesman came back with the secret: "Explosives. In Machines."

Japan (and this is hard for the West to understand) went to hysterical self-abnegation, began to destroy her beautiful works of art, casting them on sacrificial bonfires in public places surrounding the palace moat in Tokio: virtually throwing her civilization away upon fires as on a funeral pyre, a national form of *hara-kiri* also incomprehensible to the West. A young American at that time helped save many of these wonderful proofs of great culture from wanton destruction. His name was Ernest Fenollosa.

Japan, whose religion Shinto—the severe "be clean" religion—was overlaid with colorful Chinese Buddhism, had reached the parting of the ways. She had "lost face," an Oriental spiritual tragedy, a collapse, which again we fail to understand. Centuries of severe interior discipline, more severe in mundane poverty than any the world has seen, all had gone for naught? The culture of Dai Nippon—Land of the Rising Sun—must have been wrong if a crude barbaric people like these Western men with cold white skins, cruel noses and white eyes that frightened their little children into hysterics, had this power to destroy them; these coarse men who had no power of thought, no true spirit of

548

courage, so the Japanese believed. But could they destroy them because they were masters of explosives in engines of destruction!

Soon after Count Ito's return from his mission to study the West, Japanese schools were modeled on the German school system. A German military system was set up Germanizing the Japanese. Official Japanese delegations were for years and years continually traveling the West, picking up the details of the brutal new power, almost invariably finding the best applications of that power in Germany. It was such a delegation much later that picked me to build the new Imperial Hotel, a social clearing house for official Japan. This after first having heard of me in Germany. But German architects built Japan's new Parliament buildings, built the first Imperial Hotel. Built the Imperial University which now became, virtually, a German university. Japanese music on the stages of modernized Japanese theaters went "Ich liebe dich." The conviction settled deep in the Oriental breast that was official-Japan's national conscience that the Asiatic yellow peoples must some day meet the Western white-eyed peoples on a footing that would save Asia from barbarous double-dealing England and her stooge, America. They saw nothing to admire in Western culture except that as a means to an end, it would serve them better than their own in the undertaking now ahead—the defense of the East against the West.

Many years later, one day when I, an American architect (almost by accident), was building the new Imperial Hotel for them in their capital, Tokio, came the news that American politics had declared them an inferior race. The United States of America denied them privileges of a civilized nation.

Well I remember the fury of the indignation meetings at that time in Tokio at the old Imperial Ball Room.

For two weeks I was not allowed abroad without protection and until the ancient capital quieted down again. Infuriated Sons of Heaven were now completely confirmed in their belief that Asia must prepare to save herself from the international shopkeepers, murderers and peddlers of the whites, their gods and their goods: *Everywhere* on the Asiatic continent or on any sea that washed Asia's shores the Western Civilization had no place.

So they prepared with thoroughness and German efficiency: made preparations that seemed entirely to escape the military eye of the purblind dominant race except for one intelligent mind: the mind of the hunchback Homer Lea and one ruler—the Emperor Wilhelm's Yellow Peril. Lea's books *The Valor of Ignorance* and *The Day of the Saxons,* issued thirty years or more ago, should have had attention which they failed to recieve. Homer Lea's is one of the few minds—like

Napoleon's—to realize that the military mind is a dead mind. The world was ready for something else.

The largest populations of the world—about three to one—and the most ancient, were no longer innocent of a leader-nation who has mastered the great secret of cruel Western barbaric power—explosives in machines. The West was riding this new horse. Not only had Japan made that discovery but she soon learned how to ride the horse. She felt she was therefore the savior of the sleeping Orient, the unaware yellow-races of all Asia. Her leadership, even if their ignorance of danger had to be fought for among themselves, was Japan's great Destiny.

A common saying under the flag of the Rising Sun, that the East is the morning land, the West evening land. All the dirty seven hundred commercial tricks in streamlined Western commercial duplicity and practiced by the worst of Westerners found apt pupils on Asiatic shores. Soon the slant-eyed yellow-men everywhere, especially in Japan, learned another secret of Western power—the monkey moneyism of Commercial Empire, wherein sophisticated whites were pitted against the unawakened, as yet untaught, yellow-men. The yellow-man no match for the streamlined commercial experts of the West now in action. No, not yet. But coming—soon—tricks against tricks. Being a more ancient people, the Asiatics were more easily degenerate and demoralized by the West even than the relatively cold whites and the demoralization began.

THE PRINT

Two episodes seem to drop into place here of their own accord, since my persistent absorbing pursuit of the Print has so involved me with Oriental experience. The first was one for me. The second, one of them.

From time to time I had collected their superb Actor prints: Hosoye—about eleven hundred of the first rank—Shunsho, Shunko, Shunyei, Sharaku. Single sheets, diptychs, triptychs, pentatychs, and several septaptychs—iridian sheets of soft paper stained with soft colors portraying ancient famous actors in classical roles on the Japanese stage. Any collector will know what that collection means. "Wrieto-San" was already on the map of Tokio as the most extensive buyer of the fine antique print of the Ukioye. Already described to you is what an avocation the pursuit of the rare-print became in ancient Yedo. The prints were then extremely rare, expensive, still going up in price at this time. It was often said of collecting them—"It is finished, Japan has been raked with a fine-tooth comb for a quarter of a century. Give it up."

550

My friend Frederick Gookin of Chicago was the foremost reliable connoisseur in our country. A fine person in himself. When I was about to return for the fifth time to the building of the Imperial Hotel, he introduced William Spaulding and his brother John to me. The Spauldings were cultured Boston people (Beacon Street) who had got into this most absorbing, exciting and expensive pursuit known to esthetics, very late. As bride and groom, William Spaulding and Virginia Fairlie of the Chicago Art Institute had tried to start a collection while on their honeymoon in Japan but they could find almost nothing. I myself had been able to find little. Learning from Frederick Gookin of my extraordinary collection of actor prints, Mr. Spaulding came to my office in Orchestra Hall to see a group I had brought in for my own pleasure. Delighted with the portfolio of one hundred prints he offered me ten thousand dollars for them. At the time it was a fair price. For a number of reasons I accepted although, except as collections were abandoned, it was quite impossible to find such first-rate examples.

A few days later about ready to return to Japan I received a telegram from the Spauldings inviting me to come to Beacon Street for a conference. I gladly went. At dinner that evening this subject was broached by the Spauldings: "Would you consent to try to find prints for us in Japan, Mr. Wright? We are both impressed by your experience and your knowledge of the subject and what your opportunities must be in Japan. We feel we can trust you completely. We know it is no longer possible for us to find prints unless you will help us." I had expected something like this and had been trying to arrive at something but had nothing definite in mind.

Suddenly I decided. I said, "I will take whatever money you want to spend, spend it and divide what I buy. I'll keep what I think I should have and you shall have the others."

"Well," said John as he laughed, "that's hardly a business proposition, is it, Mr. Wright?"

I said, "No, I am not a business man, Mr. Spaulding."

They wanted to know why I would not do it on commission. I said, "Too much bookkeeping." We left it at that and went to bed.

Next morning John and William said they had thought it all over. "We will be glad to accept your offer. You will find twenty thousand dollars to your credit in the Yokohama Specie Bank when you arrive in Tokio."

There was no scratch of a pen to record the agreement.

Neither the Spauldings nor I thought I could find enough prints worth buying to spend that much money.

I arrived at Yokohama after the usual tedious Pacific crossing. The fifth. Directly I went to Shugio. He who was Emperor Mutsushito's "connoisseur" and now my intimate friend. Hiromishe Shugio had charge of all Japanese fine art exhibits, in the foreign expositions—a friend of nearly all the great artists of Europe, Whistler especially. He was a lover of London; he liked to compare London with Tokio. Shugio was a Japanese aristocrat (there must have been some Chinese blood in him with that name and countenance). Shugio was highly respected by everyone. He had access to court circles, enjoyed a universal reputation for integrity. I laid the case before him with twenty thousand in the Bank.

It was my feeling then that, hidden away Japanese-fashion in the *go-downs* of the court nobles and therefore beyond the approach of the merchant class, were many yet untouched collections of the (to them) somewhat "risqué" prints of the *ukiyoye*.

Shugio wasn't sanguine but agreed to talk with a few such friends. He wasn't very energetic either. But finally by tactful pursuit he was moved and soon we did hear of a private collection that might, with proper circumspection, be bought by Shugio if he had the tact. I had the Spaulding money, Shugio the confidence of the court nobles.

Well, it *was* simply amazing. I bought the first collection that turned up on that new trail for much less than I thought possible. The news (a secret) got around just how and where we hoped it would. Money was very scarce then (1915–16) in Japan. The interest rate at banks was nine per cent.

I was getting excited. Already had established a considerable buying power and now anything available in the ordinary channels first came to me. I picked up some fine things in this way. Aristocratic Japanese people lose face if they sell their belongings, even such things taboo as the prints. Evidently Shugio had found a way. Well, it had begun. The twenty thousand was soon gone and already we had priceless things. Anything unique or superior went to the Spauldings. I kept all the prints together in Shugio's own *go-down*, mounted and grouped them as I got hold of them in my workshop at the Imperial. I would cable for money from time to time as "finds" turned up during the five-month campaign. The money always came, no questions asked. Nothing from me except excited demands for more money until I had spent about one hundred and twenty-five thousand Spaulding dollars for about a million dollars' worth of prints, I believed.

Many were unique as of the record.

A superb collection, quite beyond price—most of it now in the Boston Museum of Fine Arts, a gift from the Spauldings. ·

Finally a cable: "When are you coming home?" I cabled back: "Taking next boat," mounted and boxed the prints, caught the next boat but one. I was to bring the prints to the Spaulding country home at Pride's Crossing. By this time both the Spauldings, William and John, and Mrs. Spaulding were proficient judges of Japanese *ukiyoye*. They had Gookin (as consultant connoisseur) present and several other collectors—Ficke, Mansfield, Chandler. For three days we laid out prints and prints and more prints and some more prints until neither the Spauldings nor Gookin (he was now leading expert in America) could believe their eyes. Even to me it seemed like some fantastic dream. Sated with riches in the most exquisite graphic art on earth, after three days at a marvelous feast we all sat back, marveled and rested.

William Spaulding expecially delighted—gratified was hardly the word—said, "Mr. Wright, this goes far beyond any expectations we had. You can't have much of your own after turning this over to us?"

"I have enough," I said. "I've done pretty well by myself, I assure you."

"No, I don't believe it."

He walked over to his desk and wrote a check for twenty-five thousand dollars, came and handed it to me. I genuinely hesitated to accept it but of course I did. And presently he came downstairs with an exquisite slightly toned copy of Utamaro's *Ryogoku Fireworks*—black sky—and said, "My brother and I want you to keep this treasure and never part with it. You have brought us a better copy—perfectly fresh, probably the finest in the world—but this is the next best, we believe. We bought it from Baron Sumitomo."

After luncheon we went out for a drive in the new Spaulding Stearns-Knight—top down. I was sitting on the rear seat between John and William Spaulding. Not going very fast, enjoying the relaxation, we were passing school grounds, boys playing ball there, when I heard the crack of a bat on the ball: a square hit. I glanced up just in time to see the ball sailing over us. Instinctively I leaped up, reached up for the ball, caught it and threw it back into the game.

"Well!" said William Spaulding in astonishment. "So that is it! Well, Mr. Wright, I now know how you got those prints! It's all clear at last!"

Hiromishe Shugio got some of the twenty-five thousand but not enough. I wish now I had given him all of it. He deserved it more than I did.

But now you have here before you a perfect picture of the West looting the Orient. I make no apologies. You may judge for yourself my feelings—pro and con.

A fascinating pursuit had now developed as avocation: this pursuit of the rare Japanese print—but on a scale never originally intended or imagined.

My own buying—buying for the Spauldings—for the Metropolitan, for the Buckinghams, Chicago Art Institute, had automatically, no such intention on my part, given me command of the print market in all Japan. Nothing much now got away. I had spent nearly a half million dollars in Japan at a time when money there was scarce indeed.

You may well say, the East got the money, didn't it? But what did the West get? Priceless art treasures running into millions. And it was always the same story, in either Japan or China.

Wrieto-San's "avocation" was great pastime, but profitable to him and to the West until I grew ashamed of it finally and resolved to get "collecting" out of my system.

All right. The Japanese merchants didn't like me, of course. But it went deeper than liking—they had been short-circuited.

Howard Mansfield, treasurer of the Metropolitan Museum at the time, had asked me to pick up some treasures for him next time I got back to Tokio if anything extraordinary should turn up. Emissaries used to come to me from various country places, frequently, to offer their "finds" first to me. I had leadership now in the print market.

Now "Wrieto-San" is getting to be too much of a merchant, I thought.

I lost caste a little in Japan, I believe, by way of these commercial transactions. But one more chance came from Nikko—*very, very secret!* I went by train with the well-known Tokio dealer, Hayashi-San, a name as common in Japan as Smith is common in America. Then by rickshaw to a little Japanese house hidden in the woods in the outskirts of Nikko.

There we found the "collection." My God! I thought I had seen every subject extant by now. I hadn't. There were things in that collection still unique—things like a large-size Harunobu (printed in gold leaf in heavy goffered paper) that later brought twenty-five hundred dollars at auction in New York. Kyonagas—stunning subjects I had never seen. Noble primitives: Sharaku by the dozen, Shunsho, charming Kiyonaga, Shunko, Yeishi triptychs, Toyokuni I five-piece, the Shunman black-and-white septaptych, Hokusai almost complete, the Hiroshige *Saruhashi*, the gorge, the snow-triptych, ah well . . . why go on? Suffice it to say that this clandestine collection beggared imagination, therefore description. I who had so eagerly read of Aladdin and his wonderful lamp when a boy . . . well, again this was Aladdin's luck. All the prints were of the first quality. *Ichiban.*

Still the hungry orphan turned loose in the bakeshop, I spent about two hours there and bought it all for fifty thousand dollars. Of course they needed money badly. I who had crowded out other buyers by now—practically had things my own way, accustomed to getting about three for one anyway, which was not greedy as things were going in Tokio. Ten for one is about what the West expects from the East, and takes.

Again the usual tedious return voyage across the vast Pacific. The eleventh.

But I had my treasures on board to study and gloat over. Glutton? Absolutely.

When I returned I had them all classified and properly mounted and took them to New York and Howard Mansfield. Howard, really by this time our most fastidious American collector, was the center of a group of more or less wealthy but, nevertheless, very discriminating collectors. He himself was by now a veteran. The group called in experts (several of them), excluded me from their conference, which hurt me. Why should they exclude me? I couldn't understand, but you see I was now a "dealer."

Finally Howard, pencil and paper and lists in hand, entered, offered me forty-five thousand dollars for about half of the collection. Make it fifty thousand, I said. Agreed, said he.

Some months after returning to Tokio and back to work on the Imperial, already sick of the rôle I had been playing, I received a cablegram from Howard:

WRIGHT. IMPEHO. TOKIO. KYOTO MATSUKI, NEW YORK DEALER, TURNS IN-FORMER ON TOKIO RING REVAMPING VALUABLE OLD PRINTS. SOME FROM YOU HAVE PINPRICKS SHOWING REVAMPING. BETTER INVESTIGATE. MANSFIELD.

I investigated at once and knew where to go to do it. I found that Matsuki told the truth. Several leading dealers, smartest in Tokio, had for years been keeping a famous craftsman with helpers working in the country on genuine old prints, rarities in poor condition as they turned up, putting months of work on a single rare specimen that would probably bring several thousand dollars.

First they would discharge the color—restoring the paper to normal and get genuine dips by soaking old worthless prints to obtain the proper colors, and then, by an ingenious system of pin pricks at certain angles of the drawing, guide the reprinting of the original print from blocks cut solely for the purpose of reprinting that one print. The result was not an imitation. No. It was a genuine *restoration* and valuable. But who wanted restored prints? No collector, certainly—nor did I.

The jig was up. Staying away from me until this last trip, these conspirators had previously loaded up many collectors like Sir Edwin Walker of Canada, and a half-dozen less well-known collectors in our country, but they had fought shy of me—either not daring to try me out, now emboldened by their success with others thinking it time to retaliate and "get" me.

Yes, Wrieto-San had fallen. I went after the ring, wiped it out, got the ring-leader (he was Hayashi) in jail. After he had been there a year his case came up. The court sent for me as evidence. The police brought Hayashi to me where I was sitting in court at a small table there to "judge" him. The court wanted to know what I wanted done with him. Hayashi knocked his forehead to the floor time and again, begged for mercy, tears streamed from his eyes. I said, "Take everything of the same sort he has away from him. Forbid him to ever deal in color prints again and let him go." This was done. He had very little of anything. They would have hanged him if I had said so, for the Japanese authorities were furious. Vain release. I heard of Hayashi in London—in the print business—a few years later.

He was a product of the West and belonged there.

I dare say he was successful in London.

Japanese trickery had greatly humiliated them and enraged the authorities. So I had "cleaned up the market" in quite another way than I originally intended.

Japanese authorities openly apologized. The print business, but not Japanese prints.

The court asked was I satisfied? I was. Satisfied that the East was one up on the West, and somehow, too, sorry. A sop to my own conscience?

But now I had to square myself with Howard and his friends. When I got home again, much later, we held at Taliesin what again was known as "The Print Party" but in reverse. I threw open the vault at Taliesin with its collections to Howard and his friends. They were free to choose what they would in exchange for the restored prints. About one-third of the "treasures" I had brought to them in that "collection" had been "restored."

That party cost me about thirty thousand dollars.

"Wright," said Howard Mansfield, "I knew we could count on you!" "Yes, Howard," I said, "But you are as culpable as I am. You excluded me, you called on your own experts and picked out your own prints. I had no responsibility really. But 'Wrieto-San' couldn't afford to 'lose face,' as the Japanese themselves say, with his own friends."

"Yes, Wright, I know," said the treasurer of the Metropolitan, "I know." He didn't look quite happy.

This Tokio game was all played according to a pattern set by the West: all served me right for getting into something I had no good right to be in. I woke up. There was no one now to say to me—No, you are no American! I was pretty good "American" now.

But I have always maintained, without pride, that had I ever desired to become one of the successful commercial gamblers of the West they would now be taking my money away in freight cars. It's easy.

Japanese war with Russia came. Japan, the novice, put her schooling to the test and to the amazement of the dominant race she won that dubious prize. From that time on she began acquiring stance in the Pacific that would some day stand her in good stead. Valuable coastlines and some ten thousand islands. One of those, nearby, became a vast secret training ground for trying out Western ideas with German schooling and Japanese personnel with secret improvements.

At one time—just previous to the Exclusion Act—evidently Japan looked upon the United States as an exception to her aversion for the West. Many of her people and many of her statesmen looked upon us as a possible trustworthy friend. I do not know why, unless because of our extensive (and expensive) interest in her culture. But she soon lost that hope and with it went what little respect she ever had for us when she saw us selling coveted iron to her for war purposes at the same time that we were encouraging China to resist her. That act tallied with her firm faith in Western depravity and duplicity.

Dai Nippon always adored her motherland, China, as we have adored the motherland, England. When in Peking, 1918, to let contracts for the rugs for the Imperial Hotel, I learned regarding China and Japan from Dr. Ku Hung Ming, author and editor of Peking. Dr. Ku had been secretary to the Empress Dowager of China. He was an Oxford graduate, but now wore his long black queue curled up under his red mandarin cap as a protest against what he called "The Motor-car Chinaman." While in Peking (Peiping) he wrote several famous books—one, *The Spirit of the Chinese People*. I had read that book in Tokio and it so impressed me that I determined to look him up when I arrived in Peking. I did so and had a chance to sit and learn from him, a true sage.

The sage and I went about together. He took me off the beaten track exploring the country about the capital. Since he hated the motor-car Chinaman, we took a strapping young Mongolian (six feet seven for me and another smaller for Dr. Ku—he was not very tall) and we would usually take along a guide who had attached himself to me—he, not very welcome, but useful often.

We saw old palaces, the blue-tiled Temple of Heaven, the Imperial Palaces, great Gates, dusty caravans of camels going through from the Gobi Desert—loaded with furs and branched off into the unknown. One day he took me to an ancient temple not known to tourists. He was continually showing me the obscure but significant features of China, interpreting all to me in "the Spirit of the Chinese People." This particular temple-roof was down, water coming in on the sculptured walls—one entire wall covered with pottery figures in complete relief set into niches in the wall. There were several hundred in several tiers, each figure some two and a half feet high—brilliant in color. A spectacle to make a collector sick with envy.

Dr. Ku walked away to take in the surrounding view.

Again I, the "hungry orphan turned loose in a bakeshop," coveting the sacred images. Satan in the bulky form of the guide stole up alongside me and now that Dr. Ku's attention was on the landscape that came through the fallen walls, he said in a low voice, "You like statues very much? Yes? All right—you pick out one, two, tree. I bring you your hotel tonight, you see mornin."

Tempted for a moment and then came reaction—revulsion would be it. I could bribe this fellow to plunder the place—sacred to such as Ku Hung Ming—historian and patriot. A plundering process across the years stripping China of her finest things. "Oh, no. No, I don't buy that way. Some day this temple might be restored."

"Never," said the guide. "Soon all gone. Somebody else will get."

"No, not me."

The little sage's ears must have been sharp. The dialogue had all been sotto voce, but I heard steps behind me and felt an arm laid on my shoulders as the old philosopher's voice almost down to a whisper in my ear said, "No, it is not so. *You* are no American!" This token of affection and respect, for so he meant it to be, touched me and I have never regretted abandoning those marvelous figures to the "somebody who would if I didn't."

We stood looking at the figures as Dr. Ku talked, told me about them. He too said there was not much chance of saving them. But it was better to leave them to their fate than go to perdition (or at least purgatory) with them.

The little old scholar, gray queue still curled up under little red mandarin cap, said many wise things: truly a wise man—one of the few I've ever met. He was neither old school nor new school. He was the timeless sort so far as his mind went. I remember his saying as we walked about the ruins, there were almost no original Chinese left in

China—all were now Mongolized. They had, during many, many centuries, been gradually Mongolized from the North. The only remaining original Chinese, due to an early migration by way of Korea, were the Japanese. The Japanese were Chinese who had met there on their islands the native Ainu and absorbed most of the small Ainu population. The secret of their excessive fertility was phosphorescent food, their diet of fish. And he said the rapid rate of their increase would soon raise a serious problem. A Japanese family of thirteen is a small family. A Japanese sire of sixty children to his credit was nothing unusual. Of course, this would be a rich man with several wives. But the Oriental birth rate, including Russia (more largely Asiatic than is general realized), was such as to be quite capable, were a gun put into its hand, of forming a deluge of manpower which under capable direction might easily swamp any further attempts by the West to subjugate Asia. The Asiatics would multiply faster than they could possibly be killed, even by modern mechanized warfare. They could ride the wild horses of destruction three to one! The Kaiser's Yellow Peril!

He said, now Japan looks upon herself as that "gun in the hand" of Asia. Both Japan and China worship at the shrine of India. Should India gain her independence, she is their natural spiritual leader. The Hindus—Buddha—conquered China and Japan. ·Dr. Ku said the Asiatics regard Russia as the connecting link between the East and the West. Japan, no doubt, would some day, probably by way of China as a natural bridge, join with Russia. And it was not unlikely, in the opinion of Dr. Ku, that India, freed from Western domination, would join with the yellow races led by Japan and China, and that all Asia would make a defensive treaty with Germany which would give a good four-fifths of the population and area of the world over to the power and uses of the yellow man. He said the Africans were sure to go with the Asiatics whenever the time came.

Dr. Ku's philosphic view was perhaps whatever biologic basis there was in the Emperor Wilhelm's "Yellow Peril": an overwhelming opposite, an entirely separate race genius—one which we do not and cannot, even if we cared to, understand. Dr. Ku told me that we of the West not only could not understand but would only ascribe to that genius the motives which we would ourselves have in whatever the circumstances might be, and be completely deceived every time as to whatever they might be, actually thinking or intending to do. Russia and China were already, and soon Japan would be, glacial in the human mass due to the fecundity of population and limitless natural resources when modern sanitation and arms came to them.

No Asiatic nation could ever be thoroughly conquered for long by any outsider.

Never would Japanese conquest of China be the end of China or

German conquest be the end of Russia. But Japan's conquest of China *would* be the end of Japan. As the Mongolian was the end of the original Chinese, so the Mongolian-Chinese womb would be the end of Japan. Every Japanese man covets a Chinese woman. Even a well-to-do merchant will gladly take a Chinese coolie-woman for a wife. She would add at least nineteen half-castes the first generation, who would in the second generation add at least three hundred forty-four three-quarterites, etc., etc., ad infinitum. In seven generations there would be no Japanese left in China nor probably very many left in Japan itself. "Henceforth," as said the tiger to the lady, "henceforth you ride inside." The fanaticism and cruelty of Orientals is something we can stay away from but that we can't change by fear of us or of our power any more than we can level their eyelids to a perpendicular with their noses. Because though cunning they are not afraid and they will fight, not for revenge but for their own.

1942, remembering the words that Dr. Ku had spoken a quarter of a century ago and judging from my own experience, I find it utterly wrong to classify Hirohito with Mussolini and Hitler. Japan is an entirely different racial quantity and spiritual quality. She is pro-Axis. That is all. She is really Asia for the Asiatics, dead or alive, and for whatever that may mean she will fight to the death. Anything that will serve that end she will embrace with indescribable Oriental faith and fatalistic fervor.

She feels the liberator's sword is in her hand and she feels free to use it in ways that seem treacherous to us of the Western world but which to her seem only good strategy.

She feels that but for the white bedevilment of China, the Indies and India, she would even now be secure in her position as qualified leader of what she calls and feels to be the great Emancipation.

What the Western world calls and would like to believe to be the Chinese Republic was ridiculous to Dr. Ku. The Chinese Republic in his view was only a coastal strip which the great uncounted—even, to modern times, undiscovered—masses of Chinese know little and care less about. To refer to China as a Democracy was to refer to Dr. Sun Yat-sen, his remarkable family and friends, and a few million Chinese all looking to the U.S.A. for a hopeless confirmation and support, which could in any final issue only *betray* and *not* liberate the Chinese people. There was no realistic basis, not even a commercial one, for calling our support of China our fight on the side of "Freedom." No. Freedom of the Asiatics will, he said, never come by such external means. It would gradually grow from within, Japan or no Japan. It was to be a matter of many centuries.

The West, Dr. Ku thought, failed utterly to take into account that China and Japan are of one blood. Their own natures within the range of their own fanaticism and cruelty can do best for and with each other in due course of time. He saw nothing the West could do for either nation or their collaterals except further bedevil and destroy them, postponing their inevitable future—the yellow races solidly linked by way of Russia with the West and Germany—if Germany should survive—retained as a paid schoolmaster. But the schoolmaster would probably be no longer needed.

TO LONDON

Invitation came to me at Taliesin—April, 1939, from the Sulgrave Manor Board by way of the British ambassador to the United States to take the Sir George Watson Chair for that year and deliver the lectures that a bequest from Sir George made possible. These lectures were to alternate, one year by an Englishman, the next an American. All were intended to serve better acquaintance of British and American Culture. Lord Bryce, Woodrow Wilson, Hadley of Yale, Theodore Roosevelt, the Governor of Canada and many others, had already delivered them.

The Sulgrave Manor Board, as you may know, took over the old family estate of George Washington in England to make sure good care of it would be taken. Common ground in American and English history. The chosen lecturer was free to deliver these famous lectures in any one of the English universities he might choose, and as many or as few lectures as he chose. The honorarium of twenty-five hundred dollars, and expenses, might be for but one lecture if the recipient of the honor so decided. The rights of publication went with acceptance by the lecturer. I accepted the honor, for so it was. I decided to give four evenings at London University. But the Royal Institute of British Architects, upon learning that I was to give the lectures, proposed to join in sponsoring them, asking that they be given in the new hall of the new building of the Royal Institute, Portland Place. As a preliminary attention, the Institute made me honorary member of their body so that I might not set foot on England's soil a stranger. At least I like to think that might have been one characteristic English reason for their hospitality.

So we decided to take Iovanna with us to London. Soon arriving at thirteen, the daughter of Taliesin needed educational experience. So on the *Queen Mary* we went again to London, this time staying at the historic old Garland Hotel (destroyed by the war). Standing not far from Trafalgar Square, it puts an end to Suffolk Street. On the boat we met a *Manchester Guardian* journalist who told us enough about the hotel to decide us to visit it. Henry James had stayed there to write. Whistler and his cronies often turned up there. I remembered my friend Ashbee saying he stayed at the Garland when he came up from Camden Town—to London. Lady Sandwich said people from English country estates coming up to London often registered there and found the old place delightful. English homeliness garnished by quaint ugliness: still as English as anything in *Pickwick*.

The lectures: If that is what they were, I've found that I do my best with them if I do not make preparation for them, whatsoever. When *I* get enjoyment out of delivering them, I am sure others do. Trying to remember spoils the delivery of what I want to say when at the podium on my own feet. Since I am only talking out of myself anyway, I need no rehearsal as I would if I had collected material for the occasion. The audience is usually an inspiration in itself, too, not to be forestalled. So when I wish to do my best, I always do, I am careful not to think beforehand of what I intend to say. This was the only "careful preparation" I made for the lectures—four evenings at the Royal Institute—published by Lund Humphries under the title "Frank Lloyd Wright." A well-illustrated and tastefully printed book issued while German bombs were dropping on London. The first copies reached Taliesin West, Arizona, February, 1941.

HONOR

While listening to a New Year's Eve broadcast at Taliesin West, 1941, that same winter I learned that among the King's birthday honors of that year, His Majesty's Royal Gold Medal for Architecture had been bestowed upon me. If my friends were astonished, you may imagine my astonishment. I think they were all startled except Russell Hitchcock, who seemed to know something about it as having been "in the air."

The most coveted honor in the world is this incorruptible one from the Royal Household of Great Britain. Unlike so many of our own institutions, these "honors" are equitably bestowed. They do not go by fashion, favor or prestige. They are so recognized throughout the United Kingdom. The Royal Gold Medal of the Royal Institute therefore goes a long way with any Britisher or any nation anywhere on earth. As a matter of course it should go with any American anywhere. It pointed up the honors previously received from seven other countries. This last one should have been first—but that the first shall be last and the last first is standard old prophecy?

I accepted by cablegram: "YOU PROPOSE A GREAT HONOR. I ACCEPT GRATIFIED THAT DURING THIS TERRIFIC WAR ENGLAND CAN THINK OF HONORING AN ARCHITECT. FRANK LLOYD WRIGHT."

Former American recipients had been Richard M. Hunt, Charles McKim and Thomas Hastings. I took it as remarkable evidence of the great change taking place in currents of thought in the world of modern Architecture. It pleased me that now the young lads who had worked and were now working with me should have less opposition to overcome in the years ahead than I had met. So I regarded the award as a distinct break for them through me although perhaps there are worse enemies than open opposition. Popular success, for example.

The British lectures in the Sir George Watson Chair I regard as a great experience: one of the most gratifying of my life. Young men came from Edinburgh, Cambridge, and places in between, until there was seldom even standing room in the splendid new hall. Notably, the audiences were young. These audiences increased until they were turning many away.

Said the Earl of Crawford, presiding on the platform, leaning over toward me—"What is this, Mr. Wright? The board has never seen anything like this before."

I said, "Your lordship, I can't imagine."

That same lord, the first evening on which I had taken a perhaps too gloomy view of the cultural state of things in general, got up and remarked that the proceedings had rather puzzled him. He said he felt somewhat in the position of Sandy at the funeral being held in an old Scotch churchyard. Sandy, curious to see what was going on, got too close to the edge of the grave, slipped and fell in, barking both shins on the coffin. Next day the local paper, commenting on the affair, said, "The unfortunate incident had cast a gloom over the entire proceedings."

And the good-natured laugh was on the "lecturer."

Always an affable lord was in the chair. No better nor more competent company on earth than the English gentleman, but one or two of the M. P. lords who came over to preside were, unlike the Earl, "rather a bore, don't you know." Olgivanna was present at the lectures. Many asked her if it was true that my "speeches" were entirely spontaneous—not because they didn't seem so, but because they seemed so spontaneous. She assured them they were one and all perfectly spontaneous. During post-mortem discussions at these lectures many interesting things were heard. One ponderous duchess next seat to a friend of mine raised her lorgnette to ask, "Who *is* this charlatan from Texas who comes way over here to talk *us* down?"

Iovanna, castle-crazy, was disappointed so much by the adding and patching of buildings that didn't "belong." She found a companion in John Gloag's little daughter who took her about. She was particularly offended by Sir Christopher Wren's additions because they so invariably ignored the original work as to be really not additions but subtractions. Nor could she reconcile the plumbing hanging over on or showing under the ancient dignity of the outside walls. No amount of explaining squared the facts with budding Romance. She loved the Tower—but was eager to be in Paris on the trail of François Villon.

AUDIENCE

On the whole I have the most intelligent of audiences but never such a high level of intelligence and fine character as the audiences in London—nor such outspoken awareness and purposeful heckling. I always enjoy a heckling. So does a British audience. I won't quote any of the many evidences of this, many have been published by Lund Humphries in the collected essays and because an old court reporter was present and got the whole thing down so accurately, that for once in my life there was little to correct in the copy he presented. The tasteful book, heckling and all, edited by the Secretary of the Royal Institute, Carter, came out as I have said, when London was raided, bombs exploding and the walls of London falling down or already in ruins.

There is something indomitable in British pluck and splendid in British character. It makes me wonder what England might have been like in the culture of this world were it not for her Empire—her "white man's burden." Such qualities as hers are good for far more than war and conquest or the conduct of subjugated peoples. If England had a chance to be a free England on her own, developing surely the characteristics and strength of Englishmen from within, the nation might have been small but the world would have had one mighty, genuine Democracy by now: the shining light, great exemplar, needed. Her great are among the world's greatest, irrespective of conquest. Empire will ruin England! Her successes for three hundred years did England, as England, no ideal good. The ancient disease—empire—took root and spread in the branch by way of her "Success." Dismal reflection—it is now spreading to her offspring—to us.

About a year after the London lectures a telegram came to the

Arizona desert from the *News-Chronicle* asking for 1,500 words of cabled suggestions for the rebuilding of London, January 21, 1942. The following was sent:

"Greatest creature of habit on earth is London. Slums and ugliness that would have taken centuries to overcome have been blasted out of the way in a few days, and while sentiment is entitled to its tears, the art and science of human habitation may therefore now get a good break. If English-speaking culture by way of the grit and will of Englishmen takes the break, goes ahead, and builds in line with this age of mechanical power the Empire may die, but English dominion will survive and triumph.

Power so capable to destroy is as capable to create, so we shall soon see. And we shall soon see whether England is humanitarian or only English, and whether Germany is humanitarian or only Germanic. If England is humanitarian London will proceed to decentralize. Even the bomb-load overhead points to that necessity. London reintegrated should be twenty-five times the area of old London. The new space-scale of our mechanical era is just about that—twenty-five feet now to one foot then.

Human congestion is murder; murder if not of the carcass, then murder of most desirable human sensibilities. There is room for this greater decentralized London, and crying need. The plan for it should be laid down now keeping in mind that Tradition with a capital T is greater than these manifold traditions to which it has given rise. Many traditions must die in order that the great Tradition may live. Great building begins at the beginning, so necessary items are:
1. No very rich nor very poor to build for—so no gold standard.
2. No idle land except for the beauty of common landscape—no real estate exploiters, liquidate the realtors.
3. No holding against society of the ideas by which society lives. So, no patents.

In short, no speculation in money, land, or ideas. Not one of these must be a speculative commodity but, not so hoarded, money *must be used* as actual necessities of human life like food, air and water. This true basis for what we could honestly call Democracy would be a necessary basis upon which to build a city. This mechanical sanitary age will take the place of the feudal monster now being destroyed by itself.

Liberation of human individuality is not so terrible a leveller of human fortunes as—to many—it seems to be. Life of human initiative is just basis for true capital. Base capital broad upon the ground, not as now with apex on the ground, base in the air. Except for the disabled, unemployment would be unthinkable in a State so founded. England should be that State forever impregnable.

The physical body of the Democratic city would have no one center but have many centers all well correlated; heights of the buildings increasing as the perimeter of activity was approached.

Were Old London to fairly accommodate the partial motorization it already had B.B. (Before Bombs), there could now be no building at all in London. London motorization has only begun. London should be a motor-car, aeroplane London, new spacing all laid out upon the new scale of human movement set by car and plane.

But the sentimentality of our elders blocks this path of progress, by continually begging for compromise. Make none! Make none whatever, because all the vision we have is not enough to prevent sentimentality and fear from catching up, holding us back and down again. Keep static out, and keep the traffic centers wide open. Historic London could be featured in a great general London-park-system. Conduct power from the mines. Do not cramp industrial living areas around piles of raw-material or fuel with the usual deadly-dull collateral 'housing-by-Government.' Abolish so far as possible the back-and-forth haul of people themselves—their fuel and supplies. Do not be afraid to build factories and farms as fit associates for country homes, schools, designed accordingly, churches, theaters, as well as parks for dwellings.

Railway and motor-car arterials should be elevated or underground, continuous storage space above or beneath the tracks. If at ground-level, lorry traffic should be set low on each side so that lorries may be free to take on or take off anywhere. All traffic should be fluid and planned. Yes, it can be done. Such grandomania as survives the bomb should now expend itself by extension parallel with the ground—going up into the air as activity thins out. Old building-codes should be revised or thrown away; new ones simplified and broadened in keeping with the opportunities of the new age of the 20th Century. These should be written and fearlessly re-written year by year.

There must be no such traffic problem as we suffer in our big cities. That has been solved in Broadacre City by broad streets concave instead of convex, underpasses for foot passengers, overpasses for left turns. Top-turn left intersections provided for traffic, over- and underpasses for the criss-cross streets. Traffic lights low because the roads themselves would be side-lighted ribbons, lights alternating from each side. The likelihood of accidents thus reduced to about one-tenth of one per cent. And away with poles and wires forever.

Along with life for the individual on his own ground in his own house and speech honestly free, man goes free his own way, yet in no man's way—laws made for man not man made for laws—the Democratic city comes alive.

No, not Utopia, Usonia. Just a way of building from a good modern twentieth century plan for a democratic people. That's all. By comparison, what luxury and pagan beauty the Greeks knew or medieval Christianity knew was an exterior thing. Any imitation of it today is like some stage setting.

No difference in quality of thought between the house of a man with more and the house of a man with less: difference only in extent. The *home*, real citadel of the human race in Democracy. Wherever and while the private home has the integrity I here bespeak for it—there can be no war!

All harmonizes. Individuality informs and enlivens all public buildings and private homes without mutual detriment if architecture could live again as organic. Industry should decentralize. Must people live again only because of atom bombs in official or irresponsible hands? Maybe we could all live again only because of destruction by such bombs? Who knows?

Easy all this. With fluid atomic power and integral architecture, any necessity for the old pigeon-holing aggregations of our horse-and-buggy Past belong back there with the horse-and-buggy mind and the manure pile. A new kind of beauty now comes back to life—Integrity that is Beauty, Beauty that is Integrity.

Economy integral. Integral building and economy are cement to Democratic Culture: not a mere phase. We are building it a little here and there in America in spite of ancient codes, ignorant legal interferences and wanton waste. Dictators should now be out of luck.

Why blink the fact that mechanization has outrun the social and esthetic forms and education the capacities of our society? We yet live in the philosophy and ideas of our Yesterday. Why use Yesterday's rules for To-day's laws? "If we are on the side of nature we are never lawless." Were organic planning now executed, Empire might disappear, but British Dominion would still be safe. Much safer. Were Germany to win this war it would be to lose it on any basis of any "plane-and-gun" future for this world.

Don't grieve too much, great-Great-Britain. Empire is now no essential.

Yes—"The Empire of Imagination is more enduring than any Empire of mere facts or force."

A kind note from Sir Ian McAllister said the cablegram had been published throughout the United Kingdom. In due course a *News-Chronicle* check for twenty guineas "made the crossing." In the circumstances a touching affair—that check? And how involved and far beyond in its significance anything I had to offer!

MOSCOW

May, 1937

Olgivanna and I—invited to the International Congress of Architects— made our way across five countries and the Atlantic Ocean, to join the Congress, via Paris.

This invitation to travel as Honored Guest to the Soviet Union to attend, in Moscow, the conference of Architects to which a number of the great architects of the world were invited. So once again we set out together for Moscow. We debarked from the *Queen Mary* at Cherbourg, went by way of Paris to Berlin. Then, after a short stay in both capitals, finally landed at the Russian border for customs' examination. The examination (too much like looking the gift horse in the teeth) was getting acrimonious as it grew more and more complex. But a telegram from Moscow called it all off and we were welcome to "come along." So we took the old European leftover parlor-and-dining-car from "the border"—on to Moscow.

We passed a wide blank space at the frontier, trees cut down, a kind of no-man's-land percursor of the war, barbed wire entanglements both side. Towers with sentries stood high overlooking this desolate cleared space. Russian sentries were marching up and down the station platforms on the one side, Polish sentries on the other. I ran into one such Russian soldier and was waved back by gun into the Russian section.

All this was because the famous purge trials were just over. The Russian Army had been purged of an army so it was said. In Paris they tried to scare us out of going to Russia at all. We wouldn't be scared.

I should like to write at length of our experiences in Moscow, but this chapter of *An Autobiography* for reasons, all good, must sometime end.

The enthusiastic Russian people were wonderfully kind to us, Olgivanna's knowledge of the Russian language an immense advantage. Such warm hospitality! Their works even more wonderful. Old churches and other blocks of buildings were going high up in the air, blown there, dynamited to make way for wide avenues for new Moscow: Moscow being made ready for five million more citizens! The great road-making program was now going forward toward Leningrad, young girls with white kerchiefs on their heads over fair hair were driving great steam-rollers. Tractors and trucks were everywhere. Old buildings, some good, contrasting sharply with new ones, mostly bad. Of their kind, many of the old Russian Greek Orthodox churches were fine. Of course, there stood the beautiful Kremlin: genuine, beautiful Architecture.

But modern buildings in Moscow were hard and superficial—unsympathetic, the badly proportioned. Cliché. This would apply to all but a score of them with perfect justice. I don't wonder the Russian people reacted to these cold facades as they did, rejecting them in favor of the warmer old Classic-order. These so-called modern buildings must have been hateful to the Russian mystic emotional nature: the passion of the people of Russia. Many Russian architects I met, and, writing for *Soviet Russia Today* when I came home, I described them and their work.

We went over to meet our Ambassador: luncheon with Mr. and Mrs. Joseph Davies. Joe was a University of Wisconsin boy and we enjoyed a private talk, a glance now and then by our host and hostess at the walls, because there was reason to believe that the walls had ears. Outsiders being under espionage. But that soon wore off. Not a single basis for suspicion could we see from first to last during our entire visit.

We were allowed to buy nothing for ourselves. Even our telegrams, personal laundry, went in by their insistence with the hotel bills to be paid by the Soviet. The architects carried this insistence so far that when we wanted to bring back some antique Russian musical instruments to Taliesin they wouldn't hear of anything but buying them themselves and presenting them to us.

So warmly attached did we become to the spirit of the Russian People that I came nearer to tears in leaving them than I remember in all my life.

Land of opportunity? Russia! In the street or private home, all places public or private, it was always *we, ours*: our theater, our subway, our schools, etc. Too much going into building up the defense against Germany which Russians then felt would inevitably have to be used, and perhaps just because "defense" was being built up to such proportions! But this was a subject of which no one spoke. I don't know why. But the whole world was in such a jam! Great changes were coming. There was something in the air though—May, 1937—that made every man afraid of something he couldn't define even if he wanted to.

American newspapers were nasty because I said publicly that they had not been telling us the truth over there at home about Russia, and said were I in Stalin's place I would kick out all correspondents, for the good of everyone concerned. There were but few exceptions. I named them. Walter Duranty was one.

At the Architects' Congress there were architects from Spain who told us of the restoration of old Spanish buildings undertaken as soon as the bombing ceased, and long before either side had won the war. There were architects from Turkey, Ankara, Jerusalem. From Finland, Rumania, Sweden, Norway, and, of course, the U.S.A., England and France. But most interesting were the native architects from the fifty-eight Russian States stretching off toward Tibet and toward Batum on the Black Sea. In all there was an ideality, an eagerness to observe and learn; I had never seen anything like it before in my own country. A solidarity too—difficult to believe could ever exist. Comradeship was everywhere as they filled the great circular foyer of the Hall-of-the-Nobles and gathered in groups for discussion of what had already been said or was just about to take place.

When we got further into the country I was much surprised to find the same weeds, flowers and trees that grow at Taliesin, see the Russians at the Kolkhoz fighting the very same weeds until I learned that vegetation of the latitudes is the same, and longitude doesn't matter climatically.

So horizontal belts of similar foliage, bird and animal life seem to encircle the globe according to latitude.

We were domiciled at the Metropole—historic Europeanized old caravansery—caviar for breakfast—for lunch until we were breaking out over our faces. This for weeks until we were taken to Sukhanov. Sukhanov is a kind of Russian Taliesin. Same rural loveliness—oaks, pines, white birches and the same wild flowers as in Southern Wisconsin. The same herds and birds and even architects similar. Modern architects looking out from old palaces over rolling fields.

Most of their buildings were of the ancient order. An old palace, big circular rooms: a big room with a big circular table at which the architects, young and old, sat with their families and guests, fed from provender which they themselves raised. Their herd was twice the size of ours at Taliesin on four hundred acres, whereas we have more than a thousand.

But we liked the Russians. They liked us. I had liked the Russian aristocrats so much in Tokio, 1915 to 1919, when Russian refugees came there from the Revolution (there were so many refugees in Tokio). Invited them to my apartment at the old Imperial; came these aristocratic Russians of the old Regime, true aristocrats; now in 1937 it was the Russians of the proletariat—the Soviets. Women I thought much the same in both regimes. In them all I felt the valient Russian spirit, regardless of circumstances, shine through. With the men this was the same yet quite different—in favor of the proletariat? They too were very American. So I thought.

In my Tokio apartment built by myself by the old Imperial there was that rarity in Tokio, a grand piano. (I had found a fairly good one, a Bechstein, on the Ginza.) Food at the Imperial was excellent—probably as good as anywhere in the world. So I used to invite the Russians frequently and we got to know each other pretty well. So well in fact that they would sometimes put an arm around my shoulder and say, "But no, it cannot be that you are an American! Surely you are a Russian!"

"No," I would answer, "I am very much an American and so are you!" It wasn't that we were one or the other, but alike, after all.

They would say, "But we don't like Americans."

I would say, "Well, the reason for that is that you don't really know Americans. The ones you would like don't come here often. Come to America sometime yourselves. Then see them where and as they really live and you will like Americans. The traveled ones aren't the natural or even the more cultivated ones. I can think of a dozen American men with whom the Princess (Cheremissinof) would fall in love and the Countess Lubiensky too [a remarkable beauty]. Perhaps you would like our American men better than our American women. I don't know. Our women can be awfully nice. Your men—I am sure—would like them. They aren't too much like the movie-stars you see over here. Our little

American shopgirls are taken for movie stars. But for true pattern, our American women, those not Frenchified too much nor Anglicized out of their natural seves, would resemble you Russians more than any other nationality. I assure you—you would like us at home in our own country where we are naturally ourselves. Nobody likes us abroad partly because the best of us don't go abroad so much."

Yes, and this little speech to the Russian refugees in Tokio twenty-five years ago goes as well for the proletariat in Moscow today. There is something native to the present-day Russian also native to Americans: the simplicity of Freedom. Or should I say the freedom of simplicity? Strange that I could see but little difference between the women of the old regime and the women of the new? The men? Yes, there was a difference there in favor of the women.

But I love the Russian spirit, glad my wife speaks the soft language of Russia. Olgivanna was a wonderful interpreter, frequently cleared up points for them and for me. She was educated in Russia though under the old regime. So she speaks the soft beautiful language like a native. Soviet Russia and Usonia are capable of perfect understanding and sympathy. Inevitable friendship eventually. But the Russians are richer in human content and colorful spirit owing to their Oriental heritage. I, too, think as my old Chinese sage Ku Hung Ming said, the Russians combine East and West. The best of us not only have sympathy to give them, but an experience that might show them much to avoid. I guess we ought to have a revolution over here now to make this thing more clear!

We came home by way of Vienna—say my old friend Hoffman sitting in a sidewalk café there and listened to his plaint—a discouraged disillusioned Architect he of the Wiener Werkstätte. I learned shortly after arriving home recently that Hoffman was dead.

TO RUSSIA

This honored Guest of the Russian People, 1937, going there via Paris direct from London engagement by the Sulgrave Manor Board, I delivered the following speech from the speaker's box in the great Hall of the Soviets. The famous purge trials had just been held there. The place was packed with architects from all over the world. Inasmuch as I couldn't speak the language, I wrote the speech and had the text translated by a journalist from *Pravda*. I had the translation carefully checked by Olgivanna before giving it to Collé to read. He was President of the Russian Institute of Architects. Having learned how to make a speech in a foreign language while in Rio in Brazil, I spoke the introduction and conclusion myself in English leaving Collé to read the body of the text. The place was overwhelmed by the six hundred architects. All the states of the Soviet Union were represented and many famous architects from abroad. Never have I had so great an ovation in my life. Many young architects crowded around Olgivanna, she who could speak to them, saying, "We know your husband's work well, and we even knew his face before he got here." The place resembled a convention hall electing a president. Again and again I had to go back, the applause continuing until I reappeared to take my seat beside Olgivanna in the box at one side of the hall when the entire audience rose to its feet and turned faces our way with a new burst of applause. During our stay Soviet fliers had just won the plaudits of the world by reaching Seattle across the North Pole. Great excitement in Moscow. Flares, music, triumphal marching day and night: The frontiers had changed. The Atlantic was no longer even the main highway in future. The United States, Canada and Russia were next-door neighbors.

THE ADDRESS TO THE ARCHITECTS' WORLD CONGRESS—SOVIET RUSSIA 1937

Dear Comrades: I have traveled across the frontiers of five nations, from one great hope of the world, the U.S.A., to greet another great hope of the world, the U.S.S.R., there to find that I your guest, could now go home crossing but one, and that one the frontier of my own nation. And, I can now return by traveling only one-third the distance I traveled to get here. The U.S.S.R. and the U.S.A. are both moved into a central position among the nations of the Northern Hemisphere by supreme aviation of the Soviet Union. Thanks to Science Russia and America are next-door neighbors. But the Soviets are now ready to build fine buildings: a very different matter. A Science too . . . yes, but more. Great Art. I am glad to be here with you because already familiar with your struggle to find suitable architecture for your new Soviet life. I am sympathetic because we of the new life of my own country, the U.S.A., were once ourselves quite where you stand now. We once had the great cultural opportunity—"a clean slate," as we say. We had to choose between crawling back into the shell of old cultures or going bravely forward to the new one we needed in order to become a strong new culture ourselves. In our new-found freedom, confused, we made the wrong choice. We chose the inferior path of the cultural slave. I am here to hope you do not make that mistake in Russia.

The rapid growth of Science, apparent success of mechanical appliances and industrial technique, all these achievements exploiting

572

men as well as vast natural resources, gave us wealth too suddenly. These advances had so far outrun our knowledge of principle underlying the right practice of Art that, needing Architecture as much as you do now, we freely plundered the tombs of such preceding civilizations as we liked and foolishly built upon forms we took from the world-bargain-counter of dying or decayed cultures. So today American official architecture is a disgrace to the name of freedom. Owing to that ignorant license we practiced, our official buildings now only serve to betray our achitecture by a commercial vanity. Our significant triumphs in the realms of Industry and Science are not used to build indigenous culture of our own. As it is elsewhere in the world, only now are genuine architectural forms original and suited to our new free life breaking through. We see them, if we look for them. They are there among these stage settings with which we ignorantly sought to camouflage our lack of growth from within: growth that alone is worthy to be called Culture; the cultural integrity which gave ancient nations whatever greatness they had in their day. That we have done pretty well at this kind of evasion by prostitution is poor enough consolation. What we have done is not good enough because meantime the U.S.A. has allowed herself to learn nothing of the great mother-art of architecture. It is still our national blind-spot. All the arts in our country have suffered in consequence.

Our skyscraper? What is it? The triumph of American engineering but the defeat of our architecture. Nineteenth-century steel frames standing now in the middle of the twentieth hidden by facings of thin stone tied on to the steel framework to make fascinating pictures either imitating feudal towers or making boxes of glass. Architecture is false as the civic economy that allowed these buildings to go up in congested urban areas. I have seen a dismal reflection of that falsity in your own Work Palace. This "work-palace"—only proposed I hope—is good if we only take it for a modern version of St. George slaying the Dragon: or to say—Lenin stamping the life out of a capitalistic skyscraper!

*   *   *   *   *

Elsewhere among you, I see our old architectural enemy—Grandomania: see it even in your subways. I see you repeating underground what the nobles did for themselves (and to themselves) in this hall in which we now stand. Suitable enough, no doubt, for the extravagant parasitic life they lived—but too far beneath the level of the new integrity we are learning to call Organic-architecture—an architecture naturally becoming to those ideals of freedom for which we fought

573

and you fought, and the old obsessions you as well as we must go on fighting now.

The "palatial" will not be easily destroyed among you in Russia, as I see. Cut the old grandomania down here and it lifts up its head over there (which means among you over here) when and where I least expected to find it. But I believe it is popular here only because the finer expressions of modern architecture have been betrayed or allowed scant standing-room here among you. Your "modern-architects" are good but few and therefore unpopular.

New thought comes fresh from the new freedom of humanity declared by my country, a more exacting and exciting ideal has come with these new freedoms than the old cultures ever knew. The old cultures could only flourish by elaborating externals, but the new must and may now flourish by a new sense of reality—by growth from within. Slow growth. I know. But the only growth safe for Russia or America.

So, I dread seeing the U.S.S.R. making the same mistakes made by the U.S.A. When your buildings must be built before the new culture has had time to come abreast in order to make them true to the great spirit of Architecture, it is better for the Soviets to make buildings scientifically sound with as much good sense and intelligent use of good materials as possible. Then stop there!

The left wing of our new movement toward an Organic-architecture professes to do this but did not do more than make flat-topped plain-wall surfaces ornamental. Their negation will pass.

The right wing is not content to do less than make ornament of the building itself. They are therefore bad company. But the true center of the new movement, Organic-architecture, has gone on developing scientific, sound material conditions of buildings until a higher manifestation of the human spirit is seen in Space suited to the character of freedom—the spaciousness required by modern life.

At this moment were the Soviets to concentrate on good proportion, good open planning and the new cantilever construction from inside out—building great highways and bridges, putting into effect great planting schemes, retaining walls and terraces, refraining from ornamentation of her structures not understood and from any attempt to make them in elaborate form until young Russian architects by way of genuine experiment gradually evolve new Russian types true to the New Russia as the Kremlin was true to the Old Russia—well—then the U.S.S.R. would justify new-world hope. A genuine national culture at last! I am saying here that I hope the U.S.S.R. will some day undo what it has badly done, and Russia not do less than this for herself.

Comrades in building! Do not waste yourselves upon these mere eclecticisms, these affairs of "taste." Architecture, in the advanced thought of our time, is fast becoming a matter of scientific knowledge of construction applying philosophical ideas wherein Art is again free and supreme inspiration.

You are young. So take no less than this.

Another great matter coming to light today in our modern world too is the inevitable decay of the great city. Urban life on ancient terms has served its turn, even for you. Therefore cities of the ancient pattern, cities great or cities small, are definitely dated. The factory worker's view and version of life, his vision now especially, needs the cooperation and healthy inspiration of the great wide Russian ground. The agrarian needs the industrialist, yes, but the industrialist needs the agrarian far more. In Russian Architecture the ground is the natural and national birthright of every man. More important to him than anything he makes out of it or gangs up and puts upon it. Of that fundamental ingredient of the good life—Russia has plenty for all forever. So it would seem to me she should now plan to use it for all good purposes freely, more freely and most freely.

Russians—make good use of your good ground for a new Russia! Can the Soviets not see that electricity, machines, automobiles, radio, television—the architecture of splendid highways and spacious, far-flung agronomy as good architecture—can make the old form of city (centralization) not only useless, but harmful to her Future? Vertical is vertigo, in all of human life. The horizontal line is the life-line of humankind. An entire nation will someday be one great free extended city perhaps with a tall center. Its citizens will be living broadly spaced on ground of their own in free pattern wherein workers in field and factory, art and craft, science and education, commerce and transportation, will all harmoniously intermingle and inter-build . . . widely green-spaced. Each branch of human endeavor will be related to every other on organic lines natural to all. Human life without waste motion, distraction, dissipation, interference or the impositions of authority will naturally take on new forms—better ways of doing everything—natural. If that is what Russia means to do, then I am a Russian. Everybody is Russia. Whatever his or her nation, the citizen will be a Free-man. Organic-architecture so far has already evolved the patterns of such a higher life on earth as to be able now to know and show the City of the Future. I would much like the young architects of the U.S.S.R. to see the models Taliesin has made of that future city. Some day they may see it. Broadacre City—the city that is nowhere yet everywhere.

Our United States is yet far from any such plan. Her economic waste and the attempt of production to control consumption prevents it. Private ownership and the Profit System supreme, raised to the nth degree in all branches of life still prevent it. These economic follies make not only the present city but the greater city impossible for another half-century at least. If she wanted it enough, Russia could have that freedom of democratic form now. I see her architects have the vision and the ability; Russia could do the work.

This new well-integrated freedom of life is the great integrity our modern world lacks and so much needs. This is the service Organic-architecture could render the U.S.S.R. at this critical stage in the national life of the Soviets. Later it will extend from Russia to the continental world at large—if by that time there should be any of that life left.

To you . . . architects of the Soviet Union! I, who admire and love your spirit, say, Go slowly into the higher realms of building that we call Architecture. No matter what the pressure, prepare to begin at the true beginning! Learn structure, yes, but first study thoroughly the *principles* beneath the technique and forms of organic architecture that make the building from the inside outward, and by way of your own high Russian spirit, grow an architecture true to yourselves living the new Soviet life as the forever beautiful Kremlin was true to the old life of the Russian on his own soil. This—so that the great new work you are to do will grow out of your life itself wherever it may stand.

Your great Kremlin—divested of its parasitic Renaissance—still stands as one of the human-treasures of all time.

But the Soviet must not imitate the Kremlin. The Kremlin honors the Soviet, but it is my hope that the Soviet will honor itself by growing up to be a true cultural entity in terms of Russia's great tomorrow. When Architecture is really Architecture it is timeless. Out of the young Freedom now of the U.S.S.R., other great treasures for the Future should come. But, patience. They cannot be forced. They must humbly begin at the beginning and slowly grow. What we see now among you as modern is very, very young. Therefore a great hope.

＊　　　＊　　　＊　　　＊　　　＊

I have described the reception given to this address by the Congress. Returning from Russia the American papers were openly hostile to me because of what I had said about their misrepresentations of Soviet life in Moscow. But I wrote the article here below: "Architecture and Life in the U.S.S.R.," in August, 1937, and it was published in *Soviet Russia Today*. Russia was by this time "red." Therefore to the entire United States, by press-news and radio, fearsome, the enemy of Democracy.

No one wanted to hear anything good about the U.S.S.R. even then, so the reporters told me.

576

To commend anything Russian got you in wrong with the powers-that-be. The common-man socially, the heavy interest financially, and especially morally, religiously the church: all were inimical to "anything good about Russia."

My God, of what hypocrisy is our Democracy capable. Capable!

ARCHITECTURE AND LIFE IN THE U.S.S.R.

Now unsafely back in Taliesin again, Moscow colleagues far enough away for perspective: I find I enjoyed them so much, personally, so much in sympathy with them as individuals while there, that appraisals made on the spot might easily have been overdrawn. I am now sure they were not.

As I look back across the North Pole—my friends in Moscow and their life and work regardless of their political bias appear the more extraordinary. I went to them intending to do what little I could to end the confusion in their reactionary practices in Architecture as I then saw it looming among them in the Work Palace. I particularly disliked the Work Palace of the Soviets and had hoped to alter the minds entangled with its erection. But foundations were already in, and I found that in Russia, long ago as in the United States, masses who had nothing and to whom the landed aristocracy appeared to have everything, now had come—their turn to be pleased? Nothing pleases the masses so much as the gleam of marble columns under high ceilings, glittering chandeliers, fountains playing, unmistakable signs of luxury as they were compelled to look up to it when it decided their fate, and they ate out of luxury's hand if they ate at all.

But reassurance for me lay in the attitude of Soviet architects themselves. I may mention Alabyan, Collé, Yofan, the Vesnins, Nikolsky, Chusev, Vlasov and the editor Arkin, my personal acquaintances in this connection. All of them took the present situation there with humor and a touch of fatalism characteristically Russian. Much as we do here in our own country.

Just now is no time to offer the "liberated ones" as they call themselves the high simplicity which repudiates the falsity of that sort of luxury. This is not the time to insist upon something they could not yet understand or celebrate. The higher simplicity that turned upon that same flagrant artifice as the people themselves turned upon its possessors and drove out "its" promoters. So there—now in the Soviet Union I saw again the cultural lag I have seen and fought against for a lifetime in these our own United

577

States. With the Russians, as with the Americans, several more generations must pass before a more natural way of life and building takes the place of the ancient order. Where human rights are concerned, the Russian people see the vicious in that old order, but the masses of the Russian people are yet unable to see "vicious" in the higher realm of created things of which architecture is the highest, and see that what they fought to destroy still lives on among them in the parasitic cultural-forms of the life they destroyed. If promoted now it would destroy them in a more subtle far-reaching destruction more interior than ever before.

Russian architects, however—at least those I have named—are fine manly men who realize this. But they are men who say, "Never mind—we will tear it all down ten years from now," as they assured me they would.

"It will take nearly that long to finish the Palace of the Soviets," I said.

"Never mind, we may tear that down too—even before we complete it." (They have done so.)

"But all this popular rush to get into Moscow?" I said. "Are you right when you prepare Moscow to take five million country-people, instead of sending Moscow out to the five million?"

"Yes, Russia needs for years to come a cultural center for her uneducated millions. Let the city be that cultural center for a time," said they. And they are planning to make it such a center.

Their resignation would not be possible to me. I understand it, perhaps envy it, but cannot approve. Notwithstanding the tragedy of these first essays in the direction of the new simplicity, I would see the Russian opportunity as a mighty incentive undiminished by a false start.

I believe the attitude of the Russian architects sincere: far in advance of the social consciousness of our own American architects. I do not know one architect in the A.I.A. who looks so far into the future, able to smile indulgently at his own present effort—or match this perspective given by a fine sense of humor mingled with idealism and cooperation that is distinctly Russian.

Said Alabyan: "I thought I would put all the columns I would ever have to use in my lifetime into this building (the new Theater) and have done with it." Said Vesnin, concerning his Palace of Culture and Rest (a very desirable improvement on Le Corbusier et al.), "It lacks color: only a preliminary study. It is not yet Russian." Said young Yofan, not yet disillusioned concerning his highly decorative eclecticism, Palace of Soviets, "Never mind, Mr. Wright, it will improve as we go along. We are studying it continually." And I saw proofs of this statement in Yofan's studio (Napoleon's old residence in Moscow by the Kremlin wall).

*   *   *   *   *   *

Who could resist loving such liberal, imaginative, great-hearted fellows? What colleague would not do anything he could do under heaven to help them? The result might be help *from* them. Said they to me: "Have faith in our people, Comrade Wright. We Russians are by nature artists! We love the Beautiful. Our sense of life is deep and rhythmic. We will create a new Russia. You will see."

I believe I do see in their efforts an organic Russia slowly, painfully entering into their consciousness and buildings. "Through closed doors?" Yes. But I see no necessity for Russia to die that the Soviet may live.

If Comrade Stalin, as disconcerted outsiders are now saying, is "betraying the revolution," then, in the light of what I have seen in Moscow, I say he is eventually betraying it into the hands of the Russian people in spite of himself.

In Moscow her architects enjoy a large old palace, complete, as their live Academy. There you find a gallery and supper rooms on the top floor. Libraries, studios and art collections below. Just before leaving Moscow we joined some of the architects I have named, for retreat and recreation at their Sukhanov: a four-hundred acre park, thirty miles from Moscow, where another old rural palace stands. There with their own herds and flocks around them, they are putting up new buildings. All stand in a grand forest with fine vistas of beautiful countryside. To this wooded retreat whenever they will, they may and all do come with their families and friends for recreation. At Sukhanov the architects are about to build small studios for preliminary study and shops for technical experiments.

There seems to be none but friendly rivalry among them. Why should there be other than willing cooperation? Worldly rewards cannot benefit them. They are economically independent for life and so are their loved ones. One man's success hurts no one else but is a stepping stone for his fellows. The sting has been taken out of competition and compromise. There is no humiliation in today's defeat because failure today may be retrieved by tomorrow's triumph. The road is open and their "tomorrow" is today in the sense that Eternity is Now. You will feel it so when you talk to them at Sukhanov.

Good fellowship at Sukhanov, as my interpreter, Olgivanna,

and I found, is unforgettable human experience. Have you ever known Russian hospitality? No? Well, then, be an architect and go to visit Russian architects. They will take you to their own Sukhanov.

Being a farmer myself as well as architect, I visited a *kolkhoz*—collective dairy-farm—farmers at their work in the fields and barns, sharing according to their ability to contribute. They milk three times a day—at sunrise, again at ten o'clock, and at sunset. All live together in a planned village much like the farm village of the old order except that now there for the infants is the crèche filled with babies cared for, while their mothers are at work, by the State. But the babies are nursed by their own mothers. Nearby is a kindergarten along German lines. Both crèche and kindergarten are maintained by the Soviet. The *kolkhoz*—collective farm—is a nucleus characteristic of all Soviet effort, but this agrarian effort is far less developed than Russian industrial effort, as it still is with us in the U.S.A.

The factories are better built and better run than the farms. For one thing, the farm requires so much more. This is partly because the Revolution first came from organized labor in the factories. The farms at first resisted the subsequent movement to collectivize their work. At one time the Russian farmers destroyed their pigs and crops rather than turn them over to Soviet "collectives": the *kolkhoz*. We well know how difficult it is to bring any cooperation to bear upon American farm life, or within it: even now. When I was a boy there, the Grange came the nearest of anything we had, but it does not flourish now.

Now, at last, the agrarian hurdle seems to have been taken by the Soviets. Cooperative farming likely to prove the blessing that socialization proved in factory industry. Houses of the farm-village range about a central square that may be a beautiful park, with loud-speakers there connecting each farm group with the voice of their leader and the cultural efforts of all urban centers. These farm-units, in time, are sure to become the most desirable of all places in which to work and live.

Plans for the new Moscow are still wrong, from my standpoint, but far ahead of any of our own city planning I have seen. Models of future improvements are on exhibition everywhere. There is splendid opportunity to make the city over because no private property nor sentimentality can say "no" when the great plan requires the blowing up of whole squares of old buildings or changing streets. Even sacred old landmarks are blown into the air to make spacious streets where dirty obscure lanes existed. Scope and liberal character of the proposed changes and extensions are astonishing . . . astounding.

When completed, inevitably Moscow will be the first city in the world. But to me that can only mean something already dated, outlived by the advanced thought of our today—call the advanced thought Broadacre City, its capitol a mile high?

All new Moscow will be much too high—the same premium put upon congestion there that landlordism places upon it here. I suppose this is partly because the industrialist in the U.S.A. is still clinging to his old habits ahead of the agrarian in the U.S.S.R. But still dated here in our own U.S.A. For some occult reason, there will be regimented areas here too in the "classic" manner, where inevitable freedom should be. There will be four-story school houses. Knowledge factories in Russia! Two stories, even, would be one too many. The entire outer-belt is a park area but it should be the other way around, mile-high in the center. The commodity sales of the traditional and official order should stand in a big encircling park, buildings growing wider as they extend outward into countryside . . . residences way off somewhere, anywhere.

But much that is splendid is already done—wide avenues and large park spaces. The ancient Moscow River is being walled with cut granite blocks sweeping in a fine curve from the bottom of the water to a parapet on the upper levels. The wonderfully beautiful ancient Kremlin walls and domes stand nobly above these great new granite-slopes: fine historic Architecture.

Moscow subways are a succession of well-planned palatial stations. What grandomania! I like the more simple ones, built first, with columns containing lights, the shafts rising and spreading into overhead. Later ones are richer and more spacious, but less beautiful to me. The Moscow subway makes the New York subway look like a sewer, which I suppose it is, in human terms.

In Russia cutting across the road to culture there is a great barrier—the same barrier is here with us. Popular demand for spiritually unearned increment, that is to say, luxury. But in their case, neither wonder nor reproach. Russians, outside the aristocracy and the bourgeoisie, had less than nothing. Now their turn, millions are looking toward Moscow as a Mecca—able to go there at last! Of course, they go and want to stay, because the lash of unrequited toil on the land has left its scars. How long to heal?

Concerning new construction: Moscow buildings are no better or worse than the best work of other countries. Misfortune befell Moscow when her modern architects took on the modern "left wing." That mistake in direction left some very negative and foreign results—indeed, drab, lonesome; technically childish. Popular reaction from that fiasco could only be in going back to luxurious picture-making in the antique, which Russian older people learned as children to admire and covet.

Chusev and I stood together in his great new Soviet hotel, a huge constructed thing, done in what I told him should be called "Metropolitan Russian" because you could see it with such virtues as it has and all faults in New York, Philadelphia, Chicago or any big city of the world. A comfortable hotel . . . and I exaggerated a little because in many respects it was better done, with more comfort provided for the occupant. But still, the building was the type of hotel we Americans are learning to hate . . . or are we?

Mere size seems to captivate the Soviets as it seduces our princes-of-the-provinces. All this is the reaction I was afraid I would see.

The Palace of the Soviets is to be the crowning glory of new construction. The Palace suffers likewise from grandomania of the American type in imitating Skyscraper effects way up to the soles of the enormous shoes of Lenin, where the realistic figure of that human giant begins to be three hundred feet tall. Something peculiar to the present cultural state of the Soviet is to be seen in the sharp contrast between thick shoes and workman's clothes and this attempt at skyscraper elegance. These perpendicular skyscraping motives are surmounted à la New York setbacks and by gigantic sculpture.

So, enormous Lenin treads upon the whole skyscraperism, regardless. Nothing more incongruous could be conceived I believe, nothing more distasteful to the man Lenin if he could see. Yet Yofan, the young architect whose design seven years ago was accepted for this work, has this year built the most dramatic and successful exhibition-building at the Paris Fair. The general motive of that building is not dissimilar to that of the Palace of the Soviets. It too is a building surmounted by better gigantic sculpture.

But the Paris Fair building is a low, extended, and suitable base for the dramatically realistic sculpture which it carries, whereas the Palace of the Soviets itself has a base of a thoroughly unsuitable, badly over-dramatized character to carry realistic, undramatic, enormous sculpture.

With Yofan I went to see a sanatorium he had done near Moscow. That, too, was a very well-designed, well-built structure. Any Soviet citizen needing medical attention and care may go there to enjoy a luxury seen only on trans-Atlantic liners. An ingenious arrangement of balconies and rooms gives outdoor enjoyment to indoor comfort. On the whole, here is performance that has not been excelled. The building occupied by *Pravda* I saw as the more creditable of the "modernistic" attempts by the Russians. But, because of its negative and unconstructive precedents, such building is not for Russia—it is too laborious a stylization, of too little spirit and small content. I see the Russians discontented with less than something more humane and profound. When culture catches up—say, in ten years?

Their extensive Palace of Culture, recreational center for the studious or artistically minded citizens, was better in many respects. It contains as good a design for an auditorium as I, specialist in auditoriums, have ever seen. The scope and extent of the whole is good in conception, not bad in execution. I liked its architects. I will like their work better when it is more like them, and that means more Russian in spirit and character. Both architects are capable, invaluable to the Soviets as are many others, besides all the friends I have mentioned. The Soviet Union had more than four hundred Russian architects at this Congress in Moscow: invited as many more from other countries and paid their expenses.

I take it Petrograd—Leningrad now—is to be the Soviet showpiece in cities. Nikolsky showed me his design for the new stadium: a spacious, monumental, broad treatment employing masses of trees in an architectural way I much liked. Sensible relief from ponderous masonry. A fine work on a grand scale.

The Russian cinema has made its buildings the finest goodtime-places for "the people" to be seen anywhere in the world. The Vesnin brothers have designed some of them. Collé, my interpreter at the Congress, President of the Architects' Society—A.I.A. of the U.S.S.R.—has a fine sense of proportion and style, at present leaning classic-ward, however. Alabyan, President of the Congress, shows himself a competent designer of the new theater, giving some life to the old mode. So it goes, tremendous social construction intelligently calling upon Architecture for help and direction. Competent architects able to build great buildings are there. Alongside are sympathetic employers, critics, editors like Arkin and the editors of *Pravda*. Many others, among whom the heads of fine arts academies may be included although now, as here, all on the side of reaction. I hope temporarily, but modern architecture has been prematurely and badly represented.

What a pity that architecture in Soviet Russia is not free—so the millennium might be born at once there where the road is still more open than anywhere else. Without all this wasteful wearisome controversy and temporizing with the old time-lag and cultural back-drag. Hard for me to be reconciled to the delays Russia is experiencing, as we ourselves have experienced them, no matter how cheerfully, in getting our architecture characteristic of our new freedom.

I saw admirable models for Soviet Russia's new towns and cities in various places—better than good but too many concessions to the time-lag. I suppose the marvel of it all is that a country so backward as Russia has been should now have these fine things at all—at least, have them so soon. Perhaps too soon?

I grant that possibility and still regret the drag.

But I saw something in my glimpses of the Russian people themselves which makes me smile in hopeful anticipation: the Russian Spirit!

There is nothing like that spirit anywhere in the world today, unless our own.

I felt it in the air, saw it as a kind of aura about the wholesome maleness of her men and femaleness of her women; saw it in this new gospel of work; saw it in the glad open expressions of the faces of workmen and workwomen, their children. Freedom already affects them. Unconsciously proud, they are so carrying themselves. Especially the women. I could not help feeling, "What a mother this new Russia is going to have!"

So a kind of new heroism, one integral with all humankind, is surely growing up in the Soviet Union where men are men and women are women; where God has ceased to be an expensive detachable abstraction; where there is no illegitimate child and where the resources of the state stand behind the mother to reinforce her in the care of her sons and daughters if necessary. In Russia, there is a place in the sun ready for the newcomer *when conceived!* Wherever and whenever the child is born—there, really, is another citizen with rights guaranteed—education ready, waiting; and future opportunity to work. No discrimination between sexes in social matters that I could see.

All this surely wise?

How wise too the premiums placed upon *quality* in work— integral industrial rewards which build up the man in his effort— the "Stakhanov Principle," they call it. Rewards of a social and substantial character devised by a wise leader to develop an entirely new Success-ideal. It is hard for us *here* in our society, our Success-ideal what it is, to conceive this new freedom for the individual without grasping several fundamentals totally changing the human objective. I find myself continually needing a simpler viewpoint than our complex order of "meum and tuum" yet allows. Until we get that viewpoint we cannot understand Russia. Of the greed of the grasping West, we may marvel at her vitality and strength, heroic growth and richness of expression; admire especially her colorful individuality, never knowing the secret of such happiness as seems to be hers.

That secret is too simple for us because it does not longer consist in our "to have or to hold," but in the acceptance of a life consisting in neither, except insofar as having or holding may have human benefits each to each and each to all. The relief of such release from ignoble fear, economic anxiety and false shames, you may already see in Soviet faces; Soviet acts. Heroes and heroism will glisten naturally in the fabric of the new Soviet life if her dictatorial government is equal to this opportunity.

Having now seen and sensed the Russian spirit, I should say that enemies interfering with the Soviet Union would not only have to reckon with the whole male population bearing arms, but with the women too, and every child above nine years of age.

Nothing less than total extermination could conquer Soviet Russia now.

A true poet and philosopher, Dr. Ku (I have quoted him when talking about Japan) had the faculty of thinking and speaking "in simples." One day, while sitting on the edge of an old stone terrace overlooking a lotus pool, he summed up and characterized the various nations of the world with what seemed to me a great insight and with justice—especially with regard to America. "Soul," said he, "seemed to be the element most lacking in all nations—the French having a substitute: Delicacy."

But, he said, it was Russia who would give soul to the world!

At the time—1919—I knew Tolstoy, Turgenev, Dostoevsky, Pushkin and Gogol; I knew Russian music, theater too, somewhat, and I thought I now saw what he had meant.

Today I believe what he said. It is true. Russia may yet give to money-minded, war-minded, quarreling, senile Western nations that make up the Western world the soul they are failing to find within themselves—and, I hope, in time to prevent the suicide Western nations are so elaborately preparing to commit where the East and intermediate Russia are concerned.

Taliesin, August 10, 1937

Many repercussions to the foregoing article, copied by the *Capital Times* of Madison, one of which was this letter:

AN OPEN LETTER TO FRANK LLOYD WRIGHT

In the many years that your name has been associated with excellence in Architecture, you have won a reputation for honesty and fearlessness, and your opinions are listened to by many Americans. It is therefore regrettable that you should have seen fit to couple a favorable account of the Soviet Union with a serious slur on the Communist Party of the United States.

We, who have visited your Taliesin and have seen your buildings with uncompleted floors, without light, and without heating facilities, have witnessed a melancholy illustration of how art is forsaken by an economic system whose one God is profit. We have admired the integrity which has kept you from accommodating your talents to the erection of the kind of structures Capitalism is willing to buy and has bought.

We wondered what you would have to say of the land of socialism where art as well as industry belongs to the *whole* people, and a great architect's creations do not need to stand about without electricity, gloomy symbols of the enchainment of art under capitalism. And we were not mistaken in your integrity. You came back with frank praise, you gave the lie to the distortions of the press, you said: "If Stalin is 'betraying the Revolution' as people are constantly shouting, he's betraying it into the hands of the Russian people." We are therefore completely at a loss to fathom your assertion that the Communists in America are racketeers. Can it be that you have momentarily forgotten your distaste for "Grandomania" and disdain us, merely because as yet there are only fifty thousand of us and we are not quite in a position to do the things the Communist Party in Russia can do?

Or can it be that even after learning that a first-hand knowledge of Soviet Russia is quite different from what the capitalist press supplies us with, you are still content to get your information about the *American* Communist Party at secondhand from the same press? If the statement in the *Capital Times* was not an error, we hope that you will find time to make an accusation more explicit and that the fairness you have shown in your description of Russia will prompt you to give us a chance to answer. We feel convinced that only a lack of direct acquaintance with American Communists—coupled perhaps with the all too common mistake of confusing some campus bohemians with Communists—can be responsible for your statement.

The Faculty Branch of the
Communist Party,
University of Wisconsin

586

REPLY:

TO OUR UNIVERSITY COMMUNISTS: I have read your open letter. First, let me assure you that I have not said Communists in America were Racketeers. That was a slip between the Press and the lip—over the telephone. To say that would be as foolish as untrue. I did say, Trotskyites and campus intelligentsia in mind, that the Communists in our country seemed to me, now that Racketeers were in among them as they are among the labor unions, the worst enemies of the U.S.A. as of the U.S.S.R.

I do not really know what *your* "communism" is. This I confess. I do not believe it is like that, but I am inclined now to see any "ists" or "isms" as alien and I shun the "ites."

I have lived to see the Organic-architecture into which I put my life exploited in the name of an "ism" and made "istic" by "ites." I refer to "internationalism," the "modernistic." Etc. So perhaps I am too ready to believe that whatever Communism may once have been, it too has been exploited by "campus sharp-wits," flourishing on the lazy, irreverent ignoramus: inevitable "ites" that curse truth by living *on* it as parasites instead of living *for* it like men. Theirs is the kiss of Caiaphas. For that reason, what does the term Republican mean now, or Socialist, or Democrat or Communist? Yes, or Architect? Any ideal or movement is more vulnerable from beneath and within that it ever is from outside or from above. Communism in these United States is a conspicuous example. Or that term Progressive? Already as ambiguous. Let's drop corrupted and corrupting labels and be specific!

"Social Justice" sounds better to me than any "ism," but that too is only a label. I could march under a banner that stood squarely upon that idea if made definite enough.

The United States might some day unite under the banner of an unequivocal idea, and win honest social objectives our people might have.

Like Social-Credit, Democracy itself aims to be no more or less than inspired Social Justice. But even the grand term, Democracy, has been bought and oversold by party politics and fakirs until it too is now merely "Americanistic."

TO YOU, AMERICAN COMMUNISTS

To the United States from Russia and back again to Russia . . . As to "Form":

1. Every man be guaranteed the right to work for fair compensation.

2. No able man to eat unless he works or serves his society according to his ability.

3. Ground free, a single-tax, and a free medium of exchange.

4. General decentralization. Everywhere less crowding, and less government except as government consists in transacting the impersonal business of the whole people and renders essential Police-services.

5. No speculation in natural resources of utilities common to all and

by way of which our people live. No private exploitation of earth, water, air or sky or of natural resources like oil, gas, coal, common carriers—ships, planes, cars—or intercommunications like radio; nor any speculation in telephone and telegraph, post or press. Reasonable education and medical help free.

This as a short cut for a country owning itself; in debt to itself only; government *from within itself*. Far greater simplicity, this proposal, than Russia's. A new Success-ideal that would soon supplant the one that went with the profit-motive, one more organic, and therefore more *humane*.

How could this be brought about? Gradually. By wise taxation like the single-tax and some form of purchase by capitalizing the country itself over and above a fair living for every man, women and child in it—selling the margin back to the people as stock in their own country.

A genuine system of private-ownership, a system of capital with its broad base on the ground in the lives of the whole people, instead of standing precariously on its apex, for the enterprising few. Is this communism I am describing? No. Well, gentlemen, if you must have an "ism" I see it as true Capitalism—organic capital of an organic Democracy: the only basis of Organic-architecture or indigenous Usonian culture.

N.B. Comrades, please don't put my plight at Taliesin up in favor of Russia as a reproach to my country. I've been pretty trying, you know, and I am still "trying." Trying to emerge with a valuable contribution to the young man in American Architecture.

Taliesin, August, 1937

SAFETY OF THE SOUL DEPENDS ON COURAGE

The long view is not always the cool view; in fact that view depends on adequate heat.

But, "Experiment, Tolerance and Change give culture strength." Strength is Reality.

Life rides to victory by strength, not through any "ism," "ist" or "ite": Only through direct responsibility of the individual as such—never signing away his sovereignty. Victory implies a characteristic called Initiative. Where initiative is Individual and inspired, Bold and operative, there you see the mainspring of the life of man in abundance, Democracy in operation.

Nature has placed this premium upon Individuality. It applies to Nations as well as individuals because Nations are only the Individual raised to a mass power which should act as a check upon the personal idiosyncrasy. But the fact that a Nation does not so act is the weakness of that Nation.

588

Democratic FORM is essentially organic: TRUTH ever fresh come to our Civilization. Though we now have the sorry spectacle of a venal world substituting money, or blows, for ideas. A whirlpool of hate and destruction into which our leaders were drawn and have drawn us with too great ease: these wars—all of them—of no good omen. No—

When we returned from Russia, friends, reading what I had written and hearing me talk of our experiences in Moscow, were all curious to know how the visit had affected my "point of view." I remember Lloyd's (Lewis), "Frank, come now, what do you really make of Communism in Moscow?" "Oh," I said, "the Russians have done remarkable things considering their start: such tremendous illiteracy. But their 'Revolution' was only partial: they've kept our idea of Money—even the profit-System that is destroying us will therefore destroy their 'Communism' too. Russians still believe in great concentrations of human beings on hard pavements—if not of capital—but for educational purposes (it will all probably prove to be for military purposes). Russia is falling for machine-worship, too—so this will turn and rend her as it has turned and is rending us." "Then," said Lloyd, "you don't come home a convert to Communism?"

I answered, "Of course not. No 'isms,' private or international, for me. I believe in a Capitalist-system. I only wish I could see it tried some time in our own country."

Book Five of *An Autobiography* ends here. A STUDY OF FORM.

Like Sinan centuries ago, the famous Ottoman architect of Agra, he who built a City for Babar, I wish to build a city for Democracy: the Usonian city that is everywhere yet nowhere.

His omnipotent ruler called for the prophetic architect to reward the marvel of his performance. To make certain that nothing so splendid should ever happen again elsewhere, the Omnipotent-ruler condemned his faithful architect to the immediate loss of both his eyes: merely Royal Insurance. Even should that happen to me in consequence I wish to build a true modern capital for these United States of America.

But this search for freedom of FORM must end here in the new Usonian City. Broadacres is that City of the Future and will be the sixth book of *An Autobiography*.

/| "KEEP THE YOUNG GENERATIONS IN HEALTH AND BEQUEATH TO THEM NO TUMBLED HOUSE" is the message of this fifth book—FORM.

BOOK SIX □ BROADACRE CITY

BROADACRE CITY

PREAMBLE

I am not fond of thinking: preferring to dream—until circumstances force me to think, which the circumstances in which I live are perpetually doing.

Previous to 1929, so far as I was concerned "Economics" had been confined to professors and a few well-read men.

I knew that the Declaration of Independence, the "Rights of Man," and the "Pursuit of Happiness" did not result in the people's obtaining independence or rights or happiness. I saw clearly enough that not Economics but Religion was what the people themselves were expected to turn to for relief from their inevitable lot of suffering and deprivation.

Charity was a virtue chiefly because it was a *necessity*.

Myself the son of a minister who came down a long line of ministers extending back to the days of the Reformation in England, I was quite familiar with deprivation and knew where to turn for relief—to my imagination, which supplied me with all good and forbidden things.

I knew that the very idea of Liberty was a danger to the State and to Church if the individual took it in earnest and not religiously.

I could never believe that the Declaration of Independence meant that all men were born free and equal because what sense I had told me it was not so and could not be so. But I thought it meant that all men, independent of the circumstances of their birth, should be given an equal chance to prove themselves equal.

I began to think of Democracy somewhat when I began the practice of Architecture. I was twenty-four. Before that I had not thought so much about it. As a boy I was taught that a vote was a political power and that because each man had a vote he would have an equal share in determining the powers of the government. But the people who had real power, as I soon saw, were those who knew how to take advantage of the hunger, fear and weakness of the voters.

593

Democracy stood in my mind for the growth and protection of individuality: stood for the rights of man as against authoritarians and all open or secret dictatorships. Gradually I came to see that the Christianity of my forebears, by way of their own sentimentality and credulity, had done a lot of harm in the world as well as a lot of good—but the harm was increasing and the good diminishing as science proceeded.

I had always been rather backward where political ideas were concerned—but idealizing Thomas Jefferson, Tom Paine and our statesmanlike forebears.

Shelley and Goethe (by way of Carlyle) contributed much to my early sense when I was about fourteen years old. As I have described, at that time I read Rousseau's *Emile* and Carlyle's *Sartor Resartus*, Victor Hugo and Voltaire, among other things an omnivorous reader. I had been interested in the Arabian Nights. Of course Jules Verne and—secretly—the "Nickel Library."

The War of Independence fascinated me but all I knew of it was what the stock-and-shop historian wrote for colonial consumption. The Civil War got to me in similar channels. I later realized that I knew little of either if I really wanted to know the truth.

The power of the "conservative" as I myself soon had good reason to know, is tremendous.

I grew up a rationalist. My religion, so far as it went, was Unitarian. After I became old enough to discriminate between dogmatism and principle, philosophy came to me gradually and mostly by way of experience on the farm, care of animals, etc.—the mysterious beauties and obvious cruelties of Nature. These interlocking interchanges of the universe began to fascinate me more then and were with with me when I began to build.

It was then that I became a seeker after Truth of Form from the inside out.

Well along, though still young in the practices of Architecture, I met Mazzini, Meredith, Tolstoy, William Blake and Walt Whitman and the great humanitarians. I must have had that quality of feeling and thought—a pretty strong undercurrent from my pioneer forebears—because none of their radical thought seemed to me other than the most natural thing in the world.

Victor Hugo's *Notre Dame* had affected me deeply.

But not until I had a home of my own and an independent practice as an architect did I realize the beneficent nature of the Law of Change—or see life as one continued flux of becoming, as Heraclitus, stoned in the streets of Athens for a fool, saw it. Then and there were laid the foundations of the philosophy of a new architecture. That philosophy arrived in my mind, as Architecture, ten years before I knew Laotze in his own words.

I met none of all this in school.

I have often told of my meeting with the philosopher who had said what I was myself trying to build—Laotze, who lived and taught five hundred years before Jesus was born.

Capitalism, Socialism, Communism, these political faiths were all so much water on the duck's back so far as I was concerned. There seemed nothing organic in them. Nothing began at the beginning where all thinking must begin—for itself and our own sake. If anything good was to happen.

As an Architect I saw that financial prosperity and the Law of Change, so far as growth went, had little or nothing in common—were indeed enemies—and that I must choose between them. It cost me nothing to choose. My forebears and upbringing as well as my innate feeling were all on the side of the change called growth, with the onward movement that is upward, toward the light. My faith in that was always a happiness to me.

Force and compulsion on the part of the State or any individual in it seemed hideous to me. Thoreau's "That government is best government which governs not at all" I accepted as a truism and felt that if men were not prepared for it yet they soon would be where they were free to feel and think for themselves as they were in my country.

I saw cooperation all around as the natural or normal thing, and not selfishness and violence. The anarchist's idea, faith in the commonwealth based on voluntary instinctive respect for the other fellow's rights, I saw as the normal thing and could never understand why it was not recognized as ideal even though unattainable in present-day society. I did realize that it was as incompatible with false capitalism as with authoritarianism.

But all the various "beliefs" were so blended at the edges that it was hard for me to tell just where and when one slid into the other. The labels so confused me. And there seemed always to be a soiled fringe of disreputables clinging to every fine faith or great thought when it started to move. But the people who were "wrong" I liked. And the people who were "right" I seldom did.

What happened to Malatesta in Italy seemed usually to happen to people who really got things moving ahead. Jail seemed always there to put a stop to anything that really meant a step up and a step forward. If not the civil-jail then it was the money-jail.

Resentment and violence seemed to attach to the law of change where human nature was concerned, although change is natural and perpetual in the nature of the Cosmos. Inextricable "interests" so involved nearly everyone in his present situation that any real forward movement was made painful beyond endurance. I began to understand why.

Karl Marx never appealed to me because he seemed to see the world as a factory for factory workers and his view of society, with all its reality, seemed to me the worm's-eye-view. After all, the industrial revolution was a passing phase—not God.

It seemed folly to assume that a greater measure of life for all could be had by exalting valleys so that hills, big and little, would all disappear. He seemed to me, as Christianity did at about the same time, to be the enemy of the rhythm, beauty and premium that nature places upon the quality she lays her plans, and is most patient, to secure: Individuality. Marx, notwithstanding, seemed to reduce everything to the level of crowds on hard pavements with a union card in its vest pocket versus the fat paunch of capital, silk-hat on its head and a big cigar in its teeth as presented by the popular cartoons of the day.

The Marxist revolution was probably necessary if the Industrial Revolution was to continue wrong side up by way of a false Capitalism. Necessary enough. But it was not the revolution I was concerned with, and in which I wanted to fight. I never cared to sing the "Internationale." I wanted to sing the work-song of Democracy.

The science of chemistry and machines and the Industrial Revolution I accepted as new tools in the Artist's hands, a great blessing—but if the Artist were to fall into the hands of these new tools, a curse put upon life that would soon destroy human happiness. I firmly believed the aesthetic-sense to be the saving clause in a Religion, a Society, a Factory, a Store or even a Government. Especially if Democratic Government.

About this time I wrote "The Art and Craft of the Machine" and, urged by Jane Addams, read what I wrote to the group at Hull House, as you probably have learned from an earlier passage of this autobiography.

Always I have loved the ground. And it interested me more than it seemed to interest Karl Marx or any of the socialists who subsequently grew up around his scientific analysis of a human economy . . . chiefly

596

industrial. I always felt the ground would be the proper universal basis for social life. Not the factory or the store.

A struggle against nature never appealed to me. The struggle for and with Nature thrilled me and inspired my work. The Victory of new ideas that, actually or figuratively, made the proverbial two blades of grass grow where only one or none grew before, became the motive for me in the day's work. But producing things just for the sake of producing things seemed senseless than as now. The fetters of old ideas and rigid dogma were always hateful and grew more hateful as I grew of age and new, more prolific methods production took the place of more simple old ones and left the old cultural forms hideous artificialities. The Marxian view of all life as a class struggle put the inordinate strain of inorganic character upon the face of the swiftly changing Cosmic order, which seemed to me less important, even if more expedient, than the facts of life seen as concordant with the nature of Man on his own Earth in his new circumstances.

So Marx (that is to say, Socialism) seemed to me an orthodox negation or degradation of the organic character of Nature. Profane to my unitarian mind because the creative-artist was left out.

The revolutionary bayonet has little in common with the evolutionary sickle although the one is supposed to have made way for the other—apparently for the purpose of making away with it eventually?

Exploitation of mankind by way of colonization in order to keep false Capitalism and its licentious Production alive (as we now see it coming to some sort of reckoning all over the world) was to me carnal sin. Coming to what conclusion? Capitalism in principle is old and strong. It is wrong only if wrong-end-to—or selfishly exploited by those who abuse it by using it for Empire instead of using it for indigenous human growth and happiness. Every age, of course, rots with its own Success. The richer a false capitalistic society becomes, the nearer bankruptcy it is. Its prosperity is a tragic thing. "Leave me undisturbed to create and cancel the financial credit of the nation and I don't care who makes its laws" said one of the great bankers.

And I could never see that what we did in the U.S.A. ever gave capital a chance to spread its base on the ground and rise naturally to an apex. Certainly it did not do so as we knew it and still know it with its apex on the ground, base up in the air—a topsy-turvy Capitalism against which Socialism and many other isms are directed for special justice and relief. Nor could I believe that Agriculture necessarily meant ignorance of beauty and a peasantry any more than I could believe that Industrialism necessarily meant ugliness and a wage slave. Unless the creative artist was left out.

Cooperation and Freedom and a great Art are certainly possible to the order of true Capital. But no Capitalism is true or tolerable where cooperation and freedom of the workers and creative art do not exist and flourish. Private human initiative flowers as prosperous public enterprise only under such conditions of Capital. This I firmly believed: an artificial society based upon capital wrong-end to and minus Art must end in weariness and war.

The elections of our Democracy have been described as "a public auction where all manner of promises are made." But that is the false democracy of the false Capitalism under which the people are content only so long as prosperity is enjoyed. Meanwhile how prosperity is had and passed around is no great matter. Apparently. The time of reckoning comes and it's always war-time. Almost all our wars are waged to keep prosperity, that is to say Success, at home under the false conditions of a false Capitalism which exploited (and now is itself exploited by) big money power. What can be worse than the deification of money by a whole people? Herodotus when asked why civilizations died, said, "First Success. Then as a consequence of Success, arrogance and injustice. Then as the consequence of arrogance and injustice—overthrow!"

Probably a false Socialism or a false Communism would work just as well, or just as badly, if similarly situated in similar circumstances which would probably arise were they put in place of Capitalism. Government in either case would become an aggressive form of egotism infecting an insolent bureaucracy. Nothing would have really happened to organize the true sources of all real wealth—the creative work of a happy people.

The great money-lender nation of the world was first England but now the United States. And it is easy to see that "God has been put in his place away from earthly matters" by our System so that this supremacy of finance might happen and prosper. Religion is become a silent partner in such top-heavy prosperity as ours. But its tolerance is really only a matter of indifference. On both sides. As a matter of fact, no Science-worshipping Nation really cares much what happens to Religion. And we might go on to say that no Western nations care much either, what happens to creative art. Except as the Artist can prettify a

598

commercial product for the eye of some prospective buyer. We may see where we stand in this throughout the world today by visiting with appraising eye the various mortuaries for the prophetic, indicative remains of ancient civilizations that we call our Art Museums. The record that is dead and not read.

And this indifference though concealed by superficial means, eventually came to me as a profound disillusion.

True Wisdom is no earthly thing. Wisdom is a spiritual state attained by refraining from selfish competition, imitation or moralizing And, most of all, by living in love and harmony with Nature.

But the exaggeration of false industrial-capitalism has intensified itself more and more as an empire within the empire of the colonial expansion of ruthless Imperialism. All over the Earth today you may see the fierce cruel grasp for this empire within the Empire by the Whites, now the Yellows, perhaps soon by the Blacks.

The English sang of the White Man's Burden; the French of the Mission Civilisatrice; the Germans of Kultur. "No one sings of the black-man's or the brown-man's burden"—not yet. But all of the Western Peoples seem to have lost the secret of true creative energy and, because of grossly exaggerated scientific means of production, to batten upon others less "productive" for raw materials to feed into the maw of the machine to make more and more machinery. But, actually, alchemy is turning sea-water, the air we breathe, and the mud under our feet into all any nation needs for independence as a basis for true world cooperation.

What cooperation is desirable without independence? Or possible?

DEMOCRATIC FORM

Although only begun, mechanized use of these brutalizing forces of the Industrial Revolution, and now more especially those of the Chemical Revolution, have already gone so far that no reform, nor any mere modification of these empirical systems of Capital now battening on colonies and milking them as a farmer does his cows, can do more than join the drab recessional that drags us, by force, toward the same tomb reached by ancient civilizations. Though we do reach our end by an ultra "Scientific" and so a different road: the Life-Vicarious is our degeneracy and our doom.

THE NEW DISCRETION

If we are not satisfied with this impending disintegration, we must go to painful, unpleasant Work, my Usonians. We must go to work at a beginning that has been far too long overlaid and so long delayed by our own very best people: go to more destructive work than bombs and mass-murder can effect—go toward organic construction.

At last we ourselves, discounting all our false starts and false alarms, we, the people, although we may not be the very best, must begin. We must go by, or cast out, our popular warped-heroes and all standardized Rulers. We must get down to work at the honest beginnings of Democracy with far higher and finer courage than any courage which may be bedeviled into going to War! The consequences of constructive destruction are so much more far reaching than destructive construction. So much more devastating and beneficent.

If this Democratic future, for which because of designed miseducation we are now to toil and plan all over again, harder than ever before, is going to be realized, our first need is for a New Discretion: true humility succeeding these excited, ignoble, angry fears.

"Whom the Gods would destroy they first make mad". That madness is fear and fear madness—is true as it ever was. And it is this peculiar consequence of Success—arrogance, that is destroying us! We need the national and rational humility that is not afraid. True humility (faith instead of fear) might serve to open the doors and windows of the Spirit of National-life to what constitutes the Democratic spirit. But, while our people are conscious of being virtuous when they are honest or conscious of being charitable when they love their neighbor—they are not virtuous nor charitable nor honest. We must begin at the beginning with a New Discretion which is not Fear nor related to it—but is Intelligent faith.

THE DEMOCRATIC SPIRIT

As a creative artist, at first in disillusionment followed by anger and resentment but now with somewhat more humility, I have been seeking, in what I have called these Broadacre City studies of our civilization, the organic-form of such Democracy.

And as a builder I have been long enough and far enough afield to know that true FORM is and must always be, Organic. I myself have actually prophesied FORM with that integrity throughout this vast undeveloped country of ours in revolutionary bricks, boards, and mortar whereever the lives of our Usonian people have come to me for a remedy. And for that matter, abroad over the whole earth.

That is why I know now that the true architect of a social order— we would not name him an Architect but call him a Statesman—could in one lifetime lay down outlines on which we could build the Democratic State for which I would be happy to build organic buildings. For one, I would like to build these life-giving buildings as normal, no longer as revolutionary. The life of a revolutionist is not easy to sustain.

At this groaning moment of all isms—Internationalism—might we not afford a statesman with the vision and personal responsibility that characterized a Thomas Jefferson or a Thomas Paine? If only we might soon find him in the terms of our own new day!

Most of all, we ourselves need the inspiration of such vision and personal-responsibility as was theirs where the humanities are concerned.

But the mind that goes with vision of that broad humane type we do not seem to have produced by our established systems of self-interest in thought, emotion, and education—all of which have been misdirected or carried away to "produce" for the sake of inordinate Production. We have been exalting a profit-motive pretending to work both ways. Indeed we seem to have abolished the creative mind on suspicion, or by insult or neglect.

MISEDUCATION

The first thing our Broadacre studies taught me to see is that it is solely upon our own personal initiative as a people that we, what there is left of us, must now turn to the young. In their behalf we must politely but firmly ask higher education to get down off its stilted horse. First of all we must Decentralize and Nature-ize the education of the very young: the same effort but opposite the direction taken by State-Socialism. We must get popular and especially higher education, down on native ground somehow. Anyhow. And keep both higher and lower education down there long enough to learn these truths: first the truth concerning this medium-of-exchange thing we keep on calling sound-money; second, this matter of the good ground. Both are neglected by us down to the present moment. And here we find Henry George for the ground and Silvio Gesell for the money.

The analysis of the basis of human poverty made by Henry George has never been refuted. His expedient for bringing a remedy to bear caused more controverts than converts because expedients are more important to academic thinking than principles. As usual the means is taken for the end. Pigeon-hole thinking.

Silvio Gesell's *Natural Economic Order* was as necessary to Henry George's success as Henry George was necessary to Gesell's success. The two men are opposite but harmonious sides of the same shield.

The preface to the *Natural Economic Order* and the preface to *Progress and Poverty* are two of the finest things in recorded English. Both are an exposition of Principle rather than panaceas: both dealing with Land and Money with a simplicity seeming naive to the prestidigitators of interest: our professional economists.

MAMMON

"Why the conscription and control of everybody and everything except the banks and their produce?" There must be a reason. What is it? And we must hold education's nose down to the native ground long enough for teachers to see that in money, that vulgar, moot root-matter, corrected lies one of the most important elements under the sun if the fundamental footing of our social structure is to reach the ground instead of the rubbish heap of bought-and-sold, dishonest Finance on which it now rests and upon which no footing can be safe. We the people can no longer afford to take "Finance" (this matter of granting a special privilege to create money out of nothing at little or no cost) for granted by way of such an education as we have received at the hands of present Education. On this basic matter of social structure we have received less than no enlightenment at all. This matter-of-ignorance might even be considered the result of designed miseducation.

We can no longer afford to regard this affair with Mammon as a sacred superstition as good old Karl Marx did, or as did the Russians, unfortunately following him by way of Lenin his disciple. Why must all Revolution be only partial and then start all over again the other way? Is it because Revolution is either ignorant of organic-law or is an explosion under too great pressure which must proceed to recover lost equilibrium?

But so far as we are concerned we cannot afford to take Money as it is now set up as any valid abstraction whatsoever. Or from God, unless we want to keep on going to War or toward Revolution, meantime maintaining Poverty as a cherished national institution decorated by "Housing."

THE TIME HAS COME

Not for nothing is the challenger of Money in its present form soon a socio-political outcast. He is suspect. "But there is a greater service to be rendered by him," as G. Hickling of British born Reality says, "than to die for his country." At bottom it is a choice between dying to retain the disastrous illusion that money is more important than men or adopting a financial policy that will serve men by enabling them to live in conditions of good will and mastery over the abundance of their own Earth.

All public offices and our entire educational system are so deeply committed and geared to the idea that Money plus Authority can rule the World, that any careful examination of this money-rot of our sociology is subversive activity. Especially if the search be at all sincere, the F.B.I. will appear. Like Sex, Money has remained the slum quarter of our human social-consciousness except when and as we realized its importance sufficiently to rebel. I found this rebellion on the trials of the Broadacre search—1929—as you too will find it when you begin to tramp those devious trails in search of either justice or organic proportion.

Long habitual mis-association of ideas kept in circulation by selfish interests conceals the vicious-character of this public enemy number one and hides from us its enormous demoralizing influence on our destiny. Our secret molders of public opinion have been skillfully concealed.

So, Power-finance now has control of our national destiny. But it has control only because designed miseducation has left us, as a Nation, ignorant. Even yet but few among us understand the imperative necessity for consumption to control production and for production to control Finance, nor do we understand also the "must" that the Credit of the

603

Nation must belong to the people to be used by them according to their will.

Democracy must get these fundamentals straight in mind so that this Nation may be forever stopped from creating a special class living on Money; Money as something in itself. Money promoting Money as an interest-bearing speculative commodity. Thus creating not only specious values but continually building barriers against the normal creative powers of a great people: barriers that must be perpetually maintained, or destroyed, by Wars.

MAMMON'S WIFE

It is always our business—is it not—to give an account of ourselves to ourselves? Is it not time for that accounting now? Official arrogance and the bureaucratic-nincompoops of National arrogance have been doing that all-important job for us so long that "Mammon's Wife" may be the proper name for our own Nation no less than for Byron's "Perfidious Albion" for which nation the term "Mammon's Wife" was originally designed by Meredith.

As we are financially established now, we are so squarely up against this affair with Mammon that in the Broadacre search for a structure and Plan-form natural to native Usonian freedom (Democracy), it soon became apparent that every man of God or man of Art or man of Benevolence in this country as things were with us then, was, first of all, and must be, a time-server, and money-raiser—or else go to Jail, go to the poor-house, go mad with frustration, or go to War.

THE NET MISTAKE

Although results at the moment do seem far enough away from the cause to confuse it, the economic tribulation we are really in over our heads, as in England, is at bottom the net social result of the unwisdom of taking away from the people their own Credit; legalizing that theft by act of Congress, and thus enfranchising endless specious occupations, raising a special class (the banking class) to whom we have given money-creating privileges.

604

Thus, Money becomes by these acts a speculative commodity not only created by a privileged few but controlled by them. Extended by them. Contracted by them.

And on this too-easy road to subversive financial power, our so-called Capitalistic-system soon became no true Capitalistic-system at all. By way of the pool of money which has been forming behind the successful industrialists, the great industrialist himself has become a pawn of the greater money-power system, itself a great cartel with endless sub-cartels. And that power-system has gradually reduced to mere speculative commodities all the natural means we have to live by . . . including our own lives.

Is it easier for "rulers" to deal with human life when thus reduced to commodity status? Preferably in herds on hard-pavements. Or in factories?

HELL

Well . . . to get back again a little out of breath but still in "simples," I hope, to this Broadacre City research undertaken soon after the nation broke down A.D. 1929. In the search for the basis for Organic FORM I could not fail to see this despotism, Power-Finance à-la-mode, in the place where a foundation ought to be. And though as yet, it seems practically invisible to our very-best miseducated manhood we can see that it is really Despotism triumphant. I soon found, as I have said before, that because of its now autocratic (now virtually automatic) power, we have no sound economic foundation whatever for our pretension to Democracy, except by this strong-arm. That is to say, exterior props and braces familiar to the ideologies that even the wielders of that power profess to despise.

We have no fundamental interior support whatever, outside the natural good intent, at heart, of the people at large to bear their burdens with blind patience. I could see that the official safeguards (external props and braces) which the administration of government set up over this privileged organ of legalized theft, were only serving to multiply popular economic-confusion until economic-fear had come as unwelcome guest to sit down at every table in this land. And now, at a time when any further concentration of humanity is mass-murder, the machine and the bomb (the industrial revolution) are carrying the work to its logical conclusion: the great war nature seems to have herself staged in the survival of the fittest—the war between white and colored.

THE BUREAU KNOBS AND DRAWERS

The tragedy in all this terrible sacrifice of a great new nation's vitality and originality perhaps ending in its premature obsolescence or destruction, lies in the fact that just because Salvation is so simple, salvation seems politically all but impossible!

What blind absurdity this pretention to democratic government has become by putting the nation's credit in pawn to a privileged Money-system! No truly democratic nation would ever so assert self-interest of a privileged class at the expense of its own people to gain a temporary advantage.

Such Statesmanship as we have been able to put in practice here has, for many years, consisted chiefly in employing Federal Crats to take more or less money from one pocket on the one side in order to put more or less of it into another pocket on the other side by force of law! Meantime, "the rectifiers of the law keep on making three laws to cure one flaw." Where it will all end is not so far ahead.

It must all end in war after war, each war laying the foundation for the ultimate war, our resourses wasted, perhaps the race itself ended, in vain attempts to end war by War? Probably. But, our partisan-minded legislators keep on making more laws to avert impending catastrophe until the various cogs that are the antagonistic administrations of government are already as pervasive, extensive and destructive in action as any plague of locusts. War or no war.

So many and so pervasive are they while the increasingly complicated mechanized sources of production mount (and not only in wartime) that the great Melting-pot is rapidly becoming the ultimate Grindstone.

INTEGRITY

We have at last reached the point in this naive preface when it is to the public integrity of those troublesome few who insist upon understanding the symbols before they will consent to use the symbols that we must look for the enlightenment that is salvation.

True revolt is always founded upon the acceptance of a principle. Any hope for a true Capitalistic Democracy must therefore begin by our realization that we, the people, haven't got the proper Principles in prac-

606

tice, and that we are not asking ourselves the right questions.

"Ideas precede and generate facts." It is our nature so to trust in the power of Truth. With this faith at heart the people themselves must manage to proceed.

THE SAVING CLAUSE

The original intent of the founders of our Nation was clear enough. Their intention was to found a nation of free men themselves in common possession, as individuals, of the natural resources of their nation as a Nation. Their considered statement is found in the Constitution of these United States: "Congress shall issue money and regulate the value thereof."

So, Money as a speculative commodity in itself (money as we know it) was never accepted by the pilgrim founders of this nation when making our Constitution. Imperfect as that property-loving instrument originally was, some of our statesmen forefathers must have seen ahead this impasse we are now in. Because, to enable the people independently to establish themselves by free use of their own credit, a vital clause was put into the constitution of these United States by the forefathers. Wisely they stipulated: "Congress shall have the right to issue money and regulate the value thereof": a provision for economic independence indispensable to Democracy.

But in that parlous time, Alexander Hamilton, under pressure of the ragged new republic's lack of initial faith in itself, himself sincerely imbued by the idea that Money-plus-Authority was inevitable, smiled, sailed over and sold us back again to the powerful money-changers of monarchic old England.

Thus English domination of these new United States was, by Hamilton, refounded upon our own Revolution. In the very name of Democracy, English domination was set up again to influence our destiny, gradually undo our Democratic Republic and precipitate wars. Unchallenged to this hour this money-power is now an invisible but none the less cruel despotism guided only by such peculiar, flexible, English conscience as we have ourselves inherited. And we are now ruining ourselves to perpetuate this old English doxology that Authority-plus-Money can rule the world?

In these bewildering reactions of a despotic era wherein under the influences of secret molders of public-opinion all ideologies swap sides or straddle the fence, the Chemical-revolution and Machine-production are pushed to a runaway artificiality which may never come back to earth on the white side of this planet.

SO WHAT OF THE NIGHT

Sound economic foundations are simply not there to be reached.

Consequently the artificial money-props and braces now employed instead of foundations were more than merely confusing to me as they must be confusing to anyone who tries seriously to understand Money as an organic instrument, not to say basis, of human establishment.

As an Architect, never before much interested in Economics, I was compelled, now, to read much of the amazing conflict that constitutes such Science and Ethics as "Economics" assumes. And taking heed, as you have already heard (might hear to much better advantage from a less amateurish source) I have nevertheless reached views that seem to validate the Broadacre studies. The variables that are variables only because no fundamental principle appeared necessary to them, we have set aside.

The Broadacre conclusion was to dig deeper, untangle and decentralize everything—except Government, to simplify and organize Government as a matter of the people's business directly, and chiefly, then try to put all back together again in more free, flexible Form planning to use our vast mechanical powers and processes for truly humane purposes.

I believe that once we do establish ourselves as organic on organic foundations and are therefore independent of external props and braces, we can afford a far more flexible, natural and free social FORM than has ever been known. And Architecturally, therefore we will have the practical social-basis for the great, beautiful, healthy buildings of genuine human Freedom. Actual Democracy will be ours.

There new Plan-forms were neither urban nor rural, but were the outgrowth of use of the ground as a common human right equally for the tiller of the soil, the poet, the preacher and the makers of things, the shop-keeper and the trader. So the forms were into the light out of the ground and were harmoniously established each in all, all in each.

Whereas the present order is Monarchic, Feudal and from the top-down. As the matter now stands to fall our Nation will be, probably, the shortest lived on record because of the deadly accelerations afforded by inordinate use of machinery: the consequence of man's control of Monstrosity before he had obtained control of himself.

608

We, the people, have been hoping against hope to see the fine things our politicians have been saying to us about ourselves coming true because we wished them to be true. They have not come true. We have gone from our early hope to early bad on the way to far worse. We are concealing the worst from ourselves as we are able.

AND YET

I believe that our Usonian society is, at heart, still sound. I believe that if we, the people, waken to our responsibility to ourselves as men and women, first; then to ourselves as a people, and therefore not only learn to know but actually realize the immediate need of a better (because an Organic instead of a Monarchic) world-order—we might expect to have the organic social FORM we could honestly call Democracy visible to all men within a generation or two. Say three generations at most if we began at the beginning in earnest.

This belief is not peculiar to me. It is, I believe, the growing conviction of the entire World of Thought.

As a Hope, a Dread, or a Fear this belief has incidentally reached and touched the lives of many millions of our own people. And, though more backward here in the United States than anywhere else in civilization, we too are about ready to go to work for an honest Organic Order.

My own quarrel, and I have one, with this money-affair of our own government is, as I have tried to describe it to you here, not that I have, myself, been unable to make money (I do not say "earn," because no one earns money as things are) but that to do anything at all worth doing I must be a shop-keeper whatever else I aspire to be. "As things are" who knows, today, what is really his own except that what a man does, that he has. Or we might say, that has him. He merely plays at a game to win or lose in a gamble with cards now stacked against him. In spite of the police he can no longer play a fair game. Or is it because of them?

Had I, myself, been free of the impositions of "the game" what might I not have accomplished for my people?

AN ANSWER

Nevertheless, The Taliesin Fellowship has proceeded to work and plan with me the erection of a great three dimensional model for a true Capitalist Society. We sought a valid Democratic FORM for our modern mechanized-society that was honestly and essentially Democracy, recognizing that the Nationalism of a true Democracy would be tolerant,

609

humanitarian and progressively liberal toward the individualities of other nations because it greatly cherished its own. It would regard its own individuality as its supreme asset and entertainment. Not only preserving its own but vitally concerned above all with improving its quality. A fairly certain way of improving the World.

Unless such constructive effort as this is made educational and effective at this time, what but Revolution or obsolesence has ever, or can ever come of such complete abnegation to money-power as ours has now become?

The compelling tide of invisible money-power dispelling our best thought and secretly aborting our honest original national-intent cannot, by way of our Science, or by singing hymns, Christmas Carols, or Cradle-songs continue to keep us wrong side up and upside down Revolution or no revolution, if we will dig down to begin at the beginning and put in a good Foundation.

TO GATHER THE SIGNIFICANCE OF ALL THIS TOGETHER

I wish to avoid the accusation that I am too vague about it all.

So in case some too academic or too impatient reader has skipped the foregoing characterization of our economic "tribulation" and a wandering eye or two should hit the page at this point, simply as I can, let me state the fundamentals (they are all Architecture) involved in these amateur chapters on organic social-welfare: social structure as seen by one whose chief study and interest is structure: an Architect.

Unfortunately, because the so-called Science of Economics has so far been only a variable in human reactions to material things instead of the working of a known principle, all simples must seem naive to the professional economist and Broadacres will have no real help from him.

Nevertheless this summation:
Democracy cannot become a vital force until:
One, APPROPRIATE LAND IS FREE TO THOSE WHO CAN AND DO CHOOSE TO USE IT CONSISTENTLY WITH THE COMMON GOOD;

Two, THE CREDIT OF THE PEOPLE IS THEIR OWN, SO ESTABLISHED BY THEIR CONSTITUTION, AND THEIR FINANCIAL ESTABLISHMENTS ARE SUCH THAT THEY THEMSELVES CONTROL AND FREELY USE THE CREDIT THEY ALONE CREATE.

Until these two conditions are established we can have no sound economic basis for this highest form of Aristocracy the world has yet to know and that we have here been calling Democracy. Democracy is the highest form of Aristocracy this world has ever seen because it will have Quality integral. It is Manhood upright and unafraid, achieved fresh, free, and true with each and every generation, freely choosing to be governed by its Bravest and Best.

When a genuine order of Capital is honestly tried, our national economic freedom of both Land and Money will be the safest basis yet devised for the creative imagination of human life in this mad world because that order of Capital will be founded in the true nature of human egoism: founded upon intelligent self-interest and honest selfhood encouraged, instead of the worthless by-product, egotism and selfishness, constantly restrained.

Meanwhile, "sound-money"? Yes, absolutely sound. Why not? What makes money "sound money"—the only true security for the Investment of Work as Idea and Idea as Work—what, indeed, except the Nation behind it?

What makes Land valuable to mankind and constitutes its only true Ownership except appreciative use and development; no makeshifts allowed to be devised as a substitute.

Building-construction is the most important organic single feature of such development. Therefore building, too, should be integral. All this put together: Building, Money, Ground and Government is Organic Architecture. All are Economics, broadly speaking, as we use the term at Taliesin. We see it so developing around the World.

Stripped of all Academic confusion and makeshift, fundamental freedom of both Land and Money is not only most important to you as a citizen home-builder and to me as a creative-architect but even more important to the yet unborn because both freedoms are indispensable to the creation of a great popular Architecture for popular Life. Such an Architecture is the real proof of quality in any civilization.

Meantime the new Integrity, let us say knowledge of Organic-law, must begin with our children so they may learn to hammer heated iron but not a stick of dynamite. And this new Integrity must reach them in time to teach them to be suspicious of what any educated, or habituated, "key man" is saying or may ever say. Our children must be grounded in a responsible selfhood; Individuality no longer to be confused with mere Personality. Theirs must be an essential Character, humanitarian, liberal, tolerant, and conciliatory. We, a truly liberal people, are learning that world-unity as the military supremacy of one people over all or any other people is impossible. But we have not learned well enough that commercial-supremacy is just as mischievous and just as impossible if we really desire Peace.

Here, then, gathering all this together follows in simple outline the bare Basement of the organic Capitalist Republican that I am calling BROADACRE CITY: THE CITY THAT IS A NATION FOUNDED IN COMMON SENSE and that subsequent chapters will present in more graphic FORM: this great reflex concerned chiefly with what an organic co-operative capitalistic society would look like were we ourselves one.

Politics, and therefore Politicians, should take a very different place in our affairs. It is probable that no politician as such could make a living were our laws organic. Only the idiosyncracies of individuals and their quarrels would require lawyers. As one item we might well dispense with five hundred thousand of our six hundred thousand lawyers. As for future wars, any occasion for them could scarcely be trumped up by the secret molders of public-opinion. And, the Bureaucrat would actually be a public servant, say an engineer, accountant, an architect or qualified agriculturist, scientist or artist. A poet? It is probable.

Because matters of policy would rise and rest fairly and squarely with the people, powers, foreign or domestic, would change completely.

THESE PARAGRAPHS, A TO G, OUTLINE THE BASEMENT:

A

ALL LAND WILL BE HAD AND HELD ONLY BY APPROPRIATE USE AND IMPROVEMENTS BUT LAND MAY BE DEVISED AND BEQUEATHED SO LONG AS BOTH USE AND IMPROVEMENTS ARE MAINTAINED BY HEIRS. SOCIAL SECURITY, INSURANCE AND INHERITANCE WOULD BE REGULATED BY THE STATES THEMSELVES.

B

THE CREDIT OF THE NATION WILL BE FREE TO THE WHOLE PEOPLE OF THE NATION, AND BE EXTENDED OR CONTRACTED AT WILL BY THE NATION.
CAPITALIZED BY CONGRESS THE NATION WILL ISSUE A CONVENIENT MEDIUM OF EXCHANGE. A DEMURRAGE-CURRENCY HAVING NO COMMODITY STATUS. THE VOLUME AND VALUE OF THE MEDIUM TO BE REGULATED BY A SPECIAL BRANCH OF CONGRESS.

C

CONSUMPTION SHALL CONTROL PRODUCTION: PRODUCTION SHALL CONTROL FI-
NANCE. NO TRADE BARRIERS. The infant Hercules has already strangled the
serpent. And pretty much everything else.

D

INVENTIONS (IDEAS) BY WAY OF WHICH THE PEOPLE FUNCTION AS A SOCIETY BELONG
TO THE PEOPLE. IDEAS THUS APPLIED TO POPULAR USE ARE TO BE APPRAISED AND
COMPENSATED BY CONGRESS.

E

THE AIR, LIKE THE WATERS, IS COMMON TO ALL BUT WHEN USED AS A HIGHWAY SHALL
BE SUBJECT TO THE WILL OF THE PEOPLE, AS ARE LIKEWISE ELECTRO-MAGNETIC
CURRENTS USED AS COMMON CARRIERS OR FOR COMMUNICATION. ALL PROPAGANDA
IN WHATEVER FORM WILL BE OPENLY PRESENTED AS SUCH.

F

ONLY BY TWO-THIRDS POPULAR VOTE INSTRUCTING THEIR OWN CONGRESS MAY WAR
BE DECLARED. AND EVERYONE VOTING FOR WAR IS THEREBY SELF-ENLISTED RE-
GARDLESS OF AGE OR AUTHORITY. WARS NOT FOUGHT VOLUNTARILY WILL BE IMPOS-
SIBLE.
CONSCRIPTION IS FOREVER ABOLISHED AS THE MODERN CRIME OF CRIMES.

G

IN ORDER TO MAKE MECHANIZATION AND ALCHEMY A HUMAN-ADVANTAGE, THE DE-
CENTRALIZATION OF ALL LIFE-CONCERNS SO FAR AS POSSIBLE IS THE MODERN PRESS-
ING NEED AND SCIENTIFIC OPPORTUNITY. THEREFORE MEASURES CONCERNING THE
PUBLIC WELFARE SHOULD BE DETERMINED WITH THE END IN VIEW OF REINTEGRA-
TION OF THE CONCERN, OR THE INDIVIDUAL WITH THE GROUND.

SELF-DEFENSE FOR USONIA

THIS SHOULD BE INTEGRAL, MILITANT BUT NOT MILITARY, BECAUSE DEFENSE WOULD
CONSIST IN THE INTEGRITY OF THE PATTERNS OF DEMOCRACY EQUIPPED IN PERFECT
TIME, TUNE, AND CHARACTER WITH ALL-OUT MECHANIZATION TO BE USED ONLY BY
FREEMEN IN EMERGENCY.

Education will be free and for freemen and develop popular ability
to resist the lies that "key men" devise and in whatever circumstances,

thus enabling Youth to stand up to the realities of events. Authority, instead of arising from the make-shifts of party politics and the policies of scheming traders, would become, more and more, the administration of well understood *principles* which the Nation would willingly defend if necessary.

And now we come to these models which the Fellowship in 1932 began to put into tangible form. They were, for the first time so far as I know, an entire cross-section of a complete Civilization: three dimensional models devised in relation of every part to the whole showing in detail a better way of doing nearly everything that we now do. A "better way" meaning one more in keeping with our character and the Science that is our opportunity. These models of Broadacres, making good and appropriate use of new means to escape outworn Expedients, were designed as a broad-way into Democratic future-life for Usonians. Direct, practicable employment of organic Principles in creating the multiplicity of new forms now essential to modern civilization, it should be unnecessary to add, therefore strong from within to defend itself against any external attack. A great instance of Art employing Science.

These new "Broadacre" ways should now be so modeled and presented that not only could the ideas of a fresh plan-formation be seen by our people but the various parts be seen in actual perspective in relation to each other by those unaccustomed to reading plans. The scheme as a whole should be adequately presented so that the details, as well as the whole, might not only be touched and intelligently studied by whoever was interested. The plans and models themselves should be so extended and supplemented by recordings and cinema.
Severely limited as it was originally set up in New York, Philadelphia and Pittsburgh, seen but by only several hundred thousand people, the idea of the new City that was nowhere except everywhere had not been carried far enough in explanation to be easily understood as a true basis for a Capitalism consistent with Democracy: that is to say Capitalism consistent with the freedom, individuality and personal initiative of a grand Nation such as ours of essentially intelligent, emotional, free individuals.

So "the organic City" was as freely misunderstood as it was variously criticized by professional experts, criticized by some few as Communism, by many others as Socialism or even as Fascism. By only the few was the City recognized for what it really was, Democracy relaxed, resilient, safe, fundamentally a free, structural FORM for the life that will, some day, become Usonia, the one great free City so founded

614

in uncommon sense as to make human life not only more beautiful but more secure. More secure and beautiful because more natural to present and future human Life, free from these feudal hang-overs from which we seem striving in vain to escape, held back by a false sentimentality masquerading as Sentiment. We exhaust ourselves trying to defend what has become indefensible.

This true Capitalist system—base on the ground instead of apex there and base in the air—when we decide in our own behalf to try it honestly with the independence we once declared, July 4, 1776—will surely eventuate into new living structural Forms together making a Plan-form something like Broadacre City (the free City) the consequence of a perception and enlightened acceptance of the new forces that have already changed or are rapidly changing our lives for better or for worse. Obsolesence has already been terrific. But the cultural back-drag is a growing menace to the life of Usonia itself.

If only we had permitted ourselves as a people to learn what Organic Architecture could do to make of our private and national life great unexampled beauty by way of our own manifold resources, a greater harmony than has yet existed anywhere would now be our constant recourse and delight. But because we have fed upon already degenerate phases of the great art of Architecture which were casually washed up on our Atlantic shores instead of developing an organic culture of our own cast in the alloy of the great melting-pot, well suited to our own time, place, and changed circumstances, we have missed the greatest, most fruitful happiness of all in any civilization: a great Architecture.

For solace we have turned away from the things of the creative spirit, seeking satisfactions derived from an eclecticism ill fitted even to material things. The greatest security for those satisfactions being money as the present brokerage banking-system has established it. A false expedient we have fought to maintain.

And, since, for the moment, Science gives us more of these so-called "realisms" than Art or Religion gives, both Art and Religion languish together.

Meantime the Democratic Spirit that has waited and hoped must go to work.

Victor Hugo, the great Modern of his time, in a chapter of *Notre Dame,* prophesied that Architecture, already some five hundred years moribund, would in the latter end of the nineteenth century or the beginning of the twentieth, come alive again.

This prophecy is beginning to be realized.

In the concept of Architecture as organic we not only grasp the center-line of the true indigenous Culture for this era of the machine in Usonia, but we have the beginning of a better world and a more humane racial order.

INDEX

For the writing of this work I have long ago consulted and occasionally remembered Pythagoras, Aristophanes, Socrates, Heraclitus, Laotze, Buddha, Jesus, Tolstoy, Kropotkin, Bacon, William Blake, Samuel Butler, Mazzini, Walt Whitman, Henry George, Grundvig, George Meredith, Henry Thoreau, Herman Melville, George Borrow, Goethe, Carlyle, Nietzsche, Voltaire, Cervantes, Giacosa, Shelley, Shakespeare, Milton, Thorstein Veblen, Nehru, Major Douglas, and Silvio Gesell.

Louis Sullivan's writings I have not read: he whose thought was, in his own person and presence, an open book to me for many years.

And innumerable are the various collaterals, diagonals, and opposites that went into the place where this book might have come from but did not. I said at the beginning that the real book was between the lines. It is true of any serious book concerned with culture.

Gene (Masselink) of the Fellowship and his helpers have untangled day by day, month by month, the mass of inter-lined and defaced scripts that would tease anyone, especially myself. Gene is the only one who could read them.

PHOTOGRAPHERS' CREDITS

MRS. HENRY ADAMS	H.H. Richardson
JOHN AMARANTIDES	Hillside Home School, Taliesin exterior, Taliesin West living room, Taliesin West entrance, Beth Sholom Synagogue
H. WILLIAM ATKINS & ARTHUR H. DICKEY	Lovness Guest House
CHICAGO ARCHITECTURAL PHOTO COMPANY	Frank Lloyd Wright Studio, Coonley House garden front
JOSHUA FREIWALD	Feldman House
HENRY FUERMANN	Larkin Building, Unity Temple, Midway Gardens
FUJIN-NO-TOMO	Frank Lloyd Wright at Giyu Gakuen
P.E. GUERRERO	First Unitarian Society Meeting House
HEDRICH-BLESSING	Fallingwater, Lloyd Lewis House, Greek Orthodox Church
BILL HEDRICH HEDRICH-BLESSING	Taliesin living room
W. ALBERT MARTIN	La Miniatura
HELEN MORRISON	Mrs. Wright, 1945
RICHARD NICKEL	Robie House
OBMA STUDIOS	Frank Lloyd Wright (portrait in white suit)
MAYNARD L. PARKER	Coonley House living room

619

Type set by Cemar Graphic Design Ltd., Rockville Centre, New York
Paper by Perkins and Squier, New York
Manufactured by Noble Offset, New York